The Encyclopedia of
VICTORIANA

VIEW ON WINDSOR CASTLE TERRACE
EASTERN FRONT

The Encyclopedia of
VICTORIANA

Preface by
Marcus Linell
Director of Sotheby's Belgravia

Edited by
**Harriet Bridgeman and
Elizabeth Drury**

Country Life

© Rainbird Reference Books Ltd 1975.

Designed and produced by Rainbird
Reference Books Ltd, Marble Arch
House, 44 Edgware Road, London W2.

Published 1975 for Country Life by
The Hamlyn Publishing Group Limited
London · New York · Sydney · Toronto
Astronaut House, Feltham, Middlesex,
England.

House Editor: Peter Faure
Picture Research: Harriet Bridgeman Ltd
Designer: Pauline Harrison
Indexer: F. T. Dunn

ISBN 0 600 331237

Set and printed by
Jolly & Barber Ltd, Rugby, England

Contents

Colour Plates

Editors' Note

This Encyclopedia is intended to be read as the story of the decorative arts in Britain and the United States between 1837 and 1901. It is also meant to be used as a reference book, containing as it does definitions and descriptions of Victorian artifacts and biographies of the principal designers and makers. The dual character of the work should be evident in the manner in which the material is presented.

Britain and the United States, though constitutionally independent and geographically remote, were linked culturally in the nineteenth century in many ways. Fashions and details of manufacturing techniques are always, in time, communicated from one country to another, to be accepted, adapted and developed, or ignored. The strongest links in this interchange of influence in the Victorian period were the great international exhibitions, the publication on both sides of the Atlantic of pattern books and American craftsmen visiting England in search of technical advice corresponding with the migration of European craftsmen to the New World in search of a better life. The design relationship between the two countries is described in the Introduction, with special reference to interior decoration and comparative standards of living.

Nonetheless, there were many dissimilarities; these arose principally from the need or desire for wares to suit a specific purpose or environment and the availability of particular materials. To demonstrate this, the output of Britain and the United States – the furniture, pottery, silver etc. – is described separately, though the glossaries which follow these texts, for purposes of comparison, relate to both. The glossaries are of necessity not definitive but contain entries on what is regarded as important and interesting, and are designed to provide enough basic information on the subject to make further reading easy to deal with. Cross references to other glossary entries in the same chapter are printed in capital letters.

There is an index at the end of the Encyclopedia which will indicate to the reader the diverse activities of a designer or maker, such as William Morris or Tiffany & Co., the different materials used in the making of, for example, tea services, and the range of influence of a style such as the Gothic Revival.

The intention has been to illustrate unique pieces, many in the safekeeping of museums, and also artifacts of humbler origin produced in large numbers which are almost as easy to acquire now, as antiques, as they were when purchased new. The contradictions of a period when exaggeration and functional simplicity were simultaneously admired, and mass-production methods were studied as closely as the techniques of Medieval craftsmen, we hope have been fully described and illustrated.

It is also our hope that this book, the first of its kind, will encourage further research on the various subjects and, above all, that it will prove useful and enjoyable.

Acknowledgments

For their assistance in compiling the Glossaries, we would like to thank John Culme, Philip Curtis, Mary Girouard, Geoffrey Godden, Flora Gill Jacobs, Martina Margetts, Fiona Pilkington, Sally Rousham, Edward Saunders, Paul Spencer-Longhurst and Cynthia Talbot. Particular thanks are due to Clive Wainwright, of the Victoria and Albert Museum, for his advice on Victorian pattern books.

We are extremely grateful to all those authors who helped to provide illustrations or who made helpful suggestions; also to Glennys Wild, of the City Museum and Art Gallery, Birmingham, E. P. Hogan, of the International Silver Co., Burr Sebring, of the Gorham Co., and Emanuel Levine, of Samuel Kirk & Son Inc., and, especially, we are indebted to Harold L. Peterson. The co-operation of the relevant people and departments at Christie's, London, Greenfield Village and Henry Ford Museum, Dearborn, the Metropolitan Museum of Art, New York, Sotheby Parke Bernet, New York, and Sotheby's Belgravia, London, is much appreciated. We would also like to thank Gordon Roberton, of A. C. Cooper Ltd.

Gillian Allan and Caroline Sykes were responsible for the line drawings for the Silver and Militaria Glossaries, and Mr F. Howe, of Hastings, made the panel of woods for the Furniture Glossary.

To Sarah Palmer-Tomkinson we are especially grateful, and to Peter Faure, of George Rainbird Ltd.

Preface

Victoriana, so I am told, has one fundamental and insurmountable flaw. It is said that it has no true style of its own. Yet to demonstrate this point the Anti-Victorian will stand in the middle of a room and identify with only a glance any objects of nineteenth-century date, and experience has shown that even the most singleminded devotee of the eighteenth century is unlikely to make any mistake in this self-appointed task, as the pieces are so distinctive that they could not possibly pass unrecognized.

Over the years certain categories of Victoriana of special interest or appeal have been separated from the main body of material and in this way have been elevated from what might be viewed as the morass of Victoriana to the status of Works of Art. Although this piecemeal process has concentrated a great deal of interest on the period, so many areas have been neglected that a casual observer might be excused for thinking that only the popular subjects are worthy of attention.

The object of this book is to present the period from 1837 to 1901 as a whole and in such a way that every subject, whether of wide appeal or of a more specialist nature, can be assessed both in the context of the period and in its own right. It is hoped that the enormous breadth of the subjects covered will open the eyes of any reader to the scope and interest of the nineteenth century. It should be stressed however that art-historical research into this period is still in its infancy and many exciting discoveries can be expected as research currently under way is completed and printed. To be able to collect in an area where original research is still possible is one of the attractions of the nineteenth century. Conversely it must be remembered that while the information in this encyclopedia is as up to date as possible, there is no doubt that in the future new facts will come to light.

The plan of the book is such that each main subject has an introductory passage to outline its development with particular attention to the sources of designs, the designers, contemporary pattern books and the innumerable technical innovations which so affected the manufacture and availability of high-quality products to the ever increasing and affluent middle classes. The interrelation of these introductory chapters is fascinating, particularly as it shows clearly how closely American styles followed those fashionable in Europe but none the less achieved an individuality and vitality which is quite unmistakable.

The book is brought to life with hundreds of photographs, all fully captioned and arranged with the relevant text, together with reproductions from contemporary trade catalogues, design books and other sources.

But the ingredient which may in the long run prove the most useful to any enthusiast is the full bibliography for each chapter. Until very recently it has been necessary to rely on source books which are not only scarce but little known, so to have a catalogue of these works arranged subject by subject together with details both of specialist articles which have appeared in various periodicals over the years and of modern reference books should prove most valuable and time saving.

MARCUS LINELL
Director of Sotheby's Belgravia

Introduction

The evolution and development of all branches of design during the nineteenth century were far removed from the relatively straight course that they had previously taken. The most difficult factor in any study of this century is the manner in which the mainstream of design, which was apparent at its beginning, had already split into many different directions after the first twenty-five years.

By 1825, several trends are discernible, developing concurrently; first one nation took the lead, then another, and this situation continued throughout the remaining seventy-five years. The variation in standards of craftsmanship and quality, due to increasing machine production, is another matter which makes an objective and balanced appraisal extremely hard, and it is therefore common for any study of nineteenth-century design to reflect merely the writer's own personal area of preference.

It is probably for these reasons that undue emphasis has been placed on what are now seen to have been progressive and influential schools of thought, those which made little immediate impact on contemporary opinions. Many historians have carefully chronicled the wilder fantasies of the Gothic Revival, the Arts and Crafts Movement or Art Nouveau, but the middle-of-the-road work, which makes up the bulk of the century's production, has remained largely undocumented and unappreciated.

Drawing room at 43 Harrington Gardens, London, photographed in 1897 by Bedford Lemere. The English interpretation of the Neo-Renaissance involved the revival of many Flemish architectural details, and a group of houses in Kensington, built by George & Peto during the 1880s, displays this style particularly happily. The photograph shows the informality of furniture arrangement and the mixture of objects that characterized middle-class taste at the end of the nineteenth century.

It is also necessary, in order to obtain a comprehensive view of the nineteenth century, to glance briefly at the social and economic forces which were responsible for the vital difference of this century from any other and to appreciate the shift of influence from one country to another, with the consequent bearing on contemporary output. Probably the most important continuous thread which joined the diverse elements of the century together was the factor of middle-class ascendancy.

The vast industrial and mercantile expansion in England during the first part of the century, and in the United States in the latter part, placed the growing middle class firmly in power in a manner hitherto unknown, and to this can be traced so much of the design ethos of the Victorian period. The middle classes are generally not creative. They are ambitious and imitative, and for these reasons so many Victorian designs have a strong feeling of 'aping their betters'. Acquisition of possessions, concern with outward display, insistence on solid quality, are all middle-class characteristics, while the confusion between elaboration and worth, the insistence that cheap materials should imitate costly ones, the preference for re-interpreted, old-established forms rather than new ones, all express the dilemmas of a changing social structure, the uncertain participants of which require reassurance.

By the time that Queen Victoria had come to the throne of England in 1837, many of the factors which suggest the High Victorian style had already become established. France had dropped behind from her traditional position as leader of fashion, and England, backed by her expanding, worldwide influence, was in the ascendant. In fact the culmination of the High Victorian, or at any rate most of the trends of the second quarter of the nineteenth century, did not materialize until the Great Exhibition of 1851, where all the best, and the worst, that taste, ingenuity, workmanship and technology could produce at this time were gathered together in incredible array; but already a number of different styles were currently popular at the beginning of Queen Victoria's reign.

Early Victorian Styles

The stricter kind of Neoclassicism, as proposed in such books as Thomas Hope's *Household Furniture and Interior Decoration* (1807) or even Peter and Michael Angelo Nicholson's *Practical Cabinet Maker* (1826), was beginning to look old fashioned and had become overlaid with the enriching elaboration of the Italianate style. The chief exponent of the Italianate in England was the architect Charles Barry, and his brilliant essays in the revived Italian style set the architectural fashion for middle-of-the-road taste until the 1870s.

A strong rival to the Italianate or Classical for interior decoration was the revived Rococo, and the two were often used together, with varying success. Certainly in furniture design the Neo-Rococo overtook the Classical in popularity towards the middle of the century, and its universal acceptance may be gauged by the fact that it has a specific name in most languages – *Neobarocco, Zweite Rokoko* – and, with slight regional variants, it can be traced in every country of the civilized world of the time, while all other nineteenth-century revivals are dismissed in Europe as the Romantic style.

It seems that the renewed interest began in England, where the brilliant interiors at Lancaster House, designed by Benjamin Wyatt for the Duke of York in 1825, deployed the richness, variety and luxury of the whole Neo-Louis vocabulary. It is not unreasonable to suggest that the style itself had a strong monarchical flavour, which accorded with the spirit of the second quarter of the century, when the old world hoped to return to the old ways after the upsets of the French Revolution and the reign of Napoleon.

At the same time Neoclassicism came to be associated in some countries with revolutionary and progressive ideas, and certainly its continued popularity in America well into the second half of the century is but a manifestation of its associational qualities. While English design had come to lead the world by 1837, and continued to do so for the next twenty-five years, it must also be admitted that there were not many contemporary challenges to its position.

In France the restored Bourbons, 'tired, reactionary and bigotted', gave little encouragement to the arts; Italy and Germany were both hampered by their fragmentation; the United States was still too busy establishing the necessities of civilized life to be concerned with leadership in this field, not that American design did not already have its own strong character in its single-minded Neoclassicism. Encouraged by such prophets as the architect Asher Benjamin, whose *American Builder's Companion* ran to six editions between 1809 and 1827, or Minard Lafever and his influential *Modern Builder's Guide* of 1833 and *Beauties of Modern Architecture* of 1835, building throughout the country followed the Neo-Greek almost without exception.

Industrialization of the American Furniture Industry

The prevailing and popular style for furniture had moved away from the American Empire style of Duncan Phyfe and Charles-Honoré Lannuier, and a number of new designers had emerged. Furthermore, the growing industrialization of the furniture industry had an effect on the appearance of furniture itself, and the use of steam sawing machinery led to the adoption of designs which made use of large flat elements with flat veneer instead of the carved and decorated members which were typical of earlier styles.

The firm of Joseph Meeks & Sons turned out furniture of this type, which had affinities with the Louis-Philippe style in France although of a less sophisticated order. Meeks' famous advertisement of 1833 shows no less than forty-one pieces of furniture which the firm was making at the time. Even Duncan Phyfe produced some of this sort of furniture, although his pieces were more closely based on contemporary French models and might therefore be considered as less native American.

In 1840, John Hall, an English immigrant working in Baltimore, published America's first furniture pattern-book, *The Cabinet Maker's Assistant* and this contained 198 plates of characteristic form. The shapes, which were easy to cut with steam saws, and the large areas of flat veneer over them, provided massive but practical pieces which were adopted by manufacturers all over the country, remaining popular well into the 1850s. Andrew Jackson Downing, America's first great taste-maker, strongly advocated such furniture in his *The Archi-*

TOP Library *from* Designs for Ornamental Villas *by P. F. Robinson, London, 1827. The character of the design is backward-looking and suggests the work of Henry Holland (1745-1806) rather than that of the more progressive architects and designers of the period.*

ABOVE *Library at Cranbury Park, Hampshire, England, incorporated in the existing house by the architect J. B. Papworth (1775-1847), 1831. Rosewood, yellow sienna scagliola, a moss-green carpet and brown leather are the dominant elements in this calm interior, which is still firmly based on the late Neoclassical vocabulary and carries no hint of the Italianate or the Neo-Louis.*

tecture of Country Houses published in 1850, although his selection of suggested designs also contained examples of Neo-Rococo and Neo-Elizabethan.

It is nevertheless the Neo-Rococo which seems to characterize the Victorian style, and it was certainly the most pervasive and long lasting of all the various stylistic experiments of the first half of the nineteenth century. Although, as has already been mentioned, the Neo-Louis fashion started in England quite early in the century, the corresponding style in furniture took somewhat longer to develop and did not really become

RIGHT *Stairway at the Alsop House, Middletown, Connecticut, 1838. The pure, early Neoclassical style remained popular in America for considerably longer than it did in England, but this example is unusual in that the painted decoration of many rooms in the house resembles the Italian Empire manner of the first ten years of the century. The stair has simulated stone-courses painted on the walls and* trompe-l'œil *figures in niches.*

BELOW RIGHT *Music room at Lancaster House (formerly York House), London, designed by Benjamin Wyatt (1775-1850), 1825. This forms part of the sumptuous Neo-Louis decoration, which was executed in all the main rooms and which is a very early example of what was to become a most popular Victorian style.*

widespread until the 1840s. Its frivolity seemed to accord happily with a reaction against the severity of the Neoclassical, and the curving shapes and the scrolls and volutes provided a luxuriant product which could be executed by indifferent craftsmen and successfully lent itself to machine production and mechanical carving. The expanding markets of the second quarter of the century reflected the increasing middle-class demand, and the Neo-Rococo supplied exactly the kind of opulence that would appeal to an ambitious and at the same time socially insecure clientele.

It is particularly interesting to note that the Neo-Rococo always remained a 'decorator's style', disliked by most architects and progressive designers. It seems to epitomize the products of what Dr Siegfried Giedion calls 'The Reign of the Upholsterer' and this relates to a situation that overtook interior design in the nineteenth century. Due to the vastly increasing demand for modish furniture and decoration, furniture makers and contracting decorators began to take over a great deal of the design work that might have been considered to be the province of the architect in the eighteenth century; not that there was anything new in the practice of a furniture maker supplying the whole interior decoration, but, as the nineteenth century moved into its second quarter, this practice became increasingly widespread.

The large numbers of prosperous middle-class families who moved into the new terraced houses of London, Brighton, New York and Boston were hardly likely to consult a top-flight designer, but they all required ready-made backgrounds which were showy, durable, respectable and not too outrageously modern: a look over the shoulder

ABOVE Bathroom suite *from the catalogue of the firm of George Jennings. It won a gold medal at the Paris Exhibition of 1889. Bathrooms had been standard provision in the better middle-class houses on both sides of the Atlantic since the early 1850s, but lavish equipment, such as this, did not make its appearance until the last fifteen years of the century, and such elaboration was hardly commonplace.*

RIGHT *Double washbasin in the middle bedroom at the Morse-Libby House, 109 Danforth St., Portland, Maine, 1858. America led the world in the development of technological comforts in the later nineteenth century.*

at the styles of the past to suggest stability as well as, of course, all the comfort that the new technology could provide them with.

Comfort and Technology

Throughout the century, technological progress affected production and changed the quality of life in a manner which had never previously been known.
The invention of the coil-spring, for

OPPOSITE *Queen Victoria's railway carriage, English, 1869. The interior of this sumptuous vehicle was furnished in a variety of styles – Neo-Louis, Neo-Gothic – which, although already a trifle old fashioned, reflected the Queen's conservative taste. Most of the larger movable pieces had in fact been designed for an earlier saloon in 1861. The silk-quilted walls and ceiling and double cork filled floor and twelve wheels were intended to reduce the rigours of travelling.*

instance, had a fundamental effect on the comfort of seating furniture, and a considerable effect on its appearance. Patents for this invention had been taken out in the 1820s, but by the 1840s and '50s its use for comfortable chairs was universal.

The typical form of mid-century overstuffed armchair (known to the French as a toad chair) derived entirely from the use of coil-springs, and these were often combined with deep-buttoned upholstery, another mid-Victorian device, the use of which some writers have even tried to ascribe to psychological forces. Attention has been drawn to the similarity of an upholstery button to the navel, which might be regarded as the emotional

centre of a bourgeois and domestic society, but it seems much more likely that buttoning was a commercial device to use up the short-staple cotton and wool combings which are the by-products of mechanical spinning. Furthermore, it is an ingenious method of keeping in place the large quantities of filling that are required in overstuffed furniture.

Throughout the nineteenth century the enjoyment of everyday life was drastically altered and improved at nearly all levels of society and in nearly all areas of design. The cast-iron cooking range, replacing the inefficient open fire, had become commonplace in most households by the 1840s, and the United States was well ahead in developing it. Efficient water closets, replacing the noxious night man of the eighteenth century, began to be a standard piece of equipment in new houses built from the 1820s onwards. (Main drainage and sewage disposal, curiously enough, lagged somewhat behind, and in many large cities there was little municipal provision for these public services until the middle of the century or even later.)

Practical methods of piping a supply of hot water to various parts of the house had been devised by the middle of the century, although many curious methods were to be adopted before the mechanics of the operation were stabilized into the hot-water systems that we know today. This amenity, above all others, remained a privilege of the rich, and one in which America's need to adopt labour-saving devices much earlier than

in Europe led to its earlier appearance in that country. An English visitor in the 1890s wrote: 'In America these fixtures are used in every mansion and in every dressing room. Domestic labour-saving appliances are much more thoroughly appreciated on the other side of the Atlantic than with us.'

A Revolution in Lighting

Perhaps the field in which the major revolution took place was that of lighting. The first real breakthrough in lighting devices, superseding candles, was the invention of the Argand lamp by a Swiss named Ami Argand in *c.* 1784. His lamp perfected the successful and practical consumption of a heavy colza oil, made from the crushed seeds of the *brassica* or kale plant, but such lamps were expensive and tended to be costly to run. Their use was mostly limited to rich households and to public buildings, but they were common until the 1840s in both Great Britain and the United States, and a great deal of care was lavished on their design.

The characteristic form of hanging lamp consisted of a ring of burners above an ornamental drip dish (essential for catching oil spillage) and a highly wrought container, often urn shaped, placed centrally, higher than the burners, to feed the heavy oil down by gravity to

the wicks. A modification of the gravity principle was the Moderator lamp, in which the heavy oil was forced from a low container up into the wick by either clockwork or spring pressure.

Towards the end of the first quarter of the century coal gas began to be produced in most urban centres, and its first application was primarily for lighting. It was not until the late 1850s that gas was put to other uses such as heating water and cooking. At first, the light was obtained purely from the flame itself, and various improvements were made to the burners throughout the century to ensure a combustion that gave the maximum light.

The discovery of abundant supplies of paraffin oil in Pennsylvania in 1859 completely revolutionized the use of oil lamps. This oil would rise by capillary action up a wick from a container below the burner, and paraffin lamps were

Kitchen at Keele Hall, Staffordshire. The mechanization of cooking developed throughout the nineteenth century, from the 1820s onwards, and although this photograph was not taken until the 1890s it shows a typical interior from a wealthy household of the 1860s with a cooking-range with mechanical spits, rational arrangement of shelves for utensils and hygienically tiled wall surfaces. The University Library, Keele.

OPPOSITE ABOVE The Hatch Family *by Eastman Johnson (1824-1906), commissioned 1871. Oil on canvas, 48 in × 73⅜ in (121.9 cm × 185.8 cm). A complete Neo-Renaissance decorative scheme is shown in this proud multiple portrait, forming a rich and solid background to a prosperous way of life. Metropolitan Museum of Art.*

OPPOSITE BELOW Interior *by Charles Frederick Lowcock (fl. 1860-1904), 1860s. Oil on canvas, 20 in × 24 in (50.8 cm × 60.9 cm). This sparsely furnished room is unusual at a period when most English interiors had a rich, object-filled appearance. Typical of the time, nevertheless, are the plate-glass sashes set in a three-sided bay window, the gas brackets projecting from the wall at either side of the fireplace, the massive marble-cased clock, the highly polished surface of the table and the door, the needlework-covered fireside stool with a receptacle beneath for slippers or knitting. Fine Art Society Ltd.*

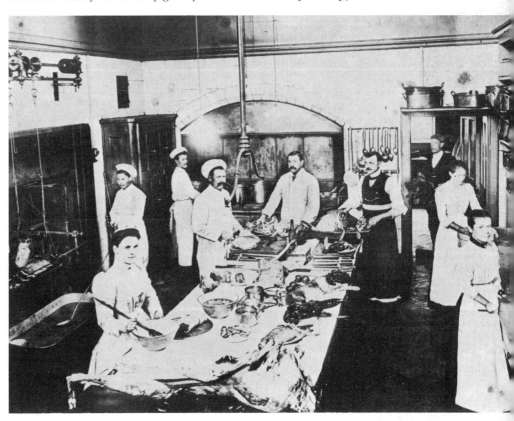

Dining room at Abney Hall, Cheshire, decorated by the Crace firm assisted by A. W. N. Pugin (1812-52), 1851. While Pugin's Gothic furniture bore little resemblance to true Medieval pieces, his design skill, coupled with that of J. G. Crace, produced an interior scheme of impressive richness.

Dining room at Lyndhurst, Tarrytown, New York, by A. J. Davis (1803-92), 1865. Davis was the architect of the original house in 1838 but did not add the dining room for a new owner, George Merritt, until nearly thirty years later. Davis also designed the furniture and he hardly based it on historical precedent.

clean, easily maintained, simple in construction and cheap to run. This development brought to the country dweller the benefit that had only been enjoyed by the gas-lit city dweller in the earlier part of the century, and much attention was expended on the form and ornamentation of the lamps themselves and their glass shades.

In the 1890s, the development of the incandescent mantle, consisting of a gauze hood impregnated with cerium and thorium oxide and fitted over gas burners, held back for a time the popularization of electricity. The incandescent glow which the heated mixture gave off was of a particularly livid greenish colour however, and the fragility of the mantles, combined with the disadvantages of gas in other ways, meant that as soon as a practical and robust electric lamp using a tungsten filament became available in about 1910, electricity rapidly superseded all other forms of lighting wherever it was obtainable.

The Mid Century

It is small wonder that, concerned as they must have been with adapting constantly to the rapid changes in con-temporary technology, the taste of the average person should have turned to the type of reassurance that the styles of the past could afford them, and that the average designer, swamped with new demands, new techniques and a hugely increasing clientele, should also have made use of re-interpretations of the comfortably established in an effort to keep up with other requirements in his constantly expanding programme. The tradition of drawing inspiration from the past had existed throughout the Renaissance; it was simply that during the Victorian period the interpretations were rather more literal.

Although the Neo-Rococo seems to have been the most popular style of the mid century, it was by no means the only one. Neo-Gothic, while increasingly favoured during the years 1840 to 1880 as the style for public buildings and churches, never found popularity on the domestic level, and Gothic furniture and decoration was fairly rare, especially in its extreme manifestations.

A. W. N. Pugin designed the magnificent Gothic interiors for the new Houses of Parliament in London during the years 1844 to 1852, and he supplied sketches and designs for furniture and textiles to the firm of Crace in Wigmore Street, London, in the 1840s. In the United States Alexander Jackson Davis produced some delightful Gothic furniture in 1841 for Lyndhurst, the romantic house that he was building for William Paulding. These examples are not typical, however, and often interiors in the most strict Gothic were furnished with what were known as either the Elizabethan or the Jacobean style. Both of these styles had more actual archaeological correctness than the so-called Gothic.

In Great Britain it was hoped that the high-water mark of design for the first half of the nineteenth century would be the Great Exhibition of 1851, but it was a disappointment to its organizers. Although it emphasised Britain's material ascendancy over the rest of the world, a comparison of the quality of the exhibits from other countries served to underline the fact that British standards of design were generally poor, and this was made very clear in all the official reports. By the time of the exhibition of 1862, a marked change had taken place. Size and elaboration, especially in furniture, had begun to be replaced by simpler outlines and more controlled forms, and this trend is noticeable whatever the style that the object purported to follow.

Quality and Reform in Britain

As the new middle class settled down with more confidence to its rôle of patronage, demand began to grow for quality rather than quantity, and restraint, of a kind, rather than elaboration.

Black oak bedroom at Abney Hall, Cheshire. The furniture here is copied much more closely from historical examples than the suite in the dining room (see far left), but the precision of the ornament and accuracy of construction could only have been achieved by craftsmen in the nineteenth century copying the originals.

Drawing room at Osborne House, Isle of Wight. This photograph was taken in the 1880s, but little would have been changed since the 1850s. Much of the furniture, which is approximately in the Louis Seize style, was made by Holland & Sons. Though richly polychromatic, the decoration is relatively restrained.

Furniture made in the middle part of the century, in the years 1855 to 1870, often in a style approximating closest to that of the period of Louis XVI, represents perhaps the high point in quality production.

Firms such as Gillow's, Holland & Sons, Wright & Mansfield or Howard & Sons, consistently turned out pieces of beautiful workmanship, and the standards that such firms helped to establish inevitably found their way down to the more humble, commercial manufacturers.

These fifteen years also saw the emergence of a number of prophetic reformers, determined in some cases not only to improve general standards of design but also every aspect of life itself. In most instances their ideas had only an immediate local influence, although in the long term there is no doubt but that the course of creative thought was decided by them for the next hundred years.

The foremost of these men was William Morris, who towers above his contemporaries in ability, energy and imagination. His desire for reform in the field of domestic artifacts was closely connected with his ideas of Socialism, satisfaction in work, beauty through craftsmanship

in everyday objects, and a return to Medieval working methods as an escape from what he regarded as the horrors of industrialization and machine production.

In many of his aims he failed completely, since the handmade products that were turned out by the firm that he started in 1861 were much too costly for any but the rich, and much too unusual for any but the sophisticated. On the other hand, his rejection of mass production in favour of craftsmanship, of standardization in favour of individuality, and of elaboration in favour of simplicity, all had an immense effect eventually on the development of taste throughout the world. The furniture, wallpapers, carpets and textiles produced by Morris, Marshall, Faulkner & Co. during the firm's long existence have remained some of the most enduring productions of the whole Victorian period.

Owen Jones, an architect and colour theorist, slightly older than Morris, can also be considered a key figure of the second half of the century. Although he had published *Plans, Elevations, Sections and Details of the Alhambra* in 1842 and '45, and designed the decoration for the interior of the Crystal Palace in 1851, his great *œuvre*, *The Grammar of Ornament* did not appear until 1856. Its influence was felt all over the world, and Jones' advocacy of flat geometric ornament was brilliantly explained by the colour plates of this sumptuous work.

Bruce Talbert was another influential theorist, architect and writer. His *Gothic Forms* (1867) and *Examples of Ancient and Modern Furniture* (1876) were both,

within his terms of reference, pleas for rationalism, solidity and fitness for purpose.

And finally Charles Eastlake, whose book *Hints on Household Taste* (London, 1868; Boston, 1872), suggested a style of furnishing reminiscent of Talbert, but cruder, more rustic, more basic. His name has been adopted in the United States to describe a whole range of furniture and decoration, although in fact most of what is nowadays known in America as Eastlake is much more easily associated with the style of Talbert, or is at least somewhere between the two.

There are in any case a number of differences between the course of taste in the United States and that in Great Britain during the Victorian period. The development of the two countries did not run parallel, and it was not until the very end of the century that American design began to be influential in England.

Elaboration to Mechanization in the United States

As the enthusiasm for the Neoclassical began to wane in America, much later than it had done in England, taste turned towards the Neo-Rococo much as it already had in Europe. The man who seems to symbolize the Rococo Revival in America is the New York cabinet-maker Henry Belter, whose furniture, often composed of curved laminated rosewood sections, is of an elaboration and exaggeration which are almost unknown elsewhere and which give it a uniquely American flavour. Various other American furniture-makers such as Charles A. Baudouine, in New York, and Prudent Mallard, in New Orleans, were making similar pieces in the 1850s, but none of them, or any maker outside the United States, displayed anything approaching Belter's virtuosity.

The American Civil War (1861–65) brought about the closure of many of the smaller manufacturers of furniture for economic reasons, and the eventual recovery in terms of industrial expansion completely revolutionized the composition of the furniture industry. Mechanical processes overtook even more of the traditional skill of the craftsman than they had before the War. By the 1870s manufacturers in the Mid West had virtually eliminated the smaller East Coast firms, and Grand Rapids, Michigan, and Cincinnati, Ohio, had become the principal centres of the trade, supplying their goods to the whole of the continent.

During the middle years of the century, a curious and characteristic American development took place in furniture manufacture, in the attention given to mechanical pieces, and also in ones which made specific use of the new technology. Cast iron, papier mâché and laminated wood had all been used experimentally in Europe as well as the United States, but no country's industry took such an interest in dual-purpose and convertible pieces. Several factors appear to have contributed to this, and undoubtedly the development of long-distance railway travel played a large part. Trains which could be lived in for several days required numerous space-saving devices which were unknown even on shipboard, together with provision for extra comfort in adjustable and well-sprung seating.

America's social structure was a great deal more democratized than its European equivalent, and the idea that travelling comfort should be within the reach of everyone found much earlier acceptance. The first American sleeping-cars appeared in 1857, whereas there were no regular services in the British Isles until 1873. Probably the greatest influence, however, was the enormous influx of people into the cities during the period

Front bay window of the music room at the Morse-Libby House, 109 Danforth St., Maine, 1858. A characteristic detail showing a fully developed Neo-Rococo decorative scheme.

of industrial expansion which followed the end of the Civil War.

Large numbers of families had, of necessity, to occupy small apartments in rapidly expanding towns, and chairs that would convert into beds, sofas which could turn into tables, or chests of drawers which concealed washing arrangements all helped to maximize space standards that were basically inadequate. It is interesting to observe the way in which the social and psychological climate of the period sometimes led to the acceptance of subterfuges that were curious and even rather ridiculous. This was particularly apparent in furniture that was designed to conceal beds. The bed was a suggestive and rather doubtful object to the developing bourgeois mentality, but while it might be acceptable to disguise it when raised end-on against the wall as an elaborate wardrobe-cupboard, to make it look like an upright piano seems to our present-day thinking to be venturing into the realms of idiotic fantasy.

Certain types of furniture which made use of new technical processes were equally popular on both sides of the Atlantic. Tables with cast-iron bases were first made in England in the late 1830s, and became very popular throughout the remainder of the century, especially where they were to receive particularly hard use, in cafés or pubs, or out of doors. Metal beds, popular from the 1850s onwards, were made in cast and wrought iron, and later in brass or steel tubing. They provided a sanitary answer to the tendency of wooden bedsteads to harbour vermin, and there was a period between the middle of the century and its end during which a very considerable prejudice existed against wooden beds and thick, dusty hangings.

22

One type of 'technological' furniture which was a particular favourite with the American public, and which found little parallel in Europe, was the specially designed 'comfortable' chair. Numerous devices were perfected for 'digestive' chairs, adjustable chairs, reclining chairs and rocking chairs, and most of them made use of metal springs, ratchets, levers, cast-iron bases or revolving supports. The influence of the railway is very apparent, and many of the pieces might have been taken straight out of a Pullman drawing-room car. There was little equivalent enthusiasm in England, and most English patent furniture was intended solely for the use of invalids.

Bentwood furniture, the most famous example of technical specialization in this field, is one of the best instances of nineteenth-century ingenuity properly applied to practical uses. Although it was used in homes and business establishments all over the United States, it was neither an American invention nor was it made there until after the original patents had expired in 1869.

The technique of bending wood sections in application to furniture manufacture was first developed by a German named Michael Thonet, who started a small factory for making conventional furniture at Boppard on the Rhine, and who began experimenting with methods to economize on labour and materials in 1830. After an unsuccessful start, he moved to Vienna in 1842 and set up another factory in 1849. From then on he never looked back.

The opening up of the United States after the middle of the century provided an insatiable market for pieces of furniture which were cheap, strong, light and easily transportable, and bentwood fulfilled all these requirements perfectly. Furthermore, the pieces themselves, mainly chairs (including the famous 'American' rocking chair) but also tables, stools, hat stands, all displayed a delightfully inventive elegance, and the snaky convolutions of the circular sections exerted an appeal to the senses which, coupled with their qualities of strength and durability, have ensured the popularity of this furniture right up to the present day. It was Thonet, not the idealist William Morris, who created something approaching the 'decorative, noble, popular art' which Morris hoped to produce.

The Influence of the Collectors

By the mid 1860s the taste for the Neo-Rococo was on the decline in the United States as well as in England and the Belter firm, almost synonymous with the revived Louis Quinze, went bankrupt in 1867. In England the influence of Bruce Talbert and the designs of such Medieval or traditional stylists as the architects William Burges, Philip Webb and Norman Shaw was evident in the increasing rectangularity of decoration and ensembles throughout the 1860s and '70s. This was accompanied by a revival of interest in Gothic, Medieval and Elizabethan styles of furniture, which were thought to be especially appropriate to the large numbers of country houses that were then being built; and this interest in its turn reflected the ideas and attitudes of William Morris and his circle. The new enthusiasm for the artifacts of the past which was fostered by so many of the progressive designers at this time led, though indirectly, to the stimulation of a passion which was to grip many people in the western world during the last third of the nineteenth century, and this was for the collection of antique furniture and works of art.

King George IV was one of the first notable connoisseurs to acquire antiques, and he amassed a large number of splendid seventeenth- and eighteenth-century objects, many of which were bought specially for him in Paris during the difficult years around the end of the eighteenth century. Nevertheless, most early collectors tended to amass oddments and curios rather than old furniture specifically for use. Two leaders stand out in the new cult, however, each of a rather different kind. One is, William Morris, whose love for old craftsmanship and admiration for the pre-industrial way of life naturally led him to want to surround himself with objects from the past. His knowledge and taste spread to the other members of his circle, and it could be said that a whole generation of collectors in the last third of the century followed where they led.

The other important figure was the Empress Eugénie of France, whose admiration for Marie Antoinette directed her interest towards eighteenth-century decoration and furniture. Her rooms in the imperial palaces were redecorated as accurate, though elaborated, copies of eighteenth-century models, and much genuine eighteenth-century furniture was brought back and sometimes embellished with extra ormolu mounts or new inlay to bring it into line with the current lavish preference. The *mobilier* was then supplemented with new pieces which copied the originals much more closely than had previously been the practice.

In both the United States and Great Britain the decorating and furnishing trades began to turn their skills increasingly towards the production of interiors, furniture and textiles which followed precedent much more accurately than before, and in some cases even making copies of such exactitude that it is now difficult to distinguish them from the genuine article. The comparison of, say, an English chair in the Elizabethan style of the 1840s and one in the Adams manner of the 1880s shows vividly how much attitudes had changed. The first bears no resemblance whatsoever to a genuine Elizabethan chair (although it is no worse for that), and merely has a few grafted-on architectural ornaments to give it 'period'. The second is a close

Side elevation of a dining room in the Jacobean style from the influential book, Examples of Ancient and Modern Furniture, *by B. J. Talbert (1836-81), 1876. Much of the furniture in what is known as the Eastlake style has much more in common with the designs of Talbert than with those of its namesake and assumed originator, Charles Eastlake (1836-1906).*

Blue drawing room at Thoresby Hall, Nottinghamshire, built by Anthony Salvin (1799-1881), 1873. A rich example of the English Neo-Renaissance style, which was usually rather closer to the original than was generally the practice in America.

Dining room at Marble House, Newport, Rhode Island, to the designs of Richard Morris Hunt (1827-95) for William K. Vanderbilt, completed 1893. Towards the end of the nineteenth century several millionaires on both sides of the Atlantic had interiors created for them that were fairly accurate interpretations of seventeenth- or eighteenth-century French palaces. Hunt created such a room here, the point being emphasised by the portrait of Louis XIV as a young man hanging above the fireplace.

interpretation of the original, albeit sometimes with a few noticeable differences.

A particular and curious habit of the makers of commercial copies in the latter part of the nineteenth century was to increase the general size of the piece while making the parts thinner or smaller, and although much of the carving and detail would be accurate and well made, the eventual result would frequently appear spindly when compared with the original model.

The London firm of Gillow's specialized in making copies of antique furniture, and they would also undertake to reproduce historic interiors with panelling, plasterwork and fittings. The fashion was also adopted in the United States, perhaps a little later than in England, and many firms on both sides of the Atlantic began to supply the growing demand. It is interesting to observe that of all the trends and fashions set by the nineteenth century, that of collecting antiques and furnishing the home with them remains universally acceptable in all the English-speaking countries.

Tendencies towards Fussiness

In England, by the mid 1870s, even middle-of-the-road taste had moved from the Neo-Louis Seize style of the '60s into a highly eclectic phase, based more closely on Renaissance precedent than any other. The main characteristics of furniture in the last twenty-five years of the century are an increasing reduction in the size of the parts, often leading to flimsy construction, and an ever-growing elaboration of small details and contrasting inlay, often composed of several different coloured woods.

The late Charles Handley-Read and the late H. S. Goodhart-Rendel have respectively called these styles 'Free-Renaissance' and 'Bracket and Overmantel' and it is certainly evident that whatever the so-called provenance (and this could be Renaissance, Adams, French or what you will) the profusion of small turnery, the introduction of little shelves and brackets, the proliferation of panels of bevelled mirror-glass or decorative inlay, were all universal in application. The whole scale of interior decoration became progressively smaller, wallpaper and textile patterns tighter and less flowing, mouldings less bold and more fussy, structural elements thinner and more attenuated. It might, incident-

ally, be suggested that the emancipation of women and their increasing say in the decoration of the home had a bearing on the frequent use of the words dainty, quaint or artistic to describe desirable attributes in contemporary literature about the fashionable middle-class interior. Even progressive designers such as the architect E. W. Godwin, whose furniture in an Anglo-Japanese style exerted a strong influence on advanced taste in the 1870s and '80s, was still not free of the general trend towards fragility and spindliness, although his standard was far above contemporary commercial output.

The early and mid-Victorian desire for massive quality and boldly defined shapes seems to have completely dissipated itself by the 1880s, and the illustrations in *Decoration and Furniture of Town Houses* by Robert Edis, first published in 1881, show the end-of-the-century English domestic interior with great vividness. The Art Nouveau style, although it had to a certain degree been absorbed into textile and glass design by the late 1890s, was never part of the English scene to the extent that it was on the Continent. Not even the most advanced designs of Voysey, Mackmurdo, Ashbee or Mackintosh displayed the free-flowing, sinuous forms to be found in contemporary and slightly later productions by Majorelle, Horta, Guimard or Gallé in France. Rather did the English school develop a style of rectangular forms, upon which the flowing elements of the Art Nouveau vocabulary were applied as decorative additions.

Prosperity and the Renaissance Revival

The development of design in the United States during the years after the end of the Civil War in 1865 until the end of the century, took a somewhat different course from that in England. The revived Louis Seize style, very similar to its English equivalent, superseded the Neo-Rococo during the 1860s, as it did in Great Britain, and the New York firm of Marcotte was prominent in the production of high-quality furniture in this style. Gaining in popularity alongside this, however, was a particularly American type of revived Renaissance style, further from the original than its European counterpart, and therefore much more truly of the nineteenth century.

Massive, elaborate, rectangular rather than flowing, pieces in this style were ornamented with projected panels of contrasting veneers, gilded, incised lines and a profusion of turned ornamental

ABOVE *Drawing room at 18 Stafford Terrace, London, furnished for himself by Linley Sambourne, an artist who worked for* Punch, *1870s. The fashionable clutter of the closing years of the nineteenth century is much in evidence, but Sambourne's advanced taste led him to collect genuine antiques rather than the usual copies.*

LEFT *Drawing room at the house of D. G. Rossetti, 16 Cheyne Walk, London, painted by H. Treffry Dunn, 1882. Rossetti's close contact with the Arts and Crafts Movement and the Pre-Raphaelites naturally led him to favour a scheme of furnishing that was somewhat out of the ordinary at the time. Within the house, which was early eighteenth century, he collected antiques and objets d'art for their artistic and intrinsic value, and in his drawing room he assembled seventeenth-century chairs, Chinese tables, Georgian silver and Eastern rugs in an aesthetic unity that had little in common with contemporary taste.*

25

knobs. It seems to have been a style which was perfectly in accord with the growing prosperity of the post Civil War years, and when set in an interior that was fitted up in the same manner, this furniture was undeniably impressive.

The Lockwood Mansion, at Norwalk, Connecticut, was decorated in this fashion in 1864; the Hatch family were portrayed by Eastman Johnson in 1871 (see p. 18) seated in the Renaissance drawing room of their Park Avenue mansion. These were the houses of men who had 'arrived' and their interiors achieved a sumptuous unity which seems quintessential of the American scene at the time. The style was exactly suited to the ideals of railway magnates, expanding frontiers, industrialization and progress.

It is nevertheless interesting to compare the best examples of such furniture, made by John Jelliff of Newark, Berkey & Gay, of Grand Rapids, Thomas Brooks or Leon Marcotte, with some of the crude and perfunctory productions of the less reputable Grand Rapids firms, and one can see that its very adaptability in terms of bastardisation must surely have been one of the most important factors which led to the fall of the Renaissance style from favour. Furthermore, a new generation of buying public was growing up in the United States by the 1880s and '90s and they had not the same need for the ostentatious and massive display that their parents required to demonstrate their position in society.

Simplicity versus Elaboration in the United States

Innovators such as William Morris and, later, Charles Eastlake, had had a following in the United States all through the 1860s and '70s, and the notion gradually dawned that quality does not reside in mass, that taste bears little relation to elaboration, that good design is not achieved merely by mingling many materials.

A considerable swing was evident during the last quarter of the century, and it led to a general tidying up and simplification in almost all fields of design. The Eastlake style was much popularized by firms such as Kimbel & Cabus and Mitchell & Rammelsberg, and the Centennial Exhibition of 1876 in Fairmount Park, Philadelphia, featured many examples of this style.

While the beautiful furniture produced by the New York firm of Herter Bros in the 1870s and '80s was not to everyone's taste, these lovely, bland pieces are indicative of the general trend towards simpler outlines and less elaboration of

TOP Octagon Boudoir Adams Style, *furnished by Gillow's for the Princess of Wales' Pavilion at Paris, illustrated in* Decoration and Furniture of Town Houses *by Robert W. Edis (1839-1927), 1881. The mid-century enthusiasm for heavy mass and bold shape had largely given way by the 1880s to an interest in the kind of feminine elegance that the revived eighteenth-century styles, with the appropriate satinwood furniture, seemed to offer.*

ABOVE *Entrance hall at the Carson House, Eureka, California, built by the architects Samuel and Jos. C. Newsom of San Francisco, 1884-85. Like the Neo-Italianate in England, the Neo-Renaissance had a long period of popularity in America. Whatever stylistic allegiances this interior might have, however, it richly expresses the taste of its lumber-baron owner.*

ornament. Further evidence of a desire for a return to simplicity is shown in the influence exerted by the architect H. H. Richardson, whose brilliant, though self conscious, essays in reformed decoration had tremendous impact. His designs relied on the use of exposed and expressed natural materials, which might be carved, but which carried little applied ornament, and his furniture was designed to harmonize into such surroundings. Judicious, small areas of elaborate carving were used to offset adjacent contrasting areas of linear incision, repeat pattern or flat plank, and all were executed with the utmost precision in 'honest' native woods – it must have seemed revolutionary.

The ideas of Richardson and his contemporaries and followers were not universally accepted, however, and much of the average taste remained firmly anchored to revival styles for at least another twenty years. A great deal of contemporary literature, and especially the magazines such as *The Decorator and Furnisher* and those specifically aimed at a female readership, went on advocating various interpretations of past styles in decoration very similar to those which were popular in Great Britain. All through the 1880s and '90s, furniture firms, especially the more mass-market orientated Grand Rapids companies went on turning out pieces and suites which can only be considered as spindly caricatures of Chinese Chippendale, Louis Seize or whatever models that they purported to follow.

The interest in elaboration for its own sake, which might have been dismissed merely as the expression of the unsure but expanding society of the immediate post Civil War years, still held a firm place in the preferences of the increasingly prosperous middle class right up till the early 1900s and beyond. At the World's Columbian Exposition, held in Chicago in 1893, some 'dying but dogged holdouts of High Victorian design' were still to be found among the exhibits. Particularly excessive were some overstuffed chairs and sofas, which were fringed, tufted, buttoned and ruched in a manner that can only be described as hysterical, and which make curious contemporaries to the early furniture of Frank Lloyd Wright or the elegant sophistication of the output of Tiffany & Co.

Wallpaper and the New Methods of Production

It is difficult to suggest a complete picture of the appearance and feel of any period, and to isolate the objects which

exert the most influence over it. Furniture, which forms the largest group of movable items, plays a very important part and certainly has a most conclusive rôle in defining character. Colour and pattern on painted surfaces, applied decoration, textiles or natural materials are equally important, and indeed throughout the nineteenth century all the industries connected with furnishing and decoration kept their productions in line with the general trends of contemporary taste.

The characteristic of totality seems more evident during the nineteenth century than at any other period in history, and it has the effect of compensating to a great extent for the decline in quality that mechanization brought to certain fields of design.

Technological modifications in production methods were nevertheless essential

Library at Château-sur-Mer, Newport, Rhode Island. The Neo-Rococo decoration is much closer to the original models than many contemporary interiors and was possibly intended as a setting for a collection of genuine eighteenth-century French furniture.

to enable output to keep pace with the constantly growing world markets for furniture, textiles, glass, china, metalwork and domestic appliances. The wallpaper industry, for instance, was transformed in the late 1830s by the English invention of a machine to supersede traditional hand-printing methods. It made use of rollers of the type that had already been perfected for calico printing, and, together with 'endless' paper produced by the Fourdrinier method, allowed almost unlimited cheap produc-

tion and variation of designs. Indeed, it seemed as though 'a new race of wallpaper men took the field, and for a time the mechanics who had launched the new methods of production were more important than the artists who created the designs'.

During the 1840s and '50s there was a definite decline in wallpaper design. Many *trompe l'œil*, three-dimensional effects were produced showing landscape views, simulated panelling or tapestries, even groups of carving or trophies which deceived the eye of the viewer until he moved close to them. None of this concentration on technique gave proper exploitation to the flat-pattern and repeat potentialities of a necessarily flat material.

A. W. N. Pugin's designs for the papers in the new Houses of Parliament in London and for the firm of Crace, by

Turkish room (opposite) and dressing-room (above) from the John D. Rockefeller House at 4 West 54th Street, New York. When Rockefeller bought the house from Mrs Arabella Worsham in 1884, these interiors had been there probably since about 1880. While the surface decoration and the colouring are still of the utmost richness, a distinct trend towards simplification can be observed in the forms that are basically rectangular and the lighter scale of the furniture. Museum of the City of New York and Brooklyn Museum.

whom he was retained, are in marked contrast to the general trend of the '40s, and he displayed a fine appreciation of the limitations of the medium which lifts his productions high above those of many of his contemporaries.

The name of William Morris stands out as the best-known leader of the revolution in wallpaper and textile design of the last third of the century, and he produced his first wallpaper, *Rose Trellis,* in 1862 for manufacture by his firm. Morris was not the only important figure however, and Owen Jones, E. W. Godwin, Bruce Talbert, Walter Crane and Lewis F. Day were all designing papers for most of the important firms during the 1870s and '80s. Their various styles, though reflecting the individual talents of each of them, nicely emphasized their appreciation of the two-dimensional character of paper and the effects which may best be achieved by repetition of pattern.

The opening up of Japan to Western trade in 1856 permitted the importation into Europe of a particularly tough paper, the fashion for which led to the invention of a wall covering which combined repeat pattern with an embossed surface. *Lincrusta* was first produced in 1877 and *Anaglypta* in 1887, and both became very popular towards the end of the century.

Wallpaper making was, of course, not by any means the only industry which was influenced by technical changes in production methods during the nineteenth century, but it certainly exerted a great influence over the appearance of interior decoration, especially that which was favoured by the great, growing middle classes. Nearly every branch of the domestic and fine arts underwent some drastic upheaval during this fascinating century, and this will be clearly evident from the following chapters.

'The Devaluation of Space'

While the changes, improvements and advances in the technology of domestic appliances fundamentally altered the physical quality of life, they had little effect on the appearance of average domestic surroundings. One of the fundamental differences in appearance, and that which makes a nineteenth-century interior so unlike any other, was caused by the phenomenon called by Dr Giedion 'the devaluation of space'. A comparison of contemporary views of Victorian interiors with those of previous centuries will show a completely altered arrangement in the disposition of furniture which became progressively more untidy and informal as the century advanced, with pieces standing about in the centre of the floor in such eventual confusion that it must have been difficult in some cases even to cross the room.

During the seventeenth and eighteenth centuries, and even in the early nineteenth century, furniture had been placed round the walls in a formal and symmetrical manner, but this had changed completely by the 1830s. A number of reasons can be found for this radical change in the taste of the average person towards the character of his habitat.

In the first place, in a philosophical context, the early nineteenth century saw a major attack on the old, static, aristocratic idea, with its attendant formality and set codes of behaviour. The emerging middle classes inevitably felt little connection in their own lives with the past in this form, and the changed appearance of their background reflects these changing values.

Secondly, the Romantic Movement brought in its wake a different set of attitudes, and emotional relations began to be considered more valuable than formal etiquette; revolutionary ideas of change came to threaten previously immutable notions of social order. Contemporary fashions in clothes, architectural styles and literature all show the trend, as did the new fashion for romantically leaning and lounging. Madame Recamier could never have reclined so interestingly without her *chaise longue,* and new ideas of posture required new types of furniture placed in convenient positions. While *chaises longues* and other comfortable, relaxing furniture had of course been produced in the eighteenth century, it was only during the nineteenth century that it became permissible to relax in romantic attitudes in the drawing room, which hitherto had been regarded as an apartment of the strictest formality.

In the grandest rooms a new piece of central furniture known as the ottoman (or *borne* by the French) began to be placed in the middle of the floor, for the repose of the guests, and this piece achieved an extraordinary degree of monumental importance in the second half of the century. The days when only titled ladies were permitted to sit in an armchair, and only princesses could sit by the fire (as was the practice at the eighteenth-century French court) were over, never to return.

Finally, of course, technology also helped to break down the old, rigid codes. The development of the coil-spring and methods of overstuffing made really comfortable seat furniture a possibility within the reach of all levels of society. New methods of constructing chairs facilitated the production of *chaises volantes* (literally, flying chairs), light pieces made of one of the lightweight timbers from Africa, or from bentwood, which could easily be moved by a guest to enable him to join another conversational group.

It became the practice to supplement the furniture in existing formal interiors with a whole host of light chairs, basket chairs and sprung chairs on easily moving castors. These were in turn complemented by 'occasional' tables, whatnots, reading tables, bookstands and sewing tables. All these in their turn could be loaded with the ever-increasing collection of objects and ornaments with which the nineteenth-century middle classes needed to surround themselves in order to display their taste, wealth, success and permanence.

The advancing century eventually saw the complete breakdown of the principle of formal furniture arrangement, and by the 1880s and '90s the tendency was for no piece to match another, nothing to be placed squarely in position, and everything to be informal, casual, crowded and irregular.

Colour, an Indication of the Victorian Mentality

Colours and tone values changed gradually throughout the century, and in order to appreciate Victorian colour schemes it is desirable to understand the thought processes behind them. One of the most important factors in design during the whole period was a desire at every level of society to imitate the one above. To this end everything was made to look as rich, costly and showy as it could be, and any method of increasing this would be pressed into service. Brick would be stuccoed to simulate stone, softwood would be grained to imitate hardwood, plaster would be marbleized, brass would be silverplated. Is this dishonest or merely expressive of a desire to improve the world as we find it? We are in no position to pass judgment, but the fact remains that this ingenuity had a fundamental and deep effect on every aspect of design.

During almost the whole of the Victorian period hardly any decorated surface was ever painted white: that would have suggested pigsty limewash and was not to be entertained for a moment. Even progressive and openminded men such as Owen Jones or the encyclopedist J. C. Loudon merely advised the use of small areas of white to set off other, richer, more attractive and more interesting colours.

Hall at the Bell House, Newport, Rhode Island built by McKim, Mead & White, 1882-3. The architects McKim and White were pupils of H. H. Richardson (1838-86). At the Bell House they carried on their master's principles in the flat, carved decoration of the panelling, the expression of natural materials and the absence of applied ornament.

Although the interiors which were produced by the famous London firm of Liberty & Co. in the 1890s made great use of white paint, particularly on their fitted furniture and cupboards, this was always contrasted with patterned and strongly coloured wallpapers and textiles. It was not until the very end of the century that the influence of innovators such as the architect Philip Webb began to filter down to the mass public, and white paint began to be used on interior woodwork and panelling in the manner that became so universal in the twentieth century.

Ian Grant

Glossary

Institutions, styles and events referred to throughout the encyclopedia are listed here with definitions.

Art Nouveau
International style evolving simultaneously in various European and American capitals in the 1890s. It might be regarded as the only truly original Victorian decorative style, characterized by a graceful, attenuated interpretation of natural forms and the use of materials and techniques neglected in previous decades of the nineteenth century.

Art Union
In 1836 the Art Union of London was inaugurated, recognized by Parliament in 1846; this was followed by the establishment of similar organizations elsewhere in Great Britain. Members drew lots for works of art, principally reproductions in bronze or parian, or prints of Royal Academy exhibits, commissioned by the Art Union. The objects from these editions often bear Art Union inscriptions.

Art Workers' Guild
Founded in 1884, by W. R. Lethaby (1857–1931) among others, to promote contact between craftsmen working in various media. Their activities were taken over and enlarged upon by the Arts and Crafts Exhibition Society.

Arts and Crafts Movement
Essentially English manifestation which began in the 1880s as a direct result of the beliefs of William Morris (1834–96), principally that there should be greater co-ordination between the various branches of the applied and decorative arts and that the quality of design and craftsmanship should not be subordinated to the requirements of mass production. Major contributions to the doctrines and practices of the Movement were made by A. H. Mackmurdo (1851–1942), C. R. Ashbee (1863–1942), W. R. Lethaby and W. A. S. Benson (1854–1924), who was largely responsible for

the foundation of the Arts and Crafts Exhibition Society in 1888.

Eastlake style
American style of interior decoration based on the interpretation of *Hints on Household Taste* by Charles Lock Eastlake (1836–1906), first published in Great Britain in 1868 and in the United States in 1872. Contemporary with and related to the ARTS AND CRAFTS MOVEMENT.

Exhibitions
Uniquely Victorian in conception were the international expositions held in Europe and the United States to display the arts, manufactures and natural resources of the contributing countries. Some were government sponsored, others were paid for privately or through public companies; at some prizes were awarded. The Great Exhibition in Hyde Park, London, was the first of its kind, and the Crystal Palace, designed by Sir Joseph Paxton (1801–65), was the prototype for later exhibition constructions elsewhere. Much of the most elaborate and exaggerated in Victorian design resulted from a desire for display at the exhibitions, and they were also responsible for the dissemination of styles and new methods of manufacture. They were an important factor in the interchange of ideas between the two continents. The principal exhibitions held during the reign of Queen Victoria were:

1851 London Great Exhibition
1853 Dublin International Exhibition
1853 New York Crystal Palace Exhibition
1855 Paris Exposition
1862 London International Exhibition
1867 Paris Exposition
1871 London International Exhibition
1872 London International Exhibition
1873 London International Exhibition
1873 Vienna International Exhibition
1876 Philadelphia Centennial Exhibition
1878 Paris Exposition
1887 Manchester Royal Jubilee Exhibition
1889 Paris Exposition
1893 Chicago World's Columbian Exposition
1900 Paris Universal Exposition
1900 Vienna Secession Exhibition
1901 Glasgow International Exhibition

Glasgow School
Charles Rennie Mackintosh (1868–1928), Herbert MacNair (1868–1955) and their respective wives, Margaret Macdonald (1865–1933) and Frances Macdonald (1874–1921), known as The Four were the isolated creators in the 1890s and 1900s of a style of decoration in architecture, interior design, furniture, metalwork, jewelry and textiles. Ignored in London, they were claimed elsewhere as early exponents of ART NOUVEAU. A plain, elongated fragility is a characteristic of their style.

Guild and School of Handicraft
Founded in 1888 by C. R. Ashbee to encourage 'traditional workshop knowledge,' co-operation between the designer and craftsmen and between craftsmen in various trades – silversmiths, jewelers, metalworkers and furniture makers. Its products were first shown at the exhibition of the Arts and Crafts Exhibition Society in 1889. In 1898 it became a limited company and in 1902 moved from London to Chipping Camden, Gloucestershire. It was wound up in 1907. A Guild of Handicraft was founded in Birmingham in 1895 by Arthur Dixon (1856–1929).

Shakers
The United Society of Believers in Christ's Second Appearing, whose members lived in self-sufficient celibate communities of farmers and craftsmen in New York, New England and the Mid West. The Society was founded in 1776 by Mother Ann Lee (1736–84), whose beliefs regarding simplicity, cleanliness and usefulness are apparent in their furniture and woodwares.

Houses Open to the Public with Victorian Interiors

Great Britain
Alnwick Castle, Alnwick, Northumberland
Brodick Castle, Isle of Arran
Cardiff Castle, Cardiff, South Glamorgan
Castell Coch, Whitchurch, South Glamorgan
Felbrigg Hall, near Cromer, Norfolk
Knebworth House, Knebworth, Hertfordshire
Osborne House, Isle of Wight

Thoresby Hall, Ollerton, Nottinghamshire
Waddesdon Manor, near Aylesbury, Buckinghamshire
Wightwick Manor, Wolverhampton, West Midlands

United States of America
Asa Packer House, Jim Thorpe, Pennsylvania
The Breakers, Newport, Rhode Island
Château-sur-Mer (Wetmore Mansion), Newport, Rhode Island
Munson-Williams-Procter Institute (Fountain Elms), Utica, New York
Gallier House, New Orleans, Louisiana
Lansdowne, Natchez, Mississippi
Lockwood-Mathews Mansion (Norwalk Mansion), Norwalk, Connecticut
Lyndhurst, Tarrytown, New York
Morse-Libby House (Victoria Mansion), Portland, Maine
Roosevelt House, New York City, New York

Bibliography

Art Journal Illustrated Catalogue of the Industry of All Nations, London, 1851

DAVIDSON, MARSHALL B. (editor). *The American Heritage History of American Antiques from the Revolution to the Civil War,* New York, 1968

DAVIDSON, MARSHALL B. (editor). *The American Heritage History of American Antiques from the Civil War to World War I,* New York, 1969

DOWNING, A. J. *The Architecture of Country Houses,* New York and Philadelphia, 1842

EASTLAKE, CHARLES LOCK. *Hints on Household Taste in Furniture, Upholstery, and Other Details,* London, 1868, Boston, 1872

EDIS, ROBERT W. *Decoration and Furniture of Town Houses,* London, 1881

HITCHCOCK, HENRY-RUSSELL. *Architecture, 19th and 20th Centuries,* London, 1958

KERR, ROBERT. *The Gentleman's House,* London, 1871

LOUDON, J. C. *An Encyclopedia of Cottage, Farm, and Villa Architecture and Furniture,* London, 1833

Metropolitan Museum of Art. *19th-Century America,* Catalogue of the exhibition held 16 April – 7 September, 1970, New York, 1970

Furniture

BRITISH

The Victorian period witnessed the unprecedented economic and social changes of the Industrial Revolution and an extraordinary increase in the population of England and Wales which doubled every fifty years after the first official census of 1801, when nine millions were recorded. A vast new market for furniture was thus created, for never before had so many English people the means to acquire and furnish a place of their own. A new class of patron, new materials and new production methods all came at a time when the long reign of Classical taste was ending.

To fill the vacuum a number of historical revivals, characterized by considerable eclecticism, came into fashion, most of them lasting until the end of the century. They reflected in part the Romantic Revival in literature and in part the vogue of the Picturesque, which encouraged asymmetry and a multiplicity of styles and helped to break down the formal arrangement of furniture.

Historicism also had a sentimental basis: the association of ideas, which saw the beauty of an object not in its intrinsic qualities but in those associated with it. The Gothic, Tudor and Elizabethan Revivals, for instance, were held to recall stirring periods in English history when the national character – and the nineteenth century was the age of nationalism – was at its sturdiest. The association of ideas underlies the Victorian craze for symbolic ornament which, with increasing elaboration, reached its peak at the Great Exhibition in 1851. After that date progressive designers applied themselves to the task of developing styles that would more truly meet the needs of the new industrial society. As England was the birthplace

OPPOSITE *Side chair, Charles Rohlfs, Buffalo, New York, c. 1896. Oak, ht 4 ft 6 in (1·37 m). A unique high-style American Art Nouveau piece. Art Museum, Princeton University.*

of the Industrial Revolution, their efforts were watched with great interest by foreign designers.

English furniture manufacturers, however, continued to cater for a largely undiscriminating mass market, exploiting novelty for its own sake. There is thus a constant division in Victorian furniture between the large-scale output of commercial producers, prompted mainly by considerations of cheapness, and the attempts of reforming designers to face the challenge of the nineteenth century. Until about 1860 there was also another important factor in furniture design: the search for comfort, common to all classes. Upholstery materials, now available in abundance, concealed the former graceful lines of seating furniture, and heavy patterned fabrics covered tables and formed draperies in the increasingly cluttered-up interiors. In the words of the Juries' Report on the International Exhibition of 1862, 'It would be an absurdity to sacrifice convenience to elegance.'

The Furniture Industry

In spite of a vast increase in output there was surprisingly little alteration in the structure of the furniture industry in Queen Victoria's reign. There were naturally important changes in the scale of production and in location as the new industrial cities developed their own furniture firms and challenged London's traditional lead. But Victorian mass production of furniture must not be equated (as it often has been) with the fully mechanized factory system of the twentieth century. Woodworking machines of all kinds had been invented by Sir Samuel Bentham as early as 1793 and these had long been used for the preliminary processes of furniture making. Yet until the 1870s the circular saw was the only machine that could be said to be in general use, and then only in urban areas. Various shaping machines pro-

duced the decorative details on furniture and from 1845 Jordan's carving machine turned out repetitive carved ornament cheaply, though its use was countered to some extent by a revival of handcarving. But essentially Victorian furniture was a hand product, whether from the high-class London and provincial shops or from the numerous small workshops of Shoreditch, the home of cheap ready-made articles.

The high regard accorded by foreigners to English furniture in the Victorian period surprises those accustomed to consider the age as representative of a generally abysmal standard of design. By the end of the century the prestige of English designers stood very high indeed. From 1896, for instance, Hermann Muthesius was attached to the German Embassy in London for seven years to study English architecture and domestic design, and his appreciative reports form the first serious investigation ever made of the subject. Muthesius was later, in 1907, to help found the Deutscher Werkbund, forerunner of the famous Bauhaus.

The interest of other countries is confirmed by the considerable export trade in English furniture. Naturally the Colonies offered a ready market for furniture from home, but exports went to all parts of the world and significantly there was a steady rise in the trade with Europe, where competition could be expected to be keenest. The value of furniture exports in 1885, at a period of low prices, reached the very considerable sum of almost £650,000, Europe's share being then about one third.

The Grecian, Elizabethan and Louis Quatorze Styles

Early Victorian furniture styles are described and illustrated in John C. Loudon's monumental *An Encyclopedia of Cottage, Farm and Villa Architecture and Furniture*, first published in 1833 and

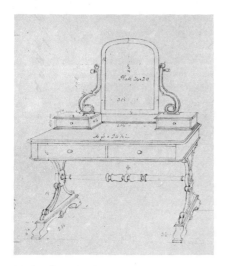

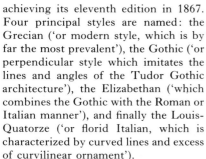

Design for a birch dressing table, Gillow & Co., 1865. Founded in 1695, the firm made all types of furniture in the Victorian period, most of it marked and numbered. Westminster Public Library

Chiffonier and detail from a drawer showing the marks of the maker, James Lamb of Manchester (1840-99), c. 1870. Hungarian-ash veneer with balusters and stringing of ebonized wood, ht 4 ft 3½ in (1·3 m). A commercial piece in light-coloured wood. Victoria and Albert Museum.

Armchair in the Louis Quatorze style, Holland & Sons for Osborne House, Isle of Wight, 1845-50. Satinwood, carved and gilded. The firm also supplied furniture to Balmoral. Osborne House.

achieving its eleventh edition in 1867. Four principal styles are named: the Grecian ('or modern style, which is by far the most prevalent'), the Gothic ('or perpendicular style which imitates the lines and angles of the Tudor Gothic architecture'), the Elizabethan ('which combines the Gothic with the Roman or Italian manner'), and finally the Louis-Quatorze ('or florid Italian, which is characterized by curved lines and excess of curvilinear ornament').

Grecian was the accepted term for the final phase of Classical taste, influenced by Regency forms. The description sub-Classical has been coined for debased ornament in this style, but much admirable furniture continued to be made, and simple, unobtrusive pieces were designed for dining rooms, clubs and public buildings, especially for rooms intended mainly for men's use. Anthemion crestings, astragal mouldings, fluting and Classical columns remained typical decorative features. The architect, Philip Hardwick, designed some fine mahogany furniture in this taste for Goldsmiths' Hall, London, in 1834. His dining chairs have broad shoulder boards with carved anthemion decoration, front legs of sabre form, and leather seats and back rests. Henry Whitaker designed Grecian furniture in the mid 1840s for the Conservative Club, London, and for Osborne House on the Isle of Wight, and leading firms, including Gillow's and Holland & Sons continued to produce pieces in this style until after 1850.

The Elizabethan style was in vogue from about 1825 to 1855 and incorporated, in the loose interpretation of the time, many features of late Stuart as well as of Tudor and Jacobean furniture. Spiral and ball turning and carved strapwork were particular features of the style. Attempts were made to apply the results of serious antiquarian research to this revival, seen in the Elizabethan suites at Mamhead, Devon, and at Scotney Castle, Kent, designed by the architect, Anthony Salvin, and some furniture was influenced by T. F. Hunt's scholarly *Exemplars of Tudor Architecture* (1830) and by Henry Shaw's *Specimens of Ancient Furniture* (1836).

Many firms made pseudo-Elizabethan furniture cheaply by reconstructing it from genuine old fragments with modern additions. The low cost of spiral and ball turning also encouraged manufacturers. Elizabethan designs predominate in Robert Bridgens' *Furniture with Candelabra and Interior Decoration* (1838) in which strapwork is a favoured decoration. This was another cheap form of ornament, described by George Fildes in 1844 as 'open work in panels, friezes, etc., which modern improvement in mechanics renders easy of adoption'. Nearly one-third of the illustrations in Henry Whitaker's *Treasury of Designs* (1847) is devoted to the Elizabethan taste. The style was much in evidence at

the Great Exhibition. The dining room at Charlecote Park, Warwickshire, has well-known examples, the chairs and firescreen, dating from the 1850s, having the spirally turned uprights universally associated with the style. A type of high-backed chair resembling late Stuart specimens became known as the Scott or Abbotsford chair.

Louis Quatorze was the name given to the somewhat indiscriminate revival of French eighteenth-century styles which were also variously described as Louis Quinze, Rococo, or, quite simply, the Old French style. These French revivals were the only ones of the time which were based on eighteenth-century styles, and the only ones which formed an integral part of the construction of furniture and were not merely decorative trimmings added to current forms. Early examples were the opulent chairs and settees introduced in the 1820s in the drawing room at Tatton Park, Cheshire.

While some competent designers – H. W. and A. Arrowsmith, for instance, in *The House Decorator and Painter's Guide* (1840) – distinguished between the 'ponderous and massive elegance' of the Louis Quatorze Baroque and the 'lightness, grace and variety' of the Louis Quinze Rococo, most pattern books borrowed freely from both reigns,

OPPOSITE *Longcase clock, signed on the dial, Gaze Bros, London, c. 1880. Silvered regulator with dead-beat escapement, the oak case in the Gothic Revival style, inlaid with birch and ebony, ht 8 ft 2 in (2·49 m). Christie's.*

as in Thomas King's *The Modern Style of Cabinet Work* (1829) in which 'as far as possible the English style is carefully blended with Parisian taste.' Scrolls and curves, often of massive proportions, and gilded decoration were features of this style.

The French taste was, however, attractively adapted for drawing rooms and ladies' bedrooms and boudoirs. When Hardwick designed Grecian furniture for Goldsmiths' Hall in 1834, he also designed for the drawing room there, to which ladies were admitted, dainty 'fly' chairs with curved shoulder boards and cabriole legs, painted white with gilded enrichments. Louis Quatorze was one more instance of French influence on English furniture styles which had been exercised for generations and was to continue, through exhibitions and immigrant craftsmen (especially after the French political troubles, of 1848, 1851 and 1870–1) until the end of Queen Victoria's reign.

The Gothic

Gothic was a truly national style, now receiving fresh impetus through the Romantic Movement in literature. Gothic furniture was usually produced by adding crockets, pinnacles, tracery and gables to existing forms or, as with other antiquarian revivals, by composing it from old panelling and carving. But while commercial producers remained obsessed with ornament which had an adverse effect on design, antiquarian study, fostered by Roman Catholics after the Catholic Emancipation Act of 1829, and by Tractarian Anglicans, yielded much accurate information on Medieval crafts and ornament.

The Gothic Revival was instrumental in producing the first great reformist furniture designer of the nineteenth-century, A. W. N. Pugin. In 1827, Pugin, aged fifteen, first began to work in the Gothic style, designing furniture for Windsor Castle. He later criticized his pieces as 'a complete burlesque of pointed design'. A significant change occurred after 1835, the date of his conversion to Roman Catholicism. Thereafter he devoted himself with tremendous energy to building churches,

OPPOSITE *Columned clock, Seth Thomas, Thomaston, c. 1860. Rosewood case with ringed gilded columns, panel of flowers and a game bird; rare double-decker striking wall clock with eight-day lyre movement. Strike One.*

ABOVE *Settee attributed to A. W. N. Pugin (1812-52), 1827-30. The pair to this parcel-gilded settee, part of the Windsor Castle Suite, is in the Queen's robing-room, Westminster. Pugin was the* first Gothic Revival designer in the nineteenth century to make a serious study of Medieval art. Sotheby's Belgravia.
BELOW *Gothic card table, English,* c. *1830-50. Sotheby's Belgravia.*

writing books and pamphlets, and designing furniture, wallpaper, textiles, jewelry, metalwork and stained glass.

Pugin was the first designer of the century to study the fundamental principles of Medieval art and he applied to furniture the two great rules of design laid down in his *The True Principles of Pointed or Christian Architecture* (1841): '1st, that there should be no features about a building which are not necessary for convenience, construction and propriety; 2nd, that all ornament should consist of enrichment of essential construction.' He emphasized rational structure and, contrary to established cabinet-making practice, he made no attempt to conceal all constructional elements. In his *Gothic Furniture in the Style of the Fifteenth Century* (1835) and in his architectural drawings, he often reveals the structural framework of furniture, marking the pegs, for instance, in framed construction. Moreover, his Gothic ornament is derived from natural forms, his *Floriated Ornament* (1849) identifying the original plants on which Gothic carvings were modelled.

Pugin's emphasis on honest construction openly displayed, itself an attractive feature of furniture, was to be repeated in the work of Burges, Morris, Webb, Lethaby, Voysey and other prominent Victorian furniture designers. The furniture designed by Pugin for Abney Hall, Cheshire, and for Scarisbrick Hall, Lancashire, illustrate his vigorous grasp of constructional and decorative detail, far removed from the imitation Gothic of his contemporaries.

The Great Exhibition

Though Pugin's Medieval Court at the Great Exhibition was widely admired, his views had little immediate effect on furniture design. The Exhibition itself showed all too clearly the proliferation of styles and decorative media which had become fashionable in the 1840s. Whitaker's book *Treasury of Designs*, one of the chief pattern books of the time, listed no less than seven different styles on its title page: Grecian, Italian, Renaissance, Louis Quatorze, Gothic, Tudor and Elizabethan, to which he added François Premier in the book, while his contemporaries also designed in the Moorish, Pompeian and other styles. Exhibitionism was indeed the keynote to much of the furniture shown in 1851. Overloaded with carving, indicating little grasp of the historical revivals which they were supposed to interpret, too many pieces showed a sad lapse in standards of design. Indeed, by 1850, the

Kenilworth Buffet, Cookes & Sons of Warwick, exhibited at the Great Exhibition, 1851. Oak, carved with scenes from Scott's novel. There was a revival of the skills of handcarving in England in the 1840s.

Balloon-back dining chair, English, mid-nineteenth century. Mahogany with moulded back, leaf-carved strap and upholstered seat. The popular balloon-back chair was of English origin and manufactured in a variety of slightly differing forms. Sotheby's Belgravia.

love of opulent curves, mounds of upholstery and above all of naturalistic carving had produced the first original Victorian style, named, appropriately, Naturalistic, which owed much to the Louis Quatorze and was eagerly taken up by manufacturers.

Exhibition furniture was not, however, typical of the time, though it has often been regarded as such. If the general

Table, Jennens & Bettridge, mid-nineteenth century. Papier mâché with mother-of-pearl and painted decoration. This Birmingham firm specialized in papier-mâché wares, from small articles to sizeable pieces of furniture. Sotheby's Belgravia.

standard remained undistinguished, it was often executed with skill and with the aid of first-class materials. An important factor in furniture design between 1830 and 1860 was the development of rounded forms, in both woodwork and upholstery, a measure of the growing concern for comfort. The right angles and straight lines of earlier Classical furniture went out of fashion. Sideboards, for instance, acquired rounded ends and a semi-circular mirror at the back. The most famous example of this trend is the balloon-back chair, an English invention, which seems to have emerged from a gradual blending of Grecian chairs in which the characteristic shoulder board took on a curved form, and chairs of Louis Quatorze style with their component curves and scrolls. The balloon back, acquiring cabriole legs in about 1850, became the standard dining- and drawing-room chair until about 1870. Another innovation was the *priedieu* chair, with tall back and low seat.

The Exhibition illustrated the willingness of designers to experiment with new materials, processes and technical devices. Metal bedsteads were replacing the traditional wooden four posters. Birmingham was rapidly becoming the main centre for the production of these and of brass fittings; it was also the principal centre for the production of papier mâché, the best known of the new materials. The most important makers, Jennens & Bettridge, produced a range of papier-mâché furniture as well as a mass of smaller articles such as trays and letter-racks. They also patented in 1825 their famous method of pearl-shell inlay. Papier mâché is not itself a satisfactory structural material and furniture made from it was mounted on a wooden or metal frame. Some chair backs, however, showed a novel handling of moulded plastic forms, heralding future developments. In 1851 bentwood furniture was also exhibited, made by the Austrian firm of Thonet and this was to enjoy a considerable vogue later in the century.

The Reformers

The depressing standard of taste shown by so many exhibits in 1851 provoked widespread criticism, and the International Exhibition of 1862 in London was intended to remedy the situation. It first brought to notice the name of William Morris through the exhibits of his firm, Morris, Marshall, Faulkner & Co., founded in 1861 (see p. 61). Morris' influence probably did more than anybody else's ultimately to re-

Buffet designed by Philip Webb (1831-1915) and made by Morris, Marshall, Faulkner & Co., founded in 1861. An illustration from Decoration and Furniture of Town Houses *by Robert Edis, 1881.*

form Victorian design though, ironically, he was not himself particularly interested in furniture. His aim was to counter the excesses of commercial manufacture with the production of well-designed household articles at a low price for the masses (in practice most of his firm's products

Sussex chair, Morris, Marshall, Faulkner & Co., after 1865. Stained oak with a rush seat. This is one of several patterns adapted for 'the Firm' from a traditional country chair and made in various stained woods. Sotheby's Belgravia.

were far from cheap). His views gradually became known through his writings and speeches, summed up in his famous dictum, 'have nothing in your house that you do not know to be useful or believe to be beautiful'. The firm's exhibits in 1862 were awarded a medal and were 'in the style of the middle ages'. This confirmed that the Gothic style was to remain the reformers' medium.

Morris divided his firm's furniture into two classes, 'the necessary workaday furniture . . . which should be of course well made and well proportioned, but simple to the last degree', and 'state furniture'. The latter – sideboards, cabinets, etc. – could be made elegant and elaborate with carving, inlay or painting. The celebrated St George Cabinet of mahogany and pinewood on an oak stand is perhaps Morris' best-known piece of 'state furniture'. It was designed by Philip Webb in 1861 and has panels painted by Morris with scenes from the life of St George. Painted surfaces, a significant swing away from heavy carving, were to be adopted by reformist designers. Webb also designed simpler pieces. His oak table, now in the Victoria and Albert Museum, London, fully reveals his constructional methods (in, for instance, the pegs which secure the framing of the legs) in the manner of Pugin. But it was Ford Madox Brown who designed some of the firm's most popular workaday pieces, including cottage-type chairs with rush seats and green-stained or ebonized frames, though he was not responsible for the Sussex chair, made from about 1865, which was based on a traditional country type and became the most famous of all the firm's products.

In the 1860s the hitherto neglected eighteenth century returned to favour among some of the best furniture designers. Curves and carved ornaments were replaced by rectilinear forms and inlay. Holland & Sons specialized in remarkable reproductions of French furniture of the *ancien régime*. Wright & Mansfield, also of London, gained a medal at the Paris Exhibition of 1867, for a superb satinwood cabinet in the Adam style. At the same time Art Furniture Manufacturers employed designers in the current fashion of applying art to furniture as an ornamental addition and, although this practice led to the usual debased commercial dissemination, it did produce a number of progressive designers. The most influential of these was probably Bruce Talbert, who was one of the earliest professional designers to gain a national reputation. Trained as an architect, he moved to London in 1865 to design furniture for Holland & Sons, for whom he designed

Cabinet on stand, Gillow & Co., late nineteenth century. Walnut with decoration carved and painted en grisaille. *This and the cabinet below right demonstrate the return to favour after 1860 of eighteenth-century styles. Sotheby's Belgravia.*

ABOVE RIGHT *Pet sideboard designed by Bruce Talbert (1838-81) and made by Gillow & Co. for the 1873 London International Exhibition. Oak with carved boxwood panels. Talbert's adaptation of the Gothic is generally massive. Victoria and Albert Museum.*

RIGHT *Cabinet, Wright & Mansfield, exhibited at the Paris Exhibition of 1867. Satinwood with marquetry of coloured woods, gilded mouldings and Wedgwood plaques. Victoria and Albert Museum.*

the 'dressoir' (sideboard) which won a medal at the Paris Exhibition of 1867. This piece has a smaller companion, the Sleeping Beauty Cabinet, so called from the metal reliefs decorating the upper centre; it is made of walnut, carved and inlaid with various woods, and has enamel plaques of birds.

In 1867 Talbert published *Gothic Forms Applied to Furniture,* in which the Early English style (mainly of the twelfth and thirteenth centuries) is recommended for 'its great breadth and simplicity'. He praised furniture of this period for 'the construction honestly shown'. His own furniture is generally massive, employing framed construction and rich surface decoration, often combined with carved panels or low-relief

Bed designed by William Burges (1827-81), for his own house, Tower House, Kensington, 1879. Gilded wood, the head inset with mirrors and the Judgment of Paris. Victoria and Albert Museum.

metal panels and inlaid geometrical patterns. His celebrated Pet Sideboard has inset panels of carved boxwood which set a distinct fashion. J. Moyr Smith states in his *Ornamental Interiors* (1887) that drawing-room designs in Talbert's *Gothic Forms* 'were without doubt the cause of the new style of decoration taking hold of the public'.

William Burges was another notable designer in the early Gothic style. His furniture displays a massiveness derived from his researches into Medieval architecture and particularly into Medieval French chests. It has a bold and simple structure with little carving, its chief effect being obtained from painted and gilded decoration and insets of various materials. A cabinet of his design in the 1862 Exhibition is completely covered with paintings by E. J. Poynter representing the Contest between Wines and Beers. For his own house in Kensington he designed in 1879 a gilded bed of which the headboard is inset with two large and ten small mirrors and has a painting of a Medieval version of the Judgment of Paris. In 1880, also for his house, he designed a well-known wash-stand with masterly use of polychrome and rich materials. Burges worked for wealthy patrons, not, like Talbert, for commercial producers. He made his furniture

known through exhibitions, writings and lectures. A certain amount of attractive make-believe was combined with his researches, as can be seen in the fairy-tale Castell Coch, Glamorgan, which he recreated, complete with furniture, from 1875 onwards for Lord Bute. He was also one of the first designers in England to become interested in Japanese art.

Another important propagandist of the Early English style was Charles L. Eastlake whose *Hints on Household Taste* (1868) had immediate success in England and the United States. This book, illustrating simple and largely undecorated furniture of plain rectangular form and Medieval construction, gave rise to the so-called Eastlake Style, which had a considerable following in America.

Burges' friend, E. W. Godwin, was one of the most original of Victorian furniture designers and the first to make important adaptations of Japanese designs. In 1867 he transferred his architectural practice from Bristol to London and designed furniture for private commissions and for leading firms, including Gillow's, William Watt, W. A. Smee and Collinson & Lock. His many notebooks and sketches illustrate material taken from numerous sources – Egyptian, Greek, Gothic, 'early fifteenth century', Renaissance and Japanese – but in his eclecticism he differed completely from his contemporaries in refusing to reproduce exactly any historical style. In his own words (in Watt's Catalogue, 1877) he sought 'a modern treatment of certain well-known and admired styles'. He may be considered the first Victorian designer

to be concerned primarily with function and not style, and the simplicity of his furniture, based on considerations of utility and economy, contrasted strongly with the elaborately carved, gilded and painted furniture of his time.

He was interested in what he called 'the grouping of solid and void', and this approach is seen in the remarkable sideboard which is illustrated in Watt's Catalogue. Of ebonized wood, its Japanese character is emphasized by the inset panels of embossed Japanese leather, the only other decoration being the startlingly simple keyhole motif on the silverplated fittings. A walnut cabinet, made in about 1876 to Godwin's design, has Japanese carved boxwood panels and carved ivory handles in the form of monkeys. A so-called Greek chair, designed by Godwin and made by Watt in about 1885, shows Japanese influence though the legs are inspired by Greek examples; it is of ebonized oak and has elongated uprights. An oak chair, described as Jacobean in Watt's Catalogue, has a circular cane seat and rectilinear supports. This again shows Japanese influence and seems to have been widely plagiarized.

Ebonized pieces of Godwin inspiration are often mentioned in the *Art at Home* series of small books published in the late 1870s to keep middle-class householders in touch with current trends. Godwin's functionalism had a considerable following abroad. To some extent his work was closely followed in England by T. E. Collcutt who designed for Collinson & Lock a much admired ebonized cabinet exhibited at the International Exhibition, London, in 1871. This had many of the features which were fashionable at the time – slender turned supports, painted and inlaid decoration, an abundance of shelves, bevelled glass panels and a coved canopy.

Arts and Crafts Furniture and the Rural Tradition

The ideas of William Morris began to exercise a potent influence on furniture design in the 1880s through the Arts and Crafts Movement. This movement sprang from the formation of various guilds and societies of designers and craftsmen, directed by architects, which aimed to unite good design and skilled, honest craftsmanship with social reform. The pioneer group was the Century Guild founded in 1882 by the architect, A. H. Mackmurdo. The Guild presented its furniture (and other products) as a co-operative effort, so that it is difficult to distinguish individual contributions. In 1883 the St George's Art

Sideboard designed by E. W. Godwin (1833-86) and made by William Watt (1865-85), c. 1867. Ebonized wood with embossed leather panels and silver-plated fittings, ht 5 ft 11 in (1·8 m). An early and influential essay in the Anglo-Japanese style developed by Godwin. Victoria and Albert Museum.

Society was founded, and in 1884 the Art Workers' Guild, followed in 1888 by the Arts and Crafts Exhibition Society (after which the whole Movement was named) and C. R. Ashbee's Guild and School of Handicraft. Through exhibitions of their work, in 1888, 1889, 1890, 1893, 1896 and 1899, a wider public became aware of the Guilds' ideals.

Arts and Crafts furniture was by no means all of the austere cottage type of the early Morris period, but showed increasing interest in Georgian furniture and sometimes incorporated decorative work in brass, ivory and stained glass. Lewis F. Day exhibited in 1888 at the first Arts and Crafts Exhibition an oak cabinet inlaid with ebony and satinwood, with painted panels of the signs of the zodiac, and its simple and attractive proportions, effected with great skill, typify one aspect of the Movement's work. Morris' own firm began, in about 1890, when George Jack succeeded Philip Webb as chief designer, to produce mahogany and rosewood furniture decorated with marquetry. A well-known example is a rosewood cabinet of about

1899 inlaid with purplewood, tulipwood and ebony, with metal mounts designed by W. A. S. Benson.

The vernacular tradition of the early Morris phase was preserved by the Arts and Crafts Movement through the Cotswold School. This began in 1893 when the architects Ernest Gimson and Sidney and Ernest Barnsley, moved from London to the Cotswolds and began to make simple but beautifully finished furniture in the rural tradition. Gimson carried Morris' principles into workshop practice as well as into design, and it is through him more than anybody else that traditional English rural craftsmanship and the highest standard of hand skill have survived to the present. He is associated with rush-seated, ladder-back chairs of ancient lineage, made of local woods, with turned spindle legs, stretchers and uprights. Restrained adaptations of traditional forms and a sensitive feeling for materials were keynotes of Gimson's designs. He had an important influence on two outstanding designers of the twentieth century – Sir Ambrose Heal and Sir Gordon Russell. A permanent exhibition of Gimson's work can be seen at the Museum and Art Gallery, Leicester, the city of his birth.

The architect W. R. Lethaby, who had been a partner of Gimson in the short-lived Kenton & Co. in 1890, showed the same devotion to tradition when he designed furniture as Principal of the Central School of Arts and Crafts, London. The sideboard of oak inlaid with ebony, sycamore and bleached mahogany which he designed in about 1900 is a fine example of unpolished furniture in the best Arts and Crafts manner; the inlaid decoration is inspired by Morris, for whose company Lethaby also designed pieces.

Meanwhile one branch of traditional, rural furniture making had made significant developments through a combination of business enterprise and the concentration of manufacture in one area. Since the beginning of the nineteenth century the production of Windsor chairs had become centred in small workshops in and around High Wycombe, Buckinghamshire, where the prime material, beech, grew in abundance. The workshops assembled and finished the chairs from components made by the 'bodgers' in the neighbouring woods. There was a remarkable expansion of the industry after the introduction of the Wycombe chair vans which travelled about the country selling their loads and taking orders for further supplies. One of the earliest pioneers of this trade, Benjamin North, was already reaching the industrial cities of the Midlands and North by the beginning of Queen Victoria's reign. When he set up his own chair-making business in High Wycombe in 1853 his market was a national one. His firm produced many variations of the stock Windsor type, and some of his designs were registered at the Patent Office. Another well-known High Wycombe maker, Edwin Skull, issued a trade card in about 1870 which illustrated over one hundred varieties of the chair. The three High Wycombe firms of Skull, Birch and Glenister, were given a very large order for rush-seated chairs for the coronation of Edward VII in 1901. Birch also made chairs for Liberty's of Regent Street, London, and built up a considerable export trade to Europe and the United States.

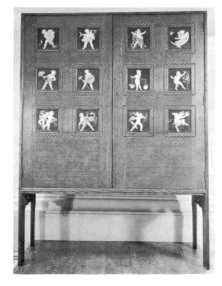

TOP *Cabinet designed by Lewis F. Day (1845-1910), exhibited at the first Arts and Crafts Exhibition in 1888. Oak inlaid with ebony and satinwood, with panels depicting the signs of the Zodiac by George McCulloch. Victoria and Albert Museum.*

ABOVE *Cabinet on stand probably designed by Ernest Gimson (1864-1919) for Kenton & Co., c. 1891. Ebonized wood with ebony veneer and ebony, orange, holly and palm inlay. Gimson was a founder of Kenton & Co. in 1890. Christie's.*

Art Nouveau Furniture

Contemporary with the Arts and Crafts Movement in the 1890s, and owing much to it, was Art Nouveau, a style which deliberately sought a new art form for the coming twentieth century and, eschewing historical revivals, based its ornament on sinuous curves and undulating forms taken from plants, waves or flame-like shapes. In this movement, destined to spread throughout Europe, English designers played a vital part. Among its pioneers was A. H. Mackmurdo, the founder of the Century Guild. In about 1892 he designed for the Guild some mahogany dining-room chairs with brilliantly original fretwork backs of undulating flame- or tendril-like curves which rank as one of the very first examples of Art Nouveau in applied art. Mackmurdo's other designs display a basic conservatism of form and simplicity of structure. Severe vertical lines are evident in a small oak writing desk which he designed for the Guild in about 1886 but the Art Nouveau influence is evident in the flat-capped uprights rising clear above the rear of the desk. A selection of Mackmurdo's furniture, exemplifying his love for simple lines and careful proportions, is on display at the William Morris Gallery, Walthamstow, Essex.

On the Continent the most widely admired and imitated of all English designers of Art Nouveau furniture was the architect, C. F. A. Voysey. His work is a happy fusion between the ideals and practices of Art Nouveau and of the Arts and Crafts Movement. Greatly influenced by Mackmurdo, Voysey joined the Art Workers' Guild in 1884 and exhibited furniture for the first time in 1893 at the Arts and Crafts Exhibition, where his sideboard commissioned for Lady Lovelace combined sinuous curves with simple traditional craftsmanship and attracted much attention abroad as well as in England. But while Voysey's designs were regarded as the fountainhead of Art Nouveau, he himself retained a highly personal interpretation of furniture based on traditional English forms. He disliked the Victorian revivals and pleaded for a re-assessment of design 'by discarding the mass of useless ornaments'.

Typical features of his work were the use of plain unvarnished oak, the emphasis on verticality in attenuated members, ending in flat cappings on chairs and desks, and the employment of heart-shaped decoration in varied forms, in pierced wood, for instance, or elaborate metal hinges. The oak writing desk which was made in 1896 to his design has four slender legs rising as detached columns above the writing surface to support the cornice; the strong vertical feeling of the whole is confirmed by interesting spatial interplay between uprights and cabinet with which the copper hinges and ornamental plate make a marked contrast. 'Simplicity', in Voysey's own words, 'requires perfection in

LEFT *Side chair, Liberty & Co., c. 1900. Oak with a drop-in rush seat. Liberty's, of Regent St., London, was founded as an Oriental warehouse in 1875. Sotheby's Belgravia.*

RIGHT *Writing-cabinet designed by C. F. A. Voysey (1857-1941) and made by W. H. Tingey, 1896. Oak with copper hinges incorporating a pastoral scene, ht 5 ft 6 in (1·7m). Voysey was an advocate of simplicity and natural, untreated materials. Victoria and Albert Museum.*

BELOW LEFT *Piano designed by M. H. Baillie Scott (1865-1945), c. 1898. This dates from the period when he was living on the Isle of Man, before he moved to Bedford. Twentieth-century built-in furniture is prefigured in this piece. Sotheby's Belgravia.*

BELOW RIGHT *Armchair designed by Voysey for the Essex and Suffolk Insurance Co., c. 1900-10. Oak with leather upholstery. A subtle combination of rectilinear and curved forms. Sotheby's Belgravia.*

all its details while elaboration is easy in comparison.' Voysey designed a number of houses on a moderate scale, informally comfortable and intimately related to their surroundings. The interiors, which he designed in detail, were refreshingly simple and marked a complete break with the long-established crowded Victorian household. The Orchard at Chorley Wood, Hertfordshire, designed in 1900, is his best-known house.

H. M. Baillie-Scott also made important contributions to the European Art-Nouveau style. He built and furnished houses in Germany, Switzerland, Poland, Russia, the United States and throughout the British Isles. The furniture which he designed for the New Palace, Darmstadt, in 1898 was made by the Guild of Handicraft. Basically simple and well proportioned, it marked a new approach with its lavish decoration in colour and relief, including inlay in various woods and in ivory, pewter and pearl.

The British designer whose name is most readily associated with Art Nouveau furniture is the Scottish architect, Charles Rennie Mackintosh, leader of a group of designers centred on the Glasgow School of Art. This group held many exhibitions abroad but had significantly less success in England. Mackintosh designed and furnished the Glasgow School of Art (1897 onwards), a number of tearooms for Miss Cranston in Glasgow (1897–1910), and several houses. He is particularly remembered for his very tall chairs, some having backs 5 ft (1.5 m) high. This exaggerated elongation earned his group the title of the Spook School in England. But some of Mackintosh's work was of great interest. He favoured a predominantly white setting which his furniture was painted to match, with touches of silver, pink or mauve. The rose was his favourite motif, inlaid in coloured glass or ivory, or stencilled in upholstery. Yet a damaging general criticism of his furniture, particularly the white-painted pieces, is directed at their unsound construction, despite the fact that on occasions – exemplifying the considerable variety of his designs – his work could be sturdy and practical.

With their usual misinterpretation, many manufacturers produced spindly-legged pieces in cheap stained woods, inlaid with motifs of pseudo-Art Nouveau character, which were designated as being made in the Quaint Style. But Art Nouveau furniture of high quality was made by a number of firms, including Liberty's, J. S. Henry, the Bath cabinetmakers and William Birch, and a considerable quantity of their pieces were exported.

Edward Joy

AMERICAN

In the first years of Queen Victoria's reign American furniture showed the predominant influence of the Late Classical style, in its popular interpretations often called the pillar and scroll style. Based on designs of the French Restoration as illustrated by La Mésangère in the periodical *Journal des Dames et des Modes* (later published in one volume as *Meubles et Objets des Gouts*), as well as those of the late English Regency seen in the illustrations of Ackermann's *Repository* and the pattern books of George Smith and the brothers Nicholson, this style was illustrated in America in the earliest surviving American published pictorial representation of furniture, an 1833 broadside of Joseph Meeks & Sons of New York. More than twenty of the forty-four furniture and drapery designs in this lithograph were, in turn, directly taken from Smith's *The Cabinet-Maker and Upholsterer's Guide* (1828). The Meeks, by this period enjoying an extensive trade to the South, had a branch office in New Orleans, as did their competitor, Henry Weil.

The Late Classical Style

The massive proportions of the Late Classical style were as well suited to the cavernous interiors of Greek Revival Plantation houses, as to the high-ceilinged double parlours of the town houses which belonged to a rising mercantile aristocracy in the North, where a sophisticated clientele favoured the style. In 1837, a depression year, Duncan Phyfe, the most fashionable cabinetmaker in New York since the early nineteenth century, furnished the New York lawyer, Samuel Foot, with a complete parlour suite comprising a pair of *méridiennes* with curving backs, scrolled ends of unequal height and heavy straight legs, four *chaises gondoles* with straight splats and cresting rails, four stools with saddle seats on curule bases, a pair of card tables and a pair of oblong window benches supported at either end by paired scrolls on a plinth.

A year earlier, in 1836, the first Mid-Western publication for the trade, the *Book of Prices of the United Society of Journeyman Cabinet Makers of Cincinnati*, had listed furniture forms in the Late Classical style. Perhaps the most important publication, however, was America's first pattern book, John Hall's *The Cabinet Maker's Assistant*, published in Baltimore, Maryland, in 1840 with the avowed intention of presenting 'the most modern style of furniture in an economical arrangement to save labor'.

Designs were based almost entirely upon single and double scrolls. These could be cut with the bandsaw, which was introduced in a steam-driven version in that same year, though originally patented in the first decade of the century. Of equal importance to production in the Late Classical style, with its emphasis upon expanses of highly figured mahogany, was the increasing use of the circular saw, which could produce larger, thinner and more economical sheets of veneer.

The 1840s saw other styles challenge the pre-eminence of the Late Classical, but vestiges of it remained well into the 1850s. *The Architecture of Country Houses* (1850) by Andrew Jackson Downing illustrated a group of highly archaeological Grecian chairs and cited the Classical style as the most popular for homes, while the notes and sketches of the nineteenth-century cabinetmaker Ernest Hagen (now in the Winterthur Museum, Delaware), indicate that simple French chairs, pillar and scroll sofas, French bedsteads and pillar and scroll lyre card tables and lyre-fronted bureaux continued to be made in large quantities in New York in the 1850s. It was to these last vestiges of the pillar and scroll style that Professor Benjamin Silliman undoubtedly referred when, in reviewing

furniture at the Exhibition at the New York Crystal Palace in 1853, he condemned the 'ponderous and frigid monstrosities of the Classical style'.

Historical Revivals

By 1840, as a reaction against the rigid balance of Greek Revival architecture and the ponderous quality of Late Classical furniture, picturesque houses and furnishings were becoming popular in America, as they had in England more than a decade earlier. One of the most significant English books was J. C. Loudon's *An Encyclopedia of Cottage, Farm and Villa Architecture and Furniture* (1833), which named the principal styles of furniture: Grecian, Gothic, Elizabethan and Louis Quatorze. In the same tradition in America were the works of the landscape gardener, Andrew Jackson Downing. The first, *Cottage Residences* (1842), expressed the hope that 'our country residences may rival the "cottage homes of England",' while *The Architecture of Country Houses* featured furniture as well as architecture, advising what was proper for various rooms. Like Loudon, Downing cited the Gothic and the Elizabethan as two of the predominant styles.

The earliest Gothic Revival American furniture is generally one of two kinds: a Late Classical form upon which Gothic ornament is superimposed, or an architect-designed piece showing a closer adherence to real Gothic furniture or a fanciful adaptation of Medieval motifs and architectural elements. An example of the first is a cabinet bookcase with a pillar and scroll base surmounted by a bookcase with glass doors, with clustered columns, Gothic tracery and a pediment rising to a trefoil. In this same tradition were numerous chairs based on a Gothicized French Restoration *chaise gondole*, featuring arcaded backs and pierced trefoils in the cresting rail. Oak versions labelled by Alexander and Frederick Roux exist, as do walnut versions attributed to the Meeks. This type of furniture was first illustrated in America in Conner's *The Cabinet Maker's Assistant*.

Less clearly derived from European prototypes was the Gothic furniture which Downing's friend and colleague, the architect Alexander Jackson Davis,

Bookcase, Brooks Cabinet Warehouse, Brooklyn, presented by New York firemen to Jenny Lind with a set of Audubon's Birds of America. *Rosewood, ht 6 ft (1·8 m). A combination of Rococo, Elizabethan and Renaissance elements. Museum of the City of New York.*

designed for the homes of his clients, such as a 'country mansion in the pointed style' (now Lyndhurst) for the mayor of New York, William Paulding. Probably dating from 1841, a pair of hall chairs have round backs loosely based upon a rose window. Another great Gothic house by Davis was Joel Rathbone's Kenmore, near Albany, a room from which was illustrated in *The Architecture of Country Houses*. In the same book Downing named the leading New York cabinetmakers specializing in Gothic furniture as Burns & Trainque, Roux and George Platt. According to A. J. Davis' diaries and notes, William Burns and Peter Trainque executed some of his early Gothic furniture designs.

In addition to these, several other prominent cabinetmakers are known to have made Gothic furniture: Thomas Brooks of Brooklyn, New York, who may have made the furniture for the Gothic cottage, Roseland, at Woodstock, Connecticut; John Jelliff of Newark, New Jersey, who successfully worked in all the historical revival styles; Richard Byrnes of White Plains, New York, who executed many of Davis' designs; and Daniel & Hitchins of Troy, New York. The Gothic style in furniture continued throughout the 1850s but began to wane in the 1860s, recurring in the late nineteenth century as it had in the late eighteenth.

Concurrent with the Gothic, from the late 1830s to the late 1850s, was a style called, somewhat inaccurately, Elizabethan. Inspired, like the Gothic, by both English Romantic novels such as those by Sir Walter Scott, and works on antique furniture by Hunt and Shaw, it sometimes featured ornament derived from Elizabethan strapwork. Its salient characteristic, however, was spiral or bobbin turning, which derived from furniture, not of Queen Elizabeth's reign, but of the period of Charles I and Charles II. Cabinetmakers noted for work in the Gothic style often favoured the Elizabethan. At present the only known labelled piece of furniture by the New York partnership of Burns & Trainque is an Elizabethan rosewood side chair of *c.* 1850 with upholstered back and seat and spiral turning on the stiles and front legs and bobbin turning on the rear legs and stretchers. Side chairs of this general type, sometimes with turned spindles or panels of carved

Desk and bookcase, J. & J. W. Meeks, New York, 1836-50. Rosewood with satinwood interior, ht 7ft 7¾in (2·3m). The firm that made this Gothic Revival piece was founded by Joseph Meeks (1771-1868) in 1797. Metropolitan Museum of Art.

Side chair in the Gothic Revival style, New York, c. 1850. Walnut. This type of Gothic furniture was first illustrated in America in The Cabinet Maker's Assistant *by Robert Conner, 1842. Greenfield Village and Henry Ford Museum.*

strapwork forming the backs, were popular, as was a *prie-dieu* type of chair with low seat, high back and padded cresting rail.

The Elizabethan style was most commonly manifested in America in sets of inexpensive, painted cottage furniture with turning, not only on chairs but table supports and stretchers, and split spindles on dressers. At the opposite end of the style spectrum, was the use of Elizabethan spiral columns on the lower section of an elaborate rosewood bookcase made in 1850 by the Brooklyn Brooks Cabinet Warehouse for presentation by New York firemen to the 'Swedish Nightingale,' Jenny Lind. This bookcase clearly incorporates several of the historical revival styles popular in the mid-century, not only the Elizabethan, but, in the pediment, the Renaissance Revival, and in the moulded and carved aprons, curving legs and scroll feet, the dominant style of the 1850s, the Rococo Revival.

The Rococo Revival

Sometimes called the antique-French style because of its origins in eighteenth-century Rococo, sometimes the modern-French style because it had been popularized at the court of Louis Philippe and was currently in vogue, the Rococo more than any other historical nineteenth-century revival style expressed the expansive, optimistic, even ostentatious, prosperity of mid-century America. Although many of the characteristics of the earlier style appeared, such as the cabriole leg, C- and S-scrolls and naturalistic carving with a shell or cabochon and foliage, the Rococo Revival developed its own character. New forms became prominent, such as the *étagère*, with shelf, table or cabinet base, sometimes designed for a corner, surmounted by stepped shelves, often with mirrored backing to improve the display of objects.

New shapes in seating furniture included sofas, called sociables, often with

Étagère in the Rococo Revival style, Alexander Roux (c. 1812-86), New York, c. 1850-7. Roux was born in France and was first listed in the New York directories, as an upholsterer, in 1837-8. Metropolitan Museum of Art.

a low centre back flanked by chair backs, and *tête-à-têtes*, having the S-curve in the form itself, two armchairs attached so that they faced outwards in opposite directions. Usually, like other sofas, mounted on castors for movability, these innovatory forms sometimes had cabriole front legs ending in traditional scroll feet. Often, however, sofa and chair front legs terminated in a tapered cylinder, while rear legs formed a reverse curve which gave an appearance of stability. With a new concern for comfort, and the increasing use of the coil spring, upholstery became deeper and more pronounced and was usually tufted or deep buttoned. On high-style upholstered pieces, elaborate carving of flowers, grapes and foliage ornamented the backs, while factory-produced seating furniture, including the popular balloon-back chair, had finger-moulded frames.

Mass produced in these simpler versions by firms not only in the East, but also in Mid-Western cities such as Cincinnati and Grand Rapids, the Rococo Revival in its elaborate form was often associated with cabinetmakers of French birth or background. According to

Hagen's notes, the leading cabinetmaker in New York in the mid-1850s, when the style reached its peak, was Charles Baudouine, who employed about seventy cabinetmakers and, including carvers, varnishers and upholsterers, nearly 200 hands all told.

Also important was Alexander Roux, whose brother and sometime partner, Frederick, was a prominent cabinet-maker in Paris. The most famous name associated with the style was that of the German-born John Henry Belter (see p. 62), who patented a process of laminating and steam-bending wood, subsequently copied by Baudouine. Other major cabinetmakers working in the style included Ringuet Leprince and Marcotte of New York and Paris, Joseph Meeks & Sons, Henry Weil, Bembé & Kimbel, Rochefort & Skarren and E. W. Hutchings of New York City, Elijah Galusha of Troy, New York, John Jelliff of Newark, New Jersey, Daniel Pabst and George Henkels of Philadelphia, Auguste Eliaers of Boston, and Prudent Mallard of New Orleans. Important in the 1840s and dominant in the 1850s, the Rococo Revival waned in the 1860s, when its exuberant excesses perhaps no longer met the mood of a nation torn by civil conflict.

The Louis Seize Revival

As an alternative to the curves of the Rococo, the straight lines of the Louis Seize Revival appealed to some of the fashion-conscious customers of larger American cities. On the Continent the style was especially favoured after Louis Napoleon became president of France in 1848 and emperor in 1852. Because the Empress Eugénie identified herself with Marie Antoinette and selected Louis Seize furniture and decoration for the private apartments at the Tuileries and St Cloud, the Louis Seize Revival, which was prominent at the Paris Exhibition of 1855, is often called Second Empire, as is the architecture of the era.

Furniture has straight tapering legs, usually fluted or channelled. Chairs and sofas with square backs, straight arms and ribbon cresting followed the forms of the late eighteenth century, but were often ebonized and trimmed with ormolu mounts and beading, rather than being carved and painted in pastel colours. Porcelain or bronze plaques were often added to case pieces. New York more than any other area seems to have produced high-style Louis Seize furniture, perhaps because so many major New York cabinetmakers had strong connections with France.

Louis Seize Revival furniture. The seating furniture and firescreen form part of a suite in ebonized maple and fruitwood purchased for the John Taylor Johnston House, New York, from Leon Marcotte (c. 1825 – c. 1886/7) in c. 1860. The marquetry library table was probably acquired from Marcotte & Co. (founded in 1861) in 1872, though it may be of an earlier date. Metropolitan Museum of Art.

The style reached its height in New York in about 1860: in 1878 Harriet Spofford in her book *Art Decoration Applied to Furniture*, stated: 'At present the Louis XVI furniture is made in America with a nicety and a purity equal to that which characterizes the best examples'. Although, as this quotation indicates, the Louis Seize style continued to be made, its early ebonized phase of the 1850s merged somewhat in the 1860s with the style called the Renaissance Revival.

The Renaissance Revival

At the exhibition at the New York Crystal Palace of 1853, as at the Great Exhibition of 1851 in London, the style favoured for massive case pieces was the Renaissance style. It appeared in numerous buffets exhibited in New York, including an oak one by Alexander Roux, another designed by Gustave Herter and made by Thomas Brooks, and one by Bulkley & Herter. The Renaissance Revival had been known in the United States as early as the late 1840s; Down-ing's *The Architecture of Country Houses* (1850) stated: 'The French, in their Renaissance style, at present in high favour on the continent, offer the best example of it as applied to modern uses . . . French furniture in the same plain modern classical taste is almost universally preferred in this country.'

The majority of the pieces surviving from the early period of the Renaissance Revival, however, are elaborate, incorporating decorative elements from the fifteenth to the eighteenth centuries. The principal characteristics were rectangular shapes and massive proportions on case pieces, which usually rested on the floor and had panels of high-relief carving and a broken arch pediment centred with a cartouche or sculptural bust. Consoles, columns and colonnettes appeared, as did Neoclassical motifs such as palmettes, scrolling leaves and urns.

By the 1860s, as Renaissance characteristics were increasingly combined with those of the Louis Seize style, porcelain and bronze plaques were often added to case pieces, while seating furniture had carved crestings decorated with enamel, bronze or mother-of-pearl plaques. By this period the Renaissance Revival was the most fashionable style, and had changed character in the interpretations of such large manufacturers as Mitchell & Rammelsberg of Cincinnati and Berkey & Gay of Grand Rapids, Michigan. A table from the latter shows the addition of angular, non-structural elements and a flattening of decorative detail.

Some of the same characteristics can be seen on a Wooten Patent desk of 1874, which, although innovatory in its mechanical aspects, follows the prevailing taste in its Renaissance Revival ornamentation: large panels of burled wood, contrasting surfaces of light and dark, incised linear patterns and a cresting decorated with small knobs. In the next few years the Renaissance Revival style began to decline in popularity, although it was still the favoured style for furniture at the 1876 Centennial Exhibition, when critics lamented the 'vulgar renditions of the French Renaissance'.

The Reform Styles

Although most American furniture makers who exhibited at the Centennial Exhibition of 1876 showed pieces in the style of the historical revivals, two companies showed new reform styles. An oak sideboard and hallstand by Mitchell & Rammelsberg, illustrated in *The Masterpieces of the International Centennial Exhibition*, features the straight lines, chamfered supports, grooved boards, incised linear decoration, large ornate strap hinges, and coved cornice of contemporary English designs. Similar in character to the sideboard was the cabinet in a room by the New York firm of Kimbel & Cabus, illustrated in 1876 in both the *American Architect and Builder* and *Harper's Monthly* and subsequently in many other publications, including Mrs Spofford's book of 1878 and the 1880s catalogue of the Lang &

LEFT *Secretary bookcase, Mitchell & Rammelsberg, Cincinnati, founded in 1836 or 1844, c. 1860. Rosewood, ht 10 ft (3 m). In the late nineteenth century the name was changed to Robert Mitchell Furniture Co., and the firm was still in existence in 1923. Newark Museum.*

BELOW LEFT *Table, Berkey & Gay, Grand Rapids, founded in 1862, 1870s. Founded as Berkey & Mather, they made furniture in the Renaissance Revival style. Grand Rapids Public Museum.*

Armchair, Meriden, c. 1869. Rosewood, ht 3 ft 8½ in (1·1 m). Part of a suite of Renaissance Revival furnishings in the house of Jedediah Wilcox in Meriden. Metropolitan Museum of Art.

Nau furniture company. Both of these groups of furniture might be called Modern Gothic in contrast to the earlier Gothic Revival which was more preoccupied with ornament than structure.

Modern Gothic had roots in the work of A. W. N. Pugin, with its emphasis on solidity and honesty of construction, and, in the mid century, the theorizing of Ruskin and Carlyle, with their fears of the effects of industrialization. It made its first major appearances in the late 1850s and early 1860s in the furniture designs of architects such as William Burges, Philip Webb and Norman Shaw. In the late 1860s it was popularized in books by Bruce J. Talbert and Sir Charles Eastlake.

Talbert's *Gothic Forms Applied to Furniture* (London, 1867; Boston, 1873) and Eastlake's *Hints on Household Taste* (London, 1868; Boston, 1872) were rapidly assimilated in the United States. The Philadelphia-born cabinetmaker Isaac Scott, working in Chicago by 1873, shows the influence of Talbert in an ambitious bookcase which, according to research by David Hanks, the prominent Glessner family purchased in 1875. The name Eastlake, however, was adopted by Americans more thoroughly than that of any other English advocate of furniture reform. In J. Wayland Kimball's commercial catalogue, the *Album of Design* (1876), numerous companies illustrated or described suites of furniture designated as Eastlake.

On the whole Eastlake in the United States became synonymous with inexpensive, mass-produced, straight-line furniture, sometimes with turned supports, legs, or balusters in galleries, and often with ebonized finish, shallow geometric carving, and incised lines. Clarence Cook in *The House Beautiful* (1878) warned that 'Eastlake furniture must not . . . be judged by what is made in this country, and sold under that name'. That more sophisticated furniture designs, as well as cheap factory productions, were influenced by Eastlake's book is shown, however, by a buffet made in 1877 by Daniel Pabst of Philadelphia for the John Trevor House in Yonkers, New York. Research by M. J. Madigan cites the source of the sideboard's carved panels of Aesop's fox and crane fable as the *Hints on Household Taste* illustration of a *portière* design by C. Hinton. Pabst, whose work was so well known and regarded that clients from other states came to him, may have executed some of the distinctive furniture designs of the Philadelphia architect Frank Furness.

In New York the prominent decorator was Christian Herter, head of Herter

BELOW *Bookcase, Isaac Scott (1845-1920), 1875. Walnut with inlay of various woods, ht 7ft 2¼in (2·2m). Scott displayed some examples of his furniture at the Centennial Exhibition of 1876 in Philadelphia. This piece is in the Modern Gothic style. Chicago School of Architecture.*

RIGHT *Wardrobe, Herter Bros., New York, made for the actress Lillian Russell in c. 1880. Cherry, inlaid and ebonized,*

ht 7ft 5in (2·3m). The Japanese influence is evident in this piece in the colour and stylized decoration. Metropolitan Museum of Art.

BELOW RIGHT *Detail of a door panel from a buffet in the Eastlake Style, Daniel Pabst, Philadelphia, c. 1877. Hudson River Museum.*

Bros, which had been founded by his older half brother Gustave. During the 1860s, under Gustave's leadership, Herter Bros had become one of New York's leading firms and had decorated the music room and several bedrooms of the LeGrand Lockwood Mansion in Norwalk, Connecticut, the greatest house of its era. According to the *American Architect and Builder*, Herter Bros was not represented at the Centennial Exhibition except by piano cases and display

cases made for other companies. Had they been present, wrote a critic, superiority would not have been credited solely to English manufacturers for their art furniture, as was evinced for example, by two ebonized cabinets which evoked great admiration and were published in several reviews. One of these, designed by Collcutt and made by Collinson & Lock, may have had considerable influence on American art furniture. Herter and his designers, however, were clearly more influenced by the work of E. W. Godwin. Japonism, which was so much a part of Godwin's highly advanced designs, is evident in one of Herter Bros' masterpieces, the wardrobe made for the actress Lillian Russell in about 1880.

The Anglo-Japanese style of Godwin was evident in numerous other Herter designs, including a bedroom suite made for a railroad magnate, Jay Gould, and decorated with hand-painted Japanese tiles. The culmination of Herter's work in this idiom, however, was the Japanese parlour which he designed for the Fifth Avenue home of William H. Vanderbilt. Although it in some ways presaged Japanese influence on American architecture and interiors at the close of the century, this room with its concentration upon elaborate decoration rather than Oriental sparseness, related far more closely to the 1870s and 1880s rage for the exotic.

Eclecticism
and Continuing Reform

At the Centennial Exhibition, Americans showed strong interest in the Japanese Pavilion and the Turkish Bazaar. The influence of the Orient could be seen in the newly fashionable bamboo or pseudo-bamboo furniture, the former either imported or made by such New York

ABOVE LEFT *Japanese parlour from the William H. Vanderbilt House, New York, designed by Christian Herter (1840-83), 1882. From Edward Strahan's The William H. Vanderbilt House and Collection, 1884.*

LEFT *Desk, probably New York, c. 1885. Bird's eye maple. Exotic bamboo or imitation-bamboo furniture became fashionable after the Centennial Exhibition. Metropolitan Museum of Art.*

RIGHT *Clock, Tiffany & Co., 1882 patent. Mahogany with brass dome, finials and dial plate, ht 8ft 9in (2·7m). An exotic mixture of Near Eastern and Indian motifs. Metropolitan Museum of Art.*

firms as Nimura & Sato of Brooklyn, the latter with turned maple simulating bamboo supports and flat panels of bird's-eye maple. Some Oriental rooms appeared in *Artistic Houses*, a book published in 1883–4 to illustrate the houses of the country's wealthy and prominent. Moorish or Persian rooms also appeared, often showing the new importance of upholstered furniture. The 'Turkish Corner' replete with pillows and secluded by draperies was emulated in simpler houses, and a type of deeply cushioned easy chair with a wire frame supporting the upholstery and deep fringes decorating it, was designated a Turkish chair.

From Near Eastern bazaars came such decorative accessories as screens, copper and brass ornaments and small hexagonal tables, usually inlaid with mother of pearl. One of the most successful rooms in the Moorish taste was the parlour (now in the Brooklyn Museum) of Arabella Worsham's house, which subsequently became the home of John D. Rockefeller. During the early 1880s Louis Comfort Tiffany decorated his own drawing room in the Moorish style, and in the early 1890s his decorating company carried out an exotic scheme for the house of H. O. Havemeyer.

Concurrent with the fashion for exotic styles, was a renewed interest in the furniture of America's colonial past. Colonial Revival furniture was long called Centennial furniture. Although it is now thought that little authentic American eighteenth-century furniture was exhibited at Philadelphia, a few pieces have turned up with Centennial Exhibition labels, including a settee and a lowboy, which was shown at Machinery Hall. *Gems of the Centennial* mentioned the 'extraordinary prices' of old furniture. Whatever the cause of the Revival and the part the Centennial played in it, reproductions of early furniture began during the last quarter of the nineteenth century and continued, often in highly eclectic versions, into the twentieth.

The reform movement which had begun in the United States in the 1870s, continued through to the end of the nineteenth century along with exotic trends, historical revivals and the Colonial Revival. In the late 1870s, the 1880s and 1890s the reform impulse could be seen in a continuing interest in the precepts of the Arts and Crafts Movement, often reflected in furniture designed by architects such as H. H. Richardson of Boston, Frank Lloyd Wright and others of the Prairie School of Chicago and, by the first decade of the twentieth century, the brothers Charles and Henry Greene of Pasadena, California. Several art

Print table designed by Frank Lloyd Wright (1867-1959) for Francis W. Little. Stained white oak, ht 3ft 9¼in (1·1 m). Metropolitan Museum of Art.

RIGHT *Dining table, Tobey Furniture Co., founded in 1875, c. 1890. Cherry, 4ft 5¾in (1·4m). This and the table above are closely related to the architectural style of the Prairie School of Chicago. Metropolitan Museum of Art.*

guilds emulated those established in England in the 1880s, one being the Art Workers' Guild, of Providence, Rhode Island, whose members were Sydney R. Burleigh, Charles W. Stetson and John G. Aldrich.

In other cities there were numerous workmen creating fine furniture. One of the most impressive was Charles Rohlfs, who established a workshop in Buffalo, New York, employing no more than eight men. Highly original, the work of Rohlfs clearly shows the influence of the Arts and Crafts tradition in its tenoned construction and visible pegs, and the influence of Art Nouveau in its decoration. A side chair created for Rohlfs' own residence in about 1896, though it has traces of Gothicism in its base, has a purely Art Nouveau pierced and scrolled

back, making it, at present, the only known high-style piece of American furniture which is basically Art Nouveau in design (see p. 32).

After the turn of the century, Rohlfs sometimes lectured at the East Aurora, New York, craft community founded by Elbert Hubbard, an admirer of William Morris. Hubbard's Roycrofters produced work in leather, metal, glass and wood, the last being simple oak furniture which brought the ideals of the Arts and Crafts Movement within the reach of the common man. The chief competitor of Hubbard's Roycrofters was the Craftsman Workshop of Gustav Stickley which began producing furniture in 1898 in Eastwood, New York. Plain, undecorated oak furniture, sometimes with honest (revealed) construction in the style of Hubbard and Stickley, became popular in the first decade of the twentieth century and was often called Mission furniture. Before going bankrupt in 1915, Stickley extended his enterprises to create a craft empire and to become the most influential force in the American Arts and Crafts Movement. At the turn of the century, however, this influence was just beginning. Stickley's work was first exhibited to the public in a 1900 Grand Rapids furniture exhibition. In 1901, the last year of Queen Victoria's life and of the Victorian era, Stickley patented his first three designs and began spreading his gospel through the initial issue of his magazine *Craftsman*. His words in this and other publications presaged the twentieth century's preoccupation with functionalism. His purpose was, he stated, 'To make furniture which would be simple, durable, comfortable and fitted for the place it was to occupy and the work it had to do.'

Functional Design
1837–1901

Throughout the nineteenth century furniture was made that belongs outside the mainstream of design and presaged the functionalism important in the twentieth century. This included vernacular furniture, mechanical patent furniture, furniture made of various materials hitherto not generally used in its manufacture and built-in storage furniture.

Vernacular furniture is the simple, unpretentious furniture which meets the everyday needs of common people. Although it may bear some resemblance to high-style furniture, its flat undecorated surfaces and serviceable qualities often make it appear to lack a dominant style. Chairs are the most obvious examples, and in the nineteenth century there were two principal types, originating in the eighteenth century, which continued to be important: ladder-back and Windsor chairs. These and other vernacular forms were in general use and they were also taken over by some of the religious separatist communities which arose as nineteenth-century Utopian experiments, and in the hands of the separatists they developed their own character. Unquestionably the most important of these groups was the Shakers.

From the late eighteenth century the Shakers lived in communities which spread to eight states. Their dwellings and other buildings showed an emphasis upon simplicity, order and cleanliness. Furniture forms evolved from the vernacular furniture of New England, but they developed a distinctive character in

ABOVE and OPPOSITE ABOVE *Invalid chair designed by C. B. Sheldon and made by Marks Adjustable Folding Chair Co., New York, founded in 1875, 1876 patent. Cast iron, walnut and cane with plush cushions. The firm won a gold medal at the Paris Exposition of 1889. Greenfield Village and Henry Ford Museum.*

their proportions and in the strict elimination of all ornament and superfluous parts. Austere, uncurtained rooms with polished wooden floors and whitewashed walls usually had a high peg rail. Here chairs could be hung when the room was cleaned. Low, ladder-back chairs with two slats could be slid under tables to make a room appear uncluttered, while beds often had large wooden castors for movability. Rocking chairs were favoured. Cupboards and chests that were free standing were made without feet and mouldings at their base and with simple peg handles rather than elaborate brasses. Often, however, drawers and cupboards with narrow doors were constructed as part of a wall, anticipating the built-in storage units of the twentieth century.

The Shakers were not alone in their preoccupation with better, movable furniture and a more practical use of space. Built-in storage, flexibility of working areas and careful planning of space were all emphasised in *The American Woman's Home* (1869), written partly by Harriet Beecher Stowe, author of *Uncle Tom's Cabin,* and partly by her sister, Catherine Beecher, who hoped to reform kitchens and make it possible for women to work efficiently without the aid of servants.

The same kind of preoccupation with the efficient organization of working space can be seen in a piece of furniture such as the Wooten patent secretary, which was advertised in 1876 in *The*

BELOW *Platform rocker, American, 1880-90. Wicker. An American invention, the platform rocker dates from c. 1870. In England the type is known as a swing rocking chair. The base remains immobile while the chair rocks on its axle. Greenfield Village and Henry Ford Museum.*

Queen, the Lady's Newspaper by Francis and James Smith of London and Glasgow. They called it 'Of all American inventions . . . the most useful, elegant and convenient desk' with 'every particle of space practically utilized'. American patent furniture, which was most generally produced from the 1840s to the 1870s, shows a consistent emphasis upon efficiency, flexibility, movability and convertability. Many forms prevalent in the twentieth century, such as the convertible sofa-bed and chairs which revolve and recline, often designed for specialized purposes such as typing, were explored in the mid- to late nineteenth century.

Together with new forms, makers explored new materials, including a variety of organic substances: animal horns, rattan, cane, wicker, bamboo and natural wood for rustic furniture, as well as various metals, in particular brass and iron. Cast-iron furniture for both interior and exterior use was extensively made from the 1850s onwards, and wire garden furniture, chiefly lacy chairs, settees and fanciful plant stands and arbours became important in the 1870s. Some patent furniture, such as the Marks folding chair, shows both the interest in new materials – in this case a strap-iron frame which has been caned and loose cushioned – and multi-purpose use and flexibility.

Marilynn Johnson Bordes

Pattern Books Influential in the Victorian Period

ARROWSMITH, H. W. and A.

The House Decorator and Painter's Guide; containing a series of designs for decorating apartments, suited to the various styles of architecture, London, 1840. Supplying the need for a work on interior decoration, this book was aimed at improving the average decorator's taste, usually untutored by the study of Antiquity, the principles of taste and the best modern examples. Most of the sixty-one lithographs (thirty coloured) are designs of wall elevations and details of their carved decoration. Designs in the Elizabethan, French (Louis Quatorze and Louis Quinze) and Grecian styles are the most common. The Arrowsmiths admit, however, that the period had no style of its own, but boast that 'it will ever be known that the talent of the age was not confined to the bare imitation of any one style, but that all were used and employed.' The text of 120 pages consists of descriptions of the plates with suggestions for materials to be used in their execution, and a history of the styles and a definition of their characteristics. Furniture is only mentioned briefly, with the recommendation that it should always be appropriate to the style of architecture and decoration. As the first book specifically on interior decoration, and issued by decorators to the Queen, it was undoubtedly popular, particularly on account of its unbiased attitude to style.

Art at Home

London, 1876–8. Series of about ten books, each containing approximately 100 pages of text with accompanying illustrations, published under the direction of William John Loftie, an architect. The majority of the authors were female amateurs. The most popular titles were *A Plea for Art in the House* by Loftie himself, *The Dining Room* by his wife, *Suggestions for House Decoration in Painting, Woodwork and Furniture* by Rhoda and Agnes Garrett, *The Drawing Room* by Mrs Orrinsmith, *The Bedroom and the Boudoir* by Lady Barker and *Dress* by Mrs Oliphant. They are written in an unscholarly, chatty style, full of useful advice and aimed chiefly at the middle-class householder rather than those with well-staffed homes. The authors advocate comfort, durability,

cleanliness and beauty. Generally the texts show a preference for the Queen Anne style in furniture, although plain, rectangular pieces without much decoration are also illustrated, and an echo of the late eighteenth century is found in some designs. Most of the interiors illustrated are refreshingly sparse, although the 'quaint beauty' of 'cosy little corners' is admired. The illustrations in *The Dining Room, The Drawing Room* and *The Bedroom and the Boudoir* are taken from the American book, *The House Beautiful* (1878) by COOK, whose influence is also found in the texts.

Armchair designed by E. W. Godwin (1833-86) for production by William Watt & Co. and listed in the catalogue, Art Furniture, *of 1877. An example of an Anglo-Japanese piece designed by Godwin. Sotheby's Belgravia.*

Art Furniture

From designs by E. W. Godwin and others, with hints and suggestions on Domestic Furniture and Decoration by William Watt, London, 1877. An illustrated trade catalogue of the furniture manufactured in William Watt's Art Furniture Warehouse in Grafton Street, London. It provides a comprehensive survey of Godwin's Anglo-Japanese designs, and includes some other designs and Watt's introduction on furnishing and decoration. The preface consists of a letter from Godwin to Watt, from which it is apparent that most of the pieces had already been in production for some time, for Godwin mentions the extensive copying of his furniture by other manufacturers to the detriment of its proportions. Although unlike furniture used in Japan, Godwin's designs show strong Japanese characteristics. His simple, elegant pieces, with their attenuated supports, were based on the arrangement of solid and void without additional decoration. The firms of Jackson & Graham, and Collier & Plunkett were among the most important in manufacturing his designs after Watt's initiative. While Godwin's furniture was a personal interpretation of Japanese form, his flat patterns for wallpapers, chiefly manufactured by Jeffrey & Co., were far closer to the Japanese original. This book, with its twenty black and white plates, the majority illustrating uncluttered interiors supplied with Godwin's furniture, did much to acquaint the public with his original ideas, and it provided the answer for those designers who were endlessly searching for a new style. The vogue for Anglo-Japanese furniture reached its height in the 1880s, but in the trade version, Japanese details were usually applied to essentially Victorian furniture, and imitation bamboo and fretwork panels flourished.

Artistic Houses

Being a series of interior views of a number of the most beautiful and celebrated homes in the United States, with a description of the art treasures contained therein, New York, 1883–4. Printed for the subscribers by D. Appleton & Co., the edition limited to 500 copies.

BATLEY, H. W.
A Series of Studies for Domestic Furniture Decoration, London, 1883. H. W. Batley was a pupil of TALBERT and designer to James Shoolbred & Co., which specialized in 'Japanese' and 'Old English' furniture. The ten large-scale etched plates are printed in sepia, and the descriptions, with instructions on which woods to use, have a Gothic typeface. The designs are for rooms and their furniture and textiles, some of which had already been executed. The majority are in the early seventeenth-century style with Jacobean panelling and carving, stamped leather and stained glass. Batley's earliest design, dated 1872, attempts 'to adapt Egyptian ornament and detail to the modern dining room'. Japanese influence is evident in some of his textile and wallpaper designs, in one of the clockcases and in the fretwork decoration on a cabinet, and Moorish influence in the design for a flower stand. There is perhaps an echo of Talbert in the hanging corner cupboard and a hint of Art Nouveau in his treatment of plant forms.

BISHOP, J. LEANDER
A History of American Manufacturers from 1608-1860; exhibiting the origin and growth of the principal mechanic arts and manufactures, from the earliest colonial period to the adoption of the Constitution; and comprising Annals of the industry of the United States in machinery, manufactures and useful arts, with a notice of the important inventions, tariffs and the results of each decennial census; with an appendix containing statistics of the principle manufacturing centres, and descriptions of remarkable manufactories at the present time, 3 vols, Philadelphia, 1861–4; 3rd edition Philadelphia and London, 1868. The first volume of Bishop's scholarly history covers manufacture in the Colonial period. He used every available source in his research: contemporary records and periodicals, local histories, State papers, volumes of law and the minutes of assemblies and councils, resulting in a wealth of precise and valuable detail. Although he collected most of the material for Volume II in 1862, when he joined up for the Civil War, Bishop entrusted the completion of his work to Edwin T. Freedley (1827–1904) and Edward Young (1814–1909), who may have been partners together in the publishing firm of Edward Young & Co. Young had been head of the Census Office in Washington, and supplied the statistical material. Volume II covers the period from the birth of the new constitution to 1863. During these years, despite the effects of three wars, manufacturing expanded enormously, changing 'from a general system of isolated and fireside manual operations . . . to the more organised efforts of regular establishments with associated capital and corporate privileges'. The new government encouraged all forms of manufacture. The authors mention among other developments the use of rubber and the exploitation of petroleum, as well as such inventions as the power, carpet and stocking looms; patents are recorded, and the development of every type of manufacture from gas lighting to hats. Volume III consists of chapters on the main industrial towns with a survey of their respective industries. The many statistical tables are taken from the census returns of 1860. Bishop was among the first to appreciate and record the history of American industry, and his work remains an important reference book.

BRIDGENS, ROBERT
Furniture with Candelabra and Interior Decoration, London, 1838. Of the sixty plates, there are twenty-five designs in the Grecian style, twenty-seven in the Elizabethan and seven in the Gothic, although the majority seem merely typical early Victorian pieces with the appropriate ornament applied. Wall elevations, window cornices and draperies, doors, chimneypieces, and fire dogs are included, although most of the designs are for furniture. There is no text. Of the Elizabethan pieces illustrated, only the tables from Penshurst and Christ Church Cathedral, and the furnishings from Haddon Hall, appear genuine. Many of Bridgens' Elizabethan designs were engraved by SHAW. Apart from the two original examples, his Gothic furniture is noticeably less correct than PUGIN's, but it is generally less extreme than either his Grecian or Elizabethan designs. It was widely influential as a source book of ideas, although it is unknown whether any of his designs were directly copied.

The Cabinet Maker's Assistant
A series of original designs for modern furniture, with descriptions and details of construction. Preceded by practical observations on the materials and manufacture of cabinet work and instructions in drawing adapted to the trade, London, Blackie & Son, 1853. Beginning with a section on geometry and drawing, the next section contains advice on cabinet-making, with a detailed description of thirty-nine of the most popular woods and directions for their selection, cutting and seasoning, instructions on the most economical methods of constructing a piece of furniture and on carving and veneering. This is followed by 100 black and white engraved plates covering all types of furniture including such unusual items as rails on steam-boat berths, and a portable all-in-one bed chair and ottoman seat. The descriptions to the plates contain very detailed instructions to the cabinetmaker, illustrated by diagrams, including the comparative merits of different constructional methods, the tools to be used and the exact measurements. The furniture represented is typically mid-nineteenth century in shape, generally adapted stylistically by its ornament. The majority of the designs are in the Elizabethan style. Some of the most remarkable designs are for chairs: the National Emblem chairs have backs not only decorated with carved roses, shamrocks or thistles, but shaped accordingly. Most extraordinary are some of the details taken from the Great Exhibition which include massive table supports of 'fantastic combinations of animal and vegetable forms'. They well represent the enthusiastic search for the novel.

CONNER, ROBERT
The Cabinet-maker's Assistant, New York, 1842. There were numerous adaptations of Gothic design in American Victorian furniture, although the style was not as popular as in England, where its historical and romantic significance had greater meaning. According to Helen Comstock in *American Furniture: Seventeenth, Eighteenth, and Nineteenth Century Styles*, published in New York in 1962, SMITH illustrated a Gothic state bed as early as 1808 in his *A Collection of Designs for Household Furniture and Interior Decoration* and he also introduced Gothic plates in his *Guide* of 1826. His pupil, Robert Conner (active 1842-58), left England for New York, and in 1842, Conner's *The Cabinet-maker's Assistant* became the first book of Gothic designs to appear in America. The use of Gothic detail in American furniture had not waited for this, however. Smith's work was available, as was LOUDON's standard guide, the *Encyclopedia*. The Gothic style influenced American architecture considerably more than it did furniture design.

COOK, CLARENCE
The House Beautiful; essays on beds and tables, stools and candlesticks, New York, 1878. Composed of Cook's articles written for the magazine *Scribner's Monthly*, it contains chapters on the entrance, living room, dining room and bedroom, with a final chapter on general matters to help people furnish their homes in their own taste, relying less on the whims of fashion, the past or professionals. That it is written for the

average middle-class home is shown by Cook's stress on the 'living room', not the 'parlour' of those wealthy enough to have a room set apart for idleness; his preference for an informal way of life; his belief that no belongings are too good for daily use and in the stupidity of keeping up useless ceremonies. His aim is usefulness united with beauty, and simplicity made charming. Bearing in mind the lack of space in most New York apartments, he recommends the use of corners and walls where possible and the avoidance of anything super-fluous. He writes, 'there is hardly any-thing this time of ours enjoys less, less knows how to value, than a clear space of blank wall. . . . We have to admit in the face of all evidence that the designing faculty is not very active in this age; we weaken what we have . . . by perpetually and persistently copying the designs of those who have gone before us.' Though admiring seventeenth-, early and late eighteenth-century furniture, he says that if genuine articles cannot be ob-tained, it is preferable to have furniture made from good modern designs, not copied from past styles. The 111 black and white engravings also illustrate pieces showing Chinese or French influ-ence, and there are modern pieces with plain, rectangular shapes, some derived from Godwin's ideas and others showing EASTLAKE's influence. He mentions the names of New York firms where such pieces might be purchased, and com-pares New York with Paris and London, praising 'England, with its absolute perfection in the art of domestic living'. This book was influential not only in America but also in England. Engrav-ings from it were used to illustrate books in the ART AT HOME series.

DOWNING, ANDREW JACKSON

Cottage Residences ; or, a series of de-signs for rural cottages and cottage villas, and their gardens and grounds adapted to North America, New York and London, 1842. In 1842, Andrew Jackson Downing (1815–52) presented the rural public of America with ten designs for cottages in his desire to contribute something to 'the improve-ment of the domestic architecture and the rural taste of our country' so that 'at no distant day our country residences may rival "the cottage homes of England" so universally and so justly admired.' In his introductory chapter, Downing dis-cusses the importance of the principles of appropriateness, beauty, unity, har-mony and variety, and the different styles of architecture. Disliking the hypocrisy of using Greek temple forms for dwellings, he advocates 'The Rural Gothic' and Italian styles for country residences. He also includes designs in the Tudor style, and in the 'bracketed mode' with projecting roofs, supported by decorative brackets, which he thought highly suited to America. Chiefly con-cerned with the picturesque appearance, his designs show a concentration on the superficial ornamental details rather than any true understanding of the original style. Each set of designs is accompanied by measurements, descriptions and, of-ten, Downing's reasons for choosing such a style. He includes a design for a water closet, taken from LOUDON's *En-cyclopedia*, without which he considered no dwelling complete, and also for a rising cupboard or dumb waiter, and other labour-saving devices. Downing's extensive knowledge of horticulture is shown by elaborate plans for the lay-out of the grounds, ornamental and kitchen gardens and orchards, as well as his suggestions for planting, greenhouses, fences rendered ornamental, garden sculpture and fountains. In addition to the debt he owes to Loudon's *Encyclo-pedia*, he is indebted to the architect Alexander Davis and J. Notman for two of his designs, both of which had already been executed. This book of 187 pages, copiously illustrated with black and white engravings, was immediately suc-cessful. Downing was particularly in-strumental in establishing the Gothic style in America. His book sold well in England and his reputation spread to Denmark, Germany and the Low Coun-tries. It was republished in 1844, 1847, 1852, 1856, 1866, 1873 and 1887.

The Architecture of Country Houses in-cluding designs for cottages, farm houses and villas, with remarks on interiors, furniture and the best modes of warm-ing and ventilating, New York and Philadelphia, 1850. Determined to im-prove public taste, Downing published this, his most ambitious and best-known work, with thirteen designs for cottages, seven for farm houses, and fourteen for villas, believing that 'so long as men are forced to live in log huts and follow the hunter's life, we must not be surprised at lynch law and the use of the bowie knife. But, when smiling lawns and tasteful cottages begin to embellish a country, we know that order and culture are established.' Downing prefaces each section with a definition of the characteristics and uses of the type of dwelling concerned, and his general ideas on them. Each design is accom-panied by plans, measurements, de-scriptions of its accommodation and explanations for its construction, as well as an estimated cost; he also considers the varying supply of raw materials, climatic conditions and habits of different areas. In his concern for the picturesque, he advocates vine-covered verandas and advises on the cultivation of creepers. In the chapter on decoration, Downing dis-cusses the main current styles: the Grecian, Italian, Gothic (he includes a sketch of a room in his own house), Romanesque or Norman, Elizabethan or Renaissance, Louis Quatorze and the 'bracketed' style. He condemns the 'tasteless temples' of the Grecian style, and the Louis Quatorze as unsuitable for country dwellings. He shows a wide selection of furniture in current supply, designed by such well-known cabinet-makers as Platt and Roux of New York, and Hennessy of Boston, with other designs taken from the encyclopedias of LOUDON and WEBSTER. He writes that 'modern furniture has the merit of being simple, easily made and very moderate in cost', and that well designed, simple Gothic furniture is hard to find. He thinks that the surprising popularity of Elizabethan furniture is due to its 'picturesque charm' but, realizing its expense, advocates a simple and cheap modification with bobbin-turned sup-ports for cottages and farm houses in the 'bracketed' style. In others, he recom-mends cheap, plain, painted furniture, and he includes suggestions for his poorer readers of home-made furniture, made from boards and barrels, stuffed with hay and covered with chintz. This book of 484 pages, with approximately 300 black and white engravings, was enormously influential, and the results may still be seen in the eastern states and the Mid West. It was republished in 1851, 1852, 1853, 1856, 1861 and 1866. Downing remained the chief arbiter of American taste until EASTLAKE's book arrived in the 1870s. By then his dream of simple and tasteful dwellings for everyone was beginning to fade, replaced during the building boom following the Civil War by ostentation, although the Societies of Rural Art and Rural Taste in many towns were still trying to pro-mote similar ideas.

EASTLAKE, CHARLES L.

Hints on Household Taste in Furniture, Upholstery & Other Details, London 1868; Boston, 1872. Originally pub-lished as a series of articles in contem-porary journals. Charles Lock Eastlake (1836–1906), the chief theorist of the art movement, deplores the uneducated, commonplace taste, the endless search for novelty, the lowering of standards due to inferior mass production and the impossibility of buying from stock 'good artistic furniture of modern date and moderate price'. He condemns the tran-sient quality of furniture, the excessive curves and decoration of the Rococo

Revival and the dishonest methods of craftsmanship, especially veneering, French polishing, varnishing and staining. Betraying the influence of Morris and Ruskin, he advocates simplicity of design and sincerity of craftsmanship, and his resultant style is rectangular, sparsely decorated and functional, with a rude, Medieval quality. He discusses the rooms of a house and their furnishings, advocating simplicity, the uniformity of one style throughout and the artistic design of even the humblest articles. The book is illustrated with thirty-one plates and numerous smaller engravings, the majority drawn by Eastlake himself, either of antique pieces or of his own designs. Eastlake's ideas were revolutionary at the time and enormously influential. Although little furniture is directly attributable to him, his sane ideas and the greater suitability of his designs to domestic life than those of previous Gothic reformers did much to stimulate the demand for art furniture and led to three further editions of his book in 1869, 1872 and 1878, the latter with revised illustrations showing simpler pieces with a greater emphasis on turned supports. His book was most influential in America, giving rise to the Eastlake style, in effect, a parody of Eastlake's designs, although unmistakably founded on his ideas.

EDIS, ROBERT W.

Decoration and Furniture of Town Houses ; a series of Cantor lectures delivered before the Society of Arts, 1880, amplified and enlarged, London, 1881. In the 285 pages and twenty-nine black and white illustrations, Edis aims at showing how the decoration and furnishings of an average house could be improved economically, for he condemns many contemporary products as 'incongruous in design, bad in taste and often utterly commonplace and uncomfortable', partly the result of having been designed by upholsterers. In the first of the six lectures, he says that beauty is independent of any particular style, and that past or foreign art should not be slavishly imitated but studied profitably for its merits. Deploring the current love of novelty, pretentious show and dishonest craftsmanship, he praises the attempts made to improve taste by the establishment of the South Kensington School of Design, and by the Society of Arts and the Royal Academy. In the following four lectures, he discusses the decoration and furniture of various rooms of the house. In dealing specifically with town houses, he recommends fitted cupboards in recesses to save space and the avoidance of dust traps. He describes, and sometimes illustrates, the products

of contemporary firms, among which he particularly admires wallpapers by Morris. Edis' own designs, often surprisingly badly proportioned, are in the free Renaissance style with copious shelves, brackets and cupboards dominated by an architectural framework decorated with Renaissance ornament. He also admires the style of the late-eighteenth century. The last lecture covers general articles of domestic use.

HALL, JOHN

The Cabinet Maker's Assistant, embracing the most modern style of Cabinet furniture ; exemplified in new designs, practically arranged on 44 plates containing 198 figures: to which is prefixed a short treatise on linear perspective, for the use of practical men, Baltimore, 1840. America's first pattern book, the forty pages of text include a treatise on linear perspective. In his commentary Hall says 'his designs are Grecian, and that the style of the United States is blended with European taste'. In fact the designs are in the debased Classical style derived from the French Restoration period. The forty-four plates show furniture with plain veneered surfaces with scroll-shaped supports. There is no unnecessary ornament, for Hall aimed at designing furniture which could be produced economically. Many of these designs had been included earlier in the important broadsheet issued in 1833 by

Bedroom Furniture *made by Holland & Sons in light-stained or lacquer-painted wood, an illustration from* Decoration and Furniture of Town Houses *by Robert W. Edis, London, 1881.*

Joseph Meeks & Sons, the leading cabinetmaking firm in New York, which was the centre of production for this type of furniture. Hall's designs were taken up throughout the eastern half of America and another edition of his book appeared in 1848.

HOPE, THOMAS

Household Furniture and Interior Decoration, London, 1807. An illustrated record of the interior of his house in Duchess Street, London, rather than a pattern book. Hope illustrates the rooms he had remodelled to form appropriate settings for his collection of Egyptian, Greek and Roman antiquities and the furniture he designed from antique models with an archaeological accuracy that was hitherto unknown. The sixty black and white plates show not only interiors and furniture but Greek vases, details taken from antique pieces, mosaic borders of floors and ceilings and sets of silver vessels. He was indebted to his friend Percier who, with Fontaine, published *Recueil de Décorations Intérieures* (1801 and 1812) which provided the prototype for his book. The most important publication of the early nineteenth century, it established the English Empire style and the designs were widely copied. GEORGE SMITH's publication in 1808 with the same title is a direct imitation of Hope's, although his designs are less accomplished and less archaeologically correct. Hope's rectilinear furniture, either of solid wood or with veneered or painted surfaces, and its decoration, chiefly of applied ormolu ornament, was well suited to the new industrial methods of the nineteenth century. His son wrote in 1861: 'He, the first of Englishmen, con-

ceived and taught the idea of art-manu-
facture, of allying the beauty of form to
the wants and products of common life.'
In his deliberate search for a new style
and his insistence on symbolical details
to portray the function, he anticipates
the attitudes of later nineteenth-century
designers.

HUNT, THOMAS FREDERICK
Exemplars of Tudor Architecture; adapted to modern habitations with illustrative details adapted from ancient edifices
and observations on the furniture of the
Tudor period, London, 1830. First
publication prompting the Elizabethan
Revival. In the thirty-seven black and
white plates, Hunt adapts Tudor and
Elizabethan architecture, which he considers on a level with that of Ancient
Greece and Rome and the most applicable to English dwellings, to modern
habitations. In the section on furniture
he illustrates and describes the furniture
of the Tudor and Elizabethan periods,
bemoaning the loss of their splendour,
but comforting himself with the greater
comfort, convenience and cleanliness of
his own time.

JONES, OWEN
*Plans, Elevations, Sections and Details of
the Alhambra;* from drawings taken on
the spot in 1834 by the late M. Jules
Goury and in 1834 and 1837 by Owen
Jones. With a complete translation of the
Arabic inscriptions, and an historical
notice of the Kings of Granada, from the
conquest of that city by the Arabs to
the expulsion of the moors, by Mr
Pasqual de Gayangos, London, 1842 and
1845. Volume I contains a scholarly
history of the Kings of Granada by Mr
Pasqual de Gayangos and fifty-one
large-scale plates, many of them beautiful chromo-lithographs, which show
views, plans and sections of the many
different parts of the Alhambra. Each
plate is accompanied by text, written in
both English and French. Volume II has
no text, and the fifty plates illustrate
decorative details of the palace. The
plates are drawn mostly by Jones himself, in extraordinary detail. A plaster
cast was taken of every ornament to ensure complete accuracy in the drawings,
and the exact scale is usually given. In
the colour plates the decoration has been
restored to its original brightness. Its
publication was largely responsible for
the adoption of the Moorish style as an
ornamental alternative for designers.
Another edition appeared in 1847–8.
The Grammar of Ornament: illustrated
by examples from various styles of ornament, London, 1856. In the twenty
chapters, illustrated by 100 lithographs,
Owen Jones (1809–74) covers the ornamentation of savage tribes, the Egyp-

Elizabethan Ornament, *detail of a page
from* The Grammar of Ornament *by
Owen Jones (1809-74), London 1856,
showing (top) a late James I wood carving,
and (above) a wood diaper. Both from
Aston Hall, Warwickshire.*

tians, Assyrians, Greeks, Pompeians,
Romans, Byzantines, Arabs, Turks,
Moors and Persians, continuing with
that of the Indians, Hindus, Chinese and
Celts, and of the Middle Ages, Renaissance, Elizabethans and Italians. The
last chapter is devoted to leaves and
flowers and ornament taken directly
from nature. He presented it in the hope
that designers would study these decorations, compare them with natural forms,
and then create new styles instead of
reproducing the works of the past. At
the beginning he states thirty-seven
general principles which cover the
relationship between decorative arts and
architecture, design, proportion and
colour. In particular, he stresses that
natural forms should be idealized, not
copied exactly. In the text, illustrated by
small black and white engravings, he

outlines the circumstances of the races
who produced each style. The plates,
mainly sub-divided into numerous examples, show decorations taken from
buildings, museums and publications.
Jones acknowledges the assistance of
among others, James Wild, J. B. Waring,
C. Dresser and Digby Wyatt in supplying illustrations and essays. The most
distinguished work in its field, it was
widely used by designers as a source
book of ornamental motifs. Further
editions appeared in 1865 and 1868.

KING, THOMAS
The Modern Style of Cabinet Work;
exemplified in new designs, practically
arranged, London, 1829. Seventy-two
plates of designs, seventeen coloured,
illustrating furniture in the debased
Classical style with heavy, often rather
clumsy shapes, generally decorated with
carved foliage of a luxuriant nature. He
also included a Gothic hall chair and
two Gothic bookcases, reflecting the
current opinion that the Gothic style was
suitable only for halls and libraries. In
his use of plain, veneered surfaces,
scroll-shaped supports and his consideration of economy, he may well have influenced HALL in the United States. The
book was republished five times before
1863, in 1840 with twenty-eight supple-
mentary plates including designs for
adaptable pieces.

(continued on page 66)

OPPOSITE ABOVE *Morris, Marshall, Faulkner & Co. period room, the oak table and
copper candlesticks, wardrobe with paintings by Sir Edward Burne Jones (1833-98),
settle and the St George Cabinet with
paintings by William Morris (1834-96) all
by Philip Webb (1831-1915). The wallpaper is* Pomegranate *and the carpet* Lily.
Victoria and Albert Museum.

OPPOSITE BELOW *Mantelpiece from the
Lawrence House, Beverly, Massachusetts,
c. 1870, the pair of chairs made by Pottier
& Stymus, New York, c. 1875, and the
stained-glass screen, American, c. 1880.
Metropolitan Museum of Art.*

OVERLEAF *Parlour suite in the style of J. H.
Belter (b. 1804), New York, 1850-60.
The centre table, étagère, tête-à-tête and
chairs are in the Rococo style. Metropolitan
Museum of Art.*

1 Birch	2 Yew	3 Burr yew	4 Laburnum	5 Sycamore	6 Mahogany
7 Tuliptree	8 Olive	9 London plane	10 Burr plane	11 Ebony	12 Scotch pine
13 Apple	14 American walnut	15 Pear	16 Macassar ebony	17 Satinwood	18 Cedar
19 Palm	20 Box	21 Bog oak	22 Ash	23 English walnut	24 Sapele
25 Elm	26 Purpleheart	27 Lime	28 Jacaranda	29 Oregon pine	30 Padouk
31 Palm endgrain	32 Holly	33 Lignum vitae	34 Maple	35 Oak	36 Pollard oak

Woods used in furniture making

Apple (13)
Hard, pinkish, fine-grained fruitwood used in the manufacture of country furniture and suitable for turned work.

Ash (22)
Tough, elastic and light brown with yellowish veins, the English variety was found to be suitable for wheels and the working parts of machinery. It was also used for the seats of traditional country chairs and for the interior fittings of chests of drawers and wardrobes (for which its lack of smell was considered desirable). In the United States its principal use was for strong upholstery frames.

Birch (1)
Varying from hard to soft, with an undulating grain, it has a sparkling, translucent appearance. Sometimes stained, though seldom satisfactorily, to resemble MAHOGANY and WALNUT, it was more often polished unstained and used as a VENEER on bedroom furniture. It was extensively used for cheap mass-produced pieces and in the manufacture of plywood after 1890.

Box (20)
Hard, fine-grained yellow wood, turning brown when polished, used in the solid for snuff-boxes and for STRINGING and MARQUETRY.

Cedar (18)
From North America, the reddish wood of the pencil cedar is soft and light, has an agreeable smell and takes a smooth, silky finish. Its use was primarily for the linings of small drawers and for the interior fittings of cabinets. The wood of the cedar of Lebanon is inferior in quality and has never been used successfully in furniture making.

Ebony (11 and 16)
Tropical, hard, heavy, dense black timber, which takes a fine, silky finish and is not liable to shrinkage, extensively used in MARQUETRY and STRINGING and for piano keys and knife handles. Macassar ebony (16), distinguished by stripes of orange and dark brown, is an inferior wood.

Elm (25)
Lightish brown, strongly grained wood native to England and North America, it was used early in the nineteenth century in conjunction with BURR elm for drawing-room furniture. Later in the century it was used chiefly for traditional forms of country chair. The example is of English elm.

Holly (32)
Hard, white, close-grained wood, which takes a good polish. When dyed black it was used for STRINGING, and it was extensively used in the manufacture of TUNBRIDGEWARE (see MISCELLANY GLOSSARY).

Jacaranda (28)
Fine, South American rosewood, heavy and used throughout the nineteenth century in the solid, sometimes for billiard-table legs, and as a VENEER.

Laburnum (4)
Hard, durable timber, whose conspicuous striped character is produced by the sudden natural change in colour from the dark brown of the heart wood to the yellow of the outer annual rings. It was used principally as a VENEER on tables, mirror frames and bureaus.

Lignum vitae (33)
Tropical wood, dark brown streaked with black, very hard when seasoned and used in turnery and in the manufacture of utilitarian objects such as bowls and mortars.

Lime (27)
Pale, fine and straight grained. Because of its even texture and capacity for sharp outline, it was found to be suitable for carving and, like PEAR, as a ground for japanning.

Mahogany (6)
Used for all types of furniture, notably chairs, bedposts, table tops and legs, and as a VENEER, it was imported into England and the United States throughout the nineteenth century. Mahogany from San Domingo is hard and dark in colour; from Cuba, as illustrated, dark but tending to show a more varied FIGURE; from Honduras lighter and easier to work. A similar but inferior wood is native to West Africa.

Maple (34)
Whitish in colour, close grained, easily

worked and not liable to warp, it was principally used in turnery and for such everyday domestic objects as cutting boards. BIRD'S EYE maple was one of the most admired of nineteenth-century ornamental woods used, often in conjunction with gilding, for mirror and picture frames and as a VENEER for such purposes as the interior fittings of DAVENPORTS to contrast with the darker wood of the exterior.

Oak (35, 21 and 36)
Hard, heavy and varying in colour from white to brown, favoured for hall, dining-room and library furniture, usually unstained and polished. It was also employed for drawer linings and rails in pieces of good quality. The unnatural swelling that forms at the end of branches when the tree has been pollarded produces fine VENEERS (36). Bog oak (21), stained black by long immersion in water or peat bog, is used in the solid and in MARQUETRY and as an inlay.

Olive (8)
Hard, close-grained Mediterranean wood of yellowish-green colour with dark, cloudy markings, used as a VENEER.

Padouk (30)
Imported from Burma and the Andaman Islands and known in the United States as vermilion wood, it is hard and heavy, varying in colour from golden brown to deep red when first cut. It was used in the solid, especially for fretwork, and less often as a VENEER as an expensive alternative to MAHOGANY.

Palm (19 and 31)
Used in both long and cross grain as a decorative VENEER especially for table tops, often manufactured in the West Indies for the European and American markets.

Pear (15)
Strong, pale, fine-grained wood, slightly pinkish in colour, used in MARQUETRY and often EBONIZED.

Pine (12 and 29)
Softwood native to Europe and North America, cheap and readily available. It is easily carved and was extensively used as a carcase wood. It was often treated to simulate other, more expensive, woods and as a base for painting. The examples are of *pinus sylvestris*, or red pine (12), and Oregon, or yellow, pine (29).

Plane (9 and 10)
Tough and close grained, often used in England, like beech, for the frames of painted chairs. The burrwood (10) was sometimes used as a VENEER.

Purpleheart (26)
Hard, rigid wood of purplish colour, regularly grained with narrow, black streaks, from South and Central America. In the United States it is also known as amaranth. It was used principally for decorative details in furniture.

Sapele (24)
Imported towards the end of the nineteenth century from Africa as a cheap alternative to MAHOGANY, with which it has much in common. The large size of the tree made it suitable for table tops.

Satinwood (17)
Light, fine-grained, delicately veined wood, its rich yellow colour fading to a pale gold. Imported in the eighteenth and early nineteenth centuries from San Domingo, an inferior variety was imported later in the century from Singapore and Bombay. It was used principally as a VENEER, in the 1890s painted with floral cartouches and borders in imitation of late eighteenth-century furniture of the Sheraton period.

Sycamore (5)
Close-grained white wood, yellowing with age and often occurring with the rippling FIGURE also found in SATINWOOD and MAHOGANY. When used as a VENEER for small table tops and polished, it turns a greenish grey. It is sometimes stained dark green and used in MARQUETRY, when it is known as harewood, and it is also frequently EBONIZED.

Tuliptree (7)
Cheap, soft and easily worked, it varies in colour from white, through grey-green, to pale brown and was often EBONIZED. It should not be confused with tulipwood, an exotic timber related to rosewood.

Walnut (14 and 23)
Native to England and North America, it is uniform in texture and pale brown in colour streaked with lines of black and darker brown. Easily carved and with an interesting FIGURE, it was employed both in the solid and as a VENEER.

Yew (2 and 3)
Durable, close-grained wood, notable for its elasticity and toughness of fibre. Windsor chairs are traditionally of yew with ASH seats. BURR yew (3) is expensive as the slow-growing excrescence from which it is derived is comparatively rare. It is found as a VENEER and is sometimes difficult to distinguish from amboyna.

Pattern Books Influential in the Victorian Period
(continued from page 60)

LOUDON, JOHN CLAUDIUS
An Encyclopedia of Cottage, Farm and Villa Architecture and Furniture; containing numerous designs for dwellings, from the cottage to the villa, including farm houses, farmeries, and other agricultural buildings; several designs for country inns, public houses, and parochial schools; with the requisite fittings-up, fixtures, and furniture; and appropriate offices, gardens and garden scenery; each design accompanied by analytical and critical remarks, illustrative of the principles of architectural science and taste on which it is composed, London, 1833. Issued in monthly parts during 1832, it was written chiefly for the rural populations of Britain, America and Australia. A single volume of 1,138 pages and more than 2,000 engravings, it is divided into four parts: the first three cover the architecture, exterior and interior finishings and furnishings of cottages, farm houses and their out-buildings, country inns and schools, and villas; the fourth is a serious and analytical discussion on art and taste. Unlike most previous pattern books, Loudon included designs for cheap, utilitarian pieces for the humblest quarters as well as designs for the wealthy. Designs in all the currently approved architectural styles were included. In the preface to villa furniture, Loudon describes the four main styles: the Grecian or modern style, by far the most common, Gothic, Elizabethan, and the 'style of the age of Louis XIV or the florid Italian'; the latter he dismisses as

too expensive and unsuited to the present age. In many ways, Loudon seems in advance of his time with his revolutionary ideas for cast-iron furniture, bathrooms in inns and 'cheerful' country school rooms, and in his anticipation of cooking by gas and oil. Himself responsible for the text, the illustrations are the work of others, including SHAW for many of the Elizabethan designs and Robert and William Mallett, Dublin engineers, for the cast-iron furniture and tubular steel chairs. Some designs resemble those in earlier pattern books. The encyclopedia had enormous influence on public taste, and it remained the principal copybook for builders and furniture makers for at least fifty years, being republished in 1835, 1836, 1839, 1842, 1846, 1847, 1850, 1853, 1857, 1863 and 1867. It left a permanent mark on the rural and suburban architecture of England, and lodges and gatehouses, cottages, farm buildings, inns, schools and railway stations were copied from its illustrations. It was also widely influential in America where Loudon had arranged for 5,000 prospectuses to be distributed before its publication in 1833, and it was republished there as late as 1883. DOWNING, in particular, acknowledged a debt to Loudon.

Gothic Chairs, *an illustration from* Gothic Furniture *by A. W. N. Pugin (1812-52), London, 1835. After his death the influence of Pugin's designs for furniture were strongly felt in the carved pieces made by J. G. Crace & Sons.*

NASH, JOSEPH
The Mansions of England in the Olden Time, 4 vols, London 1839, 1840, 1841, 1849. Romanticized but fairly accurate views of English country houses by the water-colourist and draughtsman, Joseph Nash (1808–78). Each volume contains twenty-six tinted plates of interiors with contemporary furniture and exteriors, illustrating fifty-four houses from the Medieval to the Jacobean period. They were enormously influential on the romantic Victorian who, though he may not have been able to build a complete house in the Tudor or Elizabethan style, could afford to decorate his rooms with oak panelling, stained-glass windows and elaborately carved oak furniture.

NICHOLSON, PETER and MICHAEL ANGELO
The Practical Cabinet-Maker, Upholsterer and Complete Decorator, London, 1826. Most accomplished of the late Regency pattern books, planned by the Scottish mathematician and architect, Peter Nicholson. He wrote the introduction, a long illustrated treatise on geometry with mathematical instructions for cabinetmakers and the glossary of technical terms. His son, Michael Angelo, an architectural draughtsman, was responsible for the eighty-one plates (many coloured) of furniture designs, the Classical orders and ornament. Although the Grecian style predominates, there are a few examples of Gothic pieces. Another edition was published in 1835 with some different plates, which had been issued separately during the

intervening period. They showed similar pieces with a tendency towards more profuse decoration.

PUGIN, AUGUSTUS WELBY NORTHMORE
Gothic Furniture in the Style of the Fifteenth Century, London, 1835. Making a change from the sentimental Medievalism of his father, and of his own earlier designs, to a more serious and archaeological approach, this pattern book has been considered as the first reformist manifesto. Besides the beautiful frontispiece and endpiece, there are twenty-three black and white engraved plates and, unlike most contemporary pattern books, there is no text or commentary, and no plans or scales are given. A. W. N. Pugin (1812–52) was a superb draughtsman, and every detail of the elaborate tracery and the stylized foliage is beautifully delineated. The pieces are on the whole so ornate that they would have been extremely costly to execute and difficult to accommodate in a domestic environment. However, the plainer chairs and bed, the tables, chests, stools, fire screen and *prie-dieu* were adapted by the commercial firms for mass production. Although these designs were probably less influential than the furniture designed by him and made by J. G. Crace of Wigmore Street, furniture which had its origins in his designs was extremely popular over a long period.
The True Principles of Pointed or Christian Architecture; set forth in two lectures delivered at St Marie's, Oscott, London, 1841. Based on two lectures given by Pugin at the College of St

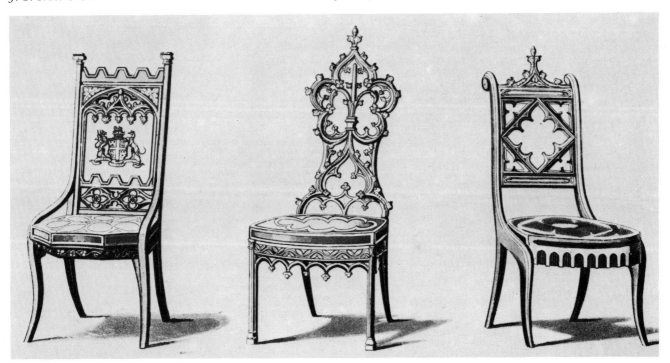

Marie, Oscott, where he was Professor of Ecclesiastical Antiquities, it sets forth the two basic principles of design: 'that there should be no features about a building which are not necessary for convenience, construction or propriety' and 'that all ornament should consist of enrichment of the essential construction of the building.' He says that the current decline in architecture is due to the neglect of these rules, and that only in Gothic architecture are they obeyed. Pugin deplores the misuse of Gothic decoration by manufacturers, especially in the metal trade, and their practice of disguising, rather than beautifying, objects of utility. He also condemns interior designers and furniture makers who lavish ecclesiastical detail on domestic articles with unsuitable and uncomfortable results. Pugin concludes by urging his countrymen to overthrow 'modern paltry taste and paganism' and 'restore the Christian ideas of our Catholic ancestors'. The sixty-seven pages are illustrated by ten black and white plates and seventy-eight smaller engravings, mostly of Gothic buildings and constructional details, carving and metalwork. It was one of the major influences behind the Gothic Revival and encouraged William Morris and others in their dislike of dishonest craftsmanship.

Floriated Ornament, London, 1849. In his introduction Pugin says that Gothic foliage is, in fact, natural foliage adapted and arranged. He contrasts the decorative use of nature by past and present designers: the former arranged them in well-defined geometrical patterns, so shaped as to fill up the specified area, while the modern artist uses shadow and foreshortening to give a dishonest appearance of relief to a flat surface. In producing these designs composed of natural flowers and foliage, he hoped to reverse these practices and to counteract the current debased and spiritless copies. The thirty-one chromo-lithographed plates illustrate geometrical designs in rich colours. Many different types of flowers and foliage are used, both cultivated and wild, including thistles and ears of wheat. His designs were widely influential, particularly in the ecclesiastical field for textiles, stained glass and tiles.

SHAW, HENRY
Specimens of Ancient Furniture, from existing authorities – by Henry Shaw, with descriptions by Sir Samuel Rush Meyrick, London, 1836. This work first appeared in part issues from 1832 to 1835. Its publication was probably due to the antiquarian and writer, Sir Samuel Rush Meyrick (1783–1848), who wrote

the learned introduction, in which he discusses furnishings of the past, and the descriptions of each plate. Henry Shaw (1800–73), an accurate and prolific draughtsman, was responsible for most of the beautiful and detailed engraved plates which illustrate all kinds of furniture from the thirteenth to the late seventeenth century, particularly Gothic and Elizabethan, as well as various other objects. Most of the illustrations were taken from examples of English furniture in private ownership, but a few are of foreign pieces, and others were copied from Medieval, particularly French, illuminated manuscripts. Some of the plates show articles that are obviously not genuine, revealing the fairly common nineteenth-century practice of concocting an Elizabethan piece of furniture from a few original carvings. *Specimens* was widely influential in the adoption of the Elizabethan style during the early Victorian period. In particular, it may have influenced the architect Anthony Salvin in his Elizabethan suites for Mamhead, Devonshire, and Scotney Castle, Kent. As the first English book on antique furniture, it probably encouraged the fashion for collecting, and it was an important source book for designers.

SMITH, GEORGE
The Cabinet-Maker and Upholsterer's Guide, drawing book and repository of new and original designs for household furniture and interior decoration, in the most approved and modern taste including specimens of the Egyptian, Grecian, Gothic, Arabesque, French, English and other schools of art, London, 1828. In the introduction to this lengthy work of 220 pages, with 153 plates, Smith dismisses his designs of 1808 (see under HOPE) as wholly obsolete due to the rapid change in taste during the past twenty years. Realizing new forms must be found to replace the dying Regency style, he illustrates interiors in the Egyptian, Grecian, Etruscan, Roman, Gothic and Louis Quatorze styles. There is also one entitled English 1827 which shows a medley of Classical and Louis Quatorze decoration. Generally, the furniture is heavier and clumsier, and its decoration coarser, than earlier Regency pieces, and, compared with the NICHOLSONS', his designs lack elegance. This book, the most important of the late Regency publications, was influential not only in England, but also in America, where it soon became available.

SMITH, JOHN MOYR
Ornamental Interiors, Ancient and Modern, London, 1887. General account of contemporary interiors, containing a

survey of decoration from the earliest times to the present. Smith is interesting on the subject of his contemporaries, and discusses the contributions and publications of various designers including William Burges, EASTLAKE, TALBERT, William Morris, Voysey and the work of G. E. Street, Alfred Waterhouse, W. Butterfield and Gilbert Scott. He describes the interiors of famous buildings such as the Houses of Parliament, the Royal Palaces, Manchester Town Hall, with its paintings by Ford Madox Brown, and rooms in the Town Halls of Antwerp and Brussels, as well as the principal London theatres. He claims that due to the enormous advance made by manufacturers during the last twenty years, they have surpassed architects in design, and that as a result of the wide choice now available, the decoration and furnishing of houses is easier than ever before. The book has thirty-two plates and ninety-two smaller illustrations, and includes only three of his own designs.

Hanging corner cupboard of ebonized wood with painted decoration after a design by John Moyr Smith (active 1870-89). Smith designed art furniture for Collinson & Lock. Sotheby's Belgravia.

SPOFFORD, HARRIET PRESCOTT
Art Decoration Applied to Furniture, New York, 1878. Appearing first in *Harper's Bazaar* in the United States, it comprises a brief history of Ancient and Early English decoration and furniture, chapters on the types of furniture, tracing their ancestry, on the ornament of the recently adopted styles: Gothic, Renaissance, Elizabethan, Jacobean, Louis Quatorze, Louis Quinze, Louis Seize, Pompeian, First Empire, Moor-

ish, Eastlake, Queen Anne and Oriental, and on modern furniture and furnishing. She praises EASTLAKE's *Hints on Household Taste*, 'a volume that has done a great work towards revolutionizing the manufacture of furniture', and advocates the Gothic. The majority of the 109 engravings are from TALBERT's *Gothic Forms Applied to Furniture*. Mrs Spofford (1835–1921) believed that 'provided that there is space enough to move about, without walking over the furniture, there is hardly likely to be too much in the room,' and her consideration of so many different styles reflects the attitudes of her time. As one of the first American books on decoration, it became enormously popular.

TALBERT, BRUCE J.

Gothic Forms Applied to Furniture, Metal Work and Decoration for Domestic Purposes; illustrated with thirty pages of geometrical and perspective sketches, London, 1867; Boston, 1873. Influenced in his ideas by Webb, Burges and SHAW, Bruce Talbert (1838–81) rejects the High Victorian Gothic of PUGIN as undesirable in cabinet work, and like EASTLAKE, offers a more practical style of Gothic to the public. Characterized by its lack of curves and florid carving, it relies mainly on basic framed construction, decorated with piercing, inlay, low-relief carving or decorative panels with bold metal hinges. Despite his recommendations of simplicity, his designs seem ornate. The book was much acclaimed and his designs were imitated by commercial firms. JOHN MOYR SMITH in *Ornamental Interiors* (1887) says that Talbert's design for a drawing-room, with its panelled walls and ceiling, coved frieze and vast Gothic chimneypiece, and its Gothic furniture, was 'without doubt the cause of the new style of decoration taking hold of the public'.

Examples of Ancient and Modern Furniture, Metal Work, Tapestries, Decoration, London, 1876; Boston, 1877. Published as a continuation of *Gothic Forms,* the 1867 introduction is reprinted, but Talbot's earlier progressive ideas, with the exception of designs for a drawing room and for a sideboard, both drawn in *c.* 1870, are replaced by unoriginal designs in the style of the late sixteenth and early seventeenth centuries. Several plates illustrate flat patterns for wallpapers and draperies consisting of heavy designs of flowers, fruit and foliage, sometimes including Oriental motifs, and others show beautifully drawn examples of medieval metalwork. The book exerted little influence for it merely offered additional designs in the late Elizabethan and Jacobean styles, which had been widely employed for some time.

Sleeping Beauty Cabinet designed by Bruce Talbert (1838-81) and made by Holland & Sons, 1867. Talbert encouraged the imitation of first the Early English and later the Jacobean styles. Victoria and Albert Museum.

WEBSTER, THOMAS

An Encyclopedia of Domestic Economy; comprising such subjects as are most immediately connected with house keeping: as, the construction of domestic edifices, with the modes of warming, ventilating and lighting them; a description of the various articles of furniture, with the nature of their materials; duties of servants; a general account of the animal and vegetable substances used as food, and the methods of preserving and preparing them by cooking; making bread; the chemical nature and the preparation of all kinds of fermented liquors used as beverage; materials employed in dress and the toilette; business of the laundry; description of the various wheel-carriages; preservation of health; domestic medicine, etc., etc., London, 1844. Initiated by LOUDON, although Webster was responsible for the majority of it, it is 1,253 pages long, comprising twenty-six sections, and covers every possible subject connected with housekeeping. It has nearly 1,000 black and white engravings. In the section on housing, Webster writes that modern Grecian architecture 'is admirably suited to our present domestic habits, and is considered, by the greater number of well-educated architects and amateurs, as excelling every other style in the most important parts'. In the section on furniture, Webster gives a history of Classical and English furniture, borrowing from the publications of HUNT and HOPE; DOWNING in turn borrows from Webster in *The Architecture of Country Houses.* Webster praises Hope for a revolutionary improvement in the design of furniture. Discussing the contemporary fashion, he writes, 'it is difficult to say what it is, and indeed it does not admit of any accurate description'. He regards the Louis Quatorze 'with its abundance of light, ornamental scrollwork and foliage' as admirably suited to the drawing room and unequalled in splendour. The encyclopedia also contains separate chapters on cabinetmaking and upholstering, the materials used in furniture, gilding, bronzing, japanning and varnishing, lacquering, the history of furniture, contemporary furniture and the complete furnishing of rooms. Mrs William Parkes was responsible for the section on servants, and some of those on cookery, while her son, a surgeon, contributed most of that on health. Amended to conform to American needs by D. Meredith Reese, it appeared in America in 1845, with a further publication in 1849. Another appeared in both countries in 1852.

WHARTON, EDITH, and CODMAN, OGDEN, JR

The Decoration of Houses, New York, 1897; London, 1898. Scholarly book, maintained by the authors to be the first book on 'house decoration as a branch of architecture' to appear in America or England for fifty years. Written for the very wealthy in the hope that their poorer neighbours would follow, only the most exquisite decoration, usually on a grand scale, is discussed, with examples taken from the *palazzi*, *châteaux* and mansions of Europe from the time of the Renaissance onwards. The 198 pages, divided into sixteen chapters, trace the historical traditions of the main elements of a room: the walls, doors, windows, fireplaces, ceiling and floor, and the origins and growth of the various rooms of a house from the beginning of the sixteenth century in Italy, the time of Louis XIV in France, and that of Inigo Jones in England. The authors stress that a building and its decoration should be appropriate to its function, and that the furniture and decoration should harmonize. The fifty-six black and white photographs illustrate pieces of antique, particularly French, furniture. The authors advocate the plainest possible furniture when antiques or good copies cannot be obtained, with lamps and books as embellishments.

WHITAKER, HENRY

The Practical Cabinet Maker & Upholsterer's Treasury of Designs, House-Furnishing & Decorating Assistant; in the Grecian, Italian, Renaissance, Louis Quatorze, Gothic, Tudor and Elizabethan styles; interspersed with designs executed for the royal palaces, and for some of the principal mansions of the nobility and gentry, and club houses, London, 1847. Designs for stair railings, chimneypieces, stoves, grates, wallpapers, window cornices and draperies, china and silver are included in an attempt to show that beauty may be achieved as cheaply as ugliness, although most of the 111 black and white engravings are for furniture. Though Whitaker boasts 'original designs in the Grecian, Italian, Renaissance, Louis XIV, Gothic, Tudor and Elizabethan styles', the pieces represented are merely ornate versions of typical mid-century products, and variations in ornament,

not basic structure, are responsible for the stylistic differences. In his accompanying notes, he recommends adaptability: discussing a design for a marquetry table top, he says it is equally applicable to a ceiling, and a design for an upright piano 'could do very well for a writing table and bookcase united'. Most of the designs are over elaborate, and he admits an Elizabethan sideboard 'is perhaps richer than a work of general utility would justify, were it not for the carving companies who very much now facilitate the boosting of carvings' and could execute such a design at moderate cost. Whitaker's book is important for illustrating the Italian pieces he had designed for Osborne, and those for the Conservative Club in the Grecian style. Other executed designs include pieces for Chatsworth, the Duke of Northumberland and the Duchess of Sutherland.

Glossary

Bird's eye
Circular FIGURE produced by cutting through small growths in the wood, especially of the MAPLE.

Boston rocker
American rocking chair with a curving seat and scrolled top rail often bearing painted or stencilled decoration.

Burl, or burr
Abnormal growth common to ASH, MAPLE, WALNUT, ELM, OAK and YEW, cross sections of which are used for decorative VENEERS.

Canterbury
Stand with divisions for music, usually on castors. In the late Victorian period the term was also used to describe a box music seat with a hinged lid. Alternatively, it has been used to describe a supper tray with partitions for plates and cutlery.

Chesterfield
OVERSTUFFED sofa, usually with buttoned upholstery.

Cheval glass
Full- or three-quarter-length dressing mirror, suspended on screws from a pair of supports so that it is free to swing and generally on long feet.

Confidante
Sofa or settee with separate seats at each end with upholstered divisions. It was sometimes used in the nineteenth century as a general term for multiple seating.

Davenport
Small writing-desk with a sloping lift

lid, often with a gallery, and drawers beneath that pull out from one side. The original model was made by Gillow's for a Captain Davenport in the eighteenth century and many versions of it were made in the early and mid-Victorian periods.

Davenport, English, mid-nineteenth century. Mahogany with a galleried fretwork superstructure. Sotheby's Belgravia.

Davenport bed
American, late-nineteenth-century couch that may be transformed into a bed.

Divan
Turkish-inspired seat without arms or back. A divan easy chair is the nineteenth-century name for an armchair with a long seat and rolled over arms.

Dwarf bookcase
Small bookcase, after the mid-nineteenth century usually square, table height and sometimes revolving.

Ebonized wood
Stained and polished wood resembling EBONY. Employed in the eighteenth century, it was popular for Arts and Crafts furniture.

Endgrain
Grain of a cross section of a tree.

Étagère
Whatnot or tiered stand, often of fragile construction, popularly used in the nineteenth century for the display of curios and memorabilia.

Fiddleback
Parallel curly FIGURE such as is found in SYCAMORE, used for violin backs. It is characteristic also of MAHOGANY, MAPLE and WALNUT veneers.

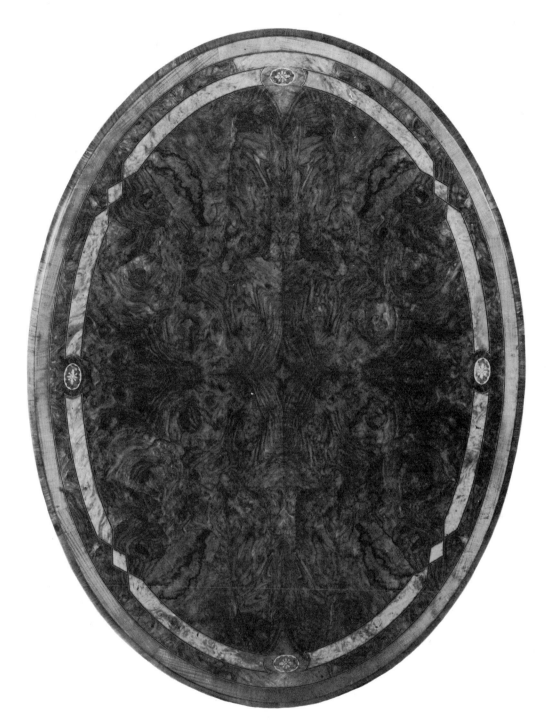

Figure
Characteristic markings of wood such as
FIDDLEBACK, BURL, OYSTERSHELL.
French polish
Introduced into England from France
in about 1820. A solution of shellac (thin
plates of dark-red resin) dissolved in
spirit is applied to a wood surface on a
pad. Several coats are added at intervals
until a hard, glossy film of shellac
covers the surface.
Gondola chair
Chair with arms that continue in a down-
ward curve from the back, also known in
the United States as a *chaise gondole*.

*Breakfast Table, English, mid-nineteenth
century. This has a burr walnut marquetry
top with maple and harewood banding and
ebony stringing ; the base is mahogany.
Sotheby's Belgravia.*

Hourglass stool
Characteristically Victorian seat resem-
bling an hour glass in form, often with
sides of pleated fabric.
Jardinière
Flower stand.
Library steps
Mobile or folding ladder or steps, often

converting into a chair, used for reaching the high shelves of a bookcase.
Marquetry
Decorative, pictorial, inlay of contrasting woods set into a VENEERED surface.
Méridienne
French Empire style short sofa with one
arm higher than the other.
Ottoman
Upholstered seat in the Turkish style
with or without back and arms popularized in the nineteenth century by
LOUDON and DOWNING. Circular and
octagonal models often had pot plants or
a decorative object in the centre.

Sofa in the Renaissance Revival style attributed to John Jelliff (1813-93), Newark, c. 1860. Deep-buttoned upholstery was popular in Britain and the United States from the beginning of the Victorian period. Newark Museum.

LEFT *Tête-à-tête, New York, 1850s. Laminated rosewood with carved decoration. Seating furniture of this type, allowing for private conversation between two people, was Victorian in origin and popular on both sides of the Atlantic. Metropolitan Museum of Art.*

Overstuffing
Thickly padded upholstery disguising the framework of seat furniture, common in the Victorian period for reasons of comfort and economy.

Oystering or oystershell veneer
Veneer with a FIGURE of concentric rings cut at right angles to the length of a root or small branch, usually of the WALNUT, LABURNUM, LIGNUM VITAE or OLIVE.

Parquetry
Similar to MARQUETRY, and often used in conjunction with it, but forming a geometric pattern. It may be inlaid into

Prie-dieu chair, American, 1840-55. Walnut with needlework and velvet upholstery. The chair is in the Elizabethan Revival style. Greenfield Village and Henry Ford Museum.

solid wood, set into a VENEERED surface or form a veneer.
Prie-dieu
Praying desk of Medieval origin, which became popular in the mid-nineteenth century.

Prie-dieu chair
Upholstered chair with a low seat and tall back derived from a kneeling or prayer chair popularized in the mid-Victorian period partially because of its suitability for ladies with voluminous skirts.
Stringing
Narrow band of inlay.
Teapoy
Small table on a single support, after the mid-nineteenth century usually with a box or tea caddy forming the top.
Tête-à-tête
Two-seated sofa with an S-shaped arm, also known as a *Siamoise* or *vis-à-vis*. A three- or six-seated version is sometimes known as a companion chair.
Veneer
Overlay of thin wood glued to the carcase for decorative effect and for economic use of expensive woods and those that are difficult to work.

Bibliography

ANDREWS, EDWARD DEMING and FAITH. *Shaker Furniture*, Yale, 1937; New York, 1964

ASLIN, ELIZABETH. *Nineteenth Century English Furniture*, London, 1962

BIRD, ANTHONY. *Early Victorian Furniture*, London, 1964

BORDES, MARILYNN JOHNSON. 'Furniture 1790–1910' in *The Britannica Encyclopaedia of American Art*, Chicago, 1973

BUTLER, JOSEPH T. *American Antiques 1800–1900*, New York, 1965

COMSTOCK, HELEN. *American Furniture*, New York, 1962

DAVIDSON, MARSHALL B. (ed.) *The American Heritage History of American Antiques, from the Revolution to the Civil War*, New York, 1968

DAVIDSON, MARSHALL B. (ed.) *The American Heritage History of American Antiques from the Civil War to World War I*, New York, 1969

DREPPERD, CARL W. *Victorian the Cinderella of Antiques*, New York, 1950

EASTLAKE, CHARLES L. (introduction by J. Gloag). *Hints on Household Taste*, New York, 1969

FLOUD, PETER. 'Furniture: the Early Victorian period 1830–60,' edited by Ralph Edwards and L. G. G. Ramsey in *The Connoisseur's Complete Period Guides*, London, 1968

FLOUD, PETER. 'Victorian Furniture' in *The Connoisseur's Guide to Antique Furniture* edited by L. G. G. Ramsey and Helen Comstock, London, 1969

GIEDION, SIEGFRIED. *Mechanization Takes Command*, New York, 1948

GILBERT, CHRISTOPHER. *Loudon's Furniture Designs*, Wakefield, Yorkshire, 1970

HANDLEY-READ, CHARLES. 'England: 1830–1901' in *World Furniture* edited by Helena Hayward, London, 1965

Hudson River Museum. *Eastlake-influenced American Furniture*, Catalogue of the exhibition held November 1973, New York, 1973

JERVIS, SIMON. *Victorian Furniture*, London, 1968

LICHTEN, FRANCES. *Decorative Art of Victoria's Era*, New York, 1950

McCLINTON, KATHARINE MORRISON. *Collecting American Victorian Antiques*, New York, 1966

Metropolitan Museum of Art. *19th-Century America*, Catalogue of the exhibition held 16 April–7 September 1970, New York, 1970

OTTO, CELIA JACKSON. *American Furniture of the Nineteenth Century*, New York, 1965

Princeton University Museum of Historic Art. *The Arts and Crafts Movement in America*, Catalogue of the exhibition held October 1972–September 1973, Princeton, New Jersey, 1972

ROE, F. GORDON. *Victorian Furniture*, London, 1952

SCHAEFER, HERWIN. *Nineteenth Century Modern*, New York, 1970

SYMONDS, R. W. and WHINERY, B. B. *Victorian Furniture*, London, 1962

Victoria and Albert Museum. *Victorian Furniture*, London, 1962

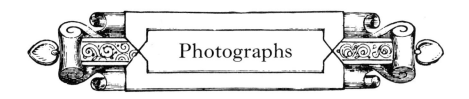

Photographs

BRITISH

No one man invented photography. During the early years of the nineteenth century and, indeed, before that, scientists had appreciated the possibility of using light-sensitive chemicals to fix images captured through a camera obscura, or pin-hole camera. This idea was a natural extension of the use of the camera obscura (literally 'dark room'), which had been conceived centuries before as a device to facilitate drawing – as a rudimentary copying-machine. Tom Wedgwood and Humphry Davy were among several who experimented with various chemicals and bases with no real success. Impractically long exposures, lack of permanency and the reversal of light and shade were three major technical drawbacks.

When finally ways were found of fixing images, two distinct processes were evolved, one in England and one in France, and, although the French process was the first, it was the English that ultimately enjoyed greater success and led the way for the development of photography as we know it.

The Birth of Photography

The earliest surviving fixed photographic image was made by Joseph Niépce in 1826 or 1827. It was a direct positive image on a coated pewter plate showing the view from his attic workroom across the courtyard. He claimed in a Notice to the Royal Society, London, to be 'the inventor of this discovery', but cautiously guarded the secrets of his new skill. Niépce's plate required an exposure of about eight hours. It was Louis Daguerre, his partner after 1829, who discovered that exposure time could be

OPPOSITE *The Reading Establishment, Fox Talbot's photographic printing establishment, c. 1845. Calotype. An engraving is photographed while in the foreground a man sits for his portrait. Science Museum.*

cut down to about twenty minutes and that the latent image thus produced could be developed with mercuric chemicals. (See colour plate p. 335.)

This important discovery was made in 1835; within two years Daguerre had also discovered the means of permanently fixing the image thus achieved. By 1839, when problems of payment and protocol had been ironed out between Daguerre, Niépce and the French Government, the *Historique et Description des Procédés du Daguerréotype et du Diorama* was published. By all accounts, *'daguerréotypomanie'* seized Paris like a plague and every would-be man of science and many wealthy amateurs took to the streets with their cumbersome tripods and equipment.

The Open Door by William Henry Fox Talbot (1800-77). Calotype. Photographed at Lacock Abbey, where he made the first negative. Sotheby's Belgravia.

Daguerreotypes, made on polished and silvered copper plates are generally small, their surfaces are delicate and they need to be kept sealed behind glass, but, above all, being direct positive images, each one is unique and the image cannot be multiplied, a disadvantage by comparison with the process perfected in England by William Henry Fox Talbot. In England in 1835 W. H. Fox Talbot made a great step forward when he produced the first paper negative. Dissatisfied at first with his inability to produce a direct positive, he spent the time on further experiments until, hearing in 1839 of Daguerre's advances, he determined to lay full claim to the discovery of an effective photographic process in England. The result was the hurried preparation in February 1837, and publication in 1839, of *Some Account of the Art of Photogenic Drawing*.

Talbot's discoveries met with a disconcerting indifference in contrast with the excitement inspired in Paris by Dagu-

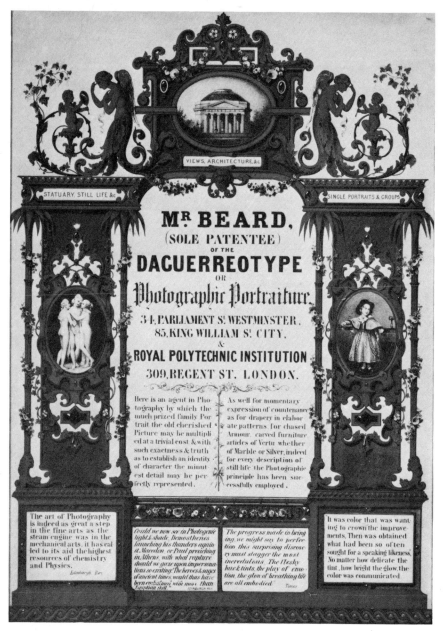

Trade card of Richard Beard (1801/2-85), the sole patentee of the daguerreotype in England from 1841. Science Museum.

erre, who was raised almost to the level of a national hero. This was in part due to the soft, grainy texture of Talbot's prints, a painterly quality which, while much appreciated today, was considered by his contemporaries a poor second to Daguerre's crystal-sharp images. Talbot's bitterness at this lack of appreciation caused him to become very troublesome over enforcing the rights of the process, which he patented under the name calotype (from the Greek for beautiful) on 8 February, 1841. Between his photogenic drawing and his improved process, the calotype, Talbot had made

independently the vital discovery of the latent image which could be developed out of the camera. Exposure time was reduced from about half an hour to a minimum of half a minute, making portraiture possible. Thus, by a series of largely chance discoveries was photography born.

The Daguerreotype in Britain

Cross-Channel rivalries, whether as a political throwback or for reasons of profit, were kept very much alive by photographic pioneers. We have seen Talbot and Daguerre race to the finishing post (to be correct we should call it the starting line), but when the first

round was over, Daguerre's spirit was not spent. Daguerre, supposedly, was presenting his invention as a gift to the world through the intermediary of the French Government, which granted him a pension as a token of gratitude. The perfidious Frenchman, however, manacled poor Albion by furtively but effectively patenting his process in England.

The first daguerreotypes to be taken in England were probably those taken in October 1839 by M. de Saint Croix and exhibited at the Royal Adelaide Gallery, West Strand. Whether he worked in ignorance or defiance of Daguerre's patent, we do not know. An injunction soon put an end to his career.

The first patentee in England was the Frenchman, Antoine François Jean Claudet. He was the only man to buy a licence before the rights were bought exclusively by a profit-conscious speculator, Richard Beard, who in March 1841 set up the first British professional portrait studio on the roof of the Royal Polytechnic Institution. How Claudet's success must have aggravated Beard! He put legal pressure on this, the only fish to escape his net, but Claudet managed to stay safely outside Beard's monopoly. A comparison of their progress is a pure Victorian moral allegory. Claudet's concern as a scientist and a photographer brought him great success, and the rich and titled flocked to him. Beard's greed, however, led him down the road to ruin. After an initial flush of success with new, speedier portrait photography, he lost the fortune he had won in protracted lawsuits as he fought to protect his exclusive rights. He was granted a certificate of bankruptcy on 5 June, 1850.

After 1846, Beard eased his hold on the capital by granting a number of licences. William Kilburn and John Jabez Edwin Mayall were two who distinguished themselves as portrait photographers. The fashionable district in which to open a studio was Lower Regent Street, between Vigo Street and Swan & Edgar. To capture all available light, photographers built glass studios on the rooftops. From the air the cluster of studios must have looked like fruitless greenhouses, and Glasshouse Street owes its name to this fashion which was given the final seal of approval when Claudet opened his 'Temple to Photography' at 107 Regent Street in 1851, and in two years became Photographer-in-Ordinary to the Queen.

1851

The year 1851 marked a significant turning point in the history of photography in England. The year in which Daguerre died saw the introduction of a new process which had many advantages over both the daguerreotype and the calotype. Not least of these was that, not being subject to patent restrictions, photographers could try the new wet-plate collodion process without the bickerings and squabbles that had become, sadly, so characteristic of photography in the 1840s. Frederick Scott Archer's collodion process involved making negatives, pin sharp in detail, on glass plates, the sensitized surface adhering to the glass by the use of collodion.

The great advantage was speed – this, the fastest process so far devised, reigned supreme till about 1880. The disadvantage was that the sensitizing, exposure and subsequent development of the plates had to be done as one process, for the plates could only be used wet. Photographers in the field were, as a result, obliged to operate from mobile dark tents, and the endurance of men who trekked around the world with their workshops on their backs, so to speak, is to be admired. Collodion photography opened up what had been a very restricted field, though not effectively until 1854, when the loss by Fox Talbot of a test case, in which he claimed the new process to be covered by his calotype patent, removed the last crotchety obstacle from its path.

1851 is significant on another count. The Great Exhibition of that year, the celebration by excess of Victorian success, was a major showcase for the ad-

Half-plate wet collodion camera by Horne & Thornwaite, c. 1860. The wet-plate process, the most popular mid-century photographic technique, was devised by Frederick Scott Archer (1813-57) and made public in 1851. Sotheby's Belgravia.

vances made in the field of photography; and, in addition to assembling the first major international display of photographs (seven hundred from six nations), it was the first major exhibition to be fully recorded and documented by photographers.

Frederick Scott Archer died penniless and without an obituary in 1857. He was unable even to provide for his family because he had sunk what little money he had into his researches on photography. His altruism left the Victorian age with a gift for which he barely received recognition.

The Popularization of Photography

The collodion period saw a number of innovations which helped to popularize photography. The first was the introduction of the ambrotype in 1852. This was a small collodion negative, bleached and backed with black paper to create a positive which, when put in a gilded and plush-lined leather case, became a cheap and effective substitute for the daguerreotype. Ambrotype portraits enjoyed popularity with a very wide public for about ten years.

Even more popular during the late 1850s and the 1860s were carte-devisite portraits. The idea of photographic visiting-cards was suggested as early as 1851. Disdéri in 1855 patented his method of cutting costs by taking ten small photographs on one large negative plate, which could then be trimmed and mounted and sold for a good profit. Their popularity dates from May 1859, when Napoleon III, to promote his public image, stopped at Disdéri's studios for multiple portraits to be taken which could be cherished by all Frenchmen, especially by his troops. From his first

excited successes, through his parvenu extravagance as France's wealthiest photographer (taking £48,000 per annum in his Paris studio alone), to his decline with the waning of interest in the carte-de-visite to beach photographer in Nice and death, half blind and deaf, in the poor house, Disdéri's is a typically Balzacian story.

In England the most successful carte-de-visite portraitist was J. J. E. Mayall, who wisely abandoned the daguerreotype in favour of this new craze. Cartes-de-visite were cheap and highly collectable. The Queen herself was a keen patron with a collection of one hundred and ten albums, thirty-six of which were devoted to cartes of royalty.

'The Optical Wonder of the Age', however, was stereoscopic photography. The idea was simple: two images should re-create the images seen by the human eye and when viewed one by each eye, simultaneously and independently, they should give the three-dimensional effect of human vision.

First Sir David Brewster, then Antoine Claudet became pioneers of stereoscopic photography, working towards the most effective methods of producing and viewing images. Queen Victoria marvelled at the stereoscopic daguerreotypes exhibited at the Great Exhibition. By 1858 the demand was so great that the recently founded London Stereoscopic Company could optimistically advertise a stock of a hundred thousand different photographs taken in England and abroad by staff photographers. 'Stereoscopomania' reached a peak with the 1862 International Exhibition, where the London Stereoscopic Company, having paid £1,500, made a proverbial killing with the sale of over a quarter of a million stereo slides, and it seems also to have made a genuine killing, for they had fed their own market to saturation and the fickle public began to disdain stereoscopic in favour of carte-de-visite photographs.

Great Victorian Photographers

The most fascinating aspect of Victorian photography is that its possibilities as a medium of artistic expression were soon realized, and, after certain misguided attempts to create images with the camera more suited to the medium of oils, a number of photographers showed great skill in giving atmosphere to the subjects they chose to photograph.

As early as 1842, Sir David Brewster, a scientist deeply involved in the progress of photography, could claim to have dis-

ABOVE *Carte-de-visite of Queen Victoria by J. J. E. Mayall (1810-1901), 1861. The collecting and exchanging of cartes began in France and was popularized in Britain by Mayall with his portraits of royalty. Science Museum.*

LEFT *Cartes-de-visite, mid-nineteenth century. Science Museum.*

BELOW LEFT *Stereoscopic daguerreotype portrait by M. Millet, 1850s. Sotheby's Belgravia.*

covered an artist 'several [of whose] photographs have all the force and beauty of the sketches of Rembrandt'. The reference was to Robert Adamson, younger brother of Dr John Adamson, who was a colleague of Brewster at St Andrew's University and had taken the first calotype in Scotland. Robert Adamson set up a portrait studio in Edinburgh in 1842 and, judging from contemporary reports, met with great success. Adamson is always remembered, however, for those photographs he took after 1843, when he was introduced to David Octavius Hill. Hill was primarily a painter and it was as an aid to his painting that he decided to consult Adamson, for he thought that if he could first capture the likeness of his sitters through the camera, the task he had set himself of depicting the Assembly of the Free Church of Scotland would be greatly facilitated.

As a team, they took the necessary photographs for the painting, then continued working together till Adamson's death in 1848. They photographed their friends, and celebrities, and went out to

photograph the local fishermen and their families in the settings of St Andrew's and Newhaven. Their work has a warmth, a mellowness which is accentuated by the rich, broad quality of the calotype technique. In addition, one can see in certain of their photographs, especially in their morbid fascination with Greyfriars churchyard, Edinburgh, traces of the romanticism which was so strong in the 1840s.

Roger Fenton, a member of the Calotype Club and founder of the (Royal) Photographic Society, was an energetic publicist for photography and took a great number of very sensitive photographs, especially during the 1850s. He opposed the general practice of creating artificial backgrounds for portraits or of using backdrops, preferring to photograph his subjects in natural settings. His outdoor compositions have a serenity and calm which are strongly evocative. Fenton photographed the Royal Family and, under royal patronage, made the photographic expedition to the Crimean War which was to ensure his fame. Working with wet-collodion plates from his photographic van, he took some three hundred and sixty photographs of scenes of battle, of the allied camps and supply bases and of the men involved in the War, from the privates to the generals. These were published in five portfolios on his return in 1855 and make a moving record. Fenton was the first successfully to attempt war reportage. He was followed in the Crimea by James Robertson and his assistant Felice Beato. The latter deserves individual acclaim for his photographs of the 1860 Chinese Opium War.

The first great wet-plate topographical photographer was perhaps Francis Frith. He set sail for Egypt in 1856 to record on glass plates the magnificent relics of Ancient Egypt which previous travellers could merely describe. This was to be the first of several visits, for the publication of his work on his return by Negretti & Zambra and by Agnew caused such excitement that his backers begged for further photographs. The result was a series of large folios of photographs of Egypt, Sinai, Palestine and the Middle East. Frith's early work is full of interest, but he became a mechanical photographer

TOP *David Octavius Hill by Robert Adamson (1821-48), c. 1845. Calotype. Sotheby's Belgravia.*

ABOVE *Master Miller by David Octavius Hill (1802-70) and Robert Adamson, c. 1845. Calotype. The combination of Hill's artistic sense and Adamson's technical skills after they started to work together in 1843 was to result in some outstanding examples of Victorian genre photography. Sotheby's Belgravia.*

RIGHT *Photographic Van by Roger Fenton (1819-69), 1855. Albumen print. Fenton used this van for his wet-collodion equipment in the Crimea. Science Museum.*

and very over-commercialized in later years.

Julia Margaret Cameron was given a complete set of photographic equipment by her daughter in 1863 to amuse her while at Freshwater on the Isle of Wight. It became more than a hobby for Mrs Cameron. Photography became a driving force till 1875, when she and her husband left England for Ceylon. Mrs Cameron's work falls into two categories – straight portraiture and symbolic or allegorical composition. For the latter she would enlist any young women, children and friends to play the parts.

These photographs, Pre-Raphaelite in mood, are to modern eyes both wooden and sentimental. In her soft-focus portraits of celebrated men such as Herschel, Tennyson or G. F. Watts, however, she captured all the strength of 'the inner man' (her words).

Viscountess Clementina Hawarden is known for a small group of exceptionally good studies which depict women or girls, alone or in groups, and distil a strong, slightly strange mood. Her work was much admired by Lewis Carroll, author of *Alice in Wonderland*, who was an exceptionally sensitive photographer

in his own right. His speciality, not surprisingly, was little girls, and the rapport which he evidently enjoyed with his subjects is evident in the charm and character of the images. Among Lewis Carroll's best achievements are the numerous portraits of the young Alice Liddell, model for his own magical Alice.

Such then are a few of the names which distinguished themselves when Victorian photography was at its strength and before excessive popularization led to a deadening uniformity and monotony.

Philippe Garner

OPPOSITE Façade of the Temple of Rameses II at Abu Simbel *by Francis Frith (1822-98), 1857. Albumen print. Frith made a number of photographic expeditions, his first visit to the Near East dating from 1856. Like Fenton, he had to overcome the difficulties of taking collodion plates away from the studio. Sotheby's Belgravia.*

G. F. Watts *by Julia Margaret Cameron (1815-79), c. 1870. Gold-tinted albumen print. This print of the English painter was formerly in the collection of Virginia Woolf. Julia Margaret Cameron's photographs are recognizable by their sentiment and by the softness of the impression. They are often signed and dated on the mount. Sotheby's Belgravia.*

AMERICAN

Visitors to the Great Exhibition of 1851 were full of admiration for the fine quality of the American daguerreotypes on display. There was, however, an undercurrent of resentment at this American superiority, and bitter commentators ascribed their quality to nothing more than the cleanness of the American air, claiming that the photographers were 'seconded by all that climate and the purest of atmospheres could effect'. This suggestion seems far-fetched. The explanations are more practical.

The Daguerreotype in America

The technical superiority of the American daguerreotype was in part attribut-

able to the fact that the metal plates had a particularly smooth surface, which was the result of mechanical as opposed to hand buffing. Another logical explanation lies in the fact that during the 1840s, and even the 1850s, the daguerreotype was effectively the only photographic process employed in America. The calotype process was virtually unknown. A few amateurs worked with waxed-paper negatives, but there was no popular enthusiasm for William Henry Fox Talbot's discovery. It seems ironical, therefore, that Talbot, almost as an afterthought, should patent his invention in America in June 1847, over six years after taking out his English patent. Talbot even found professional photographers, the Langenheim brothers of Philadelphia, prepared to pay $6000

for the patent rights. Theirs was a disastrous speculation; for the few amateurs who had already been taking calotypes for a number of years simply ignored the patent, and the patent-free daguerreotype was enjoying such popularity that no commercial rival seemed possible.

The daguerreotype was introduced to America by Samuel F. Morse, perhaps better known to posterity for his electromagnetic telegraph system. In early experiments, Morse had met with the same difficulties encountered by so many others: 'light produced dark' on his silver-nitrate paper, and exposure times were impractically long. He abandoned the idea of fixing a positive image. His interest was revived, however, when on a visit to Paris he heard that Daguerre had overcome these basic problems.

ABOVE LEFT Margaret Fuller *by Albert Sands Southworth and Josiah Johnson Hawes, before 1846. Daguerreotype. These two Boston photographers produced some of the finest-quality early daguerreotypes in the United States. Metropolitan Museum of Art.*

ABOVE Emerson School *by Albert Sands Southworth and Josiah Johnson Hawes, mid-nineteenth century. Daguerreotype. Metropolitan Museum of Art.*

LEFT *Daguerreotype camera and tripod, c. 1845. Greenfield Village and Henry Ford Museum.*

Morse returned to New York flattered that the Frenchman should communicate his process to him and greatly encouraged by this new incentive to make further experiments.

In April 1840, Morse, together with his equally keen colleague Dr William Draper, set up New York's second roof-top portrait studio. The first had been opened a month earlier by Alexander S. Wolcott, who had been experimenting for a mere six months. On sunny days New Yorkers would flock to have their likenesses taken. On cloudy days they were invited to attend lessons on the art of photographic portraiture. In America the daguerreotype was in no way a jealously guarded secret. We even find Draper publishing suggestions for photographic portraiture in the September 1840 issue of the *London and Edinburgh Philosophical Magazine.*

The daguerreotype rapidly became popular throughout the United States, and this lasted during the 1840s and '50s and even into the '60s. The process was applied to every type of photography, unlike in Europe, where it was primarily a portrait technique. We find many daguerrean landscapes and urban studies and we find a more extensive use of large-size plates. The Langenheim

INSET *Carte-de-visite of Francis E. Brownell, the Avenger of Ellsworth, by Mathew Frady (1823–96), 1861–5. Sotheby's Belgravia.*

TOP *Three Confederate Soldiers by Mathew Brady, c. 1865. Library of Congress.*

ABOVE *Union case, American, c. 1858. Thermoplastic, 7¼ in × 9¼ in (18·6 cm × 23·6 cm). Sotheby's Belgravia.*

brothers of Philadelphia are celebrated for a series of panoramas of the Niagara Falls, one set of which was presented to, and praised by, Daguerre. Charles Fontayne, Robert Vance and S. N. Carvalho also became celebrated as landscape daguerreotype photographers. Platt D. Babbitt became possibly the first tourist photographer when in 1853 he acquired the monopoly to photograph groups on the American side of the Niagara Falls. Few visitors could resist purchasing the portrait groups which Babbitt would take, his subjects unaware, their eyes fixed on the spray.

An interesting side product of the American daguerreotype was the Union case. These small, hinged presentation cases, cast in dark brown thermo-plastic with elaborate baroque designs, sometimes patriotic in subject, were first patented by Samuel Peck in October 1854. A more substantial side product was the town of Daguerreville, which

grew up on the Hudson River around the production plants for photographic materials.

The Collodion Period and Photography in the Field

When Christopher Columbus discovered America, it was indeed the 'New World'. Yet even by the middle of the nineteenth century, to most Europeans and, in fact, to most Americans, this 'New World' was still very much an unknown quantity. Settlers had congregated in towns down the East Coast, and vast tracts of land were still virtually uncharted.

Photography enabled Americans and others to familiarize themselves with the wonders of the American landscape. The first decades of the collodion period produced a quantity of superb topographical material; they also, sadly, produced some of the most poignant war reportage in the photographs of Mathew Brady, Alexander Gardner and others who recorded the American Civil War (1861–5).

Mathew Brady would appear to have won for himself the reputation of being America's greatest portrait photographer during a working life of almost fifty years spanning the daguerreotype and collodion eras. Certain critics note that his reputation depends on sheer bulk of output (at their peak his studios in New York and Washington were producing over thirty thousand portraits annually). Nonetheless, Brady was a masterful organizer, and was well aware of the camera's rôle as the 'eye of history'. He made it his duty to record the features of every American of note. At the outbreak of the Civil War in 1861 Brady, having been refused Government backing, decided to finance the photographic coverage himself. He equipped twenty photographers and organized their operations in every major campaign. Brady's foresight in producing this photographic document of major national importance was not appreciated by his contemporaries and the fortune which he invested in the venture was never recuperated. Alexander Gardner, formerly the manager of Brady's Washington studio was able to compile *Gardner's Photographic Sketchbook of the War*, while he was carrying on his duties as photographer to the Ordnance Department of the Army

of the Potomac. George N. Barnard's *Photographic Views of Sherman's Campaign*, published in 1866 was another key contribution to the coverage of the War.

Possibly the best-known photograph of the war is *The Harvest of Death*, a scene of the carnage after the Battle of Gettysburg, by Timothy O'Sullivan, assistant to Gardner but better known for his outstanding topographical work. Between 1867 and 1874 he took part in various Government-sponsored expeditions and produced stunning, large-format prints of scenes in the Colorado River Valley, in Arizona, New Mexico and Panama.

Carleton E. Watkins travelled with his photographic van from his base in San Francisco, taking photographs in the Yosemite Valley. His studies of cascading waterfalls, of breathtaking rock structures, captured with great sensitivity the vastness of the American landscape and caused considerable excitement when shown at the Paris Universal Exhibition of 1867. Watkins' pupil Eadweard Muybridge was appointed in 1868 chief photographer to the United States Government and is best remembered for the topographical work done in connection with the Pacific Mail Steamship Company and the Central Pacific Railway Company. The camera and the railroads simultaneously extended the horizons of the United States, the one always at hand to record the other.

Muybridge's reputation rests more solidly, however, on the series of photographic investigations into the sequences of human and animal locomotion which he undertook full time after 1877. He first became involved in this work when

asked to settle absolutely, by photographic means, an argument as to whether or not in any stage of galloping a horse had all its feet off the ground at the same time. This was in 1872. In 1887 he published *Animal Locomotion, an electro-photographic investigation of consecutive phases of animal movement*. The eleven-folio series of 781 prints sold for $600 and is a major contribution to the history of photography.

Finally, mention should be made of a characteristically American area of photography – the recording of the features, the rituals and the customs of ethnic domestic civilizations before their strength was eroded by the pervasiveness of imported cultures. Edward Curtis' camera recorded what had become a corner of the American conscience. His twenty volumes of photogravures, *The North American Indian*, published at the very beginning of the twentieth century, form a significant tribute to a phase of American history and constitute a major work of photographic social history.

Philippe Garner

Photographers

ADAMSON, ROBERT (1821–48)
Scottish calotypist, proprietor of a portrait studio in Edinburgh, who first collaborated with HILL in 1843 over the latter's painting of the formation of the Free Church of Scotland. His first CALOTYPES, made independently of Hill, date from 1842, but it was during their five-year association that his best work was done, taking advantage of Hill's artistry in posing the sitters and choosing the angle from which to photograph seaside and architectural scenes.
ARCHER, FREDERICK SCOTT (1813–57)
Inventor of the WET-COLLODION PROCESS, first described in *The Chemist* and

Photogravure plate from Animal Locomotion *by Eadweard Muybridge (1830-1904), copyright 1887. He was the first to study human and animal movement by photography. Sotheby's Belgravia.*

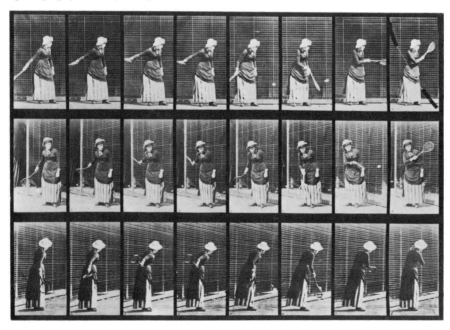

OPPOSITE ABOVE Sioux Chiefs *by Edward Curtis (1868-1952). Photogravure plate from* The North American Indian, *1907. New York Public Library.*

OPPOSITE NEAR RIGHT Quarles Mill, Virginia *by Timothy O'Sullivan (c. 1840-82), 1864. A member of Brady's Civil War photographic team and topographical photographer. Library of Congress.*

OPPOSITE FAR RIGHT Mirror Lake View of El Capitan *from an album of landscape studies by Carleton E. Watkins (1825-1916), of San Francisco, and others, 1860s and 1870s. Sotheby's Belgravia.*

made public in *Manual of the Collodion Photographic Process* (1851). As a sculptor he learned to make CALOTYPES to help obtain likenesses of his sitters. He did not patent his invention and, unlike FOX TALBOT, received no material reward and little recognition for his brilliant work. None of his own photographs survives.

BEARD, RICHARD (1801/2–85)
London coal-merchant and early speculator in photography who set up the first British professional portrait studio, on the roof of the Royal Polytechnic Institution, in 1841. In that year he became the sole patentee in England, Wales and the Colonies of the DAGUERREOTYPE, though he was unable to restrict the activities of CLAUDET. He used the equipment invented by the American WOLCOTT. In 1842 his business expanded as he sold licences for other studios in London and in the provinces, and in the same year he purchased a CALOTYPE licence from FOX TALBOT and patented the colouring of daguerreotypes. He also made STEREOSCOPIC PHOTOGRAPHS. As a result of lawsuits concerning his patents, he was declared bankrupt in 1850.

BRADY, MATHEW (1823–96)
Leading American portrait photographer and recorder of the Civil War (1861–5). Learning the DAGUERREOTYPE process from MORSE, he opened his own studio in 1844 and won a silver medal at the first photographic competition. With the interests of a historian, he made daguerreotypes of Washington celebrities, some of which appeared as lithographs by François D'Avignon in *Gallery of Illustrious Americans*, published in 1850, and collected portraits by other photographers. The scope of the project and the historical importance of the portraits is considered to be more remarkable than the quality of his daguerreotypes. So famous was he, and so profitable his business, that by 1860 he had a studio in Washington as well as impressive premises in New York and employed several assistants, notably GARDNER, George N. Barnard, O'SULLIVAN and George S. Cook. During the Civil War he sent a team of photographers to the front to record, by the wet-plate process (see WET-COLLODION PROCESS), scenes of war, some of which appeared as engravings in *Harper's Weekly*. Ruined financially, he lived thereafter, and died, in poverty, for recognition came too late. In 1911 some of the 7,000 negatives were used for the publication of *Photographic History of the Civil War*. The Library of Congress, Washington D.C. is in possession of a major collection of his work.

CAMERON, JULIA MARGARET (1815–79)
English amateur photographer who learned the art at the age of forty-eight on being given a camera by her daughter. At Freshwater, Isle of Wight, she took close-up portraits of famous Victorians, including Tennyson and Darwin, and allegorical and religious compositions inspired by the painter G. F. Watts, the Pre-Raphaelites and Tennyson's poetry. Her studies of heads are usually 12 in × 16 in (30·5 cm × 40·6 cm), and with this exceptionally large format many technical deficiencies are exposed. It is, however, for the quality and softness of the characterization, that her work is so much admired. Her prints are often signed and dated on the mounts.

CARROLL, LEWIS (1832–98)
Nom de plume of the Rev. Charles Lutwidge Dodgson, professor of mathematics at Christ Church, Oxford, and author of *Alice in Wonderland*. An amateur photographer between 1856 and 1880, principally of romantically posed children. He also wrote *Photography Extraordinary* (1855), *Hiawatha's Photographing* (1857), *A Photographer's Day Out* (1860).

CLAUDET, ANTOINE FRANÇOIS JEAN (1797–1867)
French glassware importer resident in London who, in 1839, purchased direct from DAGUERRE in Paris, for a fee of £200, the first licence to practise the DAGUERREOTYPE in England. His rights were upheld by the courts despite the fact that BEARD, his greatest rival, bought his rights as the sole patentee in England. He also imported daguerreotypes, selling some examples to Queen Victoria and Prince Albert, and daguerreotype equipment, and he mounted exhibitions at the Royal Society. In 1841, after introducing and publicizing various modifications to the process, he set up a studio on the roof of the Adelaide Gallery. In 1851 he moved to a 'Temple to Photography' at 107 Regent Street, constructed for him by Sir Charles Barry, and in 1853 he was appointed Photographer-in-Ordinary to the Queen. Interested in STEREOSCOPIC PHOTOGRAPHY, he improved the stereoscope and designed a pocket model.

CURTIS, EDWARD (1868–1952)
American genre photographer principally known for his studies of North American Indians, their appearance and way of life. In limited editions of 500, he published twenty volumes of photographs on this subject.

DAGUERRE, LOUIS JACQUES MANDÉ (1787–1851)
French stage-designer and co-deviser of

Alice Liddell as a Beggar-girl *by Lewis Carroll (1832-98), early 1860s. Albumen print. The sitter was the subject of Carroll's literary masterpieces. Private collection.*

the Diorama, a scenic show operated by diminishing and increasing the light from skylights on either side of a painted-glass screen so that the picture seemed to 'grow' realistically. His interest in optics and experiments with a CAMERA OBSCURA in painting scenes for the Diorama led him to enter into partnership with NIÉPCE in 1829. Having learned the secrets of HELIOGRAPHY, his researches resulted in the accidental discovery of the first successful photographic process, named after him, the DAGUERREOTYPE. In claiming recognition for his invention, he was assisted by François Dominique Arago, scientist and member of the Chamber of Deputies. Very few of his daguerreotypes are known to survive.

DAVY, HUMPHRY (1778–1829)
Joint publisher in 1802 of WEDGWOOD's important paper in the *Journal of the Royal Institution*, 'An account of a method of copying paintings upon glass and of making profiles by the agency of light upon nitrate of silver'. By different

means, NIÉPCE was to succeed where Wedgwood and Davy had failed.

FENTON, ROGER (1819–69)
Early calotypist and founder of the (Royal) Photographic Society, London, in 1853, renowned for his photographs of the Crimean War in 1855. Travelling with a horse-drawn van containing his bulky WET-COLLODION equipment, he took a series of photographs of the militia and of battlefields, purposely avoiding the action as the exposure time was too long. Previously he had made a photographic tour of Russia using the WAXED-PAPER PROCESS, and he was also responsible for a number of informal studies of the Royal Family, some of which are in the Victoria and Albert Museum, London.

FOX TALBOT, WILLIAM HENRY (1800–77)
Inventor of the first negative-positive photograph, the CALOTYPE, and earlier of PHOTOGENIC DRAWING. Developed contemporaneously with the DAGUERREOTYPE, it was the basis for all later improvements in photographic technique, principally because it was possible to produce more than one positive image and to fix permanently the image. He rigorously guarded his invention, patenting it in England (but not Scotland, where HILL and ADAMSON were able to make calotypes without a licence) and the United States. Starting his experiments with a CAMERA OBSCURA in 1833, by 1835 he had produced a photograph taken with a camera. Although more interested in the scientific aspects of photography, he made a number of fine calotypes, some of which were published in *The Pencil of Nature* in 1844, the first book with photographic illustrations. In 1843 he set up studios and offices at Reading for demonstrations and the sale of equipment.

FRITH, FRANCIS (1822–98)
English topographical and architectural photographer, noted for his views of the Middle East distributed in albums, singly or as stereoscopic slides. Using a photographic van and encountering the same difficulties with the WET-COLLODION PROCESS as FENTON in the Crimea, he attempted always to introduce an artistic as well as a documentary element into his work. The name of the firm of printers and publishers he founded, Francis Frith & Co., sometimes appears on his prints. He was among the first to make photographic post-cards. Some of his photographs are exceptionally large for their date, in particular the 20 in × 16 in (50·8 cm × 40·6 cm) prints published in *Egypt, Sinai and Palestine*.

GARDNER, ALEXANDER (1821–82)
Scottish scientist and journalist who arrived in the United States in 1856; photographic assistant to BRADY and manager of his Washington studio. In 1863 he set up independently, principally for CARTE-DE-VISITE photography. He was one of the team organized by Brady to take photographs of the Civil War (1861–5), results of which were published in two volumes in 1866: *Gardner's Photographic Sketch Book of the War*. In 1867 he made a photographic record of the frontier for the Union Pacific Railroad.

HILL, DAVID OCTAVIUS (1802–70)
Scottish painter and calotypist. In 1843, determined to paint a gigantic canvas of the signing of the Deed of Demission depicting all the participants in the founding of the Free Church of Scotland, he approached ADAMSON, who was already an established calotypist. Having recorded together photographic likenesses of the dissenting ministers, the partnership thrived for five years. The combination of an accomplished artist and a good technician produced some of the most sensitive examples of early photography. Their CALOTYPES are of distinguished Victorians and of local scenes. Their albums of photographs are uniquely important historically and artistically. After Adamson's death, the quality of Hill's photography declined.

LANGENHEIM, FREDERICK (1809–79) and WILLIAM (1807–74)
American photographers of German origin, purchasers in 1848 of CALOTYPE rights in the United States. Because of the popularity of the DAGUERREOTYPE and the licensing fees imposed on the would-be calotypist, they failed to interest American photographers in the process. Probably the first in the United States to make commercially STEREOSCOPIC PHOTOGRAPHS, Frederick Langenheim published in Philadelphia in 1856 *Photographic Views at Home and Abroad*, an album of landscapes on salted paper. In 1849 they introduced hyalotypes (from the Greek for glass), magic lantern slides made by the ALBUMEN PROCESS.

MAYALL, JOHN JABEZ EDWIN (1810–1901)
Daguerreotypist in Philadelphia from 1842 to 1846, when he arrived in London and worked briefly for CLAUDET. Using his American pseudonym 'Professor Highschool', he set up a portrait studio in West Strand, where he also composed large-scale 'art' DAGUERREOTYPES. Though these were much praised at the Great Exhibition, he soon decided that it was not the purpose of photography to ape the style and subject-matter of contemporary painting. He concentrated on portraiture and it was he who popular-ized the CARTE-DE-VISITE in Britain, taking photographs of the Royal Family.

MORSE, SAMUEL F. B. (1791–1872)
American painter and inventor, and visitor to DAGUERRE in Paris. He introduced the daguerreotype into the United States, describing the photographs in a letter to the *New York Observer* in 1839, as 'Rembrandt perfected', and opened a commercial studio with Draper in New York in 1840.

MUYBRIDGE, EADWEARD (1830–1904)
Photographer of English origin who analysed, by photographic means, the movement of animals. While making a photographic survey for the United States Government of the Pacific Coast, he was commissioned by Leland Stanford, Governor of California, to show that, at the gallop, all four feet of a horse are simultaneously off the ground. Experiments took place between 1872 and 1887 and some of the photographs were put on sale entitled *The Horse in Motion*. In 1880, mounting the prints on a revolving disk, which he named a zoopraxiscope, he anticipated motion-picture photography. The images were taken with a battery of cameras placed at intervals along the path of a horse. The first photo-finish was recorded in 1888. Eventually, using the DRY-PLATE PROCESS instead of the more ungainly WET-COLLODION PROCESS, and sponsored by the University of Pennsylvania, he recorded a series of studies of humans and animals in motion. The publication in 1898 of *Animals in Motion* and 1901 of *The Human Figure in Motion,* which succeeded his original work, *Animal Locomotion, an electro-photographic investigation of consecutive phases of animal movement,* published in 1887, was intended to make his experiments widely known: he also lectured in the United States and Europe.

NIÉPCE, JOSEPH-NICÉPHORE (1765–1833)
Maker of the earliest surviving fixed photographic image from nature. French lithographer and inventor of HELIOGRAPHY. In 1816 he began to experiment, advised by his brother Claude; with a CAMERA OBSCURA and paper sensitized with chloride of silver, he succeeded in producing an impermanent photographic negative on paper. It was probably in 1826 that the fixed positive impression of the view from his studio was made on a pewter plate 8 in × 6½ in (20·3 cm × 16·5 cm) after an exposure of about eight hours. The plate was treated with bitumen of Judea dissolved in white petroleum and contained in a camera obscura fitted with a meniscus prism to correct the lateral reversal of the image. In 1829 Niépce went into partner-

The Two Ways of Life by Oscar Rejlander (1813-75), 1857. Composite carbon print. Symbolizing Industry and Dissipation. A copy was bought by Queen Victoria for Prince Albert. Victoria & Albert Museum.

ship with DAGUERRE with the intention that was to be unfulfilled of further developing heliography.

O'SULLIVAN, TIMOTHY (*c.*1840–82)
American Civil War and expeditionary photographer, who started working for BRADY in his New York and Washington studios. Until he became official photographer to the Army of the Potomac, he was attached to Brady's photographic team covering the Civil War. Later he took part in Government expeditions of exploration on the American continent, using, in the Black Canyon, a boat as his darkroom. Lithographs were made from his photographs to illustrate the reports.

REJLANDER, OSCAR GUSTAVE (1813–75)
Swedish painter famous for his combination printing: up to thirty separate negatives were used in the composition of some of his allegorical photographs, for example, *The Two Ways of Life,* of which a print was bought by Queen Victoria for Prince Albert. His studies of children were an inspiration to CAMERON and CARROLL, and his later genre photo-

graphs are noteworthy. In 1872 he illustrated Charles Darwin's *The Expression of the Emotions in Man and Animals.*

ROBERTSON, JAMES (active 1852–65)
Superintendent and chief engraver at the Imperial Mint, Constantinople, and amateur photographer. Arriving in the Crimea in 1855, and working in partnership with the Venetian Felice Beato, he recorded the aftermath of the fall of Sebastopol, after the departure of FENTON. Printing blocks could not at that time be made directly from a photograph and in order to make speedy engravings for publications such as *The Illustrated London News,* the blocks were divided into sections and worked on by more than one engraver. With Felice Beato again, Robertson covered the Indian Mutiny. He employed principally the ALBUMEN PROCESS.

WEDGWOOD, THOMAS (1771–1805)
Son of Josiah Wedgwood the potter and protagonist of the first recorded attempt in England to produce photographic images. Using a silver nitrate solution, upon which sunlight has a darkening effect, he succeeded in obtaining outlines and silhouettes on a white leather base, but he was unable to fix the images and had, therefore, to view his achievements by candlelight; nor did he manage to obtain images using a CAMERA OBSCURA.

WOLCOTT, ALEXANDER S. (1804–44)
With William S. Johnson, opened the first DAGUERREOTYPE studio, the 'Daguerrean Parlor', in New York in 1840. He was the inventor of a mirror camera which accelerated exposure time, used in Great Britain by BEARD, and of a successful system for studio lighting.

Glossary

Albumen paper
Positive paper coated with albumen (white of egg) originated by Blanquart-Evrard in 1850 after the invention of the ALBUMEN PROCESS. It had a smooth, shiny surface that retained much of the detail of the negative. Early prints on albumen paper were apt to yellow, and to counteract this disagreeable effect they were often toned with chloride of gold. The sensitized albumen paper was exposed behind the negative until an image emerged which was then fixed. The production of albumen paper required quantities of eggs: a Dresden manufacturing company used 60,000 a day. Until the introduction of bromide

paper after 1873, it was the principal positive paper.

Albumen process

Photography on glass, the silver salts adhering to the glass base by means of albumen (white of egg). Experiments with photography on glass had been made by NIÉPCE and it was his cousin, Abel Niépce de Saint-Victor (1805–70) who invented the albumen process, details of which were published in 1848. Lengthy exposures were required, and this, coupled with the fact that FOX TALBOT succeeded in taking out a patent that covered the process, meant that it never found popularity in Britain. In the United States, the LANGENHEIM brothers made magic-lantern slides (hyalotypes) by the albumen process.

Ambrotype

Collodion negative on glass, bleached and set against a dark background, giving the appearance of a positive, introduced in 1852 by ARCHER, the inventor of the WET-COLLODION PROCESS. They were patented, however, by the American James Cutting in 1854. Used almost exclusively for small-scale portraits, ambrotypes were a substitute for the DAGUERREOTYPE and are often found in similar cases. Exposure time could be as little as five seconds. They were popular in Britain and the United States until c. 1865.

Cabinet portrait

Posed photographic portrait, usually $6\frac{1}{2}$ in × 4 in (16·5 cm × 10·2 cm), fashionable after the CARTE-DE-VISITE, produced by similar methods and often by the same photographers.

Calotype

First photograph made by a negative-positive process and dependent on the chemical development of a latent image produced by the effect of light on silver salts. Developed in the 1830s by FOX TALBOT, the process was patented in England (but not in Scotland) in 1841 and in the United States in 1847. The name derives from the Greek word meaning beautiful. It was so-named by its inventor, after whom it was also called the Talbotype. A sheet of paper was prepared in a solution of potassium iodide, washed and dried and then sensitized with gallo-nitrate of silver; it was then exposed in a camera for one to three minutes. Gallo-nitrate of silver was again applied to the exposed, but apparently blank, sheet to produce the negative image, which was then fixed. Positives were obtained by the same method as with PHOTOGENIC DRAWINGS. The calotype, reddish-brown in colour, is characterized by a painterly quality, with broad effects of light and shade. Apart from Fox Talbot himself,

the principal photographers in Britain who adopted the process were ADAMSON, HILL and FENTON. In the United States the LANGENHEIM brothers purchased a licence, but in general the patent-free DAGUERREOTYPE, developed simultaneously but without the advantage of multiple images, was more popular. The patent lapsed in England in 1855.

Camera obscura

Copying-device used by artists and a precursor of the photographic camera. A dark room with a small aperture through which light enters to project on to a plain surface opposite an inverted image of external objects. The immobile camera obscura, large enough for a man to stand in, was known in Europe from before the time of Leonardo da Vinci, who described in his notebooks the making of pinhole images. By the seventeenth century, a lens had been fitted at one end of a small box and the image cast on to a ground-glass plate or oiled paper at the other. From this a model, with an adjustable diaphragm resembling a reflex camera, was developed in which the image was projected the right way up on to the glass or paper at the top of the box by means of an internal mirror set at an angle of 45°. Artists traced the image on a thin piece of paper laid over the glass.

Carte-de-visite

Portrait photograph, usually full length, mounted on card, taken in a multi-lens camera so that between eight and twelve exposures could be made on a single collodion plate, thereby considerably reducing costs; the negative was cut up to make the equivalent number of prints. They were the first photographs within financial reach of the masses. Cartes-de-visite became fashionable in France after Napoleon III was photographed, halting his troops as they departed for Italy, by André Adolphe Disdéri (1819–c. 1890). They were popularized in Britain by MAYALL, who published in 1860 an album of cartes of the Royal Family. It was the Queen herself who set the vogue for collecting them. In the United States, Major Robert Anderson, the Union commander in the Civil War, was one of the first celebrities to sit for a carte. More than 1,000 prints a day were made by E. and H. T. Anthony & Co. Cartes of the famous could be purchased in shops or begged from their subject. They were also exchanged between friends. 'Cartomania' was international and lasted from 1859 to c. 1865. Passport and identity photographs, first used in 1861 by the Chicago & Milwaukee Railway Co., derive from these card photographs.

Daguerreotype

Named after its inventor DAGUERRE, the first practical and commercial photo-

graph taken with a camera. The image obtained was a direct positive on a metal plate and laterally reversed. Each image was unique. The impression was taken on a copper plate coated with silver which was polished and sensitized with iodine and, after 1840, bromine. After an exposure time of up to forty minutes, the latent image was developed by vapour of mercury and fixed in a solution of sodium hyposulphite. The first successful daguerreotype, a still life, was made in 1837, although the process was discovered, accidentally, after mercury from a broken thermometer had fallen on to an exposed plate, in 1835. Daguerre's *Historique et Description des Procédés du Daguerréotype et du Diorama* was published in 1839 after the process was given 'free to the world', though patented in England, Wales and the Colonies. It was brought to England by St Croix who, on account of the patent, was ordered to cease his photographic activities. CLAUDET purchased a licence direct from Daguerre before exclusive rights for England were acquired by BEARD. Portrait-daguerreotypes became possible after it was realized that the exposure time, virtually impossible for the sitter at half an hour, could be reduced to less than a minute by the application of bromine to the plate. In addition, a lens designed by Josef Petzval and manufactured in Vienna by Peter Friedrich Voigtländer permitted considerably more light to enter the camera. The first daguerreotypists in the United States were MORSE, Draper, and WOLCOTT; later, and of considerable note, were the LANGENHEIM brothers, Fontayne, Carvalho, Vance and Babbitt. Soon after they made their first experiments, François Courand, Daguerre's agent, arrived in New York to give demonstrations. He also published a booklet. Daguerreotypomania was international in the 1840s and 1850s and American photographers, making adjustments of their own, excelled. Unlike their counterparts in Europe, they took landscapes and urban views as well as portraits; they also favoured larger size plates. Travelling daguerreotypists visited towns too small to deserve a permanent studio. Their products are usually small, $2\frac{3}{4}$ in × $3\frac{1}{4}$ in (7 cm × 8·3 cm). The images were often enclosed in presentation, or Union, cases of thermoplastic, while European daguerreotypes of smaller dimensions are usually to be found in leather cases.

Dry-plate process

Gelatin emulsion succeeded wet collodion as the agent for binding the sensitizing chemicals to the glass plate. Following experiments by the Englishman

Richard Leach Maddox (1816–1902), Charles Bennett, John Burgess and Richard Kennet fully realized the potential of the process, and by 1878 gelatin dry plates were manufactured in commercial quantities. By 1881 it had generally superseded the WET-COLLODION PROCESS, its principal recommendation being that the plates could be prepared, or bought, long before they were exposed, and development could be equally delayed. In 1880, the American George Eastman, opened one of the first dry-plate factories in the United States, and this was followed in 1888 by his invention of the Kodak, the first camera to take roll-film designed specifically for the amateur photographer.

Ferrotype

Collodion positive producing, like the DAGUERREOTYPE, a unique laterally reversed image on a metal base, introduced in 1852–3 by the Frenchman, A. A. Martin. The photographing procedure was quick and cheap as a multi-lens

camera was employed. They were mounted on card, in frames or in jewelry. They are commonly found in the United States. Also known as American gem photographs and tintypes.

Heliography

Sun-drawing, a process invented in 1882 by NIÉPCE of photo-engraving, which was a crucial step towards photography. Oiled, transparent engravings were placed on a zinc, pewter or glass plate coated with a light-sensitive varnish of bitumen of Judea dissolved in

LEFT Ferrotype Photographer at Golders Green, *English, 1896. Bromide print. Ferrotypes were collected in albums and even incorporated in jewelry. Private Collection.*

Contrebands on Mrs Fuller's Farm *by James F. Gibson, 1862. Stereoscopic print distributed by E. & H. T. Anthony of New York. Chicago Historical Society.*

white petroleum, which bleaches and hardens when exposed to sunlight for several hours. When the engraving was removed the varnish under the light areas was white and fixed and, under the dark areas, soluble in oil of lavender and white petroleum. In the 1820s several of these plates were etched and from them prints were made. By 1826 Niépce had made improvements to the process so that he achieved a direct positive image of nature on the plate. A view from his window taken in that year should probably be regarded as the first photograph.

Photogravure
Photo-etching using a stippled screen.

Photogenic drawing
Photographic process invented by FOX TALBOT in 1835. At first he succeeded in making a negative on paper sensitized with a solution of silver nitrate and common salt. The image was fixed in a solution of common salt, converting the silver nitrate into halide salts, still used today in processing. Between 1835 and 1839, positive photogenic drawings were achieved by placing a sensitized sheet of paper on top of the negative on to the fresh sheet, the positive. Exposure time in the camera was approximately one hour. In 1839 the technique of photogenic drawings was described in a paper to the Royal Society, and subsequently published, *Some Account of the Art of Photogenic Drawing ; or the Process by which Nature's Objects may be made to delineate themselves without the Aid of the Artist's Pencil.*

Silverprint
Albumen print based on silver iodide as opposed to silver bromide.

Stereoscopic photograph
Binocular picture viewed in a double-sighted apparatus called a stereoscope: two photographic images of the same subject taken from slightly different viewpoints producing a three-dimensional effect. Stereoscopic DAGUERREO-TYPES were made by CLAUDET, BEARD, MAYALL and Kilburn, and FOX TALBOT and FENTON made stereoscopic CALO-TYPES, but it was the WET-COLLODION PROCESS that was most satisfactorily and cheaply adapted to it. The photographs were immensely popular in the 1850s and 1860s. The London Stereoscopic Company, founded in 1854, sold stereoscopes and slides of subjects such as Blondin walking the tightrope over Niagara Falls and the 1862 International Exhibition. Their principal photographer was William England (d. 1896), whose series entitled *America in the Stereoscope* gave an unprecedentedly vivid picture of the landscape and architecture on the other side of the Atlantic

Interior of the Barrack Battery, Sebastopol *by James Robertson (active 1852-65), 1855. Albumen print from a wet-collodion negative. Victoria and Albert Museum.*

to an astonished public in Britain. Bell & Bros took stereoscopic photographs in Washington in the 1860s, and Underwood & Underwood, the Keystone View Co. and H. C. White & Co. captured the American market for stereoscopic photography in the 1890s; soon after that it ceased to have a commercial appeal.

Waxed-paper process
Photographic process invented by the Frenchman, Gustave le Gray (1820–82) and made public in 1851. The negative paper was waxed before it was iodized, rendering it almost as transparent as a glass negative. An alternative to the CALOTYPE process, it was particularly favoured by, for example, FENTON for landscape photography as the detail was clear and development could take place up to three days after exposure.

Wet-collodion process
Also known as the wet-plate process, a photographic method originated by ARCHER and made public in 1851. A glass plate was coated with collodion (gun cotton dissolved in ether) containing iodide of potassium and sensitized in a solution of nitrate of silver. Exposure had to be made while the plate was still wet and the time necessary varied from five seconds to a minute and a half. Photographers had to equip themselves with a tent or caravan if they wished to work outside their studios. Archer never

patented the invention, though FOX TALBOT tried to claim that it fell under his CALOTYPE patent. A collodion positive on glass is known as an AMBRO-TYPE. The wet-collodion process, despite the difficulties involved in preparing and using the plates in a single operation, was used successfully by all photographers for at least twenty years, including the travelling photographers FENTON, FRITH and O'SULLIVAN and portrait photographers such as CAMERON.

Bibliography

The Arts Council of Great Britain. *'From today painting is dead.' The Beginnings of Photography,* Catalogue of the exhibition held at the Victoria and Albert Museum 16 March–14 May 1972, London, 1972.

BAIER, WOLFGANG. *Geschichte der Fotographie,* Leipzig, 1966.

CAMERON, J. M. (introduction by Virginia Woolf). *Victorian Photographs of Famous Men and Fair Women,* London, 1973

GERNSHEIM, HELMUT. *Julia Margaret Cameron,* London, 1948

GERNSHEIM, HELMUT and ALISON. *L. J. M. Daguerre,* New York, 1968

GERNSHEIM, HELMUT. *Lewis Carroll Photographer,* New York, 1969

GERNSHEIM, HELMUT and ALISON. *The History of Photography,* London, 1969

RINHART, FLOYD and MARION. *American Miniature Case Art,* New York, 1969

SCHARF, AARON. *Art and Photography,* London, 1968

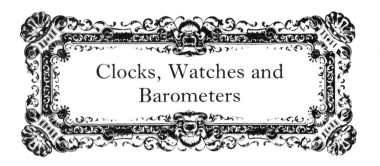

Clocks, Watches and Barometers

BRITISH

The long and somewhat painful process by which Britain eventually became, during the nineteenth century, the first primarily industrial country in the world gave rise to many quite unpredictable anomalies. For example, factory systems of manufacture, the existence of railways and all the other paraphernalia of industrialization foreshadowed a universal need for cheap clocks and watches such as can never have existed in a hitherto mainly agricultural community. Yet the earliest experiments in making clocks and watches by mass-production methods took place in America, and were rapidly assimilated by the French and the Swiss. In Britain, the traditional craft took a firm stand against any and every attempt to emulate them. By 1842 England was the largest market for cheap foreign clocks in the world; by 1854, the annual figure for imported clocks had reached 228,000, with the home industry in chaos and unemployment widespread.

As for barometers, the increased wealth resulting from industrialization placed these hitherto expensive status symbols within the reach of a much wider buying public. Yet those available to the average Victorian consumer were mediocre instruments, unoriginal in design and unreliable in operation.

Clocks

Despite all commercial considerations, English clockmakers and watchmakers refused to lower their standards and produce a cheaper clock or watch; since the days of Thomas Tompion, Britain had excelled both in horological invention and in maintaining the excellence of its craftsmanship, and the hard core of

OPPOSITE *Aesthetic Movement mantel clock, possibly by Howell & James, c. 1875. Oak with pottery mounts. Sotheby's Belgravia.*

those employed in the trade would yield nothing to the cause of mechanization. So it is a sad fact that the vast majority of clocks – and watches – that existed in Victorian Britain came from abroad. The French, for instance, had standardized a clock mechanism contained within small circular plates which was perhaps the most accurate factory-made movement to appear during the century; it fitted well into every kind of case, including those of polished slate, which the later Victorians liked to call black marble. From France also came the prototype carriage clock, or *pendule de voyage,* much copied elsewhere.

Carriage clock, English, 1860. Gilded metal. Sotheby & Co.

From the 1840s onwards, American makers flooded the British market with cheap clocks, many being of brass and derived from an original German design, which sold for as little as $1.50. There were also the so-called postman's alarm clocks and other designs of similarly

rudimentary construction, in which, so far as was practicable, expensive metal components were replaced by wooden ones. These emanated from the Black Forest – and not, as is the popular misconception, from Switzerland – from where also originated the ubiquitous cuckoo, trumpeter and similar clocks. Last but not least, the Vienna Regulator clock started to appear in quantity during the last quarter of the century. Although not a regulator in the English sense of the term, these clocks were excellent timekeepers in domestic service; of Austrian design, as the name implies, they were subsequently much copied in Germany and America.

So what was the indigenous product? Not the traditional long-case, or grandfather clock, which seems to have become extinct in about 1820 and not to have been reintroduced until after 1900. British skill did, however, continue to turn out plenty of fine handmade movements, many of which went into so-called three-quarter length clocks, which either hung from, or rested upon, a bracket on the wall and which resembled a long-case clock without its base. These cases offered enormous scope for ornate decoration, with the revival styles variously denoted as Egyptian, Gothic, Elizabethan, Jacobean, Louis Quatorze or Quinze, and so on. Also revived were two decorative materials – buhl and papier mâché – which were once again much used in clock cases, often in original eighteenth-century designs.

Probably most representative of the best in Victorian clockmaking, is the type known as the English dial. This is the spring-driven clock so well known on station platforms, in booking halls and in other public rooms. Consisting of a painted iron dial with a 12 in or 14 in (30·4 cm or 35·4 cm) diameter, protected by a convex glass set in a hinged-brass bezel, the whole within a turned mahogany surround, these clocks contain substantial movements with comparatively heavy pendulums. Variants

FAR LEFT *Mantel clock designed in the Greek Revival style of the 1860s and 1870s, English, c. 1870. Brass with pottery mounts and malachite pilasters. Sotheby's Belgravia.*

LEFT *Drop dial clock by Backett, c. 1835. Case veneered in coromandel wood and inlaid with mother of pearl. This clock has a striking mechanism which is unusual in English movements of this type. Strike One.*

BELOW LEFT *Mantel clock, English, c. 1850. Ebonized and decorated with gilded bronze mounts. Sotheby's Belgravia.*

OPPOSITE *Skeleton clock with eight-bell chiming movement and lever escapement by J. Lowe, Over-Darwen, Lancashire, c. 1850. So-called because the movement is wholly visible at all times, the skeleton clock was designed to stand under a glass dome, an essential protection against dust damaging its delicate mechanism. Aubrey Brocklehurst.*

of this pattern sometimes utilize a longer pendulum, so that a short trunk has to extend below the dial to accommodate it. The English dial clock has a long history, extending back into the eighteenth century; as is usually the case, quality tends to deteriorate in time.

The skeleton clock, which is usually displayed under a glass dome, probably started out as an English dial movement with its frame elaborately pierced and decorated to satisfy Victorian taste. Also, of course, the mechanism could be seen working. Skeleton clocks were once thought to be the masterpieces of apprentices in the craft; there may be isolated instances of this, but as a general assumption it is unjustified. The French skeleton clock is much less solid in appearance, and there were also major mechanical differences. The British version, in fashion in about 1860, may therefore be considered a distinctive type.

As its French name implies, the carriage clock is a travelling clock rather than one fixed inside a carriage. The style was adopted by a few of the best London makers, not in order to compete with the imported French product, but as a vehicle for their high-grade movements. Although it does not necessarily follow that a carriage clock with an English name on the dial is of English provenance, in other respects there can be no mistaking the genuine article. Among English makers of repute, Vulliamy, Dent, McCabe, Kullberg, Frodsham and a few others made carriage clocks of great excellence. The imported French product, on the other hand, can

be found in every degree of quality from the highest to the lowest.

Although the domestic long-case clock was in eclipse, the scientific version – the regulator clock – was still made, in small numbers but to the highest standards, as is the case today. Mainly used by clockmakers when regulating their stock or for timing astronomical phenomena in observatories, the regulator was made totally devoid of decoration, hence it would have had little appeal for Victorian domestic consumption.

Victorian horological prowess achieved some notable distinctions. Following pioneer work in the 1840s, it eventually became possible by electrical means to synchronize a number of 'slave' clocks in distant locations, a system quickly utilized to synchronize regulators with observatory time. In the same period, clocks were designed which were powered by electricity, generally from a rather primitive battery; these were never made in any quantity, however, and the common electric clock is a product of the twentieth century. On another level, the Victorians are responsible for some of the finest tower clocks ever made, notably Big Ben, the most famous of them all, erected in 1859.

There is one special clock which is closely associated with the Industrial Revolution, and that is the tell-tale, or watchman's clock. Of earlier origin but still made in Victorian times, it is generally found in a long, narrow, plain oak case, the time being told by a rotating dial registering against a fixed hand. Around the edge of the dial, at half-hour intervals, is a series of metal pins, one of which the night watchman depressed each time he went on his rounds, thus recording the moment of each visit.

Watches

From the middle to the end of the nineteenth century, an enormous number of Swiss watches, mainly of the cheaper varieties, were imported into England; there was no equivalent homemade commodity. Indeed, more in respect of watches even than clocks did the 'quality versus quantity' argument rage among Victorian craftsmen; the death-throes of the English hand-finished watch continued, at least until the Depression of the 1930s, and certainly long after wholly craftsman-made clocks had disappeared from the retailer's shelves.

The Victorian watchmaker, working at a time when the mechanical arts had reached a zenith, exercised his skill and ingenuity to produce complex, small-scale, multi-component assemblies with

LEFT *Minute-repeating lever watch by Edward Ashley of Clerkenwell, 1890.* RIGHT *Gold watch with an 'up and down' dial by French of the Royal Exchange, 1890. British Horological Institute.*

a greater degree of precision and to lower tolerances than ever before. Yet, the English watch had already reached a most advanced state of development by the end of the eighteenth century, so the Victorian craftsman was mainly concerned with refining even further, the basic inventions which existed; such problems as still defied solution were fairly minor ones.

The most important feature governing the time keeping qualities of a watch is the escapement – so-called because it is a device for allowing the driving power stored in the mainspring to 'escape' in measured amounts which are commensurate with the passage of time. The lever escapement, used to this day in most mechanical watches, had been invented and rejected in the eighteenth century, rediscovered in the early nineteenth century, and by Victorian times, was firmly established as the escapement *par excellence* for the high-quality pocket watch. Nevertheless, several of the best inventors among practising London craftsmen – men of the calibre of James Ferguson Cole, for instance – continued to experiment with it. Watches of lesser quality, based on older escapement designs, continued to be made; thus duplex and cylinder escapements became obsolete only in about 1860, and the robust verge escapement, the oldest of them all, continued to be made into the 1880s.

The pocket watch, *per se*, offered nothing like the scope of the domestic clock for enthusiastic Victorian embellishment, so that Victorian watches tend to be plain and provide a considerable contrast to those made even as late as 1820. Some early Victorian makers

favoured the metal dial decorated with multicoloured gold flowers while engine-turning on the dial and case was not considered out of place. However, soon after 1850 the white enamel dial returned to universal favour.

As for cases, the so-called hunters and demi-hunters, which had first put in an appearance around 1802, remained popular, with only minor improvements throughout the remainder of the century. In the former, a solid metal, spring-operated cover protects the dial, while in the latter this cover incorporates a central glazed window revealing the dial centre and those parts of the hands nearest to it, through which the time can be estimated. Open-face watches – the name given to those with nothing except the protective glass over the dial – still constituted the majority of all those made.

The principal preoccupation of Victorian watchmakers, unlikely as it may seem, was to find an alternative to the inconvenient key with which to wind up the watch. Starting with a system devised by Thomas Prest in 1820, there were many attempts to perfect keyless winding; some depended upon a pump action, that is a push-pull applied to the pendant boss, or, in other versions, upon a lever projecting from the edge of the movement. This preoccupation reached its greatest heights of absurdity as late as 1870, when watches were provided with keys which, when not in use, were concealed within the pendant of the watch case, being then disguised with a ribbed crown like the winding button of a keyless watch. Well before the end of the century, keyless work had become a standard facility.

The other main concern of Victorian watchmakers was to increase the range of additional facilities available on a watch. Several variations of chronograph work, which is a kind of stopwatch mechanism, were produced, while repeating work, by which at will the time could be made to sound on tuned wire gongs inside the watch-case, was sufficiently refined as to strike to the nearest minute. The means of actuating these additional mechanisms were also improved. At the end of the century two watchmakers – Nicole Nielsen, in London and Bonniksen, of Coventry – started to employ the principle of a travelling escapement in their finest watches, thereby taking another step forward towards even greater timekeeping accuracy.

Group of watch movements, English, nineteenth century. Gold. Although many mass-produced watches were imported, London makers remained concerned with improvement. Author's collection.

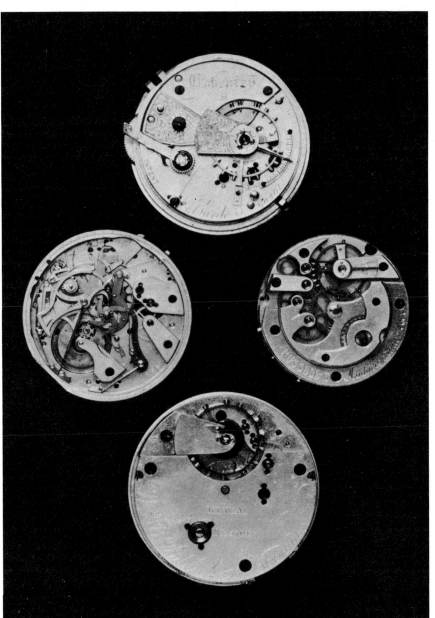

Barometers

The nineteenth century saw a peak in the huge influx into England of Italian barometer-makers. In reality, these were shopkeepers – hardware, mirror and picture-frame dealers, carvers, gilders, glassblowers, print-sellers and the like – who had started to move into England in the 1760s. Although their names appear on thousands of Victorian instruments, most of them had no part whatsoever in their manufacture. They were simply retailers, which explains why it is possible to find barometers of this period which are identical in appearance – and which must have originated from the same workshop – and yet which bear different names. The barometers were mass produced, by whom it is impossible to say, the names added afterwards, often in an inferior style of engraving.

By 1840, Italians dominated the industry. There were a few old-established English firms still in business, although often making meteorological barometers for scientific use. This was to all intents and purposes a different industry, having separated from domestic manufacture in the previous century. What was available to the domestic consumer was an undoubtedly inferior product.

The most characteristic barometer throughout the whole of the nineteenth century was the banjo wheel barometer. This design seems to have originated in France in the 1760s, arrived in England in about 1780, and by the time of Queen Victoria's accession, it was already starting to degenerate. Apart from the barometer dial, such instruments are customarily fitted with a selection of other facilities from a range which includes a thermometer, an oatbeard hygrometer – to demonstrate the state of humidity of the surrounding atmosphere – a spirit level, and, perhaps rarest and most desirable for present-day collectors, a clock.

Throughout the nineteenth century and irrespective of design, barometers were all actuated by the same principle, namely measuring atmospheric pressure in terms of the height of a column of mercury in a glass tube. The principle of measuring pressure by movement of the walls of an evacuated vessel – the aneroid barometer – did not make real headway until the beginning of the twentieth century.

Much evidence of the best domestic barometers of Queen Victoria's reign comes from the catalogue published in 1859 by Negretti & Zambra, well-known instrument makers in both the domestic and scientific fields. While many designs which the firm made were of the wheel type, it still advertised a number of patterns based on the older stick, or pediment barometer, as it is still called in the trade, pediment probably being a corruption of pendant. Stick barometers, crowned by a scroll or broken pediment, appear to have gone out of fashion around 1840, to be superseded by those with a round top or, occasionally, with some typical Victorian extravagance such as Gothic castellated cresting.

Not all the wheel barometers of the nineteenth century were of banjo design, although the operating principles were the same. The term wheel refers to a pulley behind the dial, on the same axle as the hand, over which a cord passes between a float resting on the surface of mercury in a syphon tube and a carefully contrived counterpoise. As the height of the mercury rises or falls, so does the

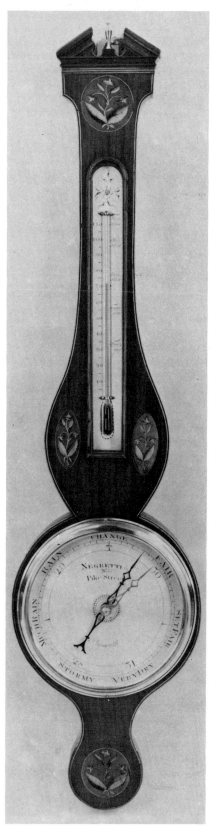

Wheel barometer with mercury column, Negretti & Zambra, 1850. Mahogany inlaid with satinwood. This barometer is based on the firm's 'Pergolese' design. Negretti & Zambra Ltd.

float, turning the pulley and also the indicating hand on the barometer dial.

Finally, brief reference should be made to those barometers named after Admiral Fitzroy, which mainly date from the latter half of the nineteenth century. Despite their cleverly devised air of efficiency, they were cheap and hardly worthy of even the disparaging remarks made of wheel barometers by J. H.

Belville who, writing in 1849, remarked that the wheel barometer 'from its construction, cannot be trusted for correct heights; it merely shows if the mercury be in a rising or falling state; it may rather be considered as an ornamental piece of furniture than as having the slightest pretensions to a scientific instrument'.

Cedric Jagger

AMERICAN

World leadership in both clock and watch manufacture was achieved in the United States during the Victorian period. The ingenuities and contributions of many individuals and details of the development of automatic precision machinery are beyond the scope of this chapter. Studies of the products do, however, reveal considerable information concerning the 'free competitive system', technological growth and artistic achievement in the United States.

At the beginning of the nineteenth century, clockmakers and watchmakers relied largely on apprentices, and both crafts involved considerable hard work. After 1860, business interests dominated both industries and a wide range of standardized timekeeping mechanisms were developed. Such artifacts became available to practically all families. In retrospect, perhaps more important than these products were the manufacturing techniques derived from these activities and the development of machinery which subsequently contributed to industrial supremacy in the United States.

Clocks

When Queen Victoria ascended the throne, the principal centres of clockmaking in the United States were Bristol and Plymouth, Connecticut. Mass production of wooden clock movements, employing interchangeable parts and largely made by contract labour, had commenced there early in the nineteenth century. Two types of shelf clocks were made in 1837; one with a thirty-hour wooden movement and the other with an eight-day wrought-brass movement. Clockmaking had virtually been brought to a standstill in other

areas. With the exception of limited production in Massachusetts and at a few other locations, it simply was not competitive with the effective manufacturing system developed at Connecticut.

Two basic types of case were being produced at this time: the first had half-round columns with stencilled, carved or gilded top splats; the second, combinations of various cornice tops with round columns, generally veneered. Such cases were consistent with American Empire styling, employing such features as 'crotch' veneer mahogany, bronze-powder stencilling and painted-glass tablets. These cases were usually between 24 in and 36 in high (61 cm–91·5 cm) and their design was similar to frames for looking-glasses. Sales were made mainly in the Mid-western and Southern states. These clocks were too bulky for export and the designs were not suitable for foreign markets.

Competitive price reductions and surplus production by 1836 resulted in decreased manufacture of wooden-movement clocks. A serious economic condition resulted from over-extended credit in 1837. Thus clock sales were further curtailed, particularly the sale of the more expensive eight-day brass clocks.

The famous clockmaker-entrepreneur, Chauncey Jerome, who had been in the business since 1816, was sensitive to the prevailing financial conditions and instrumental in the introduction of a cheap one-day weight-driven brass clock. This became a popular alternative by 1840. The movement of this clock was assembled between frames and with wheels that had been stamped from thinner wrought-brass sheet than that used previously for the wheels of eight-day clocks. This less expensive movement was commonly offered in a rectangular

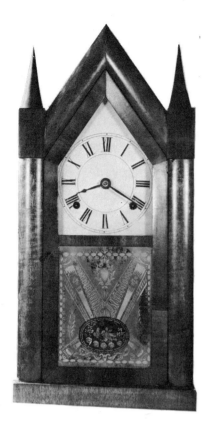

case, about 25 in (63 cm) high, the front being framed with an ogee moulding to which a thin layer of mahogany veneer had been applied. The dial was painted on a square zinc sheet, and the glass door at the base of the clock had a decoration in decalcomania, simulating a painted tablet.

It is difficult to determine whether it was Chauncey Jerome or a New York exporter who first introduced this clock into England. Jerome claimed in 1842 that it was he, stating: 'It was a long and tedious undertaking to introduce my first cargo in England'. In any event, thousands of such clocks were to be exported from the United States during the subsequent sixty years.

About this time, the art of hardening and tempering steel springs became known to Connecticut manufacturers. New case designs were sought for potential markets in England. Elias Ingraham, a cabinetmaker, adapted two Gothic styles of cases previously used in England: a round Gothic case that was similar to the 1810 lancet design; the other, a sharp Gothic, which had conical finials mounted on pilasters at each side and in between the centre spire. These cases were both about 20 in (55·8 cm) high. They were first offered by the firm of Brewster & Ingrahams.

Many competitors soon copied both these popular designs, which remained in fashion throughout the twentieth century. The 1840 to 1860 models are today much sought after by Victorian antiquarians. The firm of Birge & Fuller, also of Bristol, adapted the same motif but produced a much larger, more extreme Gothic design containing the famous cantilever-spring movement designed by Joseph Ives. Many of these clocks were exported to England. Two other unique styles, resembling the form of an acorn, were introduced by Jonathan Brown, another Bristol cabinetmaker who had entered the clock business. He was also famous for the 'ripple' front style with its machine-cut finish, which he adapted to the Ingraham case designs.

Improved processing techniques enabled Connecticut manufacturers to produce by 1850 smaller and more accurately regulated spring clocks. A balance wheel with detached lever movements for portable operation was developed for railway and sea transportation. The cases of these marine clocks were usually octagonal or circular in shape, often of rosewood or mahogany veneer, and the dials varied from 4 in to 12 in (10·2 cm – 30·4 cm) in diameter.

The Great Exhibition of 1851 exerted considerable influence on subsequent

TOP *Gothic clock with thirty-hour fusee movement by C. Boardman and J. A. Wells, 1847. Mahogany veneered case. Author's collection.*

ABOVE *Round Gothic clock by E. C. Brewster, 1847. Mahogany veneered case. Author's Collection.*

TOP *Acorn clock by the Forestville Manufacturing Co., c. 1847. Glass tablet decorated with the State House, Hartford, Connecticut. Philip Hammerslough.*

ABOVE *Acorn clock with eight-day fusee movement by J. C. Brown, c. 1848. American Watch and Clock Museum.*

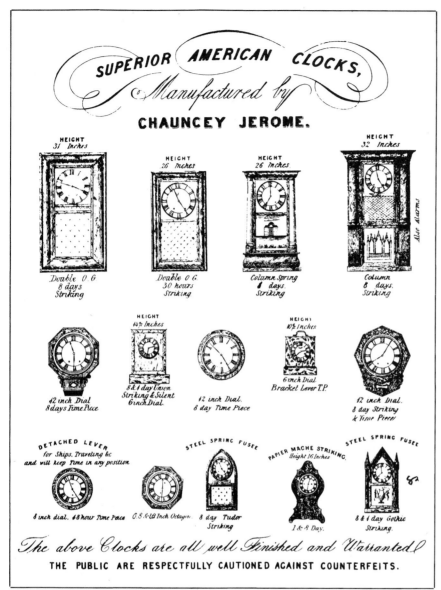

Early advertising circular from the Jerome Manufacturing Co., 1852. Circulated in England. The Company was at pains to point out the superiority of American clocks over English and the risk of fakes.

American clock-case designs; not that the United States firms exhibited clocks at this exhibition, but visiting exporters, agents and merchants must have noted the artistic and elegant statuary, porcelain, ormolu, silver, bronze and carved clock cases of French and English manufacture. During the subsequent forty years, many American firms imitated such designs with inexpensive, substitute materials and by mass-production methods succeeded in bringing such art within the reach of the middle classes.

Trade catalogues and design patents of clock cases provide the best chronological records. Unfortunately such cata-logues from the period 1850 to 1875 are now rare, particularly issues prior to 1860. The earliest known example is the 1852 catalogue of the Jerome Manufacturing Co. which illustrates forty different clocks. From about 1875 catalogues frequently illustrating over one hundred designs of clocks were issued annually by such manufacturers as Seth Thomas, the Ansonia Clock Co., Gilbert, Ingraham, the New Haven Clock Co., and the Waterbury Clock Co.

The clocks offered in the Jerome Manufacturing Co.'s 1852 catalogue varied in size from the 8 in (22·5 cm) Tom Thumb enclosed in an iron, pearl-inlaid case, to the 33 in (83·8 cm) high Gilt Top and Column Three Decker, which had an eagle top and an eight-day brass weight-operated movement with roller pinions. Wooden materials for cases included painted and decorated pearl inlay and veneers of mahogany, walnut, zebra-wood or rosewood. Some had iron frames, and papier mâché was also used. Models were frequently named after well-known public figures: Queen Victoria, Prince Albert, President Washington and Benjamin Franklin, General Lafayette, the Hungarian patriot Kossuth and the singer, Jenny Lind. Actually the Jerome Manufacturing Co. was not the manufacturer of all the clocks featured in the catalogue, for stock was included from the newly formed New York sales organization, the American Clock Co.

Jerome issued another catalogue in 1853, probably for the International Exhibition at the New York Crystal Palace. Cast-bronze and marble cases appeared for the first time as American products. Many of the first attempts to simulate Continental Baroque styling were featured in bronze and the carved rosewood base also dates from this period. Somewhat crude and grotesque designs, were soon to follow. Shell castings, made from composition bronze or cast iron, were used to decorate the wooden frames which contained the clock movements. It is estimated that from 1850 to 1875 over two hundred different designs of cast-front cases were produced.

Wooden cases decorated with veneers remained the most popular for both shelf and wall clocks until the last quarter of the century. Elias Ingraham introduced several patented designs between 1857 and 1871. These bore trademarks such as Venetian, Doric, Ionic, Grecian and Oriental. Rosewood, mahogany and often mosaic patterns of various inlaid woods were the most common materials used. Numerous new case designs followed with the introduction of solid walnut around 1867. A full-length door with a single glass permitted a full view of the pendulum below the dial. Trade advertisements would note that the pendulum bobs were imitations of either French or Mercury Ball designs.

Early in the 1850s a wall-clock design appeared. This was a modification of the English Act of Parliament clock introduced in about 1797–8. This was an eight-day spring-actuated clock with a 12 in (30·4 cm) diameter dial and an octagonal top. Later it became known as drop octagon and was also made in various sizes with a round top. These clocks were produced by the thousand for offices, banks, schools and homes with little change until 1940. Present-day collectors refer to them as school-house clocks. Currently, a reproduction case is made with an electric movement; this also drives an imitation non-functional pendulum which serves to create the oscillating period effect.

In 1863 the Seth Thomas Clock Co. introduced a line of weight-operated wall timepieces, known as regulators. The movement had been designed some years earlier by Silas B. Terry, youngest son of the celebrated Connecticut clock-maker, Eli Terry. These regulators became very popular for commercial use,

Eight-day regulator clock by the Seth Thomas Clock Co., 1863. Rosewood veneered case, ht 34 in (86 cm). Ken Roberts Publishing Co.

especially for railway stations. They were among the most accurate time-keepers produced in Connecticut, or indeed in the United States, during the nineteenth century, and continued to be made with few modifications until the 1950s. It was not long before similar styles were produced by competitors, but the regulator is strictly speaking the original Seth Thomas model.

The same Seth Thomas 1863 catalogue illustrated for the first time three models of calendar clocks. The firm had purchased the right to manufacture a calendar movement the previous year from a company in Ithaca, New York. The catalogue attested: 'They require the winding of time movement only to secure the required change at midnight, showing the day of the week, the month and the day of the month, (including the

29th day of February of leap year) perpetually and with unfailing certainty.' This idea was soon copied by many other firms.

E. Howard & Co., of Boston, Massachusetts, marketed a line of wall clocks. The style was similar to the banjo design of Simon Willard of *c.* 1802. Edward Howard had been apprenticed to Aaron Willard Jr, a nephew of Simon. The Howard firm, which was established in 1857, produced clocks of a very high quality, and also watches.

Tower, or turret, clocks became very popular during the latter part of the nineteenth century. The firms of Seth Thomas and E. Howard became the leaders in this field. Each produced a wide range of sizes of both strikers and quarter-hour chimers as well as time-pieces and side-walk clocks. This suited the individual pockets of the many builders of churches, and public and commercial buildings throughout the country.

Distinct changes in case designs and the application of materials began to appear in the 1870s. Marble cases with artistic cast-bronze decorations, frequently in the form of statues, were imported from France. In order to cater for large, low-price demand, imitation marble was offered which utilized enamelled iron with gilded and brass ornamentation. The Seth Thomas Co. noted in an 1872 catalogue that such clocks were 'fully equal in beauty and design of finish, superior in timekeepers, yet at lower prices than the imported French marble clocks'.

Awards for industrial art in ornamental cast bronze were presented to the firm of Mitchell, Vance & Co., of New York, N.Y., for their exhibits at the great Centennial Exhibition at Philadelphia in 1876. Other Connecticut firms soon developed less expensive imitations which made use of japanned wood. In 1880 the Seth Thomas Clock Co. developed a patented enamel which bore the trade name Adamantine. With this technique, variegated marble or onyx or tortoiseshell finishes could be reproduced on wood, and countless cases with different patterns, designs and ornamentations were manufactured by these methods – though most of them, judged by contemporary taste, are hideous.

The first metal case, known as the Nickel and the Nutmeg Lever, was brought out by the Seth Thomas Clock Co. in 1876. This pattern was the forerunner of the bedside alarm clock. Imitation carriage clocks, noted as 'lever novelties', soon followed. These were cheap reproductions of high grade French clocks with gilded fronts and nickel-plated side frames.

After 1880 black walnut, cherry and ash became increasingly used as case materials. Each year new designs continued to appear. While these were undoubtedly popular during their limited production period, for the most part they were sadly lacking in any art worth the name. Machine stamping and automatic

Kitchen alarm clock by Elias Ingraham (1805-85). Made in about 1880. Walnut case. Greenfield Village and Henry Ford Museum.

carving simply could not match the individual craftsmanship formerly accomplished by hand. The door glasses were decorated by transfer printing and stencil techniques, with much repetition in the patterns.

Towards the end of the century oak became the chief material for cases. The so-called kitchen clock was the product. Around 1900 ceramic cases became popular. Domestic movements were cased in imported cameo and Royal Hanover, frequently richly decorated with raised floral patterns and Rococo sashes and fitted with porcelain dials. Though these imported cases were an exception, the century as a whole ended with the production of a stereotyped and monotonous selection of wood cases and a general deterioration in artistic standards.

Watches

It was in the 1840s that the greatest technical skills of watchmaking were to be found for the first time not in England but in Switzerland, and from then on Switzerland was to become the world's largest producer of watches. Before this period a few Swiss watches had been imported and sold in the United States. There had in fact been a rudimentary watchmaking trade since the days of the early settlers; nevertheless, the great majority of products which bore the signatures of local craftsmen had been assembled, finished and cased from parts imported from England. An attempt in 1809 by Luther Goddard of Shrewsbury, Massachusetts, to manufacture his own watches had failed by 1817. The first machine-made watch in America was produced by the brothers Henry and James Pitkin, at East Hartford, Connecticut, in 1838. However, they were unable to master the prices of imported models and this venture too was unsuccessful and ended in 1841, though it is possible that the 1837 economic recession may have been a contributing factor.

Aaron Dennison is generally regarded as the father of American watchmaking. In association with Edward Howard, the Boston clockmaker, and Samuel Curtis, who put up the capital, Dennison was the prime mover in what was to become a prosperous American industry. After a series of early setbacks he established in 1859 the American Watch Co. at Waltham, Massachusetts, which in 1885 became the American Waltham Watch Co., the largest watch-manufacturing concern in the world. There is no doubt, however, that Dennison's success owed much in the early days to the technical progress achieved by the Pitkins in their own company's short existence.

The development of precision automatic machinery made possible a high-quality watch assembled from mass-produced and interchangeable parts. This was among the greatest technological achievements in the United States during the nineteenth century, and it occurred over an amazingly short space of time. It says much for the enterprise and resource of the industry's pioneers. They were quick to take advantage of capital, freely available at this period.

Watches from a catalogue produced by Otto Young & Co., Chicago, Illinois, 1883. The advertisement offers solid gold watch cases to which movements of the buyer's choice could be fitted at any stage. Ken Roberts Publishing Co.

They also trained and directed a willing and adaptable workforce. So, by 1875, only sixteen years after the founding of the American Watch Co., previously unskilled operators, many of whom were women, were producing low-priced but good-quality watches unrivalled for value anywhere else in the world. The designer of both the cheap watch movements and the machinery to make them was N. P. Stratton, who in his youth had been apprenticed to the Pitkins. The rapid growth of the American watchmaking industry also owed much to the talents of immigrant Englishmen and to close studies of English watchmaking techniques.

When the American Watch Co. started business in 1859 about two hundred workers were employed producing fifty watches a day. The start of the Civil War in 1861 caused a sharp rise in demand for watches and by the time the War ended in 1865 the work force had increased to 640 and output to 250 watches a day. The first lady's watch to be made in America was produced by this firm in 1861.

Of various attempts to start up in competition with Waltham, none survived with the exception of E. Howard & Co., Mr Howard having parted company with Dennison in 1857 and returned to Boston.

The first serious challenge to Waltham came from the National Watch Co., of Chicago, Illinois, which was incorporated in 1864, changing its name in 1874 to the Elgin National Watch Co. By 1886 there were seventeen watch companies in the United States, though only seven of these survived to the end of the century.

The foreign market was still dominated by the Swiss. It was not until 1876 that United States production overtook imports from Switzerland where manufacturers would not compete with the cheapness but reliability of the American product. In England, too, American watches were earning an increasing reputation. An article published in the London *Times* of 21 August 1884, gives an account of the rapid progress which had been made at Waltham.

An 1883 Chicago Jewelry catalogue listed twenty-four grades of movements made by the American Watch Co. These were priced between $9.74 and $333.34 (at that date $5 was equivalent to £1); in the same catalogue there were forty Elgin movements ranging from $9.00 to $180.54. The same firm's 1889 catalogue listed 'Swiss imitation American Movements', engraved with such names as The Richmond, The Grangin, The Bridgeport, and The Ohio or Bristol and were priced from $3.50 to $7.50. Whereas the Waltham firm supplied movements with or without silver or gold cases, the Elgin firm supplied only movements to jewelers who fitted their own cases. Stem winding had been introduced in Switzerland in about 1840. The first stemwatches made in the United States appeared from Waltham in 1868. By the end of the century all American watches were stemwind, but key-wind movements were still in production as late as 1890.

Standard time had been adopted in 1883. The introduction of strict train schedules brought demand for reliable timekeeping instruments from the railroad companies. The Railroad Time Inspection System was established in the early 1890s. This included standard specifications for railroad watches, under which requirements for accuracy and dependability were of a high order. These railroad watches were produced by the nation's six leading watch firms: E. Howard, Waltham, Elgin, Hampden, Illinois and Hamilton.

Throughout the period demand for the truly cheap watch was growing every year. In 1880 the Waterbury Watch Co. marketed a $4.00 non-jeweled watch having only fifty-eight parts, about half the number in a conventional watch. The mainspring was 9 ft (2·75 m) long and the watch became known as the 'never wind'. Eventually the price came down to $2.50. Robert H. Ingersoll placed his initial order for watches with this firm in 1892. A great success with these was experienced at the Chicago World's Columbian Exposition in 1893. They were the forerunners of the famous Dollar Watch which first appeared in 1908.

Barometers

Domestically manufactured mercurial barometers were indeed rare in the United States before 1850. In fact, throughout the remainder of the nineteenth century, these instruments were not produced in large quantities. For the most part the limited supply had been imported from Europe. The earliest significant U.S. Patent, No. 18,560, was issued to T. R. Timby in 1857 for a bottle barometer. This was the second barometer patent to be issued in the United States, the first being to R. Hopkins, Patent No. 1,951, 27 January 1841. This was not very significant as the instrument was not particularly reliable. Although barometers were made by a few other manufacturers, perhaps the most frequently noted were those

made by Charles Wilder, of Peterborough, New Hampshire, under the L. Woodruft, U.S. Patent 36,872, issued on 8 June 1860. In comparison to furniture of the period, the design of barometer cases remained relatively simple, decorations being limited to modest carving frequently embellished with a beaded moulding.

Kenneth D. Roberts

Clock and Watchmakers

AIRY, GEORGE BIDDELL (1801–92)
Astronomer-Royal from 1835 to 1881; K.C.B. 1874. He died aged ninety having devoted much of his life to the perfecting of timekeepers.

AMERICAN CLOCK CO.
Founded in New York in 1849 to succeed the Connecticut Protective Clock Co., the 1850 credit report reads, 'A Clock Co. consisting of John Birge, Brewster & Ingrahams, J. C. Brown, E. Manross, Smith & Goodrich, Terry & Andrews and Chauncey Jerome and William L. Gilbert of Winchester. Large dealers in clocks: have opened a repository in N.Y.C. for the sale of clocks, and I understand that it is there called The American Clock Co. They have a factory in Bristol, where they make 30,000 clocks annually. They must be and are good and safe to trust.' There are many extant clocks.

AMERICAN WATCH CO.
Based in Waltham, Massachusetts, from 1859 to 1885. In 1862 the American Watch Co. absorbed the Nashua Watch Co. The factory was rebuilt and enlarged from 1878 to 1883 and became the American Waltham Watch Co. in 1885.

ANSONIA CLOCK CO.
An American company started by Anson G. Phelps (and named after him) as a subsidiary of the Ansonia Brass Co. to augment the use of brass: both names were used in Connecticut, where the Company was based from 1851 to 1878. The Company produced the usual style of Connecticut clocks, WALL and SHELF, some weight- but mainly spring-driven, with or without alarms. After the factory moved to New York where it was based from 1879 to c. 1930, it produced gallery, SHELF and MANTEL CLOCKS in wood and china cases, as well as such unusual clocks as the Bobbing Doll and Swinging Doll clock.

ATKINS, GEORGE (1807–98)
Operated from Cornhill, London from 1840 to 1842, and succeeded by his son Samuel Elliott Atkins. He became Clerk of the Worshipful Company of Clock-

makers, resigning this office in 1878 to serve as Master in 1882.

BAIN, ALEXANDER (1810–77)
Scottish inventor of ELECTRIC CLOCKS active in Edinburgh from 1838 to 1858, the first to utilize electricity as a motive force for a clock and to transmit electrical impulses to a series of dials.

BARRAUD & LUND
Barraud family firm based in London which was founded in the middle of the eighteenth century reaching a peak under Paul Philip Barraud (d. 1820), a famous chronometer-maker. It was joined in the nineteenth century by members of the Lund family who had expertise in chronometers and also in electrical horology. The firm was finally wound up in 1929.

BARWISE, JOHN
In 1841, John Barwise was associated with BAIN in an ELECTRIC CLOCK patent; his firm also spanned the eighteenth and nineteenth centuries. Barwise was Chairman of the BRITISH WATCH CO. and died in 1842.

BENNETT, SIR JOHN (1816–97)
Jeweler and watch and clock retailer in Cheapside, London, with a large business, from 1846. He was Sheriff of London in 1872, by virtue of which he was knighted upon the occasion of a Royal visit to the City.

BENSON, JAMES W.
Manufacturer of a wide range of wares, from TURRET CLOCKS to watches and an exhibitor at the International Exhibition of 1862. His premises were located at 58/60 Ludgate Hill, London. In 1875 he wrote a small book on horology, *Time and Time-Tellers*.

JOHN BIRGE & THOMAS FULLER
Successful American partnership from 1844 to 1848 which was terminated by the death of Fuller. They specialized in the steeples on the cases of STEEPLE CLOCKS, fusee and one- and eight-day WAGON-SPRING power plants.

BREWSTER & INGRAHAMS
Operating from 1843 to 1852 this American company became one of the most prolific producers of the period. INGRAHAM's design for the STEEPLE CLOCK was widely copied and the Company boasted a large export trade to England.

BRITISH WATCH CO.
Formed in c. 1840 to manufacture watches by mass-production methods using machine tools designed by the Swiss craftsman P. F. Ingold. The Company failed owing to total opposition from the trade.

BROWN, JONATHAN CLARK (1807–72)
Active in the United States from c. 1832 to 1855, in 1832 Jonathan Brown purchased the interests of INGRAHAM and

William G. Bartholomew in clock cases, the name of the firm subsequently changing to Bartholomew, Brown & Co. From 1835 to 1839, the firm became partners in the FORESTVILLE MANUFAC-TURING CO. Owing to a bad fire and the approaching depression of 1857, all Brown's enterprises had failed by 1855 and were purchased by E. N. Welch, who combined them with various Birge and Manross firms.

CAMERER CUSS & CO.
Founded in Bloomsbury in 1788 and active to the present day. Described as 'wooden clockmakers', producing clocks in the style of the Black Forest crafts-men, the Company subsequently turned to quality clocks and watches of its own and other makes.

COLE, JAMES FERGUSON (1799–1880)
Able London watchmaker and expert springer, Cole devoted much attention to the lever escapement of which he de-vised several forms. For some time, he was vice-president of the Horological Institute.

CURTIS, LEMUEL (1790–1857)
Described as 'one of the best known and finest makers' (H. G. Rowell), Lemuel Curtis originated one of America's most typical designs, the GIRANDOLE CLOCK.

CURTIS, SAMUEL (1788–1879)
Brother of LEMUEL CURTIS and son-in-law of AARON WILLARD, Samuel Curtis specialized in the production of dials, tablets, mirrors and paintings.

DENNISON, AARON L. (1812–95)
Described as 'the father of the American watch industry', son of a shoemaker and with little schooling to his credit, he in-vented the Dennison Standard Gauge in 1840. Aaron Dennison and HOWARD were the first to use successfully inter-changeable parts and machinery to make watches.

DENT, EDWARD JOHN (1790–1853)
English clockmaker originally appren-ticed to a tallow chandler, but lodged in the house of a London watchmaker from whom he learned the art of making re-peater mechanisms. Worked as a finisher of repeating mechanisms until 1830 and later turned his attention to the com-pensation of chronometers and secured the confidence of AIRY, the Astronomer-Royal. On his recommendation, Dent supplied the clock for the Royal Ex-change in 1844 which led to his being asked to quote for the great clock of the Houses of Parliament, which order he subsequently obtained. He died in 1853 and it fell to his eldest step-son Fred-erick, to complete the contract.

DENT, FREDERICK (d. 1860)
Since Frederick Dent had no great in-terest in the trade, the supervision of the work on the Westminster clock was left

largely to the barrister, E. B. Dennison, who acted for AIRY in his absence. Dent's contract did not include the dials and the hands which were designed by the architect Charles Barry, nor the provi-sion or fixing of the bells. The clock was set going in May 1859.

FORESTVILLE MANUFACTURING CO.
One of BROWN's trade names, the fac-tory operated in Bristol, Connecticut, from 1835 to 1853. It specialized in eight- and thirty-hour marine clocks (see SHIP's CLOCK), Jenny Lind's, Prince Albert's and Victoria's, etc.

FORESTVILLE HARDWARE CO.
In Bristol, Connecticut, from 1852 to 1853, joint stock company and another operation of BROWN, the name was changed in 1853 to the Forestville Hard-ware & Clock Co., when it is reputed to have produced 100,000 clocks a year. One of a long line of continuous com-panies, the present company is called the Sessions Clock Co.

FRODSHAM, CHARLES (1810–71)
Son and apprentice of W. J. FRODSHAM, and a skilful and successful London watchmaker, Charles Frodsham experi-mented with the compensation balance and the balance-spring, and wrote sev-eral papers on technical subjects. For some time he was vice-president of the Horological Institute.

FRODSHAM, WILLIAM JAMES, F.R.S. (1778–1850)
One of a line of English clockmakers who brought up four sons to the trade, Wil-liam Frodsham entered into partnership with William Parkinson, was admitted to the Clockmakers' Company in 1802 and was Master in 1836 and 1837.

GILBERT, WILLIAM LEWIS
First operated with his brother-in-law, George Marsh, as Marsh & Gilbert at Bristol, Connecticut, from 1828 to 1834 and at Farnington, Connecticut, from 1830 to 1835. William Gilbert then went into partnership with BIRGE as Birge, Gilbert & Co. at Bristol from 1835 to 1837, successors to Birge, Case & Co. In partnership with Lucius Clarke the Company became Clarke, Gilbert & Co. at Winsted (Winchester), Connecticut from 1841 to c. 1850 when it became the William Lewis Gilbert Co. until 1866 when it renamed itself the Gilbert Manufacturing Co.

GLASGOW, DAVID (1824–1911)
Worked for LOSADA and afterwards at 20 Myddelton Square, London. Vice presi-dent of the Horological Institute and an authoritative figure in the field of tech-nical horology.

GODDARD, LUTHER (1762–1842)
Preacher and evangelist, Luther God-dard was responsible for the first quan-tity production of watches in America.

He set up a small shop in Shrewsbury, where he employed European-trained immigrants and produced about 500 watches before production ceased in 1817, when the lifting of the Jefferson embargo resulted in a flood of imported watches.

HAMPDEN WATCH CO.
Founded at Springfield, Massachusetts, in c. 1877, the Hampden Watch Co. was one of the largest makers of watches in America until 1925.

HOWARD, EDWARD (1813–1904)
Apprenticed at sixteen to AARON WIL-LARD JR, a mechanical genius who made many inventions and had a particular interest in mass-production machinery. He was famous for his BANJO, REGU-LATOR, tower and WALL CLOCKS for offices and factories.

ILLINOIS SPRINGFIELD WATCH CO.
Founded in 1869 at Springfield, Illinois, and reorganized in 1875 when it retained the same name. It was reorganized again in 1879 as the Springfield Illinois Watch Co.

INGRAHAM, ELIAS (1805–85)
Foremost clock-case designer of the period, the most famous of Elias Ingra-ham's innovations was a sharp Gothic SHELF CLOCK, called a STEEPLE CLOCK. In 1852 he founded a clock business which became one of the largest in the world and was carried on to the fifth generation.

Advertisement for a Marbleite clock by the Ingraham Co., Bristol, Connecticut, c. 1888. Case of ebonized and enamelled wood with gilded metal trimmings, ht 16½ in (42 cm). Ken Roberts Publishing Co.

IVES, JOSEPH (1782–1862)
In business from 1812 producing tall, wooden-movement clocks, Joseph Ives invented and patented the mirror clock and roller pinions. He went to Brooklyn, New York, in 1825, where he produced the famous WAGON-SPRING CLOCK in which a laminated spring was firmly fixed to the clock case and tensioned by drawing up its two ends by cords connected with the winding devices. In 1830 Ives found himself in financial difficulties and was bailed out by BIRGE who took him back to Bristol. He produced his best wagon-spring movements between 1850 and 1856; they ran for a month on one winding.

JEROME, CHAUNCEY (1793–1868)
Successful, prosperous and a colourful figure in Connecticut clockmaking, Jerome was more efficient as a salesman than a businessman. He claimed to have made the first pillar and scroll case for ELI TERRY in 1816 and in 1842 he shipped clocks to England which the customs authorities seized and paid for, believing they were undervalued. Shortly afterwards he started the Jerome Manufacturing Co. at New Haven, Connecticut.

JUMP, JOSEPH (d. 1899)
Son of Richard Thomas Jump, who had joined VULLIAMY in 1812, Joseph Jump was himself apprenticed to Vulliamy in 1827, remaining with him until his death in 1854, after which he worked in Bond Street and Pall Mall, London.

LOSADA, JOSÉ R.
Immigrant Spaniard who set up as a watchmaker and clockmaker in the vicinity of Euston Road, London, in 1835; later in Regent Street. He dealt mainly in the highest-grade timekeepers. After his death he was succeeded by his nephew Riego, at 105 Regent Street, London, until c. 1890.

MCCABE
English firm famed for its fine watches and clocks, especially in India. They operated from 32 Cornhill, London, from 1838 to 1883 when the current member of the family, Robert McCabe, closed the shop, declining all offers to purchase the business. McCabe's best watches were engraved James McCabe, the second grade McCabe and the lowest quality Beatson. The firm were also specialists in duplex escapements.

MURRAY, JAMES
James Murray founded his business at Cornhill, London, in c. 1814, and became a celebrated chronometer maker and watchmaker. He was succeeded by his two sons, James and John.

NATIONAL WATCH CO.
Founded in 1864 at Elgin, Illinois, the firm took the name Elgin National Watch Co. in 1874.

NEW HAVEN CLOCK CO.
Founded in 1853 at New Haven, Connecticut, the firm made movements in the first instance for the Jerome Manufacturing Co. Its own clocks date from 1856 and were made with both one- and eight-day brass movements. The firm also made smaller, spring-driven SHELF CLOCKS.

PITKIN & BROS
In partnership with various others, the two American brothers, Henry and James, produced approximately 1,000 movements from 1837 to 1841.

ROTHERHAM & SON
Coventry firm who exhibited the only display of machine-made British watches at the Great Exhibition of 1851. The father died in 1864, aged seventy-four, to be succeeded by his son John. The latter died in 1905, aged sixty-seven.

S. SMITH & SON
London makers of highly complicated watches and timepieces for observatory use. Forerunners of the present-day Smith's Industries Ltd.

STRATTON, CHARLES
Operating from Worcester and Holden, Massachusetts, Charles Stratton specialized in looking-glass clocks from c. 1830 to 1840.

TERRY, ELI (1772–1852)
Eli Terry was the first American to introduce the mass production of clocks into his country. He invented and perfected the wooden movement in the SHELF CLOCK and was a master of difficult horological principles taking out eight patents from 1797 to 1845. Terry specialized in TALL, SHELF, tower and REGULATOR CLOCKS with brass and wooden movements, taking his sons Eli Jr and Henry into his business which continued from 1823 to 1828. He worked with his brother as Eli & Samuel Terry from 1824 to 1827 and retired with a fortune in c. 1834, when he turned his business into a hobby. His success in Connecticut encouraged a large influx of clockmakers and many new factories started up.

TERRY, SILAS BURNHAM
Inventive American clockmaker, active from 1828 to 1876, who specialized in clock springs and many new types of movements, particularly early models of the marine clock (see SHIP'S CLOCK), Connecticut clocks with a balance wheel instead of pendulum control.

SETH THOMAS, CLOCK CO.
Joint stock company founded at Plymouth, Connecticut, in 1853 to continue the business of the founder, Seth Thomas. The Company made calendar clocks from c. 1863, lever escapement clocks from c. 1866 and round alarm clocks from c. 1875 (see p. 36).

THOMAS, SETH (1785–1859)
Connecticut clockmaker who worked with ELI TERRY on an order for 4,000 clocks and later with Silas Hoadley on thirty-hour wooden movements. In 1860 Seth Thomas was employing 125 workers.

VULLIAMY, BENJAMIN LOUIS (1780–1854)
Eminent London clockmaker, active from 1810 to 1854, B. L. Vulliamy was the son of Benjamin and grandson of Justin, both celebrated in their time. Between them they held the Royal Warrant as clockmakers for 112 years, under five sovereigns. B. L. Vulliamy's reputation as a designer of TURRET CLOCKS led to his being asked to produce a design for BIG BEN which he duly submitted but withdrew when it was not accepted outright.

WATERBURY CLOCK CO.
Founded in 1857 at Waterbury, Connecticut, as a branch of Benedict & Burnham, the Company grew rapidly, producing all types of popular SHELF CLOCKS and some TALL CLOCKS.

WELCH MANUFACTURING CO.
E. N. Welch consolidated his clock companies under this name in 1864. It subsequently became one of the largest Bristol companies and continued in successful production until E. N. Welch's death in 1887.

WILLARD, AARON (1757–1844)
Member of a famous Massachusetts clockmaking family, Aaron together with his brother Simon, was the most successful member of the family making a considerable fortune. He specialized in magnificent WALL, TALL, Massachusetts SHELF, gallery and BANJO CLOCKS.

WILLARD, AARON JR (1783–1864)
Son of AARON WILLARD, Aaron Jr continued to make large numbers of clocks after his father's retirement from the Boston factory. His clocks tended to be less expensive than those of his uncle, SIMON WILLARD, and he was inclined to use more gilding, commonly adding a base piece.

WILLARD, SIMON (1753–1848)
Simon Willard showed early mechanical skill, initially producing long-case clocks. In 1802 he patented his eight-day BANJO CLOCK calling it an 'Improved patent timepiece'. He made little profit from his inventions and sold his tools and goodwill to his favourite apprentice, Elnathan Taber, allowing him to use the Willard name on his own clocks.

WILLARD, SIMON JR (1795–1881)
Apprenticed to his father, from whom he inherited great mechanical skill, Simon Jr was given charge of the Boston tower clocks, also clocks at Harvard University. Financially he was highly successful.

Watch Parts

Note: where two names are given for a part the first is
the British name, the second the American.

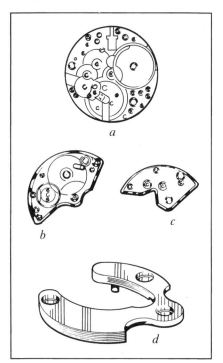

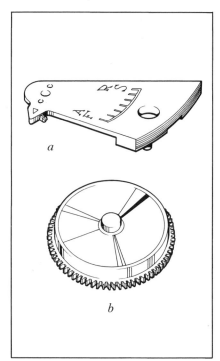

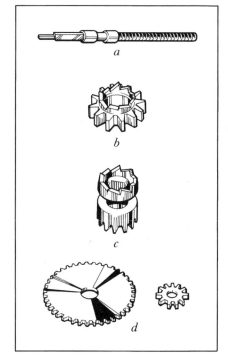

a. Bottom plate – Pillar plate
b. Barrel bar – Barrel bridge.
c. Train bar – Train bridge.
d. Pallet cock – Pallet bridge.

a. Balance cock.
b. Barrel (complete).

a. Winding shaft – Winding arbor.
b. Crown wheel – Winding pinion.
c. Castle wheel – Clutch wheel.
d. Intermediate wheels – Setting wheels.

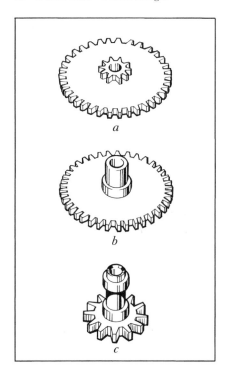

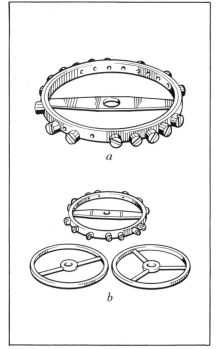

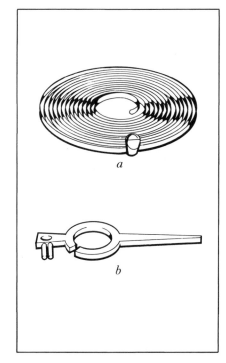

a. Minute wheel.
b. Hour wheel.
c. Cannon pinion.

a. Compensation balance – Bi-metallic balance.
b. Plain balance – Mono-metallic balance.

a. Flat balance spring – Flat hair spring.
b. Index (for flat spring) – Regulator (for flat spring).

Glossary of Types

Acorn clock
Type of American SHELF CLOCK made in Connecticut in the mid-nineteenth century, roughly in the form of an acorn. The only maker was the FORESTVILLE MANUFACTURING CO., of Forestville, Connecticut.

Albert
Watch chain used to attach a pocket watch to a garment, named after Prince Albert.

Alpha clock
Clock made for the Great Exhibition of 1851 in the shape of the letter A.

Appointment clock
Originated in 1891 by an inventor called Davidson, when it was called a memorandum clock, appointments were written on ivory tablets and placed in the slots of a drum which were marked with hours. At the designated hour, a tablet was ejected and the alarm bell rang.

Bain's clock
First electric clock, invented by BAIN in 1840.

Balloon clock
Clock, so-called after its balloon shape, introduced in c. 1760 and particularly popular towards the end of the eighteenth and the beginning of the nineteenth centuries.

Banjo clock
Clock of American origin, introduced by SIMON WILLARD of Massachusetts in c. 1800 and named after its resemblance in shape to a banjo. The English Act of Parliament clock possibly provided Willard with inspiration for its design.

Barograph clock
Mechanical instrument introduced for recording changes in atmospheric pressure by inking upon a chart which is fixed to a rotating drum. The drum is fitted with an eight-day movement.

Battery clock
Clock powered by an electric battery invented by BAIN in 1840. Also known as BAIN'S CLOCK.

Big Ben
One of the most famous English Victorian clocks, so-called after its big bell or, others maintain, after Sir Benjamin Hall, the then Chief Commissioner. The bell is 14 tons in weight, the hour hand made of gun metal is 9 ft (2·7 m) long and the minute hand, of sheet copper with reinforcing strips, is 14 ft (4·2 m) long. Edmund Beckett designed the clock for Charles Barry's clock tower for the new Houses of Parliament in 1859.

Bookmaker's bag clock
Devised in 1890 as a precaution against dishonest dealings prior to the introduction of the Betting Act. A special bag which was used for the collection of betting slips from the bookmakers' assistants. It was closed just before the start of the race, thus starting the clock mechanism and when opened by the bookmaker at the end of the race, indicated the exact time of the closing of the slot.

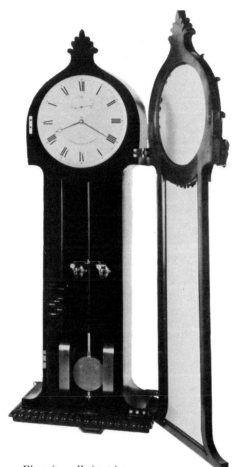

*Electric wall timepiece
by Alexander Bain (1810-77),
c. 1845. Mahogany case, ht 58 in (146 cm).
An early example of Bain's work. He was
the first person to utilize electricity as the
motive force for a clock. Science Museum.*

Boudoir clock
Brass clock, engraved and gilded, introduced in c. 1860 probably with a lady's bedroom or sitting room in mind. Often made with a strut or swivel foot so that the clock can be made to stand up or fold flat for travelling, they are usually beautifully made with eight-day movements and engraved silvered dials.

Bracket clock
Name applied in the late eighteenth and early nineteenth centuries to clocks specifically designed to stand on a bracket, the latter usually having a drawer for the winding key. The term is now generally used to describe any of the larger wooden clocks designed to stand on mantelpieces and other ledges.

Carriage clock
Originally a clock designed for the rough coach and carriage travel of the late seventeenth and early eighteenth century. They were highly popular in England in the latter half of the nineteenth century, when they were nearly all French imports and called *Pendules de Voyage*. The case usually consists of a brass base having four vertical corner pillars holding mainly glass panels at the front, sides and back.

Chess clock
Invented in about 1860 as a successor to the sand glass. The chess clock was designed to control the amount of time a player could spend on a move. Two linked clocks were used by the players each independent of the other; when a move was made, the player depressed the knob or push button on the clock nearest him, thus automatically stopping his own clock and starting his opponent's.

Crystal ball clock
Large clock designed to stand on a desk, invented in c. 1900, with a half-spherical front and back of glass forming a ball and often decorated with a surround of coloured pastes.

Cuckoo clock
First made by Anton Ketterer of Schönwald in the Black Forest, Germany, its feature is that the hours and half hours are struck on a gong which signalizes the emergence of a wooden model of a cuckoo through a door at the top of the case. The call of the cuckoo is simulated by the sound made by two pipes. Very popular in the Victorian period, all brass movements were introduced from the mid century.

Demi-hunter
Watch with a hole cut into the full HUNTER cover so that the hands can be observed without opening the cover. The design is attributed to Napoleon I (hence also called a Napoleon), who is said to have cut a hole in the cover of his own hunter to facilitate observation.

Dial clock
Circular clock also sometimes referred to as a kitchen or office clock, very popular from c. 1875.

Drop dial or trunk dial clock
Similar to the DIAL CLOCK but with an extended lower section to the case to accomodate a longer pendulum. Usually of English, American or German make, the American drop dial clock being sometimes fitted with a striking mechanism.

Drum clock
Drum-shaped brass case into which the clock movement fits, generally set into an outer case of wood. Introduced in *c*. 1875.

Drumhead clock
Similar in its drum shape to the DRUM CLOCK but introduced about ten years earlier, it is usually fitted with a timepiece and rarely a striking movement, and was generally favoured for use in libraries, banks and offices.

Electric clock
First introduced in *c*. 1840, the description refers to a clock which is wholly dependent upon electric force either from the mains or battery; clocks with mainsprings or weights wound by electricity cannot accurately be described as electric clocks.

Engine clock
American clock in the form of a railway engine introduced in *c*. 1890, on which the hours are sounded on the bell of an engine.

English four-glass clock
Clock with wooden case introduced in *c*. 1850, whose name derives from the glass panels at the sides, back and top. Standing some 6 in to 10 in (15·3 cm–25·6 cm) high, the clock is fitted with a fusee pendulum movement, sometimes with a platform escapement.

English regulator clock
Weight-driven long-case timepiece clock designed to be specially accurate, with temperature compensated pendulum, jeweled pivots and possibly pallets. For the best results, regulators should be fixed to the wall. Although invented in 1750, they continued to be made to a high standard in the nineteenth century.

Fob
Decorative attachment for the pocket watch used in place of the ALBERT, in the twentieth century it has sometimes been used to describe a lady's pendant watch.

Girandole clock
Development of the BANJO CLOCK away from its original simplicity of design.

Grandfather clock
Long-case clock of about 6ft 6in (195 cm) or more.

Grandmother clock
Long-case clock similar to the GRANDFATHER CLOCK but not so tall and less frequently made.

Hunter
Watch with the face hidden by a cover or lid.

Koosen's clock
ELECTRIC CLOCK invented in 1862 by Koosen.

Lancet clock
Clock with a pointed top like a Gothic lancet arch particularly favoured at the end of the eighteenth century but made also in the nineteenth century. In the Victorian period carrying handles, used originally for this purpose, were moved to the sides as decoration, since, with the increase in cheaper clocks, there was no longer the need to move the same clock from room to room.

Lighthouse clock
Table clock in the form of a lighthouse, introduced in *c*. 1850. A clock is fitted in the tower under the lamphouse in which a cylinder of glass prisms rotate.

Lyre clock
Clock with the case in the form of the musical instrument, the pendulum bob forming the body and the rods of the gridiron pendulum forming the strings of the instrument. Of French origin, clocks of this type were imported into America after the Revolution and developed into a simplified version known as the banjo lyre.

Mantel clock
English term for a clock which roughly corresponds to the American SHELF CLOCK.

Mantel clock by Thomas Smith & Sons of Edinburgh, c. 1890. Oak. Chiming clock. Sotheby's Belgravia.

Nef clock
Clock incorporated in the model of a ship, usually a galleon. Earliest examples date from the sixteenth century; it was reintroduced in *c*. 1875.

Open face
Watch not fitted with a HUNTER or DEMI-HUNTER cover over the dial.

Pediment barometer
Type of barometer where the readings are taken directly from the level of mercury in the tube. The case is usually parallel with the bulbous end of the tube to accommodate the 'bag' of mercury.

Sometimes referred to as a stick barometer on account of its stick-like appearance.

Picture clock
Type resulting from a fashion starting at the end of the eighteenth century, for painting a village or town scene incorporating a church clock and putting a watch movement in the church tower. Since they usually had to be wound daily, the picture was hinged forward in the frame allowing it to swing outward for winding.

Postman's alarm clock
Simple dial clock made from 1850. Designed as a WALL CLOCK, it is made without a glass dial cover and it is pendulum controlled and weight driven.

Railway clock
In the mid-nineteenth century clocks in railway stations were set to show local time and leaflets were distributed showing the conversion of Greenwich Mean Time, i.e. railway time to local time. With the expansion of the railway, clocks were unified and Greenwich Mean Time was generally adopted.

Shelf clock
American term for a clock roughly corresponding to the English MANTEL or BRACKET CLOCK. The first shelf clocks were made by ELI TERRY and Eli Whitney and the main part of the mechanism was of wood. Rolled brass was first employed in *c*. 1837 and with it came mass production.

Ship's bell clock
Clock similar in appearance to a SHIP'S CLOCK which strikes the time at each half hour to denote watches. Introduced *c*. 1850.

Ship's clock
Simple timepiece clock with lever escapement also known as a marine clock. It is usually fitted into a round brass case with a flange to enable it to be screwed to a bulkhead or panel.

Skeleton clock
Clock in which the movement is visible from all angles, usually kept under a glass dome to exclude dust and fixed to a plinth. Some fine examples were exhibited at the Great Exhibition, which subscribed largely to their popularity.

Slave clock
Clock or dial driven from a master clock.

Steeple clock
Used in the nineteenth century to refer to an American type which is ornamented with two or more sharp conical finials.

Synchronome clock
Invented by F. Hope-Jones in 1895, the word Synchronome – the name of the firm of makers – has become synonymous with a type of master clock which can operate a great number of subsidiary or slave dials.

Skeleton clock, English, c. 1870. Fretted brass on marble plinth. Powered by a going train, this type of striking clock is known colloquially as 'one at the hour'. Strike One.

Tall clock
American term for a long-case clock also described as a hall and floor clock.

Torsion clock
American clock with unique striking system, probably patented in 1829 by Aaron D. Crane.

Trumpeter clock
Type of Black Forest clock in which the cuckoo is replaced by a trumpeter who plays a tune.

Tubular chiming clock
Chiming clock invented in *c.* 1870 in which tubes are employed in place of bells, gongs or rods.

Turret clock
Large clock erected in a tower or church steeple. Frequently the clock was a later addition to the tower.

Vienna Regulator
Weight-driven pendulum clock designed to hang on a wall and first made in Austria in *c.* 1875. Not a regulator in the English sense of the word, they were fitted with timepiece and striking movements, were weight driven and usually had a wood rod pendulum which was shorter than a seconds pendulum. Much copied in America and Germany, many were also widely imported by the English clock retailers in the last quarter of the century.

Wall clock
Clock, as the name denotes, that hangs on the wall, also known as a hanging clock.

Wagon-spring clock
Leaf spring similar to that used in wagons (and other vehicles) employed as the motive power for a SHELF CLOCK in place of a mainspring or weight.

Wag-on-the-wall-clock
American term for a WALL CLOCK, namely any clock designed to hang on the wall. Frequently fitted with a pendulum, both the weights and the pendulum are exposed.

Watchman's clock
Also known as a tell-tale clock. It was invented by Whitehurst of Derby in 1750 and originally consisted of a large rotating disk operated by a clock movement. Pegs were pushed in by the watchman around the edge of the disk to note the time of his visit. The more modern version consists of a small portable clock which the watchman can carry.

Wheel barometer
Type of barometer where the reading is indicated by a hand on a dial. A cord attached to a glass float in the mercurial tube passes over a pulley and the hand is fixed to an extending pivot also attached to the pulley. Referred to also as a banjo barometer, although not all wheel barometers of the nineteenth century were of banjo design.

Bibliography

ABBOT, HENRY G. *Watch Factories of America*, Exeter, New Hampshire, reprinted, 1888

ALLIX, CHARLES. *Carriage Clocks*, London, 1974

American Watch Company's Catalogue of New Orleans Exposition 1884-5, Bristol, Connecticut, reprinted, 1972

BEESON, C. F. C. *English Church Clocks 1280-1850*, London, 1971

BELL, G. H. and E. F. *Old English Barometers*, Winchester, Hampshire, 1952

BRUTON, ERIC. *Clocks and Watches 1400-1900*, London, 1967

BRUTON, ERIC. *Clocks and Watches*, Feltham, Middlesex, 1968

CAMERER CUSS, T. P. *The Country Life Book of Watches*, London, 1967

CLUTTON, CECIL and DANIELS, GEORGE. *Watches*, London, 1965

DE CARLE, DONALD. *Clocks and Their Value*, London, 1968

Elgin Reminiscences, Bristol, Connecticut, reprinted, 1972

GOODISON, NICHOLAS. *English Barometers 1680-1860*, London, 1969

JAGGER, CEDRIC. *Clocks*, London, 1973

JOY, EDWARD T. *The Country Life Book of Clocks*, London, 1967

LLOYD, H. ALAN. *Some Outstanding Clocks Over Seven Hundred Years 1250-1950*, London, 1958

MIDDLETON, W. E. K. *The History of the Barometer*, Baltimore, Maryland, 1964

NEGRETTI & ZAMBRA. *A Treatise on Meteorological Instruments*, London, 1864

ROBERTS, KENNETH D. *Contributions of Joseph Ives to Connecticut Clock Technology, 1810-62*, Bristol, Connecticut, 1970

Eli Terry and the Connecticut Shelf Clock, Bristol, Connecticut, 1973

ROYER-COLLARD, F. B. *Skeleton Clocks*, London, 1969

ULLYETT, KENNETH. *Clocks and Watches*, London, 1971

ULLYETT, KENNETH. *Watch Collecting*, London, 1970

Queen of England

Pottery

BRITISH

There were many distinctive types of pottery produced during the years of Queen Victoria's reign. The variety of wares is itself a reflection of times which the Victorians considered were, above all else, changing. But in terms of industrial output, probably the greater part of all the pottery made during the period was the cheap, strong and attractive white earthenware which had been introduced by Josiah Wedgwood in the late eighteenth century, and which remains today the staple production of the Staffordshire potteries.

Throughout the Five Towns, numerous firms were engaged in the manufacture of this transfer-printed tableware, which was exported to the Colonies, the Continent and the United States. Some services were still hand painted in enamels, but during Queen Victoria's reign, the form of decoration generally employed was transfer-printed designs. Among these designs, topographical, architectural, Classical and commemorative subjects predominated, and these were surrounded by ornamental borders. From the 1840s, polychrome printing was sometimes used, but this comparatively expensive process was generally restricted to ornamental vases and the lids of pots in which luxuries such as toilet preparations and gastronomic delicacies were marketed. A rare instance when this cheap tableware was designed and decorated in an *avant-garde* style was a tea service manufactured by Minton's in the 1840s; the shapes were designed by Henry Cole and they were printed with Gothic ornament, designed by the architect A. W. N. Pugin.

Cole and Pugin were among a handful of reformers who from the 1840s at-

tempted to bring artistic principles to bear on factory-made goods. These men objected to early Victorian design on the grounds that it was inappropriate (design and decoration were not adapted to the function of the object) and, in its imitation of nature and historical styles, incorrect. At the same time there was emerging a middle class which took pride in its knowledge of the natural and historical world. Ruskin praised Turner because the painter accurately portrayed the forces of nature, and his praises were given in terms of morality.

Plate printed with Gothic ornament designed by A. W. N. Pugin (1812-52), Minton. Exhibited at the Great Exhibition of 1851. The shape was designed by Henry Cole. Victoria and Albert Museum.

Moulded Jugs and Staffordshire Figures

A genus of Victorian pottery, produced in quantity during the 1830s and '40s and to a lesser extent in later decades, was the jug with moulded decoration. These jugs do not compare in quality with china tableware and were probably used mainly in catering establishments. Their style of decoration reflects the shifting emphasis of Victorian taste. The

swing is away from light-hearted incident and broadly sketched *mise en scène* to a moral and artistic earnestness expressed literally and precisely. Greater variety and originality of design were encouraged by a piece of legislation enacted by Parliament in 1842; this set up a Design Registry at the Patent Office. Designs registered were protected from copyists for a number of years. Manufacturers were thus given the incentive to employ competent designers, for, if any design was commercially successful, profits went exclusively to the manufacturer who had commissioned it and not to all the other manufacturers who would otherwise have copied it. It became viable to pay considerable fees to leading contemporary artists for ornamental designs.

Moulded jugs were slip cast in either earthenware or stoneware. To give definition to the moulded decoration, earthenware jugs were only slightly glazed on the outside and stoneware jugs were salt glazed. In shape, the earlier jugs were usually given a wider lower half which tapered to the neck, above which the lip was flared upwards. Many later jugs were also of this form, but in 1847 T. & R. Boote introduced a jug with straight sides slightly tapering inwards towards the rim. There subsequently appeared many straight-sided jugs, with or without a foot. The spouts on later jugs were generally lower, and the profile at the rim tended to be more level.

Victorian Staffordshire figures were manufactured in huge quantities throughout Queen Victoria's reign. Their manufacture was almost without any technical sophistication, and their appearance had scarcely any artistic merit. Nevertheless, they have some attraction as a gallery of the Victorians who captured the popular imagination, and their simple press-moulded forms, their flat, undecorated backs and their bright overglaze and underglaze colours make them acceptable art-objects through their very lack of artistic pre-

OPPOSITE *Figure of Queen Victoria, Staffordshire, c. 1850. Pottery. Figures of the Queen and other prominent personalities were often modelled from portraits and illustrations current at the time. Private Collection.*

tension (although this is of necessity a twentieth-century viewpoint). Royalty, politicians, soldiers, entertainers, clergy, criminals and sportsmen were all depicted. Some Staffordshire figures of this period were modelled and coloured in the round.

Apostle jug, Charles Meigh, Hanley, Stoke-on-Trent, c. 1850. Smear-glazed stoneware. Moulded jugs were slip cast and stoneware often salt glazed to give definition. City Museum and Art Gallery, Hanley.

The Classical Revival

In the 1840s there was a Classical Revival. Significantly, by that time, the original Wedgwood jasperware designs had lost their appeal, and the new range which was produced for the Great Exhibition of 1851 was heavier in its shapes and more cluttered in its ornament. The Classicism was pointed and didactic where, half a century before, it had been light and suggestive.

Much of the pottery exhibited at the Crystal Palace in 1851 was of Classical inspiration. It was, as it remains, the safest style to adopt when offering expensive goods, and it was known to be the style favoured by Prince Albert who had been enthusiastic and energetic in the conception and planning of the Exhibition. In 1848 the Consort had purchased a massive 'Etruscan' vase, 4 ft (1·2 m) high, from Messrs F. & R. Pratt & Co. This firm had pioneered the polychrome transfer-printing process and produced a wide range of Classical Revival wares decorated in this technique. Messrs Copeland & Garrett also produced Classical Revival pottery, called Etrurian ware, and another firm to do

Vase in the form of a Classical amphora, F. & R. Pratt, c. 1850. Pottery, ht 22½ in (57 cm). This vase is colour printed with Classical scenes. Sotheby's Belgravia.

so was Samuel Alcock & Co. A good Alcock vase from the Handley-Read Collection bears on its base the transfer-printed inscription: 'Fac-simile of an antique vase, in the coll[n] of M. Le Comte de Lamberg. Subject: A sacrifice at Delphos'; it demonstrates well the learned approach to Classical Antiquity which characterized this Victorian revival. Thomas Battam, a London decorating firm, exhibited a complete Etruscan tomb in 1851, which was a cave packed

with pottery decorated in the Classical taste.

Since Classical Greek pottery had been unglazed, many of the imitations were appropriately made in terracotta. Minton and Copeland both produced terracotta ware about the middle of the century, and Blanchard of Lambeth and J. Pulham of Broxbourne specialized in architectural work and garden ornaments in the same material. The Watcombe Pottery, founded in 1869, produced terracotta vases and urns which were successfully shown at the South Kensington Exhibitions of 1871 and '72. But these were in a much simpler, more refined, Classical taste, often embellished with areas of turquoise-blue glaze, and decorated with ornament which characterized the Aesthetic Movement of the 1870s rather than Greek or Roman Antiquity. The Classical Revival of the 1840s and '50s, with its impressive displays of archaeological learning, had passed.

Figure of a seated girl reading, Watcombe, Torquay, 1875. Terracotta. The pottery was founded in 1869 and renowned for its terracotta vases and urns. City Museum and Art Gallery, Hanley.

Historicism in Majolica

In the second half of the nineteenth century the production of pottery known as Majolica or Faïence was undertaken by numerous firms in Staffordshire and elsewhere. Minton exhibited their Majolica at the Great Exhibition of 1851. Herbert Minton, apparently, saw some flower pots decorated with a green glaze at Rouen in 1849. On his return to Stoke, he instructed a Frenchman, Léon Arnoux, who was the son of a porcelain manufacturer at Toulouse and who, at Stoke, was experimenting with new porcelain bodies, to produce a new ware along the lines of the Rouen pots. Arnoux developed glazes in a range of rich colours which were used to decorate the new, highly sculptural products. To make the original models after which the ware was cast, Minton employed a succession of French sculptors, Émile

Jeannest, Albert Carrier-Belleuse and Hugues Protat.

In Majolica, Minton produced close imitations of Palissy ware (appropriately, since the sixteenth-century French potter had used a similar decorative technique) and Henri Deux ware. The latter,

Tea service, Minton, 1868. Majolica. Minton introduced their Majolica at the Great Exhibition of 1851, Herbert Minton having first seen this type of body at Rouen in 1849. Sotheby's Belgravia.

Ewer, probably by Charles Toft, exhibited in 1862. Henri Deux ware, ht 15 in (38 cm). Henri Deux ware was closely based on sixteenth-century designs, Victoria and Albert Museum.

now generally called St Porchaire ware, involved Minton's craftsmen in a complicated process of clay inlays, a technique in which Charles Toft particularly excelled. Some Majolica was embellished with underglaze paintings in the Renaissance and Mannerist styles; for example, at the International Exhibition of 1862 a ewer was shown painted by Thomas Allen with Classical deities after Polidoro da Caravaggio. Some of the finest Majolica pieces made by

Minton's were the vases and chargers, decorated with painted ornament in the style of the Italian Renaissance, which were designed by the sculptor Alfred Stevens.

Minton's produced Majolica in many styles other than Renaissance, for in-

stance a Gothic breadplate designed by A. W. N. Pugin, and many items in the form of fruit and vegetables. Majolica soon became widely popular and was produced by other firms, notably George Jones and Adams & Co. Without the technical supervision of Léon Arnoux, the products of these firms lacked the depth of colour in the glazes which characterizes Minton's Majolica. Wedgwood's revived a ware they had made in the eighteenth century which was moulded in leaf or vegetable forms and decorated in a translucent green glaze. They also produced plates with moulded and countersunk decoration covered in coloured glazes, a process which gives a remarkable three-dimensional appearance to the design.

The Aesthetic Movement: Art Pottery

From the late 1860s, a spate of books were published which dealt with the 'artistic' decoration of the home, beginning with Charles Eastlake's *Hints on Household Taste* (1868). The general admonition of their authors was to avoid over-elaboration and excess of detail in décor and furnishings. The underlying aesthetic attitude was an emphasis on effects of form and colour rather than on historical and literary allusion or mere technical sophistication. Japanese artifacts, which were after centuries of obscurity appearing at international exhibitions, set standards of excellence by these criteria, and thoughtful Western designers and decorators were not slow in their attempts to achieve the same results. Another characteristic of the Aesthetic Movement, as this artistic development was called, was a prevalence of geometric motifs both in form and decoration. Abstract geometrical pattern and the geometrical stylization of plants and animals are to be found both in Japanese and Gothic art. To many Victorian designers the attraction of the Japanese style, as had been that of the Gothic, was that it was traditional and represented a Medieval spirit unaffected by the Renaissance and other subsequent developments which, to their mind, had reduced Western art to stylistic formulae.

From the late 1870s, there sprung up a number of potteries, not, significantly, situated in Staffordshire, though often drawing their technical experts from there, which produced wares answering to the principles of the Aesthetic Movement. At the Linthorpe Pottery in Middlesbrough, much of the ware produced was designed by Dr Christopher Dresser, who had visited Japan in order to make a close study of its decorative art. Many of the shapes he designed for the Linthorpe Pottery were related to Japanese ceramics, although in his pursuit of pure form he also based designs on Classical, Moorish, Anglo-Saxon, Celtic and Peruvian originals. The ware was slip cast and decorated with coloured glazes, including a rich honey tint and *sang-de-boeuf* in emulation of Oriental glazes; pieces were usually covered in two or more colours of glaze, which were allowed to mingle, giving a streaked or mottled effect similar to that found on some Oriental wares. Under the glazes, some pieces were incised with geometrical ornament, which was also designed by Dresser.

In Barnstaple, North Devon, Charles Brannam began making art pottery at his father's works which had been producing traditional domestic slipware for many years. Decorative designs in the Japanese taste were supplied by Owen Davis, a well-known ornamentalist, and carried out in *sgraffito*. The ware was stocked by Howell & James, a leading London retailer. Another West Country enterprise was that of Edmund Elton, who built his kilns on the family estate at Clevedon Court, Somerset. His ware was decorated with marbled glaze effects and raised flowers, birds and insects in coloured slips; in this instance, too, the Japanese influence was strong.

Another form of Victorian ceramic which is connected with the Aesthetic Movement is the painted pottery produced during the 1870s and '80s. In 1869 Minton's asked W. S. Coleman, a water-colour artist, to paint on china. The idea of employing professional artists to paint on pottery was that the finished piece should be a work of art with the same intrinsic merits as an easel-painting or a water-colour drawing. The artists were given pottery to work on which provided a large flat area, usually either dishes or flat-sided vases in the form of pilgrim-flasks; painted tiles were *de rigueur* in the 'artistic' home. There were usually no ornamental borders.

In 1871, Minton's opened an art pottery studio in South Kensington under the supervision of W. S. Coleman where artists painted on biscuit pottery sent from Stoke, and where there were kilns

Dish, Minton, 1870. Pottery painted in over and underglaze enamels by W. S. Coleman, diam. 11¾ in (29 cm). Coleman was a professional artist specializing in water colours. Sotheby's Belgravia.

for firing their work. Students from the nearby Art School were invited to work there, and for a fee amateurs were given tuition in the techniques of underglaze and overglaze painting. Coleman left the Studio in 1873 and two years later the buildings were destroyed by fire, but facilities for china painting were soon afterwards provided by Howell & James, who organized annual exhibitions of work by professionals and amateurs. The biscuit ware was available from Howell & James, who had it specially made in Staffordshire. The painted subjects were varied but predominantly floral, Japanese or Medieval.

Some of the professional artists who competed at these exhibitions were employed by Messrs Doulton & Co. Ltd of Lambeth who from 1873 produced painted pottery called Lambeth Faïence. It is similar in character to Minton's Art Pottery Studio work (some artists worked for both concerns), but ornamental borders were often incorporated; sometimes the painting is entirely of ornamental patterns. In 1878 Doulton's took over the Pinder Bourne works in Burslem, Staffordshire, and china blanks were sent from there to be painted at Lambeth.

Stoneware and Studio Pottery

Doulton's had produced cheap stoneware, mostly industrial and sanitary ware, until the late 1860s when, at the instigation of John Sparkes, headmaster of the Lambeth School of Art, they began to employ art students to decorate art pottery. The stoneware produced under this arrangement was at first inspired by the fifteenth- and sixteenth-century *grès de flandres*. The buff stoneware was decorated with incised or carved designs, and beads and florets were applied. Blue was used to colour

part of the designs. The treatment of Doulton stoneware, which was salt glazed, soon became more varied as new techniques were developed and, at the same time, other artistic styles, such as Japanese, influenced the decoration. But the young art students were encouraged to show originality, and corporately developed a style of their own which was essentially Doulton. Among the more talented decorators was a sculptor, George Tinworth, whose stoneware and terracotta reliefs of biblical scenes were outside the normal run of Doulton ware.

Artistic salt-glazed stoneware was also produced from *c.* 1870 at the Fulham pottery of C. J. C. Bailey. The work was similar to Doulton's but reflects the influence of the *émigré* French artist and potter J.-C. Cazin who worked at Fulham from 1871. His vases are decorated with more relief modelling than most Doulton pieces, and the same is true of the work of Edgar Kettle, Bailey's leading artist. Cazin must also have been working at the Fulham Pottery at the same time as R. W. Martin, to whom he left his throwing wheel when he returned to France. Martin set up his own pottery in 1873 where he was joined by his three brothers who had been taught at Lambeth by Cazin. They decorated their salt-glazed stoneware in a variety of styles over a period of about forty years. The importance of their enterprise was that, although they had assistants, each

TOP Christ riding into Jerusalem *by George Tinworth, c. 1890. Pottery plaque. Birmingham Art Gallery and Museum.*

ABOVE *Wall plaque, Martin Bros, c. 1890. Martin ware. The brothers are depicted at work in their Southall pottery. Southall Library, Middlesex.*

Pair of vases, Messrs Doulton & Co. Ltd, with incised decoration by Mary Mitchell, 1880. Stoneware, ht 12¾ in (32 cm). Sotheby's Belgravia.

of the brothers could manage most of the potter's various crafts, throwing, modelling, decorating and firing. The Martin brothers were the first studio-potters in England.

The teaching of Ruskin and Morris emphasized the moral benefit, both to maker and to user, of the handicrafts. They despised factories where men toiled as mindlessly as the machines beside them, and where commercial compromise thwarted any truly artistic endeavour. It suggests the wide acceptance of these precepts that at the new art potteries each craftsman had opportunity of expression and freedom of choice, and that the public demanded these firms' products despite their frequent lack of technical sophistication or high finish.

William de Morgan was a close friend of Morris and began making pottery in around 1870. He and the artists working for him, first in Chelsea, then at Merton Abbey and ultimately in Fulham, decorated the ware with designs which in style are related to, but distinct from, the work of Morris. The decoration was painted in lustres, predominantly copper, but sometimes silver and gold, or in Persian colours, blue, green and red. Grotesque animals, fishes, common flowers and leaves were the usual motifs. De Morgan had an inventive mind and he overcame technical problems which might have defeated more experienced potters. After years of dwindling commercial success, his firm ceased in 1907.

Another firm closely connected with the core of the Arts and Crafts Movement was the Della Robbia Pottery Co. of Birkenhead, founded in 1894 by Conrad Dressler, a sculptor, and Harold Rathbone, who had been a pupil of Ford Madox Brown. In its short existence (about a dozen years), Rathbone directed a small group of inexperienced potters and decorators. The shapes were often inspired by Renaissance or Persian originals and the decoration was generally *sgraffito* as well as painted. Although

LEFT *Fountain, Martin Bros, late-nineteenth century. Salt-glazed stoneware. Having started his career as a sculptor, R. W. Martin frequently modelled animals and birds. Southall Manor, Middlesex.*

BELOW *Vase by William de Morgan (1839-1917), painted in the Persian style by Edward Porter, c. 1890. Pottery, ht 19¾ in (50 cm). Sotheby's Belgravia.*

the designs were occasionally reminiscent of the Italian Renaissance, their style was original and contemporary. Formalized leaf and flower motifs prevail, arranged in sinuous patterns which are not remote from Continental Art Nouveau. Execution was never good, but this was almost a merit in view of the ethics underlying the work, and it gives the pottery a quality of direct artistic expression.

By the end of Queen Victoria's reign, production had begun at the Pilkington Pottery works near Manchester, and, at Smethwick near Birmingham, W. Howson Taylor had started the experiments which led to his achievements in *flambé* glazes. Pilkington's, under the direction of William Burton, an able ceramic chemist who had started at Wedgwood's, and his brother Joseph, produced tiles designed by such eminent artists as Walter Crane, Lewis Day and the architect C. F. A. Voysey. The Burtons also experimented with glaze effects, but production of the firm's lustre ware did not begin until 1903. Howson Taylor's efforts were directed towards the emulation of Oriental glazes, and his successes were acclaimed by Eastern as well as Western connoisseurs. His work represents a step between the Japonism of the Aesthetic Movement and the identification with the Oriental ceramist, which was fully achieved by Bernard Leach in the 1920s.

Malcolm Haslam

Lead-glazed redware and salt-glazed stoneware were made during the late eighteenth and early nineteenth centuries. Redware was made wherever there was a good deposit of common red clay and a viable market in the locality, a distance of about thirty miles generally separating one redware pottery from the next. Stoneware was only made in the eighteenth century in those areas where stoneware clay was found, such as South Amboy, Middlesex County, New Jersey. Because of the high temperature necessary for firing stoneware, salt glaze was utilized instead of lead glaze. After the beginning of the nineteenth century, New Jersey clay was transported to potting centres all along the East Coast and stoneware replaced redware in urban locations. In addition, the interiors of the pots were coated with Albany slip and only the exteriors were salt glazed, unlike eighteenth-century pots which were salt glazed both inside and out.

Early Traditions in Redware and Stoneware

Charlestown, Massachusetts, was one of the places which had a redware tradition dating back to the seventeenth century, and the area provided a ready market for stoneware clay. Several potteries made the new ware, but the oldest was that of Barnabas Edmands & Co. Edmands had been a brass founder who sold his foundry in 1819 to buy a pottery with his brother-in-law, William Burroughs. They engaged the services of a potter named Frederick Carpenter and marked their ware with the name of the town. Later their mark was EDMANDS & CO., and in some rare instances the town name was also added. Many potteries throughout New England made thrown stoneware, such as Franklin T. Wright & Son, in Taunton, Massachusetts, who were in business from about 1868.

In New York State, potteries principally made redware until the opening of the Eerie Canal in 1825 which enabled New Jersey clay to be transported across the State and into the Mid West. It has been said that the quality of New York State pottery varies in direct proportion to the distance of the pottery from Perth Amboy and South Amboy, New Jersey.

Some potteries supplied specialized markets, such as William Hare's Pottery in Wilmington, Delaware, which principally produced Albany slip-lined, salt-glazed stoneware snuff bottles for the snuff mills of northern New Castle County, Delaware. These snuff bottles are relatively common but other objects with Hare's mark are rare.

Moulded Earthenware

In 1828 David Henderson and his brother bought the defunct Jersey Porcelain & Earthenware Co. in Jersey City, N.J., and founded in 1833 the American Pottery Co. They owned the first American pottery to make earthenware in moulds. Their body was a refined stoneware covered with lead glaze and coloured by Albany slip: small amounts of it made the glaze yellow and larger amounts brown. The shapes they used were copies of Ridgway and Turner pieces, such as hunting-scene pitchers, hexagonal pitchers, octagonal cuspidors, teasets, and toby jugs, as well as ordinary utilitarian yellow ware. One rare type of pottery made by the firm was blue transfer-printed white earthenware in the Canova pattern. The Pottery continued until 1845 when David Henderson was killed in a hunting accident in the Adirondack Mountains.

From the late 1830s into the 1840s, two Frenchmen, Henry de Casse and Michel Lefoulon operated a pottery named the Salamander Works, in Woodbridge, New Jersey, making a variety of moulded pottery pitchers, water coolers and other objects, as well as fire brick. They had a sales room in New York City on Cannon Street.

A redware pottery in Bennington, Vermont, was run by Captain John Norton in the late eighteenth century. After the turn of the century it was taken over by his offspring and the production of the pottery changed to salt-glazed stoneware. Captain Norton's descendants ran the pottery until its closure in 1906.

Experiments in Ceramics

In 1845 Christopher Weber Fenton of Dorset, Vermont, married Louisa Norton and went into partnership with his brother-in-law as Norton & Fenton, located in East Bennington, Vermont, now known simply as Bennington. In 1847 the partnership was dissolved by mutual consent. Norton continued to make stoneware in the pottery while in 1848 Fenton acquired two new partners, Alanson P. Lyman and Calvin Park, and arranged financial backing for a new venture called the United States Pottery Co. In 1849 Park withdrew from the partnership and the firm became known as Lyman, Fenton & Co.

The firm continued to make mottled brown-glazed earthenware pitchers in many different shapes and sizes as well as sanitary pottery and other utilitarian ware. In 1849, Fenton applied for and received a United States patent for Fenton's Patented Enamel. The patent was granted for a new method of applying powdered coloured-glaze materials by means of a shaker to the surface of a previously glazed object. In the kiln, the powder melted and ran so that the finished glaze looks feathery instead of blotchy and streaked as does the same mottled brown glaze when applied using a liquid base.

Fenton continued to experiment with new bodies and glazes. He made parian and glazed porcelain following the lead of such English potteries as Mayer, Copeland and Ridgway, whose products were fashionable in the United States. Fenton made figurines, ewers, vases, jewelry and trinket boxes from both materials. The pottery also produced solid agate ware, experimental pink, tan and blue porcelain as well as the iridescent glazed porcelain popularly called Belleek. For the Crystal Palace Exhibition held in New York in 1853, the pottery made an 8 ft (2·4 m) tall statue using various of its bodies and glazes and surmounting the statue by a parian porcelain Madonna and Child. The early 1850s saw the heyday of the United States Pottery Co. for by 1858 it was forced to close its doors because costs had risen to the point where prices could not follow.

During the 1850s other potteries made earthenware in moulds, competing with Fenton's works in Bennington, Vermont. One was the Edmands Pottery in Charlestown, Massachusetts, which made Albany slip-covered jars and another was the John T. Winslow Pottery, of Portland, Maine, which operated between 1846 and about 1874.

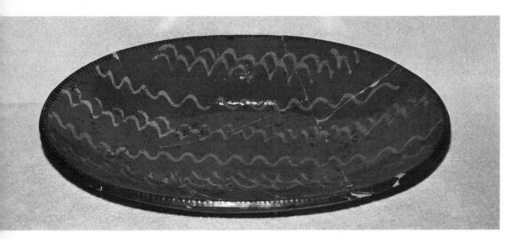

Platter, J. McCully, Trenton, New Jersey (1799-1852). Lead-glazed redware. New Jersey State Museum.

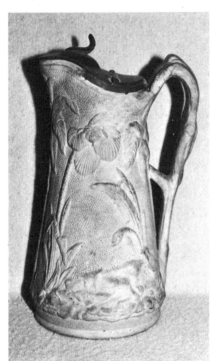

Pitcher, American Pottery Co., c. 1835. Brown-glazed earthenware. Carborundum Museum of Ceramics.

OPPOSITE *Jar and snuff jar, Barnabas Edmands Pottery, Charlestown, Massachusetts, c. 1830. Salt-glazed stoneware. Author's Collection.*

BELOW *Poodle, Lyman, Fenton & Co., Bennington, Vermont, c. 1850. Mottled brown-glazed yellow ware. Metropolitan Museum of Art.*

Crock, J. Fisher, Lyons, New York, c. 1850. Salt-glazed stoneware. Author's Collection.

Syrup pitcher, United States Pottery Co., Bennington, Vermont, c. 1853. Solid agateware. Author's Collection.

Mould, Ira W. Cory of the Mill Street Pottery, New York, c. 1869. Yellow earthenware. Author's Collection.

In South Amboy, New Jersey, the Congress and the Swan Hill Potteries made the same mottled, brown-glazed earthenware as was made at Bennington. In Trenton, New Jersey, William Young founded a pottery in 1852 and Taylor & Speeler a year later. Young's pottery claimed to have made the first white ware in Trenton and the piece still survives. It is a smaller edition of a hexagonal pitcher made by Taylor & Speeler, who closed their doors in 1859. Young's sons joined him in business and continued after his death until 1879, when they sold their Excelsior Works to the Willets brothers. Willets Manufacturing Co. made ironstone china and Belleek porcelain until 1908.

One minor pottery was Ira W. Cory's Mill Street Pottery which operated between 1866 and 1870. The only objects known to have been made by him are yellow ware moulds.

Another centre of pottery production in the 1850s was in and around East Liverpool, Ohio, where a number of potteries made mottled, brown-glazed earthenware in the same manner as the potteries in Bennington, Vermont; South Amboy, Jersey City and Trenton, New Jersey.

The Potting Centres

The distance from Trenton, New Jersey, to East Liverpool, Ohio, is approximately 300 miles. Trenton is on the opposite side of the Delaware River to the State of Pennsylvania in the East and East Liverpool, Ohio, is on the opposite side of the Ohio River to Pennsylvania in the West. Pioneers and new immigrants travelled across Pennsylvania seeking the new lands in the Mid West and potters formed part of their company. However, when things did not go well in Ohio, the potters would often return to New Jersey attempting to continue to seek their fortunes. As a result, such names as Bloor, Speeler, Taylor, Coxon and Thompson are part of the history of both potting centres.

There were, of course, potteries making brown-glazed yellow ware in various locations in the United States other than in such centres as New Jersey and East Liverpool, Ohio. In Baltimore, Maryland, for example, Edwin and James Bennett had a pottery on Canton Avenue between 1849 and 1856 making oil-resistant brown-glazed yellow earthenware.

W. H. Farrar of Bennington and Jersey City established a pottery in 1856 called the Southern Porcelain Manufacturing Co. at Kaolin, Mitchell County, South

Mug, Edwin & William Bennett, Baltimore, Maryland, c. 1848. Mottled brown-glazed earthenware. Author's Collection.

Pitcher, Southern Porcelain Co., Kaolin, South Carolina, c. 1860. Mottled brown-glazed earthenware. Author's Collection.

Carolina, which continued in production until 1862. It specialized in glazed and parian porcelain as well as mottled brown-glazed earthenware.

In 1868 J. E. Jeffords established a pottery in Philadelphia, Pennsylvania, which made mottled brown-glazed yellow ware, white-lined yellow ware and plain yellow ware, continuing in production until 1906.

Prior to the Civil War (1861–5), the most popular inexpensive American body was a yellow earthenware usually referred to then as cream-coloured ware. White granite ware was more expensive to make but was a more practical purchase since it was less porous than cream-coloured ware. As time passed the cheaper ware became so good that only an expert could distinguish the cheap from the expensive, and the Mayer Pottery Co. of Beaver Falls, Pennsylvania, proclaimed this fact in their advertisements.

After the Civil War, English ironstone

china became popular in the United States and American potteries followed the English lead and also made the fashionable ware. However, American consumers were accustomed to English goods representing a standard of excellence. In order to sell American ironstone china, the potteries in Ohio and New Jersey copied English coats-of-arms, substituted their own initials for English ones and sold their ware without informing the consumer that it was made in the United States rather than in England.

One early piece of white earthenware was a pitcher made in 1863 by Millington, Astbury & Poulson of Trenton, New Jersey, to commemorate the assassination of Colonel Elmer Ellsworth of the 24th New York Zouaves. A detachment of men under his command was ordered by President Abraham Lincoln to remove a rebel flag from a hotel across the Potomac River in Alexandria, Virginia, visible from the White House. After lowering the flag and while leaving the hotel, Colonel Ellsworth was shot and killed by the proprietor, who in turn was bayoneted by a Zouave. The act is pictured on one side of the pitcher while the other side is devoted to an iconographic depiction of Union Victory.

Changes in Partnership

Millington, Astbury & Poulson was one of many American pottery firms which survived only a few years during the nineteenth century but which was part of a long series of different establishments covering a number of years. For example, in 1857 Richard Millington and John Astbury went into business in Trenton. In 1859 they were joined by a Mr Poulson, who sold his portion to a Mr Colclough in 1863. Ten years later Thomas Maddock bought out Colclough with the resulting partnership of Millington, Astbury & Maddock, which lasted one year until Richard Millington retired in 1874. Astbury and Maddock made pottery until 1878, when Astbury died and Maddock's sons replaced him, causing the partnership to be named Thomas Maddock & Sons. In 1890 Mr Maddock retired and the firm became Thomas Maddock's Sons' Co.

OPPOSITE *Ceramics, Rookwood, late nineteenth century. Left: Vase with portrait of Chief Joseph of the Nez Percés, ht 14in (35cm). Right: Bowl with Japanese flower-motif. Metropolitan Museum of Art.*

Crock, Western Stoneware Co., Monmouth, Illinois, c. 1880. Stoneware. Author's Collection.

The sons continued in business until 1929 when the pottery was sold to the American Radiator & Sanitary Pottery Co. This firm is still in operation but is now named the American Standard Inc.

Many firms sprang up across the United States as the troubles in the Mid-West and Far West were settled. They made a wide variety of wares but principally thrown stoneware such as that made about 1850 by the Belmont Pottery in Belmont, Wisconsin. Between 1870 and 1890 the largest stoneware pottery in the United States was the Western Stoneware Co. in Monmouth, Illinois.

At the end of the century, the influence of Art Nouveau coupled with the Arts and Crafts Movement spawned art potteries throughout the United States. The Hampshire Pottery, for example, owned by J. S. Taft & Co. and operated from 1871 to 1917 in Keene, New Hampshire, made a variety of art wares including those with solid-colour matt-finish glazes.

Pottery and porcelain made in the United States between 1837 and 1901 was, with some exceptions, either made in a vernacular tradition or as a conscious effort to copy and reproduce styles and material from Europe so as to secure part of the market for such wares made in the United States.

James R. Mitchell

OPPOSITE *Selection of tiles, English, nineteenth century. Pottery. Set of tiles of the Four Seasons, Minton. Four-tile panel with lily design, hand-painted by W. B. Simpson & Sons, c. 1869. Richard Dennis Antiques.*

Manufacturers

ADAMS, WILLIAM (1798–1865)
Member of the famous Adams family who specialized in blue TRANSFER-PRINTED wares, hand-painted earthenware and bone china. Continued in the family tradition but also specialized in ware decorated in sponge-applied colour and painted with conventional bird.

AMERICAN POTTERY CO.
Incorporated in 1833 by David Henderson and others in Jersey City. Manufacturers of YELLOW WARE, ROCKINGHAM WARE and white EARTHENWARE, they were instrumental in introducing a number of innovations to the United States and also in providing a springboard for several immigrant potters, who made their names elsewhere. They produced the first successful American TRANSFER-PRINTED wares from 1840. Mark: American Pottery Manufg. Co. (1833–40) and American Pottery Co., Jersey City (1840–5). They were succeeded in 1845 by Rhodes, Strong & McGeron, Jersey City Pottery.

BARUM WARE
ART POTTERY produced by C. H. Brannam in Barnstaple, Devon, from 1879. Decoration was in SGRAFFITO or painted SLIP. It was normally dated and signed with the initials of the decorator.

BROAD STREET WORKS
Works famed for Mason's Patent Ironstone China in addition to most varieties of useful earthenware. The original patent was taken out in 1813 by Charles James Mason and the manufacture carried on under the styles of G. & C. Mason & Co., the partners being Charles James Mason and his brother George Miles Mason.

CHELSEA KERAMIC ART WORKS
Art pottery in Massachusetts owned by the Robertson family. Founded in 1866 for the production of brown EARTHENWARE, the plant was enlarged and the new name adopted in 1872. Much of the work was in the Greek style, but high-relief decoration was also employed. From 1884 the firm was under the sole direction of Hugh C. Robertson, who concerned himself with the search for the Oriental *sang-de-boeuf* GLAZE, a search which forced the factory to close in 1888. A new company, the Chelsea Pottery with Robertson as manager, was formed in 1891, successfully producing Oriental crackled and high-fired glazes. It moved to Dedham, south west of Boston, resuming work there in 1896 under the name of the Dedham Pottery.

CINCINNATI
Focal point of emergent ART POTTERY production in America following the Philadelphia Centennial Exhibition of 1876. Between 1879 and 1889 six art potteries were founded, but only the ROOKWOOD POTTERY survived the decade to achieve international recognition.

MESSRS COPELAND & GARRETT
Successors to Messrs Spode in 1833, becoming W. T. Copeland in 1847. Producers of a wide range of fine EARTHENWARE.

MESSRS DOULTON & CO. LTD
Pottery founded in 1815 at Vauxhall by John Doulton, moving soon afterwards to Lambeth with John Watts becoming a partner until his death in 1858. Initially producing utilitarian STONEWARE, the factory was brought into close contact with the Lambeth school of Art under the management of Doulton's son, Henry Doulton. Students from the school used the facilities of the factory to produce ART POTTERY and their SALT-GLAZED STONEWARE decorated with SGRAFFITO filled in with colours proved a great success at the exhibitions held at South Kensington in 1871 and 1872. Other decorative techniques were developed, including impasto stoneware, and Lambeth FAÏENCE. All wares were marked with the name of the firm and the initials of the decorator. Among the Doulton decorators were Hannah B. Barlow, her sister and brother, Florence and Arthur Barlow, George Tinworth, Emily Edwards and Frank Butler.

EAST LIVERPOOL
Pottery centre in Ohio, which between 1840 and 1900, produced the bulk of YELLOW WARE and ROCKINGHAM WARE in the United States, particularly the simpler types. The pioneer was James Bennett, an English immigrant potter, who built a small pottery there in 1839 to make yellow ware. This concern was sold in 1844 to Thomas Croxall & Bros, becoming one of the most important concerns in East Liverpool. Other early potters, whose output became large and important, were Benjamin Harker and Isaac W. Knowles.

ELTON WARE
Work of the Somerset art potter, Sir Edmund Elton, who commenced experiments in 1879 and continued production until his death in 1920. Decorated mainly with asymmetrical floral patterns built up in coloured SLIP, the ware was made from dark native CLAY and showed a strong Japanese influence.

GRUEBY FAÏENCE CO.
ART POTTERY established in Boston, Massachusetts, in 1894 by William H. Grueby. Inspired by the work of the French potter, Auguste Delaherche, the

characteristic leaf-shaped forms, designed by George P. Kendrick, were covered with a matt GLAZE, generally dark green, developed by Grueby. Production of art pottery ceased in 1910.

LINTHORPE POTTERY

Established near Middlesbrough, Yorkshire, in 1879 by John Harrison with initial designs provided by Dr Christopher Dresser, some reminiscent of pre-Columbian American pottery. It closed in 1889.

LONHUDA POTTERY

Founded in 1892 by William A. Long in Steubenville, Ohio, for the production of UNDERGLAZE decorated ART POTTERY in imitation of ROOKWOOD POTTERY. Among the decorators was Laura A. Fry from Cincinnati, who had been in MCLAUGHLIN's group and at the Rookwood Pottery. The company was bought in 1895 by Samuel A. Weller, who introduced art pottery to ZANESVILLE, Ohio.

MCLAUGHLIN, MARY LOUISE

Early exponent of ART-POTTERY decoration in CINCINNATI. Mary Louise McLaughlin sought to discover the technique of UNDERGLAZE DECORATION following the Philadelphia Centennial Exhibition of 1876: her first successes were achieved in the following year. In 1879 Miss McLaughlin organized the Women's Pottery Club in the city which played an important part in developing Cincinnati as an art-pottery centre.

MARTIN BROS

Association of four brothers, led by Robert Wallace Martin, formed in 1873 to produce SALT-GLAZED STONEWARE, first in London and then at Southall, Middlesex. The decoration and shapes often show Oriental influence. They also produced jugs and jars in shapes of grotesque faces and birds. The last firing of Martin ware was in 1914. Mark: R. W. Martin with the place of production (Fulham and later London and Southall).

MINTON & CO.

One of the foremost porcelain and pottery producers of the nineteenth century, the firm was founded in 1793 by Thomas Minton at Stoke-on-Trent. At the forefront of Victorian eclecticism, Minton's introduced MAJOLICA in 1850 under the guidance of Léon Arnoux, followed by Della Robbia and Palissy wares, both of which were made of EARTHENWARE with semi-translucent coloured GLAZES inspired by Renaissance originals. Their most ambitious pottery creations were copies of the French sixteenth-century Saint-Porchaire, called Henry Deux ware. In 1869 the firm engaged William Stephen Coleman, under whose direction Minton's Art Pottery Studio was established in

1871 in Kensington, London. Wares from Stoke were decorated there, often by art students, both in UNDERGLAZE and OVERGLAZE techniques. The Studio products usually have a printed mark, Mintons' Art-Pottery Studio Kensington Gore, as well as the factory marks.

MORGAN, WILLIAM DE (1839–1917)

Art potter most closely associated with the Arts and Crafts Movement. He started a small pottery in Chelsea in 1872, moving to Merton Abbey in 1882 but returning to Fulham in 1888 to 1907 in partnership with Halsey Ricardo. He sought to reproduce Moorish and Gubbio LUSTRES on a variety of ornamental vases, tiles and dishes decorated in greens and blues with animals, birds, flowers and fishes. A range of fanciful and decorative marks were used.

NEWCOMB POTTERY

ART POTTERY promoted at Newcomb College, New Orleans, in 1896 by Professor Ellsworth Woodward and Mary G. Sheerer. Characteristic decoration is of indigenous flora and fauna in the Art Nouveau idiom.

NORTON, CAPTAIN JOHN

Established one of the earliest potteries in Vermont in 1793, originally producing red EARTHENWARE and STONEWARE. He was succeeded by his son. Lyman, in 1823 and by his grandson Julius in 1840. Under Julius Norton the firm entered into a brief partnership (1845–7) with Christopher W. Fenton, who introduced ROCKINGHAM WARE and YELLOW WARE to the range of pottery. The firm finally closed in 1894. Wares were marked from 1823, usually impressed with the name of the respective owner and Bennington or East Bennington.

MESSRS F. & R. PRATT & CO.

Established in Fenton, Staffordshire, in 1803 by Felix Pratt, they produced all classes of ordinary EARTHENWARE but are particularly associated with POT LIDS, decorated with polychrome printing by the engraver, Jesse Austin, and also with Greek Revival vases.

ROOKWOOD POTTERY

Established in Cincinnati, Ohio, in 1880 by Mrs Maria Longworth Nichols (later Mrs Bellamy Storer). One of the first successful ART POTTERIES in the United States, much of its early decoration is characterized by asymmetrical arrangements of flowers in the Japanese manner painted under the GLAZE in coloured SLIP on a dark ground. Among its prominent decorators were Albert R. Valentien and Kataro Shirayamadani. In 1900 the pottery achieved international recognition when it was awarded a Grand Prix at the Paris Exhibition. From 1883 to 1913 the pottery was under the management of William Watts Taylor, who

took over the ownership in 1889. It was declared bankrupt in 1941. Up to c. 1910, all pieces were signed by the decorator and usually impressed with Rookwood and the date in code. (See p. 121.)

MESSRS J. S. TAFT & CO.

Established in 1871 in Keene, New Hampshire, to produce STONEWARE, REDWARE and MAJOLICA. Mark: Hampshire Pottery with J. S. Taft in script, printed.

TRENTON

Established as a pottery centre in New Jersey after William Taylor and Henry Speeler set up a factory there in 1852 for the manufacture of ROCKINGHAM and YELLOW WARE. Called the 'Staffordshire of America', a number of renowned firms began by producing pottery and later turned to porcelain. These include Millington & Astbury (later Thomas Maddock & Sons), William Young & Sons (later the Willets Manufacturing Co.) and Messrs Bloor, Ott & Booth (later Ott & Brewer).

VAN BRIGGLE, ARTUS (d. 1904)

Foremost American Art Nouveau potter, decorator at ROOKWOOD POTTERY from 1896 to 1899, having previously been sent by them to Paris on a scholarship. He moved to Colorado Springs in 1899 because of ill health, establishing a pottery there under his own name in 1901.

WATCOMBE POTTERY

Devon potters, founded in 1869, producing refined small TERRACOTTA wares mainly in the Greek Revival idiom.

MESSRS WEDGWOOD

Most celebrated of English potteries, founded by Josiah Wedgwood at Burslem in Staffordshire in 1759. Throughout the nineteenth century all classes of ware as initiated by the founder were manufactured; the same moulds were used; the same skill and craftsmanship applied. They continued to produce JASPER WARE, BASALTES, TERRACOTTA, CREAMWARE, PEARL WARE, ROCKINGHAM WARE and TRANSFER-PRINTED WARE. From 1858 until his death in 1876, the gifted French pottery painter, Émile Lessore, was employed.

ZANESVILLE

Turn-of-the-century ART-POTTERY centre in Ohio producing wares in imitation of ROOKWOOD. Commercial undertakings include those of Samuel A. Weller and J. B. Owens, successively influenced by William A. Long, formerly of the LONHUDA POTTERY, and the Roseville Pottery Co.

OPPOSITE *Selection of pottery marks. For further information see Bibliography p. 127.*

American Pottery Marks

American Pottery Co., established 1840

The Chelsea Keramic Art Works, c. 1890

The Grueby Faïence Co., established 1897

Chelsea Pottery, established 1892

M. L. McLaughlin, established 1876

Newcomb Pottery, c. 1896

Norton & Fenton, Bennington, VT.

Norton & Fenton, c. 1845

J. NORTON
BENNINGTON
VT.

Julius Norton, c. 1845

Owens Pottery Co., 1890 (See Zanesville)

Rookwood Pottery Co., c. 1880

Van Briggle Pottery Co., established 1901

Rookwood Pottery Co., 1886

S. A. Weller, c. 1890 (See Zanesville)

Reproduced from *Dictionary of Marks: Pottery and Porcelain*, Ralph M. and Terry H. Kovel, Crown Publishers Inc., 1971

British Pottery Marks

William Adams & Sons, 1879

Samuel Alcock
This version of the Royal Arms mark occurs on Alcock wares with or without the initials S. A. & Co. or the name below it

W. T. Copeland

Impressed mark, 1850-67. An impressed mark of a crown and 'Copeland' occurs on earthenware. Sometimes 'Copeland' was impressed in curved form without the crown. These marks were used into the 20th century

Impressed mark, 1851-85

Printed mark, 1875-90

Della Robbia Co. Ltd (see Minton & Co.)

Printed mark c. 1894-1901. The initials above vary and relate to the decorator. These initials include C. (Charles Collis), C.A.W. (Walker), R.B. (Ruth Bare).

Messrs Doulton & Co. Ltd

Impressed mark, c. 1877-80. The year of production is normally incised in the clay

Impressed or printed mark on earthenware (not stoneware), c. 1872+

Impressed mark on stonewares, c. 1880-1902. 'England' added from 1891
From 1872-88 the year of production was impressed or incised on each piece, with the mark of the artist

Sir Edmund Elton

Painted or incised mark, 1879-1920. The date may occur on some specimens

Martin Bros

Incised name and address mark, 'Fulham' occurs only in the 1873-4 period. B.4 refers to the object

'Bros.' or 'Brothers' added in 1882. Mark continued in this form to May 1914 when 'London' was deleted
The month and year of production appears incised, with the mark on most specimens

Mason's Patent Ironstone China (see Broad Street Works)

Former Mason mark continued

Name Ashworth added 1862+

William de Morgan

Name-mark, c. 1882+. Many name-marks occur in various forms: De Morgan, W. De Morgan, Wm. De Morgan, D.M.
'& Co.' added to most marks after 1888

Impressed or painted mark 1882+

Sands End address mark. Others were used, all may be dated from 1888 onwards

Messrs F. & R. Pratt & Co.

Rare printed mark, c. 1847-60. Found on fine quality Prattware, Etruscan pattern vases, and fine printed wares

F. & R. PRATT & Cº
349
FENTON

Printed mark, on multi-coloured printed wares, of pot-lid type (a speciality of this firm). Most examples are un-marked, c. 1850+. These marks with 'England' are subsequent to 1891 and usually of 20th-century date

Wedgwood's impressed year letters

Occuring in sets of three (from 1860), the last shows the year of manufacture

O = 1860	X = 1869	G = 1878
P = 1861	Y = 1870	H = 1879
Q = 1862	Z = 1871	I = 1880
R = 1863	A = 1872	J = 1881
S = 1864	B = 1873	K = 1882
T = 1865	C = 1874	L = 1883
U = 1866	D = 1875	M = 1884
V = 1867	E = 1876	N = 1885
W = 1868	F = 1877	

From 1886 to 1897 the letters used from 1860 to 1871 are repeated
From 1898 to 1901 the letters used from 1872 to 1875 re-occur
From 1891 'England' should occur on specimens

Minton year marks

From 1842 onwards small year cyphers have been impressed into the body. Such marks occur in sets of three: month letter, potter's mark and the year cypher

1842	1843	1844	1845	1846	1847
1848	1849	1850	1851	1852	1853
1854	1855	1856	1857	1858	1859
1860	1861	1862	1863	1864	1865
1866	1867	1868	1869	1870	1871
1872	1873	1874	1875	1876	1877
1878	1879	1880	1881	1882	1883
1884	1885	1886	1887	1888	1889
1890	1891	1892	1893	1894	1895
1896	1897	1898	1899	1900	1901

Key to Month Letters

J	January		H	July
F	February		Y	August
M	March		S	September
A	April		O	October
E	May		N	November
I	June		D	December

Reproduced by courtesy of Geoffrey A. Godden from *Encyclopædia of British Pottery and Porcelain Marks*, Barrie & Jenkins, 1964, and *The Handbook of British Pottery and Porcelain Marks*, Barrie & Jenkins, 1968

Glossary

Agate ware
Pottery made of variously tinted CLAYS, the colours extending through the BODY in imitation of agate.

Anglo-American pottery
CREAMWARE decorated with TRANSFER-PRINTED designs relating to American events. Made originally in Liverpool and by Staffordshire potters from *c.* 1815 for the American trade.

Art pottery
Inspired initially in England by the Arts and Crafts Movement, the catalyst in both Europe and the United States for original wares was the influence of Japanese art in the last three decades of the nineteenth century. Reacting against the industrialization of commercial pottery, workshops arose where either a team of experts sought to achieve group creations or the artist-potter strove alone to master every stage of the process. In such undertakings the wares could range from everyday objects to unique creations.

Basalt
Uniformly hard, black, unglazed STONEWARE developed by WEDGWOOD in the 1760s.

Bennington ware
REDWARE, STONEWARE, ROCKINGHAM and YELLOW WARE, but particularly refers to WHITE GRANITE and FLINT ENAMELLED WARE made at Bennington, Vermont.

Body
Composite material of which the potter's CLAY is made. Generally used in relation to EARTHENWARE and STONEWARE, whereas paste is used when referring to porcelain and bone-china.

Cadborough ware
Red EARTHENWARE coated and streaked with a LEAD GLAZE. It was introduced in 1790 by the Smith family of Rye, Sussex.

Ceramics
Derived from the Greek word *keramos*, meaning clay. A general term applied to all articles made of fired CLAYS, embracing pottery and porcelain.

Clay
Stiff, viscous earth which forms a tenacious paste when mixed with water. Usually with a green or blue hue in its unfired state, it becomes red when fired because it contains oxide of iron. The purest clay, however, becomes nearly white in the kiln.

Coloured bodies
Self-coloured body obtained by the use of oxides or ochreous earths.

Creamware
Ivory- or cream-coloured EARTHENWARE developed by WEDGWOOD and made by most potteries from 1770. Also called QUEENSWARE in honour of Queen Charlotte.

Earthenware
Opaque pottery which is porous after the first firing, and requires to be glazed and refired before use. Decoration can be under or over the GLAZE.

Faïence
Originally the French term for tin-glazed EARTHENWARE, misappropriated in the nineteenth century for UNDERGLAZE decorated earthenware.

Firing
Process of transferring CLAY into pottery by burning it in a kiln.

Flambé
GLAZE, often streaked or mottled, first produced in China and imitated by artist-potters in Europe and the United States in the latter part of the nineteenth century.

Flint-enamelled ware
Fine quality ROCKINGHAM WARE with a hard, brilliant GLAZE containing flint, mottled in brown, yellow, olive or blue. The process was patented in November 1849 by Christopher W. Fenton of Bennington, Vermont.

Glaze
Glassy preparation applied to the surface of CERAMICS to make them impervious to liquids, to give them brilliance, and to act as a base or cover for painted decoration.

Ironstone china
Strong, fine EARTHENWARE closely resembling porcelain. It was patented in England in 1813 by Charles J. Mason and used for utilitarian as well as decorative wares.

Soup tureen, cover and stand, Ashworth/Mason, c. 1865. Pottery decorated with a hand-coloured transfer print. Sotheby's Belgravia.

Jasper ware
Fine unglazed STONEWARE developed in 1774 by WEDGWOOD. The body is often coloured throughout by metallic oxides.

Jet
Glossy black body, a late-nineteenth-century successor to Jackfield ware, favoured by small manufacturers of teapots, etc.

Lead glaze
Transparent GLAZE used on CERAMICS, applied either as a dry powder or as a liquid.

Lustre
Shiny metallic coating of silver, copper, gold or platinum which by means of a reducing atmosphere in the kiln is not allowed to oxidize.

Majolica
Nineteenth-century misuse of the Italian term *maiolica* for tin-glazed EARTHENWARE. Applied to earthenware with relief decoration under coloured GLAZES, it was introduced by MINTON'S in 1850 and widely adopted, particularly by two other Staffordshire firms, George Jones and Adams & Co. In America it was taken up by E. & W. Bennett of Baltimore and by the Pennsylvania pottery of Griffen, Smith & Hill.

Mark
Name, monogram, letter or other device, impressed, raised, scratched, painted, printed or stencilled on CERAMICS. It indicates the factory where the piece was made, its date, maker or decorator.

Mocha ware
Tree-like decoration on EARTHENWARE resembling ornamental quartz known as mocha-stone. An inexpensive ware.

Overglaze decoration
Painted or printed designs on a glazed surface.

Pearl ware
White EARTHENWARE containing more calcined flint and china clay than CREAMWARE. First made by WEDGWOOD in 1779, it was extensively imitated in the nineteenth century being used mainly for tableware with painted or TRANSFER-PRINTED decoration.

Pot lids
White EARTHENWARE lids decorated with multi-coloured TRANSFER-PRINTING. Mainly produced by MESSRS F. & R. PRATT & CO., of Fenton, Staffordshire, whose chief engraver, Jesse Austin, perfected the process in 1848.

Pottery
All articles made of clay, powdered rocks and water which have undergone the chemical changes produced by a heat of 600°C. or more. The term covers both EARTHENWARE and STONEWARE, which are opaque, as opposed to porcelain, which is translucent.

Snake devouring a toad, William Brownfield, Stoke-on-Trent, c. 1885. Majolica. Majolica is the nineteenth-century misuse of the Italian term maiolica *(tin-glazed earthenware). City Museum and Art Gallery, Hanley.*

Queensware
See CREAMWARE.

Redware
First pottery made in the American Colonies. First produced in the late 1600s and continued well into the nineteenth century, the CLAY used was identical to that used in red brick and roof tiles, the colour coming from traces of iron oxide. Redware is LEAD GLAZED and decorated with SLIP or SGRAFFITO.

Rockingham ware
White EARTHENWARE covered with a brown GLAZE obtained from an admixture of manganese. Originated in the Rockingham factory at Swinton in England in the late eighteenth century, it was subsequently used for a range of ornamental wares. Considerably developed in the United States, it became one of the most widely used types of American CERAMIC. The principal centre was EAST LIVERPOOL, Ohio. In contrast with English Rockingham, the American ware was usually given a deliberately brown and yellow mottled appearance.

Salt glaze
Transparent hard GLAZE produced by throwing salt into the kiln at the maximum degree of heat, and thus creating a pitted surface on the ware.

Sgraffito
Incised decoration, usually through a layer of SLIP on EARTHENWARE.

Slip
CLAY diluted with water to the consistency of cream, used for decorating or casting pottery.

Stoneware
Opaque, vitrified pottery fired at a very high temperature and so named because of its extreme hardness, which renders it practically impervious to water without glazing.

Terracotta
Unglazed refined red EARTHENWARE.

Transfer printing
Process of applying engraved patterns and designs to the surface of CERAMICS by means of tissue paper and prepared ink. The decoration can be OVERGLAZE or UNDERGLAZE. Initially of one colour, multi-coloured printing was perfected by MESSRS F. & R. PRATT & CO. in 1848 and soon adopted by other Staffordshire firms.

Underglaze decoration
Painted or printed decoration applied to the fired BODY prior to the firing of the GLAZE. Extensively used for blue-printed designs by the large English potteries.

Variegated wares
EARTHENWARE made by the use of different coloured CLAYS extending throughout the body as in AGATE WARE or by the mixture of colours in the slip GLAZES as in mottled, sprinkled, freckled, marbled and tortoiseshell wares.

White granite
Hard white opaque pottery bearing a close resemblance to porcelain. It was much used for tableware. See IRONSTONE CHINA.

Yellow ware
Utilitarian EARTHENWARE of a yellow or cane colour.

Bibliography

BARBER, EDWIN ATLEE. *The Pottery and Porcelain of the United States,* New York and London, 1901

BARRETT, RICHARD CARTER. *Bennington Pottery and Porcelain,* New York, 1958

BIVINS, JOHN, JR. *The Moravian Potters in North Carolina,* Chapel Hill, North Carolina, 1972

BLACKER, J. F. *The A.B.C. of XIX-Century English Ceramic Art,* London, 1911

BLACKER, J. F. *The A.B.C. of English Salt-Glaze Stoneware,* London, 1922

CLARK, ROBERT JUDSON. *Catalogue of the Exhibition of the Arts and Crafts Movement in America 1876-1916,* Princeton, 1971

EYLES, D. *Royal Doulton 1815-1965,* London, 1966

GAUNT, W. and CLAYTON-STAMM, M.D.E. *William de Morgan,* London, 1971

GODDEN, G. A. *British Pottery. An illustrated guide,* London, 1974

JEWITT, L. *The Ceramic Art of Great Britain,* London and New York, 1878, revised 1972

KETCHUM, WILLIAM C., JR. *Early Potters and Potteries of New York State,* New York, 1970

MADDOCK, A. M. II. *The Polished Earth,* Trenton, New Jersey, 1962.

MITCHELL, JAMES R. *New Jersey Pottery to 1840,* Trenton, New Jersey, 1972

MITCHELL, JAMES R. 'Ott & Brewer: Etruria in America', *Winterthur Portfolio 7,* pp. 217-28, 1972

Newark Museum. *The Pottery and Porcelain of New Jersey 1688-1900,* Newark, New Jersey, 1947

Philadelphia Museum of Art. *Tucker China 1825-38,* Philadelphia, 1957

QUIMBY, IAN M. G. (ed.) *Ceramics in America,* Charlottesville, Virginia, 1973

RAMSAY, JOHN. *American Potters and Pottery,* Clinton, South Carolina, 1939

SCHWARTZ, MARVIN D. and WOLFE, RICHARD. *A History of American Art Porcelain,* New York, 1967

SPARGO, JOHN. *The Potters and Potteries of Bennington,* Boston, 1926

WAKEFIELD, H. *Victorian Pottery,* London, 1962

WATKINS, LURA WOODSIDE. *Early New England Potters and Their Wares,* Cambridge, Massachusetts, 1950

YOUNG, JENNIE J. *The Ceramic Art,* New York, 1878

Porcelain

BRITISH

In general terms the porcelain body is more refined and expensive to manufacture than earthenware and, when the Victorian era commenced in 1837, only the upper and middle classes would have owned porcelain services and even then, for everyday use, the family may well have eaten from pottery, reserving their porcelain services for special occasions.

By the 1830s the English porcelain body had become remarkably standard, containing a high percentage of bone-ash which has given rise to its current name, 'English bone-china'. This fine and pleasing white bone-china was translucent and acted as a near-perfect vehicle for the rich enamelling and gilding with which it was embellished.

Supremacy of English Porcelain

The Victorian era saw the rise of the English porcelain manufacturer to a position where he led the world. Previously, in the eighteenth century, English porcelains were made mainly for the home markets and, although in many ways attractive, they can have posed little threat to the leading Continental manufacturers. Now the situation was reversed: the Sèvres and Dresden factories were on the decline, while the excellence of English wares and the strength of English world markets meant that leading Continental designers, artists and modellers were attracted across the Channel. As far as larger English firms were concerned, their products can be summed up by the one word, quality.

However, our present-day picture of Victorian porcelain is distorted by the

OPPOSITE *Covered vase on stand, Minton, c. 1860-70. Porcelain, ht 16 in (41 cm). This vase is decorated in the Sèvres style with typical figure painting, rich gilding and a turquoise-blue ground. Author's Collection.*

tours de force exhibited by the leading manufacturers at the numerous international exhibitions which were such a feature of the Victorian period. Some nine-tenths of the porcelain produced by the Victorian manufacturers in the 1840s and even in the 1850s comprised tablewares, often bearing quite restrained decoration. Ornamental pieces were relatively few; similarly, figures and groups are extremely scarce – this market would seem to have been left largely to the importers of Dresden and other Continental porcelains, although the British manufacturers certainly excelled and pioneered the market for the unglazed, off-white parian figures. Since porcelain was always relatively expensive and designed for the drawing rooms and dining-rooms of the wealthy, no attempt was made to compete with the Staffordshire potters in producing ornaments suitable for the cottage-trade.

Variety of Victorian Design

It is remarkably difficult to summarize the general styles of decoration favoured in the Victorian era by the porcelain-buying public. Factories in different parts of the country tended to specialize in their own styles so that what the Worcester porcelain manufacturers were making bears very little relation to what Minton or W. T. Copeland & Sons were producing in Stoke-on-Trent at the same period.

For at least ten years after Queen Victoria came to the throne in 1837, the general taste in porcelain changed remarkably little; it showed none of the fussiness of later wares and in fact some teaware shapes displayed in the 1851 Exhibition could well have been introduced in the 1820s.

Fine porcelain dinner-services were in general modelled on eighteenth-century French shapes which had originated at the Sèvres factory, outside Paris. Tea-

wares were usually Neo-Rococo in style, the teapots having low, moulded feet and the teacups being low and wide so that the tea chilled almost at once. Individual plates were not issued in tea-services and are somewhat rare, even in sets of the 1860s. Although sets included coffee-cups, coffee-pots were almost never made in porcelain; presumably the buyer was expected to own a silver coffee-pot.

In decoration, the French style was favoured, although the international floral designs were also popular. When landscapes were employed as the decorative motif, it was usually on dessert-services.

After tea-services, dessert-services were the most favoured by the Victorians, those of the 1830s and 1840s comprising low-shaped dishes with a relief-moulded ornate edge and a pair of covered cream- and sugar-tureens as well as the centre-piece and plates. By the 1850s, the comports tended to be of circular form, resembling plates and supported on single-footed stems of 2 in, 4 in or 6 in (4·8, 9·6, 14·4 cm). The dessert-plates and the three sizes of footed comports were hand painted with fruit, flowers, landscapes or figure subjects. With the more expensive sets, the comports were supported by ornamental bases or by parian figures. A Victorian table dressed with a rich dessert-service must have presented a magnificent appearance and it is little wonder that today such services tend to be divided when they come on the market and the plates and comports sold separately for wall or cabinet display.

Turning from tablewares to ornamental objects, mention must be made of the vogue for Japanese designs in the 1870s and '80s which developed into the Art Nouveau style of the 1890s. The Japanese influence, which is to be found in all aspects of the Victorian arts of this period, was disseminated in porcelain by undoubtedly the leading manufacturer, the Royal Worcester Porcelain Co. Superb vases and figures were modelled

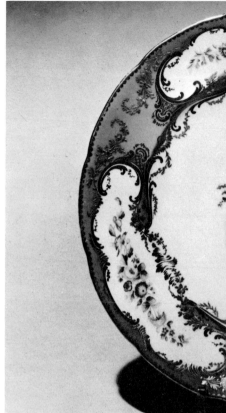

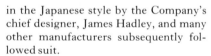

in the Japanese style by the Company's chief designer, James Hadley, and many other manufacturers subsequently followed suit.

Ceramic Innovations

The basic types of Victorian ceramics must also be singled out for mention. First, there is the parian body which was undoubtedly the most typical of Victorian ceramic bodies. It was introduced in the 1840s and subsequently adopted by every porcelain manufacturer. Mass-produced from plaster-of-Paris moulds, figures by the tens of thousands were made – groups, numerous ornaments, butter dishes, jugs and a multitude of knick-knacks. At its best parian is superb; at its worst, when produced by firms endeavouring to cut production costs, it is tasteless and ugly.

In contrast to the mass-produced parian wares there are the individual hand-modelled masterpieces in the *pâte-sur-pâte* technique, where white slip is slowly

TOP *Minton ware displayed in a contemporary photograph from* Reports by the Juries Presented by Her Majesty's Commissioners for the Exhibition of 1851. *Westminster Public Library.*

ABOVE LEFT Clorinda *modelled by John Bell for the Summerley Art Manufactures. Parian. Made originally by Minton in 1848, this example was made for the Victoria and Albert Museum in 1865.*

ABOVE *Menu-holder figure, Minton, c. 1875. Porcelain, ht 4¼ in (11 cm). This figure is in the Oriental style popularized by the Aesthetic Movement. Author's Collection.*

ABOVE RIGHT *Plate, Coalport, c. 1850. Porcelain. Sèvres style showing a mock Sèvres mark with the initial C. Painted with birds in the manner of John Randall. Author's Collection.*

RIGHT *Comport from a dessert service, Copeland, c. 1850. Porcelain, ht 8 in (20 cm). Decorated with typical Victorian flower painting and gilded borders. Author's Collection.*

built up layer by layer and modelled and carved until a cameo-like effect is formed by the dark body showing through the added decoration. The master of this technique was the Sèvres-trained artist-modeller, Marc Louis Solon, who joined Minton's at Stoke in 1870. Several of the other leading firms produced essays in *pâte-sur-pâte* with varying success.

Considering only Victorian porcelain, the major English manufacturers were the Coalport factory, Messrs Copeland & Garrett, subsequently W. T. Copeland, of Stoke, the Derby factories, Minton & Co. of Stoke, Messrs Ridgway of Hanley and the Worcester factories.

Coalport

The Coalport factory was picturesquely situated on the banks of the River Severn in Shropshire and for most of the nineteenth century it was owned by the firm of John Rose & Co. It had been founded in the 1790s and soon built up a reputation for the excellence of its porcelain; by the beginning of the Victorian period the Coalport factory had become one of the largest porcelain manufactories in Europe. It looked to the Continent for inspiration, for the main influence at Coalport was undoubtedly the rich eighteenth-century Sèvres porcelains with their ground colours and reserved panels of flowers or exotic birds in landscapes as well as the characteristic Watteauesque figure designs. These Coalport porcelains are of superb quality and highly prized in their own right, although it must be said that some examples bear a close copy of the Sèvres crossed L mark. The Sèvres styles were favoured at Coalport for a long period, from the 1840s to at least the 1880s.

From the 1880s the porcelains, both fine table-services, dessert-sets in particular and vases, were richly painted with British landscapes, panels of fruit or floral designs. At the time of the 1893 Chicago Exhibition, richly jeweled pieces were being made and, in contrast, the less expensive wares were decorated with coloured-over printed patterns such as the traditional Indian Tree design.

Copeland

Messrs Copeland & Garrett, a partnership of the 1833 to 1847 period, succeeded the famous firm of Spode at Stoke in the heart of the Staffordshire potteries. These Copeland & Garrett porcelains underline the point that before the late 1840s the ornate, typically Victorian taste had not been generally

Covered jug, Coalport, c. 1890. Porcelain, ht 8 in (20 cm). Richly gilded and jeweled, this example was displayed at the 1893 Chicago Exhibition. Author's Collection.

adopted. The post-1847 wares are generally of fine quality and often quite restrained in their design. Tasteful gilded decoration and flower studies were a feature of the table-services, while vases and other decorative objects were, in contrast, richly decorated, often with painted scenes. Messrs Copelands led the field in the most typical of all Victorian wares, the white, unglazed parian body. Copeland products throughout the whole range of ceramics were of the finest quality, and the firm continues to the present day under the new name of Spode Ltd.

Derby

The original eighteenth-century Derby factory had been forced to close down in 1848 after the somewhat uninspired managements of Robert Bloor, James Thomason and Thomas Clarke, all of whom tried to trade on past glories. However, on the closure of the factory, a

group of the workmen banded together to carry on the old Derby porcelain tradition. These persons purchased a small factory at King Street, Derby, and concentrated largely on the production of close copies of old Derby models and designs, and also adopted a close copy of the old mark. Several different proprietors owned this company until it was taken over in April 1935 by the Royal Crown Derby management but the wares are usually called Stevenson & Hancock after one of the intervening partnerships.

The now internationally renowned Royal Crown Derby Porcelain Co. did not come into being until 1876, the leading light in its success being Edward Phillips from the Royal Worcester Porcelain Co. The prefix Royal was granted by Queen Victoria in 1890 and consequently most pieces that bear this famous mark were made after the period under discussion. Although some pieces were superbly painted and richly gilded by leading Victorian ceramic artists, the name of Royal Crown Derby will probably forever be associated with their stock 'Japan' patterns which are characterized by bold formal, floral designs in blue, red and gold. Such articles range from large dinner-services to charming little miniature trinkets.

Various pieces from a dinner service, Minton, the design of which was registered in June 1846. Porcelain. The white bone-china is free of crazing and is gilded. Author's Collection.

Minton

The world-famous firm of Minton in Stoke-on-Trent was founded in 1793 and continues to the present day. Undoubtedly its fame was built up in the Victorian era and with the help of talented French and German artists and modellers who were attracted to Minton partly because since 1848 Minton's art director had been a noted French potter, Léon Arnoux (1816–1902), but probably more on account of the renown and standing of this firm, perhaps the leading porcelain manufacturers of the Victorian period. Whatever Minton produced, it was the best, and notably the fine porcelains sumptuously decorated in the fashionable Sèvres manner with delicate ground-colours and finely painted reserve panels.

It is difficult not to single out these expensive, richly decorated porcelains, but one must remember that much of the output of any factory is for everyday use and often a dinner-plate having only a simple gilded border design is more practical to eat from than an ornate plate in the Sèvres style. Taking as an example, representative pieces from a simple Minton service of a design registered in June 1846, the bone-china is white and devoid of any blemishes, the covering glaze is transparent and free of crazing. In short, for practicability and attractiveness such a set nears perfection. If it has one fault, it is that shared by so much Victorian pottery and porcelain: its reticence to be Victorian. The designers continually referred to earlier styles and

borrowed many old Sèvres porcelain forms and designs.

Ridgway

A third Staffordshire porcelain manufacturer who deserves to be mentioned separately is John Ridgway, of the Cauldon Place works at Hanley, who, after separating from his brother William in 1830, was later to be appointed 'Potter to Queen Victoria'. John Ridgway's fine porcelains are, however, little known, for a large percentage of his output is unmarked. As a result of research in the original factory pattern-books, many of his standard shapes have now been identified and, armed with this information, one can attribute other superb quality porcelain to this royal potter.

John Ridgway & Co. succeeded in 1855 to the new partnership of Ridgway & Bates, to be followed in 1859 by Bates, Brown-Westhead & Moore, a trading style amended to Brown-Westhead, Moore & Co. in 1862. This partnership continued until 1905 and issued some late Victorian ceramics in Minton's manner such as the vase made to commemorate Queen Victoria's Jubilee in 1887. Other more utilitarian wares also display the same high quality of workmanship.

Worcester

The city of Worcester has been the home of many famous porcelain manufacturers. When the Victorian era opened in 1837 there were – Messrs Chamberlains, Messrs Flight, Barr & Barr and Messrs George Grainger. In 1840, Chamberlains and Flight Barr & Barr combined to form the new firm of Chamberlain & Co., which gave way in 1852 to Messrs Kerr & Binns, a partnership which continued until 1862. During this ten-year period, Kerr & Binns produced a delightful range of fine-quality porcelains, tastefully decorated on shapes that have a Classical elegance.

In 1862 the famous Royal Worcester Porcelain Co. was established under R. W. Binns. Quality was the target for every type of object ranging from porcelain thimbles to huge exhibition vases. The Royal Worcester Porcelain Co. was the leading manufacturer in England of glazed figures and groups, some models rivalling the best eighteenth-century classics. The charming series of boys and girls in Kate Greenaway-style dress are a delight, and they were incorporated in a bewildering

ABOVE *Plate from a dessert service, John Ridgway, c. 1850. Porcelain. These orange and gold bordered plates are each hand-painted with a different design in the centre panel. Author's collection.*

ABOVE RIGHT *Vase, Worcester, made in the Kerr & Binns period with shield-shaped mark and year numbers for 1857. Porcelain, ht 12¾ in (32 cm.). This vase is painted in the Limoges enamel style on a blue ground by Thomas Bott (1854-1932). Author's Collection.*

RIGHT *Vase, Royal Worcester Porcelain Co., 1891. Porcelain, ht 7½ in (19 cm). Richly gilded and decorated, this vase is a fine example of high Victorian taste. Author's Collection.*

array of semi-useful ornaments, candlesticks, centre-pieces, fruit-baskets, menu-holders and candle-snuffers. The artist-modeller responsible for these and other Royal Worcester shapes was James Hadley, who, in 1896, was to establish

his own rival factory in Worcester.

The Grainger factory at Worcester had been taken over by the Royal Worcester Porcelain Co. in 1889, although production continued there until 1902. In 1895 the factory of Locke & Co. was established which continued to manufacture products very similar in style to those of the main company until it closed in 1904.

Although it is possible to mention only the leading firms, it must be borne in mind that numerous lesser firms produced a vast variety of inexpensive wares for everyday use and a fascinating selection of novelties to catch the public eye.

The finest pieces from the major firms represent the ultimate in quality, quality which can never be repeated, for we cannot return to the low wages paid to the workers and artists of the period and the consequent lack of concern over the time spent decorating a single plate or vase. Victorian porcelain represents the ultimate in painstaking concern for quality.

Geoffrey Godden

133

AMERICAN

American Preference for European Porcelain

The major obstacle to the production of porcelain was more psychological than physical. To the American mind, the popularity of European porcelain had always exceeded that produced in the United States. The foreign stamp of design and subsequent approval was necessary for public acceptance. While Americans took pride in their industrial and commercial advances, they preferred European arts. The prejudice in favour of imported goods was based on the erroneous belief that there was little truly American art of genuine aesthetic value.

Economic factors also influenced the popularity of native porcelain. Because of the lack of an adequate protective tariff, European porcelain could be imported into the United States and sold for a lower price than American porcelain. As a result, most porcelain manufacturers in the United States, in order to achieve financial solvency, produced an auxiliary line of earthenware, fire brick, tile or white ware to support the growing American mania for amateur china decorating after the Civil War.

Pitcher, William E. Tucker, c. 1835. Porcelain, ht 9½ in (24 cm). Gilded and enamelled, this is one of the earliest examples of American porcelain. Greenfield Village and Henry Ford Museum.

During the nineteenth century the quality and quantity of household and industrial earthenwares and stonewares manufactured in the United States achieved such magnitude that one major centre of American ceramic production, Trenton, New Jersey, was known as the 'Staffordshire of America'. While the United States excelled in the manufacture of earthenwares, the production of porcelain remained largely underdeveloped.

Numerous American factories attempted the production of porcelain, but very few were able to sustain their operations for more than a few years. The production of porcelain has never been simple. It is an expensive manufacture requiring specialized materials, adequate fuel supplies, sophisticated equipment, transportation facilities and skilled artisans.

The United States abounded with a wealth of the raw materials necessary for the production of porcelain. Extensive kaolin deposits were worked in New Jersey, Delaware, Pennsylvania, Maryland, North and South Carolina, Florida, Illinois, Indiana and Missouri. Feldspar, the second necessary ingredient for porcelain manufacture, was obtained from locations in Connecticut, Maine, Pennsylvania and Maryland.

Although the raw materials were readily available, the scarcity of skilled potters presented a substantial barrier to successful porcelain production. The lack of a porcelain tradition and the absence of an established apprenticeship system meant that many potters were self taught. Immigration of trained English and Continental potters, many expressly invited by American porcelain manufacturers, compensated for the shortage of native craftsmen. These European craftsmen introduced new styles and techniques of production.

Four United States cities – Trenton, New Jersey; East Liverpool, Ohio; New York and Philadelphia, Pennsylvania – possessed all the prerequisites of porcelain manufacture and as a result they became the leading centres of American porcelain production. All four cities were located near major market areas, superior railways, canal and river transportation and extensive clay deposits.

In the attempt to influence the American consumer, newspapers and pamphlets extolled the virtues of American porcelain and encouraged the public to believe that it was their patriotic duty to buy American goods. In numerous American cities organizations for the encouragement of domestic manufacture were formed. The Franklin Institute, organized in Philadelphia, Pennsylvania, in 1824, held an annual competition for American products. These competitions provided much-needed publicity for American porcelain, and the awards furnished a stamp of excellence to a struggling industry. Despite the ardent publicity campaign, consumers most often let the dollar sign outweigh their feelings of nationalism. While many of the early American porcelain factories were founded on the principle of supplying an American market with American-made goods, they were, nevertheless, totally dependent on European styles and practices. With few exceptions, commercial manufacturers were content to copy the wares of European establishments.

First Indigenous Wares

It was only after the middle of the nineteenth century that porcelain factories in the United States began to manufacture purely American wares that had no recognizable European counterparts. Although the production of household porcelain and figurines enjoyed brief periods of success, it was not until 1876 that a definite production of art porcelain was developed in the United States. This development was partly due to the Centennial Exposition of 1876 held in Philadelphia. The celebration of the hundredth anniversary of the United States presented a record of the progress and expectations of the American people.

As one of the first great fairs in the United States, the Centennial Exposition recorded the industrial and artistic advances made during the country's first hundred years. After approximately seventy-five years of porcelain production, the American public was beginning to accept the artistic merit of its own native porcelain. Another result of this period of development was the increased supply of trained craftsmen. Mature potters possessed the necessary talent and confidence to produce superior art porcelain for a home market. During this period of production, the American public recognized native porcelain as equivalent in quality to European imports.

By the end of the nineteenth century, the Arts and Crafts Movement with its emphasis on naturalism and hand craftsmanship exerted its influence on the ceramic production of the United States. The new movement saw its artistic expression in earthenware rather than porcelain. The impact of the Movement caused a decline in the production and demand for art porcelains. By 1900 the production of porcelain in the United States had reverted to the manufacture of tea-, toilet-, and dinner-services.

Early Production

The factory of Dr Henry Mead, a New York physician, is credited with producing the first attributed example of nineteenth-century United States porcelain. Utilizing native American materials, Mead's factory experimented with the production of porcelain between 1813 and 1820. In an effort to encourage the manufacture of porcelain and as a means of combating the dearth of porcelain craftsmen in the United States, Mead proposed to the New York Common Council that paupers and criminals be utilized as workers in his factory. The Mead Vase, a Classical urn shape with

Vase attributed to the factory of Dr Henry Mead, New York City, c. 1816. Soft-paste porcelain, ht 13 in (33 cm). Philadelphia Museum of Art.

moulded caryatid handles, features a paper label stating that it was completed in 1816. Because of the similarity between the Mead Vase and French vases of the period, and the lack of any factory marks, it is very likely that there are Mead examples masquerading today as European porcelain.

Further attempts at the production of porcelain did not occur until 1824. In that year, two separate Pennsylvanian earthenware potters manufactured porcelain on an experimental basis. Abraham Miller, a successful Philadelphia manufacturer of red- and black-glazed household wares, exhibited a 'specimen of porcelain' at the 1824 Franklin Institute competition. While Miller's experimental production of porcelain was one of the earliest in the United States, he never manufactured it on a commercial basis. John Vickers, a member of an established family of Chester County earthenware potters, produced a small quantity of experimental porcelain which he signed 'August/1824' and 'September/1824'. The few pieces that survive are heavily painted with foliate and fruit forms on a stark white body. These designs were amateurish attempts to approximate the decoration found on imported European porcelain. While the quality of the body and glaze are decidedly inferior to European counterparts, Vickers' wares represent the first dated porcelain manufactured in the United States.

The Jersey Porcelain and Earthenware Co. of Jersey City, New Jersey, extended the production of porcelain beyond the experimental stage to become the first commercially successful manufacturer in the United States. Incorporated on 10 December 1825 under an Act of the New Jersey Legislature, the Company received a silver medal in the Franklin Institute competition of 1826 for the 'best china from American material'. The production of porcelain does not seem to have continued for more than three years. No extant examples of the factory's wares are known. In 1829 the porcelain works were sold to D. and J. Henderson, who changed the production to earthenware and stoneware.

Concurrent with the development of the Jersey Porcelain Co. was the production of porcelain by the Tucker factory of Philadelphia, Pennsylvania. Founded in 1826 by William Ellis Tucker, the factory produced a sizeable quantity of porcelain in the Classical, or Empire, style until its closure in 1838. William Tucker, born in 1800, first experimented with the production of creamware before turning his talents to the production of porcelain. After experimenting with over

Vase, Tucker & Hemphill, c. 1835. Hard-paste porcelain, ht 20½ in (52 cm). The ormolu handles of this vase of Classical shape were designed by F. Sachse. Philadelphia Museum of Art.

twenty different porcelain recipes, Tucker selected one combination as his 'secret formula'. The recipes for glazes and enamels, while secretly coded by Tucker, were copied from various printed sources and books available in the library of the Franklin Institute.

As with most early attempts at porcelain production, the Tucker factory was burdened with financial problems. Attempting to alleviate this, Tucker acquired a succession of three partners: John N. Bird, April 1826 to January 1827; John Hulme, April 1828 to June 1828; and Joseph Hemphill, 1832 to 1838. Because the heavy financial requirements outweighed the profits, the first two partners withdrew after brief periods of partnership. In 1828 William Tucker's younger brother, Thomas Tucker, joined the factory as chief decorator; he created the floral sprays and extensive use of gilding that became the factory's trademark. In 1827, and again in 1828, the Tucker factory received a silver medal from the Franklin Institute for 'the best Porcelain made in the U.S., gilt, painted and plain'. William Tucker died in 1832, but the factory continued production under Hemphill's

OPPOSITE *Pitcher, Tucker & Hemphill, c. 1832. Hard-paste porcelain, ht 9½ in (24 cm). Philadelphia Museum of Art.*

RIGHT *Pitcher, Charles Cartlidge & Co., Greenpoint, New York, c. 1850. Porcelain, ht 6 in (15 cm). Designed by the English immigrant potter and modeller, Josiah Jones, with a maize or corn pattern selected by Cartlidge as a distinctively American design motif. Brooklyn Museum.*

FAR RIGHT *Pitcher, American Porcelain Manufacturing Co., Gloucester, New Jersey, c. 1854-7. Porcelain, ht 8¼ in (21 cm). Brooklyn Museum.*

ownership with Thomas Tucker employed as manager. The eventual closure of the factory in 1838 was a result of the national tariff controversies, the bank failure of 1837 and the personal financial problems of Hemphill.

The factory produced a complete line of household wares in plain white and decorated porcelain, basing most of its designs on English and French prototypes. It was the factory's intent to copy European porcelain so exactly that customers would not be able to differentiate between the imported porcelain and that produced by the Tucker factory. The complete factory papers, preserved in the collection of the Philadelphia Museum of Art, include account books, formulae and price-books, letter books, line-drawings of the factory equipment and two elaborate pattern-books. With its high arched handle and reeded moulded base, the vase-shaped pitcher is the most distinctive of the factory's wares. As the most significant of the early nineteenth-century porcelain factories, the Tucker porcelain company is honoured by being the first large-scale manufactory of porcelain in the United States.

Rococo Revival: 1840–60

While early porcelain production was based exclusively on the imitation of European wares, the middle period of manufacture, while following European prototypes, experienced the development of an American consciousness and an attempt to produce purely American designs.

Christopher Weber Fenton of Bennington, Vermont, established a porcelain works in 1847. In 1848, with the assistance of John Harrison, brought over from the Copeland works in Stoke-on-Trent, England, Fenton produced the first parian ware to be manufactured in

the United States. Until its closure in 1858, Fenton's factory, reorganized in 1852 as the United States Pottery Co., was the major producer of American parian ware. The factory produced functional porcelain as well as decorative items in plain white parian or statuary porcelain and coloured porcelain.

The shapes utilized by the factory were simplified versions of English parian designs executed in the Rococo Revival style. Fenton also produced certain designs that were distinctly American. The Niagara Falls, or Cascade Pitcher had no English or European counterpart. The naturalism of the Pitcher is typical of the romantic virtues popular throughout the period. Another distinctly American design, the corn or maize pattern, extols corn as a unique American symbol. While the factory experienced a period of economic success, increased production costs and the rising price of fuel forced its closure in 1858.

Naturalistic Rococo Revival forms with intricate moulded shapes were also produced by Charles Cartlidge & Co. of Greenpoint, New York (now a part of Brooklyn). Organized in 1848 by Charles Cartlidge, a potter and former American agent for John Ridgway, the Company produced a sizeable quantity of hard-paste, or true, porcelain. The factory's production included tablewares, buttons, ornamental figures, parian ware and hardware trimmings. A gleaming white-glazed body often devoid of any decoration became the factory's distinctive trademark. Cartlidge also selected the corn pattern, designed by his chief modeller, Josiah Jones, as a distinctly American expression. Because Cartlidge was more interested in artistic excellence than financial success, the factory ceased operations in 1856.

Cartlidge, one of the foremost of the

nineteenth-century American potters, was referred to as the 'American Wedgwood'. It was the contemporary feeling that Cartlidge was several decades in advance of public taste which resulted in an insufficient demand for his porcelain. After the Cartlidge factory closed, Josiah Jones assumed the management of the Southern Porcelain Manufacturing Co. of Kaolin, South Carolina.

The American Porcelain Manufacturing Co., incorporated in Gloucester, New Jersey, in 1854, continued the production of American porcelain in the Rococo Revival style. The Company produced a remarkably translucent porcelain which featured moulded floral forms. There are believed to be only three examples of the porcelain which have survived.

Financial problems forced the factory to close in 1857. The Gloucester China Co., a continuation of the former company, was incorporated in 1857 for the manufacture of 'porcelain, china, chemicals, drugs, and other articles'. The quality of the porcelain was excellent but the workmanship and the glazing were inferior to that of European wares. All the finished examples were sold unpainted. After the factory closed in 1860, many of the workers joined other porcelain factories in New Jersey.

Art Porcelain: 1860–1900

Beginning in the 1860s, American porcelain entered a new phase of self-awareness and excellence. This new awareness was evident in the extensive production of art wares, which lifted the status of American porcelain from the realm of dinner wares and figurines. While historical revivalism continued to influence design, it was no longer expressed in one particular style. The new period of

eclecticism was a borrowing and blending of several historical styles to suit the particular needs of the manufacturer. American art wares were greatly encouraged by the Centennial Exposition of 1876. Factories produced distinctively American wares for display and Americans became aware, for the first time, of the quality of native porcelain.

The development of American art porcelain reached its height with the wares of the Union Porcelain Works established in Greenpoint, New York, in 1862. The factory, founded by Thomas C. Smith, was a continuation of the Boch Bros firm established in 1845. Until its closure in 1910, the Union Porcelain Works produced a superior quality porcelain noted for its applied decoration and gilding. Smith continued the earlier bone composition of the Boch factory until 1864 when he introduced the use of a new kaolin body.

In addition to art wares, the factory manufactured a standard line of porcelain tablewares, tiles, hardware trimmings, electrical insulators and parian ware. Karl Mueller, a German sculptor and artist who was employed as the factory's chief designer and modeller, produced designs for the factory's Centennial exhibit, which featured motifs that were of purely American origin. The Century Vase, a masterpiece of Mueller's design and modelling, features scenes from American history as well as moulded bison-headed handles. A teaset, also designed by Mueller, depicts a Negro head finial on the sugar bowl and a Chinese head on the teapot.

The firm of Ott & Brewer (Etruria Pottery), Trenton, New Jersey, continued the art porcelain tradition of the Union Porcelain Works. Established in 1863 as Bloor, Ott & Booth, the name of the firm was changed to Ott & Brewer

ABOVE LEFT *Century Vase designed by Karl Mueller for the Union Porcelain Works, Greenpoint, New York, c. 1876. Porcelain, ht 22¼ in (56 cm). Decorated with bison handles and relief scenes from American history. New Jersey State Museum.*

LEFT *Tea-service designed by Karl Mueller for the Union Porcelain Works, Greenpoint, New York, c. 1876. Porcelain, teapot ht 6¼ in (17 cm). The finials, handles and applied feet of this service are unique. Brooklyn Museum.*

OPPOSITE *Vase, Ott & Brewer, Trenton, New Jersey, c. 1900. Belleek porcelain, ht 9½ in (24 cm). The first Belleek ware manufactured in America was produced by Ott & Brewer in 1882. Metropolitan Museum of Art.*

when John Hart Brewer acquired a controlling interest in 1865. From 1863 until 1875 the factory produced creamware and granite ware, but in 1875 the factory began the successful production of parian figures and portrait busts. These parian pieces were the work of Isaac Broome, a noted American sculptor and modeller, engaged by Ott & Brewer to design a series of works in parian for the Centennial Exposition of 1876. One of his most successful designs, the Baseball Vase, was a unique American statement. In 1882, with the assistance of William Bromley and several other workers imported from the Belleek factory in Ireland, Ott & Brewer produced the first Belleek porcelain made in the United States. The thinness of the body and the detailed decoration was equal to that manufactured by the Irish. In 1893, after a brief period of artistic and financial success the firm was dissolved.

In 1889 Jonathan Coxon, former superintendent of the Ott & Brewer company, and Walter Scott Lenox, Ott & Brewer's chief decorator, formed the Ceramic Art Co. of Trenton, New Jersey. The Company brought the manufacture of Belleek to the highest state of perfection in America. The factory also produced a type of cameo ware carved by Kate B. Sears, the factory's chief artist. Coxon withdrew from the partnership in 1896 and Walter Lenox continued alone, changing the name of the Company to Lenox, Inc. and subsequently became the foremost producer of porcelain in the United States.

While the majority of porcelain manufactured in the United States was produced in cities along the East Coast, one Mid Western town, East Liverpool, Ohio, managed to become a leading centre of ceramic production. The firm

of Knowles, Taylor & Knowles founded in 1854, produced a sizeable quantity of porcelain including Belleek ware and parian. Its original design, Lotus Ware, was a translucent bone-china with a soft, velvety glaze. By 1893 the factory had reached gigantic proportions with thirty-five kilns and over seven hundred employees.

Aftermath of Nineteenth-century Production

By the beginning of the twentieth century, porcelain production in the United States had become a major industry rather than an art. Growing markets and the impact of mass production reduced porcelain manufacture to functional tea-, toilet- and dinner-wares. With the financial decline of many small companies, American porcelain production was increasingly controlled by larger companies who ignored the production of art wares in favour of more lucrative products. The days of small factories concentrating on limited artistic production were over.

While porcelain development in the United States was never comparable to that of Europe, the phenomenal achievements of American factories brought porcelain manufacture from the experimental stage, through a dynamic period of artistic development, to the production of porcelain for a world market in less than one hundred years.

Philip H. Curtis

Manufacturers

ABOVE RIGHT *Baseball Vase designed by Isaac Broome for Ott & Brewer, Trenton, New Jersey, 1876. Parian porcelain, ht 34 in (86 cm). This vase was modelled by Isaac Broome for the 1876 Centennial Exhibition at Philadelphia. New Jersey State Museum.*

RIGHT *Vase with cameo reliefs carved by Kate B. Sears for the Ceramic Art Co., Trenton, New Jersey, c. 1891. Porcelain, ht 9¼ in (24 cm). Greenfield Village and Henry Ford Museum.*

OPPOSITE *Figure in the Japanese style, designed by James Hadley for the Royal Worcester Porcelain Co., 1874. Porcelain, ht 16½ in (42 cm). This design was exhibited at Vienna in 1873 and epitomizes the 1870s. Author's Collection.*

ALCOCK, SAMUEL
One of the leading early Victorian producers of porcelain at Cobridge and Burslem in the 1828 to 1859 period.

ALLEN, GEORGE
Manufacturer of PARIAN between 1857 and 1858 in Philadelphia, Pennsylvania. Many of his moulds were obtained from the GLOUCESTER CHINA CO., Gloucester, New Jersey.

AMERICAN ART CHINA WORKS
Established 1 December 1891 at Trenton, New Jersey, and formerly known as the Washington Pottery. Producers of Belleek art wares for professional and amateur china painters.

AMERICAN CROCKERY CO.
Manufacturers of BISQUE and white GRANITE WARE from 1876 to 1890 at Trenton, New Jersey. The Company also produced porcelain on an experi-

mental basis. Mark: printed American China/A. C. Co.

AMERICAN PORCELAIN MANUFACTURING CO.
Factory operating from 1854 to 1857 at Gloucester, New Jersey. It produced a thin, translucent moulded porcelain. Mark: impressed A.P.M. Co.

ARNOUX, LÉON (1816–1902)
French ceramic chemist and potter. Art director at MINTON from 1848 until his retirement in 1895, his presence at Stoke attracted many leading Continental artists.

ARSENAL POTTERY
Founded in the 1890s at Trenton, New Jersey, by Joseph S. Mayer, the company produced a general line of decorated porcelain.

ASSANPINK POTTERY CO.
Organized by Henry Speeler at Trenton, New Jersey, the factory produced Belleek ware during the 1860s and 1870s.

ASTBURY & MADDOCK
Founded after 1853 at Trenton, New Jersey, on an earlier company. They experimented with porcelain production using kaolin from Missouri and Pennsylvania.

BAGALY & FORD
Produced porcelain at Philadelphia, Pennsylvania, on an experimental basis c. 1843. They exhibited articles at the 1843 Franklin Institute competition.

BELL, JOHN (1811–95)
Noted English Victorian sculptor who produced models for MINTON and other ceramic firms from c. 1845 into the 1860s.

BELLEEK
Irish manufactory of delicate, thinly potted glazed-PARIAN wares, very often modelled after marine-forms such as shells. Openwork baskets were a feature. Established in about 1863, the factory continues to the present day.

BENNETT, EDWIN (1818–1908)
From 1855 to 1908 Bennett produced PARIAN busts, pitchers and figurines. Born in Derbyshire, England, Bennett came to the United States in 1839 to join his brother James' pottery in East Liverpool, Ohio. In 1844 Edwin Bennett established his own manufactory in Baltimore, Maryland. Awarded a gold medal at the 1876 Centennial Exposition, Bennett became a major producer of parian ware. By 1886 the factory was also producing Belleek ware. In 1890 the company was incorporated as the Edwin Bennett Pottery. Trademark: A globe showing the western hemisphere with a sword driven through the United States. Initials of the company are printed on the sword guard.

BIRKS, ALBOINE (1861–1941)
Pupil of M. L. Solon at MINTON, who worked in the PÂTE-SUR-PÂTE technique into the 1930s. Signature and/or initials incorporated in design.

BLOOR, WILLIAM
Formerly of Bloor, Ott & Booth of Trenton, New Jersey, Bloor moved to East Liverpool, Ohio, in 1865, where he introduced the manufacture of PARIAN ware.

BOCH BROS
Company founded in 1845 at Greenpoint, Long Island, New York, by a family of German potters, William, Anthony and Victor Boch. They manufactured porcelain pitchers, mugs, vases, furniture knobs and funerary images until 1862, when the factory was purchased by Thomas C. Smith, who continued the factory under the name UNION PORCELAIN WORKS. The Boch brothers were also connected with the EMPIRE POTTERY CO. of New York. Boch exhibited a selection of its plain and gilded porcelain door plates at the 1853 New York Crystal Palace Exhibition. Noah Boch, a grandson, was employed in the knob department of the GREENWOOD POTTERY CO.

BOTT, THOMAS (1829–70)
Noted Worcester artist who worked for KERR & BINNS and for the ROYAL WORCESTER PORCELAIN CO. up to his early death at the age of forty-one. He specialized in a Limoges enamel style of painting.

BOTT, THOMAS JOHN (1854–1932)
Son of THOMAS BOTT, succeeded his father at the ROYAL WORCESTER PORCELAIN CO. and subsequently worked independently and as art director at the COALPORT PORCELAIN WORKS.

BOULLEMIER, ANTONIN (1840–1900)
Sèvres-trained figurative painter, working for MINTON from 1872. A superb artist of charming compositions.

BOULTER, CHARLES J.
United States modeller employed by Tucker & Hemphill's porcelain factory from 1832 to 1838. When the factory closed in 1838, Boulter became the foreman of the MILLER factory. After Miller's death Boulter continued in the production of porcelain until 1872.

BREWER, JOHN J.
See OTT & BREWER (Etruria Pottery)

BROMLEY, WILLIAM
Trained as a potter at Belleek in Ireland, where he established a porcelain works, Bromley was brought over to America in 1882 by the firm of OTT & BREWER to produce the first Belleek wares made in the United States. Bromley later instructed the WILLETS MANUFACTURING CO. of Trenton, New Jersey, in the production of Belleek.

BROOME, ISAAC
American sculptor and artist employed by OTT & BREWER for the Philadelphia Centennial Exposition in 1876. Previous to his employment by Ott & Brewer, Broome was affiliated with several terracotta manufacturers near Pittsburgh, Pennsylvania, and Brooklyn, New York. In 1878 appointed a special commissioner on ceramics to the Paris Exposition.

BROWN-WESTHEAD, MOORE & CO.
Noted partnership working RIDGWAY's former Cauldon Place Works at Hanley in the 1862 to 1905 period. A little-known firm closely rivalling the leading houses.

BROWNFIELD, WILLIAM
Manufacturer at Cobridge in the Staffordshire Potteries, who made quality porcelain in the 1871 to 1891 period.

BULLOCK, R. B.
In 1865 Bullock organized a new porcelain company at Kaolin, South Carolina. After twelve years of varying success, the factory was sold to McNamee & Co. of New York. The kaolin clay proved to be too fine for the production of porcelain and was exported for use in the manufacture of wallpaper.

BURROUGHS & MOUNTFORD
Established in 1879 at Trenton, New Jersey, the company manufactured porcelain tables and toilet-sets. The company also manufactured ornate copies of DOULTON, ROYAL WORCESTER, and Limoges in addition to ornamental tiles in the Japanese taste.

CERAMIC ART CO.
Organized in 1889 at Trenton, New Jersey by Jonathan Coxon, former superintendent of OTT & BREWER and by LENOX, the former director of Ott & Brewer's decorating department. The Ceramic Art Co. brought the production of Belleek china to the highest state of perfection in the United States. The

Vase, Ott & Brewer, Trenton, New Jersey, c. 1880. Belleek porcelain decorated with ivory painted flowers. James R. Seibert Collection.

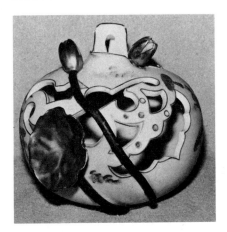

Company produced both decorated and plain wares.

MESSRS CHAMBERLAINS & CO.
Manufacturers of fine porcelains at Worcester before 1852, when they were succeeded by the firm of KERR & BINNS. Clear name-marks employed.

CHARLES CARTLIDGE & CO.
Founded in 1848 by Charles Cartlidge at Greenpoint, Long Island, former American agent for the English pottery of RIDGWAY. Cartlidge manufactured porcelain tableware, buttons, hardware trimmings, and PARIAN ware. In 1848 JONES joined the firm as the chief modeller. At the 1853 Crystal Palace Exhibition in New York, Cartlidge was awarded a silver medal for the superior body and glazing of his wares. The firm also excelled in its painted decoration and gilded trim. The foremost decorators imported from England, were George Washington, Frank Lockett, Daniel Smith and Elijah Tatler. In 1854 the firm was dissolved and reorganized under the name, AMERICAN PORCELAIN MANUFACTURING CO. Because Cartlidge was more interested in artistic excellence than financial success, the factory was forced to cease operating in 1856.

CHEVERTON, BENJAMIN (1794–1876)
United States inventor of a reducing lathe used for making models for mass production of the PARIAN body. The inscription Cheverton Sc. is found on such pieces.

COALBROOKDALE
Name given to nineteenth-century Coalport porcelains encrusted with relief-moulded and coloured flowers. Name-marks Coalbrookdale or C'Dale occur.

COALPORT PORCELAIN WORKS
Noted ceramic centre from the eighteenth century which was based on the banks of the River Severn in Shropshire. It moved to Staffordshire in 1926 and continues there to the present day.

COLUMBIAN ART POTTERY
Established by W. T. Morris and F. R. Williamson at Trenton, New Jersey in 1893, the year of the World's Columbian Exposition in Chicago, Illinois, producing both domestic china and Belleek art wares. The company specialized in small porcelain trinkets. Both Morris and Williamson had previously been employed by OTT & BREWER of Trenton, New Jersey, and the ROYAL WORCESTER PORCELAIN WORKS, England.

COOK POTTERY CO.
Founded in 1894 at Trenton, New Jersey, by Charles Howell Cook and F. G. Mellor, the factory produced porcelain dinner-ware and Belleek art wares. In 1894 the Company succeeded to the former factory of OTT & BREWER.

Page from a Coalport shape book showing typical late Victorian forms. These plain pieces would later have been richly embellished in different styles.

MESSRS COPELAND & GARRETT
British manufacturers of fine porcelains, the company succeeded Messrs Spode in 1833 continuing until 1847.

MESSRS DAVENPORT
Producers of porcelain and various earthenwares at Longport, Staffordshire, in the 1793 to 1887 period. Clear name-marks employed.

DELAWARE POTTERY CO.
Factory operated between 1884 and 1895 by Oliphant & Co. at Trenton, New Jersey, and producers of a limited amount of Belleek art wares.

DERBY
Home of several noted porcelain manufacturers, the original factory closed in 1848. The new factory opened at King Street, Derby and continued on a small scale until 1935. The present Royal Crown Derby Porcelain Co. dates from 1876. The prefix Royal was granted in 1890.

MESSRS DOULTON & CO.
Porcelain made at the Burslem factory, Staffordshire, from 1884 to the present day. Some superb wares were made and decorated by leading late-Victorian ceramic artists. Clear name-marks employed.

EAST MORRISANIA CHINA CO.
Organized in the 1880s by D. Robitzek in New York City for the manufacture of porcelain door knobs and hardware.

EMPIRE POTTERY CO.
Established in 1863 by Coxon and Thompson in Trenton, New Jersey. The factory was acquired by Alpaugh and Magowan in 1883. The Company produced porcelain dinner-, tea-, and toilet-sets.

FAÏENCE MANUFACTURING CO.
Established in 1880 at Greenpoint, New York, the factory produced true, or hard-paste, porcelain under the trade name Royal Crown. Edward Lycett, the noted American china painter, served as superintendent and principal decorator as well as regulating the composition of the body.

FENTON, CHRISTOPHER WEBER
In 1847 Fenton organized the Fenton's Works at Bennington, Vermont, and produced the first PARIAN ware to be manufactured in the United States. Fenton was assisted by John Harrison, a modeller from the COPELAND Works in Stoke-on-Trent where parian was first introduced in 1842. In 1848 Fenton acquired two partners, Alanson P. Lyman and Calvin Park, and the firm's name became Lyman, Fenton & Park. In 1849 Park withdrew from the partnership and the firm's name became Lyman, Fenton & Co. The Company became the major producer of parian ware in the United States. While the Company copied English parian, it also created several purely American designs. In 1852 the firm's name was changed to the United States Pottery Co. Continuous financial instability forced the factory to close in 1858.

FRENCH CHINA MANUFACTURING CO.
Organized in 1868 by William BOCH, Jr at Corona, Queens, New York, the factory produced porcelain tableware and furniture knobs for a period of two to three years before the factory was abandoned. In 1879, it was rebuilt after a fire destroyed the buildings. The new factory, the Corona Manufacturing Co., closed in 1882 after a short period of production.

GLOUCESTER CHINA CO.
Organized in 1857 at Gloucester, New Jersey, as a continuation of the AMERICAN PORCELAIN MANUFACTURING CO., the

factory produced porcelain on a limited scale. While the quality of the porcelain was good, the workmanship and glazing were inferior. All pieces were sold undecorated. The factory ceased to operate in 1860.

MESSRS THOMAS GOODE
Leading London retailer in South Audley Street. A mark or name often occurs on wares sold by this firm.

GOSS, W. H.
Manufacturer of PARIAN wares at Stoke from 1858, best known for the mainly twentieth-century Goss Ware armorial trinkets. William Goss was personally responsible for some fine art productions, including floral jewelry, busts and figures.

GRAINGER, GEORGE
Noted manufacturer of porcelain and PARIAN at Worcester. The works were established in 1800 by Thomas Grainger and taken over by the ROYAL WORCESTER PORCELAIN CO. in 1889.

GREENWOOD POTTERY CO.
Established in 1861 at Trenton, New Jersey, under the name of Stephens (James P. Stephens), Tams (James Tams) and Co., the firm's name was changed to Greenwood in 1868. Producers of porcelain hardware trimmings and electrical supplies as well as tablewares, their decorations in the style of the ROYAL WORCESTER PORCELAIN CO. featured extensive use of silver and gold enamel. Mark: printed G.P. Co.

HADLEY, JAMES (1837–1903)
Talented modeller and designer employed by the ROYAL WORCESTER PORCELAIN CO. until 1875 after which he worked on his own account selling designs to the Company. He established his own works in 1896. (See colour plate p. 140.)

J. HAMBLETON & SON
Extensive porcelain decorating firm established at Philadelphia, Pennsylvania, in 1876. The factory was specifically known for its barber's mugs.

D. F. HAYNES & CO.
Established in 1881 at Baltimore, Maryland, in 1887 the name was changed to the Chesapeake Pottery Co. The original modeller, Haynes, produced PARIAN ware as well as GRANITE WARE and majolica. By 1890 the factory had ceased production.

HURTEN, C. F. (1818–97)
Talented German flower-painter, famous for his paintings while employed in the 1859–97 period by W. T. Copeland & Sons.

INTERNATIONAL POTTERY CO.
Established in 1878 in New York City by Edward Clarke, formerly of the Lincoln Pottery Co., the Company was purchased in 1879 by William Burgess and

John Campbell. It specialized in the production of porcelain toilet and dinner wares until its closure in 1888.

JENSEN, JAMES L.
Formerly employed by the UNION PORCELAIN WORKS, Jensen purchased the Empire Pottery in New York City (previously established by the BOCH family) and manufactured porcelain hardware trimmings and industrial wares between 1873 and 1900.

JONES, JOSIAH
Potter, designer and modeller, Jones emigrated to the United States in 1847 from Staffordshire, England. He was employed by CHARLES CARTLIDGE & CO. until the factory closed in 1856. He was then employed as the manager of the SOUTHERN PORCELAIN MANUFACTURING CO. At the outset of the Civil War he moved to Trenton, New Jersey, as a modeller for the MILLINGTON & ASTBURY and Poulson Co. for whom he designed a pitcher in 1863 depicting in relief the assassination of Colonel Ellsworth at Alexandria, Virginia.

KERR & BINNS
Successors to MESSRS CHAMBERLAINS & CO. at Worcester in the 1852 to 1862 period. They made superb quality porcelain before the firm was succeeded by the present-day ROYAL WORCESTER PORCELAIN CO.

KNOWLES, TAYLOR & KNOWLES
Founded in 1854 by Isaac W. Knowles and Isaac Harvey at East Liverpool, Ohio, in 1870 Knowles purchased Harvey's

Vase, Worcester, made in the Kerr & Binns period, 1852-62. Porcelain, diam 4⅛ in (10 cm). This was one of the best periods in the history of the Worcester factory. Author's Collection.

partnership and was joined by John N. Taylor and Homer S. Knowles. In 1887 the factory imported an Irish potter to manufacture Belleek wares. The factory was destroyed by fire in 1889, rebuilt, and continued in operation until 1898, producing a sizeable quantity of art wares and originating Lotus Ware, a translucent BONE-CHINA with a soft, velvety glaze. White decoration was built up on the surface in a PÂTE-SUR-PÂTE technique.

KURLBAUM & SCHWARTZ
Founded in 1851 by Charles Kurlbaum and John T. Schwartz at Philadelphia, Pennsylvania, the factory produced true, or hard-paste, porcelain closely resembling French porcelain. A German potter named Reiss was employed as factory manager. The factory ceased production in 1855 and Reiss was subsequently employed by the AMERICAN PORCELAIN MANUFACTURING CO. In 1853, Kurlbaum & Schwartz were praised by the Franklin Institute of Philadelphia as producers of the 'best American porcelain we have ever seen'. Mark K & S impressed.

LENOX, WALTER SCOTT (1859–1920)
By 1887 Lenox was art director for OTT & BREWER of Trenton, New Jersey. With Jonathan Coxon he established the CERAMIC ART CO. in 1889 for the production of Belleek wares, in the interests of which they imported two craftsmen from Ireland. In 1895 Lenox was stricken with paralysis and blindness. In 1906 the firm's name was changed to Lenox Inc. and was subsequently to become one of the foremost producers of porcelain in the United States.

LOCKE & CO.
Small factory established at Worcester by Edward Locke in 1895 which closed

in 1904. The wares are very similar in general style to those from the ROYAL WORCESTER PORCELAIN CO.

LOUISIANA PORCELAIN WORKS
Established in 1880 at New Orleans, Louisiana, by Hernandez and Saloy, the factory produced a general line of porcelain in imitation of Limoges utilizing French workers and materials. All wares were sold undecorated. By 1890 the factory had ceased to operate.

LYCETT, EDWARD
Foremost American china decorator, trained in Staffordshire, England. Lycett arrived in New York City in c. 1861 and established an extensive decorating business employing thirty to forty decorators. In 1884 Lycett joined the FAÏENCE MANUFACTURING CO. where, under his direction, a fine grade of porcelain in the Moorish style was produced. In 1890 Lycett retired and joined his son William in Atlanta, Georgia. William Lycett and two other sons Joseph and Frederick continued the family tradition of china painting.

MERCER POTTERY CO.
Established in 1868 at Trenton, New Jersey, the factory claims to have produced the first semi-porcelain in the United States. They also manufactured white earthenware, GRANITE WARE, and porcelain table- and toilet-wares. John Pope was employed as designer, and James Moses as modeller.

MILLER, ABRAHAM
Noted American potter from Philadelphia, Pennsylvania, who experimented with the production of porcelain as early as 1824. Miller served as the ceramics judge for the annual competition of the Franklin Institute. In 1838 when the Tucker & Hemphill factory closed, Miller purchased the machinery and many of the moulds.

MILLINGTON & ASTBURY
Established by Richard Millington and John Astbury at Trenton, New Jersey, in the 1850s for the manufacture of porcelain, the company was purchased by Thomas Maddock & Co., who continued the business into the twentieth century.

MINTON
Established at Stoke-on-Trent in 1793, the name of the firm was changed from Minton to Mintons in 1873. Leading manufacturers of fine porcelains and other wares, the firm employed a large staff of able artists and designers, many of whom were permitted to sign their work.

MOORE BROS
Manufacturers of porcelain at St Mary's Works, Longton, from 1872 to 1905. Raised floral motifs or hops were a characteristic motif.

MORRISON & CARR
Established in 1853 in New York City by James Carr, who was born in Hanley Staffordshire, as the New York City Pottery Co. The Company produced BONE-CHINA in addition to PARIAN busts and figures. The partnership dissolved in 1871, although Carr continued production until 1888 when the factory ceased operation.

MUELLER, KARL
German sculptor, educated in Paris and employed as a modeller and designer by the UNION PORCELAIN WORKS. He designed exhibition pieces for the Philadelphia Centennial Exposition of 1876.

NATIONAL LEAGUE OF MINERAL PAINTERS
National association of ceramic clubs and professional china decorators established in the United States in 1892. The organization was founded to provide a closer relationship between china decorators and to develop a national school of ceramic art. A national exhibition was conducted each year. Founded by Mrs S. S. Frackelton of Milwaukee, Wisconsin.

NEW ENGLAND POTTERY CO.
Founded in 1854 by Frederick Meagher at Boston, Massachusetts, the Company were producing PARIAN and porcelain by 1862.

OHIO VALLEY CHINA CO.
Established in 1890 at Wheeling, West Virginia, the factory produced a general line of porcelain tablewares, figures and cuspidors. Shortly after 1893, the factory was closed for a few years and then re-opened for the production of sanitary wares until 1900, when the factory ceased operation.

ONONDAGA POTTERY CO.
Established in 1871, at Syracuse, New York, the factory commenced the production of porcelain in 1888. Receiving a gold medal and the grand prize, the Company attracted public notice at the 1893 Chicago World's Fair. In 1897 the Company produced the first American made ceramic decalcomania.

OTT & BREWER (ETRURIA POTTERY)
Established in 1863 by Bloor, Ott & Booth at Trenton, New Jersey, in 1865 John Hart Brewer bought the interest of Bloor, who subsequently moved to East Liverpool, Ohio, changing the firm's name to Ott & Brewer. The production from 1863 to 1875 was limited to GRANITE WARE and cream-coloured wares. In 1875 PARIAN ware was introduced consisting largely of busts and figures modelled by BROOME. The first Belleek ware manufactured in America was produced by Ott & Brewer in 1882 (see colour plate p. 139). BROMLEY and other workers from Belleek, Ireland,

were persuaded to work in the United States and direct the Belleek production for Ott & Brewer. Henry Saunders directed the production of PÂTE-SUR-PÂTE. In 1871, the firm was re-organized with special emphasis on production for exhibition and display. Isaac Broome's works featured a series of original parian designs. Throughout its history Ott & Brewer remained one of the largest ceramic producers in Trenton, and the firm was finally dissolved in 1893.

OWEN, GEORGE (d.1917)
ROYAL WORCESTER craftsman-designer famous for his reticulated or pierced designs. Examples are normally signed but other firms such as GRAINGER's produced inferior essays in Owen's style.

PHOENIX POTTERY CO.
In 1872 the factory at Phoenixville, Pennsylvania, was leased to W. A. H. Schreiber and J. F. Betz. Until it closed in 1899 the factory manufactured PARIAN ware and porcelain LITHOPHANES.

RIDGWAY, JOHN (1785–1860)
Noted porcelain manufacturer at Cauldon Place, Hanley, in the 1830 to 1865 period, and potter to Queen Victoria.

ROBINSON & LEADBEATER
Leading Staffordshire manufacturers of mass-produced PARIAN figures and groups in the 1864 to 1924 period. R & L initial marks employed.

ROCKINGHAM
Famous Yorkshire pottery managed by the Bramelds on the estate of Earl Fitzwilliam, Marquis of Rockingham. Porcelain was first produced in the mid 1820s and the works closed in 1842 so that this factory was only active for the first five years of Queen Victoria's reign. The wares are often unmarked.

ROYAL CROWN DERBY PORCELAIN CO.
See DERBY.

ROYAL WORCESTER PORCELAIN CO.
See WORCESTER.

SOUTHERN PORCELAIN MANUFACTURING CO.
Founded in 1856 at Kaolin, South Carolina, by William H. Farrar of the United States Pottery Co. of Bennington, Vermont. In 1857 JONES, formerly the chief modeller with CHARLES CARTLIDGE & CO., assumed management and succeeded in producing porcelain. The pottery works continued in operation until the start of the Civil War, when the finer grades were discontinued and the factory limited its production to porcelain telegraph insulators. In 1864 the factory was destroyed by fire.

SPIEGEL, JOHN
Between 1880 and 1890 Spiegel produced BISQUE vases and plaques under the trade name Barbotine Ware. The

biscuit was decorated with three-dimensional floral designs, but many pieces were also produced for china decorators working outside his company.

STAFFORDSHIRE POTTERIES
In the Victorian era the Staffordshire centre of the English ceramic industry contained numerous potteries of which the majority were quite small and producing low-priced wares. The main towns making up the complex were Burslem, Cobridge, Fenton, Hanley, Longton, Stoke and Tunstall, now incorporated in the present city of Stoke-on-Trent.

STEVENSON & HANCOCK
Main Victorian partnership working the King Street, Derby factory, the name is often erroneously subscribed to the total output of this small factory in the 1848 to 1935 period.

SUMMERLY'S ART MANUFACTURES
Name adopted by Henry Cole in 1847 for his wares designed by leading designers of the day and mass produced under licence by major British firms such as MINTON.

TUCKER PORCELAIN FACTORY
Established by William Ellis Tucker in 1826 at Philadelphia, Pennsylvania, the factory produced both plain white and decorated porcelain of excellent quality and decoration. The factory was awarded a silver medal by the Franklin Institute in 1827 and 1828. In 1832 William Tucker died and the factory was continued by his partner Joseph Hemphill until 1838, when the factory was closed. William Tucker's younger brother Thomas Tucker served as chief decorator and manager of the factory under Hemphill's ownership. The factory was the most significant of the early United States manufacturers and is noted for being the first large-scale manufactory in the United States, playing an important rôle in the subsequent development of the ceramic industry within the Victorian period.

UNION PORCELAIN WORKS
In 1862 Thomas Carll Smith acquired the pottery of BOCH BROS at Greenpoint, New York. After several years of experimentation, Smith became one of the major producers of porcelain in the United States, and one of the few manufacturers of true, or hard-paste, porcelain, soon abandoning the bone body of the Boch brothers in favour of a kaolin body. In 1875 MUELLER joined the firm as chief decorator and modeller. In addition to art works the company produced tiles, furniture, hardware and industrial wares. Thomas Smith's son C. H. L. Smith continued as manager of the factory until its closure in 1910. Marks: K.L., H.M. and U.P.W., N.Y.

VICKERS, JOHN V.
In 1824 Vickers, an earthenware potter from Chester County, Pennsylvania, produced porcelain on an experimental basis. He decorated the hard white surface with enamelled fruit and foliate forms, but his output was never very considerable.

MESSRS WEDGWOOD
Earthenwares, basalt and jasperwares were the main concern of this leading Staffordshire firm. Porcelain was made only in the c. 1812 to 1822 period and again from 1878 onwards. Clear name marks were employed.

WHEELING POTTERY CO.
Established in November 1879 at Wheeling, West Virginia, by George K. Wheat, William A. Isett and Edward Meakin Pearson. The factory produced a general line of porcelain tablewares. Charles Creddock, head of the decorating department, was a native of Burslem, England, where he had previously been employed by MINTON of Stoke-on-Trent. He joined the American firm in 1882.

WILLETS MANUFACTURING CO.
Established in 1879 at Trenton, New Jersey, by Joseph, Daniel and Edmund Willets, it became a major manufacturer of American Belleek ware. William Bromley, formerly with OTT & BREWER, directed the Willets production. They supplied white wares for china decorators. Mark printed 'Belleek/Willits'.

WORCESTER
The home of several important porcelain manufactories in the Victorian period, namely, Flight, Barr & Barr (1813–40), CHAMBERLAINS (1840–52), GRAINGER (1800–89), KERR & BINNS (1852–62), ROYAL WORCESTER PORCELAIN CO. (1862 to present day), HADLEY (1896–1905), LOCKE & CO. (c. 1895–1904), as well as several independent decorators. They made useful wares in blue-and-white and polychrome enamels and very highly decorated wares in BONE-CHINA. The Royal Worcester Porcelain Co. has produced many fine decorative pieces, figures, groups, and vases, etc.

WILLIAM YOUNG & SONS
Established in 1853 at Trenton, New Jersey, the company first made ROCK-INGHAM and white wares. In 1857 the factory became known as the Excelsior Pottery Works. In 1870 William Young retired from the firm, and management passed to his sons William Jr, Edward and John. The factory won a bronze medal for porcelain hardware trimmings at the Centennial Exposition in 1876. In 1879 the factory was acquired by the WILLETS MANUFACTURING CO.

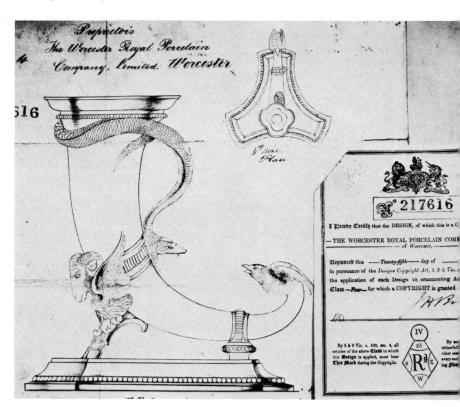

Page from the Design Registration Books of the Royal Worcester Porcelain Co. showing details of the shape of an ornament registered on 25 March 1868. To the right of the vase is shown the diamond-shaped registration mark with the letters and numbers corresponding to the date of registration at the Design Office.

American Porcelain Marks

Reproduced from *Dictionary of Marks : Pottery and Porcelain*, by Ralph M. and Terry H. Kovel, Crown Publishers Inc., 1971

Isaac Broome

Ceramic Art Co., established 1889

Edward Lycett

Lyman, Fenton & Co., 1849

Millington, Astbury & Poulson, 1859-70

Ohio Valley China Co., *c.* 1890

Ott & Brewer, 1867-92

Union Porcelain Works, *c.* 1880

Wheeling Pottery Co., established 1879

Willetts Manufacturing Co., established 1879

British Porcelain Marks

Reproduced by courtesy of Geoffrey A. Godden from *Victorian Porcelain*, Herbert Jenkins, 1961

For British Registration Marks see Glass Marks p. 170

Coalport Porcelain Works

c. 1851-61   *c.* 1861-75   *c.* 1881-1939. 'England' added from 1891. 'Made in England' from *c.* 1920.

Most wares of the 1830-50 period were unmarked

W. T. Copeland & Sons

COPELAND
c. 1851-85   *c.* 1875-90   *c.* 1894-1910

The addition of the word 'England' with any mark denotes a date after 1891

Derby

King Street mark, *c.* 1862-1935

Early Crown Derby mark, *c.* 1876-90

Royal Crown Derby mark, 1890+. Normally with the word 'England' or 'Made in England' after *c.* 1921

Mintons

c. 1850-70

c. 1863-72

c. 1873-1912. Note the 's' added in 1872. 'England' added after 1891

c. 1912-50

John Ridgway

Royal Arms mark, *c.* 1840-55

Worcester

1852-62. The shield-shaped mark includes the last two digits of the year placed in the central cross-bar

c. 1862-75. With year-numbers

Amended mark, *c.* 1876-91

Revised post-1891 trade mark

For further information on marks see Bibliography p. 149.

Main British Victorian Porcelain Manufacturers

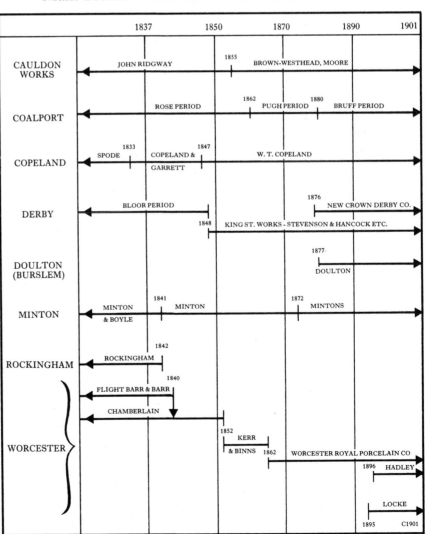

Glossary

Acid gilding
Process patented in 1863 and first adopted by MINTON. Part of the sections to be gilded were eaten away with acid, so recessing some of the gold. This resulted in certain parts being left matt when the surface gold was burnished.

Amateur work
Many blanks made by the leading manufacturers were decorated by amateurs – normally females. Such non-factory decoration lacks a gilded border and is often fully signed and dated.

Bisque, or biscuit
PORCELAIN after its first firing but before glazing. Some charming figures and groups were made in this medium in the nineteenth century.

Figure of Prince Albert, English. Biscuit porcelain. This type of unglazed porcelain was used for many figures and groups in the nineteenth century. City Museum and Art Gallery, Birmingham.

Bone-china
Standard English porcelain body in the nineteenth century containing bone-ash. A good white body, strong and translucent. Reputedly introduced at the Spode factory, the firm's old pattern books indicating that the first sales took place in *c.* 1794.

Centre-piece
Ornate flower or fruit stand. Some magnificent Victorian dessert-services had a centre-piece supported by PARIAN figures.

China
Loose term which, when found in marks, normally indicates a type of pottery rather than PORCELAIN; examples are stone china or ironstone china.

Comport
Footed, high dish, a component part of a Victorian dessert-service: they normally occur in three sizes, – some 6 in, 4 in and 2 in high (14·4, 9·6, 4·8 cm).

Crazing
Break-up of a glaze into a network of fine cracks rendering it both unsightly and prone to staining and the body absorbent.

Granite ware
Name used from the 1840s onwards for a hard, serviceable ironstone-type body. Much used for dinner services and other useful wares and widely exported, being both cheap and practical.

Ground-colour
Wide coloured border or other main painted ground to an object. Reserve panels are normally left clear to be painted with views, flowers, figure compositions, etc. General style mainly associated with the French Sèvres factory.

Japan pattern
Rich, formal design normally incorporating underglaze blue with overglaze red and green enamels and gilding. These patterns are normally associated with the DERBY factories but most porcelain manufacturers used these gay and colourful designs, which were universally popular in the nineteenth century.

Lithophane
Moulded PARIAN or BISQUE plaque or

Plate decorated by L. Solon, Minton, c. 1880. Tinted parian porcelain decorated in the pâte-sur-pâte *technique. Author's Collection.*

panel forming a picture when held to the light on account of the varying thickness and therefore translucency of the different parts.

Lustre
Shiny surface produced by using metallic pigments, generally in emulation of silver or copper. Mainly used on pottery rather than PORCELAIN.

Opaque porcelain
Contradictory term for a type of pottery.

Parian
Cream-white porcelaineous body – sometimes glazed – introduced in the early 1840s and much favoured for figures and groups.

Pâte-sur-pâte
Painstaking method of building up by hand a white design in slip over a tinted, PARIAN ground. Introduced into England by Solon of MINTON in 1870.

Pattern numbers
Identifying number placed on stock-designs, mainly tablewares, to help in the reordering and identification of the design by recourse to the factory pattern-books.

Porcelain
Semi-translucent fired compound basically of two types, true, or hard paste and artificial, or soft paste. However, several other types were made, notably BONE-CHINA. True porcelain contains petuntse (china stone) and kaolin (china clay). Artificial or soft-paste porcelain contains a large proportion of glass or frit.

Registration mark
Diamond-shaped device showing that the design or basic form had been protected by registration. The system was in use between 1842 and 1883 and subsequently superseded by registration numbers. The date of registration but not manufacture can be decoded with the aid of modern mark reference books.

Registration number
From January 1884, protected designs or shapes were given a number which appears on the ware. These numbers were normally prefixed with the abbreviation Rd No. (See p. 170.)

Statuary porcelain
Early name used by MESSRS COPELAND & GARRETT and W. T. Copeland & Sons for their PARIAN body.

Toy
Term normally used in the ceramic industry for a figure or image.

Underglaze blue
Blue pigment – cobalt – applied to the BISCUIT body before glazing.

Year-cypher
Factory marking by which the year and sometimes also the month can be ascertained. Some need reference to standard mark books to decode, others are self-evident, i.e. 6.87, or $\frac{6}{8\,7}$, for June 1887.

Bibliography

BARBER, EDWIN ATLEE. *Historical Sketch of the Green Point Porcelain Works of Charles Cartlidge & Co.*, Indiana, 1895

BARBER, EDWIN ATLEE. *Marks of American Potters*, Pennsylvania, 1904

BARBER, EDWIN ATLEE. *The Pottery and Porcelain of the United States*, New York and London, 1901.

BARRETT, RICHARD CARTER. *Bennington Pottery and Porcelain*, New York, 1958

BEMROSE, G. *Nineteenth Century English Pottery & Porcelain*, London, 1952

BLACKER, J. F. *The A.B.C. of XIX Century English Ceramic Art*, London, ND (c. 1911)

CLEMENT, ARTHUR W. *Notes on American Ceramics 1607–1943*, New York, 1944

CLEMENT, ARTHUR W. *Our Pioneer Potters*, New York, 1947

CURTIS, PHILIP H. *Tucker Porcelain 1826–38 ; A Reappraisal*, Delaware, 1972

GODDEN, G. A. *Victorian Porcelain*, London and New York, 1961

GODDEN, G. A. *Encyclopedia of British Pottery & Porcelain Marks*, London and New York, 1964

GODDEN, G. A. *Illustrated Encyclopedia of British Pottery and Porcelain*, London and New York, 1966

GODDEN, G. A. *Minton Pottery & Porcelain of the First Period*, London and New York, 1968

GODDEN, G. A. *British Porcelain, An Illustrated Guide*, London and New York, 1974

HOLLAND, EUGENIA CALVERT. *Edwin Bennett and The Products of His Baltimore Pottery*, Maryland, 1973

HUGHES, G. B. *Victorian Pottery & Porcelain*, London, 1959

JEWITT, L. *The Ceramic Art of Great Britain*, London and New York, 1878, revised, 1972

Newark Museum. *New Jersey Potteries 1685–1876*, New Jersey, 1914

Newark Museum. *The Pottery and Porcelain of New Jersey 1688–1900*, Newark, New Jersey, 1947

Philadelphia Museum of Art. *Tucker China 1825–38*, Philadelphia, 1957

RHEAD, G. W. and F. A. *Staffordshire Pots & Potters*, London, 1906

SANDON, H. *Royal Worcester Porcelain, from 1862 to the present day*, London, 1973

SCHWARTZ, MARVIN D., and WOLFE, RICHARD. *A History of American Art Porcelain*, New York, 1967

SHINN, C. and D. *The Illustrated Guide to Victorian Parian China*, London, 1971

SPARGO, JOHN. *Early American Pottery and China*, New York, 1926

State Museum of New Jersey. *The American Porcelain Tradition*, New Jersey, 1971

YOUNG, JENNIE J. *The Ceramic Art*, New York, 1878

Glass

BRITISH

The development of lead-crystal glass in the seventeenth century in England had a traumatic effect on the future of glass experimentation. The heavy, transparently clear and satisfyingly sonorous metal appealed to an increasingly large public, and more and more glass manufacturers turned to its production. The technique for decorating lead crystal involved faceting by deep criss-cross cuts, the fashion over the years leading to more intricate patterns. The popularity of cut lead crystal spread to the Netherlands, France and Bohemia, where factories were established to produce glass in the English style. By the early nineteenth century cut-glass techniques had ossified into traditional patterns.

New Styles and Techniques

The increasing wealth of the Victorian middle classes inspired a demand for more elaborate confections, and the flamboyant Bohemian techniques of glass cutting were adopted in England, the brilliant-cutting multiplicity of facets in a vase, decanter or bowl becoming the bowl-of-fire centre-piece of every fashionable table or sideboard.

In 1825, the Bakewell factory, of Pittsburgh, Pennsylvania, took out a patent for pressed glass. Within a few years a number of American and English firms had developed their own techniques. By pressing molten glass into a mould, it was possible to produce quickly and cheaply a reasonable facsimile of cut glass. Such glass is readily identifiable by the fact that it is less brilliantly reflective than cut lead crystal, the facets are rounded, not sharp, and a

OPPOSITE *Cameo plaque, George Woodall (1850-1925), late-nineteenth century. Translucent red glass overlaid in opaque white, diam. 18 in (45 cm). The plate is carved with the figures of Venus and Cupid. Sotheby & Co.*

central mould mark indicating the join is usually visible. The firms of Stevens & Williams Ltd, George Bacchus & Sons, Green & Gammon and Rice Harris & Son of Birmingham, as well as Apsley Pellatt of Blackfriars, in London, all pioneered this technique.

The decline of interest in cut glass between 1860 and 1880, after which there was a considerable revival, encouraged the production of press-moulded ornaments more suited to the technique than the sadly imitative vases. These ornaments often have considerable charm and some grace.

In the late 1840s cut glass was criticized by such eminent figures as Ruskin, who considered it to be a betrayal of the nature of the metal which was molten and fluid and hence it was barbarous to negate this by rigid planar patterns. The purists maintained that the only acceptable decoration should be on the surface and for this the ideal technique was wheel engraving, capable of sustaining the most elaborate designs, and involving great skill.

This method employed a shallow intaglio cut, minimal variations in depth producing fine effects of light and shading. The Neptune Jug is a famous example, as is Frederick Kny's Elgin Claret Jug inspired by a frieze of riders on horseback from the Elgin Marbles in the British Museum. A two-handled amphora, inspired by the same scene from the Marbles was made by John Northwood. Frederick Kny, at Thomas Webb & Sons, of Stourbridge, in Worcestershire, also created bowls and vases engraved and polished in imitation of Chinese rock-crystal carvings, as did Northwood for Stevens & Williams Ltd, another Stourbridge firm.

William Morris, who rejected everything that was elaborate or machine worked, encouraged Philip Webb to design a series of glasses for him. These were manufactured by James Powell & Sons, of Whitefriars, London, in 1860, and exhibited by Morris, Marshall,

Faulkner & Co. at the International Exhibition of 1862 in London; they were of great simplicity and purity of design. Powell, inspired by the Arts and Crafts Movement, produced fine hand-made glass until the end of the century.

Coloured and Fancy Glass

The Excise Act of 1745 imposed a tax of 9s 4d per hundredweight on materials used in the manufacture of glass. This meant that glassmakers had either to increase the price of the finished product or to reduce its size in order to use less glass. Increasingly, efforts were directed towards the surface or interior decoration of thin-walled glass. Metallic oxides were added to molten glass to give it colour; the surface was decorated by gilding or enamelling. Blue and green glass were produced in quantity in Bristol, while other factories in the Midlands and the North concentrated on popular, coloured wares for sale at country fairs. These included not only jugs, bottles and bowls, but also bells, rolling pins, walking sticks, pipes, candlesticks and toys, the latter often inaccurately attributed to the Nailsea factory. They are in flecked, striped or plain coloured glass and are often decorated with coloured pulled loops, stripes, spirals, or *latticino* patterns.

The repeal of the Excise Act in 1845, combined with the opportunities for showing off new wares in competition with those of other countries afforded by the great international exhibitions held throughout the second half of the nineteenth century, led to an explosion of productivity. Factories became increasingly concentrated around Stourbridge, Birmingham and Dudley, and mid-Victorian prosperity encouraged designers to migrate to these factories, which were producing numerous new patterns and styles. From 1845, Benjamin Richardson exhibited layered, opaline, and frosted vases overpainted in

TOP LEFT AND TOP RIGHT Punch *and* Judy, *John Derbyshire, Manchester,* c. 1875. *Press-moulded figures in colourless glass, ht 6¼ in (16 cm). Victoria and Albert Museum.*

TOP CENTRE *Well Spring Carafe, designed by Richard Redgrave R.A. for Henry Cole's Summerly's Art Manufactures, made by John Fell Christy, Stangate Glass Works, Lambeth, 1847. Clear glass decorated with enamels and gilt. Victoria and Albert Museum.*

ABOVE *Bell, Nailsea,* c. 1860. *Victoria and Albert Museum.*

RIGHT *Amphora, Francis Wollaston Moody,* c. 1860. *Clear glass with wheel-engraved decoration on a silverplated tripod base, ht 11½ in (29 cm). Victoria and Albert Museum.*

ABOVE CENTRE *Neptune Jug, blank possibly by W. H. & B. & J. Richardson,* c. 1850. *Clear glass with wheel-engraved decoration, ht 13¼ in (33 cm). Victoria and Albert Museum.*

ABOVE *Vase, Sowerby's Ellison Glassworks, Gateshead-on-Tyne, 1879. Press-moulded in opalescent glass, marked with peacock crest head, ht 3½ in (9 cm). Victoria and Albert Museum.*

Table service, designed by Philip Webb for William Morris, made by James Powell & Sons, 1859, embodying the purist principles of the Arts and Crafts Movement. Clear Glass. Victoria and Albert Museum.

enamel colours with Classical scenes. He called these vitrified enamel, and similar pieces were produced by George Bacchus & Sons. This technique was later used on clear glass, with elaborate enamel-painted and gilded decorations of leaves and flowers which are often very beautiful. Richard Redgrave, R.A., designed the very fine Well Spring Carafe for Henry Cole's Summerly's Art Manufactures in 1847.

Chinese Peach Bloom porcelain vases inspired Thomas Webb & Sons and Stevens & Williams Ltd to produce so-called Peach Bloom glass consisting of two glass layers, an outer one shading from a pale pink to deep red, and an inner one of pale cream, the outer surface being either polished or matt (using acid) and often gilded. Other glass was made in imitation of hardstones.

In 1885, the American Mt Washington Glass Co., of New Bedford, Massachusetts, patented an opaque single-layer type of glass which shaded from yellow to pink, and was made by fusing the glass with uranium oxide, fluorspar and feldspar. A set of glasses made by this technique and decorated with a floral pattern designed by Albert Steffin was presented to Queen Victoria and Prince Albert, and the design became known, inevitably, as Queen's Design. In 1886 Webb bought the licence to manufacture this ware in England, and re-named it Queen's Burmese. Decorated in a variety of patterns, sometimes with gilding, the surface is normally acid-finished. The decoration was usually carried out for Webb by the workshop of Jules Barbe. Variations include Bronze, Old Roman and Tricolour, all with some iridescence.

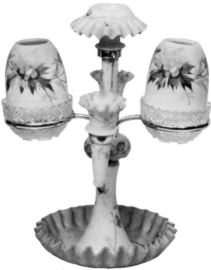

Fairy Pyramid, English, late-nineteenth century. Enamelled with flower sprays, with two shaded lights set in cut glass and three trumpet-shaped vases. A typical Victorian parlour lamp. Christie's.

Curious silvered vases were also produced. Frederick Hale Thompson and Edward Varnish, of E. Varnish & Co., patented a decorative process in 1849 in which double-walled glassware, somewhat similar in shape to a vacuum flask, was silvered on the inside and layered on the outside with coloured glass which could then be cut intaglio to produce contrasting coloured and silvered patterns. An almost identical process was patented a year later by Thompson and Thomas Robert Mellish. Most of the blanks were manufactured by James Powell & Sons, of Whitefriars, London, and both E. Varnish & Co. and Thomas Mellish produced a variety of such vases, which are sometimes found marked with the name of the retailer, such as W. Lund. Mellish exhibited his cut-silvered and coloured glass at the Great Exhibition of 1851.

In 1878 Paul Raoul de Facheux d'Humy patented a method of blowing a glass vessel, whereby he coated it in silver or gold foil and then blew it up to full size inside an outer layer of glass. This resulted in splitting the foil to give the glass a crackled, decorative appearance. In the same year the French Pantin Glass Works patented a similar process in England. In 1900, John Northwood II devised a layered glass with enclosed silver foil in which the inner vessel was blown virtually to full size before being coated with the foil; it was then dipped into fluid glass for the outer, transparent layer and finally coloured glass trailings were dripped over the surface of the piece. The outer layer was allowed to split and the air bubbles to explode, portions of the enclosed foil being exposed to the atmosphere so becoming oxidized and discoloured. This spectacular if somewhat sinister pattern was called Silveria and was produced by Stevens & Williams Ltd.

New types of glass were also introduced. One such is Moss Agate glass which has a streaked, multi-coloured appearance and was also made by Stevens & Williams Ltd. Similar glass was produced in the United States by the Steuben Glass Co., whose co-founder, Frederick Carder, had been a leading designer for Stevens & Williams Ltd and in France, by Rousseau and Leveillé. Another variant is Clutha glass, an old Scottish word meaning cloudy – a glass which is bubbled and streaked throughout. Made by James Couper & Sons, in Glasgow, the majority of the pieces were designed by Dr Christopher Dresser or George Walton.

Dresser was one of the most forward looking of the commercial designers of the period and an important art theorist, turning his hand to a variety of products including metalwork and ceramics for the Linthorpe Pottery in Middlesbrough. His glass shapes are based on simple, antique models, sometimes of floral inspiration. Though often clumsy and primitive, at their best they have a sturdy honesty that anticipates the development of modern glass after 1920. Webb's launched a similar line, Old Roman, which raised fierce opposition from Couper's, who considered it to be a deliberate imitation of Clutha.

In 1857, Benjamin Richardson patented a process for manufacturing pearl satin glass by blowing into a mould which produced hollows in the surface, then coating the surface with another layer. The air traps between the layers provided the decoration. Variations of this technique were patented in the United States. One such patent was taken out by Mt Washington Glass Works and licensed to Thomas Webb & Sons. A similar glass called Verre de Soie was produced by Stevens & Williams Ltd. The pearly, slightly iridescent surface in various colours generally had a diamond or *moiré* pattern which in later pieces was often decorated with glass applications. In 1889, Thomas Webb & Sons patented a process by which an additional opaque outer layer of glass was added and then cut away to produce a cameo relief design (see colour plate p. 173).

In 1876, William J. Hodgetts, of Hodgetts, Richardson & Sons, Wordsley, patented a machine enabling glass threads to be applied to glass objects. Similar machines were patented by other firms, one of the most advanced being devised by John Northwood in 1885. These machines enabled glass not only to be decorated on the surface, but also to have the glass threads sunk into the metal to give a smooth decorated look. Examples of these patterns include *Moiré* and Tartan glass (different combinations of coloured glass threads arranged into plaid patterns manufactured by the Wordsley Flint Glassworks and other firms); Jewell glass (in which the applied threads were combed into various patterns by blowing into a ribbed mould) registered by Stevens & Williams Ltd in 1886; and Tapestry ware, for which a regularly threaded glass vessel was painted in enamels to simulate tapestry. It was first made by Stevens & Williams Ltd in the 1890s, the decoration in many instances being by Oscar Pierre Erard. Glass threads were also used in the manufacture of intricate novelty objects, such as models of ships, which were so delicate that they were displayed under glass bells.

Cameo Glass

The Victorian revival of cameo glass was directly attributable to the notoriety surrounding the Portland Vase. This was a first century A.D. Roman amphora which had been purchased from the Palazzo Barberini, in Rome, and sold to Sir William Hamilton, the British Ambassador to the court of Naples, for £1,000. Sir William had then resold the vase for £1,800 to the Duchess of Portland. Soon after this purchase, the careless Duchess of Gordon damaged the vase, which was later loaned to the British Museum. In 1845, a young man entered the museum and succeeded in smashing the vase into more than 200 fragments. By a quirk of the law he could only be prosecuted for damage to the case in which the vase had been exhibited, thus he was fined only £3. Fortunately, the Scot who had originally bought the vase had had some sixty copies of it made from a mould before selling it to Sir William Hamilton. One of the copies was used as a model in the restoration of the original by John Doubleday.

Vase, Thomas Webb & Sons, late nineteenth century. Green glass overlaid in white, encased in green and decorated with a cameo relief of a mermaid teasing a fish in a marine setting. Christie's.

Josiah Wedgwood had made a famous copy of the Portland Vase in stoneware, so that it was associated in the popular mind with pottery. Now, suddenly, it was realised that the deep blue amphora with a white frieze of Classical figures was actually a two-layered glass vase with carved decoration. Some years before the incident, Apsley Pellatt had produced an imitation of cameo glass, which he called *crystallo-ceramie* or cameo incrustations, in which the glass vessel was decorated with Classical profiles and other motifs made of ceramic paste embedded in the glass. The craftsmen of Stourbridge were now encouraged to experiment with true cameo work. Benjamin Richardson, who pioneered so many of the new directions in glassmaking techniques in the nineteenth century made a dramatic offer of £1,000 to the first craftsman able to copy the Portland Vase in cameo glass. The prize was won some years later by John Northwood.

Born in Wordsley, John Northwood was twelve years old when he became an apprentice at the Richardson firm after being a prize pupil at the Stourbridge School of Art. He acquired a thorough grounding in glass – painting, enamelling, etching and all other aspects of glass manufacture and decoration, later designing several tools and devising new processes which were widely adopted. Temperamentally, he was greatly drawn to Neoclassicism and admired such artists as John Flaxman, so that when he began to experiment with elaborate decoration on glass, it was to Classical design that he turned for inspiration. His first essay in cameo glass was completed by 1860, a small vase depicting Perseus rescuing Andromeda from the dragon, but this was accidently smashed some years later.

In about 1861, John Northwood set up the decorating workshop of J. & J. Northwood with his brother Joseph, gathering around him men who were to become some of the finest glass craftsmen of their time. In 1864 Northwood was commissioned by J. B. Stone to produce the Elgin Vase, a clear glass amphora decorated in intaglio. He completed this vase in 1873, and Stone presented it to the City of Birmingham Art Gallery. In 1873 Philip Pargeter, of the Red House Glassworks and a cousin of Northwood, commissioned him to carve a replica of the Portland Vase. Three years later the vase was completed, and Northwood had won Richardson's prize. The vase was displayed on R. P. Daniell's Stand at the Paris Exhibition of 1878.

Two other Northwood cameo vases were displayed at the 1878 Exhibition: the unfinished Pegasus, or Dennis Vase, commissioned by Thomas Wilkes Webb, director of the Dennis Glassworks (a subsidiary of Thomas Webb & Sons) and exhibited on the Webb Stand; and the Milton Vase, an amphora depicting a scene from *Paradise Lost*, the expulsion

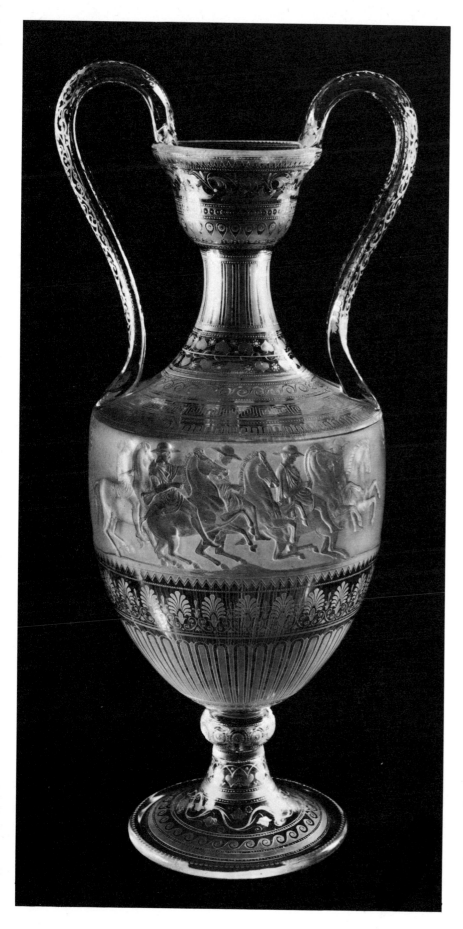

of Adam and Eve from the Garden of Eden by the Archangel Michael, displayed on J. G. Green's stand.

The Pegasus Vase was Northwood's last great cameo piece. Begun in 1876, it won a Gold Medal at the Paris Exhibition in its unfinished state, and was only completed in 1882, when it was sold to Tiffany & Co. of New York. After some time in Mrs Pierpont Morgan's collection, it eventually found its way to the National Collection of Fine Arts at the Smithsonian Institution, Washington, in 1929. The firm of J. & J. Northwood increasingly carried out decorating work for Stevens & Williams Ltd, John Northwood eventually becoming art director of that firm and training what was to become one of the great teams of glass craftsmen. The team included his son John Northwood II, who later became director and technical manager for Stevens & Williams Ltd; his nephew, William Northwood, who won a national bronze medal in 1889; Joshua Hodgetts, who specialized in floral decoration and also produced cameo-style work on engraved crystal, and Frederick Carder, who emigrated to the United States in 1903 and there co-founded the Steuben Glassworks at Corning, New York.

The Stourbridge firm of Hodgetts, Richardson & Co. also exhibited cameo glass at the 1878 Exhibition in Paris. They had brought the French sculptor and medallist Alphonse Eugène Lechevrel to Wordsley in 1877 to train their workmen, and he too worked in a Classical idiom, with the vases *Raising an Altar to Bacchus, Hercules Restoring Alcestis to her Husband, The Birth of Venus* and *Venus Rising from the Sea.* Lechevrel's most able pupil was Joseph Locke who carved a second copy of the Portland Vase, which was awarded a Gold Medal at the 1878 Paris Exhibition. Locke later worked for Philip Pargeter and then for Webb & Corbetts, before emigrating to the United States, where he developed several types of glass for the New England Glass Co., of East Cambridge, Massachusetts, examples of which include Pomona, Agata and Amberina.

The Woodall team probably constitute the most celebrated of the cameo workshops. George Woodall and his brother Thomas received a thorough grounding in all aspects of glass decoration, first from their uncle, Thomas Bott, a former Richardson employee who had moved

Elgin Vase, John Northwood, commissioned in 1864, completed in 1873. Clear glass decorated in intaglio. Northwood employed some of the finest glass craftsmen. Birmingham City Museum & Art Gallery.

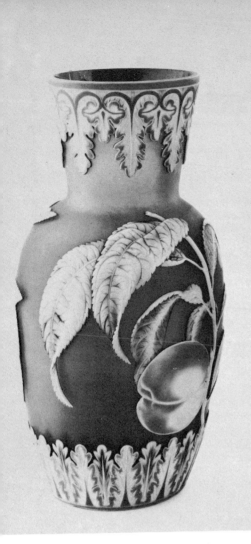

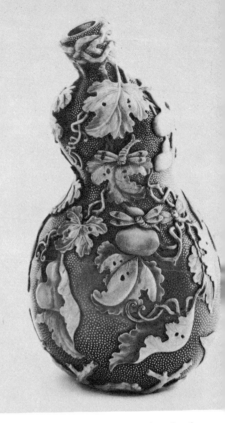

to the Worcester Porcelain factory, then at the Stourbridge School of Design and finally from John Northwood. Thomas Wilkes Webb hired the brothers for Thomas Webb & Sons in about 1894, later sending George to tour the glassworks of Europe and to study at the South Kensington Museum and Art School. The Woodalls, together and separately, worked on plaques and vases, and assembled a superb team which included Daniel and Lionel Pearce, J. T. Fereday and William Fritsche. George Woodall was a consummate craftsman, who tempered his Classicism with a tempestuous Romanticism very close in mood to the paintings of the Pre-Raphaelite Brotherhood.

Cameo glass is made by blowing a sandwich of two or more layers of glass called the blank, then partially removing the outer layer or layers to reveal the different coloured glass beneath, and using these combinations of colour to form the design decorating the surface. To do this, the intended design was first roughed out on the surface of the blanks, those portions of the outer layer to be retained being coated in a resin resist. The blank was then placed in a solution of hydrofluoric acid for a predetermined

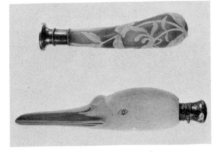

TOP LEFT *Cameo vase, English. Four-colour cameo vase in olive-green glass decorated in triple overlay with carved peach sprigs, the stalks and leaves in opaque white, ht 10½ in (27 cm).* TOP CENTRE *Cameo vase, designed by George Woodall for Thomas Webb & Sons. Velvet-blue glass overlaid in opaque white and dark blue, ht 12 in (30 cm).* TOP RIGHT *Cameo double-gourd vase, carved in the Chinese style by F. Kretschman and coloured by Jules Barbe. Ht 9 in (23 cm). Sotheby & Co.*

ABOVE *Cameo seal in the shape of a powder flask (*TOP*) and Cameo scent bottle in the shape of a duck's head, English, glass with silver mounts. Ht of scent bottles 4½ in (12 cm) and 5¾ in (15 cm) Sotheby & Co.*

time. Once this was completed, the craftsman would carve the decoration in relief using minute metal rods and chisels, often made to his own design. By placing a layer of clear glass over one of dark glass and then thinning it, it became possible to model and highlight the design. Since the decorative process was always complex and time consuming and made great demands on the ability, technique and patience of the craftsman, the cameo items which were produced tended to be rare and costly, and were usually commissioned exhibition pieces.

The originality and sober magnificence of cameo glass by comparison with the gaudy excesses of Victorian decorated coloured glass, made it highly desirable to the rich and it became virtually impossible to satisfy the demand. George Woodall responded by introducing some simplification and standardization. Simpler designs, mostly of a stylized floral nature were devised, thinner glass layers were used so that less effort was needed to obtain the relief; acid was employed increasingly in the forming of the pattern and it was George Woodall himself who pioneered the use of the engraving-wheel to aid in the carving.

Individual cameo items are often found

signed by the decorator although several people sometimes worked on a single item. Cameos decorated by the Woodall team are usually signed Webb's Gem Cameo. The lack of a signature is not very important as each of the great Stourbridge craftsmen probably worked for several firms in his lifetime.

In 1887, Webb patented a new form of cameo which simulated carved ivory. The vessel was made of an opaque ivory-coloured glass which was etched and engraved with the design in shallow relief, then rubbed with a brownish stain which darkened the recesses. This technique greatly appealed to Queen Victoria, who purchased the first ivory

cameo vases which were produced, and they later became very popular. Another shallow technique used was *dolce-rilievo*. Here a transparent, coloured outer layer was etched away leaving shallow highlights over a white or ivory ground. In 1899 Webb launched a new line of carved crystal engraving which was similar to cameo, but lacked the contrast of colour.

In addition to the figurative scenes and floral designs, vases and plaques were produced in imitation of Peking glass, as well as Chien Lung designs. The padding technique was sometimes used, in which blobs of coloured glass were applied and then carved as flowers, fruit

or fish. Depictions varied from Classical scenes to such modern ones as horse races, or the stunning Antarctic Vase by George Woodall, carved in 1912 to commemorate Scott's ill-fated expedition.

Individual craftsmen continued to produce fine cameo glass into the 1920s but the great demand for it disappeared with the First World War. Ludwig Kny, at Webb's, designed some acid-etched items in transparent coloured glass over an etched crystal ground in the Art Nouveau style, but these never became popular.

Victor Arwas

AMERICAN

The First Art Glasses

Silvered glass (sometimes called mercury glass) and opal glass, as opaque white or 'milk' glass was called by glassmakers, may be considered as the first art glasses, or as forerunners of the later, more elaborate art glasses. In England, several methods for producing silvered glass, which consists of a double-walled glass vessel whose interior wall is coated with a mercury deposit, were developed in the 1840s, but the process discovered by Hale Thompson in about 1850 proved the most practical and successful. E. Varnish & Co. of London produced a number of fine glasses of this type, sometimes cased and cut, at the time of the Great Exhibition in London in 1851.

The process spread rapidly to America. Thomas Leighton, who came from England in 1826 to become superintendent of the New England Glass Works in East Cambridge, near Boston, was granted a United States patent for silvering glass door knobs on 16 January 1855. The company, however, produced silvered glass before that date, for it exhibited 200 such door knobs (claimed by Leighton to 'possess the colour and lustre of polished silver, without liability to tarnish') at the New York Crystal Palace Exhibition of 1853. Among their other exhibits were:
Three plated glass goblets, cut and silvered
One glass globe on foot, plated, cut and silvered

One glass pyramid plated, cut and silvered
One large silvered glass bowl on foot, very richly engraved.

Bohemian influence, which was first exerted on American glass in about 1850 or 1851, is evident in the grape and vine engraving on a compote which is a counterpart of, or may actually be, the engraved and silvered glass bowl on foot exhibited at the Crystal Palace in New York City. Obviously, their production of silvered glass was well developed before Leighton received his patent.

Silvered glassware proved to be popular and in great demand. It was produced by numerous other companies, including the Boston & Sandwich Glass Co., of Sandwich, Cape Cod, Massachusetts, which was noted in 1871 as being the largest producer of this type of glass in the country; the Mt Washington Glass Co., of New Bedford, Massachusetts; the Union Glass Co. of Somerville, Massachusetts; the Dithridge Flint Glass Works, at Martins Ferry, Ohio, and later New Brighton, Pennsylvania; and the Boston Silver Glass Co., which specialized in silvered glass. As in Britain, some of it was cased or plated, especially by ruby-coloured glass and then cut and engraved. It seems to have been less frequently, if ever, enamelled in America. The production of silvered glass continued until about the end of the nineteenth century, when art glass went out of fashion.

When the first opal glass was made and decorated is less certain, but production

Art glass – colourful, ornate, often appearing to be something other than glass – was an effusive expression of the late Victorian era, as popular in the United States as in Britain. It resulted chiefly from two factors: the taste of the day and technological developments, which included a greater knowledge of the chemistry of glass and improved melting techniques.

British and Bohemian styles and decorative techniques exerted a strong influence on the development of art glass in the United States. Bohemian colour technology, which, along with fine engraving and cutting, resulted in that country's dominance of the glass industry in the mid-nineteenth century, was the technical basis for art glass. Following the repeal of the Excise Tax in 1845, which resulted in a renaissance of glassmaking in Britain, British glassmakers fully exploited this technology. Within a short time, much of this knowledge and many of these influences were brought to America by glassmakers migrating from Britain as well as from Bohemia and Germany. In addition, importation of glass from Bohemia and Britain also exerted a strong influence upon the development of decorative glass in America. Despite these influences and the difficulty of distinguishing the origins of some art glasses, American glassmakers developed a number of singular and distinctive glasses in this style which were in the height of fashion in the late Victorian period.

157

of this type of glassware was well established by 1870, and it was probably begun in the early 1850s. Among other glasswares listed as part of the New England Glass Co.'s exhibition at the New York City Crystal Palace were 'smoke bells, richly decorated and gilded'. These were undoubtedly of opal glass. To a large degree, the form and style of decoration on opal glasses was strongly influenced by the similar wares made by W. H. & B. & J. Richardson & Co., of Birmingham, England. William L. Smith, who worked for twelve years as a glass decorator in Birmingham before coming to America in 1851 to set up and manage a decorating shop at the Boston & Sandwich Glass Works, was undoubtedly familiar with their products. At Sandwich, he gilded and enamelled lamps in the 1850s before moving to Boston to set up his own shop. He taught his two sons, Alfred E. and Harry A. Smith the decorating trade, in which they subsequently played an important rôle at the Mt Washington Glass Works, in New Bedford, Massachusetts, and later in their own business.

Decorated Art Glass

In 1871 William L. Libbey, agent for the Mt Washington Glass Works, established a decorating department there, indicating a growing demand, or an anticipation of such a demand, for decorated glass. He engaged the Smith brothers to operate this shop, which they did, starting with eight or ten workmen. Two years earlier, decorated cone shades had been introduced and continued to be in great demand. The decorating department there was a success from the outset.

In 1874, the Smith brothers leased the shop from the Mt Washington Glass Works and worked there for several more years until they moved their operations to 28-30 William Street, New Bedford. They decorated a wide variety of tablewares, vases and lampshades, obtaining some of their blanks from the Mt Washington Glass Works but also importing some from abroad. Their display of decorated glass at the Centennial Exposition in Philadelphia in 1876 aroused great interest, and they received awards for their work. A photograph of their exhibit at an unidentified exposi-

Compote, probably New England Glass Co., c. 1850. Engraved silvered glass, ht 18¼ in (48 cm). Elaborately engraved with a vine and grape motif, this compote demonstrates the new Bohemian influence. Corning Museum of Glass.

TOP *Contemporary photograph of Smith Bros display of decorated glass at an unknown trade exposition, probably* c. *1885. The Smith family pioneered decorated glass in America. Mrs Frank McKenzie Collection.*

ABOVE *Two vases and sugar sifter, decorated by the Smith Bros, 1875-90. Opal glass. The firm introduced the decorated 'ring' vase which became popularly known as the Smith vase. Corning Museum of Glass.*

tion or trade fair illustrates the diversity and scope of their work. A sugar sifter is characteristic of the delicacy and quality of their decorations, which included a wide variety of flowers, birds and natural settings. They introduced the decorated 'ring' vase which became popularly

known as the Smith vase. Relatively few pieces of their work are signed. When they are, they bear either a rust-red shield enclosing a rampant lion, or simply the name Smith Bros.

Advertisements of the Mt Washington firm of 1875 and 1877 and later continued to offer for sale, among other things, opal ware and decorated goods. Other firms were also producing these wares during this period. Stereoscopic views of the New England Glass Co.'s showrooms, dating from about 1875, show large quantities of opal decorated glass. Many of the forms indicate both British and Bohemian influences and many of these pieces were handpainted, although some were decorated by means of transfer prints and decalcomania.

Among the earliest of the art-glass wares, other than silvered glass or decorated opal glass, was Lava glass.

Frederick Shirley, an Englishman, who became agent of the Mt Washington Glass Works in 1874 and who was largely responsible for the predominance of the company in the art-glass field, was granted a patent for this glass on 28 May 1878. Little of it exists today, and its rarity suggests that it was either difficult to make or was so unpopular that little was produced. Essentially, it was a glass with a dark, almost black body brought about by the use of volcanic lava in the batch (or a substitute for it), decorated with insets of coloured glasses in either a haphazard or a predetermined pattern. A second patent dated 30 September 1879, covered this type of decoration which was also developed by Shirley.

Coloured Art Glass

One of the earlier and most successful art glasses was Amberina, developed and patented by Joseph Locke of the New England Glass Co. on 24 July 1883. It is a transparent glass shading from a light amber colour at the base to a ruby-red or fuchsia colour at the top. In addition to this subtle shading, caused by a thermal reaction to the gold oxide in the batch, the many forms produced in this bi-partite coloured glass are almost always further decorated by pattern moulding. Amberina proved to be such a success that it was copied and produced by the Mt Washington Glass Co. A threatened lawsuit was amicably settled when this firm agreed to call its products Rose Amber. Advertisements and catalogues of the Company show, however, that at least occasionally, it continued to use the name Amberina, or Rose Amberina. Regardless of terminology, it is difficult to distinguish today between the products of these two glasshouses.

The development and production of other bi-partite coloured glasses followed quickly upon the success of Amberina. Chief among them was Burmese glassware patented by Frederick Shirley on 15 December 1885. This is, in effect, an opal glass coloured by oxides of uranium and gold in the batch. The uranium produces a delicate lemon-yellow colour while the gold causes those parts of the piece which are reheated during the manufacturing process to 'strike' and turn to a salmon-pink colour. This glass was produced with a natural or 'glossy' finish, and a matt, acid-finished surface. The latter type, referred to by collectors as 'satin' finish, was termed 'plush' in the Mt Washington Glass Co.'s catalogues.

Burmese proved to be very popular. Its commercial success was certainly due in a large measure to Shirley's business acumen. Among other promotional efforts, he sent a present of Burmese glassware to Queen Victoria and Princess Beatrice, bearing enamelled decorations he named the Queen's Pattern. After acknowledging her pleasure through her secretary, Queen Victoria ordered a tea-set of Burmese. Subsequently, Thomas Webb & Sons, a noted English glass-making firm in the Stourbridge district, was licensed by the Mt Washington Glass Co. to produce Burmese glass-ware. This glass is always marked with an acid stamp: 'Thos. Webb & Sons, Queen's Burmese Ware, Patented'. The Mt Washington Co.'s Burmese ware was never marked except with paper labels.

Shirley also promoted this glass by presenting the wife of President Cleveland with a pair of Burmese vases. The popularity of this glass is indicated by the fact that more than 250 forms appear in the Company's printed catalogue and price list, to which additions were later made. A portion of the wide variety of forms – some inspired by the Far East, some derived almost directly from Classical shapes and others which can only be described as Victorian – may be seen in two catalogue photographs of Burmese.

Peach Blow, an opaque glass shading from a light pinkish white to a deep bluish pink was another product of the

Mt Washington Glass Co., for which a trademark was filed on 20 July 1886. Based upon the lesser quantities which exist today, this glass seems to have been less commercially successful than Burmese. Nevertheless, it was closely imitated by the New England Glass Co., which, after an infringement was charged by the makers of Peach Blow, agreed to call their product Wild Rose. This bipartite glass shaded from a delicate light pink at the base to a much deeper pink at the top of the object. It, too, was produced with glossy and matt surfaces, both of which were sometimes enamelled and gilded.

A variation of Wild Rose, patented on 18 January 1887 by Joseph Locke and produced by the New England Glass Co., again made in apparently limited quantities, was Agata. This was simply

Wild Rose decorated by applying a metallic stain to the surface, then splashing it with a volatile solution such as naptha, benzene or alcohol. When this liquid evaporated, it left the surface with a mottled effect, which was then made permanent by heating it in a kiln, or muffle. This same type of stained decoration is found, but even less frequently, on opaque light-green glass, usually confined to the rim of the object.

Cased, Crackle and Spangled Glass

The most successful of the Peach Blows was that produced by Hobbs, Brockunier & Co., of Wheeling, West Virginia. It was termed Coral by them, and produced in a wide variety of forms, with

RIGHT *Burmese glass, patented by Frederick S. Shirley, 15 December 1885. The success of Burmese glassware in America was largely due to Shirley's commercial enterprise. Smithsonian Institution.*

Agata glass, patented by Joseph Locke, 18 January 1887 and made at the New England Glass Co. until 1888. Diam of centre bowl 5¼ in (13 cm). Corning Museum of Glass.

both glossy and matt finishes. Unlike the Mt Washington Peach Blow and the New England Glass Co.'s Wild Rose, which were homogeneous glasses, Coral was made by casing or plating opaque white glass with a thin layer of transparent, heat-sensitive glass which shaded from a deep amber at the base to a rich orangey-red at the top. The best-known form of Coral or Wheeling Peach Blow, as it is commonly called by collectors today, is the Morgan Vase. It was designed after the Chinese porcelain vase in the collection of the late Mrs Pierpont Morgan, which was sold on 8 March 1886 for the astounding sum of $18,000, a fact which aroused much public interest and awe. Undoubtedly, this had much to do with the successful sale of Coral glassware.

A product closely related to Coral glassware is Plated Amberina, patented on 15 June 1886, by Edward D. Libbey of the New England Glass Co. and produced by them only until 1888, when Libbey moved the works to Toledo, Ohio. Again an opal glass was plated with a transparent, heat-sensitive amber glass containing gold which 'struck' when re-heated to produce a rich ruby colour. Despite their production by the same method, Plated Amberina and Coral glass each have distinctive shaded colourings; the former is much rarer than the latter.

A number of other art glasses were made by Hobbs, Brockunier & Co., between 1882 and 1891. Among them were crackle or ice glass, spangled glass and a variety of baskets and vases of different forms of coloured glasses with elaborate applied decorations, usually of glass of another colour, often representing clinging limbs, vines, fruit and flowers. Such glasses closely parallel English examples of the same era.

Pressed and Satin Glass

The same firm also produced colourful and ornamental pressed glass during this period, for example a type called Rubina Verde which shades from a yellowish green to a ruby red, and was achieved by laying a band of red glass partially over the green, then pressing it or blowing the gather into a mould to form the object. This Company also made various coloured glasses, termed satin or mother-of-pearl satin glass by collectors.

These satin glasses were also made by other firms in America, as well as in England, and it is usually impossible to distinguish their origins. Several pieces of this type of glass were presented to the Smithsonian Institution, Washing-

ton, in 1888 by the manufacturer, the Phoenix Glass Co. of Monaca, near Pittsburgh, Pennsylvania. Their quality compares favourably with English examples of the period, as well as with pieces attributed to the Mt Washington Glass Co., which was granted a trademark for such glass under the name of pearl satin ware and which licensed Thomas Webb & Sons to produce this glass in England.

Other glasshouses in America which produced satin glass include the Boston & Sandwich Glass Co. and the Cape Cod Glass Works, both located in Sandwich, Massachusetts, though few specifically identified pieces can be traced to either factory. Nevertheless, quantities of fragments dug up at their sites attest to this type of production. Both factories also made several other varieties of art glass.

Mechanically threaded glass, most frequently of transparent pink or amber colour, and often engraved, was apparently a major product of the Boston & Sandwich Glass Co. in its later years. Its catalogue also indicates the production of a variety of frosted glass, called crackle, overshot or ice glass today.

The Cape Cod Glass Works, established by the well-known glassmaker Deming Jarves in 1858 after he left the Boston & Sandwich Glass Co., produced primarily pressed glassware until it closed at the time of his death in 1869. Subsequently Dr Flower organized the Vasa Murrhina Art Glass Co. for the manufacture of variegated coloured glasses. He leased and reopened the inactive Cape Cod Glass Works to produce his glass, though his headquarters was in Hartford, Connecticut. Again, few pieces of this glass can be definitely identified as products of this firm, but thousands of fragments of it have been found on the factory site. They are usually thick, of several layers of different coloured glass, frequently with inclu-

LEFT *Morgan Vase and stand, Hobbs, Brockunier & Co., 1885-91. Coral or Wheeling Peach Blow, ht 9⅞ in (25 cm). One of the most successful of the Peach Blows was produced by this company. Corning Museum of Glass.*

BELOW LEFT *Craquelle or ice-glass pitcher, Hobbs, Brockunier & Co., 1882-91. Amber-coloured glass. This company produced a number of art glasses closely parallel to English examples of the same period. Oglebay Mansion House Museum.*

Covered chalice or large goblet and pitcher, Boston & Sandwich Glass Co., 1870-88. Colourless glass decorated with applied threads of ruby coloured glass, ht of pitcher 8 in (20 cm). Private Collection.

sions of mica, aventurine and pieces of multi-coloured glass. Another type known to have been made there has a deep brownish-red interior covered with streaks and flecks of deep-red, white and pale-blue glasses, encased by colourless glass. A vase of this type, along with fragments found at the site of the Cape Cod Glass factory, is attributable to this firm, which closed in 1882.

The Mt Washington Glass Co.

In May 1882, the Farrall Venetian Art Glass Manufacturing Co. was established in Brooklyn, New York, to manufacture Vasa Murrhina. This glass incorporated gold or silver leaf, or granules of these two metals, as well as various coloured glasses within the body of the piece. The Reading Art Glass Co. in Reading, Pennsylvania, also produced at least a limited amount of art glass during the period of its operations in the late nineteenth century. But it was the Mt Washington Glass Co., which claimed in its advertisement to be 'Headquarters in America for Art Glass Wares', that was the major producer of this type of glass in the United States.

In addition to the art glasses already noted as part of its production, it produced many other richly decorated wares. Among them were Albertine, Crown Milano, Ivory Decorated glass, Royal Flemish, Cameo glass, Napoli glass and a wide variety of opal decorated glasses, some in the form of novelties such as eggs and tomatoes. The latter were used as salt and pepper shakers and sugar sifters and as *bonbonnières* and marmalade jars, respectively. Many of these art glasses were made to fit ornate silverplated (electroplated) stands or the baskets which were so popular in the late nineteenth century, or, as biscuit and marmalade jars, were fitted with silverplated rims and covers. The Mt Washington Glass Works which became the Mt Washington Glass Company in 1876, produced many of these glasses for the Pairpoint Manufacturing Co., a silverplating firm established next door to it in 1880. In 1894 the two firms merged, the glassworks becoming a subsidiary of the Pairpoint firm. Many of the art glasses made by the Mt Washington glasshouse appear in Pairpoint

catalogues but their glass was also widely used by other silverplating companies, such as Reed & Barton and the Meriden Silver Plating Co.

It is often difficult to distinguish some of the opaque decorated glasses made by this company from one another. In fact, in some instances, the same glasses and designs are offered for sale by the Company under different names, such as Ivory Decorated glass and Crown Milano. The latter name also seems to have been a new term applied to what had earlier been called Albertine glass. To further confuse the issue, some pieces are marked, while the majority are not. Though trademarks were received for some of these glasses, they are not always meaningful with regard to the initial production of that particular type of glass. For example, trademarks for Crown Milano and Royal Flemish glass were issued in January 1893 and on 27 February 1894, respectively, yet both products were advertised in the *Crockery and Glass Journal* as early as 1889.

Royal Flemish glass is much more readily distinguishable than the opaque decorated glasses from this firm. It is a colourless glass which usually has a thin, almost transparent, stained background, on which is superimposed a design, often gilded, in fairly high relief. Many pieces of Royal Flemish glass are characterized by both exotic forms and decorations, whose origins are often based upon Far Eastern designs. Napoli glass is also a colourless glass, but its background is usually not stained and its enamelled and gilded decoration is applied partly to the interior and partly to the exterior of the vessel. A patent granted to Albert Steffin dated 22 May 1894 describes this manner of decoration but does not name it. In view of its rarity, it apparently was produced only

TOP *Cameo berry bowl on silverplated stand, Mt Washington Glass Co., c. 1885. Opal glass with pink glass casing decorated with griffins made with stencils, resist and acid immersion, width 8 in (20 cm). Corning Museum of Glass.*

CENTRE *Bottle, Mt Washington Glass Co., c. 1889-95. Royal Flemish glass, ht 13 in (33 cm). A characteristic piece of Royal Flemish glass, the exotic decoration being based on Far Eastern design. Corning Museum of Glass.*

LEFT *Lamp and shade, marked on both parts, Tiffany Studio, New York, late nineteenth century. Copper and stained glass, the domed shade with a border of lotus foliage, the body of conical form. Christie's.*

OPPOSITE *Cracker jar, signed on the base 'Napoli', Mt Washington Glass Co., c. 1894. Silverplated mounts, enamelled and gilded decoration partly on the interior and partly on the exterior. Private Collection.*

in limited quantities. Another appealing art glass decorated by acid etching and staining is Pomona glass, first patented by Joseph Locke on 28 April 1885, and produced in quantity by the New England Glass Co. until 1888. A second patent for a less expensive method of producing this glass was granted to Locke on 15 June 1886.

The art of carving cameo glass, which was highly developed by luxury glass-makers during the Roman Empire, was revived in Britain in the 1860s by such artists as John Northwood and Joseph Locke, each of whom made a copy of the famous Portland Vase. Cameo glass was greatly admired and became much in demand in Britain, despite the painstaking efforts and time required to produce it and its comparatively high cost. With the exception of a few pieces made by Joseph Locke after he came to the United States and a limited number of pieces made by the Gillinder Co., true cameo glass was not produced in America, but cameo glass, more or less mass-produced by using stencils and acid, was made and advertised by the Mt Washington Glass Co. The decorative motifs were often of a pseudo-Classical nature, and most of the pieces consisted of a delicate pink glass cased over opaque white glass, but examples were also made of light blue and a delicate yellow cased over white glass.

The heyday of art glass was from about 1880 to 1895 – the height of the late Victorian era in America. Its production declined rapidly after that time; in part, because several of the major producers of this glass went out of business, but primarily because of changing taste and styles. Art Nouveau glass was emerging as the new art glass, and the dazzling cut glass of the brilliant period – with which art glass shared the stage for almost a decade – became even more popular as the turn of the century approached.

Kenneth M. Wilson

Designers and Manufacturers

GEORGE BACCHUS & SONS
Birmingham firm, known by this name after 1840, associated with the manufacture of PRESSED GLASS in the 1830s in England. Leading producers of CASED, OPALESCENT and vitrified ENAMEL glassware in the mid-nineteenth century, the firm specialized in decanters and urn-shaped vases, exhibiting skilled CUTTING, ENGRAVING and GILDING techniques, and in MILLEFIORI paperweights, first made there in 1848. The catalogue of the Great Exhibition records the profusion of styles, colours and techniques already mastered by the firm in 1851.

BAKEWELL, PEARS & CO.
One of longest active American glasshouses, known by this name after 1836 and previously by the names of its other proprietors, and commercially successful manufacturer of FLINT GLASS in the United States. The firm was also a pioneer of machine-PRESSED GLASS in 1825 and by the late 1830s had a reputation for every type and article of glassware. Its mid-nineteenth-century experiments in colour and design presaged later ART GLASS processes.

BARBE, JULES
Noted enameller and gilder, Barbe spent twenty-one years at the Dennis Glassworks before joining the WOODALL team at THOMAS WEBB & SONS. Here he achieved special decorative effects in CAMEO and gold on CAMEO GLASS and also specialized in the decoration of Queen's BURMESE.

BOSTON & SANDWICH GLASS CO.
Founded in 1825 at Cape Cod, Massachusetts, the firm was one of the largest and most famous American glasshouses and an immediate success under the management of JARVES. A major award-winning producer of PRESSED GLASS for over sixty years, they also manufactured free-blown, MOULDED, CUT and ENGRAVED glass. In the 1850s and '60s they produced many CASED or PLATED wares in the Bohemian style, especially for lamp fonts. The Company was also noted for its large-scale production of SILVERED, SATIN, CRACKLE and THREADED glassware in the 1870s. In 1888 the Company was forced to close under pressure from Mid Western competitors and striking glassblowers.

BOSTON SILVER GLASS CO.
Established by A. E. Young at Cambridge, Massachusetts, in 1857, the Company was in operation until at least 1871. The firm specialized in SILVERED-GLASS and FLINT-GLASS tableware and lamps.

CAPE COD GLASS WORKS
Well-equipped, small fifty-man company, founded in 1858 by JARVES at Sandwich, Massachusetts, its site and personnel being closely linked with the BOSTON & SANDWICH GLASS CO. The firm produced a wide variety of glassware, especially PRESSED and CUT GLASS. The factory closed in 1869 when JARVES died, but it was later purchased by a Dr Flower who operated it until it finally closed in 1882. During these later years, numerous ART GLASSES were produced, including VASA MURRHINA.

CARDER, FREDERICK (1863–1963)
Famous, English award-winning glass technologist and designer, Carder 'typifies the searching open-minded spirit of the art glass movement' (Papert). In 1881 he was apprenticed to NORTHWOOD at STEVENS & WILLIAMS LTD. Carder emigrated to America in 1903. Here he co-founded the Steuben Glass Works, where he developed Aurene, Cluthra, Cintra, Verre de Soie, and MILLEFIORI glass and produced a multitude of coloured glasses in many forms and styles. After his retirement as art director of Corning Glass Works Carder continued to design and make glass. As one authority puts it, 'there are few achievements in glass manufacture which Carder has not either pioneered or matched' (Revi).

COLE, SIR HENRY (1808–82)
British politician and entrepreneur closely associated with the principles of the Arts and Crafts Movement. He commissioned designs for uncut glassware with simple painted decoration particularly by REDGRAVE, for his firm, Felix Summerly's Art Manufactures.

JAMES COUPER & SONS
Important Glasgow firm, noted for its pioneering development and production of CLUTHA glass in the 1880s. The firm was proud and fortunate to employ leading designers such as the architect, WALTON, and DRESSER, which explains the appearance of the latter's signature or initials on the base of much of the glass. Examples can be seen in the Victoria and Albert Museum, London.

GEORGE DAVIDSON & CO.
Tyneside firm, founded at Gateshead in 1867 by Alderman George Davidson, J.P. He achieved early success with the manufacture of glass lamp chimneys, and by the 1880s was exporting the full range of domestic tableware to Australia. Purple SLAG GLASS was very popular at this time and successfully appealed to both the glass and pottery market. The Company still thrives, producing both coloured and PRESSED ware, the latter often marked with a turret and a lion.

DAVIS, GREATHEAD & GREEN
First mechanized glasshouse founded in England in 1809 and operating from Brettel Lane, Stourbridge; the firm produced PRESSED GLASS from the 1830s. One of the five main glass exhibitors in 1851, its specialities were MILLEFIORI paperweights, black FLINT and CASED. The firm also exhibited a myriad of coloured glassware, particularly vases and scent jars in ancient styles. Its painted glass versions of Greek pottery

were universally admired in London at this time, but the firm's prestige declined after its Exhibition triumph.

DRESSER, DR CHRISTOPHER (1834–1903)
Prominent British designer whose taste for simplicity of form and lack of ornament was alien to the majority of his contemporaries. Best known in the glassware field as the designer of CLUTHA ware for JAMES COUPER & SONS, Dresser was strongly influenced by Japanese linear form.

ERARD, OSCAR PIERRE
Famous French painter on glass, producing distinctive enamel work with its own trademark of origin. In the 1890s Erard decorated tapestry ware at STEVENS & WILLIAMS LTD, the THREADED, ENAMELLED vases and bowls being good examples.

FEREDAY, J. T. (1854–1942)
Accomplished designer in the WOODALL team, working at THOMAS WEBB & SONS for forty years until 1922. The borders and detail of Woodall CAMEO plaques, often in his favourite colour, yellow, are his work, a good example being the medal-winning vase designed by Thomas Woodall in 1884 which was entirely cut by Fereday. His geometric designs are characteristic and with the decline in popularity of cameo glass in the 1890s, Fereday successfully adopted the ENGRAVING technique and developed the Dynasty crystal line using Egyptian motifs for Webb's. A set of this was given as a Royal wedding present in 1922.

FRITSCHE, WILLIAM (1853–1924)
Bohemian engraver, Fritsche came to England in 1868 and by 1879 had established his own workshop at THOMAS WEBB & SONS, where he worked until his death. With THOMAS WILKES WEBB and GEORGE WOODALL, he discovered how to mass produce ROCK CRYSTAL GLASS, the ENGRAVING of which became his workshop's main concern.

GREEN, J. G.
This London firm exhibited some of the most significant ENGRAVED GLASS at the 1851 Exhibition, particularly the famous Neptune Jug with its Greek shape and engraved figure composition. Its MILLEFIORI paperweights were popular from the 1840s. However, the firm's main interest was in manufacturing both novelty CUT CRYSTAL and PRESSED GLASS as well as CAMEO GLASS, since in 1866 the firm registered the first design for a flower stand with hanging baskets and in 1878 exhibited NORTHWOOD's Milton Vase on their stand at the Paris exhibition.

HENRY GREENER & CO.
Major Sunderland manufacturer of PRESSED GLASS after its foundation in 1850. It was the first to produce stippled LACY GLASS in England in 1869 and in a successful attempt to appeal to both the glass and pottery market Greener's produced SLAG GLASS advertised as OPAL, Malachite and Black Majolica. Its pressed glassware is usually marked on the base with a lion facing left, bearing a halberd. The Company exists today as James A. Jobling & Co.

RICE HARRIS & SON
Birmingham firm, noted in the 1830s for its PRESSED flatware and in particular for its tumblers, which were a novelty when exhibited at the International Exhibition of 1861, together with the Exhibition's largest variety of coloured and opalescent glassware. Other achievements include black CASED vases and MILLEFIORI paperweights, first made by the firm in 1849, and VASA MURRHINA GLASS.

THOMAS HAWKES & CO.
Worcestershire firm operating in Dudley where RICHARDSON and William Greathead of DAVIS, GREATHEAD & GREEN began their careers. Known for MILLEFIORI paperweights and PRESSED GLASS, the firm had perfected gold ENAMEL wares, often with ETCHED decoration, by 1834. From this date, the use of the etching technique was extended to other wares and, during the same period, the work of the Herbert family established Hawkes' enduring reputation for ENGRAVED glassware.

HOBBS, BROCKUNIER & CO.
Founded at Wheeling, West Virginia, in 1820 as the Virginia Green Glassworks, the firm operated under the above name after 1863, during its most successful period. By 1879 the firm was heralded as the largest in America, sales of CUT GLASS alone totalling $300,000. Prolific producers of PRESSED coloured glassware, the Company was made famous in the 1880s by William Leighton's CORAL PEACH BLOW (called by collectors today Wheeling Peach Blow), SPANGLED and opalescent wares, particularly lamps. A dozen patents for new pressed processes and techniques further enhanced its prestige.

HODGETTS, JOSHUA (1857–1933)
Famous British engraver, Hodgetts worked under JOHN NORTHWOOD at STEVENS & WILLIAMS LTD, where he stayed for forty years. With Northwood, he developed INTAGLIO ware and managed this department until his retirement in 1929. He specialized in floral designs ENGRAVED on CAMEO and CRYSTAL GLASS, which are characterized by a high degree of accuracy, since as an amateur botanist Hodgetts delighted in using actual floral specimens.

Cameo vase, Joshua Hodgetts, late nineteenth century. Deep turquoise glass overlaid in opaque white carved with tulips, the neck with an entwined rope garland below a foliate border. Sotheby & Co.

JARVES, DEMING (1790–1869)
Son of a Huguenot immigrant and initially a crockery and glass salesman, Jarves became a noted entrepreneur and glass manufacturer, using his business acumen and fertile imagination to pioneer new techniques in the industry. He was agent of the NEW ENGLAND GLASS CO. from 1818 until 1825, when he founded what became the BOSTON & SANDWICH GLASS CO. In 1828 he was issued his first patent for mechanical PRESSING of glass. He was associated with the New England Glass Bottle Co., which opened in 1827, and in 1837 he established the MOUNT WASHINGTON GLASS WORKS and finally, in 1858, the CAPE COD GLASS WORKS which he managed until his death. His book Reminiscences of Glassmaking (1854) records some of his achievements.

KNY, FREDERICK
Most distinguished engraver on glass in the 1860s to 1870s and prominent for the rest of the nineteenth century, Kny, a Bohemian immigrant, worked briefly for JAMES POWELL & SONS and then established his own workshop at THOMAS WEBB & SONS. His most famous wheel-engraved piece, the Elgin Claret Jug, made in 1873 and exhibited in Paris

in 1878, reflects the Classical influence on much of his work, although his animal scenes and imitations of Chinese carvings are noted examples of ENGRAVED ROCK CRYSTAL GLASS.

KNY, LUDWIG (d.1937)
Distinguished etcher, engraver and designer, Ludwig inherited the decorating business of his father, FREDERICK KNY, and later joined Stuart & Sons. His early travels in Greece and Italy together with art-school training in Paris and London provided him with wide-ranging ideas which are reflected in his work. He produced CASED, CAMEO, CRYSTAL and coloured ware with ETCHED and INTAGLIO decoration and although his Art Nouveau style was not popular, he successfully exported ROCK CRYSTAL GLASS designs to America.

KRETSCHMAN, F.
Engraver and enameller who worked with BARBE as part of the WOODALL team of THOMAS WEBB & SONS. He decorated plaques and vases in the Chinese and Japanese style. The design books of Thomas Webb & Sons illustrate his designs for CAMEO glassware in imitation of old ivory.

LECHEVREL, ALPHONSE EUGÈNE
French medallist and gem engraver and designer, Lechevrel was invited to England in 1877 to train glassworkers in CAMEO CARVING at RICHARDSON & CO.; his pupils included LOCKE. The Company's CAMEO GLASS shown at the 1878 Paris Exhibition was mainly Lechevrel's work, and reflects his interest in pseudo-Classical NORTHWOOD-style figurative and mythological subjects, as well as floral and geometric designs. Paris exhibits in 1900 revealed black onyx cameo work as his speciality.

LOCKE, JOSEPH (1846–1936)
Perfectionist British painter, etcher, engraver and sculptor on glass, and a prolific inventor. After early training at the Red House Glassworks and at Webb & Corbett, Locke learned the art of CAMEO GLASS cutting from LECHEVREL. With JOHN NORTHWOOD at STEVENS & WILLIAMS LTD he brought the art to its peak, his masterpiece being the medal-winning second copy of the Portland Vase. In 1882, Locke emigrated to America where, as a designer for the NEW ENGLAND GLASS CO., he developed AMBERINA, AGATA and POMONA ART GLASS. In later years he decorated many glasses by acid ETCHING, naming these delicate and intricate designs Locke Art.

MORRIS, MARSHALL, FAULKNER & CO.
Established in London by William Morris as a retail outlet for all manufactured goods designed and produced by members of the Arts and Crafts Movement. The set of glasses by PHILIP WEBB

Two-handled cameo vase, Joseph Locke, c. 1878. Deep translucent blue glass cut with a border of flutes around the shoulder, overlaid in opaque white, ht 9 in (22 cm). Sotheby & Co.

was the first work to be sold and was exhibited by the firm at the International Exhibition in London of 1862. The firm's glassware, unadorned and functional, has had a greater influence on glass design in the twentieth century than the fanciful wares prevalent in the Victorian era.

MT WASHINGTON GLASS WORKS & CO.
Advertising itself as the 'Headquarters in America for Art Glass Wares', the Company was founded in South Boston, Massachusetts, in 1837 by JARVES. In 1869 the owner, William Libbey, moved the works to New Bedford, where in 1894 the Company merged with the PAIRPOINT MANUFACTURING CO. Award-winning productions included blown, CUT CRYSTAL, OPAL and PRESSED tableware and lamps, but the firm is justifiably most famous for its ART GLASS, notably BURMESE, Rose Amber, PEARL SATINWARE and LAVA glass, all of which were patented by SHIRLEY. Other art glasswares made there include: Albertine, CROWN MILANO, ROYAL FLEMISH and numerous OPAL decorated wares.

NEW ENGLAND GLASS CO.
Originally the Boston Porcelain & Glass Manufacturing Co. established in 1814 at East Cambridge, Massachusetts, the firm was incorporated by JARVES and his associates as the New England Glass Co. in 1818. In 1888 the Company was refounded at Toledo, Ohio, by William Libbey's son, Edward, and it exists there today as the Libbey Products Division of Owens-Illinois. Major productions throughout the firm's distinguished career were CUT and blown wares; PRESSED wares from the mid-1820s onwards, SILVERED and Bohemian-style glass during the third quarter of the century, POMONA, AGATA, WILD ROSE and the phenomenally successful AMBERINA in the 1880s, the firm's financial saviour in a critical decade.

NORTHWOOD, JOHN (1836/7–1902)
Outstanding figure in the history of English glassmaking, he produced the most famous piece of modern CAMEO GLASS, the Portland Vase replica. Apprenticed to W. H. & B. & J. RICHARDSON & CO. aged twelve, Northwood came to know all aspects of glass manufacture and decoration, and himself devised new tools and processes such as the PULL-UP machine. He established the successful J. & J. Northwood Decorating Works in c. 1861 and as art director of STEVENS & WILLIAMS LTD he trained a famous team producing cameo glass. His masterpieces are the stylized Classical cameo works; the Elgin (1873), Portland (1876), Pegasus (Dennis) (1876–82) and Milton Vases, which exhibit his mastery of the cameo-carving technique.

NORTHWOOD, JOHN II (1870–1960)
Member of his father's CAMEO GLASS team at STEVENS & WILLIAMS LTD, where he became director and technical manager until his retirement in 1947. He invented SILVERIA glass in 1900 and produced a limited number of cameo pieces, notably the Aphrodite Plaque and Dancing Figures after Flaxman.

J. & J. NORTHWOOD
Established in c. 1861 at Stourbridge by businessman Joseph Northwood (1839–1915) and his brother, designer JOHN NORTHWOOD, the firm supplied decorators to local glasshouses. A skilled team was employed, including the WOODALL brothers and HODGETTS, and up until the 1880s much ETCHED and fancy glassware was produced. The firm then became preoccupied with the decoration of CAMEO GLASS for STEVENS & WILLIAMS LTD, where Northwood had become art director, but returned to etched decoration with the decline of cameo carving on glassware in the 1890s.

F. & C. OSLER
Birmingham firm founded in 1807, with a branch in London, which specialized in the production of large-scale glass fabrications. The centre-piece at the Great Exhibition of 1851 was Osler's

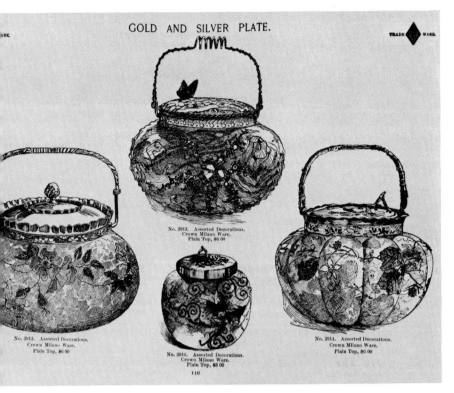

GOLD AND SILVER PLATE.

No. 3913. Assorted Decorations.
Crown Milano Ware.
Plain Top, $6 00

No. 3912. Assorted Decorations.
Crown Milano Ware.
Plain Top, $6 00

No. 3916. Assorted Decorations.
Crown Milano Ware.
Plain Top, $3 00

No. 3914. Assorted Decorations.
Crown Milano Ware.
Plain Top, $6 00

110

Page from a catalogue of the Pairpoint Manufacturing Co., dating from 1893 or 1894. Advertising Crown Milano ware it also demonstrates their use of silver mounts. Corning Museum of Glass.

three-tiered clear glass fountain. Standing 27 ft (8m) high and weighing four tons, it was a monument to Victorian craftsmanship. Although much admired, it failed to win a medal, a fountain being considered by critics such as REDGRAVE to be an unsuitable object for design in glass. However, Royal approval of Osler's style had been shown by Prince Albert's gift of a pair of 8 ft high (2·4 m) candelabra to Queen Victoria in 1849. Novelties included FROSTED, MOULDED busts of royalty and literary figures.

PAIRPOINT MANUFACTURING CO.
This silverplating firm was established in New Bedford, Massachusetts (next door to the MT WASHINGTON GLASS WORKS & CO.), in 1880. From its inception, it enhanced much of the glassware produced by its neighbour with silverplated mounts and holders, as well as providing fittings for the SMITH brothers' decorated wares. In 1894, the two firms merged and in 1900 the firm was reorganized as the Pairpoint Corporation. BURMESE, PEACH BLOW, Rose Amber, Albertine, CROWN MILANO, ROYAL FLEMISH and richly decorated OPAL glasses – as well as CUT and ENGRAVED glass – were among those

fitted with silver plate by the Pairpoint firm, which remained in business until 1937. It was later revived as a glass manufactory, undergoing several changes in management and name and continues in business today in Sagamore, Massachusetts, producing fine quality lead glass as the Pairpoint Glass Co., Inc.
PARGETER, PHILIP (1826–1906)
Cousin of JOHN NORTHWOOD and nephew of RICHARDSON, he joined W. H. & B. & J. RICHARDSON & CO. after school and there acquired a complete knowledge of the glass industry, while specializing in ENGRAVING. A partner of Hodgetts, Richardson & Pargeter from 1863 to 1869, he became proprietor of the Red House Glassworks from 1872. He brought fame to the Stourbridge glass industry when in 1876 he manufactured the blank for the Portland Vase and paid his cousin £500 to decorate it.
PEARCE, DANIEL (1817–1907)
British designer and decorator and a partner of Dobson & Pearce, later Philips & Pearce. The exhibition in 1867 of his original centre-pieces and chandeliers with hanging baskets attracted the comment – 'Pearce is unrivalled in England as a glasswork designer'. As head of the design department at THOMAS WEBB & SONS from 1884, Pearce manufactured these novelties and as a member of the WOODALL team he designed and made CAMEO pieces showing perfect linear control and carved detail.
PEARCE, LIONEL (1852–1926)
Following in his father Daniel's foot-

steps, Lionel both ran the family firm and worked with the WOODALLS at THOMAS WEBB & SONS from 1884. The CAMEO Polar Vase is a fine example of his meticulous ENGRAVING.
PELLATT, APSLEY (1791–1863)
Descendant of generations of British glassmakers, Pellatt had a high reputation as a glassmaker, traveller, inventor, writer and politician. In 1821 he inherited his father's Falcon Glassworks at Southwark and was M.P. for that area from 1852 to 1857 and in the 1860s established APSLEY PELLATT & CO. at Blackfriars. In England he pioneered the CRYSTALLO-CERAMIE technique (1819), Venetian frosted glass (1845) and the pressing machine (1831). His two books *The Origin, Progress and Improvement of Glass Manufacture* (1821) and the famous *Curiosities of Glassmaking* (1849) are important records of Victorian glasswork developments and it is largely due to his efforts that ancient and foreign styles and techniques became popular in Britain around 1851.
APSLEY PELLATT & CO.
London firm at Blackfriars, the successor to the Falcon glasshouse and known as Green & Pellatt from 1802 to 1814. Directed by PELLATT until 1852, noted productions include CRYSTALLO-CERAMIE ware, CRACKLE, ENGRAVED and CUT CRYSTAL GLASS, the latter winning a prize medal in 1851. MILLEFIORI paperweights, together with 'the largest and most modern collection of chandeliers in Europe' were advertised in the 1840s, while after 1851 THREADED glasses and Greek 'œnochoe'-shaped decanters were produced. In the 1860s the Company dealt in engraved glassware, but in 1895 glassmaking was abandoned and Apsley Pellatt & Co., the limited company dealing in wholesale tableware, was formed at Stourbridge.
PHOENIX GLASS CO.
Established by Andrew Howard at Monaca (near Pittsburgh), Pennsylvania, in 1880, the Company was noted for its MOULDED and PRESSED tableware and lampshades, often of the hobnail type. MOTHER-OF-PEARL SATIN GLASS was extensively produced after 1885. This was perfected by Joseph Webb, an etcher and member of the Stourbridge WEBB family who, as patentee of these designs and decorating processes, was largely responsible for the firm's success.
JAMES POWELL & SONS
Situated at Whitefriars, London, until the 1920s, the firm was managed from 1875 to 1915 by the writer and designer H. J. Powell. This was the only company to revive the tradition of hand-blown glass, emphasizing shape rather than decoration, in the late nineteenth cen-

tury, a tradition which was applied to the pioneering production of light bulbs in 1885. The artistic excellence of its products was exemplified by the elegant lines of glassware designs by PHILIP WEBB and Thomas Jackson, leading contemporary designers. Although many of the popular types of Victorian glassware were made and exported to the United States, Powell's reputation for diamond-point ENGRAVING, for pure jewel-like colours and for stained glass, continues to the present day.

REDGRAVE, RICHARD R. A. (1804–88) Designer and painter, Redgrave became art director of the South Kensington (later Victoria & Albert) Museum and Surveyor of the Royal Pictures. He is remembered for his Well Spring Carafe and glasses made of clear glass with painted decoration of green leaves and flower heads, made by J. F. Christy for COLE's firm. Unique in contemporary design, where form complemented function, this glassware exemplified Redgrave's principles, which led him to condemn OSLER's glass fountain in his official report on glassware at the 1851 Exhibition, as being an unsuitable object for the material used.

RICHARDSON, BENJAMIN (1802–87) Called the 'Father of the Glass Trade' because of the fame of his apprentices, his enthusiastic, wide-ranging patronage and his avid experimentation in decorative techniques. After managing THOMAS HAWKES & CO., he founded his own successful firm, W. H. & B. & J. RICHARDSON & CO. His offer of £1,000 reward to the maker of the first CAMEO replica of the Portland Vase led to NORTHWOOD's achievement.

W. H. & B. & J. RICHARDSON & CO. The Richardson family became associated with the eighteenth-century glasshouse, Bradley's at Wordsley, in 1825 and by 1851, at the Great Exhibition, recorded 278 items in current production of plain, OPALINE, gilded and richly CUT GLASS of all colours. After 1852, with two awards and a royal order to its credit, the Company, called Hodgetts, Richardson & Co., flourished under the direction of BENJAMIN RICHARDSON and his partners from 1871 to 1882. The firm perfected techniques such as ETCHING, THREADING, ENAMELLING and CAMEO CARVING and enhanced its reputation by employing LOCKE, LECHEVREL, HODGETTS, PARGETER and NORTHWOOD.

SHIRLEY, FREDERICK Agent of the MT WASHINGTON GLASS WORKS from 1874, Shirley patented several types of ART GLASS for the firm, including LAVA (1878), BURMESE (1885) and PEARL SATINWARE (1885) and was

Water jug, W.H. & B. & J. Richardson & Co., 1848. Clear glass with decoration painted in enamels, ht 9¼ in (24 cm). At the Great Exhibition of 1851, the Richardson family recorded 278 items in current production. Victoria and Albert Museum.

thus responsible for the importance of the company in this field. Burmese glass in particular achieved huge popularity after his shrewd presentation of a service to Queen Victoria in 1885.

SMITH, HARRY & ALFRED Brothers trained as glass decorators by their father, WILLIAM SMITH, a pioneer of glass decorating in America. They established the hugely successful decorating department at the MT WASHINGTON GLASS WORKS in 1871, which they later relinquished for their own premises at New Bedford. Using foreign OPAL lamp shade and vase blanks, they exhibited their award-winning skill in the GILDING and ENAMELLING of Oriental scenes, landscapes and fruit and flowers, while the ringed cylindrical Smith vase became much in demand for every American household.

SMITH, WILLIAM Pioneer of glass decoration in America, Smith emigrated to America (after twelve years in the Birmingham glass industry) to work for the BOSTON & SANDWICH GLASS CO. from 1855. Here he eventually established his own shop for GILDING and ENAMELLING lamps and trained his two sons HARRY and ALFRED SMITH as decorators.

SOWERBY'S ELLISON GLASSWORKS With the other Tyneside firms of HENRY GREENER & CO. and GEORGE DAVIDSON &

CO., this was one of the three most important manufacturers of PRESSED GLASS in England, its wares often being marked with a peacock's head. Sowerby's relinquished production of CUT, ENGRAVED and coloured glassware in the 1830s to concentrate solely on developing techniques of mechanized pressing and on the production of SLAG GLASS which won the firm a wide reputation by 1880.

STEFFIN, ALBERT
United States designer and decorator, Steffin was foreman of the MT WASHINGTON GLASS WORKS decorating department. He collaborated with SHIRLEY in the development of decorators' processes, such as OPALINE, ROYAL FLEMISH and NAPOLI, using fruit, floral and Far Eastern motifs. Gaudy BURMESE vases and kerosene lamps decorated with enamel Egyptian figures from tomb walls are exuberant examples of his work. He is famous as the designer and decorator of the floral-patterned BURMESE ware presented to Queen Victoria in 1885.

STEVENS & WILLIAMS LTD
Joseph Silvers Williams-Thomas took over the old Brierley Hill Glassworks at Stourbridge in 1847 and made his award-winning firm synonymous with the success of JOHN NORTHWOOD CAMEO glassware, making Northwood art director in 1882. HODGETTS' INTAGLIO ware and ERARD'S ENAMELLED glassware added to the firm's fame. New techniques such as ETCHING, THREADING and PRESSING were pioneered here, as well as the process for MOSS AGATE glass. CUT and ENGRAVED ROCK CRYSTAL GLASS and CASED tableware were popular products.

TIFFANY, LOUIS COMFORT
(1848–1933)
Leading American exponent of the Art Nouveau style in glassware from c. 1890 and the self-styled William Morris of America, Tiffany aimed to improve the standard of everyday design, but in producing FAVRILE, he abandoned the accepted shape and decoration of glass and exploited the organic formation and fusible properties of the metal itself (see colour plate p. 174). The son of the famous New York jeweler, Tiffany founded the Tiffany Glass & Decorating Co.

UNION GLASS CO.
This firm was established in Somerville, Massachusetts, in 1854 by Amory Houghton and associates. In 1863, Houghton sold the Company and purchased the Brooklyn Flint Glass Works in Brooklyn, New York, which he moved to Corning, New York, in 1868, where the firm became the Corning Flint Glass Works until it was reorganized in 1878 as Corning Glass Works. Products of the Union Glass Works were like those of

other large FLINT-GLASS factories of the period: PRESSED pattern glass, blown CUT and ENGRAVED GLASS and also SILVERED GLASS. Cordova took over the management of the Company in 1891 and subsequently became the sole owner. He operated the factory successfully until its close in 1924. During the 1890s and early twentieth century, the firm produced glassware in the Art Nouveau style which they designated KEW BLAS, an anagram of the superintendent's name, W. S. Blake. At about the same time, the firm also made a variety of Venetian-style glass, including encased gold-leaf decorated glasses.

WALTON, GEORGE (1867–1933)
Glasgow architect and interior decorator who, from c. 1896 to c. 1898 designed CLUTHA GLASS for JAMES COUPER & SONS. Unlike the designs by DRESSER for the same firm, Walton often included patches of AVENTURINE in the glass.

WEBB, PHILIP (1831–1915)
Leading British architect and designer, his set of uncut glasses made by JAMES POWELL & SONS in 1859 for William Morris embody the purist principles of simple form and good craftsmanship of the Arts and Crafts Movement. Webb's unique glassware designs attracted the contemporary comment that he was 'an external man intruding on a trade which knew its own job', but his belief in the beauty of outline as the essential decoration of a drinking-glass profoundly influenced glassware design in the twentieth century.

WEBB, THOMAS WILKES (1837–91)
Credited by GEORGE WOODALL with the revival of the glass industry in the 1880s, the artistically and technically gifted Webb relinquished his directorship of the Dennis Glassworks in 1869 to succeed his father as head of the parent company, THOMAS WEBB & SONS. A dedicated and enterprising manufacturer, Webb expanded production in the 1870s and '80s in the new directions of ETCHED and ENGRAVED ROCK CRYSTAL glass, and CAMEO GLASS, patenting a process in imitation of old ivory in 1887. His keen interest in cameo glass is reflected in the commission for NORTHWOOD's Pegasus (Dennis) Vase which won the only Grand Prix in Paris in 1878 (when Webb was also decorated with the Legion of Honour), and his assembly of an accomplished cameo glass team at Webb's which included BARBE, KNY, FRITSCHE and the WOODALL brothers. Always determined upon excellence in methods of production and in style and technique, Webb travelled to Australia and America to learn new ideas, to develop an export trade and to arrange exhibitions of the firm's work. He also

paid for his best employees, such as GEORGE WOODALL, to attend art school and to travel abroad, and their resultant ideas enhanced Webb's reputation. Webb's untimely death in 1891 robbed the glass trade of its leading spirit at that time.

THOMAS WEBB & SONS
Founded in 1837 at Amblecote, Staffordshire, the firm's best period was between 1869 and 1891, when directed by THOMAS WILKES WEBB. Virtually synonymous with WOODALL CAMEO GLASS, the firm's high reputation for craftsmanship is also derived from its superior ETCHED, ROCK CRYSTAL and ENGRAVED glassware, executed, for example by KNY. The fame of the firm's CAMEO Pegasus (Dennis) Vase is almost matched by its range of ART GLASS, notably PEACH (1885), Queen's BURMESE (1886), Old Roman (1888) and Tricolour (1889). The extent of the company's success is indicated by awards, by its flourishing international export trade and by the fact that between 1837 and 1900, 25,000 items from its main series of patterns were produced.

Cameo vase, Thomas Webb & Sons, the figures carved by George Woodall, the patterns engraved by J. T. Fereday, the gold and enamel decoration by Jules Barbe. Carved with figures within silver cartouches, the gilded grounds covered with green foliage, ht 7 in (17 cm). Christie's.

Cameo vase, George Woodall, late nine-teenth-century. Deep purple glass overlaid in opaque white, carved with a semi-draped figure of Syrenea playing her harp, seated on a rock in a turbulent sea. Éditions Graphiques Gallery.

WOODALL, GEORGE (1850–1925)

With JOHN NORTHWOOD who exercised a formative influence as an early teacher, George and his brother THOMAS WOOD-ALL are famous as the best designers and carvers of CAMEO GLASS in the nineteenth century. They worked jointly with their skilled team at THOMAS WEBB & SONS from the 1880s and their versatility is reflected in the plaques and vases bearing floral, Classical figurative or Far Eastern designs. In the 1870s George had worked in FLINT GLASS and ROCK CRYSTAL, but it is the cameo work, diversely inspired by Canova and the Pre-Raphaelites, which was universally acclaimed in Paris in 1889 when the future King Edward VII discussed with him the difficulties of cameo carving. George's pioneering use of the ENGRAVING wheel on cameo produced intricate perspective and pictorial effects which distinguishes Woodall's work from that of Northwood. His Antarctic Vase (1912) is an example of this work.

WOODALL, THOMAS (1849–1926)

Thomas and his brother GEORGE WOOD-ALL followed similar careers and until the end of the nineteenth century colla-borated on most pieces, a fact borne out by the price books still at THOMAS WEBB & SONS, which indicate the scope and value of Woodall CAMEO work. The Victoria & Albert Museum, London, exhibits some award-winning pieces by Thomas Woodall.

Marks

British Registration Marks

Objects made according to designs registered at the Patent Office Design Registry from 1842 to 1883 may bear a lozenge-shaped mark, by which the date of registration can be deduced from the codes (1) and (2) below. The mark also provides a key whereby other details of a registration may be obtained from official records. During this period all glassware was listed as Class III.

In 1884 a new series began which was marked on objects as a serial number, normally preceded by the letters Rd. A list of the first registrations issued in January of each year, of objects in all classes, is appended at (3). Before the beginning of 1892, however, account should be taken of a slight numerical overlap between the registrations of each December and January.

Registration marks appear often on PRESSED GLASS, but are only occasionally found on other types of glassware.

(1) 1842 to 1867

Years		Months
1842 – X	1855 – E	January – C
1843 – H	1856 – L	February – G
1844 – C	1857 – K	March – W
1845 – A	1858 – B	April – H
1846 – I	1859 – M	May – E
1847 – F	1860 – Z	June – M
1848 – U	1861 – R	July – I
1849 – S	1862 – O	August – R
1850 – V	1863 – G	September – D
1851 – P	1864 – N	October – B
1852 – D	1865 – W	November – K
1853 – Y	1866 – Q	December – A
1854 – J	1867 – T	

(R may be found as the month for 1 – 19 September 1857, and K for December 1860.)

(2) 1868 to 1883

Years		Months
1868 – X	1876 – V	January – C
1869 – H	1877 – P	February – G
1870 – C	1878 – D	March – W
1871 – A	1879 – Y	April – H
1872 – I	1880 – J	May – E
1873 – F	1881 – E	June – M
1874 – U	1882 – L	July – I
1875 – S	1883 – K	August – R
		September – D
		October – B
		November – K
		December – A

(For 1 – 6 March 1878, G was used for the month and W for the year.)

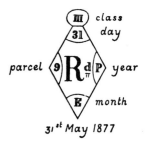

(3) 1884 to 1901

1884– 1	1890–141273	1896–268392
1885– 19754	1891–163767	1897–291241
1886– 40480	1892–185713	1898–311658
1887– 64520	1893–205240	1899–331707
1888– 90483	1894–224720	1900–351202
1889–116648	1895–246975	1901–368154

Factory Marks

Marks on hand-made glass are rare and usually self-explanatory. The following crests appear as trademarks on PRESSED GLASS in the latter part of the nineteenth century.

Sowerby, Gateshead   Henry Greener, Sunderland   George Davidson, Gateshead

Registration marks reproduced by courtesy of Hugh Wakefield from *Nineteenth-Century British Glass*, published by Faber & Faber, 1961.

American Marks

There is no equivalent dating system of registration marks for American PRESSED GLASS in the nineteenth century. Hand-made glass may bear one or more of three types of marks:

    (1) factory mark

(2) designer's mark

(3) mark indicating the specific title of an ART-GLASS process. Common examples of these categories are as follows:

(1) FACTORY MARK

TIFFANY GLASS & DECORATING CO. Signed under the base with the initials L.C.T. or Tiffany's name in full, preceded by numerals which suggest a numbering system unique to this factory
NEW ENGLAND GLASS CO. N.E.G. Co.

(2) DESIGNER'S MARK

SMITH BROTHERS Stamped rampant lion enclosed in a rust-red shield or the written words Smith Bros
FREDERICK CARDER Name written in full

(3) TYPE MARK

CROWN MILANO Initial C and/or M and a crown
ROYAL FLEMISH Initials R.F. separate or written in full underfoot

Glossary of Techniques

Acid polishing
Method of restoring the brilliance to parts of the glass that have been cut by briefly dipping the article in a mixture of acids.

Annealing
Slow cooling of hot glass to relieve a sufficient part of the strain within the metal to prevent breakage.

Applied decoration
Application on glass of such decoration as snakes, fruit, flowers, vines, frills, scrolls, beads and rope handles of different coloured glass.

Cameo carving
Roman technique. Cameo glass blank drawn with a design, carved with miniature steel rods, files and occasionally with the engraving wheel. An additional layer of clear glass over dark glass produces perspective effects and highlights.

Casing, or plating
Gather of glass blown into a shell or casing of another coloured glass. The process may be repeated with additional casings then blown to the required shape. Cased glasses were often cut or ENGRAVED.

Crystallo-ceramie
Cameo incrustations, sulphides. French process perfected by PELLATT in 1819 whereby decorative mouldings of ceramic paste, such as portrait busts and flowers, are sealed into molten glass.

Cutting back
Cutting through many-layered glass to reveal underlying colours.

Dolce rilievo
Coloured outer layer of glass is ETCHED leaving shallow highlights over a white ivory ground.

Enamelling
Hard, glossy opaque white or coloured vitreous paint which is fused on to glassware for decorative purposes. Vitrified enamel is opaque white glass resembling porcelain.

Engraving
Carved decoration obtained by the cutting action of minute copper wheels or by chasing with a diamond point. Stippled engraving produces an overall dotted pattern, by puncturing the glass surface with a diamond or steel point.

Etching
Linear decoration is bitten out of wax-coated glass by the action of hydrofluoric acid on the unprotected areas.

Fire polishing
Finished piece of glass put into the furnace where the intense heat removes mould and tool marks and imparts brilliance.

Flashing
Thin CASING of one or more coloured glasses on a coloured or colourless glass.

Gilding
Mixture of gold and honey is painted on glass and fired at a low temperature, giving a matt gold relief which may be burnished to glitter.

Intaglio
Incised relief decoration achieved by the cutting action of iron wheels and sand emery or carborundum or emery on copper wheels.

Latticino
Venetian technique whereby opaque white or coloured enamel threads are embedded in the glass in twists or panels.

Millefiori
Glass of a thousand flowers, originally a Roman process used in Venice in the sixteenth and seventeenth centuries and especially in French paperweights of the nineteenth century. Sections of multicoloured glass canes are combined to give the effect of tiny flower heads.

Moulding
Glass given final shape and/or decoration by being blown in to a full-sized mould and sometimes then worked into shape with tools.

Overlaying
Gathering over the initial gather of glass a quantity of glass of another colour directly from the pot or tank. The process can be repeated with several colours.

Pattern-moulding
Glass blown into a part-size mould to produce a pattern. The patterned glass is

then expanded to produce the finished article.

Pressing
Molten glass pressed into shape with a plunger and/or PATTERNED MOULD, the glass taking the impress of the mould on the outside, the upper or interior sides and sometimes on both sides.

Pull-up
Threads of horizontal glass on the body are pulled up by an iron hook to produce a herringbone pattern, made regular with the invention of NORTHWOOD's pull-up machine.

Ribbing
Pattern of horizontal, vertical or spiral lines formed on a glass article by blowing it in a suitable mould.

Satin finishing
Frosting. Mixture of potassium fluoride and hydrofluoric acid sprayed on a glass surface to produce a matt finish.

Threading
Ancient Egyptian decorative process whereby strands of glass are coiled round the body of an article. *Moiré*, Tartan and Tapestry were popular Victorian patterns although the technical process was entirely different to that used by the Egyptians.

Glossary of Types

Agata, 1887
Variation of PEACH BLOW, the blown glass is stained to produce a mottled effect on the glossy surface, which is seldom SATIN FINISHED; colours shade from white to rose. It was in limited production from 1887 to 1888.

Amberina, or Rose Amber, 1883
Amber lead glass containing gold which when partially re-heated shades from amber to ruby by the action of gold oxide. It was widely manufactured from 1883 as PRESSED or PATTERN-MOULDED table and ornamental ware.

Art glass
Late-nineteenth century predilection for fancier forms and colour effects, often simulating materials other than glass. Art glass includes, AGATA, AMBERINA, BURMESE, MOTHER-OF-PEARL, POMONA and PEACH BLOW.

Aventurine
Copper particles in glass producing the effect of sprinkled gold dust. It was universally produced in the 1880s and is similar to SPANGLED GLASS.

Burmese
Opaque glass shading from yellow to pink by the action of oxides of uranium

and gold, with a glossy, or SATIN FINISH. Produced in a variety of table and decorative wares and popularized in England as Queen's Burmese following the presentation of a set to Queen Victoria in 1885.

Cameo glass
Two or more layers of glass laminated together, usually having a transparent black, blue or red ground and a white OPAL CASING or plating. Made famous by the CAMEO CARVING of the WOODALL brothers and NORTHWOOD, plaques and vases depicting mythological figures and dancing maidens were among the best cameo pieces and are rare today.

Clutha
Old Scottish word meaning cloudy. Deliberately bubbled and streaked glass which is very similar to THOMAS WEBB & SONS' Old Roman. First made by JAMES COUPER & SONS, Glasgow.

Coralene
Design, usually emulating coral growths, painted on the surface of any kind of glassware and struck with CRYSTAL or opalescent glass beads.

Crown Milano, 1889
ENAMEL-painted, SATINIZED OPAL glass produced in 1889, but known earlier as Albertine or Ivory Decorated glass. White, tan or pastel-coloured floral and figurative motifs were popular.

Cut glass
Glass decorated by cutting with iron wheels and the grinding power of wet sand, emery or carborundum. After 1807 the use of mechanized cutting-wheels speeded up the process and produced deeper, more uniform cutting with more elaborate designs. Also the pontil mark could be removed.

Crystal glass
Lead-potash glass which in England contains about 30% lead.

Favrile
Trade name used by Tiffany to denominate not only his glass, but also other of his products, including metal. Characterized by organic forms and an IRIDESCENT gloss from iron salt and used for a variety of coloured table and decorative ware, including the sought-after lamps and vases (see colour plate p. 174).

Flashed glass
Plain glass covered with a film of coloured or colourless glass. Thinly CASED glass, often cut or ENGRAVED to reveal the glass beneath.

Flint glass
Term used for glass containing oxide of lead. Type perfected by Ravenscroft, in which the silica at first was calcined powdered flint.

Iridescent glass
Prismatic, mirror-like film formed on the surface of the glass. Types manufac-

tured from the 1880s were THOMAS WEBB & SONS' Bronze, FAVRILE, KEW BLAS, verre de soie, Aurene.

Kew Blas, 1893
Type of IRIDESCENT Art Nouveau glass characterized by contrasting colours of green, cream and tan with a sharp pattern and a sheen.

Lacy glass
Elaborate stipple-patterned glassware, achieved only by the PRESSING technique. Gothic, naturalistic and commemorative designs on tableware and lamps were popular.

Lava glass, or Sicilian ware, 1878
Early and rare type of ART GLASS, it was first produced by SHIRLEY in 1878. He achieved varied effects from a velvet porphyry finish to brilliant mosaic patterns by mixing flint glass potash and volcanic slag. Wedgwood ware influenced some of the designs which were often adorned with coloured glass.

Mary Gregory
Generic term, named after an artist at the BOSTON & SANDWICH GLASS CO., in the third quarter of the nineteenth century, for clear and coloured glass painted in white enamel with figures of children.

Pomona glass vase, patented by Joseph Locke, 28 April 1885, made by the New England Glass Co. until 1888. Ht 6¼ in (15 cm). An art glass decorated by staining and acid-etching. Corning Museum of Glass.

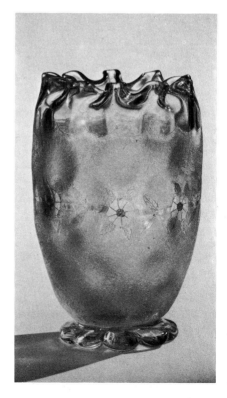

Moss Agate
Simulates the mineral moss agate. Coloured glass powders are trapped internally in the glass body in random patterns. Produced in quantity by STEVENS & WILLIAMS LTD, and in limited quantities by Steuben Glass Works.

Mother-of-pearl glass, pearl satin glass, or pearl ware, 1885
PATTERN-MOULDED opaque glass covered with a layer of transparent colour to bring out the design. The whole is sometimes covered with transparent crystal plating and SATIN finished.

Moulded glass
Glass given partial or final shape and/or decoration by being blown in a mould.

Napoli glass
Similar to ROYAL FLEMISH but here the background is not stained and the ENAMEL and GILDED decoration is found partly on the interior and partly on the exterior.

Opal, or Opaque glass
Opaque milky-white glass made by the addition of tin oxide or bone ash to the batch. A forerunner of ART GLASS, it was always popular.

Opaline glass
Crystal-coated glass, sometimes PATTERN MOULDED to produce a raised decoration of the surface, which when cooled is opalescent white in colour.

Pattern-moulded glass
Term used to differentiate between glass moulded for pattern or decoration only, in a small-dip or part-size piece-mould and then expanded, and that blown in a full-size mould.

Peach Blow, Peach glass, Coral or Wild Rose, 1886
So-called because its colouring resembles the famous Chinese porcelain Morgan Vase, it is CASED or solid glass, shading from burgundy or pink to yellow or white with a SATIN or glossy finish and ENAMEL or GILDED decoration. Overshadowed by BURMESE ware, it was nevertheless widely manufactured under various trade names.

Plated Amberina, 1886
Glass with PATTERN-MOULDED vertical ribs on the surface, it has a creamy OPAL lining and shades from yellow to red.

Pomona, c. 1884–88
Colourless glass with staining or tinting, usually a garland of flowers, against an ETCHED ground.

Pressed glass
Introduced in the 1820s, first in America,

OPPOSITE *Cameo vase and scent bottle, probably by Thomas Webb & Sons, c. 1890. Virtually synonymous with Woodall cameo glass, Webb's had a reputation for craftsmanship. Stourbridge Glass Museum.*

Group of commemorative dishes, all from glassworks in north-east England. Pressed glass. The mechanized pressing technique revolutionized the glass industry in its ability to control prices. Victoria and Albert Museum.

Footed tumbler or vase, attributed to the Boston & Sandwich Glass Co., c. 1865. Silvered glass cased with ruby-coloured glass and cut. Silvered glass is also known as mercury glass. Corning Museum of Glass.

then in England, the mechanized PRESS-ING technique revolutionized the glass industry in its ability to produce cheap glassware.

Rock crystal glass
Name given to glassware in the trade with polished ENGRAVING.

Royal Flemish, 1889
Stained-glass window effect achieved by ENAMEL-painted and GILDED raised lines dividing a background of stained transparent colourless glass. Exotic decoration, particularly Far Eastern designs and forms, was used.

Rubina Verde
Parti-coloured glassware made by HOBBS, BROCKUNIER & CO., shading from pale green to ruby red.

Satin glass
Generic term for acid-finished coloured wares having a coloured matt outer layer and usually an OPAL lining.

Silvered, or mercury glass
Twin-walled glass, the interior coated with mercury then sealed in. Sometimes CASED with blue or red glass, which by cutting reveals contrasting silver and coloured patterns. The best examples were produced by E. Varnish & Co., in the 1850s, although Hale Thompson's process was widely used until the twentieth century.

OPPOSITE *Selection of iridescent Favrile glass, Louis Comfort Tiffany, c. 1890. By producing Favrile, Tiffany exploited the organic formation and fusible properties of glass. Bethnal Green Museum.*

Silveria
Silver foil sealed between two layers of glass. Type invented by JOHN NORTH-WOOD II.

Slag, End of Day glass, or Vitro-porcelain
OPAQUE glass veined and streaked like marble, often dark purple, its main constituent being waste slag from blast furnaces.

Soda-lime glass
Traditionally glass made with lime and some form of soda ash, for which in 1864 William Leighton substituted bicarbonate of soda thereby producing a clearer, more brilliant glass which almost rivalled lead or FLINT GLASS in quality and cost one third to produce.

Spangled glass, 1883
Mica particles embedded in glass with an additional layer of coloured glass, achieving a glittering, spangled effect.

Spattered glass
Coloured fragments used to produce an effect similar to that of AVENTURINE or SPANGLED GLASS.

Spun glass
Made by spinning glass thread on a revolving wheel, it is the forerunner of modern glass fibre. A spectacular early example was a dress for the actress, Miss Cayvan.

Vasa Murrhina, 1882
Layers of different coloured glass fused with mica, AVENTURINE or coloured particles and covered with clear glass. Frequently misapplied to SPANGLED, SPATTERED or AVENTURINE glass, it is in effect a mixture of all three.

Bibliography

AVILA, GEORGE C. *The Pairpoint Glass Story*, New Bedford, Massachusetts, 1968

BARRETT, RICHARD CARTER. *A Collector's Handbook of American Art Glass*, Manchester, Vermont, 1971

BUTLER, JOSEPH T. *American Antiques 1800-1900*, New York, 1965

DARR, PATRICK. *A Guide to Art and Pattern Glass*, Springfield, Massachusetts, 1960

DAVIS, DEREK C. and MIDDLEMAS, KEITH. *Coloured Glass*, London, 1968

GROVER, RAY and LEE. *Art Glass Nouveau*, Rutland, Vermont, 1967

GROVER, RAY and LEE. *Carved and Decorated European Glass*, Rutland, Vermont, 1970

LEE, RUTH WEBB. *Nineteenth Century Art Glass*, New York, 1952

LEE, RUTH WEBB. *Victorian Glass*. Northboro., Massachusetts, 1944

MCCLINTON, KATHARINE M. *Collecting American Victorian Antiques*, New York, 1966

MCKEARIN, HELEN and GEORGE. *American Glass*, New York, 1950

MCKEARIN, HELEN and GEORGE. *Two Hundred Years of American Blown Glass*, New York, rev. ed., 1966

NORTHWOOD, JOHN II. *John Northwood*, Stourbridge

REVI, ALBERT C. *Nineteenth-Century Glass, Its Genesis and Development*, New York, rev. ed., 1967

WAKEFIELD, HUGH. *Nineteenth Century British Glass*, London, 1961

WHITLOW, HARRY. *Art, Colored and Cameo Glass*, Riverview, Michigan, 1966

WILSON, KENNETH M. *New England Glass and Glassmaking*, New York, 1972

Sculpture

BRITISH

Sculpture of the early Victorian period is characterized by sentimental marble statuary which, though based on the work of Flaxman, Banks and other tyros of the 1800s, miserably and mindlessly prolonged the Neoclassical style far beyond its natural limits. It is the independent and creative sculpture of the last quarter of the century that deserves notice. This is true on both aesthetic grounds and because the bronze statuette claimed the attention of the most interesting sculptors, rather than the life-size marble, which is less accessible to the collector.

The Victorian Neoclassicists

The hero and leader of the Victorian Neoclassical School was John Gibson, who worked towards a revival of the purities of Greek statuary and, indeed, achieved this ambition, in his terms, with the celebrated 'Tinted Venus', displayed at the London International Exhibition of 1862; Gibson completed his idealized nude Venus with the application of wax pigment to the marble in imitation of what was considered to be the practice of Antiquity. Many other English sculptors followed Gibson's Classicism, notably E. H. Baily, Richard Wyatt and Thomas Woolner, but all failed to appreciate the firmness of line and subtlety of composition of John Flaxman, their admired master, at the beginning of the century.

Other British sculptors of the mid-nineteenth century extended this underlying Classicism into a soft-centred naturalism, the fashion for which was encouraged by Queen Victoria's com-

OPPOSITE *Clytie by William Henry Rinehart (1825-74), 1872. Marble. An American sculptor in the Neoclassical manner, he lived and worked in Rome. Metropolitan Museum of Art.*

missions for sentimental portraits of the expanding Royal Family from skilful but dull sculptors such as Mary Thornycroft and F. J. Williamson. Sadly, this lack of inventive vigour in the handling of subject matter and form lived on in sculptors such as E. Roscoe Mullins until the end of the century.

In France popular sculpture suffered the same fate with purely decorative, Rococo work continuing to be produced by, for example, the Moreau family long after Jules Dalou and Auguste Rodin had lifted sculpture into strong, modern expressions of feeling and form.

Greek Hunter by John Gibson (1790-1866). A calotype from Reports by the Juries Presented by her Majesty's Commissioners for the Exhibition of 1851. Westminster Public Library.

Sculpture in Bronze

It was in France that bronze first began to replace marble as the most favoured medium. To begin with, bronze casts were made in a purely commercial operation by Parisian founders such as Barbedienne and Susse Frères. They employed the Collas method which enabled them to make mechanically bronze reproductions of a reduced size of both Antique and modern statuary. The quality of this French commercial founding was so high that no English foundry attempted to rival it in the mid-nineteenth century and the vast majority of bronze casts of the *Venus de Milo*, the sculptural bronze candelabra and decorative bronze statuettes that crowded the Englishman's home in the Victorian period were imported from France.

Prior to 1875, the only regular English production of bronze statuettes was through the Art-Union scheme, inaugurated in 1836, although not officially recognized until 1846, to influence the taste and art-morality of the British public. Heroic and morally uplifting statues were chosen for reproduction in bronze and given as prizes in national lotteries. Typical of these Art-Union bronzes was John Bell's *Eagle Slayer*, the original of which was first exhibited in 1837. It showed an heroic nude youth standing astride a dead sheep as he looses an arrow skywards at the marauding eagle. A number of John Foley's works were exhibited by the Art Union, including *Youth at the Stream*, which glorified the qualities of innocent beauty and contrasts with Bell's *Eagle Slayer*, which proclaimed the aesthetic merit of a moral theme, in this case good triumphing over evil.

Stevens and Leighton

Only one artist of this earlier generation possessed exceptional sculptural gifts, Alfred Stevens. Sadly, Stevens was

commissioned to execute just one major work, the Wellington Monument in St Paul's Cathedral, London. This one piece, begun as a competition model in 1857 and still uncompleted at the sculptor's death, immediately distinguishes him from all his contemporaries. *Valour and Cowardice* (after a group on the monument) is a remarkable achievement in its broadness of conception, rhythmic textures and Michelangelesque massiveness.

While Stevens was greatly admired by the progressive sculptors at the end of the century, he was stylistically isolated from what Edmund Gosse was in 1894 to term 'the New Sculpture', the principle aim of which was to introduce natural forms and individual human feeling into sculptural expressions and to replace the slavish stylizations and spiritless idealizations of Gibson and his admirers. In this new aesthetic there was no place even for Stevens' allegorical monumentality.

The first expression of tentative new ideals came with the exhibition by Sir Frederic, later Lord, Leighton, of *Athlete Wrestling with a Python* at the Royal Academy of 1877. Although the group, being essentially a Classical subject, could not claim to be a true expression of realism, it was distinguished in several ways: firstly by being a clay model cast in bronze and not a reduction from an original work in marble; secondly in the anatomical accuracy of the pose and the muscular tension; and thirdly in the generalized, textured nature of the surface.

In 1878 Leighton became President of the Royal Academy and was thus in a powerful position to encourage young sculptors. He quickly assessed the qualities of Alfred Gilbert and in commissioning *Icarus* from him in 1884, he was instrumental in forming the career of the outstanding English sculptor of the period.

Gilbert and 'the New Sculpture'

Already in 1882 Alfred Gilbert had exhibited *Perseus Arming* at the Grosvenor Gallery, London, which, while a Classical subject, achieved a remarkable naturalism. The culmination of this series of small *cire perdue* bronzes was *Tragedy and Comedy* of 1892, in which careful detail of the human form is combined with an almost abstract quality in the rippling surface of the bronze; and at the same time it is a poignant illustration of the human predicament. (See colour plate p. 191.)

Alfred Gilbert soon went far beyond the bounds of this early work, developing a style of sculpture that was more complex not only in its personal imagery but also in technique, introducing enamel, ivory and other media into his bronze casts. His most triumphant work in this vein was the Clarence Tomb in the Albert Memorial Chapel, Windsor, commissioned by Queen Victoria in 1892. A figure of St Elizabeth of Hungary is a variant of a sculpture from the tomb, and it gives some idea of the elaborate symbolism and involved technique of his later work; every detail of the tomb is brilliant and individual in its inventiveness, yet the overall expression of ethereal mourning is unified.

The other early leader of 'the New Sculpture' was Hamo Thornycroft, son of Thomas and Mary, both of whom were sculptors themselves, and it may well have been these connections that enabled him so quickly to win over the Academicians to his support. The most interesting part of Thornycroft's *œuvre* is devoted to representations of man at work. A bronze cast from a maquette for *The Mower* displays easy naturalism and significant generalization of detail.

The French Influence

Developments in sculpture began to accelerate quickly in England at this time, and its progress was helped by certain external factors, the most important of which was the increased emphasis placed on the teaching of sculpture at the National Art Training School, South Kensington (now the Royal College of Art), and at the Lambeth School of Art. The teaching was especially influential under Jules Dalou, in exile from Paris from 1871 to 1880; after his departure his work was continued by two Continental *émigrés*, Alphonse Legros and Édouard Lantéri. This Continental teaching brought progressive ideas across the Channel, and

BELOW Valour and Cowardice *by Alfred Stevens (1817-76), 1856. A sketch model for a group forming part of the Wellington Memorial in St Paul's Cathedral, London. Bronze, ht 2ft 1¼ in (64cm). Private Collection.*

CENTRE The Sluggard *by Frederic, Lord Leighton (1830-96), 1885. Bronze, ht 6 ft 3¼ in (1·9 m). Leighton became President of the Royal Academy in 1878. The* Sluggard *was exhibited there in 1886. Tate Gallery.*

RIGHT The Mower *by Sir W. Hamo Thornycroft (1850-1925), 1884. A bronze cast from a maquette for the lifesize original, ht 7½ in (19cm). This figure was treated in various different poses by Thornycroft. Sotheby's Belgravia.*

St Elizabeth of Hungary *by Sir Alfred Gilbert (1854-1934). A variant replica of the figure on the Clarence Tomb, Windsor. Bronze, polychrome with ivory face, ht 1 ft 6 in (45·7 cm). Kirk Session of Kippen Parish Church, Stirlingshire.*

the Grosvenor Gallery, founded by Sir Coutts Lindsay in 1877, brought contemporary French sculpture over in specially arranged exhibitions. The Grosvenor Gallery and, on its decline after 1888, the New Gallery exhibited and sold contemporary British sculpture as well.

Under these encouraging conditions, many sculptors developed their talents along naturalistic lines that would previously have been denied them. Among the developing artists were Thomas Stirling Lee, James Harvard Thomas and the only British animal sculptors of any real merit, James Macallan Swan and J. H. M. Furse. There were also peripheral figures such as G. F. Watts, who made occasional, but highly significant, contributions such as *Clytie*, 1868-78, an extraordinarily robust piece of sculpture for its date, and *Physical Energy* in Kensington Gardens, which is also remarkably progressive in its illustration of movement and muscular tension.

Variety and Quality

Perhaps the most impressive quality of 'the New Sculpture' was its unrestricted variety, the qualities of which were delightfully revealed in the work of Onslow Ford. His work varied from a naturalistic study of the nude figure of 1886, *Folly*, to the exotic, enamelled bronze figures of 1889, *Singer* and *Applause*. Most admirable of all, perhaps, is the sensitivity of *A Study*.

Although William Goscombe John did not actually work with Ford, the two men reveal many similarities in the simplicity of their response to nature, shown to charming effect by John in *A Boy at Play*.

Other sculptors followed the example of the Arts and Crafts Movement, and distinguished sculptors such as George Frampton, Frederick Pomeroy and William Reynolds-Stevens are frequently found designing and making furniture and jewelry and architectural designs. They also used mixed media in their imaginative sculptures, Frampton's *Mother and Child* of 1895 being notable.

Some of the younger sculptors found themselves becoming directly involved in Continental developments, not least Alfred Drury, who had been Dalou's most favoured pupil and worked with him in Paris from 1881 to 1885. Much of his work showed an obvious visual debt to his master and to France.

Bertram Mackennal was another Francophile, although he turned more towards the Symbolists than the Realists. His work was thought to be daringly progressive in England and although *Circe* had already received honourable mention in the Paris Salon of 1893, the overtly sexual decorations of the base were covered from view when exhibited later in England. There is nothing actually permissive about his *Truth*, but its smooth surfaces and stern symbolism differ basically from the indigenous style. Gilbert Bayes also studied in Paris and worked in a variety of media, his *Putti* being in colourfully glazed terracotta.

The development of 'the New Sculpture' in England was cut short by the outbreak of the First World War. Although many sculptors continued again after the War, by that time art styles had moved away from the basic naturalism of 'the New Sculpture'. While admiring the firmness with which Alfred Gilbert led British sculpture away from the dead Classicism of John Gibson, it must be remembered that even before 1880 in France Auguste Rodin was leading sculpture in a far more significant direction towards Abstract Expression-ism. It is appropriate therefore to conclude with Charles Ricketts, who claimed, with some justification, to have been the only English sculptor to understand Rodin.

Jeremy Cooper

ABOVE Truth *by Sir Edgar Bertram Mackennal (1863-1931), 1894. Bronze, ht 2 ft 2 in (66 cm). This shows sympathies with Symbolist movements on the Continent. Sotheby's Belgravia.*

OPPOSITE (NEAR) Clytie *by G. F. Watts (1817-1904), 1868-78. Bronze, ht 2 ft 4 in (71·1 cm). Watts, known principally as a painter, executed many of his sculptures as models for his paintings. Tate Gallery.*

A Study *by Edward Onslow Ford (1852-1901), 1897. Bronze, ht 1 ft 6 in (45·7 cm). An initiator of 'the New Sculpture', Ford was primarily a sculptor of portrait busts and monuments. John Lewis Collection.*

A Boy at Play *by Sir William Goscombe John (1860-1952), exhibited at the Royal Academy of 1895. Bronze, ht 1 ft 6 in (45·7 cm). John worked under Rodin in Paris in 1890 and 1891. Sotheby's Belgravia.*

AMERICAN

The origins of sculpture in America date back to the purely utilitarian production of gravestones, wooden ship figureheads and metal weathervanes, produced by artisans and totally unallied to a tradition of monumental sculptural expression. Only from about 1769, when Mrs Patience Wright from Bordentown, New Jersey, established herself as a wax modeller in New York City before removing to London, did the art of sculpture find recognition.

The true origins of this artistic form in the new republic lay in the need for commemorative statuary and decorative architectural carving. The former was at first satisfied by the statues and busts of George Washington and other national notables, produced by European artists, some of whom such as Antonio Canova and Sir Francis Chantrey never visited America, while others – Jean Antoine Houdon in 1785; Giuseppe Ceracchi in 1791 – did visit the new nation. Other Italian Neoclassicists followed Ceracchi and were primarily involved with the adornment of the new Capitol building in Washington which remained a focal point for sculptural activities well into the middle of the nineteenth century. Luigi Persico was the last and the most significant of these Italian *émigré* sculptors, producing for the Capitol the Neoclassical figures of *War and Peace*, between 1829 and 1835, and the *Discovery* group, unveiled in 1844.

The Italian Influence

In the early years of the century, a number of native Americans appeared to turn the tradition of sculpture in America from a craft to that of an art. William Rush in Philadelphia represents the apogee of the early woodcarving tradition, while both John Frazee and Hezekiah Augur were determined to find more enduring and more traditional expression in marble. But, despite the efforts to establish adequate instruction in all the arts in Philadelphia and New York, and the acquisition of plaster casts of the great sculptures of Antiquity by nascent American artistic institutions, Americans realized the need to pursue their studies in Europe and, more particularly, in Italy.

Only in Rome and Florence could the traditions of unbroken artistic activity and production in sculpture be found, along with a congenial group of artists of all nations, all pursuing the same goals. These goals consisted of the emulation of the forms and ideals of the Classical world, the belief in the superiority of Ancient art, and the significance of its imitation, in adopting and adapting the appearances, poses, and proportions of Antiquity, all based upon a true and proper understanding of their underlying structure and meaning. While Neoclassicism as a stylistic and philosophic approach to sculptural expression was already on the wane in Europe, it represented for young America the most advanced ideals, and was to maintain its eminence, almost undisputed, for two generations.

Italy provided more than just this tradition and its monuments: in Italy were to be found both most of the major works and most of the major contemporary practitioners of Neoclassicism. It is true that Antonio Canova was deceased when the first American sculptor arrived, but his successor in the Neoclassical pantheon, the Dane, Bertel Thorwaldsen, was active in Rome, and to Americans his work was even preferred to Canova's as more masculine, more homely in sentiment and less disconcertingly sensual. Furthermore, the materials necessary for the carvings themselves were to be found in Italy, the white marble from the quarries at Carrara and Serravezza. And it was in Italy that the artisans could be found who actually carved the stone sculptures. The artists themselves, for the most part, merely modelled their ideas in small clay statuettes which would then be turned over to their workers who would create a large clay duplicate, make a plaster cast of this and then carve it in marble, often with the assistance of pointing machines. The marble would be selected by the artist himself, who would also supervise all the stages in the process, often making changes and sometimes finishing the carving in order to achieve the proper surfaces.

This procedure had many factors to recommend it, notably the retention of the original plasters, allowing for innumerable replicas if commissions came from patrons. Thus, the American sculptors not only went to Italy to study, but for the most part to live and work there, freely receiving visiting patrons on their grand tours, Americans for the most part but also Europeans, and in particular, Englishmen. They produced not only portrait likenesses but preferably more creative, original and imaginative 'ideal' pieces, usually Classical and Biblical subjects, occasionally allegorical and historical figures (busts principally) occasionally the more ambitious and costly full-length figures, and once in a while complex groupings of two or more figures, sometimes in the round.

The first of the American Neoclassical sculptors, and one of the most cultivated, was the Bostonian, Horatio Greenough, encouraged by the doyen of Boston artists, Washington Allston, to go to Italy in 1825. His year in Rome studying sculpture almost ended in his death, but he recovered back in America and returned, this time to Florence, in 1829. Commissioned by his first major patron, the writer James Fennimore Cooper, to produce his now lost *Chanting Cherubs*, based upon two subsidiary figures in a Raphael altarpiece, he sent the sculpture on tour in America, where it received a mixed reception owing primarily to the nakedness of the cherubs. Nevertheless, the work established Greenough as an artist of professional achievement in the accepted mode, material and style. To Greenough, therefore, went the coveted commission for the heroic statue of Washington for the rotunda of the Capitol in 1833.

Greenough based his conception upon the reconstruction of the Phidian *Zeus*. The work was greeted with some derision upon its reception in 1841, primarily because of its partial nakedness and also because of the ghostly, and ghastly lighting available in the Capitol. Nevertheless, while Greenough was still working on the statue, he received a second, even more ambitious, commission from the Government, a group for the portico. Originally, the two groups planned were offered to Persico, but with the appearance of a native American able to undertake such commissions, nationalistic considerations held sway and a compromise was decided upon, each artist being offered one group. Greenough's

subject was *The Rescue*, depicting a frontier family attacked by a savage Indian. This was a native theme, and Greenough assiduously studied Indian anatomy and American costumes; but in the main his sculpture conforms to Neoclassical principles, and his theories celebrating the moral virtues of honest craftsmanship and emphasizing the principles of functionalism, do not seem to be reflected in his own art.

The second American sculptor to go to Italy to live and work was Thomas Crawford, who was the first to choose Rome as his permanent residence and who, of all the American sculptors, received the greatest number of public and governmental commissions. These include the equestrian *Washington* outside the Virginia State Capitol, 1850-7, and the 1855 Senate pediment and doors for the Capitol in Washington, as well as the gigantic *Armed Freedom* on its dome, installed in 1863.

The most famous of all the sculptors, however, was Hiram Powers, who went to Italy in 1837 and who achieved international fame with *The Greek Slave*, first carved in 1842–3, and winning renown at the Great Exhibition in 1851 (see p. 192). Several later replicas were toured throughout the United States and, de-

George Washington *by Horatio Greenough (1805-52), commissioned in 1833 and completed in 1841 for the rotunda of the Capitol. Marble. Executed in the manner of the Italian Neoclassical Sculptor, Canova. Smithsonian Institution.*

Babes in the Wood *by Thomas Crawford (1813-57), 1851. Marble, l 4 ft 0½ in (1·2 m). The work is signed and dated. Metropolitan Museum of Art.*

spite her total nudity, she was for the most part eagerly received and hailed in America. Nudity was a problem, of course, for Victorian America, but the slave was nude *against her will*, and the Greek subject brought forth expressions of sympathy from Americans as well as identification between democratic modern America and Ancient Greece. Her pure, white, virginal marble lent an element of abstraction, and Powers was shrewd enough to enlist the approval of celebrated clergymen who declared the sculpture clothed with spiritual innocence. Powers followed up the *Slave* with other busts and full-length figures such as his *California*, of 1858, and, never returning to America, became the dean of American artists in Florence.

Rome, however, especially after 1850, became the centre for American sculptural activities, and it was there that most of the second generation of American Neoclassicists worked. These included William Wetmore Story, one of the most learned and cosmopolitan of the group, whose *Cleopatra* and *Lybian Sibyl*, both sent to the London 1862 International Exhibition at the expense of Pope Pius IX, created almost as much of a sensation as Powers' *Slave* had a decade earlier. Randolph Rogers was another well-known artist of the period, whose *Nydia, the Blind Girl of Pompeii*, was the most widely reproduced full-length statue of all, over fifty having been produced; Rogers' later career was primarily devoted to public Civil War monuments.

Probably the most talented of this generation was the Baltimore-born sculptor, William Henry Rinehart, whose work retained a Classical simplicity from which his contemporaries were departing in favour of a more virtuoso treatment of textures, more dramatic Baroque carving, and themes involving movement, airyness, water subjects and even sound. To Rome also came 'The White Marmorean Flock', as Henry James called them, a group of women sculptors who achieved a modicum of fame and one of whom, Harriet Hosmer, established an international reputation, both with her grandiose figures such as her *Zenobia*, of 1858 to 1860, and her more playful conceits, such as the frequently reproduced *Puck* of 1854.

Only a few Neoclassicists chose to work for much or all of their careers back in America, but one artist, the Albany

RIGHT Nydia *by Randolph Rogers (1825-92), 1859. Marble, ht 4ft 7in (1·4m). This sculpture, of which there are over fifty replicas, was shown at the Centennial Exhibition, 1876. Metropolitan Museum of Art.*

BELOW The White Captive *by Erastus Dow Palmer (1817-1904), 1859. Marble, ht 5ft 6in (1·7m). Inspired by tales of frontier women taken captive by Indians. Metropolitan Museum of Art.*

sculptor, Erastus Dow Palmer, achieved great success in the 1850s when his reputation was second only to that of Powers. Indeed, *The White Captive* of 1859 is an obvious paraphrase of Powers' *Slave*, this time an American girl held captive by Indians – again, totally naked – and his champions did not hesitate to emphasise the superiority of his native theme.

In Washington, Clark Mills, whose *Andrew Jackson* dedicated in 1853 became the first equestrian group in America, preceding Crawford's Richmond statue, produced the first monumental bronze sculpture cast in America, though its historic fame is offset by the stiff, wooden, rocking-horse nature of the work, factors noted by critics in his own day. Nevertheless, both in Italy and in America, American artists had established sculpture as a valid artistic profession and pursuit before the Civil War, and some had achieved distinct national, and even international, reputations.

The Reaction to Neoclassicism

A reaction against alien Neoclassicism set in at the middle of the century, alien both in the derivation of its principles from heathen Antiquity and in its production upon foreign soil; and with the failure of the Adamic dream, following the civil conflict, the earlier aesthetics became outmoded and meaningless, despite the continued activity of American sculptors in Italy. This reaction took a number of forms. There were the popular genre sculptures, statuettes of grouped figures in plaster, reflecting homely situations and native scenes, often interpreted humorously by John Rogers, who first came to public notice with his more serious reflections on the Civil War in the same material and on the same scale. There were the monumental sculptures by the physician-teacher-painter-sculptor of Boston, William Rimmer, perhaps the greatest of all American sculptors of the Victorian era, whose Classical subject-matter of, for example, *Dying Gladiator* of 1861 or *Falling Centaur* of 1871 – belies the intense personal anguish and emotional power of his work, earning him the appellation of 'The American Michelangelo'. And there was the more conventional but still powerful sculpture of Thomas Ball, Henry Kirke Brown and John Quincy Adams Ward, adherents to the Realist tradition.

All three sculptors occasionally produced work in marble; Brown began in a Neoclassical manner, against which he later reacted, and Ball vacillated between Neoclassicism and Realism in his monuments throughout his career. But the majority of their most significant sculptures were in bronze, depicting historical figures with a continually diminishing dependence upon Antique models. Both Ball and Brown created major equestrian statues of Washington for Boston and New York City respectively in 1858–61 and 1853–6, but with the Civil War and the assassination of Lincoln new subjects for commemorative sculpture appeared which were interpreted with a greater freedom, culminating in their Lincoln monuments of 1874 and 1868 respectively and Ward's powerful statue of Henry Ward Beecher of 1891.

In the late nineteenth century a new generation grew up, nurtured not only on the study of the Antique in Italy, but also upon training at the École des Beaux-Arts, in Paris. They created bronze monuments in which the Realist reaction to Neoclassicism was overlain and tempered with the study of, and enthusiasm for, the Italian Renaissance.

The greatest of these artists was Augustus Saint-Gaudens. In the early 1870s he produced several marble statues in Rome, but the appearance of his monument to Admiral Farragut in New York City in 1881 heralded a new dynamic spirit in which abstract allegories were replaced by an individualism heightened by heroic idealism. The Farragut Monument is adorned by exquisite low-relief figures in a manner recalling the Florentine Desiderio da Settignano. Saint-Gaudens' most subtle and personal sculptures are his portrait medallion reliefs, but he is best known for the great public monuments in bronze which he produced – *Lincoln* for Chicago in 1887, the Shaw Memorial in Boston of 1884–96 and the Sherman Monument in New York City of 1903, as well as the very personal memorial to Mrs Henry Adams of 1886–91 in Washington's Rock Creek Cemetery.

Equal in fame to Saint-Gaudens was Daniel Chester French, who early established a reputation with his heroic *Minute Man* for his native city of Concord, Massachusetts, in 1874, the first of many major monuments he produced, of which the most notable is probably the Milmore Memorial of 1891–2. If the Philadelphia Centennial Exposition of 1876 clearly displayed the contrast of the old Neoclassicism and the newer trends in sculpture, the World's Columbian Exposition in Chicago of 1893 witnessed the triumph of the Beaux-Arts style. The Exposition was dominated by French's statue *The Republic*. Frederick MacMonnies displayed his elaborate *Barge of State*, and nearly all the major sculptors of the day were represented. MacMonnies' style, particularly, exhibited the influence of Neo-Rococo tendencies associated with the works of Carpeaux, especially in his New York monument to Nathan Hale of 1890, and his *Bacchante* of 1893, though the latter was criticized not only for its nudity but the combination of this with drunkenness and maternity. Other major sculptors in the Beaux-Arts tradition were Olin Warner; Paul Bartlett, who created the equestrian *Lafayette* for

Pan of Rohallion by F. W. MacMonnies (1863-1937), 1890. A cast made in Paris from the maquette for a fountain. Bronze, ht 1ft 3in (38cm). MacMonnies designed a fountain for the World's Columbian Exposition. Sotheby's Belgravia.

the Louvre, 1899–1907, and the final sculptural decorations for the Capitol, the pediment for the House of Representatives; and Herbert Adams, whose polychrome portrait busts were consciously in the manner of the Renaissance sculptor, Laurana.

Some of the more private and personal work of these sculptors, however, maintained an awkward naturalism comparable to that of their Italian contemporary, Vincenzo Gemito. Bartlett's *Bear Tamer* of 1887 is such a work. But naturalism was particularly strongly seen in the work of those artists that dealt with Indian subject matter – Hermon MacNiel, Cyrus Dallin and Solon Borglum, or animal sculptors, such as Edward Kemeys and A. Phimister Proctor, heirs to the French artist, Barye. The best known of the artists specializing in subjects derived from the American West, however, are the painter-sculptors, Frederic Remington and Charles Russell, whose dynamic, spirited statuettes reflect their activity as illustrators. In a more humble realist tradition should also be mentioned the rare sculptures by the major American painter, Thomas Eakins, figure and animal reliefs, and small sculptures in the round, usually related to, or studies for, his major oil paintings.

If William Rimmer was both the outstanding American sculptor of the mid-century and a solitary figure working in a personal style, his counterpart at the end of the century was George Grey Barnard. Barnard, too, worked in Paris, but his first great sculpture, *Struggle of the Two Natures in Man*, 1888-94, taken from Victor Hugo, was vastly different from most Beaux-Arts products – it did not express superficial surface brilliance nor heroic historicism but the vitality of inner struggle and emotional power, worthily reflective of Rimmer; it was, incidentally, a work much admired by Rodin. This was followed by his heroic *Hewer*, completed in 1902. The remainder of Barnard's career was dominated by his commission to adorn the Pennsylvania State Capitol at Harrisburg with a complex iconographic programme of scores of nude figures, which, though reduced in its final materialization, is still the closest contemporary American sculptural programme to that awarded to Gustav Vigeland in Norway's Frogner Park in Oslo. Again, like Rimmer, Barnard was an individualist; only Charles Niehaus, in such sculptures as *The Driller*, approached the expressive possibilities of the human form embodied in Barnard's art.

Professor William H. Gerdts

Sculptors

BALL, THOMAS (1819–1911)
American sculptor in marble and bronze, miniaturist, portrait painter and musician. Apprenticed to a wood engraver, he was active after 1837 as a sculptor in the United States and in Italy. His best-known works are an equestrian statue of Washington in the Boston Public Gardens and a monument to Lincoln. He also created a number of memorials in which some Neoclassical influence is evident.

BARNARD, GEORGE GREY (1863–1938)
Pennsylvania-born sculptor, principally in stone, trained at the Chicago Art Institute and the École des Beaux-Arts in Paris. He exhibited at the Beaux-Arts Salon in 1894. His collection of Romanesque and Gothic sculpture, which forms the nucleus of the Metropolitan Museum's collection at The Cloisters, has perhaps some relevance to the powerfully expressive figures of his own design. Admired by Rodin, his monumental works include a complex decorative scheme for the Pennsylvania State Capitol, Harrisburg.

BARTLETT, PAUL WAYLAND (1865–1925)
American sculptor trained in Paris, known for his statues of animals and for his monumental portraits. His works include the bronze equestrian statue of Lafayette for the Louvre, Paris, and *Columbus* and *Michelangelo* in the Library of Congress, Washington D.C.

BAYES, GILBERT (1872–1953)
English sculptor influenced by French art. He specialized in sculptures of horses and later in literary-inspired subjects. He was trained at the Royal Academy Schools, first exhibiting there in 1889. In 1900 he won a prize at the Paris Exposition.

BELL, JOHN (1811–95)
English sculptor born at Hopton, Suffolk. A student at the Royal Academy Schools, he first exhibited there in 1832. In 1837 he exhibited *Eagle Shooter*, a version of which was shown at Westminster Hall, London, in 1844 in the competition for decorative designs for the new Houses of Parliament. Renamed *Eagle Slayer*, it was purchased by the Art Union of London. Public monuments for which he was responsible include the Wèllington Monument at the Guildhall, 1855–6, the Guards' Memorial, Waterloo Place, 1858–60 and *United States Directing the Progress of America*, which forms part of the Albert Memorial, Hyde Park, a terra-cotta copy of which is in Washington.

Parian versions of his work were made at Minton.

BROWN, HENRY KIRKE (1814–86)
Sculptor and portrait painter born in Massachusetts. Apart from four years spent in Europe, he lived in the United States, working principally in bronze. His best-known work is an equestrian statue of Washington in New York.

CRAWFORD, THOMAS (1813–57)
New York sculptor employed by the stonecutting firm of Frazee and Launitz. In 1835 he moved to Rome and was the first American to work under the great Danish Neoclassical sculptor Bertel Thorwaldsen. He modelled portrait busts and in 1839 started work on *Orpheus*, which was to establish his reputation. The marble was purchased by subscription and exhibited in Boston. In 1849 he won the prestigious commission for a monument to Washington for Richmond, Virginia. The equestrian group and auxiliary figures were cast in bronze in Munich but were not unveiled until after his death, when completion of the monument was supervised by RANDOLPH ROGERS. In 1853 he was invited to design the sculptures for the Senate pediment and doors.

DRURY, ALFRED (1856–1944)
English pupil of the French sculptor, Jules Dalou (1838–1902) at the South Kensington School and later his assistant in Paris. Returning to England in 1886, he worked as an assistant to Sir Joseph Boehm (1834–90), the Viennese sculptor patronized by Queen Victoria. He is noted for his portrait busts and public monuments.

EAKINS, THOMAS (1844–1916)
American painter and teacher who executed a small number of sculptures, principally as preliminary studies for his paintings. They belong to the Realist tradition and are proof of his studies in anatomy.

FOLEY, JOHN HENRY (1818–74)
Dublin-born sculptor trained in the Schools of the Royal Dublin Society. Arriving in England in 1834, he entered the Royal Academy Schools in the following year and first exhibited there in 1839; an Associate of the Royal Academy in 1849, he was elected a Royal Academician in 1858. He executed three monumental equestrian statues, *Asia* and the bronze figure of the Prince Consort for the Albert Memorial, erected after his death. He designed the seal for

OPPOSITE Struggle of the Two Natures in Man *by George Grey Barnard (1863-1938), 1888-94. Marble, ht 8ft 5½ in (2·6 m). Exhibited at the Paris Salon of 1894. Metropolitan Museum of Art.*

the Confederate States of America and *Egeria* for the Mansion House, London. *Youth at the Stream* was much praised in 1844, when it was shown at Westminster Hall.

FORD, EDWARD ONSLOW (1852–1901)
English sculptor and original member with HAMO THORNYCROFT of the Art Workers' Guild, noted for his portrait sculptures. He first exhibited at the Royal Academy in 1875, became an Associate of the Royal Academy in 1888 and a Royal Academician in 1895. Casts of his work were sold by Collie, the Bond Street dealer. His best-known works include *Folly*, a bronze statuette exhibited at the Royal Academy in 1886 and the memorials to Shelley and Jowitt at Oxford.

FRAMPTON, SIR GEORGE JAMES (1860–1928)
English sculptor and participant in the Arts and Crafts Movement. Student of W. S. Frith at the Lambeth School of Art and between 1881 and 1887 at the Royal Academy Schools. He first exhibited at the Royal Academy in 1884; in 1887 he won a gold medal and travelling scholarship for *An Act of Mercy* and from 1888 to 1890 he was in Paris studying sculpture under Antonin Mercié. At the Salon of 1889 he was awarded a medal for *Angel of Death*. In the 1890s Frampton was a leading figure in the Arts and Crafts Movement and the

Mysteriarch *by Sir George James Frampton (1860-1928), 1892. Polychrome plaster, ht 3 ft (91·4 cm). This won a Medal of Honour at the Paris Exposition of 1900. Walker Art Gallery.*

attempts to revive Medieval craftsmanship; he contributed several articles on craft techniques to the newly founded magazine *The Studio*, executed designs for work in media other than sculpture and combined various different materials in his sculpture. He was also at this time inspired by the French Symbolists. Frampton was elected a Royal Academician in 1902 and knighted in 1908. He was master of the Art Workers' Guild and President of the Royal Society of British Sculptors. His public works include *Peter Pan* in Kensington Gardens, London, and sculptural details for the exterior of the Victoria and Albert Museum, London, and the Glasgow Art Gallery.

FRENCH, DANIEL CHESTER (1850–1931)
American sculptor in contact with WARD and RIMMER, noted for his monumental statuary combining realism with heroic idealism. His first important commission was *Minute Man* in 1874 for Concord, Massachusetts. At the World's Columbian Exposition in 1893 he exhibited *The Republic* and *Death Staying the Hand of the Young Sculptor*. Much admired in his own time, he executed a number of portrait busts.

Venus and Cupid *by John Gibson (1790-1866). Marble, ht 3ft 10¾ in (1·2m). Gibson, who studied in Rome under Canova and Thorwaldsen, was the leading English Victorian Neoclassical sculptor. Victoria and Albert Museum.*

GIBSON, JOHN (1790–1866)
English sculptor in the Classical tradition born near Conway, apprenticed to a Liverpool firm of cabinetmakers and then to Messrs Francis, makers of statuary. He exhibited at the Royal

Academy in 1816 and in the following year went to London, where he probably worked under the sculptor Joseph Nollekens (1737–1823). Later in that year he went to Rome, receiving instruction from Canova and Thorwaldsen and soon achieving fame. In 1844 he introduced pigmentation in imitation of Greek sculpture in a statue of Queen Victoria, a practice that was to lead to considerable comment and criticism when he exhibited at the International Exhibition in 1862 the statue known as 'The Tinted Venus'. He died in Rome.

GILBERT, SIR ALFRED (1854–1934)
Influential English sculptor, initiator of 'the New Sculpture', a style combining the realism of Italian Renaissance art with the imaginative romanticism of French sculpture and a Medieval regard for excellent craftsmanship and use of various materials. He attended Heatherley's Art School and the Royal Academy Schools, also receiving instruction from Sir Edgar Boehm. He completed his studies in Paris and Rome, where he executed *Icarus*, cast by the CIRE PERDUE method, commissioned by LEIGHTON. He was elected an Associate of the Royal Academy in 1887 and a Royal Academician in 1892; in 1901 he was appointed Professor of Sculpture at the Royal Academy Schools. From 1904 to 1926 he resided in Bruges. Among his major early works are the Shaftesbury memorial fountain in Piccadilly Circus incorporating *Eros*, cast in aluminium, and the memorial to the Duke of Clarence in the Albert Memorial Chapel, Windsor. He executed a number of bronze statuettes, mostly connected with the design of his monumental work, and also medals and precious metalwork, in particular an épergne for Queen Victoria.

GREENOUGH, HORATIO (1805–52)
American Neoclassical sculptor in marble, born in Boston. He first went to Italy to study with Thorwaldsen in 1825; in 1829 and until 1851 he lived in Florence. He won the commission for the statue of Washington for the rotunda of the Capitol in 1833 and delivered it in 1841: it was the first large-scale marble executed by an American and he was the first American sculptor to gain an international reputation. For the buttress of the Capitol portico he executed *The Rescue*. He is also known for his portrait busts, figures and groups, some of which were commissioned by American visitors to Italy. His brothers, John and Richard S. Greenough were a painter and sculptor respectively. He was an Honorary Member of the National Academy and author of *Travels, Observations and Experiences of a Yankee Stonecutter*, (1852).

HOSMER, HARRIET GOODHUE
(1830–1908)
Massachusetts-born sculptress, who studied art and anatomy in the United States before becoming a pupil of GIBSON in Rome. *Zenobia* was shown at the International Exhibition in London in 1862. She worked in Italy, England and the United States.

LEIGHTON, FREDERIC, LORD
(1830–96)
English painter and sculptor who, like his friend Watts, made sculptured models for his compositions. Educated in various European capitals, he settled in England in 1860. His first sculpture exhibited at the Royal Academy was in 1853. In 1877 he exhibited *Athlete Wrestling with a Python*, a powerful bronze illustrating a new interest in surface texture. In 1886 he exhibited *The Sluggard*. Reproductions were made of both his major works in sculpture and some of his preliminary models were cast in bronze. Elected President of the Royal Academy in 1878, he was created a baron in 1896.

MACMONNIES, FREDERICK WILLIAM
(1863–1937)
Brooklyn-born pupil of SAINT-GAUDENS and student at the École des Beaux-Arts in Paris. In 1891 he became the first American sculptor to win a medal at the Paris Salon with his statues of Stranahan and Hale. For the World's Columbian Exposition of 1893 in Chicago he designed and executed a gigantic and elaborate fountain, *Barge of State*. The influence of the French sculptor Carpeaux is evident in his work.

MILLS, CLARK (1810–83)
American sculptor, creator of the monument to Andrew Jackson, now in Lafayette Square, Washington, D.C., the first equestrian statue and the first monumental bronze in the United States. He executed numerous portrait busts and, notably, an equestrian statue of Washington and a bronze cast of *Freedom* by CRAWFORD for the Capitol dome.

MULLINS, EDWIN ROSCOE
(1848–1907)
English sculptor of marble and bronze statues, statuettes and busts. Trained at the Lambeth School of Art and at the Royal Academy Schools, he exhibited there from 1873 and at the Grosvenor Gallery and the New Gallery. He shared a studio with FORD. He executed a number of ideal and decorative works as well as portraits.

PALMER, ERASTUS DOW (1817–1904)
Cameo-cutter and sculptor born at Pompey, New York. He visited Italy late in life, exhibiting a lyricism in his work that still bore the imprint of Neoclassicism. In his studio at Albany he executed portrait busts, RELIEFS and memorials. His best-known work is *The White Captive* in which he imitates the manner of *The Greek Slave* by POWERS.

POMEROY, FREDERICK (1856–1924)
English sculptor of the Arts and Crafts Movement, a student of Dalou at the Lambeth School of Art, founded in 1854, and at the Royal Academy Schools, first exhibiting there in 1885. He became an Associate of the Royal Academy in 1907 and a Royal Academician in 1917. His contributions to the first Arts and Crafts Exhibition in 1888 were two statuettes in gilded plaster, a medium in which he often worked. Like FRAMPTON, he also used mixed media and much of his work, including his stone RELIEFS for Sheffield Town Hall, decorations in Holy Trinity, Sloane Street, and *Agriculture* for Vauxhall Bridge, London, was done in collaboration with architects.

POWERS, HIRAM (1805–73)
Most famous American Neoclassical sculptor, born in Vermont. Working first as a mechanic, his earliest surviving sculpture dates from *c.* 1830. In 1834 Nicholas Longworth, a leading figure in Cincinnati and his friend and patron thenceforward, established him in Washington, where he modelled a number of romantic and heroic portraits of eminent citizens. In 1837 he went to Florence, where in 1842 he started to work on the controversial life-size nude symbolizing the contemporary theme of

Anna B. Sinton by Hiram Powers (1805-73). Powers executed his first marble busts in Cincinnati before he was sent by his patron, Nicholas Longworth, to Washington in 1834. Taft Museum.

Turkish tyranny over the Greeks, *The Greek Slave*. The original marble was acquired by an English collector and five replicas and numerous busts were sold, while several of the replicas toured the United States. In 1859 he received an important Government commission for statues of Franklin and Jefferson for the Capitol. While the original clay models are by his own hand – from this the PLASTER CAST was made by workmen under his supervision – most of the time-consuming task of carving was done by artisans working under his direction. He was, however, meticulous in the finish he gave his works, devising a special tool to reproduce the appearance of porous flesh.

REMINGTON, FREDERICK (1861–1909)
American sculptor, painter, illustrator and writer renowned for his energetic characterizations in bronze on a small scale of American Indians, cowboys, frontiersmen and soldiers, of which many examples exist.

The Snake in the Path by Frederick Remington (1861-1909), 1900-1. Bronze. The American West was the subject of many of Remington's vigorous small bronzes. Metropolitan Museum of Art.

REYNOLDS-STEVENS, SIR WILLIAM
(1862–1943)
American-born sculptor in the tradition of GILBERT, painter and designer of metalwork and furniture. Trained at the Royal Academy Schools, he first exhibited there in 1886. He undertook several commissions from the Church and experimented with electrodeposition.

RIMMER, WILLIAM (1816–79)
English-born sculptor, painter, teacher of anatomy, drawing and modelling, and

writer, brought up in Boston. Starting as a sign painter, he worked also as a shoemaker and practised medicine. His sculptures in plaster, stone and bronze are principally of Classical subjects, executed in a remarkably vigorous manner.

RINEHART, WILLIAM HENRY (1825–74)
American apprentice stonecutter and letterer in Baltimore. Enjoying the patronage of local merchants, he first visited Italy in 1855 and was to make it his permanent home. One of the last American sculptors to derive inspiration from Neoclassicism, he is best remembered for his statue, *Clytie*, and for his massive monument to Roger B. Taney in Annapolis.

ROGERS, JOHN (1829–1904)
Massachusetts-born sculptor noted for his small-scale plaster groups of genre and topical subjects, often of a humorous nature. Employed as a store clerk and later as a draughtsman and machinist, he made clay models in his spare time. In 1858 he travelled in Europe with a view to becoming a sculptor and in 1859 set up a studio in New York. Apart from his plaster groups, which brought him fame and wealth, he executed some portrait busts and monumental statuary. In 1863 he was elected to the National Academy.

The Travelling Magician *by John Rogers (1829–1904), c. 1875. Plaster. Rogers' small groups executed after 1860 are often of a humorous character. Greenfield Village and Henry Ford Museum.*

ROGERS, RANDOLPH (1825–92)
American sculptor born in Michigan, a store clerk and amateur modeller, be-

tween 1848 and 1853 he studied in Florence and Rome, where he executed *Nydia*, a full-length marble in the Neoclassical manner, of which there exist numerous versions. One of his most important commissions was in 1853 for the bronze Columbus doors of the Capitol which he worked on in Italy. He executed a number of portrait busts and military and funerary monuments.

SAINT-GAUDENS, AUGUSTUS (1848–1907)
Irish-born American sculptor in marble and bronze. Apprenticed to a cameocutter, and a student at the schools of the Cooper Union and the National Academy of Design in New York, he went to Paris in 1868, where he studied under Jouffroy at the École des Beaux-Arts. Between 1870 and 1873 he was in Rome, after which he settled in New York City. Among his commissions for public places were the statue of Lincoln in Chicago, unveiled in 1887, and two equestrian monuments, the Shaw Memorial in Boston, 1884–96, and the statue to General Sherman at the entrance to Central Park, New York, 1892–1903, from which the winged figure of Victory was shown at the Paris Exposition of 1900. For St Giles Cathedral, Edinburgh, he designed a relief medallion of R. L. Stevenson.

STEVENS, ALFRED (1817–76)
English painter and sculptor inspired by High Renaissance art, which he studied in Italy between 1833 and 1842. From 1840 until his return to England he worked in Rome as an assistant to Thorwaldsen. He taught at the New School of Design, Somerset House, between 1845 and 1847 and in 1850 was appointed chief artist to a firm of metalworkers, Messrs Hoole of Sheffield, producing designs for industrial productions, some of which were shown at the London International Exhibition of 1862. Most of his time and energy after 1856 was spent on the Wellington Memorial for St Paul's Cathedral, London, which due to constant official interference and lack of money was still incomplete at his death. His preparatory models for the monument were later cast in bronze. His other designs for sculptures include the lions for the British Museum forecourt and decorations for Dorchester House, Park Lane. He also made designs for the Sheffield silversmiths and platers THOMAS BRADBURY & SONS (see SILVER GLOSSARY).

STORY, WILLIAM WETMORE (1819–95)
American sculptor, author and lawyer, born at Salem, Massachusetts. Having designed a funerary monument to his father, he settled in Italy in 1856 and was

a practitioner of Neoclassicism. *Cleopatra* and *Lybian Sybil* were exhibited at the International Exhibition in London in 1862.

THORNYCROFT, SIR W. HAMO (1850–1925)
English sculptor, with GILBERT a leader of 'the New Sculpture', son of the sculptors THOMAS THORNYCROFT and Mary (1814–95). Trained at the Royal Academy Schools, and a close follower of LEIGHTON, he first exhibited there in 1871. He was elected a Royal Academician in 1888. Visiting Italy as a young man, his early work is within the conventions of contemporary regard for the Antique: *Warrior Bearing a Wounded Youth from the Field of Battle*, which won a gold medal at the Royal Academy and was purchased by the Art Union of London, and *Artemis*, commissioned by the Duke of Westminster for Eaton Hall, Cheshire, in 1879, are the most notable. In the 1880s he was attracted by contemporary Realism and, influenced perhaps by the paintings of Millet, he concentrated on subjects showing man at work. His best-known public works are the memorial to Gladstone in the Strand, London, *Oliver Cromwell* for Old Palace Yard, Westminster, which (won the *médaille d'honneur* at the Paris Exposition of 1900) and *General Charles Gordon* in Trafalgar Square.

THORNYCROFT, THOMAS (1815–85)
English sculptor and pioneer of electrobronze casting. He was assisted in some of his sculptures by his son HAMO THORNYCROFT. Chief among his works are the equestrian statue of Queen Victoria shown at the Great Exhibition of 1851, of which he cast fifty reproductions in bronze for the Art Union of London and *Commerce* for the Albert Memorial.

WARD, JOHN QUINCY ADAMS (1830–1910)
American sculptor born in Ohio, for seven years a pupil of BROWN. American in training and outlook, he broke entirely with the traditions of Rome, preferring a powerful, realistic approach. He set up a studio in New York in 1861 and in 1867 exhibited at the International Exposition in Paris *The Freedman* and *Indian Hunter*, the latter erected in Central Park, New York, in the following year. He executed a number of monumental bronzes including statues of Lafayette for Burlington, Vermont, in 1883, and Henry Ward Beecher, in 1891.

OPPOSITE *Perseus Arming by Sir Alfred Gilbert (1854–1934), 1882, exhibited at the Paris Salon of 1883. Bronze, ht 15 in (38 cm). J. S. M. Scott Collection.*

WARNER, OLIN (1844–96)
American sculptor in the Beaux-Arts tradition. Best known for his portrait busts, he executed a number of studies of Indians. He designed the door of the Library of Congress, Washington D.C.

Glossary

Armature
Skeleton of iron bars on which a clay or plaster model may be built up, preventing it from collapsing.

Bronze
(See METALWORK GLOSSARY.)

Chasing
Working and texturing the surface of a bronze with chisels and punches, removing the evidence of casting. Poor detail or unskilled chasing might indicate unauthentic, modern after-casting.

Cire perdue
Method of hollow casting, also known as the lost-wax process. Practised during the Renaissance, and probably earlier, it was the method generally adopted for casting bronzes in the late-nineteenth century. The figure or object to be cast is first roughly modelled in clay, or some heat-proof material, and a layer of wax applied to it and modelled by the sculptor. Alternatively the wax may be fashioned by the founder with the aid of a mould taken from the sculptor's original. The thickness of the wax dictates that of the final bronze. To the model are attached thin wax cords, eventually to act as funnels and air vents for the molten bronze, and the whole is enveloped in plaster and grog (pulverized crockery) to form the mould. The mould is strongly reinforced, then turned upside down and placed in a kiln, baking the material of which the core and mould is made and causing the wax of the model and the cords to run out. Into the space vacated by the wax is poured the molten bronze. When this has cooled, the mould is broken away from the bronze and as much of the core as can be is removed. Finally, the bronze cords are sawn off and the sculpture is ready for CHASING and finishing. For each cast the wax model will differ slightly, for it is not a process of mass production: for this reason there will be variations in an edition of bronze casts. Large-scale bronzes were piece-moulded and cast in several sections.

Collas method
Mechanical means of making reproductions of sculpture and other objects in the round devised by the French inventor Achille Collas (1795–1859). After much experimentation he succeeded in 1836 in making a copy of the *Venus de Milo* in the Louvre two-fifths the size of the original. The machine he invented consists of a wooden structure with a soft-tipped arm, which is guided over the surface of the original. The movement of this member corresponds with that of the copying arm, which can be set to increase or diminish the movement and consequently the size of the copy, at the tip of which is a sharp point that cuts into a block of damp plaster. The plaster copy might be left in its natural state and sold at a reasonable price or from it a bronze cast made. The Parisian founders such as Barbedienne and Susse Frères, who employed the Collas method, exported a number of bronze casts to Britain in the mid-nineteenth century.

Maquette
Small-scale preliminary model, generally of clay or wax, for a marble or bronze sculpture. Roughly finished, it often indicates little more than the pose. More than one maquette may exist for a single sculpture, demonstrating different stages in its conception.

Patina
Surface texture of bronzes as affected over a period of years by the atmosphere. Natural patina is green where the bronze is altered by carbonic acid in the atmosphere, forming a protective layer of copper carbonate on the metal, or dark brown or black where copper sulphate forms on the surface caused by sulphur in the atmosphere. Patina may also be created artificially by the application of chemicals. Sculptors and bronze-founders devised their own formulae for achieving this effect of age or weathering. To prevent alteration to the colour of bronze, lacquering is sometimes employed.

Plaster cast
Plaster of Paris (powdered gypsum), and consequently fragile, cast of a bronze or marble sculpture or of a clay or wax model made from a mould. With a piece-mould the original remains intact, the mould having been made in several segments which may be placed together; a spoil-mould, made in one or a small number of segments, necessitates the destruction of the original. Numerous plaster casts were made in the nineteenth century of famous sculptures, principally for study purposes, and they were often used in the POINTING process.

Pointing
Indirect method of carving by transferring the proportions of a model to stone or for copying a sculpture. In the nineteenth century American sculptors sent or accompanied their plaster models, made by assistants from a full-size clay duplicate of the sculptor's MAQUETTE, to Italy. There, where suitable marble was available, trained assistants carved the sculpture under the sculptor's supervision, often with the aid of a pointing machine. Early pointing techniques relied on the transference of the relative position of three prominent points on the model to the block to be worked by measurement with callipers. Provided the entire subject is contained within these three points, it is possible to ascertain by reference to them the positioning of all other features; the necessity for drilling or chiselling the material is indicated when the callipers cannot be made to meet precisely on the surface of the block. Enlargements or reductions can be effected by increasing or decreasing the measurements proportionately. A similar method involves the use of a plumb-line and frame, the points of contact being transferred from the model to the copy. In the early nineteenth century, when the production of monumental marbles was considerable, a pointing machine was devised of which there are many variants: the COLLAS METHOD is an adaptation of the basic principle. In the latter the cutting edge replaces the simple point indicating a reference on the copy to the original.

Polychromy
Pigmentation of statuary or RELIEF sculpture of which there was a revival in Britain, led by GIBSON with his 'Tinted Venus', in the nineteenth century. Polychromy was practised by Greek sculptors and advocated by Pliny, who describes techniques for preserving pigmentation. Applied naturalistically or simply for decorative effect, it was condemned by John Ruskin (1819–1900), the influential critic and theorist, as trespassing on the territory of painting. In the latter years of the century, in the work of FRAMPTON, for example, it was allied to the practise of working in mixed media.

Reduction méchanique
Version of a sculpture reduced in size by means of POINTING or the COLLAS METHOD. Reductions may be made of stone, marble or bronze sculptures.

Relief
Sculpture in any medium where the dimensions of height and width are greater than that of the depth, and the

OPPOSITE *The Greek Slave by Hiram Powers (1805–73), 1842–3, shown at the Great Exhibition of 1851. The life-size marble was carved by the American sculptor in Florence. Lord Barnard Collection.*

forms stand out from a flat or curved background. The sculpture is termed high or low relief according to the scale of the projection. The reverse of relief is intaglio.

Sand-casting

Method of hollow casting, until the 1880s more popular than the CIRE PERDUE process for the casting of metalwork. A PLASTER CAST is first made from the original clay or wax model and from this are made negative moulds of manageable sections in a mixture of sand and clay. The two sides of each section are then packed tightly into frames which exactly fit together. Into the empty space is inserted an iron rod and round this more of the sand and clay mixture. This new model is then removed and a layer equivalent to the intended thickness of the metal cast scraped away to form the core of the mould. The molten metal is poured into the space between the sand core and the sand mould. With the sand-casting method evidence of the joins, often accomplished by means of a system of flanges with corresponding grooves firmly united by screws, must be removed by careful CHASING.

Scarpellino

Chiseller or carver who works on a marble sculpture, with or without a POINTING machine, copying a sculptor's model, or a cast of his model. The finishing is generally left to the sculptor.

Spelter

Alloy of copper and zinc used for brazing metalwork and as a cheap substitute for bronze in sculpture. Silvery-grey in colour, the surface may be given a coating of pigment or treated electrically to resemble the colour of bronze. It is comparatively light and brittle and easily scratched to reveal the true colour of the metal.

Bibliography

ADAMS, ADELINE. *The Spirit of American Sculpture*, New York, 1923

BENJAMIN, SAMUEL G. W. *Art in America*, New York, 1880

CAFFIN, CHARLES. *American Masters of Sculpture*, New York, 1903

CLARK, WILLIAM J. *Great American Sculptures*, Philadelphia, 1878

CLEMENT, CLARA, and HUTTON, LAURENCE. *Artists of the Nineteenth Century and Their Work*, Boston, 1889

COOPER, JEREMY. *Nineteenth Century Romantic Bronzes*, Newton Abbot, Devon, 1974

CRAVEN, WAYNE. *Sculpture in America*, New York, 1968

FINE ART SOCIETY. *British Sculpture 1850–1914*, Catalogue of the exhibition held 30 September–30 October 1968, London, 1968

GARDNER, ALBERT T. E. *Yankee Stone-cutters: The First American School of Sculpture, 1800–1850*, New York, 1944

GARDNER, ALBERT T. E. *American Sculpture*, Catalogue of the Collection of the Metropolitan Museum of Art, Greenwich, Connecticut, 1965

GERDTS, WILLIAM H. *American Neoclassic Sculpture, The Marble Resurrection*, New York, 1973

GOSSE, EDMUND. 'The New Sculpture' in *Art Journal*, pp. 138–42; 199–203; 277–82; 306–11, London, 1894

GROCE, GEORGE C., and WALLACE, DAVID. *Dictionary of Artists in America 1564–1860*, New Haven, Connecticut, 1957

GUNNIS, R. *Dictionary of British Sculpture 1660–1851*, London, 1968

HANDLEY-READ, LAVINIA. 'Alfred Gilbert: a new assessment' in *The Connoisseur*, vol. 169, pp. 22–27; 85–91; 144–51, London, 1968

LARKIN, OLIVER. *Art and Life in America*, New York, 1949

McSPADDEN, JOSEPH. *Famous Sculptors of America*, New York, 1924

POST, CHANDLER. *A History of European and American Sculpture from the Christian Period to the Present Day*, 2 vols, Cambridge, Massachusetts, 1921

SPIELMANN, MARION. *British Sculpture and Sculptors of Today*, London, 1901

TAFT, LORADO. *The History of American Sculpture*, New York, 1903

THORP, MARGARET. *The Literary Sculptors*, Durham, North Carolina, 1965

TUCKERMAN, HENRY T. *Book of the Artists*, New York, 1867

Victoria and Albert Museum. *The Wellington Monument*, London, 1970

OPPOSITE Interior of the Crystal Palace. *A photograph from* Reports by the Juries *of the transept showing some of the sculpture exhibits at the Great Exhibition of 1851. Westminster Public Library.*

Silver

BRITISH

The great silver manufacturing concerns of early Victorian England were proud of their commercial parentage. In the view of contemporary critics, however, success was not guaranteed merely by past triumphs or accumulated experience. Although Paul Storr, for instance, had been apprenticed to Andrew Fogelberg in about 1785, and had worked with Rundell, Bridge & Rundell from 1807 to 1819, the output of his workshops by the 1830s was no more promising than any other. The craftsmanship was generally beyond reproach, but thoughtful design was often sacrificed. This may be seen in a marine centre-piece of 1838, assembled from castings used in other combinations up to sixteen years previously. If this was progress, then something was wrong.

In an effort to counter such neglect in design and to stir the interest of the public at large, the Government appointed in 1835, a Select Committee of Enquiry. The witnesses had many different points of view, but the majority were unanimous in their condemnation of the current Rococo Revival. The architect and designer J. B. Papworth in his attack suggested that the absence of protection for original designs 'has induced manufacturers to seek a style of ornament capable of being executed with facility by workmen unpossessed of theoretical knowledge . . . This style has been fostered to a great extent, and erroneously termed that of Louis XIV'.

Perhaps as a direct result of the Enquiry, and certainly because of a growing involvement among the intelligentsia, the following years saw the foundations of the Government School of Design (1836), and the Patent Office Design Registry (1842). Furthermore, a 'Society for Promoting Practical Design

OPPOSITE *Tea service, Samuel Kirk & Son, Baltimore, c. 1870. Repoussé silver. The firm was noted for this type of Rococo ornament, known as the Baltimore style. Sotheby Parke Bernet.*

and Diffusing a Knowledge & Love of the Arts Among the People' held its inaugural meeting in January 1838; and nine years later, Henry Cole established the Felix Summerly's Art Manufactures scheme. The culmination of all such efforts was, of course, the Great Exhibition of 1851.

Rundell's and the Rococo Revival

The fashionable premises on Ludgate Hill in 1815 had been 'filled with riches', and 'The shop of Messrs Rundell, Bridge & Rundell, Jewellers &c. exceeds, perhaps, all others in the British Empire, if not in the whole world, for the

Coffee pot in the Rococo style, maker's mark of Paul Storr (1771-1844), of Storr & Mortimer, London, 1830. Ht 10½ in (26·7 cm). Mr and Mrs Morrie A. Moss Collection.

1. Joseph Nightingale, *London and Middlesex; or an Historical, Commercial, & descriptive Survey of the Metropolis of Great Britain*, Vol. III, p. 631, London, 1815.

value of its contents.'[1] Indeed, Rundell's was the envy of all other goldsmiths, and they are now acknowledged as innovators whose policies affected silver design until almost the end of the century. The wealth and influence of their patrons, not least the Prince Regent and the Duke of York, made it possible for them to maintain a staff of the finest designers and modellers, as well as extensive, mechanized workshops. Such an establishment, which sold both old and new plate and jewelry, could only have thrived under unique economic, artistic and managerial conditions.

Rundell's interpretation of the grand Neoclassical manner of Charles Heathcote Tatham had succeeded, and so, too, did their revival of the Rococo. The latter was inspired by eighteenth-century pieces which had passed through their hands, appearing in about 1812. The outcome of these investigations as far as Rundell's was concerned was the development of a transfigurative naturalism which, during the 1820s and 1830s, caused salt-cellars to be created in the form of sea-urchins or convolvulus' blooms and knife-rests in the form of sprays of celery. The *Art Union*, which published compatible designs by Henry Fitz Cook and T. Woodington, was still advocating such trends in the late 1840s.

With its Rundell pedigree, the Rococo Revival had quickly gained momentum. As one of the leading independent manufacturing and retail silversmiths of the next generation, Paul Storr and John Mortimer, though not alone, favoured rich Rococoesque effects. Many of their productions, in common with those of R. & S. Garrard & Co., were indeed amalgams of old designs, proved by a remarkable group of plate from the 1820s and 1830s featuring dolphins, spume and other marine motifs. On the other hand, the firm is known to have copied direct from eighteenth-century originals, or from old prints, as in a caviar pail of 1841, the design of which

Design for a vase by Jacques François Saly (1717-76), a plate from an early nineteenth-century source book, once the property of Storr & Mortimer. Sotheby's Belgravia.

ABOVE *Caviar pail based on the design for a vase by Jacques François Saly (above right), maker's mark of John Samuel Hunt, of Mortimer & Hunt, London, 1841. Ht 14½ in (36·8 cm). Sotheby & Co.*

BELOW *Silver presentation plate from the illustrated price list of A. B. Savory & Sons, 1 May 1855. Much important silver changed hands at the beginning of the reign. Bodleian Library.*

Second-hand—A very richly chased silver Vase or Soup Tureen, with Cover, tastefully shaped, with scroll and flower border, Vine handles, and ornamented with chased leaves and flowers,

weight 137¾ oz. at 10s. 6d. per oz. £72   5   6

Second-hand—A pair of silver Wine Coolers, richly chased, with twisted Vine handles, and beautiful Grape borders, (*by Rundell and Bridge*, cost 250 *guineas*,)

weight 310 oz. at 8s. 9d. per oz. £135 12   6

was based on an idea by Jacques François Saly (1717–76).[1]

The tendency to rely on old works continued, especially after the closure of Rundell's in 1842 and the subsequent dispersal of their valuable dies. Thus Flaxman's Theocritus Cup, for instance, was produced anew by Garrard's in 1864, over fifty years after its first appearance. Firms were proud to associate themselves with the former Crown Jewelers.

A. B. Savory & Sons' illustrated price list of 1855 announces that a second-hand pair of wine coolers, 'richly chased with twisted Vine handles, and beautiful Grape borders', which had originally cost 250 guineas at Rundell's in about 1815, could now be bought for £135 12s. 6d. Old collections were disposed of at auctions, while at the time of Queen Victoria's accession, works were inherited which might be the envy of all who knew them. A notable inheritance was that of Miss Burdett-Coutts, who acquired after 1837 a 'singularly elegant cruet stand' of 1804 which had come from the Duke of York's collection.

Perhaps the most important reason for interest in old rather than new productions was economic. After the Napoleonic

1. An early nineteenth-century design source book with miscellaneous prints dating from *c.* 1543 to *c.* 1780, of designs for vases, etc., inscribed 'No 201 Storr & Mortimer, 13, New Bond St'. Silver department library, Sotheby's Belgravia, London.

Centre-piece, maker's mark of Paul Storr, of Storr & Mortimer, London, 1838. Similar figures of tritons were used at Rundell's in the late 1820s and the model for the plateau appeared at Storr & Mortimer in 1822. Sotheby & Co.

Wars, depressed markets abroad and mounting agricultural output at home, promoted massive hardship and unemployment in general and economies among the landed nobility in particular. Informed clients with enough wealth to back their artistic judgments were therefore less and less responsive. Naturally, Rundell's felt the chill increasingly, particularly after the senior partner, Philip Rundell, retired in 1823, withdrawing as he did part of a fortune which amounted to some £1,500,000

when he died four years later. In 1827 and 1830 two of their most valued clients, the Duke of York and George IV, died. The former's copy of the Achilles Shield, a Rundell piece of 1822 designed by Flaxman, which had cost £2,000, was repurchased by the firm in 1827 for only £1,000.

Other establishments apparently suffered, notably Kensington Lewis', who had sold to the Duke of York the Hercules and Hydra candelabrum, a *tour de force* weighing over 1,000 oz. After 1827, the productions of its maker, and Lewis' chief supplier, Edward Cornelius Farrell, were noticeably affected. Thereafter, until his death in 1850, Farrell's workshop concentrated on reproductions of mid-eighteenth-century English domestic plate.

The twenty years after 1830 were to see the retraction or failure of further enterprises which had maintained a reputation for quality. Even Storr & Mortimer were placed in difficulties by unsold stock. Their problems were reversed only by the introduction of John Samuel Hunt in 1839 as an additional partner, bringing with him a capital of £5,000. Thomas Hamlet, on the other hand, was not as fortunate. Having been an important retail goldsmith in Regency days, he had turned his attentions to other projects which had helped to fling him into debt. When he eventually appeared in the bankruptcy courts in 1841, it was revealed that the Duke of York's estate still owed him £6,000.

Under such strained circumstances, it is hardly surprising that by the 1830s and 1840s design should have been almost wholly sacrificed to the facile

Louis Quatorze style, with its endless meanders of chased or engraved scrolls, flowers and leaves. While Henry Cole and his circle fought to improve by the example of his Felix Summerly's Art Manufactures, and through *The Journal of Design and Manufactures,* the decay had become endemic. During the 1840s, and indeed beyond the Great Exhibition, the style continued unabated.

Inevitably, the appeal for good design had its effect, if only in modest ways, as the exhibitions at Manchester in 1845 and 1846, and Birmingham in 1848 were to show. Nevertheless, quality in the Rundell tradition was now rarely equated with taste, as Benjamin Smith II, for one, was to realize. Smith, whose father's business had once been associated with Rundell's,[1] assisted Cole in the Summerly venture by making caddy spoons with cast tea-plant handles, thereby demonstrating the latter's precept that decorative design should be at one with function. As a champion of the naturalistic style, Smith was no doubt as pleased with the notion as was Cole. His attitudes, however, were not in harmony with the needs of a modern trade, a fact made uncomfortably clear by his connection with the electroplate patentees, Elkington & Co., of Birmingham. He proved unsuitable in promoting their new process, patented in 1840, and died a bankrupt ten years later.

Exhibition Silver

An improving national economy during the 1840s helped to revive the rapport between consumer and manufacturer, although this time it was to be on a much

1. Shirley Bury, 'The lengthening shadow of Rundell's', Part I, *The Connoisseur,* February 1966.

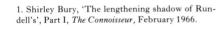

Soup tureen in the mid eighteenth-century style, maker's mark of E. C. Farrell, London, 1846. Sotheby Parke Bernet.

ment of both French and English artists was to be much publicized. Their exhibits in 1851 included work by Pierre-Émile Jeannest, Charles Grant and George Stanton. Furthermore, by the means of precision techniques, Elkington's were able to publish faithful copies, or large numbers of articles based on the designs of these men, in both silver and electroplate. The Rococo, of course, was in evidence, but Elkington's aim was diversification, and all the current styles were represented, from Gothic tea-services to naturalistic Crown Imperial fruit stands.

Joseph Angell III, whose father had worked for Rundell's, was another ambitious manufacturer; and he demonstrated at the Great Exhibition that British ingenuity and workmanship could stand alone. He was proud that all his exhibition pieces had been made in his own workshops, 'expressly for the purpose within a period of five months'. Two of his most acclaimed works, the Aesop's Fable Tea and Coffee Service and the Vintage Claret Jug, illustrated his interest in appropriate decoration. The design of both was so mixed with minute detail and Rococoesque motifs, however, that the Felix Summerly group may have been justifiably astonished at the misinterpretation of their ideas. Nevertheless, in the eyes of some critics, Angell's success in 'presenting new combinations, never before introduced in the manufacture of silver plate', was preferable to those who had 'striven to produce an overwhelming display, and have exhibited many specimens made years ago, and essentially old'.[1]

Several exhibitors were guilty of reintroducing old productions, emphasizing the point that, being 'calculated to advance our National Taste', the Great Exhibition was not an unqualified success. As successors to Storr & Mortimer, Hunt & Roskell's stand, for one, included the Tweeddale Testimonial of 1849, representing the type of plate which as early as 1844 had inspired the derision of S. Laman Blanchard. As a satirical writer, however, the latter's view was rather advanced, whereas contributors to the more conservative journals, perhaps mindful of an influential readership, continued their interest into the 1870s.

In his essay, *The Exhibition as a lesson in taste*, Ralph N. Wornum had written in 1851 that the inferiority in English silverwork to the French 'is very striking, though, perhaps, the most beautiful work of this class in the Exhibition is

1. *Descriptive Particulars of a collection of Silver, Silver Gilt and Enamel'd Plate . . . Manufactured and Designed by Joseph Angell*, London, 1851.

TOP *Ewer on stand, maker's mark of E. and J. Barnard, of Edward Barnard & Sons, London, 1859, for West & Sons of Dublin. 'Louis Quatorze, Style Irrégulier', the tritons modelled by Louis Frerêt. Sotheby & Co.*

ABOVE *Salver, maker's mark of Benjamin Smith II, London, 1840. Silver with naturalistic flat-chased decoration, diam. 11½ in (29·2 cm). Sotheby's Belgravia.*

broader basis. General public interest had expanded dramatically, and Elkington's, with an up-to-date approach, took full advantage of the situation. By attention to financial considerations, they were to be a rude example to old, established firms, the huge display of their goods at the Great Exhibition being convincing evidence. In common with some of their rivals, Elkington's employ-

TOP *Goodwood Cup of 1851, illustrating the legend of Robin Hood, shown by Charles Frederick Hancock at the Great Exhibition, 1851. Calotype from* Reports of the Juries. *Westminster Public Library.*

ABOVE The Goddess of Sleep, *from a model by Léonard Morel-Ladeuil (1820-88), maker's mark of Elkington & Co. Ltd, Birmingham, 1893. Ht 9¾ in (24·8 cm). Sotheby's Belgravia.*

Coffee pot from the Aesop's Fable Service, maker's mark of Joseph Angell III (c. 1816-91), London, 1850. Silver, parcel gilt, ht 10 in (25·4 cm). Made for the Great Exhibition of 1851. Worshipful Company of Goldsmiths.

LEFT *Tweeddale Testimonial, maker's mark of J. S. Hunt, of Hunt & Roskell, London, 1849. Ht 48½ in (123 cm). Shown at the Great Exhibition. Christie's.*

German'. Like other critics, he objected to the application of enamels, and the generally vague taste displayed. These were trends which were increasingly to be seen at the exhibitions in New York (1853), Dublin (1853) and Paris (1855), and which were further emphasized in London at the International Exhibition of 1862. Manufacturers were sometimes attacked for the mechanical brilliance of surfaces, or 'artificial' texturing devices, such as oxidization and frosting, which from the late 1850s were to gain popularity. Critics of this persuasion were precursors of the Arts and Crafts Movement and the tactile work at the turn of the century made by the Guild of Handicraft under the guidance of C. R. Ashbee.

The 1862 Exhibition showed little real advance, being chiefly remarkable for the display of testimonial plate. Elkington's exhibited Léonard Morel-Ladeuil's table, *Sleep*, which was subsequently bought by the City of Birmingham as a wedding present for the Prince and Princess of Wales. The central figure from this piece, a 'floating' Goddess of Sleep, was reproduced and sold as a separate item until the mid 1890s. Hunt & Roskell concentrated on sculptural

201

work from the artists H. H. Armstead, Frank Hunt and Archibald J. Barrett, but persisted in re-issuing wine coolers and the like from stock-dies made at least twenty-five years earlier. The important firm under the directorship of Charles Frederick Hancock, formerly at Hunt & Roskell, commissioned from the sculptor Raphael Monti designs and models for a group of vases illustrative of the poetry of Great Britain. As a serious rival to both Hunt & Roskell and Garrard's, Hancock's also employed the artists Louis Frerêt, Owen Jones, and H. H. Armstead.

The Trade versus the Innovators

The historical approach encouraged by all these firms did nothing to improve design. Contemporary manufacturers were obliged, through lack of public support, to elaborate on all the old themes, from Rococo to Gothic, to Renaissance and rustic; saving their most ambitious works for the exhibitions at Paris (1867), London (1871, 1872, 1873, 1874), Vienna (1873) and Philadelphia (1876). The Louis Quatorze style maintained its grip, although the novelty of Japanese decoration was exploited during the 1870s and 1880s in tea-services and memorandum pads with frosted or parcel-gilded surfaces engraved with birds, fans and butterflies.

Card case in the Japanese style, maker's mark of W. and J. Barnard of Edward Barnard & Sons, London, 1880. Silver, engraved, frosted and parcel gilt, 3¾ in (9·5 cm). Sotheby's Belgravia.

RIGHT *Jug based on a design by Dr Christopher Dresser (1834-1904), maker's mark of Frederick Elkington, of Elkington & Co., Birmingham, 1885. Patent Office Registry no. 22871. Sotheby & Co.*

In fact, the decorative details in Japanese design were to be a principal motif for all fashion throughout this period. Gilbert and Sullivan's *The Mikado* of 1885 reflected this, just as *Patience* in 1881 had ridiculed the Aesthetic Movement in general. In an age which trivialized the Japanese ideal, and mass produced a diluted version of the Adam style, pseudo-earnest arguments on good design could no longer hold the public interest. The nation had been offered ample encouragement for a deeper understanding of design in magazines, and by the long series of international exhibitions; but in failing to grasp in practical terms such opportunities for improvement, the consumer was finally responsible for the irreconcilable split which occurred in the silver manufacturing industry. On the one hand was a trade marketing spiritless reproductions

of eighteenth-century domestic plate, or bric-à-brac for dressing tables, and on the other the Arts and Crafts Movement with its dreamy notions of reviving craft practices.

Mass production in the silver industry at the end of the nineteenth century had reached a peak of mechanical sophistication which pushed output and profitability, if not good design, to record levels. While C. R. Ashbee and the Guild of Handicraft were labouring for work with 'feeling and character', few of the commercial firms were prepared to organize a 'house style' which might originate, rather than imitate, a current fashion. The Cymric range, launched by Liberty & Co. in 1899, with Archibald Knox among their artists, did just this. In assimilating the mood of the times, they produced articles with interlaced motifs of Celtic inspiration juxtaposed

with enamels or semi-precious stones against softly patinated, hand-finished surfaces. This commercial enterprise has proved a lasting artistic success.

If the mood of the Arts and Crafts Movement was, in a sense, commercially exploited by Liberty & Co., then the philosophy of its members was broadly put into practice by the manufacturing silversmiths and electroplaters, James Dixon & Sons, Hukin & Heath and

Elkington & Co., who, from the 1870s, worked from the designs of Dr Christopher Dresser.

Having trained at the Government School of Design during the late 1840s, Dresser was aware of the Felix Summerly's scheme and the pains to which Henry Cole went to promote good design. While the earlier experiments at Rundell's using Nature as a source for appropriate form and decoration had not succeeded,

Dresser, using his knowledge as a doctor of botany, employed the basic structure of various plants for his designs rather than using them as a decorative motif. The final results of his investigations were the production of articles of a remarkable practicality and pureness of line, which have had a profound effect on design in the twentieth century.

John Culme

AMERICAN

There are many different and conflicting influences in the design of American Victorian silver. Throughout the period the pendulum swings from the Classical to the Romantic. The styles and periods overlap with no set dates for their beginning or end and motifs associated with several styles often appear on the same vessel.

The European Influence

From the earliest days, American silver styles were influenced by those of Europe. Foreign pattern books were available and there were immigrant craftsmen who brought with them European tastes and skills. The English Regency and the French Empire styles had been established in such cities as Boston, New York, Philadelphia and Baltimore in the first quarter of the nineteenth century. When the day of the individual silversmith was ending and the silver factories were founded, the majority of the workmen were silversmiths from England and France. The chief designer at the Gorham Manufacturing Co., in Providence, Rhode Island, was Thomas Pairpoint, who came from Lambert & Rawlings in London after an apprenticeship in Paris. At Tiffany & Co., one of the chief designers was James Whitehouse, who had his training under L. Morel-Ladeuil at Elkington & Co., in England.

As the Victorian period opened, the designs for American silver continued to be dominated by influences derived from European revivals: the Greek Revival and Neoclassicism persisted from the earlier period, and the Gothic style was occasionally seen, especially in communion vessels.

Rococo

Rococo was the first important stylistic influence in American Victorian silver. It appeared initially in the 1820s and lasted many years, flourishing and intermingling with other such influences as the Gothic and Elizabethan. The early

Teapot in the Rococo style, Gorham Manufacturing Co., Providence, Rhode Island, 1850. Silver with chased and cast cast decoration. The origins of the firm date back to 1831.

repoussé pieces by Samuel Kirk, of Baltimore, were the first examples in the United States. However, it did not become generally popular until the 1840s, and the full flowering was not until the 1850s. The forms of Rococo hollowware had exaggerated shapes: teapots, coffee pots and pitchers were high shouldered with bulging bodies and heavy, rounded bases. Handles, lids and feet of articles became engulfed in curved leaf decoration.

Ornament was something added to the object not an integral part of the form, and the decorative motifs included

Salt cellar, Andrew E. Warner (1786-1870), Baltimore, 1825-50. One of a pair by the leading Baltimore manufacturer. Metropolitan Museum of Art.

RIGHT *Creamer, designed by John Chandler Moore (active 1832-51) and made by Ball, Tomkins & Black, presented to Marshall Lefferts in 1850. Part of a service in the Rococo style. Metropolitan Museum of Art.*

heavily chased C- and S-scrolls and diapers combined with bold repoussé. Naturalistic flora was raised and applied indiscriminately to all forms. Acanthus leaves were often of such luxurious growth that they overpowered the form of the object they decorated. The grape-vine with heavy bunches of grapes and gnarled oak branches laden with acorns were characteristic motifs. Oriental landscapes were enclosed in Rococo cartouches.

Other articles were decorated with scenes relating to American history: a pitcher with a scene of a Whig meeting was made by the silversmith Osmon Reed, of Philadelphia, and a monteith showing General Israel Putnam leaving his farm to go to the Battle of Lexington was made by Andrew E. Warner, of Baltimore.

In Sterling silver Tiffany and Gorham were the leaders, but there were many other important manufacturers. Among the outstanding ones in New York were William Gale & Son, Wood & Hughes and Ball, Tompkins & Black, which had by 1876 become Black, Starr & Frost. In Boston there were Jones, Ball & Poor and the Laforme Brothers, and in Philadelphia R. & W. Wilson, Bailey & Kitchen and the still existing J. E. Caldwell & Co. In Baltimore Andrew E. Warner and Samuel Kirk & Son, and in San Francisco, the firm that was to become Shreve & Co. were the pioneers.

The discovery of the Comstock Lode near Virginia City, Nevada, made a quantity of silver available. It also

produced millionaires with a desire for flashy living, and silver became a status symbol. Comstock Lode silver shipped direct from the mines to such silver manufacturers as the Gorham Manufacturing Co. and Tiffany & Co. was made into dining services and tea-sets.

The most interesting Gold Rush silver was the set made in the 1850s by Tiffany for James E. Birch, who had operated a stagecoach line to the mines. The pieces are Rococo in form and the decoration includes etched and embossed scenes of early Californian and Gold Rush days. Finials were figures of miners panning gold, and a model of an early stagecoach was incorporated.

Several other styles were also popular in the silver made in the 1840s and 1850s. The Elizabethan style was characterized by the use of heavy strapwork in both engraved ornament and heavy, applied decoration. Classical forms and ornament, based on Greek and Etruscan designs, were also revived at this time.

Renaissance

At the great Crystal Palace Exhibition of 1851 many of the French exhibits were in the Renaissance style, and from this time on there was a gradual decline in Rococo naturalistic design; an increasing vogue for design derived from Classical and Renaissance models made its appearance in American silver by the late 1850s. With its straight architectural forms, the Renaissance style became the second important influence in American Victorian silver.

Motifs of decoration such as beading and Greek key borders, anthemions, palmettes, arabesques, portrait medallions, animal heads and feet were applied to modified Classical shapes. Classical vase forms, which were Renaissance versions of Greek vases, replaced the bulbous Rococo shapes of teapots, coffeepots and pitchers. There were heavy, rounded teapots with straight, cylinder necks combining both naturalistic and formal Renaissance details, and centrepieces and dessert stands resembled the tazza, their bases decorated with swans, dolphins and groups of draped female figures. Classical friezes ornamented the more elaborate articles, and the Victorian predilection for symbolism appeared in allegorical figures of Justice, Loyalty, Agriculture, the Seasons, masks of Comedy and Tragedy and figures of Apollo and Diana. Designs combining the pictorial and the Classical resulted in the literary, story-telling silver, with scenes from contemporary literature such as Tennyson's *Daydream*.

In the 1860s, Samuel Kirk & Sons (formerly & Son) produced silver that was engraved and chased with Renaissance scroll- and leaf-designs and figures of dolphins and fauns. Elegant urn-shapes, tazze and dessert stands were ornamented with Classical figures surrounded by Pompeian arabesques. Paulding Farnham was the most important exponent of Renaissance silver in America. His pieces are ornamented with embossed fruit, flower- and vase-borders and Florentine patterns. Farnham was a member of Tiffany & Co. and the silver was exhibited at the Paris Exposition Universelle in 1900.

The 1860s marked the beginning of mass production by the silver manufacturing companies. In addition to the large companies, there were now centres of silver manufacture in North Attleboro, Massachusetts; Providence, Rhode Island; Meriden and Hartford, Connecticut, and Newark, New Jersey.

TOP *Tea service, American, c. 1875. Electroplate. The Renaissance style superseded the Rococo in the United States in the 1850s. Greenfield Village and Henry Ford Museum.*

ABOVE LEFT *Soup tureen with cover, S. Kirk & Sons, Baltimore, c. 1865. Repoussé silver with a cast silver finial of a stag, ht 10¾ in (27·3 cm).*

ABOVE *Compote, William Gale & Son, New York, 1863, W. 10½ in (26·7 cm). An amalgam of Renaissance and Classical elements not uncommon in the 1860s. Metropolitan Museum of Art.*

Other nineteenth-century centres were Baltimore, Maryland; St Louis, Missouri; and Cincinnati, Ohio. The Sterling standard was adopted in 1868 and silver was marked Sterling from that time on. Patterns of flat silver began to be patented at this period; the patent date shows when a pattern was first made.

In 1891 Tiffany was given the commission to make a vase for presentation

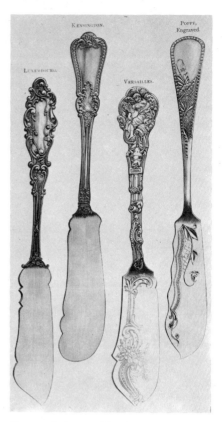

Butter knives with patterned handles illustrated in the catalogue of the Gorham Manufacturing Co. of 1894. Sterling silver. Gorham's adopted year marks on flatware in 1868.

to Edward Dean Adams, chairman of the board of the American Cotton Oil Co. The vase, which was made during the years 1893 to 1895, was designed by Paulding Farnham. It was of gold studded with pearls and semi-precious stones. The design symbolized the growth and development of the cotton industry in the United States and the cotton flower was the inspiration for the design and colour of the vase. All the materials used, including the gold and stones, were mined in the United States.

Eclecticism

The practice of reviving the styles of the past reached its height after 1870. The revivals – Classical, Medieval, Renaissance, Baroque, Rococo and Oriental – intermingled. There were combinations of Renaissance and Elizabethan, Moorish and Persian, Japanese and Jacobean. Large pieces, such as testimonials and trophies, often had mythological and symbolic decorative schemes but the domestic plate tended to be simpler. A marked angularity was characteristic of

the forms of the teapots and coffee-pots and jugs, with the body sloping inward towards the top and curving below to a flat base. Tall handles rose in a curve above the top of the vessel or at sharp right angles, repeating the angular form of the vessel. These forms were often ornamented with bands of moulding. Engraved and chased ornament replaced cast and relief decoration, and Classical designs, Persian, Indian and Egyptian motifs were used. A low dish combining a glass container in a silver framework with cupids and Classical figures was the most popular table centre-piece. A little later there was a revival of Adam urn-shapes decorated with fluting, swags and rams' heads.

Vase in the Japanese style, Tiffany & Co., New York, c. 1895. Silver with applied, engraved, pierced and chased decoration, ht 9½ in (24·1 cm). Sotheby's Belgravia.

Both Tiffany and Gorham exhibited silver at the Exposition in Paris in 1889. The Tiffany exhibit included pieces with Saracenic and native American themes decorated with American flowers, animals, sports and Indian scenes. The exhibit of the Gorham Manufacturing Co. was mainly East Indian: a huge branched candelabra supported by the form of an elephant. After-dinner coffee-pots were in exotic shapes taken from Persian and Turkish models.

The silver exhibited by both Tiffany and Gorham at the World's Columbian Exposition at Chicago in 1893 was more

impressive than that exhibited at Paris. A. J. Barrett, who had been connected with Hunt & Roskell in London, was now at Gorham and his influence was to be seen in the Gorham exhibits of the silver sculpture currently enjoying great popularity in Britain, in, for example, the vase of which the theme was Ulysses defying Polyphemus. Another elaborate piece was the Jaeger Bowl which showed a scene with figures of Neptune, sea nymphs and dolphins. There was also an extensive ecclesiastical exhibit of pieces by William C. Codman, including a large cross and vessels made for St Patrick's Cathedral, New York City. Tiffany exhibited silver with distinctive American characteristics: the impressive Magnolia Vase designed by John T. Curran was of a form suggested by the pottery of the ancient cliff dwellers of the Pueblos (see p. 210). The decoration consists of magnolias enamelled in natural colours, and below these is lattice-work of cactus and stalks of golden rod.

Presentation Silver

Presentation silver was a major product of the Victorian silver companies. Since these pieces were intended for decorative purposes, the most extreme styles and fanciful designs were employed and every technique of decoration for their enhancement. There are examples in every style.

One of the important presentation items in the Rococo style was the dinner-service consisting of 381 pieces which was made by William Gale & Son, New York, and presented to Commodore Matthew Calbraith Perry by the Chamber of Commerce and Merchants of New York City in 1855 in acknowledgment of his success in the negotiation of a treaty with Japan in 1854. The pieces are embossed with floral sprays and have rustic handles with pendant bunches of grapes. The set is now in the collection of the New York Historical Society.

There were many presentation pieces given to heroes of the Civil War but the most important item was the presentation sword. Swords made by Tiffany & Co. were given to Major General Fremont, to Major General Burnside and to Major General Halleck. The grips on these swords were decorated with mythological figures, the Goddess of Liberty or figures of officers in Civil War uniform.

The most important American Victorian piece of testimonial silver was the Bryant Vase, which was made in 1875 for presentation to the American poet, William Cullen Bryant. The vase is

Bryant Vase, designed by J. H. Whitehouse and made by Tiffany & Co., New York, presented to the poet William Cullen Bryant, 1875. Ht 33¾ in (84·8 cm). Metropolitan Museum of Art.

Classical in form with Renaissance decoration and allegorical motifs. Medallions contain the portrait bust of the poet and low-relief scenes of his life and poems. The Vase was designed by James H. Whitehouse. It was the accepted design in a contest to which Tiffany & Co., the Whiting Manufacturing Co. and the Gorham Manufacturing Co. were invited to submit designs.

Trophies and Navy Silver

Racing trophies held a place of importance in the Victorian era and, together with presentation and exhibition pieces, were regarded as major products of the silver companies. Trophies took the form of cups, vases, centre-pieces and punch-bowls. One of the best-known American racing trophies was the Belmont Cup, made by Tiffany & Co. in 1869. It is a silver punch-bowl in the Rococo style decorated with figures of horses at its base and on the cover. Race and hunt trophies often have illustrative scenes; sculptural figures of deer, and Indians and patriotic figures cling to the sides of urns, sometimes completely obliterating the form of the piece.

A considerable number of racing cups, such as the Goelet and Astor Cups of the New York Yacht Club and Commodore Bennett's Ocean Challenge Cup, were made by Tiffany's, but a group, interesting because of their indigenous subject matter, were made by the Whiting Manufacturing Co. The cup won by the *Priscilla* has a figure of the Puritan maiden and an inscription from Longfellow's poem *The Courtship of Miles Standish*; a tennis trophy made by Gorham in 1891 illustrated Cooper's *The Last of the Mohicans*.

One of the little-known categories of American silversmithing was the production of presentation pieces for battleships and cruisers of the United States Navy. In the 1880s and 1890s, when the modern navy was built, silver services were given by states or cities to ships named after them. These pieces are covered with motifs of sentimental import which relate to the history, tradition and achievements of the particular state or city. State seals, scenery including native flora and fauna mingle with characteristic naval symbols such as

207

Electroplate

Electroplate (silverplate) is one of the most characteristic products of the Victorian era. With Britannia metal, it supplied the demand of the middle classes who could not afford expensive Sterling silver for fine domestic vessels. Electroplate was a natural progression from Britannia metal since the production methods and equipment used in making Britannia wares could also be used in electroplating; in fact, many early pieces of electroplate were on a Britannia metal base. Any article that could be made in silver could be reproduced in electroplate for half the price.

The beginnings of electroplating cannot be traced to one individual. The English firm of G. R. & H. Elkington was the first to make practical use of the process, taking out a patent in 1840. A representative of Elkington had travelled to the United States to try to interest New York firms in the new process without success. However, John O. Mead, an American manufacturer of Britannia ware at Philadelphia went to England to learn the new plating technique and brought back equipment. By 1845, he had developed successful electroplating techniques. Although there were other early experimenters, John O. Mead is credited with being the first successful American electroplater.

Although Mead developed a thriving commercial trade, his firm never rivalled the larger companies. The companies which were best known in the early electroplate field in the United States were 1847 Rogers Bros, The Meriden Britannia Co. and Reed & Barton. As early as 1852 there were six or seven small Britannia ware manufacturers in Meriden, Connecticut, who combined their efforts and established the Meriden Britannia Co., which was later to become the leading spirit in the formation of the International Silver Co. in 1898. Among the many companies taken over by the International Silver Co. were the Webster Manufacturing Co., Brooklyn, New York; the Wilcox Silver Plate Co., Meriden, and the Middletown Plate Co. The International Silver Co. also manufactured flatware and hollow-ware for hotels, railways, steamships and airlines.

The firm of Reed & Barton, which had evolved from the Taunton Britannia Manufacturing Co., turned its attention to electroplate in 1848. An expert was brought over from England and initially English designs were copied. The first Reed & Barton patent, a tea-service design, was not taken out until 1858.

In 1865 the Gorham Manufacturing

Co. entered the field. In 1852 John Gorham had gone to England where he worked in the Elkington firm in Birmingham and also with James Dixon & Sons, of Sheffield. Their first electroplated wares were, however, delayed until after the Civil War. The firm of Wallace, Simpson & Co., of Wallingford, Connecticut, made electroplate in 1865 and in 1870 Tiffany & Co. acquired the Adams & Shaw factory at Newark, New Jersey, and electroplating was added to their productions.

The manufacturing of most of the electroplated wares was originally confined to New England and the north-eastern states, principally Massachusetts, Connecticut and New York, but a few manufacturers such as the Homan Manufacturing Co., of Cincinnati, Ohio, were making electroplated wares in the 1860s. Later electroplated goods were made in Rhode Island, Maine, New Jersey, Pennsylvania, Maryland, Wisconsin, Ohio, Illinois, Indiana and as far west as California.

No American manufacturers were represented at the Crystal Palace Exhibition in London in 1851, although there were displayed tea-sets, centre-pieces, fish-slices and other electroplated articles by British manufacturers. They did, however, exhibit their wares at the New York Crystal Palace Exhibition two years later, and Gorham included illustrations of electroplate in their advertisement of 1853 in *Illustrated American Advertiser*. It was not long before American manufacturers were marketing electroplated tea-sets, and from 1860 to the end of the century numerous patents were taken out. Tea- and coffee-services became the Victorian middle-class status symbol. Tea-sets comprised teapots, hot-water pots, creamers, sugar-bowls and waste bowls. There were trays and matching pieces such as swinging kettles for hot water, coffee urns, cake baskets and spoon holders.

The styles of electroplated tea-sets followed those of Sterling silver and

Commodore Bennett's Ocean Challenge Cup, Tiffany & Co., New York, 1876. In the roundel is represented an incident from Longfellow's poem, The Wreck of the Hesperus. *The figure on top is Columbus.*

anchors, cannons, flags, dolphins and eagles and an etched or cast representation of the ship. Every technique of silversmithing and all styles of traditional ornament were represented, including Egyptian, Etruscan, Oriental, Renaissance and even Art Nouveau. The first Victorian presentation pieces were given to the U.S.S. *Maine* in 1891 by the State of Maine. They are ornamented with pine cones and pine needles, and a centre panel depicts the pine-tree seal of the State of Maine.

OPPOSITE *Memorandum case, maker's mark of George Unite, Birmingham, 1882; electrotype card case, from a design by George Stanton, maker's mark of Elkington & Co., Birmingham, 1861; gilded silver spoon, maker's mark of Francis Higgins, London, 1887; gilded silver spoon, maker's mark of Atkins & Sumersall, London, 1838; electroplated wine label, Patent Office Design Registry mark for 27 March 1865, parcel 5; gilded silver shoe horn and eye mirror, maker's mark WT, FP, London, 1865. Michael Parkington Collection and Sotheby's Belgravia.*

BURGUNDY.

varied from the Classical, with beading and Greek key patterns, to the Rococo, ornamented with leafy scrolls and floral engraving. Most pieces were of large capacity, capable of holding several pints of liquid, with high-domed covers, and the designs included large lobes, heavy fluting and wide bands of cast ornament. In the 1860s pieces were often made to stand on slender goats' hoof legs ending in a goat's head where the leg joined the body of the vessel. Lions' heads and feet were also used as supports. The Classical medallion motif was popular at this time and several companies produced variations of the pattern. The historical Charter Oak pattern with vessels in the form of acorns and decorated with embossed and cast acorns and oak leaves was originated by the Meriden Britannia Co. in about 1867.

Teapots and coffee-pots were of various shapes, from tall pyriforms or pear shapes to round, ball shapes, but almost all of them stood on four short animal legs ending in a human or animal mask. By the 1880s the vessels were made smaller and squatter in shape and rested flat on the table. Repoussé floral decoration completely covered the forms or was applied in wide bands about the vessel. After-dinner coffee-pots had long necks adapted from Turkish and Persian designs and were ornamented with fluting or Oriental designs.

Electroplate was employed, too, for large exhibition and presentation pieces and quantities of these were made. There were also numerous sporting trophies made in electroplate. At first the display pieces were copies of antique originals, such as the Iliad silver in the Louvre, Paris. Original designs were made combining Classical details with symbolism relating to contemporary history. At the Philadelphia Centennial in 1876 the Meriden Silver Plate Co. exhibited an elaborate centre-piece with figures symbolizing Music, Art, Science and Commerce, and the Middletown Plate Co. exhibited the *Barge of Venus. The Buffalo Hunt,* designed by Theodore Baur and made by the Meriden Britannia Co., was exhibited a few years later at the Cotton Exposition in Atlanta, Georgia, in 1881, and again at the International Exposition in Paris in 1889. This was a figure of an Indian on horseback spearing a buffalo. The figure was originally cast

OPPOSITE *Magnolia Vase, designed by John T. Curran and made by Tiffany & Co., New York, exhibited at the World's Columbian Exposition, Chicago, 1893. Enamelled silver, ht 31 in (78·7 cm). Metropolitan Museum of Art.*

Ice pitcher and goblet, Meriden Britannia Co., 1868 Patent. Electroplate. Greenfield Village and Henry Ford Museum.

in bronze and symbolized the winning of the West. The piece was later made a standard catalogue item and could be ordered in 'old silver' or 'gold inlaid' with the Indian's body electroplated in red gold and the buckskin breeches in yellow gold.

Ornamental pieces included vases, statues of animals, Indians, and mythological gods. There was also a line in wares incorporating cut and engraved glass, such as centre-pieces and matching compotes.

Other electroplated pieces for the Victorian table and for household use included casters with sets of bottles, pickle casters, spoon holders, fruit stands, cake baskets and centre-pieces with several vases set on a plateau, ice-water pitchers and trays. The tilting ice-water pitcher set on a tray with two or more goblets reached its height of popularity in the 1880s: the Meriden Britannia Co. illustrated fifty-seven different designs in their catalogue of 1886 and in 1885 Reed & Barton had offered fifty-one styles.

A large number of vases, bowls, fruit- and cake-baskets and pickle casters were made with linings of coloured glass, and there were some with patterns of pressed glass and frilled and ripple-edged cased glass with gold and multi-coloured enamel decoration.

Katharine Morrison McClinton

Designers and Manufacturers

ANGELL III, JOSEPH
Head of a firm of manufacturing retail silversmiths founded in Clerkenwell at the beginning of the nineteenth century by his grandfather, Joseph Angell I, and his father, Joseph Angell II. Joseph Angell II and III formed a partnership in 1840 and Joseph Angell II's brother and nephew, John and George, formed a partnership in the same year. Joseph II and III moved from Clerkenwell to factory premises in Panton Street, Haymarket, before 1842, and about then to retail premises at 10 Strand. Joseph Angell III took control of the firm and entered his mark alone at the Goldsmiths' Hall in 1849. In time the factory in Panton Street closed and the firm became Angell & Brown. Joseph Angell III died in 1891. Stylistically, the Angell products are complex and interesting: far from diluting their energies, the split between Joseph Angell II and III and John and George seemed to increase them. Both firms specialized in domestic ware of a 'practical' and novel nature and were well represented at the Great Exhibition, Joseph III and George exhibiting on separate stands. Objects on Joseph III's stand included the Aesop's Fable Tea and Coffee Service and the Vintage Claret Jug, both with detachable 'jackets', minutely worked with small figures and animals set into complicated surrounds of Rococo features, exciting much comment. Joseph III also made a daring use of enamel on his tea-sets and cake baskets which was considered by the critics either the height of luxury or the extreme in bad taste.

ASHBEE, CHARLES ROBERT
(1863–1942)
English architect and designer in all media, founder of the Guild and School of Handicraft in 1887. A follower of William Morris, he was the author of *Modern English Silver* (1908). His later work is Art Nouveau in character, combining various techniques and materials.

BAILEY & KITCHEN
Philadelphia silversmiths and jewelers founded in 1833 and trading under this name between 1839 and 1846. Their successors, Bailey, Banks & Biddle Co., are still in business.

EDWARD BARNARD & SONS
Large manufacturing London silversmiths to the retail trade during the

nineteenth century who today account for a great deal of the silver made in London, from premises in Hatton Garden. Their origins can be traced to Anthony Nelme's business founded in 1689. As Edward Barnard & Sons the firm continued until 1910, when it became a limited company. In addition to a whole range of domestic plate, they were capable of producing work to special order and groups of display and presentation plate. Barnard & Sons also produced ELECTROPLATE and even supplied silvered plates for DAGUERREOTYPES (see PHOTOGRAPHY GLOSSARY).

THOMAS BRADBURY & SONS
Sheffield platers until the end of the nineteenth century and silversmiths after 1848, they made ELECTROPLATE under licence from ELKINGTON'S.

CHAWNER & CO.
London firm specializing in the manufacture of table silver. In the eighteenth and early nineteenth centuries the silversmiths George Smith, William Eley, William Fearn and William Chawner, among others were involved. William Chawner, of Hosier Lane, Smithfield, entered his first mark alone at the Goldsmiths' Hall in 1815 and died in 1834. His widow Mary succeeded to the business, then called Chawner & Co. Mrs Chawner entered a joint mark with her foreman, G. W. Adams, in 1840. Soon afterwards Adams took control of the firm, although he exhibited under his own name in 1851 and 1862. The firm continued until c. 1884, when it was absorbed into Holland, Aldwincle & Slater, formerly Henry Holland Son & Slater. Chawner & Co.'s output, struck with the maker's mark of G. W. Adams after 1840, consists chiefly of forks and spoons in all the contemporary styles. Their greatest rival during the middle of the nineteenth century was the firm of Francis Higgins, and these two concerns were the most prolific table-silver manufacturers in London, supplying most of the retail trade and large manufacturing retailers like Hunt & Roskell and GARRARD'S.

JAMES DIXON & SONS
Sheffield platers, silversmiths and electroplaters, at the International Exhibition of 1862 they showed pieces plated by both methods.

DRESSER, DR CHRISTOPHER (1834–1904)
English botanist and a leading designer and design reformer advocating simplicity, symmetry and a decorative functionalism. His interest in Oriental art resulted in a visit to Japan in 1876. He opened an Oriental warehouse in London in the 1870s and objects designed by him were displayed at the Art Furnishers' Alliance in the 1880s. He was the original

Taperstick in the form of a harebell, maker's mark of Edward Barnard & Sons, London, 1840. Barnard's were manufacturing silversmiths to the trade. Victoria and Albert Museum.

designer of Clutha glass and his silver designs were carried out by Hukin & Heath and ELKINGTON'S.

G. R. & H. ELKINGTON
Partnership formed in Birmingham in 1824 with a London branch by 1829. Patentees of the ELECTROPLATE process in 1840, they took out a patent in 1841 covering the ELECTROTYPE process and later patented improvements in electrodeposition. From 1842 the Birmingham branch traded under the name of Elkington, Mason & Co., maker of domestic and spectacular pieces; from 1848 the London branch, from premises in Regent Street, traded as Elkington & Co. Among the designers who worked for Elkington's were Pierre-Émile Jeannest, Léonard Morel-Ladeuil, A. A. Willms and DRESSER.

WILLIAM GALE & SON
New York silversmiths acquired by Dominick & Haff in the nineteenth century, and eventually by REED & BARTON. Their dinner-service of 381 pieces presented to Commodore Matthew Calbraith Perry represents the height of the Rococo style in the United States.

GARRARD & CO.
Probably founded in London in the eighteenth century by George Wickes, the firm succeeded Rundell, Bridge & Rundell as Royal Goldsmiths in 1830. They were leading makers of domestic silver and presentation pieces in the nineteenth century.

WILLIAM GIBSON & JOHN LANGMAN, THE GOLDSMITHS & SILVERSMITHS CO. LTD
Gibson, a native of Belfast, came to London and entered a joint mark with his partner John Langman in 1881, founding shortly thereafter the Goldsmiths & Silversmiths Co. Ltd, retail goldsmiths, silversmiths and jewelers with manufacturing interests. In 1952 the Company amalgamated with GARRARD & CO. LTD, and this amalgamation merged in 1963 with Mappin & Webb, Elkington & Co. Ltd, Adie Brothers and Walker & Hall under the name of British Silverware. The premises of the Goldsmiths & Silversmiths Co. Ltd in Regent Street, London, are now the designated house of Garrard & Co. Ltd.

GORHAM MANUFACTURING CO.
Trading name between 1865 and 1961 of the silver and, since 1865, ELECTROPLATE manufacturers and retailers of Providence, Rhode Island, now known as the Gorham Corporation. They were among the first to adopt methods of machine production of silver and the first, in 1868, to reject COIN SILVER in favour of STERLING SILVER. In that year they devised a system of date-marking their flatware: up to and including 1884 the letters of the alphabet from A to Q were used and thereafter until 1933 symbols were adopted. The English designers Thomas Pairpoint and A. J. Barrett were employed by them, and in the late nineteenth century William C. Codman produced a number of pieces in the Art Nouveau style using the trade name Martelé. They purchased the Whiting Manufacturing Co., makers of Sterling silverwares and jewelry in 1905, Black, Starr & Frost, the New York manufacturers and retailers, in 1929, and Graff, Washbourne & Dunn, successors to Wood & Hughes, of New York, in 1961.

SAMUEL KIRK & SON
Trading name between 1846 and 1861 and 1868 and 1896 of the oldest surviving silversmiths in the United States, since 1924 called Samuel Kirk & Son Inc. Various other trading names were used at other periods. Samuel Kirk, the founder, opened a shop in Baltimore in 1815 and it was he who introduced the REPOUSSÉ, Rococo or Baltimore style into American silver. Responsible for a number of famous trophies and presentation pieces, the firm has always responded to the newest in design.

LIBERTY & CO.
Founded in London in 1875 by Arthur Lazenby Liberty (1843–1917) as an Oriental warehouse. In addition to imported goods, they retailed wares of British manufacture and designed and

Trophy in the form of a horn, Whiting & Co., New York, awarded to the winner of the fourth annual sweepstake of the Corinthian Yacht Club of New York on 26 August 1892. Sotheby Parke Bernet.

Two Martelé vases, Gorham Manufacturing Co., Providence, Rhode Island, c. 1900. Britannia standard silver in the Art Nouveau style. Sotheby Parke Bernet.

patented their own furniture and, in partnership with W. H. Haseler of Birmingham, silver wares and jewelry (Cymric) and pewter (Tudric). Designers for Liberty's include Bernard Cuzner (1877–1956), Reginald Silver (1879–1965) and Archibald Knox (1864–1933).

MARTIN, HALL & CO. LTD
Established in Sheffield by the partners Richard Martin and Ebenezer Hall in c. 1854, by 1866 the concern had become a limited company with offices in London and Glasgow as well as Sheffield. They were manufacturing and wholesale silversmiths to the retail trade supplying domestic ware and table silver, and they were also manufacturers of ELECTRO-PLATE. The firm was dissolved in 1936. In c. 1878 their London agent James Slater joined the manufacturing silversmiths Henry Holland & Son, until 1884 known as Holland, Son & Slater.

MEAD, JOHN O.
Philadelphia Britannia ware manufacturer and gilder by the mercury process (see METALWORK GLOSSARY, BRONZE), probably the first successful electroplater in the United States. After learning the technique in Birmingham, he returned to set up his own business.

MERIDEN BRITANNIA CO.
Firm formed in 1852 by the amalgamation of several Britannia ware manufacturers in Meriden, Connecticut. By 1855 production included electroplated hollow ware and flatware and in 1862 the Company purchased 1847 ROGERS BROS. An important name in both simple domestic and elaborate exhibition pieces, it became part of the International Silver Co. in 1898.

PUGIN, AUGUSTUS WELBY NORTHMORE (1812–52)
First great Gothic Revivalist. Son of Auguste-Charles Pugin, the architect, he worked for the silversmiths Rundell, Bridge & Rundell. In 1830 he set up an independent practice and among those manufacturers who worked for him was John Hardman & Co., the Birmingham

metalworkers, who executed some of his designs for church plate.

CHARLES RAWLINGS & WILLIAM SUMMERS
London small workers, specializing in the manufacture of snuff boxes, vesta cases, many of which are finely engraved, vinaigrettes, wine labels and mounts for pipe bowls. Charles Rawlings, the senior partner, who entered his first mark in 1817, succeeded to the premises of Theodosia Ann Atkins, a buckle-maker, and Daniel Hockley & Thomas Bosworth, small workers. In 1829 Rawlings registered a mark with William Summers and they continued in partnership until Rawlings' death in 1863. William Summers continued working until the late 1870s.

REED & BARTON
Trading name probably since 1840 of a firm in Taunton, Massachusetts, with origins as pewterers and makers of Britannia wares. Evolving from the Taunton Britannia Manufacturing Co., they concentrated on electroplated wares after 1848, though in the 1890s they started to supply the renewed demand for STERLING SILVER wares. They are still in existence.

CHARLES REILY & GEORGE STORER
London makers specializing in wine labels, also makers of centre-pieces, tea-sets and other domestic and display platè. They were successors to the business of James Hyde, a working silversmith specializing in wine labels, through Mary Ann Hyde and John Samuel Reily, father of Charles Reily (b. 1803). Charles Reily & George Storer entered their first mark together in 1829,

and continued working until the early 1860s.

ROGERS BROS

Trade name in 1847 of early ELECTRO-PLATE manufacturers and distributors in Hartford, Connecticut, with origins dating back to a jeweler and silversmith in 1820. In 1862 the firm was absorbed by the MERIDEN BRITANNIA CO., though the Rogers Bros mark, prefixed by the date 1847, was retained. During the Victorian period the firm traded under various names including Rogers Bros Manufacturing Co.

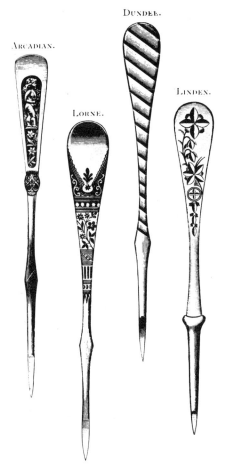

Nut picks illustrated in the catalogue of the Meriden Britannia Co. of 1893. The trademark is 1847 Rogers Bros, the name of the firm acquired in 1862 by the Meriden Britannia Co. Electroplate.

STORR & MORTIMER, MORTIMER & HUNT, HUNT & ROSKELL

London manufacturing retailers. Paul Storr, having left Rundell, Bridge & Rundell in 1819, moved to a factory in Harrison Street, Gray's Inn Lane (now Gray's Inn Road). He soon went into partnership with John Mortimer, the assistant of a retiring retail goldsmith and jeweler, William Gray, of 13 New

Bond Street. Storr & Mortimer, now manufacturing and retail goldsmiths, jewelers and silversmiths with an influential clientele, moved to 156 New Bond Street in 1838. Owing to changing economic conditions and Mortimer's supposed ineptitude as a businessman – the shop, which he managed, is said to have been overstocked – Storr brought his relative by marriage John Samuel Hunt into the firm as partner. Storr retired to Tooting in 1839 and died in 1844, and the firm continued as Mortimer & Hunt. When Mortimer left in 1843, the firm became Hunt & Roskell with Robert Roskell, of Liverpool, as the new partner. Although J. S. Hunt died in 1865, and his son John in 1879, Hunt & Roskell continued until 1889, when the firm was bought by J. W. Benson, who retained the name. It was incorporated as a limited company in 1897. An important establishment, rivalled only by GARRARD & CO. LTD, it supplied presentation pieces, racing trophies, domestic wares, table silver, writing desk furnishings and jewelry. Like Garrard's, Hunt & Roskell employed specialist makers such as the firms of Francis Higgins and CHAWNER & CO., both table-silver makers. Hunt & Roskell prominently exhibited at several exhibitions, notably in London in 1851 and 1862. Their principal designers included H. H. Armstead and A. J. Barrett.

TIFFANY & CO.

New York retailer and, after 1868, when the Company was incorporated, silver manufacturer responsible for introducing the English Sterling silver standard into the United States and for disseminating a taste for Islamic and Oriental works of art. The reputation of the Company, inaugurated as Tiffany & Young in 1837, was due in part to the contribution of Edward C. Moore as chief designer and partner from 1868 to 1891, when he was succeeded by John T. Curran.

British Silver and Electroplate Marks

SILVER

As a result of a statute enacted by Edward I, no article of silver made in England since 1300, with the exception of certain very small pieces, should be unmarked. In the case of Scottish silver, it is improbable that any marks were struck before the enactment of 1457, while no marks are known on Irish silver

before the incorporation of the Dublin Goldsmiths' Company in 1637.

The group of marks on a piece of silver vary according to where it has been assayed, or tested, and in 1837 there were ten assay offices in the British Isles: London, Birmingham, Chester, Dublin, Edinburgh, Exeter, Glasgow, Newcastle-upon-Tyne, Sheffield and York. By far the most important has always been the London Assay Office of the Worshipful Company of Goldsmiths, and between 1837 and 1901 at least four of the following five marks should be found on a piece of silver assayed in London:

London hallmark
Maker's mark
Date-letter
Assay mark
Sovereign's head.

London hallmark

The leopard's head, as specified in the statute of 1300, has always been recognized as the London mark on STERLING SILVER. Originally crowned, the leopard lost its crown in 1821 and ever since has resembled a friendly cat.

In a statute of 1363, the mark was also established as the monarch's mark, and as such it has been struck on pieces assayed elsewhere in England, but in these instances the leopard might retain its crown even after 1821.

Maker's mark

From 1363 it has been compulsory for a silversmith to strike his work with his own specific mark, registered at the assay office to which he submits his pieces which in London would be the Goldsmiths' Hall. Originally an emblem or symbol, it became law in 1739 that the mark should be the maker's initials. By the nineteenth century, this had frequently become the letter of the firm supplying the article rather than the actual craftsman who made it. (See overleaf.)

Date-letter

The system of striking a piece with an alphabetical letter, so as to establish the year in which it was assayed, was introduced during the fifteenth century. From 1560 the letter, which changes every year, has been enclosed in a shield, when struck in London, the shape of the shield and the letters themselves varying with each cycle. The number of letters used is termed a cycle, which, in the case of London, is 20: A to U or V, excluding J.

The primary purpose of the date-letter is to identify the assay master responsible for passing the piece, and since 1660 the date-letter in London has been changed on 29 May each year, the day on which new wardens are elected.

English date letters showing the year 1837 and the first mark in each new cycle.

London
1837   1856   1876   1896

Birmingham
1837   1849   1875   1900

Sheffield
1837   1844   1868   1893

Chester
1837   1839   1864   1884

Edinburgh
1837   1857   1882

Glasgow
1837   1845   1871   1897

Dublin
1837   1846   1851   1852
1853   1871   1896

Assay mark

First struck in London in 1544, the lion passant indicates that the silver is of the STERLING STANDARD, the minimum silver content being 92·5%. The mark has been in use at every British assay office since 1719. While the lion's head, when struck in London, has been in profile since 1821, it continued in certain towns to face outwards (guardant) during the nineteenth century.

Between 1697 and 1720 the standard of wrought silver in England was raised from 92·5% to 95·8%, termed the BRITANNIA STANDARD, to prevent articles being made from coin clippings. The new assay mark was the figure of Britannia and although the Sterling standard, and its lion, was restored by an act of 1719, the Britannia mark has continued in use ever since for articles made with the higher silver content. When such a piece is assayed in London, the leopard's head is replaced by a lion's head erased.

Sovereign's head

Known as the duty mark, the sovereign's head in profile should be found on every piece of silver assayed in England and Scotland between 1784 and 1890, and in Ireland between 1807 and 1890, to indicate that the requisite rate of duty has been paid. All the monarchs prior to 1837 look to the right, but the head of Queen Victoria looks to the left. With the abolition of the duty in 1890 the mark was discontinued.

Assay offices outside London

Just as the London mark on STERLING SILVER is the leopard's head, so every assay office has its own distinguishing hallmark. In 1837 there were nine other centres, their marks, with the exception of Birmingham, Sheffield and Dublin, being adaptations of the city arms:

Birmingham: Anchor. The office was established in 1773 and continues today.
Chester: Three gerbes and erect sword. The office closed in 1962.
Dublin: Figure of Hibernia. The office continues today, the sole assay office of Eire.
Edinburgh: Triple-towered castle. The office continues today, the only remaining one in Scotland.
Exeter: Triple-towered castle. The office closed in 1883.
Glasgow: Tree, fish, bird and bell. The office closed in 1964.
Newcastle-upon-Tyne: Three castles. The office closed in 1884.
Sheffield: Crown. The office was established in 1773 and continues today, the mark altered in 1975 to a Tudor rose.
York: Five lions passant on a cross. The office closed in 1858.

From 1837 to 1890 silver assayed outside London might have up to six marks: the relevant town-mark; the maker's mark; the date-letter; the assay mark; the sovereign's head; the leopard's head (the last only on pieces assayed at Exeter and Newcastle-upon-Tyne). As in the case of London, the maker's mark would be the first letters of his christian name and surname, or those of his firm, and the date-letter would change annually, without any uniformity, however, regarding the day of the year on which it was altered or the number of letters in a cycle. The sovereign's head was struck at all ten assay offices until 1890, when the duty on silver was repealed, but there was a certain tardiness in altering the punch, Edinburgh, Glasgow and Newcastle-upon-Tyne only substituting Queen Victoria for William IV in 1841.

Whereas in England the assay mark, guaranteeing that the metal is of the STERLING STANDARD, has been the lion passant since 1719, the Dublin assay mark was prescribed in 1637 as the harp crowned; the Edinburgh mark has been the thistle since 1759, and the Glasgow mark was established by an act of 1819 as the lion rampant.

Registry mark

Between 1842 and 1883 objects were sometimes stamped with a British Patent Office, lozenge-shaped mark indicating the precise date when the design was registered (see PORCELAIN and GLASS GLOSSARIES). Silver, SHEFFIELD PLATE and ELECTROPLATE were included in Class 1.

ELECTROPLATE

In addition to the REGISTRY MARK, the following marks are found on Victorian electroplate:

E.P.G.S. – Electroplated German Silver
E.P.N.S. – Electroplated nickel silver
E.P.B.M. – Electroplated Britannia metal

ELECTROPLATE

The firm of Elkington's devised a series of date marks much resembling silver marks. From 1841 to 1848 the marks numbered from 1 to 8, with the 6 reversed; from 1849 letters, starting with K, were adopted; in 1865 a new series of letters started with A, excluding B, C, I and J (in 1877 Q and R were used simultaneously). These marks were accompanied by a maker's mark which varied several times between 1837 and 1901.

American Silver and Electroplate Marks

SILVER

The comprehensive British system of marking silver so that it is generally possible to identify the maker and date of the piece, the quality of the silver and the office where it was assayed, was not adopted in the United States.

Makers' marks and trademarks

From Colonial times it was customary, though not obligatory, to mark silver with the maker's initials, sometimes accompanied by a personal device, and in the Victorian period this was often extended to include the full name and address. In the 1840s the silver and electroplate manufacturing companies began to use trademarks, some of which were registered with the United States Patent Office. These were sometimes shown with, or substituted by, the wholesaler's and retailer's marks.

Date-marks

Between 1814 and 1830 the Baltimore Assay Office date-marked silver, but until the mid-nineteenth century it was not usual to indicate date. At that time some New York silver was marked with a diamond-shaped device with a number in each corner, similar to the British registry marks. William Gale & Sons and the GORHAM MANUFACTURING CO. were among those companies that devised their own system of date marking; from 1868 TIFFANY & CO. stamped their wares with the name of the Company and the initial of the current president, which is an indication of date. Signatures and trademarks were altered periodically, and patterns, on flatware in particular, can often be dated by reference to the manufacturer's catalogues.

Quality marks

SILVER

C, Coin, Pure Coin: 900/1000 pure silver, sometimes melted down coinage and complying with the Mint Act of 1792.

D, Dollar: Coin Silver.

Sterling: 925/1000 pure silver: the English standard. The mark was in general use after 1868, when the standard was first adopted by the GORHAM MANUFACTURING CO.

ELECTROPLATE

The four common grades of electroplate were Standard Plate (usually marked A-1), Extra Plate, Double Plate and Triple Plate. They were determined by the quantity of pure silver required to coat a gross of teaspoons.

The manufacturers evolved their own systems of marking. Some used the names of the grades in full; others substituted numerals, which were related to the size of the electroplated objects and the quantity of pure silver required to plate them, e.g. a teaspoon might be marked 4 if it were Double Plate and 6 if it were Triple Plate; a dessertspoon by the same manufacturer might be marked 6 if it were Double Plate and 9 if it were Triple Plate on account of the larger size of the object. Separate brand names for the different grades were also employed.

Sectional plating and inlay and silver filling, the purpose of which was to reinforce the areas of flatware receiving the most wear, was also indicated by a mark.

For further information on marks see Bibliography p. 219.

Joseph Angell III

E., J., E. and W. Barnard of Edward Barnard & Sons

James Dixon & Sons

Frederick Elkington of Elkington & Co.

Robert Garrard of R. & S. Garrard & Co.

Gibson & Langham of The Goldsmiths & Silversmiths Co. Ltd

Gorham Manufacturing Co.

Charles Frederick Hancock

John Samuel Hunt of Hunt & Roskell (see Storr & Mortimer)

William Hutton & Sons Sheffield manufacturers of silver and electroplate

S KIRK & SON 925/1000

S. Kirk & Son

Martin, Hall & Co.

Meriden Silver Plate Co.

Meriden Britannia Co.

Charles Rawlings & William Summers

Reed & Barton

Charles Reily & George Storer

1847 Rogers Bros

Benjamin Smith II

Paul Storr of Storr & Mortimer (after 1822)

TIFFANY & CO. 295 ENGLISH STERLING 925-1000 550 BROADWAY

Tiffany & Co.

TRADE MARK STERLING

Whiting Manufacturing Co.

Glossary of Decoration

Examples illustrated are from actual Victorian pieces although the descriptions apply outside the Victorian period.

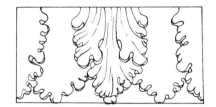

Acanthus leaf
Foliate form with stiff, often curled-over, leaf deriving from the decoration of Corinthian capitals. Incorporated principally in pieces in the Classical idiom, it commonly occurs as a linking device between the lid and the knop, or the stem and the bowl, of a piece.

Anthemion
Radiating honeysuckle motif widely used in Classical architecture. In Victorian silver it is employed principally as a surface decoration.

Arabesque
Scrolling or interlacing plant form of Hellenistic origin closely associated with Islamic ornament. A motif exemplified by TIFFANY silver in the Moorish style.

Beading
Moulded decoration of circular, half-round features simulating a string of beads.

Cartouche
Scrolled or ornate framing device surrounding a coat of arms, inscription or ornamental detail.

C-scroll
Single scroll of a handle or decorative detail, an S-scroll being a double scroll. The embellishments to the basic form might reflect a currently popular style such as the Rococo.

Fluting
Concave parallel channels, sometimes tapering, deriving from columns in Classical architecture.

Gadrooning
Border ornament of radiating lobes, either curved or straight.

Greek key pattern
Repeating pattern composed of straight lines and right angles of Classical origin, used for the decoration of friezes and borders.

Husk
Bell-shaped motif derived from a husk of wheat. It often occurs as a pendant or terminal detail in engraved or etched decoration.

Latticework
Criss-cross framework forming a diamond pattern which generally encloses other forms and motifs of decoration.

Naturalistic floral scrollwork
Uniquely Victorian decoration, often embossed, not based on a Classical form. It often occurs as an asymmetrical overall pattern on the sides of vessels and on small items such as card cases.

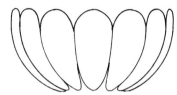

Ovolo
Convex oval form, usually moulded, often occurring in combination with an egg and dart pattern as border decoration.

Palmette
Motif of radiating leaves resembling feathers, related to the ANTHEMION, which first occurred in Classical architecture.

Reeding
Parallel convex ornament resembling reed stalks deriving, like FLUTING, from the Classical column. Melon reeding, a bulbous variant of the original form, occurs particularly in American Victorian silver.

Scrollwork
Scrolled ornament of flowing outline epitomizing the Rococo style.

Strapwork
English Elizabethan and Jacobean ornament originating at Fontainebleau in the sixteenth century and resembling pierced and interlaced straps of leather. The Victorian revival was due in part to illustrations in Owen Jones' *The Grammar of Ornament*, 1856 (see FURNITURE GLOSSARY).

Glossary of Metals and Techniques

Annealing
Reheating of the metal to make it malleable during working.

Appliqué, applied decoration
Ornament worked separately from the object to which it is then appended. Decoration that is manufactured by the CASTING process and CUT CARDWORK

may be applied in this manner for strength as well as effect.

Bright-cut engraving
Engraving with a bevelled cutting tool, which gives to the surface a faceted brilliance.

Britannia metal
Alloy of tin, copper and antimony having the appearance of silvery pewter and capable of taking a higher polish than the latter. From 1769 the newly discovered white metal was used for the manufacture of flatware by Sheffield firms such as JAMES DIXON & SONS. Exports to the United States increased and by the second decade of the nineteenth century the production of Britannia wares had begun there, shortly to supplant that of pewter. Employed as a base for ELECTROPLATE, there was also a demand for unplated Britannia wares as late as the 1890s. In Britain wares were marked with the letters E.P.B.M. to indicate electroplated Britannia metal. (See also METALWORK GLOSSARY.)

Britannia standard silver
From 1697 to 1720 the higher standard of silver obligatory in England. Since that time it has been an optional alternative to STERLING SILVER.

Buffing
Polishing by hand or mechanically with felt or leather to remove evidence of manufacturing tools and fire marks.

Burnishing
Smoothing and hardening the metal by friction to remove PLANISHING marks.

Butler's finishing
Scratching the surface of the metal with a wheel of wire to give it a dull finish, a similar effect to FROSTING.

Cast chasing
Sharpening or adding detail to the surface of CASTING, such as cannot be effected in the mould.

Casting
Fashioning an article, or parts such as the spout, handles and feet, in a mould. Details are sharpened by the process of CAST CHASING.

Chasing
Punching the metal into shape from either the front or the back, no metal being removed in the process.

Coin silver
Silver alloy, approximately 900/1000 pure silver combined with 100/1000 added metal, employed principally for flatware in the United States in the nineteenth century. The metal could be derived from melted-down coinage or it could be new metal meeting the requirements of the Mint Act of 1792.

Cut-card work
Decorative detail soldered flat on to the surface of a piece, sometimes enriched with PIERCING or BEADING.

Coffee pot, Rogers, Smith & Co., New Haven, Connecticut, 1887. The body of the electroplated pot is hand chased. The firm was absorbed by the Meriden Britannia Co. in 1854.

Damascening
Encrusting the surface of metal, usually steel or copper, with gold or silver by beating it into prepared grooves. First practised in Damascus, hence the name, it was one of the many early techniques revived by nineteenth-century metalworkers.

Electroplate
Base metal, such as copper, BRITANNIA METAL (E.P.B.M.), German silver (E.P.G.S.) or NICKEL SILVER (E.P.N.S.), coated with gold or silver by electrical deposition. The base-metal object to be plated is the cathode; the anode is pure silver; and the electric current passes through a solution of potassium cyanide in which both are placed. The first-known electroplated object is an electro-gilded silver goblet in the Royal Collection; the gilding was done by Rundell, Bridge & Rundell in 1814. In 1840 ELKINGTON'S took out a patent for electroplating and electrogilding. Although the Jury at the Great Exhibition of 1851 were careful not to recommend the process, it was evident that electroplate had supplanted the work of the Sheffield platers, some of whom had already purchased licences. In the United States MEAD, a Britannia ware manufacturer, in 1845 was the first to learn the new technique. The best-known early electroplate manufacturers were ROGERS BROS, THE MERIDEN BRITANNIA CO. and REED & BARTON. In electroplating pure

silver is used, which remains unaltered by the application of a solution of nitric acid and distilled water. When the same chemical comes in contact with STERLING SILVER, which is used in the making of SHEFFIELD PLATE, the metal turns blue. This is a test for distinguishing between the two plating techniques.

Electrotype
Copy achieved by electrical deposition. The process was developed by ELKINGTON'S in the 1830s, before the ELECTROPLATE process. In the case of a copy of a new design, a mould was generally made of the model, often of wax, and from it a metal cast was made. A negative mould was made from this and the copy made by the electrical deposition of a metal, usually copper, into this final mould. A similar technique applied to the electrocopying of antique objects, from which Elkington's received a considerable revenue. The practice was pioneered by Benjamin Schlick for Elkington's in the 1840s and the copies of famous pieces of silver from public and private collections in Britain and elsewhere were extremely popular. Alternatively, real, natural objects, flora and fauna, were coated with a conductive substance and a layer of metal electrically transferred directly on to their surface. A popular pastime for amateurs, it was a manifestation of Victorian naturalism. (See colour plate p. 209.)

Embossing
Raising decoration from the back, a form of CHASING, the reverse of FLAT CHASING, giving a domed effect. It is particularly suitable for FLUTING. REPOUSSÉ is embossing taken a stage further.

Engine-turning
Engraving geometrical patterns on a lathe.

Engraving
Incising the surface of a piece with a sharp tool, metal being removed in the process. It is used particularly for lettering and coats of arms. In the Victorian period, engraving on earlier silver is not uncommon.

Etching
Decoration, principally on Victorian machine-made silver achieved by the biting action of acid. The technique of etching on metalwork was introduced for ornamenting armour and is similar to that employed for print making.

Flat chasing
CHASING in low relief on the surface of the metal, somewhat similar in appearance to ENGRAVING, although, because no metal is removed, the edges are rounded rather than sharp. MATTING is a form of flat chasing.

Frosting
Applying acid to, or scratching with a

Coffee pot, Meriden Britannia Co., 1867. The geometrical ornament of the body is engine-turned, or engraved mechanically; the handle and spout are cast.

metal brush, the surface of silver to give it a nacreous finish.

Matting
Texturing the surface by repeated hammer blows. It was popular in the early Victorian period as a background for other decoration.

Nickel silver
Known also as German, Alaska, Alpacca and Mexican silver, a white-metal alloy of copper, nickel and zinc. A Chinese invention, it was brought from Berlin to Sheffield and patented there by Samuel Roberts in 1830. By 1840 it was replacing copper as the base for SHEFFIELD PLATE since the silver colour was less conspicuous than copper when the layer of silver wore thin. Later it was used as a base for ELECTROPLATE in Britain, where the letters E.P.N.S. were stamped on the pieces to indicate electroplated nickel silver, and in the United States. In the United States unplated nickel-silver wares were as popular as those in BRITANNIA METAL: they were less easily damaged than electroplated wares and the colour closely resembled silver.

Oxidizing
Application of an oxide or chemical substance which darkens the surface of the metal, particularly the areas in deepest relief, to give the effect of shadow. The technique was demonstrated in French and German pieces shown at the Great Exhibition, where it was much admired, and adopted thereafter in Britain.

Piercing
Hand- or machine-cutting through the thickness of the metal.

Planishing
Hammering silver with a flat-headed hammer after RAISING to give it a smooth surface.

Raising
Method of working silver hollow-ware by hand using a round-headed blocking hammer. The metal is hammered in successive rows over a stake, ANNEALING being necessary before re-hammering.

Repoussé
Technique of beating out the metal into a high-relief design from the back, the texturing and detail being worked on the front at a later stage. A late seventeenth-century technique, it was revived in *c.* 1828 in America by KIRK.

Sheffield plate
Silver-coated copper or, in the mid-nineteenth century, NICKEL SILVER achieved by fusion at intense heat: the metals were united rather than amalgamated and were worked as a single metal. The process was devised by Thomas Boulsover, a Sheffield cutler, in about 1743 and the principal centres of manufacture in Victorian England were Sheffield and Birmingham: JAMES DIXON & SONS and THOMAS BRADBURY & SONS were two of the most reputable and long-lived firms. Various techniques were employed for fashioning the plated sheets, including SWAGING and SPINNING. To counteract the effect of wear, especially at the rims and edges, and to prevent the base metal being revealed, silver reinforcements were sometimes added. At the Great Exhibition of 1851 only two firms displayed Sheffield plate and by the 1860s it was generally accepted that it had been supplanted by ELECTROPLATE.

Soldering
Uniting two metal surfaces with a fusible metallic alloy. Sections manufactured by the CASTING process have to be soldered together, as do decorative details applied to the main body of the piece.

Spinning
Working silver on a lathe, an alternative process to RAISING.

Stamping
Early, mechanical method of producing silverwares, the metal being pressed between two dies by steam pressure.

Sterling silver
The Sterling standard was introduced in the twelfth century in England by Henry II. The components are 925/1000 pure silver combined with 75/1000 added metal, usually copper, to render it sufficiently hard. In Britain the only other permissible standard is the BRITANNIA STANDARD, the use of which was enforced between the years 1697 and 1720.

Swaging
Hand forging, principally of flatware, by beating the metal into a swage, or groove.

Bibliography

BURY, SHIRLEY. *Victorian Electroplate*, London, 1971

Birmingham City Museum and Art Gallery, *Birmingham Gold & Silver 1773–1973*, Catalogue of the exhibition held 28 July–16 September, 1973, Birmingham, 1973

Brooklyn Museum. *Victoriana, An Exhibition of the Arts of the Victorian Era in America*, Catalogue of the exhibition held 7 April–5 June, 1960, Brooklyn, 1960

CULME, JOHN, and STRANG, JOHN G. *Antique Silver and Silver Collecting*, London, 1973

GIBB, GEORGE S. *The Whitesmiths of Taunton, A History of Reed and Barton*, Cambridge, Massachusetts, 1946

HILL, H. W. *Maryland's Silver Service*, Baltimore, 1962

Jewelers' Circular & Horological Review, New York, 1869–

Jewelers' Weekly, New York, 1896–1900

MCCLINTON, KATHARINE MORRISON. *Collecting American Victorian Antiques*, New York, 1966

MCCLINTON, KATHARINE MORRISON. *Collecting American 19th-Century Silver*, New York, 1968

MCCLINTON, KATHARINE MORRISON. 'American Nineteenth-century Presentation Silver', Part II, in *The Connoisseur*, vol. 167, pp 192–8, London, 1968

MAY, EARL CHAPIN. *A Century of Silver 1847–1947*, New York, 1947

Metropolitan Museum of Art. *19th-Century America*, Catalogue of the exhibition held 16 April–7 September, 1970, New York, 1970

RAINWATER, DOROTHY T. *American Silver Manufacturers*, Hanover, Pennsylvania, 1966

RAINWATER, DOROTHY T. and H. IVAN. *American Silverplate*, New York, 1968

Royal Academy of Arts. *Victorian and Edwardian Decorative Art. The Handley-Read Collection*, Catalogue of the exhibition held 4 March–30 April, 1972, London, 1972

The Spinning Wheel, Hanover, Pennsylvania, 1945–

Victoria and Albert Museum. *Victorian Church Art*, Catalogue of the exhibition held November 1971–January, 1972, London, 1971

WARDLE, PATRICIA. *Victorian Silver and Silver-plate*, London, 1963

Metalwork

BRITISH

Iron played a very large part in England throughout the nineteenth century. Availability of the metal made it possible to improve machinery for manufacturing purposes and to lay railways for distribution of the products. No wonder, then, that a writer has used the term 'the New Iron Age' in referring to the decades during which the Industrial Revolution became established. Without iron, the making of goods in brass and other metals could only have taken place on a comparatively small scale.

'The New Iron Age'

The use of iron in the earlier years of the nineteenth century had been limited largely to the workshop and outdoors, but in the 1830s there was a movement to extend its range into the realm of home furnishing. The leading advocate of this innovation, John Claudius Loudon, praised two Gothic-style chairs, one with a hexagonal wooden seat and another designated 'Etruscan' with a pierced back owing its design to honeysuckle blossom. He also illustrated iron bedsteads, which he strongly recommended for their cheapness, adding: 'The idea of having iron bedsteads will, we have no doubt, shock those who have always been accustomed to consider mahogany as essential for this piece of furniture: but we can assure them that they are to be found in the houses of people of wealth and fashion in London; sometimes even for best beds.'

The same author showed an iron kitchen armchair, which 'only wants good

OPPOSITE *Victorian Interior,* one of a pair of English stereoscopic photographs showing a scene at tea-time. Metalwork objects illustrated in the photograph include fire irons and matching stands, a cast-iron fender, a paraffin lamp and a kettle, probably made of copper. Victoria and Albert Museum.

cushions . . . to render it a most comfortable article for a cottager', and a single version of the same with an equal call for some kind of padding.

Bedstead in the Renaissance style, R. W. Winfield, Birmingham, exhibited at the Great Exhibition of 1851. Brass or iron covered with brass foil. Metal bedsteads were regarded as more hygienic than those constructed of wood.

The proposal of metal bedsteads coincided with an urge towards greater hygiene in the home, and the comforting fact that insects were unable to shelter in the framework of a metal structure, even if they continued to infest the bedding, led to their gradual adoption. At the Great Exhibition of 1851, several Birmingham firms displayed beds that were apparently of solid brass, but in fact were made of iron tubing covered in brass foil, finished with a high polish and lacquered to prevent tarnishing.

Other items of iron furniture such as chairs, benches and tables duly found their place in the conservatory and garden, for which their rugged build was more suited than indoors. Designs varied from the severe Gothic to simple repre-

sentations of twisted timber, while woven iron wire was found to be a practical means of lessening weight and introducing a style of its own.

Also to be found in the open air were fountains and ornamental vases, while attempts were made to kindle interest in cast-iron statuary. The Coalbrookdale Co., of Shropshire, produced a version of John Bell's figure, *Eagle Slayer,* standing 11 ft 6 in (3·56 m) in height with its pedestal, suggesting hopefully that it provided an acceptable and inexpensive substitute for marble or bronze.

The Coalbrookdale foundry fared better with the large cast-iron park entrance which they showed in the North Transept of the Crystal Palace at the 1851 Exhibition. The entrance comprised a pair of principal gates, two side gates and pillars 'of new construction'. The whole had a frontage of 60 ft (18·28 m) and after the close of the Exhibition it was re-erected on the border between Hyde Park and Kensington Gardens, just to the north of Kensington Road, where it may still be seen.

Certain small accessories for the home proved to be both practical and inexpensive and, once they had been put in production, continued to be manufactured throughout the period, and later. Included among these items are door stops (sometimes referred to as door porters), foot scrapers and umbrella stands. Door knockers of iron supplanted those of brass. The change was lamented by those who preferred the shine of brass to the sombre black of iron and saw the former as 'indicative of a hospitable, well-ordered house'. Designs of all the foregoing were varied. Some examples have cast on their backs the name of the foundry from which they came, and others bear the diamond-shaped registration mark of the Patent Office.

Iron was employed, too, for gaslight fittings, in the shape of chandeliers, candelabra and wall lights. One manufacturer produced what he termed an

Lantern, English, c. 1860. Red tôle (japanned tinned iron) with a circular brass internal pan and candleholder. Mallett at Bourdon House Ltd.

RIGHT *Paraffin heating stove, English, c. 1890. Cast-iron casing. Red glass in the side panels creates a warm glow. Science Museum.*

BELOW RIGHT *Fire grate and dogs designed by Alfred Stevens (1817-75) and made by Hoole & Co. for the London International Exhibition of 1862. Cast iron. Stevens also designed metalwork for Hoole & Co. for the Great Exhibition. Sheffield Museum.*

'antique candelabrum', the design of which was based on a Roman original.

The reaction which started in the 1860s against prevailing design and mass production took practical forms. Among others, there was a suggestion that wrought iron should be used in place of cast iron. C. L. Eastlake told readers of his book, *Hints on Household Taste,* first published in 1868, 'that the work of the hammer and anvil is infinitely superior in every way to the production of the mould.'

Wrought iron, which had previously been confined to the open air in the shape of gates, railings and similar erections, was proposed for the home. It proved too costly for most people and for that reason, if not also on account of its general unsuitability, failed to find many buyers. Exceptions were stands for lamps and kettles which proved popular and were made in large numbers.

Throughout the period, cast iron retained an unchallenged importance in

Candlesticks designed by Dr Christopher Dresser (1834-1904) and made by Chubb & Co., 1880. Copper and brass, ht 12¼ in (31·6 cm). The design is Oriental in inspiration. J. S. M. Scott Collection.

Cottage range, English, c. 1880. Cast iron. Victorian ovens often had turntables because the position of the fire caused one side to be hotter than the other. Science Museum.

the home as regards heating. The fireplaces of rooms, together with fire irons and fenders, were frequently made of iron whether they were intended for use in mansions or cottages. Artistic styling varied their appearance, which ranged from Renaissance to Rococo, not omitting the ever-present Gothic and essays in the manner of Louis XV. Numerous patents covered modifications in the design of grates in efforts to improve the output of heat and lessen consumption of fuel. The same considerations of efficiency and economy applied to the kitchen, where a range, of a size to suit requirements, was to be found for the supply of hot water as well as heat for cooking.

Tinned Iron Adapted to Victorian Taste

The japanned tinned iron, introduced at Pontypool in the eighteenth century, continued to be in demand, although made elsewhere and in forms acceptable to Victorian taste. The manufacture centred on Wolverhampton where, among others, E. Perry produced a range of articles listed alphabetically from baths to writing boxes, and including cake baskets, cash boxes, coal boxes, hearing trumpets, music stands, tables, trays and water cans. Hand-painted, as well as printed decoration varied as much in subject as in quality, with flowers of one variety and another frequently a prominent feature.

In the mid-century, articles of angular shape were embellished with gilded and coloured patterns of Gothic inspiration. Comparable objects had earlier drawn the epithet 'abominations' from A. W. N. Pugin, who named Birmingham and Sheffield 'those inexhaustible mines of bad taste'. On the strength of many of its products, he might well have included neighbouring Wolverhampton.

Copper for Utensils and Decoration

In the first decades of Queen Victoria's reign copper was employed, as it had been in the past, for such utilitarian articles as kettles, moulds for jellies and coal scuttles. It was used also for stew pans and other cooking utensils, but for this purpose was replaced in the 1860s by enamelled iron. The change successfully avoided any risk of the poisoning liable to occur from the use of untinned copper vessels; a danger that had been a cause for anxiety for the medical profession and the public for a century and more.

The Arts and Crafts Movement, with its emphasis on simple design and hand-methods of production, had its effect on metalwork. The colour and ductility of copper were considered admirable assets, so professional and amateur coppersmiths flourished up and down the land in the last quarter of the century. A lead was given to them by C. R. Ashbee, whose workshops at Essex House, London, produced a variety of articles with currently fashionable motifs in repoussé.

During the same years there was a liking for objects of iron ornamented with copper, the latter often in the shape of spheres or rosettes. The most popular expressions of the combination were three-legged adjustable pedestals, lightly constructed of wrought iron decorated with suitably placed copper rosettes and supporting copper oil lamps or kettles.

A further use for the metal at the close of the century was as mounts for furniture. The doors of cupboards and other pieces were supported by copper hinges of elaborate pattern, the architect and designer C. F. A. Voysey being responsible for many of them.

223

Brass Manufacture in the Midlands

The start of Queen Victoria's reign saw steam-power in wide use and the introduction of new processes to gain increased output. In no industry was this more noticeable than in that devoted to brass articles; an industry centred in the Midlands area and Birmingham in particular. The power of the new machinery often enabled pressing and punching to replace casting, resulting in a great saving of metal and a consequent lowering of cost.

Brass articles stamped from thin plates of the metal were polished by friction or immersion in acid and then coated with a tinted lacquer. This gave them a superficial likeness to gold and ensured that under normal conditions their appearance did not deteriorate for a period of years.

The 1851 Exhibition catalogue provides evidence of the enormous variety of goods on the market in the mid-century. They included finger plates for doors, fittings for curtain rods as well as hold backs for the curtains, 'outside bell pulls . . . in the Gothic, Elizabethan and other styles', buttons, candlesticks and oil lamps, and fittings for gas lighting. For the last purpose there were chandeliers, hinged wall arms and candelabra of numerous patterns, among which a

Jewel casket in the form of an early Medieval reliquary, Birmingham, exhibited in 1886. Gilded brass and enamel with velvet lining, ht 7 in (17·8 cm). City Museum and Art Gallery, Birmingham.

plain unornamented surface was seldom, if ever, to be seen.

Later in the century the styles of most articles changed towards a greater simplicity, but many of the earlier brass items continued to be made as before. This was because the moulds and dies for their manufacture had a long life, and it would have been costly to discard them before they were worn out. As Eastlake wrote: 'It is a choice not only between

good or bad taste, but between bad taste which is cheap and good taste which is certainly somewhat dear. The manufacturers state they require a larger demand before they can lower their prices. The public say they must have more reasonable prices before they can afford to buy.'

Britannia Metal and Similar Alloys

The craft of the pewterer could not withstand the competition of pottery and porcelain, and in the first decades of the nineteenth century, the long-popular alloy virtually ceased to be used. Earlier, another alloy, Britannia metal, had been put on the market, and it continued to be manufactured during most of the Victorian period. Not only was it harder than pewter, but it could be worked more thinly and would retain its polish for longer. With another alloy, German Silver or Nickel Silver, it replaced copper as a base for Sheffield plate. This occurred when electroplating was intro-

Britannia metal tableware. Coffee pot, English, late-nineteenth century; sugar basin and cream jug, with a blue pottery lining in imitation of blue glass, Broadhead & Atkins, 1840; teapot, James Dixon & Sons, 1850. Sheffield Museum.

duced in 1840, and the use of these white alloys had the advantage of not showing a pink base as the outer silver coating wore away. Examples were usually stamped with the initials E.P.B.M. (Electroplated Britannia metal) or E.P.N.S. (Electroplated nickel silver). The shapes of teapots, jugs and the numerous other items made in Britannia metal from about 1840 were most often embellished with cast and applied ornament, incorporating scrolls, shells and leaves in their patterns. For their display of tea-services in the metal at the Great Exhibition, the Sheffield firm of James Dixon & Sons were awarded a prize medal.

Zinc for Domestic Articles and Decoration

The alloy of zinc named spelter was used as an inexpensive substitute for bronze. Statuettes and other decorative objects were cast in the comparatively lightweight metal and given a coating of brown or black pigment or treated electrically so that an external similarity to bronze was obtained. Spelter is, however, brittle and any surface preparation on it will scratch easily to reveal the silvery-grey base. It was formed into castings with noticeably thin walls, and the resulting objects are therefore lighter in weight than comparable bronze ones. While a proportion of surviving spelter articles were made in England, the majority originated on the mainland of Europe.

Zinc was employed also for domestic articles such as baths, ice pails and coal scuttles. One of the latter, shown in 1851, was described as having 'been in use twenty-six years'.

Geoffrey Wills

AMERICAN

At the beginning of Queen Victoria's reign the immense mineral wealth of the United States began to be exploited to the full. Mining rapidly was expanded; cities became established in the proximity of minerals and the fuel with which they were processed, and the transport facilities for the distribution of the finished products. In the case of iron this occurred at Pittsburgh, Pennsylvania, ore being brought in from the region of Lake Superior and melted with the aid of coal obtained from nearby. The rivers Ohio, Allegeny and Monogahela, as well as the railways which were soon branching in every direction, carried raw materials as well as manufactures. As the century advanced and Pittsburgh continued to grow, it earned for itself the name The Smoky City, and by 1909 the output of iron and steel wares was in the region of $80,000,000.

The range of most metal articles manufactured in the United States was similar to that available in Europe, with designs based on the same sources. Styles fashionable in London, Paris and Berlin were to be seen in New York, Boston and Philadelphia, often with little timelag between them. However, careful study may reveal subtle differences in the details of design and construction.

Stoves and Iron Furniture

Within the home the most important use for iron was for heating appliances. The stove designed by Benjamin Franklin in 1742 was the subject of frequent improvements, although retaining the name of its originator. At first housed within the mantelpiece, it later encroached into the room. By the early years of Queen Victoria's reign it was being made in many different forms, decoration being varied to suit prevailing tastes: the cast ornament was often relieved with brass.

Stoves introduced in the 1840s were of several kinds. Among them were the two-column and four-column types, each with a fire box raised on short legs, the columns rising from the main body to a smaller box above. Their ornamentation was of relief patterns of Rococo or Neoclassical derivation, and not infrequently a combination of both with a touch of Gothic for full measure. In many instances, the name and address of the maker is present in raised lettering.

Another type of stove (patented in 1841) was surmounted by a statue of George Washington wearing a toga, while others commemorated battles. Less patriotic but probably more practical, were stoves designed to burn anthracite coal which were the subject of experiment from the 1820s. By the mid-century such 'base burners', or slow-combustion stoves, began to attain popularity as they were found to be more efficient than other types. Manufacturers embellished them to please buyers, and by the 1880s it was common for nickel plate to replace the earlier brass. The front of the stove was fitted with a pair of mica-windowed doors to reveal a glow when the fire burned, or they could be opened to throw heat rapidly into the room.

Furniture for outdoor use was indistinguishable from that made in Europe, except for the presence of a maker's name and address. In some instances, chairs, settees and tables were straightforward copies of their imported counterparts and these reproductions, with or without licences, were made in quantity by foundries all over the country. Garden ornaments in the shape of life-size or smaller figures of stags and other animals were equally similar to their imported prototypes.

More ambitious than any of the foregoing was the introduction of complete buildings constructed of cast iron. Daniel D. Badger claimed to have raised the first of them in Boston in 1842, and twenty-three years later his firm, then the Architectural Iron Works of the City of New York, published an illustrated catalogue of its stock products. The catalogue depicted office blocks, shops, warehouses and factories made of iron, as well as a selection of railings, pillars, hitching posts and ornamental vases. The catalogue listed an impressive number of buildings manufactured by the company and erected in various places. Some of them are still standing, notably the Haughwout Building, of 1857, which is at the corner of Broadway and Broome Street and is a New York City landmark.

Sheet Iron and the Blacksmith's Wares

Sheet iron coated with tin was employed for making many inexpensive objects in daily use, most of which served their purpose and were then discarded. The best remembered is perhaps the 'hog-scraper' candlestick, an article of unre-

The blacksmith was an essential member of any civilized community, and in addition to shoeing horses he supplied his locality with wrought-iron wares of many kinds. The variety included fireside fittings such as trammels and cranes for holding pots over fires, irons, spits, toasters and trivets; latches and hinges for doors; foot scrapers; swingletrees and other fittings for carts, carriages and sleighs; and working tools of all kinds. The latter were purely functional, but many of the other items permitted the smith to exercise his fancy by introducing a degree of artistry in the shaping.

Copper and Brass

Both copper and brass were worked in sheet form to make pots and pans and other domestic utensils, the makers of some of the wares being identifiable from the names and addresses stamped on them. In most instances, however, there are no indications by which they can be distinguished from imported goods, all of them following functional patterns. In the mid-century in Connecticut, kettles and other articles were being spun in quantity from brass, and this use of the machine inevitably superseded handbeating.

Sheet copper was found to be suitable for making such outdoor objects as weathervanes. The metal did not rust, and its attractiveness increased with age; some were painted and gilded to prevent their turning bright green with verdigris when exposed to the elements. The vanes were cut in the flat, like silhouettes, or were composed of two sections, each beaten to a convex shape in a cast-iron mould and then soldered together along the edges. They were made in innumer-

Pair of hogscraper candlesticks with sliding ejectors, American, impressed Hyde, ht 7 in (17.8 cm); pan candlestick, American, impressed DC. Wrought iron. Sotheby Parke Bernet.

Pantry for flour, spices, condiments and staples incorporating a flour sifter, coffee grinder and cake and bread boxes, American. Tinned iron. Greenfield Village and Henry Ford Museum.

been identified, while research has enabled examples to be attributed to particular workshops. Because of its unsophisticated appearance, the ware is sometimes referred to as country tin.

Japanned-iron wares continued to be manufactured throughout much of the nineteenth century. As late as 1872, Smith, Burns & Co. of New York, issued an illustrated catalogue of 'Stamped, galvanised and Japanned Tinware . . .'. In modern times attention has been paid to the composition of the various decorative patterns and how their effect was gained, thus enabling deceptive imitations to reach the market.

markable appearance complete with a sliding ejector to remove the candle stub. It gained its name from the allegation that the sharpened, thin rim of the base was very satisfactory for scraping bristles from the carcases of slaughtered hogs.

The same sheet metal was also employed in New England for boxes, dishes, trays, pots and other useful household articles. They were decorated with painting, predominantly of floral subjects on coloured grounds and often embellished with gilding. The work was generally executed by girls working either freehand or with the aid of stencils, their bold strokes creating effects with a minimum of skill. Despite this, the hands of some of the decorators have

Horse and sulky weathervane, American. Copper, ht 2 ft 6¼ in (77 cm). Weathervanes were often made of iron or sheet copper, the latter sometimes painted and gilded. Sotheby Parke Bernet.

OPPOSITE *Jewel casket designed and made by C. R. Mackintosh (1868-1928) for Jessie Keppie, c. 1896. Brass mounted on wood, ht approx. 6 in (15.2 cm). Victoria and Albert Museum.*

able designs, featuring horses, cockerels, fishes and so forth, and more enterprisingly, showing a complete horse-drawn sulky with driver or a racehorse and jockey.

Manufacture of cast-brass articles in the United States was a thriving industry by the mid-century, when many of the bigger cities and towns supported one or more foundries. In Philadelphia, Cornelius & Co. were among the largest in the country and in 1851 displayed some of their products at the Great Exhibition in London. There, they were awarded a Prize Medal for the chandeliers which, according to the catalogue 'were cast from patterns entirely original and new, at which the artists were employed more than six months. In style they combine the Louis Quatorze and the Renaissance.'

Lighting Devices and Lamps

Candlesticks, candelabra and oil-lamps were made in many patterns. The Argand and Astral lamps remained the most effective devices for oil burning until the 1840s, when the Solar lamp was devised in the United States. It burned lard oil and was described in 1845 as 'a late improvement of considerable importance', its supporters claiming that compared with other methods it was more economical to use and gave more light. Lamps for burning other fuels, such as camphene, were invented and patented and had varying success in their performance. Finally came the discovery of oil in Pennsylvania; paraffin became available and suitable burners were produced to employ it. All of these were, in turn, ousted by gas, which many homes were using by about 1860, and which called for further supplies of brass fittings. Designers taxed their ingenuity in camouflaging pipes and taps; an end they generally achieved by combining ancient and modern styles indiscriminately.

On both sides of the Atlantic much endeavour was directed towards enhancing the appearance of brass, either by alloying it with other metals or by treating the surface with chemicals and varnishes. The firm of Cornelius & Co. was proud of its 'damask finished' Solar lamps, while James Larkin, head of a rival Philadelphia foundry, made available to all and sundry the knowledge he had gained when working in London and

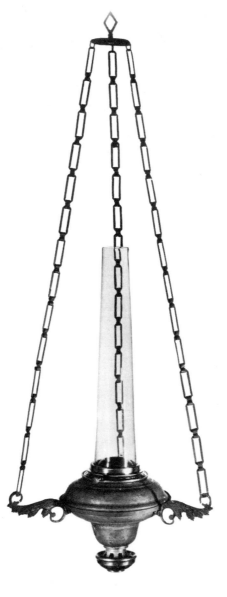

OPPOSITE *English militaria. Leopard's skin saddle-cloth, late-nineteenth century; sabretache and shako,* c. *1840; pouch and pouch belt,* c. *1850. All relate to officers of the 15th Hussars. Tradition.*

LEFT *Hanging Solar lard lamp, Cornelius & Co., 1843 patent. Cornelius & Co., of Philadelphia, were famous as manufacturers of lighting devices. Greenfield Village and Henry Ford Museum.*

BELOW *Dragonfly lamp, marked Tiffany Studios New York 367,* c. *1900. Ormolu and glass, ht 2ft 7in (79cm). Tiffany Studios became the name of the firm of L.C.Tiffany in 1900. Sotheby's Belgravia.*

Paris during thirty-four years. Larkin did this in a small volume published in Philadelphia in 1853 containing all kinds of information including formulae for making alloys for every purpose and recipes for tinted lacquers.

At the end of the Victorian period Louis Comfort Tiffany (1848-1933) often allied his brilliantly coloured glass with bronze. Among his most successful achievements in this manner were table and pedestal lamps, which were unequalled in their clever exploitation of the newly introduced electric light. Beginning his lengthy career at about this date was the architect, Frank Lloyd Wright who, along with some of his contemporaries, was no less concerned with the contents of a house than with its exterior form. For his own library in Oak Park, near Chicago, he designed and had made soon after 1893 a pair of narrow angular copper vases standing 2 ft 11 in (71 cm) in height. Other architects were allying copper with wood in making furniture, as was being done in England by Voysey.

Britannia Metal as a Successor to Pewter

At the beginning of the Victorian period pewter was displaced almost completely by the harder Britannia metal, which could be machine spun and produced cheaply in competition with chinaware and glass. The manufacture of Britannia metal began in Meriden, Connecticut, in the second decade of the century, expanding as the years progressed so that by 1845 there were at least eight firms active in the town.

Many of the Meriden craftsmen joined a fresh firm, Meriden Britannia Co., that was established in 1852. Earlier, Taunton Britannia Manufacturing Co., of Taunton, Massachusetts, had emerged from a partnership started in the 1820s. The Company endured for five years, until 1835, when the name was replaced by that of Leonard, Reed & Barton. A published list of the goods manufactured by the latter in 1838 shows that in the course of the twelve-month period they turned out 2,749 teapots, 7,416 frames for holding sets of casters, 359 coffee pots and 298 dozen coffin plates, as well as much else. In due course the style of the firm was changed once again, to become Reed & Barton.

In addition to the foregoing makers there were others, some employing only a few workers but others operating on a larger scale. They included Smith & Co. (later, Morey & Smith), of Boston, and Eben Smith of Beverly, both in Massachusetts; Sellew & Co. of Cincinnati, Ohio; William Calder of Providence, Rhode Island; T. D. & S. Boardman, of Hartford, Connecticut; Capen & Molineux, Endicott & Sumner, Yale & Curtis and Henry Hopper, all of New York, N.Y.; and John H. Palethorp, of Philadelphia, Pennsylvania. All the above were active at the beginning of the period and some of them remained in business until the late 1860s.

Largely on account of the use of mechanical methods of manufacture, designs were often restrained and superficial ornament slight or absent. Parts of objects might be made so that they could be interchanged when possible; for example, stems of precisely the same pattern are recorded as being used for a candlestick and a whale-oil lamp by the Taunton Britannia Manufacturing Co. Likewise for simplicity and economy, vessels such as teapots were made in halves of similar design, the two parts being soldered together prior to the addition of spout and handle. The plain appearance of a proportion of Britannia metal articles provides for some people a welcome oasis of simplicity amid the ostentation of much else of the time.

Among the few workers who continued using the old method of raising hollowwares from the sheet by handbeating was a Beverly, Massachusetts, man, Israel Trask, who also decorated his work with engraving. Although Trask used Britannia metal, his techniques were those of the old-time pewterer, and he doubtless regarded himself as one. He was not alone in this, for the firm of Buckley & Curtis, although they worked in Britannia metal, were described as pewterers in a Meriden directory of the 1860s.

Zinc for Garden Ornaments

Like the metals already discussed, zinc was plentiful in the United States. Its principal use was as an alloy with copper to produce brass, but it is known to have been employed sometimes on its own. Garden ornaments in the forms of human figures and animals were cast in zinc, and when painted they bore a passable resemblance to the expensive marble originals from which most of them were copied. Smaller-sized household ornaments were doubtless also made from the same metal, but the majority have been discarded in view of their comparatively breakable nature.

Geoffrey Wills

Lighting

In the nineteenth century major advances were made not only in the design of traditional lighting devices such as candleholders and oil-burning lamps, making them safer and more effective, but it was during this period that entirely new types of fuel were introduced, requiring new equipment. The principal materials employed were BRASS, BRONZE and ormolu, with glass shades for the elaborate and expensive new fittings, and IRON, TIN, COPPER and PEWTER for the humbler, more conventional varieties of lamp.

Gas
Experiments with coal gas began in the eighteenth century, and in 1807 gas lighting was exhibited in Pall Mall, London. In the United States there were gas street lights in Baltimore by 1817, but, while the London Gas Light and Coke Company was well established by the second decade of the century in Britain, few homes were lit by gas in the United States until the 1850s.

Mineral oil
In 1859 mineral oil was discovered in Pennsylvania in great quantities and was refined to produce paraffin, or kerosene. Lamps for burning the new fuel were simply constructed, comparatively safe and easily maintained, and they constituted an important development in artificial lighting, especially to the rural population on both sides of the Atlantic.

Electricity
Electric lighting was pioneered by Sir Joseph Swan in Britain and Thomas Alva Edison in the United States; in 1883 they formed in Britain the Edison-Swan Electric Co. Shortly before that, in 1880, the engineer and friend of Swan, Sir William Armstrong, had forty-five electric lamps installed in his house near Newcastle. Some of the most prized examples of early electric fittings are those manufactured by Tiffany & Co., of New York, exemplifying the Art Nouveau style of decoration. It is not uncommon to find oil, candle and gas fittings which were adapted to electricity in the last century, though many have been electrified in more recent years.

Candles and traditional lamps
Simultaneously with the use of these new lighting devices, details of which were improved and patented throughout the Victorian period, traditional forms of lighting were still employed by the less affluent and those living at some distance from a source of power or fuel. Stearine candles, cheaper than beeswax candles, had been introduced by 1840, but tallow was still in use on account of its cheapness. All forms of animal and vegetable oil were used for lamps of the simplest design, whale oil being employed to a considerable extent in the United States, where there was a flourishing whaling industry. Camphene, a mixture of turpentine and alcohol, was also popular there between 1830 and 1850, but was liable to be explosive unless correctly used. By far the most common fuel in both countries was, however, colza, rape, or carcel oil, derived from the seed of *Brassica campestris,* var. *oleifera,* and similar plants. Reasonably priced, producing a comparatively smokeless and odourless flame, it had the disadvantage of being viscous. An innovation in the design of oil-burning lamps had been made in the 1780s by the Swiss Ami Argand (1755–1803). He fitted the wick between two cylindrical metal tubes, the inner one of which carried air directly to the flame. This additional supply of oxygen greatly increased combustion and therefore the volume of light, and also reduced the quantity of smoke, qualities that were further improved by a glass chimney.

With the Argand burner it was useless to rely on capillary action alone to supply the greatly increased amount of the heavy colza oil that was required. Various methods of doing so were devised, the simplest being gravity.

Candleholders and Lamps

Astral lamp
Modification of the original Argand lamp, it was popular as a reading lamp in the 1830s and 1840s. The ring-shaped reservoir surrounds the wick, which is fed by gravity, eliminating the shadow cast by the detached reservoir on the earlier models. The glass chimney and the reservoir and wick are enclosed within a shade, often of etched glass and of smaller diameter at the top than at the base.

Betty lamp
Covered grease-burning lamp with a wick support, deriving from a seven-

teenth-century English model, in use in the United States until *c.* 1850. The wick is suspended over a spout by a metal support attached to the base of the lamp so that excess fuel is returned to the reservoir. Made principally of IRON, late examples are often of TIN, and attached to a stand, thereby converting what was originally a hanging lamp into a standing or hand lamp; the latter type is sometimes known as an Ipswich Betty, on account of its supposed place of manufacture in Massachusetts. A chained hook is supplied on some models for retrieving the wick from the reservoir.

Candelabrum

Branched candlestick or lamp-stand, principally for use on the dining table. The more expensive models were made of silver, but glass-shaded oil burners and gas and electric examples are often of BRASS or ormolu.

Chandelier

Branched, hanging lamp in any metal, or of wood, adaptable to any type of fuel. With the advent of gas and electricity supplies the basic form changed little since the inlet could be incorporated in the chain or apparatus for suspending the lamp from the ceiling; the style of decoration, however, reflected the current taste and some extremely elaborate examples were made in the mid-century, often in imitation of eighteenth-century models.

Lantern

Glass-shaded lamp, either portable or, alternatively, for hanging from a bracket or the ceiling. Originally designed to protect a candle from draught, examples were often gas-fed or electrified in the Victorian period. Some of the most popular ones, principally for use in the entrance hall, are in the Gothic style.

Mantel lamp

Version of the Argand gravity-fed burner manufactured in the United States, often in a set of three: a double lamp with the reservoir in the centre for the middle of the mantelpiece and a single lamp for either side.

Moderator lamp

Lamp-burning animal or vegetable oil with a vase-shaped base containing a spring-operated pump which, when wound up by means of a key, forces upwards and controls the supply of fuel to the wick.

Sconce

Wall light, properly with a back plate, supporting a single or branched candleholder or other light fitting. The back plate is of BRASS, PEWTER or silver so that its shiny surface, often with punched or embossed decoration, reflects the light.

Solar lamp

Similar to the ASTRAL LAMP but with the

Betty lamp attributed to J. Schmidt, Pennsylvania. Wrought iron. The Betty, lamp, of seventeenth-century origin was used in the United States until c. *1850. Greenfield Village and Henry Ford Museum.*

Zuriel Swope lamp, patented by Zuriel Swope, of Lancaster, Pennsylvania, in 1860. Tin. The funnel is for transfering heat from the flame to the lard. Greenfield Village and Henry Ford Museum.

added refinement of a metal cap and a solid circular wick, which produces a column instead of a ring of flame. It burns lard oil.

Student lamp

Colza-oil or paraffin lamp, adjustable in height and with a dark-green shade to reduce glare. Some nineteenth-century examples have a sophisticated feed mechanism, the fuel being drawn to the wick only when a valve permits air to replace it in the reservoir. This variety is commonly found converted to electricity.

Zuriel Swope lamp

Patented in the United States in 1860 by Zuriel Swope, of Lancaster, Pennsylvania, it was designed to burn lard oil, warmed by heat from the flame, transferred through a funnel to the fuel container. Lard-oil lamps are peculiar to the United States.

Glossary of Metals and Alloys

THE METALS

The following metals are those most frequently used in the production of Victorian domestic and decorative metalwork.

Copper

Soft and reddish in colour, it can be stamped and beaten and joined by soldering, brazing and welding. The practice of TINNING the interiors of domestic utensils had become widespread by the Victorian period. It takes a high polish, and when the surface is unprotected VERDIGRIS, an anti-corrosive chemical film, forms on the surface of the metal. Both these characteristics are put to decorative use. Towards the end of the nineteenth century, it found considerable popularity in England and the United States with *avant-garde* designers.

Iron

Greyish in colour, it is the most plentiful metal and was once considered more valuable than gold. Cast iron is hard and brittle and cannot be bent or welded. In the Victorian period it was used extensively for the mass production of structural and decorative architectural parts, statuary, garden furniture and fire grates. Wrought iron, the blacksmiths' metal, was used for more intricate pieces such as weathervanes, door furniture and lamps. It is tough, ductile and malleable.

Document box, two smaller boxes and a pair of pen trays, American. Tôle objects often had stencilled, or, as here, free-hand decoration. Sotheby Parke Bernet.

Lead

Heavy and bluish grey, soft, easily fusible and resistant to corrosion, it may be cast or rolled. It has been used in particular for outdoor ornaments such as cisterns and statuary.

Tin

Silvery with a slight bluish tinge, its principal use was in the manufacture of TÔLE (see MISCELLANY GLOSSARY), tin-plated IRON, of which numerous household wares were made in Britain and the United States, often with painted, japanned or stencilled decoration. The TIN-NING of the interiors of COPPER and BRASS utensils was recognized as essential by the nineteenth century. The most productive tin mines in the world until the late Victorian period were in Cornwall.

Zinc

Blue-grey when polished, lighter than iron, it was employed in the manufacture of household wares such as baths and for lining or coating objects in other metals to prevent corrosion. Particularly in the United States it was used for statuary and garden ornaments, sometimes painted to simulate marble. SPELTER (see SCULPTURE GLOSSARY) is an alloy of zinc and copper.

THE ALLOYS

An alloy is a substance composed of two or more metals that are combined or of a metal (or metals) combined with a non-metal (or non-metals), usually by fusion. An amalgam is an alloy or solution containing mercury. The following alloys are those most frequently used in the production of Victorian domestic and decorative metalwork.

Brass

COPPER and ZINC. Yellowish in colour, it takes a high polish and is easily plated with, for example, silver. Its colour and properties can be varied by the addition of other elements. It is suited to the manufacturing techniques of casting, stamping, rolling and hammering. The domestic and decorative uses are numerous and include door furniture, light fittings and kitchen utensils, fire irons and fenders. Brass bedsteads are usually of sheet brass on a cast-iron base. To prevent atmospheric corrosion it is often finished with a coating of transparent or tinted lacquer.

TOP *Gas fire, Thomas Fletcher & Co., Warrington, England, 1897. Cast iron. Metal radiants such as were used here added to the decorative effect and were long lasting. Science Museum.*

ABOVE *Dish, signed Elkington & Co., Birmingham, and dated 1875. Iron and steel inlaid with gold and bordered with silver, diam. 11¼ in (28·6 cm). City Museum and Art Gallery, Birmingham.*

Door handle, Birmingham, shown at the British Association Exhibition, Birmingham, in 1886. Gilded brass, ht 12¼ in (30·5 cm). City Museum and Art Gallery, Birmingham.

Detail of a decorative panel by Margaret Macdonald (1865–1933), 1895–99. Beaten metalwork was a speciality of this Glasgow School designer, who was the wife of C. R. Mackintosh (1868–1928). University of Glasgow.

Britannia metal

TIN, COPPER and antimony, a white metal first used in England in the eighteenth century. By the early nineteenth century, there were more than a dozen firms in Sheffield manufacturing wares of Britannia metal. Brighter, stronger and easier to work than PEWTER, with which it is sometimes confused, it was generally fashioned by spinning, a technique used in silver manufacture but unsuitable for the softer pewter. The seams run vertically and, where the various parts are joined together, are visible on the inside; parts such as spouts and handles were generally cast and of pewter. English manufacturers stamped their name on the base of the object with its catalogue number. Britannia metal wares were exported to the United States in the early years of the nineteenth century and in 1824 Babbitt & Crossman, which by 1840 had become Reed & Barton, was the first American company to manufacture Britannia metal products. In 1852 most of the small Britannia firms near Meriden, Connecticut, were amalgamated to form the Meriden Britannia Co., which

was to become one of the largest producers. Britannia metal was used extensively as a base for electroplating (see SILVER GLOSSARY).

Bronze

COPPER, TIN and generally ZINC sometimes also with small quantities of IRON, LEAD, manganese or silicon. It was the earliest known alloy and for centuries has been put to utilitarian as well as decorative purposes, particularly for statuary. Ormolu is gilded bronze, in recent times effected by electroplating but previously achieved by coating the bronze with an amalgam of powdered gold and mercury. The name derives from the French *or moulu*, ground gold. Known as mercury-gilding, the mercury was released as a vapour – poisonous to inhale, which contributed to the decline of this method – by the application of heat. The object was first cast and, in high-quality productions, chiselled by hand, the layer of gilding being so slight that every detail in the metal is retained. A skill perfected in France in the eighteenth century and by the Birmingham firm of Boulton & Fothergill, the principal use for ormolu in the nineteenth century was for CHANDELIERS, lamp stands, clock-cases and mounts for porcelain and marble, and also for the reproductions of eighteenth-century pieces which were made in some quantity. Ormolu should not be confused with brass objects that have been lacquered.

Pewter

Alloy of tin with varying quantities of COPPER, LEAD, BRASS, antimony or bismuth. When ZINC is present it is known as Ashberry metal. Grey in colour and moderately durable, it was superseded in the early nineteenth century by BRITANNIA METAL, electroplate and galvanized IRON. In the last decade of the century a revival of pewter production began in Germany with, for example, Kayserzinn, made by the firm of J. P. Kayser, of Krefeld. It was shown at the Paris Universal Exposition of 1900 and thereafter sold at Liberty's in London. In 1903 Liberty's began to manufacture their Tudric ware in pewter.

Steel

IRON and carbon, with other metals such as nickel and chromium added to obtain the properties required. A method of producing steel quickly, cheaply and in large quantities was introduced by Sir Henry Bessemer in 1856. Silvery in colour, it has always been popular for cutlery and sharp instruments as it retains an edge.

Glossary of Pieces and Processes

Andirons

Pair of supports, usually of IRON, on which the logs rest in an open fireplace; also known as fire dogs. The uprights, except of the most humble or provincial examples, bear some form of decoration and are often BRASS. In the Victorian period their design was influenced by the

Andirons, Tiffany & Co., c. 1900. Bronze, iron and glass, ht 2ft 1in (63·5 cm). The firm was founded in 1834 by C. L. Tiffany (d. 1902), father of L. C. Tiffany (1848–1933). Metropolitan Museum of Art.

Two curtain-holders, exhibited with other stamped brass objects at the Great Exhibition, 1851, by R. W. Winfield of Birmingham.

various revivalist styles, the Arts and Crafts Movement and Art Nouveau. The Tiffany andirons with bronze heads and brown glass inserts, a mixture of materials associated with the later part of the century, exemplify the latter style.

Biscuit-tin
Early type of decorated TIN associated with the beginnings of the mass production of foodstuffs and other non-durable products such as tobacco in the 1880s. Bryant & May took out a patent for offset-litho printing on tin and Huntley & Palmer, the biscuit-makers, were among the first to purchase a licence; theirs were manufactured by the local Reading firm of Huntley, Boorne & Stevens. The shape of the tins and the designs on them often reflect current fashions.

Candlebox
Sheet-metal box, usually of TÔLE (see MISCELLANY GLOSSARY) and attached horizontally to the wall. This most common type was manufactured in Britain and the United States until *c.* 1900.

Candlemould
Tapering tube, usually of TIN, with a hole at the narrower end through which the wick was threaded and held taut while the molten tallow or wax was poured in. Double moulds, or moulds for up to about twelve candles, were for home use, while the larger ones, often in wooden frames, were for the chandler. The candles were loosened by inserting the moulds in warm water. An alternative method of candlemaking was by dipping the wick into hot fat, withdrawing it

while it hardened and gradually building it up by repetition of the process.

Coal scuttle
Helmet-shaped, square with a slanting lid or elegantly urn-shaped and known as a coal vase, it was a feature of the fireplace practically unknown in the eighteenth century, when coal was brought into the room in a bucket from outside. The removable lining was often of ZINC. Made of COPPER, BRASS, TÔLE (see MISCELLANY GLOSSARY) or wood, they usually had matching shovels and tongs. After 1840 coal vases usually of tôle were introduced. More graceful in design and of smaller capacity, a number were shown at the Great Exhibition.

Curtain-holder
Tasselled cord or shaped-metal band for securing curtains at a height of approximately 4 ft (122 cm) from the floor. Often of ormolu or lacquered BRASS, they enabled long curtains to be looped back in such a way that they remained closed at the top. A number of highly decorative stamped-brass examples of these, and of other curtain fittings such as pole finials, were shown by the Birmingham firm of R. W. Winfield at the Great Exhibition of 1851.

Enamelling
Application of a layer of translucent or opaque glass to the surface of a metal, usually gold, COPPER or silver, by fusion. It was an extravagant form of decoration and was especially used for small-scale objects; in Britain the principal and most successful exponent of the technique was Alexander Fisher (1864–1936) and in the United States Louis Comfort Tiffany (1848–1933) and his associates. Characteristic of enamels of the Aesthetic Movement and in the Art Nouveau style are abstract patterns and the merging of colours with no hard outlines.

Fire mark of the United Firemen's Insurance Co., of Philadelphia, 1868. Cast iron. Originally this was attached to the exterior of a building. Abby Aldrich Rockefeller Folk Art Collection.

Fire mark
LEAD, COPPER or cast-IRON badge issued by the early fire insurance companies in Britain or the United States, notably Philadelphia, to be prominently displayed on the exterior of an insured building. Originally a fire brigade or the fire department would only deal with an outbreak at insured premises. In 1832 the various London fire brigades were amalgamated to form the London Fire Engine Establishment, but some offices continued to issue badges as advertising giveaways, and a similar situation existed in the United States.

Furniture mounts
Handles and their accompanying back plates, keys, locks, escutcheons, or key plates, and hinges, usually made of BRASS, which may be decorative as well as functional and are a possible means of dating and assigning a maker to a piece of furniture. With the Gothic Revival,

Gothic hinge, exhibited at the Great Exhibition, 1851, by Messrs Barnard & Bishop of Norwich. Their sunflower railings were shown at the Philadelphia Centennial Exhibition.

mounts became of increasing interest to the designer and maker, attempts being made to simulate Medieval metalwork, particularly on small pieces such as book ends and caskets; and with the revival of the many other furniture styles in Britain and the United States went imitations – or near imitations – of their fittings. At the end of the century there was a genuinely new approach to the design of mounts, examples of which may be seen on the furniture of C. F. A. Voysey and designers of the Glasgow School, such as C. R. Mackintosh, M. and F. Macdonald and H. MacNair, known as The Four. Using various materials, they created a delicate and graceful style of metalwork which was later to become identified with the Art Nouveau movement in Europe. (See p. 227.)

Horse brass

Horse furniture descended from the IRON and PEWTER decorations used by farmers and guilds, comparable to the BRASS charms bought by prospering barge-owners. Many bear designs of heraldic origin, and there was a fashion for commemorative and portrait brasses in the 1840 and '50s, when casting rather than hammering became the principal method of manufacture; after 1870 machine production caused a decrease in quality. Examples are often still attached to their original leather straps and show evidence of wear.

Knife grinder

Device invented in the nineteenth century and first displayed at the Great Exhibition for cleaning steel knives which were not, in those days, stainless. Cleaned by hand, each knife had to be polished with the aid of carbon powder; cleaned mechanically, the implements were slotted into a circular grinder and the blades sandwiched between carbon-impregnated pads, which were rotated by means of a handle.

Matchbox

Phosphorous-tipped matches, or spunks, came into general use in the 1830s, necessitating a metal receptacle resembling an inkwell in which the sulphur was melted. At the same time pocket and wall matchboxes were introduced, generally of TÔLE (see MISCELLANY GLOSSARY) and incorporating a striking-plate. Combined matchboxes, candleboxes and candleholders are not uncommon.

Tinning

Lining a COPPER or BRASS cooking-, serving-, eating- or drinking-vessel with tin to prevent contamination of the food, a process devised in England in 1756 which it was necessary to repeat when the tin wore thin. Previously copper-poisoning was a serious and not infrequent affliction.

Verdigris

Bright green patina acquired by COPPER and its alloys, such as BRONZE, when exposed to the elements. In some instances the green of verdigris, rather than the red-brown of polished or lacquered copper, is essential to the colour scheme of an object – some Tiffany lampshades and stands for example.

Weathervane

Feature of the roofline particularly in the United States, though often seen surmounting a clock tower on English buildings. Wooden carvings of animals were common on farm buildings, while sheet- or cast-COPPER and IRON weathervanes, mass produced in Boston and New York, were usually chosen for public buildings and meeting houses. A figure with paddle-like arms that rotate in the wind, indigenous to Pennsylvania, is known as a whirligig.

Bibliography

COMSTOCK, HELEN (ed.). *The Concise Encyclopaedia of American Antiques,* 2 vols, London, 1958

LARKIN, JAMES. *Practical Brass and Iron Founder's Guide,* Philadelphia, 1853

MASSÉ, H. J. L. *Chats on Old Pewter,* New York, 1971

MELTON, JAMES. 'Domestic Metalwork' in *Connoisseur Period Guides: Early Victorian,* edited by Ralph Edwards and L. G. G. Ramsey, London, 1956

Metropolitan Museum of Art. *19th-century America,* Catalogue of the exhibition held 16 April–7 September, 1970, New York, 1970

PEAL, CHRISTOPHER A. *British Pewter and Britannia Metal for Pleasure and Investment,* London, 1971

WILLS, GEOFFREY. *Collecting Copper and Brass,* London, 1962

WILLS, GEOFFREY. *The Book of Copper and Brass,* London, 1968

Arms & Militaria

BRITISH

Queen Victoria's reign spanned sixty-three years and during this period British society underwent many changes. In few walks of life were they greater than in the British Army. When she succeeded to the throne her troops wore and fought in bright scarlet tunics and used a smooth-bore flintlock musket which differed little from that used at Waterloo in 1815 or, indeed, at Quebec in 1759. When she died her men were fighting in drab khaki and using a high-powered, cartridge magazine rifle. These changes were not always accepted willingly and were often forced upon a reluctant War Office as the result of bitter experience in the field. Queen Victoria's reign was splattered with punitive expeditions, colonial campaigns and minor wars, as well as three major conflicts: the Crimean War (1853) the Indian Mutiny (1857) and the Boer War (1899–1902). Each had a lesson for the Command, although, in many cases, the lesson was not quickly learned.

Firearms

The Queen's accession coincided with the introduction of the first muskets incorporating the new percussion system, which had been perfected some twenty years earlier. Brown Bess muskets were adapted to use the system, but it was apparent that the poor accuracy of the weapon would not suffice and that some form of rifle would have to be adopted. The weapon chosen was known as the Brunswick rifle and had a stout barrel with two deep grooves cut on the inside. It fired a ball which had a raised belt running around it to engage with the grooves. The Brunswick was not a popular weapon and in 1853 its phasing

OPPOSITE Victorian Rifle Volunteers, *the frontispiece from* Rifle Volunteers *by Hans Busk, 1859. The uniform of volunteer units was not defined by official regulations and tended to be fanciful.*

out was begun, to be replaced by the 1851 Rifled Musket.

Supply of military weapons in the seventeenth and eighteenth centuries was largely in the hands of private contractors, but the deficiencies of this system were highlighted by the Crimean War and it was agreed that the Royal Small Arms Factory, at Enfield, just outside London, should be expanded to take over the supply of weapons. It soon got into its stride and began producing the

TOP *1853 Rifled Musket, ·577 calibre. This was the first firearm manufactured by the Royal Small Arms Factory, Middlesex, after mechanization was introduced there in 1854.* CENTRE *Martini-Henry breech-loading carbine issued to the cavalry and artillery, ·45 calibre.* BOTTOM *Lee-Metford bolt-action carbine, ·303 calibre, adopted in 1894. National Army Museum.*

1853 Rifled Musket, known generally as the Enfield rifle. This fine rifle was a muzzle loader, but developments showed that a cartridge weapon offered obvious advantages and in 1864 the Snider system of modifying muzzle-loading weapons to cartridge was adopted. A hinged, metal block was fitted at the breech and this could be opened to allow a cartridge to be inserted. Although as a stop-gap it was a reasonable weapon, it was generally

agreed that a completely new rifle was really needed. After tests the choice was made and in 1871 the Martini-Henry rifle was officially adopted. It had a trigger-guard lever, which opened the breech to allow the insertion of a brass-cased ·45 cartridge.

The Martini-Henry rifle and carbine saw action in many parts of the world, but it was limited for it was only a single-shot weapon. Tests were made to find an efficient bolt-action rifle and in 1888 the

Lee-Metford bolt-action rifle was adopted. The box magazine held eight cartridges and its action was dependable, but new propellant explosives caused wear at the breech and modifications were needed. In 1895 the Lee-Enfield rifle replaced the earlier model although, superficially, it differed but little. This was the rifle which saw action in the Boer War and remained in service until displaced in December 1902 by the Short Magazine Lee-Enfield, a thor-

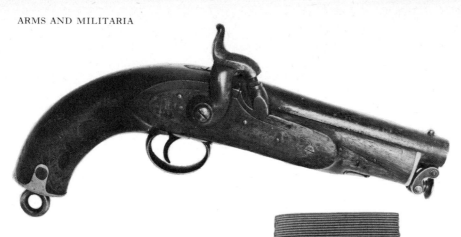

Government percussion pistol, ·58 calibre, 1855. This was inferior to the percussion revolvers already available. The ring at the base of the butt was for a lanyard. Private Collection.

oughly dependable weapon which saw service in two world wars and had few equals in the field of military rifles.

Changes in the standard infantry weapon were matched by changes in the arming of officers and cavalry. The flintlock pistol was replaced by various percussion versions, but the biggest change came after 1851. At the Great Exhibition one of the exhibitors was the American Samuel Colt, a great innovator. His exhibit, which consisted of large numbers of his percussion revolvers, aroused considerable interest and many officers privately purchased Colt revolvers. The Board of Ordnance was slower to take an interest, but some were purchased. An English revolver, the Beaumont-Adams, was preferred. Various types were tried out and in 1880 a model designed by the Enfield Royal Small Arms Factory was officially adopted. In 1887 the Webley Mark I revolver replaced it and this ·441 revolver was, subject to various minor changes, to remain standard for many years.

Campaign and Gallantry Medals

Another innovation in government policy that occurred during Queen Victoria's long reign was the issuing of campaign medals to troops. Many Indian battles were commemorated; the medals were usually given by local personages or by the East India Company, but in 1847 the Naval General Service Medal and the Army General Service Medal were struck for those who had seen action between 1793 and 1840. The fashion having been set, another general service medal, the India Medal, was issued for those with service in that country between 1799 and 1826. As these

Victoria Cross, the highest British award for bravery, instituted in 1856. Fashioned from the metal of captured enemy guns, width 1⅜ in (3·4 cm). The ribbon was crimson for soldiers and blue for sailors. Private Collection.

medals covered such a great number of battles, distinction was given by bars bearing the name of the actions and these were fitted to the clasp of the medal. During the rest of Queen Victoria's reign other medals were struck for campaigns in Africa, Asia, Canada, New Zealand and the Crimea, and the last of her reign was for the Boer War. Each medal was allocated a distinctive coloured ribbon from which it was suspended and it was during Queen Victoria's reign that the crimson ribbon of the Victoria Cross first appeared. In 1856 an order initiating this medal was signed and just over 800 were granted in the next sixty years. Among other gallantry medals instituted during her reign were the Distinguished Conduct Medal (1854), Conspicuous Gallantry Medal (1855), Albert Medal (1856), and the Distinguished Service Order (1886).

Uniforms

Queen Victoria's soldiers were probably far less concerned with their medals than with their everyday dress. Although there were numerous variations in detail from regiment to regiment, the basic uniform in 1837 consisted of a long-tailed scarlet coat decorated with various loops and buttons and a pair of greyish-blue trousers. Upon his head, the infantryman balanced a bell-topped shako, introduced in 1829. This had a small front peak and the body widened towards the crown, which was surmounted at the centre front with a tufted ball. On the front was affixed a large badge in the form of a brass star surmounted by a crown and bearing the regimental number at the centre, the officer's being a more elaborate version.

Officer of the 13th, Prince Albert Regiment of Light Infantry. *He wears with his long-tailed coats the Albert shako in use between 1844 and 1855. From Cannon's* Military Records.

In 1844 this shako was changed for a simpler type; cylindrical, measuring 6¾ in (17·1 cm) high, it had a peak at the front and a smaller one at the back. It was held on the head by a gilded chain on the officer's pattern and a leather strap on the other ranks' models. The top was surmounted by a white tufted ball which was changed in 1846 for a red and white one. The badge, too, was changed slightly with this headdress, which was known as the Albert shako. This, then, was the uniform in which the infantry marched to the Crimean War in 1853, accompanied by cavalry in even more glamorous uniforms with metal helmets fitted with drooping horse-hair plumes or shakos and busbies.

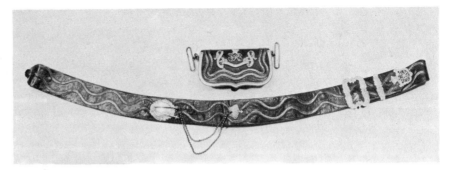

Helmet of an officer of the 5th Dragoon Guards, 1847-71. The British Cavalry rode to the Crimean War (1853-5) in metal helmets with horse-hair plumes such as this. National Army Museum.

The bitter experiences of the War hastened several changes which were under consideration at that time. Tunics replaced the coatee, trimmings were considerably reduced, epaulettes abolished and badges of rank were worn on the collar. The Albert shako was abandoned and in its place came a French-style kepi authorized in January 1855. It was in black felt, 5 in (12·6 cm) high at the front

Pouch and pouch belt of an officer of the Light Dragoons, British German Legion. The reforms of 1855 included the discarding of shoulder belts in favour of waist belts. National Army Museum.

LEFT *Shako of a soldier of the 13th (1st Somersetshire) Light Infantry, 1855-61. Also in 1855 the Albert shako was replaced by a head dress of simpler design. National Army Museum.*

7 in (17·7 cm) deep at the back, where it was moulded to the head. It had a wide peak at the front and a smaller neck peak; the tufted ball of the Albert was retained and the badge was similar in shape to the earlier versions though much smaller. In 1861 the size of the shako was reduced and a different form of construction was used, the blue cloth being mounted on a cork foundation and the back peak abandoned. The badge remained basically the same as before.

In June 1869 the last shako was adopted, similar to the earlier pattern although the chin strap was replaced by a gilded chain for all ranks. The badge was very different and in place of the star was a wreath of laurel leaves around the garter which, in turn, enclosed the regimental device or number.

Another major change which took place in 1855 was the discarding by all but the rifle regiments of shoulder belts, which had been worn since the latter part of the eighteenth century, in favour of a waist belt. This meant that one of the most attractive accessories of infantry dress was abandoned and the shoulder belt plate disappeared. During Queen Victoria's reign these were rectangular and incorporated the regimental number, name or device in their design.

Military fashion is often imitative and as the French of the Crimea influenced the shako design, so the Prussian victory over France in 1871 presumably had some bearing on the choice of a spiked helmet for the infantry. The first

steps were taken in 1877 and the General Order was issued in May 1878. The cork helmet, with a pointed peak at the front and a curved one at the back, had the edges bound with black patent leather for other ranks and gilded metal for officers. The top was surmounted with a spike for infantry and a ball for artillery, engineer and medical corps. The chin chain was worn beneath the chin or looped up across the front and side and held up by a hook on the top near the spike. Badge design reverted to the star and crown pattern with the regimental number and device at the centre. Line infantry helmets were covered in blue cloth and those for light infantry in dark green.

In 1881 the British Army was given an overhaul and the old system of regimental numbering was abandoned; each regiment was given a territorial association – a county, town or area. This change meant that all badges had to be changed and the new title incorporated.

Officers had japanned-tin boxes in which they stored their various head-dresses and these were shaped to fit the particular item. Those for guards' bear-skins were large and cylindrical; those for the shako rather like a top-hat box, and for the blue-cloth helmet they were cylindrical with a tapered lid; lance caps fitted into square tins. Most of the cases bore a brass label engraved with the owner's name and regiment.

For undress wear the infantry wore a Glengarry cap, introduced in 1874, on which was a smaller badge. These badges were produced in a great variety of regimental patterns and the commonest

Undress cap of an officer of the Norfolk Regiment. The black leather peak has a gold braid edge and the badge of Britannia is embroidered in gold and coloured thread. Private Collection.

TOP (l. to r.) *Connaught Rangers badge, after 1881; Non-commissioned officer's sleeve badge.* BOTTOM *19th Regiment of Footpouch badge, Eton (College) Rifle Volunteers shako badge. Private Collection.*

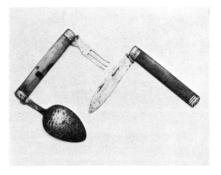

Military cutlery set, carried by an officer while on campaign. Many sets were of steel with bone handles, but they were also made in other materials, including silver. Brown Collection.

form was that of a garter enclosing the regimental number. After 1881 these badges were also altered.

Over the years there were changes in such minor items as buttons and the old pewter buttons worn by other ranks were replaced in 1855 by brass ones. Buttons, like badges, usually carried the regimental number, but this practice was discontinued in 1871 and one general service design adopted.

Victorian England was nothing if not patriotic and it is not surprising that when danger, real or imaginary, threatened the country people responded with enthusiasm. In the late 1850s it was thought that France, England's traditional enemy, was again in a warlike mood. Men rushed to form volunteer groups of riflemen, artillery, cavalry and engineers and each unit wanted a uniform and badge. Some of the units disbanded, but others were amalgamated and were later incorporated into the Territorial Army, where they were officially recognized as the Volunteer Force.

Another bitter lesson learned on several battlefields was that red was not a very suitable colour if concealment was important. Rifle regiments had always worn a less conspicuous green; in Africa and India and in the Abyssinian War of 1868, some troops had worn a drab colour known as khaki, and there was a gradual adoption of it. In 1898 an issue of khaki was made to nearly all overseas troops, although full dress was retained for ceremonial occasions.

Beside the equipment and accoutrements of the regular forces, there were numerous pieces of militaria produced for the commercial market. Post-cards, prints and picture books were published, by artists such as Orlando Norrie, Harry Paine and Richard Simkin.

Frederick Wilkinson

AMERICAN

The immense changes which took place during Queen Victoria's reign were certainly not limited to Britain and her Empire. This period saw the growth of the United States from a group of individual states into a united nation, and, for example, the development of a firearms industry second to none.

Firearms and Edged Weapons

In 1836 Samuel Colt took out his first American patent for a percussion re-

OPPOSITE *Commemorative roll to men of the 24th (2nd Warwickshire) Regiment, 1879. National Army Museum.*

volver and in so doing began to change the concept of arms manufacture, indeed the whole concept of war. In that year he produced his first revolver, the so-called Patterson, which was not a great commercial success. However, in Texas, Captain Samuel Walker of the United States Dragoons saw the potential of this type of firearm and made some suggestions for changes in design. As a result, in 1847 the Walker Colt was produced and from then on Colt was established. He went on to supply his Dragoon revolver (three models) firing a heavy ·44 bullet and appreciating the demand for a smaller, lighter weapon, he introduced in 1849, the Pocket Colt, which fired a ·31 bullet. In 1851, the year of the Great Exhibition in London,

he began the manufacture of his even more successful Navy Belt Model, which used a ·36, a slightly larger bullet.

Colt visited London and promoted his products in a forceful Yankee style and, foreseeing a great potential market, he established a London factory to manufacture his percussion revolvers. In 1855 he produced the Root 1855 Sidehammer model which was outside the mainstream of development and was designed for easy maintenance. Next came the 1860 Army Model which reverted to a ·44 bullet. What further effect Colt might have had on the firearms industry is unknown for he met an early death in 1862, but by then he had set a pattern and could lay a strong claim to being a founder of modern mass-production

Flag of the U.S. Treasury Guards displayed at Ford's Theatre, Washington, D.C., where it hung on the night of Lincoln's assassination in 1865. John Wilkes Booth's spur caught in it as he jumped from the box.

methods, using the principle of interchangeability of parts.

One firearm which took its place as essentially an American weapon was the long-barrelled rifle with a characteristic gracefully drooping butt. Known as the Pennsylvania or, popularly, the Kentucky rifle, this weapon gained a well-earned reputation for accuracy. Originally it had a flintlock, but by the 1830s to 40s, most were fitted with percussion locks.

Firearms manufacturers were constantly experimenting and developing new ideas; Smith & Wesson were responsible for one tremendously important development, a breech-loading cartridge weapon. In 1857 they produced a small metal rimfire cartridge, in which the detonating compound was deposited inside a small lip at the base of the cartridge. The cartridge could be inserted into the rear of the revolver cylinder, thus obviating the tedious business of loading in powder and ball and fitting a small percussion cap over a nipple. Needless to say, there were numerous ingenious, and often totally impractical, attempts to evade the master patent held by Smith & Wesson.

The Civil War (1861–5) and the expanding frontier both generated a great demand for firearms and in 1873 Colt's

BELOW *Spencer cartridge and Blakeslee quick loader. To speed the rate of fire of the Spencer repeating rifle, tubes loaded with cartridges were devised to slip into the butt magazine. Smithsonian Institution.*

ABOVE *Civil War drum. The drum would have been suspended from white webbing and the stocks housed in a brass case. The decoration was generally slighter than on this drum. H. K. Hayden Collection.*

factory introduced the cartridge weapon that has become more or less synonymous with the West. The Colt Single Action Army Model, known as the Peacemaker or the Frontier, proved itself a thoroughly reliable and practical weapon.

In the area of repeating weapons probably the best-known name is that of Winchester, although the origin of the famous rifle lies with a designer named B. Tyler Henry. In 1860 Henry produced his first repeating rifle with an under-barrel magazine, into which could be loaded a number of cartridges. The loading and firing mechanism was activated by a lever situated beneath the butt. It was from this weapon that the Winchester rifle was evolved under the expert management of Oliver P. Winchester, a one-time shirt manufacturer.

242

Henry repeating rifle, ·44 calibre, presented to Abraham Lincoln by the manufacturer, Oliver F. Winchester. The rifle is named after B. Tyler Henry (1821-98), who patented it in 1860. Smithsonian Institution.

There were also developments in the field of automatic weapons, the best known being that of Dr R. Gatling who, in 1865, produced a very practical, hand-operated machine gun. This weapon was developed and officially adopted by the United States Army in 1866. It was further improved and gave good service for many years.

During this period the best known of American edged weapons was undoubtedly the Bowie knife. The basic design of this famed weapon is usually credited to Rezin Bowie, who sought to produce a knife which was heavy and strong enough for general hunting purposes and capable of cutting or stabbing. The traditional Bowie knife has a fairly large blade, single edged, with a clipped point and a curved cutting edge. James Bowie, Rezin's brother, was a flamboyant character who died at the Battle of the Alamo in March 1836. This essentially American weapon was largely manufactured by British cutlers, although the blades were etched with appropriate American mottoes and sentiments. These knives varied greatly in detail but their romantic associations have made them very popular with collectors and, in consequence, they have been copied so frequently that it is now difficult to distinguish original from replica.

Uniforms

During Queen Victoria's reign the States were involved in a number of wars both large and small. First came the war with Mexico (1846–8), and already at this date the infantry were wearing a uniform which remained basically the same throughout the Civil War. Most soldiers wore a blue coatee, grey or blue trousers and a very sensible, soft cap, not unlike a civilian one and similar to that worn by British troops in undress. Compared with the uniforms of most contemporary armies this was an eminently practical and sensible garb. In 1847 stripes, or chevrons, were adopted as a simple means of distinguishing the various non-commissioned officers.

This practical approach to martial costume was somewhat modified following

Powder flasks for pistols and revolvers, mid-nineteenth century. Stamped copper and brass. Before the development of the metallic cartridge, powder flasks with patent measuring pourers were used.

the Mexican War, for the jacket was lengthened, epaulettes were fitted at the shoulders and the campaign cap was exchanged for a tall, tapering shako, topped by a pom-pom or plume. Dragoon officers wore the wide-brimmed, slouch hat with one side cocked up and held in place by a small gilded eagle clip and decorated with three small ostrich plumes.

The outbreak of the Civil War in 1861 had a great effect on uniform design and there was a trend towards flamboyance. The national standing army had been

Private Jesse Murray, Alexandria Riflemen, 6th Battalion of Virginia Volunteers, 1861, which in June 1861 became Company A, 17th Regiment of Virginia Volunteers, whose green uniform he wears. National Park Service.

very small and there was an immediate response to the appeal for volunteers. Each state, and many towns, supplied units and their uniforms were often picturesque. Influenced, no doubt, by the news of French military successes in Italy, some troops copied their uniform, and both North and South had some units dressed in the costume of the Zouaves from North Africa. These wore short blue jackets and very baggy trousers supported by a blue or red sash.

Although there were variations, the basic uniform of the Federal cavalry consisted of a short, blue jacket with gilded buttons, light blue breeches, leather boots reaching to just below the knee, a black leather belt and a low-crowned kepi. The infantryman had a coat which reached to the top of the thighs, light blue trousers with dark blue stripes down the side, a low-crowned kepi and a black leather waist belt with sundry canvas pouches suspended from the shoulders. The infantry officer wore a slouch hat, somewhat similar to the earlier version. The standard uniform of the South, although more honoured in the breach than the observance, was not dissimilar, with grey as the dominant colour.

During the Civil War there was an increasing use of standard insignia and regulation issue equipment. Buttons were yellow, mostly bearing the American eagle holding a shield with an identifying letter: I for infantry and C for cavalry. Confederate buttons differed: some also had the eagle while others bore just a single letter. Corps badges were used, especially in the North, and were generally simple geometric shapes such as the diamond, circle, heart or star.

When the War was over there still remained military demands on the frontier and although the infantry uniform changed but little the cavalry, on whom the greater part of the burden fell, became far more lax in their dress. Many of the officers wore buckskin jackets, frequently fringed, and a campaign hat with a wide brim.

Following the Franco-Prussian War (1870–1), the United States military authorities adopted a headdress closely resembling that of the victorious Prussian

Congressional Medal of Honor, authorized in July 1862. The bronze medal has the army suspension fitting and the ribbon is red and white striped with a solid blue section at the top. N. Flayderman Collection.

Knapsack and personal equipment of a soldier of Company C, 33rd Regiment of New York State Volunteers in the Civil War. 1861-5. Included are his water canteen, razor, mess plate and mug and combination cutlery set. N. Flayderman Collection.

Army. It was a cloth helmet surmounted by a spike, from which drooped a yellow plume. In 1879 a summer uniform was issued which included a sun helmet very similar to that worn by the British Army in India, but on campaign the earlier, wide-brimmed slouch hat was preferred.

The British learned from bitter experience that modern weapons were so effective that the old methods of warfare were too expensive in casualties. The idea of blending troops into the background was an obvious necessity. They found that khaki was a good neutral colour for this purpose and soon the Americans also turned to more muted colours. During the Spanish-American War of 1898 units such as the Rough Riders, Theodore Roosevelt's famous band, were fitted out with a light khaki uniform with a slouch hat. The infantryman retained his dark blue jacket and light blue trousers, although the lower part of his leg was given additional protection by a pair of khaki canvas gaiters. Over his left shoulder and encircling his body he carried a rolled blanket. Khaki was not officially adopted by the United States Army until 1902, when it was made

standard field service wear. The colour was greener than the British material.

Awards and Medals

Like the British, the Americans did not have a tradition of presenting medals. Apart from a Badge of Military Merit used during the Revolutionary War, there was no procedure for recognizing bravery until the Medal of Honor was established in July 1862. A bronze star, it had engraved on the back the recipient's name and the deed for which it was given; the ribbon had narrow red and white stripes until 1896, when the design was changed to red with a narrow central white stripe flanked on either side with blue. In 1904 the medal was completely redesigned.

The United States Navy had its own, slightly different, Medal of Honor and this was unchanged from its adoption in 1861 until 1913. One award which was rather unusual was the Certificate of Merit, which was established in 1847

and entitled the proud owner to an extra payment of two dollars a month. It was not until 1905 that the owner was awarded the right to wear a medal. In 1869 the United States Navy authorized the issue of a Good Conduct Badge, in the form of a Maltese cross until it was changed to a disk form in 1884.

Medals for specific campaigns were seldom issued by the United States. A number of private medals were awarded, but it was only in 1907 that an official award for service during the Civil War was authorized for the Army, and the Navy had to wait until 1908. Congress was equally tardy in recognizing service during the Indian Wars, which continued intermittently until 1898, for the medal was not established until 1907. However, the Manila Bay Medal was authorized almost immediately after the battle in 1898 and, following this, Congress authorized a number of campaign medals including one for service in the Boxer Rebellion in China (1900–1).

The military history of the United States in the nineteenth century has captured the imagination of the world. There is consequently a strong demand for associated items and the collector should be aware that the supply of original pieces is limited and that badges, kepis, belts, Bowie knives and even uniforms have been reproduced.

Frederick Wilkinson

Glossary of Uniform

See colour plate p. 228.

Aiguillette
Plaited cords draped from the shoulder, under the arm and over the chest, where they are looped on to a button. Also known as aiglet or aglet.

Albert shako
Cap worn by British soldiers between 1844 and 1855.

Ammunition pouch
Cartridge box. Various types and patterns of ammunition containers were used during the Victorian period, of leather, wood, metal or canvas. Because of the weight of ammunition, the load was often spread between two or more boxes and when these were suspended from the waist belt they had to be supported from the shoulders by straps.

Badge
Distinguishing mark or emblem used to denote rank or unit. They often appeared on the EPAULETTE and when this was abandoned officers' badges were moved to the collar. After the 1880s officers' rank insignia returned to the shoulder but there were many variations and some badges were worn on the cuff. Badges, other than those of rank, were worn on the arm during the Victorian period; first they were embroidered and latterly they were made of metal. These badges indicated special skills and proficiency: swordsmen, rough riders, drummers, etc. Headdress badges bore the regiment's number until after Cardwell's Army Reforms of 1881, when the name of the regiment was displayed.

Bandolier
SHOULDER BELT designed to hold ammunition.

Bearskin
Cap made from bear's skin worn by some French regiments and the British foot-guards.

Bonnet
Headdress worn by some Scottish regiments.

Busby
Fur cap, not to be confused with a BEARSKIN, worn by hussar regiments and Royal Horse Artillery.

Buttons
At the beginning of the Victorian period British officers wore domed metal buttons, often of silver, while other ranks wore flat pewter buttons. From 1855 other ranks wore brass buttons and officers wore gilded ones. After 1871 all but a few other ranks wore buttons bearing the royal arms.

Cap lines
Cords attaching a headdress to the body so that it would not be lost if knocked off.

Coatee
Short-tailed coat worn in the United States and by the British Army until 1855.

Cuirass
Armour breastplate and backplate as worn today by the Lifeguards in full dress.

Epaulette
Shoulderpiece varying from a simple cord or strap to an elaborate metal bar with an ornate fringe, often used to denote rank. The most elaborate epaulettes were abandoned during the 1850s.

Frog
Leather or webbing attachment for securing a sword or BAYONET to a SHOULDER BELT or waist belt.

Glengarry
Scottish-style side cap introduced in 1874 and worn by the British infantry in undress.

Hackle
Small bunch of feathers worn in the side of a SLOUCH HAT where the brim is pinned to the crown, or by Scotsmen or fusiliers on their headdress.

Holster
Leather container for a firearm originally slung round a horse's neck but personal holsters were worn after the introduction of PISTOLS and REVOLVERS which fired several shots after each loading.

Kepi
Cap with a flat top and peak: a low-crowned version of the British or French SHAKO.

Khaki
From the Hindu word meaning dusty, the drab-coloured uniform first worn by British troops in India and Africa. The American khaki, which was formally adopted by the United States Army in 1902, was much greener than the British khaki.

Lace
Coloured embroidery on a uniform. In the British Army it was traditionally gold for regular soldiers and silver for militia.

Lance cap
Square-topped head-dress worn by lancers.

Pelisse
Jacket worn by hussars, usually lined with fur and ornately braided; when not in use it was worn slung over the left shoulder.

Pickelhaube
German spiked helmet which was made, during the Victorian period, of leather with metal furniture.

Plate
Metal BADGE for helmets and other headdresses.

Puttees
KHAKI bandages bound around the top of the boot and part of the calf.

Rowel
Spiked wheel of a spur. For mess dress and review, dumb rowels (wheels without spikes) were worn.

Sabretache
Flat bag or pouch used by the cavalry as a despatch or map case and slung from the sword belt. Abolished in 1901.

Sam Browne
Leather belt traditionally supposed to have been designed by General Sir Sam Browne and officially adopted by the British Army in 1900.

Sash
Worn by an officer or sergeant, it was wrapped around the waist until EPAULETTES were abandoned when it was worn over the left shoulder.

Shabracque
Saddlecloth.

Shako
Peaked military cap of Hungarian origin worn by several armies during the nineteenth century. It varied from the elaborate leather headdress of the British infantryman to the simple felt cap of the American Civil War. (See p. 228.)

Shoulder belt
Leather belt worn by the British Army from the eighteenth century, when two were worn supporting the BAYONET and CARTRIDGE box, to 1855. Also known as a cross-belt.

Shoulder-belt plate
Oval or rectangular metal plate bearing regimental devices and attached to the SHOULDER BELT.

Slouch hat
Soft, broad-brimmed hat, sometimes with the brim pinned up on one side with a HACKLE.

Spatterdash
Short gaiter covering the foot and extending a few inches above the ankle.

Sword knot
Strap attached to the sword and passed around the wrist to prevent loss in combat. During the nineteenth century many regiments developed very ornate sword knots.

Tunic
Short, closely fitting coat of even length, adopted by the British Army in 1855.

Wing
Projection from the point of the shoulder of a tunic. An alternative to the EPAULETTE and worn by, for example, British drummers.

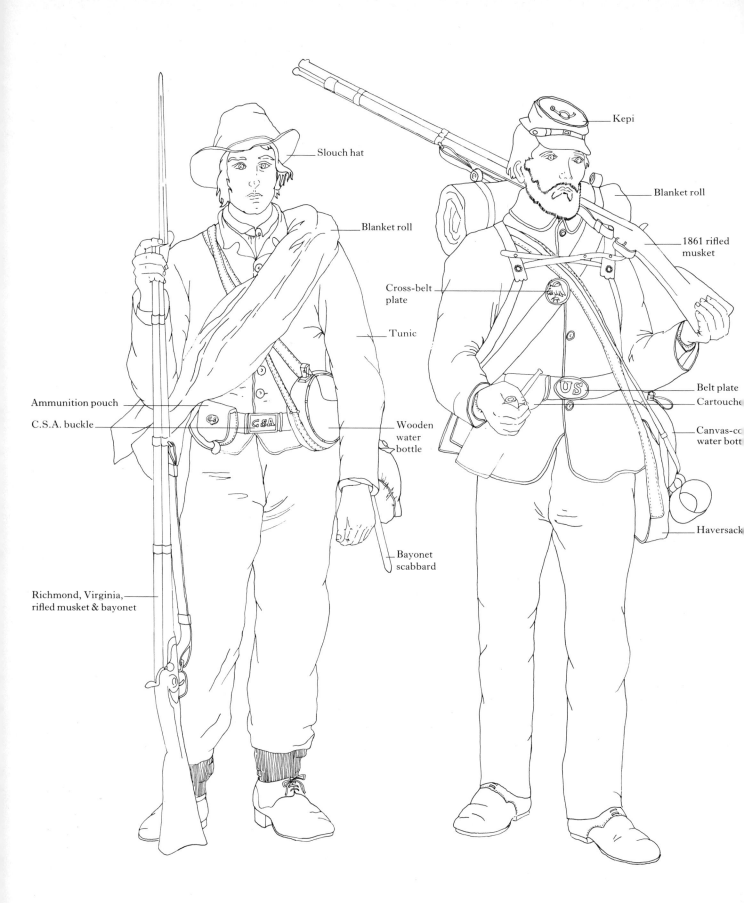

Slouch hat

Kepi

Blanket roll

Blanket roll

1861 rifled
musket

Cross-belt
plate

Tunic

Ammunition pouch

C.S.A. buckle

Belt plate

Cartouche

Wooden
water
bottle

Canvas-co
water bott

Bayonet
scabbard

Haversack

Richmond, Virginia,
rifled musket & bayonet

Glossary of Decorations and Medals

Bar
Addition to a medal on a metal strip fixed to the RIBBON giving the name of an action or campaign. One medal may have several bars.

Campaign medal
Awarded to all who took part in a particular campaign or battle.

Cartouche
Scrolled ornament which appears on many SUSPENDERS and on some BARS.

Exergue
Part of a medal separated from the main device by a line near the bottom.

Field
Background of a medal, the part not occupied by the device or the EXERGUE.

Gallantry award
Decoration conferred in respect of a specific deed of bravery or bravery sustained over a certain period of time. The most coveted of these decorations in Britain is the Victoria Cross.

Gazetted
To receive a general citation for gallantry. The term derives from the publication of the award in *The London Gazette*.

General Service Award
Instituted in 1847 for all those who had served in the British Army between 1793 and 1815 or in the Navy between 1793 and 1840. The Army medal had twenty-nine BARS and the Navy medal had 231. This type of award was used to commemorate a number of small actions in the same country or continent, for example, the India General Service Medal (1854–94) with twenty-three bars, the Canada General Service Medal (1866–70) with three bars.

Group
Term describing the medals awarded to a particular individual which may cover several wars.

Long Service Medal
Award for long service and good conduct instituted in 1830 for the British Army and 1831 for the Navy.

Medal of Honor
First American award for bravery instituted during the Victorian period (1862). The highest-ranking and best-known American decoration.

OPPOSITE *Typical dress and equipment of a Confederate soldier* (left) *and a Federal soldier* (right) *of the American Civil War, 1861–5.*

Miniature
Small replica of a medal worn on mess dress when full dress is not required.

Mounted
Term describing a GROUP of medals arranged in order of precedence.

Named
Term for a medal which bears the name of the recipient and his unit, usually on the edge of a round medal or on the back of a star. The name might be engraved or impressed.

Native medal
CAMPAIGN MEDAL awarded to natives, especially those serving with the Army of India.

Ribbon
Silk fabric of distinctive pattern associated with a medal. For ordinary wear medals are not worn but ribbons are sewn on to the TUNIC.

Suspender
Method of mounting a medal on its RIBBON. Most medals were issued with a swing suspender or slot bar, but some had ring suspenders.

Glossary of Edged Weapons

Back strap
Metal back on the GRIP of a sword, usually a continuation of the POMMEL.

Basket hilt
Broad, openwork guard, such as that on Scottish swords, designed to protect the hand.

Bayonet
Blade fixed to the MUZZLE of a firearm, primarily used as an anti-cavalry weapon.

Bayonet lug
Stud on the side or underneath of the BARREL of a firearm on to which the BAYONET slots.

Bowie knife
Most famous American knife. Supposedly designed by Rezin and popularized by Colonel James Bowie, it had a straight single-edged blade and was used for hunting and fighting.

Chape
Metal guard at the bottom of a SCABBARD.

Claymore
Scottish two-edged broadsword. The word is inaccurately used to describe later Scottish swords.

Dirk
Scottish dagger, traditionally with a one-sided blade. Each regiment had its own design, sometimes with an elaborately engraved blade. Also used by the British Navy, where it was particularly associated with midshipmen.

Elcho bayonet
Type of BAYONET with a broad spear point and a saw back developed by Lord Elcho in 1870 but not issued until 1895. It was never generally adopted.

Faible
Weak part of a blade, towards the point of a small-sword, which was used for thrusting.

Forte
Strong part of a blade, near the HILT, which was used for parrying.

Fuller
Groove in the side of a blade which makes it lighter while retaining its strength.

Grip
Part of a HILT actually grasped by the hand.

Gothic hilt
Half BASKET HILT.

Hanger
Short-bladed sword originally carried by infantrymen but only worn by pioneers and bandsmen in the nineteenth century. It was made to hang vertically from a FROG.

Hilt
Handle of a sword or dagger.

Knuckle bow
Band of metal connecting the POMMEL to the QUILLON to protect the knuckles.

Locket
Top mount of a sheath which carries the ring by which a sword is suspended.

Mameluke hilt
Style of HILT modelled on the hilt of the Turkish SABRE which was popular with Napoleon's officers in Egypt and was used by the American Army until 1859 and then again after 1875.

Point of percussion
Point on the edge of a sword where a blow may be most effectively struck and which jars the hand least.

Pipe-backed
Sword blade with its back thickened to stiffen the sword for thrusting and to give weight to the cut – in fact it succeeded in doing neither and was not much used.

Pommel
Knob at the end of a sword HILT, sometimes plain, sometimes decorated.

Quillon
Cross-guard between the GRIP and the blade of a sword or dagger.

Sabre
Cutting sword with a curved blade.

Scabbard
Sheath in which a sword is kept.

Scimitar
Sword with a curved single-edged blade with a spear point. Its wear was officially restricted to British field marshals and general officers though cavalry officers also wore it.

Shell
Disk guard between the blade and GRIP of a sword.

Shoulder
Part of a blade immediately below the HILT.

Skean dhu
Knife worn in the right stocking by Scottish regiments (from the Gaelic *sgian*, knife, and *dubh*, black).

Socket bayonet
Type of BAYONET which superseded the original plug bayonet. The blade is fixed to a short cylinder which slots over the end of the barrel.

Sword bayonet
Type of BAYONET with a QUILLON and a blade like a sword, without a neck.

Tang
Part of the blade which projects through the HILT.

Trough
Gauge into which a sword blade was fitted for inspection to ensure that it conformed exactly to the pattern.

Yatagan
Type of curved blade from the Turkish *yataghan*-dagger.

Glossary of Firearms

American rifle
Another name for the PENNSYLVANIA RIFLE.

Barrel
Tube of a RIFLE through which the bullet is projected.

Bolt-action
Sliding bolt which is drawn back to reveal the BREECH of a RIFLE. The CARTRIDGE is laid in place and the bolt rammed back.

Bore
Internal diameter or CALIBRE of a firearm.

Boxer cartridge
Brass-cased CARTRIDGE designed by Colonel Edward Boxer of the Woolwich Arsenal and used with the SNIDER RIFLE.

Breech
Section of the BARREL which holds the CHARGE or CARTRIDGE.

Breech block
Section of the BARREL which opens to admit the CARTRIDGE.

Brown Bess
British MUSKET, the Army's principal weapon for over a century. Originally it was a FLINTLOCK musket, but it was adapted to the PERCUSSION system in 1838 before being dropped in 1840.

Brunswick
RIFLE developed in the late 1830s and used by the British Army until it began to be phased out in 1853. It was designed by a Captain Berners and sponsored by the Duke of Brunswick. It had a stout BARREL with two deep grooves cut on the inside and the ball it fired had a belt which engaged the groove.

Bullet mould
Device used for casting lead bullets. First developed in the fourteenth century and used until machines were developed in the nineteenth. Hand-held scissor-type moulds are best known, but stone moulds were also used.

Butt
Heavy end of a firearm held nearest the body.

Calibre
Internal diameter or BORE of a firearm.

Carbine
Short MUSKET or RIFLE issued to cavalry or special units.

Cartridge
Case containing the charge for a firearm. Made of paper until about 1865; thereafter it was made of brass or copper.

Centre-fire
CARTRIDGE used from the 1860s with the cap fitted in the centre of a thickened base.

Charge
Load of explosive which propels the projectile from a firearm.

Cock
Part of the firing mechanism of a FLINTLOCK which holds the piece of flint. To cock a RIFLE is to make it ready for firing.

Colt
Samuel Colt (1814–62), born at Hartford, Connecticut, was an important American firearms manufacturer. His first really successful REVOLVER, the Walker Colt, was produced in 1847. He became the largest individual manufacturer of revolvers in the world and developed methods of mass production and the use of interchangeable parts.

Enfield
RIFLE produced by the Royal Small Arms Factory at Enfield, Middlesex, from 1853. It was a MUZZLE-loader and saw many years service.

Flashpan
Priming pan in a FLINTLOCK.

Flintlock
Firing mechanism in which the trigger releases a spring-operated COCK which holds a piece of flint. The flint strikes the FRIZZEN and produces sparks which ignite the PRIMING POWDER.

Frizzen
L-shaped steel hammer in a FLINTLOCK firing system which, when struck by the flint, showers sparks into the FLASHPAN.

Fulminate
Compound of fulminic acid which detonates by percussion, friction or heat.

Gatling
Early hand-operated machine gun developed by Dr R. Gatling in 1865 which was adopted by the United States Army in 1866 and used for many years.

Grenade
Small metal container filled with explosive, thrown by hand or discharged from a firearm.

Lancaster
MUZZLE-loading RIFLE which had limited use with the British Army from 1855. It had no conventional rifling but a slightly oval BORE which had a twist.

Lee-Enfield
RIFLE adopted in 1895. It was a modification of the LEE-METFORD but with fewer grooves in the rifling. This was the most advanced rifle used by British troops in the Boer War and was the precursor of the famous Short Magazine Lee-Enfield (the S.M.L.E. which saw service in two world wars).

Lee-Metford
BOLT-ACTION RIFLE adopted in 1888 incorporating the discoveries about rifling made by W. E. Metford. It had a box MAGAZINE holding eight CARTRIDGES and was the first magazine rifle adopted by the British Army.

Lock
Mechanism of a firearm by which the CHARGE is exploded.

Magazine
Storehouse for military provisions, arms and ammunition, or a case for ammunition that can be fixed to the BREECH of a firearm.

Magazine rifle
REPEATING RIFLE. The first magazine rifle to be adopted by the British Army was the LEE-METFORD.

Martini-Henry
BREECH-loading RIFLE which was adopted by the British Army in 1871. It was superseded by the LEE-METFORD.

Minié bullet
Developed by the Frenchman, Captain Claude-Étienne Minié, to permit rapid loading of a rifled gun. The CARTRIDGE contained the CHARGE and the bullet dropped down the BARREL easily, but on firing the base of the bullet expanded to fit the grooves of the rifling. Adopted by many armies in the 1850s.

Musket
Smooth-bore military firearm fired from the shoulder.

Muzzle
End of the BARREL from which the projectile emerges.

Needle gun
Percussion firearm in which a striking needle passes through the base of a

CARTRIDGE to strike a primer inside. Developed by the Prussian gunsmith, Johann Nikolaus van Dreyse.

Peacemaker
Name used on the United States frontier for the COLT Single Action Army Revolver. Introduced in 1873, it became almost synonymous with the American West.

Pennsylvania rifle
Long-barrelled American RIFLE with a drooping BUTT, originally made by German immigrant gunsmiths who settled in Pennsylvania. It was a hunting weapon but became a fighting weapon as well. Originally FLINTLOCK, it was converted to a PERCUSSION LOCK in the 1830s. The most famous American rifle, it was frequently called a Kentucky rifle.

Pepperbox
Multi-barrelled PISTOL in which each BARREL is fired separately. Usually the barrels revolve, but in some cases the firing device revolves. Because the pepperbox pistol was MUZZLE-heavy, the barrel was shortened, making it very inaccurate.

Percussion cap
Small container of copper filled with FULMINATE which is placed on the nipple of the firing LOCK. When struck by the hammer its explosive CHARGE fires and ignites the main charge.

Percussion lock
Ignition system which superseded the FLINTLOCK in the early nineteenth century. The principal pioneer of the percussion system was a Scotsman, the Rev. Alexander Forsyth, who patented a percussion MUSKET in 1807.

Pistol
Small firearm held in one hand. Military pistols were principally cavalry weapons and were used for close-quarter shooting. Officers in the nineteenth century frequently carried their own pistols or REVOLVERS rather than using the often inferior government issue.

Priming powder
Fine-grained powder used in FLINTLOCK and wheellock weapons to start the CHARGE burning.

Repeating rifle
MAGAZINE RIFLE which held several CARTRIDGES or CHARGES at a time and did not have to be reloaded between each shot. The most famous repeating rifle was the WINCHESTER.

Revolver
PISTOL with a rotating MAGAZINE. Originally the term also referred to long guns and machine guns, and sometimes it was a cluster of BARRELS that revolved. The last MUZZLE-loading revolver to be issued to the British Army was the model of 1866; it was succeeded by the WEBLEY.

Rifle
Firearm with a groove or grooves spiralling in the BARREL. This gives a twist to the bullet resulting in greater range and accuracy. The process of rifling was known in the sixteenth century but it was very costly and was only used for sporting guns. The British Army received its first rifles in 1800.

Rifled musket
Infantry firearm introduced in 1851 to the British Army which was rifled but retained the MUZZLE-loading long BARREL of the MUSKET.

Single action
Firing mechanism where the hammer has to be pulled back manually before each shot.

Snider rifle
First BREECH-loader to be on general issue to the British Army. The Snider system was a method of modifying MUZZLE-loading RIFLES for breech loading. It was developed by Jacob Snider of New York for a competition held in 1864. The Snider rifle was used by the British Army until 1871.

Stock
Wooden part of a gun.

Webley
Webley Mark I was the first really successful British BREECH-loading REVOLVER. It was issued to the British Army in 1887 and remained in service for many years.

Winchester
American repeating RIFLE, produced by Oliver P. Winchester from the developments of B. Tyler Henry. All rifles manufactured by the Winchester Repeating Arms Co. after 1866 were known as Winchesters. The firm's reputation was built on Models 1866 and 1873.

Bibliography

BLAIR, CLAUDE. *European and American Arms*, London, 1962

CARMAN, WILLIAM Y. *British Military Uniforms from Contemporary Pictures*, London, 1957

GORDON, LAWRENCE. *British Battles and Medals*, London, 1971

KERRIGAN, EVANS. *American Badges and Insignia*, New York, 1968

KERRIGAN, EVANS. *American War Medals and Decorations*, London, 1971

KIPLING, ARTHUR, and KING, HUGH. *Head-dress Badges of the British Army*, London, 1972

LORD, FRANCIS. *Civil War Collector's Encyclopedia*, Harrisburg, Pennsylvania, 1965

PETERSON, HAROLD L. (ed.). *Encyclopædia of Firearms*, London and New York, 1964

PETERSON, HAROLD L. *The American Sword 1775–1945*, Philadelphia, 1965.

WILKINSON, FREDERICK. *Militaria*, London, 1969

WILSON, R. L. and SUTHERLAND, R. Q. *The Book of Colt Firearms*, Kansas City, Missouri, 1971

WINDROW, MARTIN, and EMBLETON, GERRY. *Military Dress of North America*, Shepperton, Surrey, 1973

Jewelry

BRITISH

Victorian jewelry was international, both in terms of material and design. The British Isles had few mineral resources of use to the jeweler, and these were so little worth large-scale commercial exploitation that even the cairngorms set in many Scottish brooches were more usually mined in South America than in Banffshire, and cut and polished in Idar-Oberstein in Germany.

The Trade

Bullion, precious and semi-precious stones, pearls, shells and other materials came to England from all over the world for sale and distribution. Many fashionable shops also stocked jewelry imported from France, Germany, Italy, Switzerland, India, America, Japan and elsewhere. The trade in unmounted components was even more important. Mosaics from Rome, Florence and Venice, gem and shell cameos from Rome and Naples, carved coral from Naples and hair from the Orient (for use in cheap mourning jewelry) were among the commodities imported and set by British jewelers.

The prosperous and stable condition of British society attracted many Continental craftsmen to London, for luxury trades such as that of jewelry were especially vulnerable to the effects of revolution. The new arrivals helped to extend the technical repertory of fashionable jewelers, and they also popularized their favourite styles. During the struggle for the reunification of Italy, Alessandro Castellani, a member of the famous family of goldsmiths and jewelers in Rome, lived in exile in Paris and London. He wrote and lectured on his

firm's granulated jewelry in the antique Classical manner, which became a major source of inspiration to English and French jewelers in the 1860s and '70s.

The Castellanis' jewelry falls largely in the category of 'secondary' work, consisting mainly of gold, with stones playing a relatively minor part in the design. In this, as in 'fine' jewelry made of precious stones set in minimal mounts, English jewelers looked mainly to France and Italy for new ideas in design. But in the field of mass-produced jewelry, a new phenomenon, they pioneered the use of machine aids developed during the Industrial Revolution. Imitation jewelry produced in Birmingham reached a market which had hitherto been partially or wholly excluded from the possession of personal adornments.

Base metal, shaped by dies in steam-powered stamping presses, emerged as lockets, brooches and bracelets, the cheapest of which cost the manufacturer as little as a farthing apiece to produce. From the mid 1860s presses were sophisticated enough to form and decorate the surface of small articles at a single blow. All that was then required was the addition of pins or other attachments to make the finished article.

British machines were adopted abroad and, in time, inventions from the Continent and America were taken up in England. In the early 1860s, for instance, the first prefabricated collets were developed in France and soon afterwards were employed by British jewelers anxious to by-pass the task of making settings by hand to fit individual stones. These stamped collets were theoretically as suitable for precious as for semi-precious stones, but in practice they were more usually employed in the settings of less valuable stones and for paste jewelry.

The Birmingham jewelers were chiefly, although not entirely concerned with making secondary and imitation jewelry. Some ran small workshops in the traditional fashion; others had huge factories

equipped with the latest machinery. London was the principal centre for fine and the better qualities of secondary jewelry, which was made in workshops owned or patronized by the leading retailers in the West End. The workshops were concentrated in Soho and Clerkenwell, with a scattering of others elsewhere. Some large manufacturers in Clerkenwell, however, rivalled Birmingham in the mass production of cheap jewelry.

There was hardly a city or a town in the British Isles without its jewelers. The Whitby jet trade must be cited for example, as it flourished on a mineral found locally. Scottish jewelers in Edinburgh, Glasgow, Aberdeen and elsewhere made a speciality of traditional Celtic jewelry, reinterpreting national motifs to satisfy a demand fostered by the romances of Sir Walter Scott. Harps, shamrocks and small-scale copies of early Medieval Irish brooches formed the staple repertory of jewelry manufacturers in Dublin and Belfast, who made much use of local gems and of bog oak. National jewelry of this type was inevitably emulated by manufacturers in Birmingham. Jet, which enjoyed an almost continuous popularity as a material both for fashionable and mourning wear, was likewise taken up by Birmingham jewelers. It was expensive, however, and many substitutes were developed. One of the most effective was vulcanite, a composition of India rubber and sulphur.

A natural reluctance on the part of retailers to divulge the names of the actual makers of the goods they sold, coupled with the fact that the hallmarking laws then in force exempted many categories of jewelry from compulsory assay, means that it is often impossible to attribute pieces to individual craftsmen or even to firms. A few jewelers put their own mark on some of their goods without sending them to be hallmarked. Carlo Giuliano, who arrived in London in about 1860, almost certainly under the aegis of the Castellani firm, was one of these; many

OPPOSITE *Brooch-pendant, possibly French, c. 1850. Silver set with pastes and with articulated pendants à pampille. A magnificent mid-Victorian piece. Victoria and Albert Museum.*

Brooch, British, unmarked, c. 1850. Silver, engraved and set with polished stones and citrines. The design is probably a loose adaptation of Scoto-Irish originals dating from the eighth century. National Museum of Antiquities, Edinburgh.

ABOVE RIGHT *'Scottish Pebble' brooch, James Fenton, Birmingham, 1865. Silver set with pebbles. Fenton was a well-known manufacturer of Scottish brooches. Victoria and Albert Museum.*

of his pieces bear the initials C.G. in emulation of the crossed C mark of the Castellanis. The only other category of work that was fairly consistently marked was the stamped silver jewelry made in large quantities in Birmingham in the last thirty years of the century.

The absence of compulsory hallmarking led to widespread evasion of the legal standards for gold, even before the act of 1854 introduced three new standards of fifteen, twelve and nine carats to supplement the existing standards of twenty-two and eighteen carats. As a carat is a unit of measurement representing one twenty-fourth, it will be seen that nine carat gold contained less than a third of the precious metal. Even so, the standards in effective use probably ranged upwards from seven and a half carats.

Styles

The profusion of styles during the Victorian era was partly the result of conservatism. New fashions overlapped with the old, especially in respect of fine jewelry, now invariably made with the open, 'transparent' settings introduced before 1800. The first changes from the

Shawl brooch, G. & S. Waterhouse, Dublin, c. 1851. Parcel-gilt metal set with Irish river pearls, amethysts and minute crystals known as 'Irish diamonds'. Reduced copy of the Tara brooch. National Museum, Dublin.

rigidly axial manner of Regency work are reflected in secondary jewelry. A fanciful Gothic style, tempered by an admixture of Classical or Rococo motifs, had been introduced into England from France in about 1830. The style overtook, although it did not immediately supplant, an earlier French fashion for filigree work embellished with applied wire spirals and course granulation (*cannetille* and *grainti*). Some of this filigree was imported; a less complex variety was produced in Birmingham.

The archaeological basis of design grew more pronounced in the 1840s, partly as a protest against machine production. Techniques appropriate to the styles were revived and practised. Most of the initial experiments were conducted in France, reaching England soon afterwards. Niello decoration was one of the techniques to arrive in England, travelling the long distance from Russia and Berlin via the German goldsmith Carl Wagner, who settled in Paris in about 1830. Fashionable London goldsmiths and jewelers such as Garrard & Co., Hunt & Roskell, Hancock & Co. and Phillips Bros were happy to demonstrate their independence of the machine by taking up all the varieties of enamelling in succession, from champlevé (hitherto used mainly to decorate mourning rings) to cloisonné.

In the 1840s, the architect A. W. N. Pugin also designed Gothic plate and jewelry based on a close study of Medieval originals. He argued that Gothic was the only style fit for a Christian country and was equally happy to design for domestic or ecclesiastical purposes; his jewelry was set with cabochons and champlevé enamels. Pugin's successors in the Victorian Medieval movement, including his pupil and son-in-law J. H. Powell and the architect William Burges, shared his preference for polished cabochons rather than for elaborately cut stones, although both designers, in keeping with the changed times, were less rigorously archaeological in their approach to design.

The Naturalistic style, which flourished from the 1830s to the 1860s and was only slightly less prominent thereafter, also had historicist origins. The vine and acanthus motifs of Regency Classical began to simulate organic growth early in the century and the Naturalism, forming an integral part of the revived Rococo style, showed similar tendencies. By the 1830s, organic Naturalism was well on its way to becoming an independent style. The three-dimensional effect of floral bouquets made of precious stones was often enhanced by mounting some of the flowers as 'tremblers' on spiral wires. Hunt & Roskell showed a bodice ornament of this type at the Great Exhibition of 1851. Combined with an articulated rain of pendants known as *pampilles* (another French invention), these floral pieces are among the most characteristic manifestations of mid-Victorian jewelry. Makers of secondary jewelry were early exponents of the style, producing enamelled or chased-gold pieces simulating the growth and surface texture of plants.

The Naturalistic style underwent

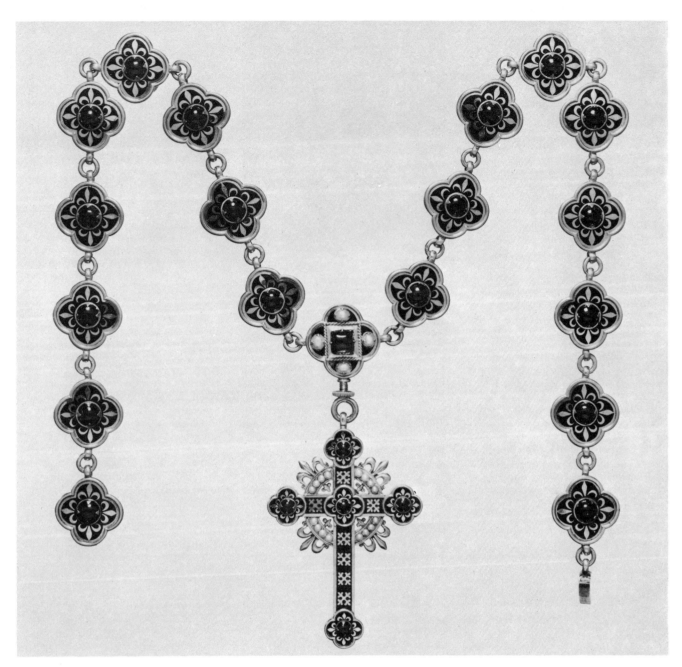

Necklace and pendant cross, designed by A. W. N. Pugin in 1848 and made by John Hardman & Co., Birmingham. Gold decorted with champlevé enamels, cabochons and pearls. Victoria and Albert Museum.

change in the 1860s. Pieces of this date were subjected to a greater degree of formalization, reflecting the new school of thought exemplified by Owen Jones' *The Grammar of Ornament*, first published in 1856. Jones' illustrations of the styles of all cultures and periods are marked by a sharply angular, two-dimensional treatment. Eclecticism was permissible, provided the result was sufficiently conventionalized, but the

Classical style, both in its Antique and Renaissance forms, lent itself particularly well to the new mode. The Castellani jewelry, shown at the International Exhibition in London in 1862 and on many occasions subsequently, exercised a profound influence on design all over Europe. The firm's prestige was undoubtedly enhanced by their claim to have rediscovered the art of fine granulation, which had been thought to have died out with the Etruscans until the Castellanis found peasant jewelers using the art in Sant' Angelo in Vado outside Rome. In London, Giuliano, John Brogden, R. A. Green, C. F. Hancock and many others were adept at the style, although only the first, as might be ex-

pected from his association with the Castellanis, executed fine granulated work.

The Classical style was still fashionable in attenuated form in the 1890s, but it had long since been overtaken by a passion for Japanese design. A few pieces of Japanese metalwork were included in the collection made by Rutherford Alcock for display at the 1862 Exhibition. Further specimens were brought to England by importers such as Londos & Co. (with whom Dr Christopher Dresser was associated), Farmer & Rogers and Liberty & Co., of Regent Street, London. In the Aesthetic 1870s and '80s no artistic home was complete without a collection of Japanese fans and knick-

253

knacks. Despite this, most major English jewelers fought shy of imitating Japanese work, unlike their French and (in the case of Tiffany) American counterparts, although a resurgence of Naturalistic jewelry in the form of flowers, butterflies and small animals is probably attributable to Japanese influence.

Anglo-Japanese jewelry was eventually launched as a mass-production exercise by Birmingham manufacturers in the latter part of the 1870s, often using the abundant supplies of silver arriving in Europe from the Comstock Lode in Nevada. For several years their stamped jewelry in the form of fans, badges or asymmetrical segments, decorated with vaguely Oriental motifs of birds and foliage often picked out with applied patches of coloured gold, was extremely popular. Jewelry of this type was not admired in the most advanced circles after the early 1880s, but production was continued for a decade or more, co-existing with Classical or Naturalistic work.

Ironically, the forms and decorations of genuine Japanese metalwork, characterized by a meticulous observation of Nature allied to skilled craftsmanship, reinforced a growing sense of dissatisfaction with commercial production which had been earlier expressed by Pugin and by Ruskin. Ruskin was especially vigorous in stating the basic need for man to rediscover a dignity in labour denied him by the great industrial enterprises. A series of lengthening trade recessions contributed to the belief that something was basically wrong with the commercial world.

William Morris, once a member of the Medieval movement was a founding

Bodice ornament in the form of a spray of flowers, probably English, c. 1850. Diamonds in a silver setting laminated with gold. Some of the flowers are mounted on springs to form 'tremblers'. Victoria and Albert Museum.

father of its successor, the Arts and Crafts Movement. The Arts and Crafts Exhibition Society staged its first exhibition in 1888, the year in which the architect C. R. Ashbee started the Guild of Handicraft in the East End of London. Demonstrating his independence of commercialism by training and using largely amateur labour and doing most of the designing himself, Ashbee produced some strikingly original jewelry. Alexander Fisher, Nelson and Edith Dawson, Henry Wilson and many others contributed to the vigour of Arts and Crafts jewelry. A few impressive pieces were designed by Charles Rennie Mackintosh

and Talwin Morris of the Glasgow School.

Commercial jewelry did not die under this theoretical and practical attack. Owing largely to the discovery of diamonds in South Africa in about 1867 diamond jewelry became more plentiful than ever before. Modestly priced specimens were mass produced, the same pattern being repeated indefinitely even when made entirely by hand and without the aid of prefabricated mounts. Settings were reduced to near-invisibility, the collets being connected by strips of metal laid edgeways; this knife-edge setting, as it was known, was popular in the 1890s. Platinum, employed to an increasing extent for diamond settings in France after 1855, was not in widespread use in England for this purpose until the Edwardian era.

The trade in general tended to ignore both the Arts and Crafts Movement in Britain and the Art Nouveau of Lalique, Vever and others in France. But some enterprises were more receptive: Liberty & Co. having expanded their business as Oriental importers to include modern Western design, launched their range of Cymric silver and jewelry in 1899. Some of the early jewelry was made in London but most was executed in the factory of W. H. Haseler in Birmingham from designs supplied by artists such as Archibald Knox, Bernard Cuzner, Jessie M. King and even Arthur Gaskin, a considerable artist-jeweler in his own right. Other commercial firms following Liberty's lead included William Hutton & Sons and Murrie Bennett & Co., the latter firm deriving some of its stock from Germany.

Shirley Bury

AMERICAN

The spoor of the individual jeweler-goldsmith is difficult to trace in the United States although the main trends are clear enough. By now it is generally conceded that despite the existence of goldsmiths and silversmiths in all the major ports along the East Coast, New York City had become the centre of the luxury trades by 1840. *The New York Business Directory,* 1840–1, lists twenty-seven names under the heading 'Jewelers and Manufacturers of Jewelry': the following year a different directory lists forty-one and these do not include all the names in the previous year's publication. The number climbs slowly to a

total of sixty in 1846-7, though one cannot help but feel that many are included for want of other categories (e.g. 'Megie, Benjamin, 43 Ann. Manufacturer of curb chains'); the dealers in 'gold & gilt jewelry' and the 'silversmith & gilder' tend to outnumber the 'manufacturer of fine articles of real jewelry only' and the (single) 'dealer in diamonds'. In the 1849–50 *Mercantile Register* an advertisement is included placed by P. B. Ruggles, dealer in 'Warranted Gold & Silver Leaf: Dentist's Gold & Tin Foil manufactured and sold Wholesale and Retail. This manufacturer, the oldest established in the U.S., having been

continued for the last twenty-three years, and has not been discontinued as reported by new competitors.' The advertisement clearly shows how recent and how small were such dealings in precious metals, even on so essential a level and, secondly, that a sudden increase in demand was simultaneously taking place.

Influence of Economic and Social Factors

The difference in supply was due to the discovery of gold in California in 1849, and the rush to exploit it. The economic factors giving rise to the increase in consumer demand coincided with the gold rush, as did the unforeseeable windfall of precious stones at bargain prices that an astute merchant, such as Charles L. Tiffany, who up until then had been a partner in a stationery and dry goods store, could obtain in the wake of the European uprisings of 1848. These upheavals, to which England also owed an influx of superior craftsmen, enabled Tiffany and others to lure goldsmiths, bronze founders and gilders, and stonecutters to the farther shores of the Atlantic.

The vogue for simplicity in dress, a striking feature of portraits in England and her colonies during the second half of the eighteenth century, happily coincided with a period in which almost no gold was discovered in North America. Until the discovery of some small veins of gold in the 1820s in South Carolina and Georgia, the supply had been limited to the coinage of other countries, obtained in trade. It is therefore easy to detect the New World jewelry of the

influence of the French Restoration under Louis Philippe is the work of F. Thibault, whose fragile bracelet of fine quality gold foil, is stamped over moulds (*cannetille*).

The difference made by Californian gold soon after its discovery cannot be better demonstrated than by a buckle with a pendant fob shaped like a horse. The buckle, cut from a sheet of the copper alloy common before 1849, is engraved with the lace-cuffed wrist of a lady writing musical notes, and inscribed 'Remember Hugh. San Francisco, Dec. 15, 1857'. Soldered to the back is a gold-wire loop of a better grade from which depends a ribbon with the horse. The latter is three dimensional and, although of indifferent workmanship, it is made of pure gold. One may deduce that the buckle was part of the stock brought by some adventurous jeweler from the East Coast to the goldfields, where some found fortune, not by panning, but as assayers (before a branch of the United States mint was established in San Francisco in 1854), and converters of

nuggets into pieces of jewelry such as this fob.

A memento of the Klondike gold rush of 1896 is provided by a lady's necklace made of a double row of tiny gold nuggets interspersed with links. The irregular smoothness of the nuggets lends itself well to the Art Nouveau style of the turn of the century.

Trade Fairs and Fashions

In 1853 to 1854 the first North American industrial fair, modelled on the Crystal Palace Exhibition in London of 1851, was held in New York City. Of the forty-five contestants in *Class 23: Works in Precious Metals and their Imitations; Bronzes, and Articles of Vertu generally*, three Americans (among others) received silver medals; Linherr & Co., New York, for hair jewelry mounted in gold; Marchand Sr, Grime, Guillemot & Co., New York, for diamond jewelry; and Tiffany & Co., – the first of its many awards throughout the century – for a

Bracelet, F. Thibaut, c. 1840. Gold. The front and back of the same bracelet made by F. Thibaut, jeweler to the Bouvier family. Fine quality gold foil stamped over moulds. Historical Society of Pennsylvania.

ABOVE CENTRE *Locket, American, c. 1850. Gold, 1⅝ in × 1½ in (4·5 cm × 3·8 cm). Jewelers, lacking a compulsory assay standard, augmented gold with copper. Yale University Art Gallery.*

Necklace, American, c. 1900. Gold nuggets. A memento of the Klondike gold rush, the irregular smoothness of the gold nuggets is well suited to the Art Nouveau style. Smithsonian Institution.

LEFT *Buckle engraved 'Remember Hugh San Francisco, Dec. 15th, 1857', with a fob in the shape of a horse. Gold. A memento of the California Gold Rush period. Maryland Historical Society.*

period 1820 to 1850; lacking a compulsory assay standard for jewelers, the gold used by them was plentifully augmented with copper, resulting in a characteristic reddish tone and a superior hardness which lends itself well to engraving, but not to repoussé. The techniques of the Colonial silversmiths could be adapted easily to this material, thus prolonging the earlier repertory of forms and decoration to the middle of the nineteenth century. A rare exception showing the

'rich silver vase supported by figures', as well as various kinds of tableware. Bronze medals went to L. & D. S. Carr, Providence, R.I., for 'superior gold lockets' and to yet another manufacturer of hair jewelry, Robert Link & Bros, New York.

Hair jewelry was extremely popular throughout the 1850s and the '60s and though some of it is documented as having been made in the homes, hospitals and prisons of the United States, it is believed that much of it, especially the tubular knotted type seemingly of horse-hair, came from Germany. This brings us to a difficult question: when does jewelry made abroad and imported, or made in North America by foreigners, become American? Perhaps the problem, which must remain unresolved, is at the root of an English criticism of the Class 23 exhibits at the New York Exhibition, as reported in 1867 by Frank Leslie, United States Commissioner for the Paris Universal Exposition: 'At present the co-mingling of totally different styles and the adoption of European designs for totally different purposes to those for which they were intended are among the least errors committed in a vague seeking after novelty.' Leslie, thirteen years later, still agreed with this criticism. If we cannot judge the jewelry, we may at least get some idea of the silverware from illustrations.

The 1850s have left us little by way of a jewelry legacy except description. A fitting present for some reformed lady sharp-shooter might have been Tiffany's 'intricate thousand dollar plaything . . . in the shape of a gold and blue enamelled pistol covered with diamonds. It was about 6 in (15·2 cm) long, and contained in its stock a watch and a scent box. Upon pulling the trigger the barrel expanded to form a bouquet holder.' A little behind the times (the vogue for Medieval gauntlets had reached its zenith in Europe in *c.* 1840) was the chatelaine, consisting of a sizeable fist holding a watch clasp and a seal masquerading as a helmet. It is made of the same materials as the pistol and in much the same taste.

Roset's account of the new Tiffany store, from which the quotation above is taken, is astonishing for the number of times it mentions opals, a stone which was not overwhelmingly popular in Europe at that time, but which was to become so by the end of the century, possibly as the result of Tiffany's influence.

Later Styles and Influences

The imminent Civil War (1861-5) must have made itself felt in the luxury industries as early as 1860: in that year Tiffany & Co. took a full-page advertisement in Wilson's *New York Business Directory* to make known the variety of its wares, which included furniture, lighting fixtures and decorative accessories; its 'superior opportunities for catering for every taste through its international connections' recently established through its Paris branch; its policy of modest markups; and – an interesting insight into the more usual conduct of the jewelry business at the time – a fixed price standard, followed by the assurance that 'a call will incur not the least obligation to purchase'.

The War between the States and subsequently Lincoln's assassination resulted in jewelry of a heavy and lugubrious style. A precedent had been set by English mourning jewelry manufactured to commemorate the death of the Prince Consort, and was to be prolonged by the French jewelry produced after the defeat of the Franco-Prussian War. The first in a series of scent bottles, although interesting as an early intimation of Japanese influence in American jewelry has little else to recommend it. If this denotes the standard of an outstanding jeweler, it comes as no surprise to learn that the lesser jewelry of the years between 1865 and 1875 was depressing although plentiful. Bracelets, stiff and formal in design

Scent bottle with belt hook, Tiffany & Co., dated 1848-73. Silver. Stamped with serial numbers, hallmark and address, it provides a fine example of Tiffany's elegance in design. Museum of the City of New York.

Chatelaine in the shape of an armoured fist holding two chains to which a watch clasp and a seal are attached, American, c. 1850. Gold, blue enamels and diamonds. Maryland Historical Society.

Scent bottle, Tiffany & Co., 1889. Glass overlaid with gold and studded with enamel forget-me-nots and small diamonds. The lid contains a watch. Museum of the City of New York.

and preferably in matched pairs resembling handcuffs, were the rage for young and old, and they came in every conceivable material to suit all pockets, from silver with bright-cut embellishment to blackened base metal with crudely worked geometric motifs on a plaque of contrasting metal. The more ambitious bracelets were made of gold, but their decoration reverted to the engraved scroll- and leaf-patterns of *c.* 1840–50, with one innovation: the incisions were coloured black with enamel, niello or plain, tinted varnish.

It was not until the Philadelphia Centennial Exposition of 1876 that an exoticism, presaged in the paintings of such American artists as Church and Heade, who had both been to South America in the previous decade, became apparent in the design of jewelry. The English artist Rossetti is supposed to have collected Peruvian feather jewelry, and actual pieces of English jewelry incorporating the heads of hummingbirds were certainly made *c.* 1870. A spectacular parure of Brazilian beetles of about this date

already possesses the combination of attraction and repulsion which was to be a signal force in Art Nouveau.

By this time, Japanese design and artifacts had been the vogue in England and France for nearly a decade; beginning with the Japanese display at the International Exhibition of 1862 in London, painters, potters, architects, jewelers and even poets tried to imitate its forms and techniques, or catch its essence. Edward Moore, an astute director of Tiffany's, was surely aware of it at a very early stage, together with other trends such as an Egyptian revival style concurrent with the building in the 1860s of the Suez Canal. Hampered by assay laws which forbade the mixing of base with precious metals, European jewelers could make little progress in this intriguing technique. It was here that Moore must have seen a possibility for America to make a profitable scoop. When the English designer, Dr Christopher Dresser, visited New York on his way to Japan in 1876, he was asked by Tiffany's to bring back not only Japan-

ese products, but also Japanese craftsmen, with the result that in *c.* 1880 the New York workshop began to produce *japonaiserie* in mixed metals that was the envy of Europeans until the turn of the century brought a relaxation of the prohibitory clauses of their own assay laws.

The decade of the 1880s was a period of great experimentation with both materials and styles, the latter ranging from bold and bizarre to mincing and fussy. After a kind of *succès de scandale* at the Paris Exhibition of 1889, Tiffany & Co., by now under the rising star of Louis C. Tiffany, whose experiments in glass were to win universal approbation in 1893 at the Columbian Exposition, lost the Moore intuition in the field of jewelry. The younger Tiffany himself made a few amazing pieces as private commissions; but after contributing many of the elements from the predilection for opals to the monstrous, which is so prominent a feature of Art Nouveau jewelry, America was almost the last to adopt the fully fledged style.

Dora Jane Janson

Fashions and Trends

	1837	1850	1860	1870	1880	1901
Gothic-style	————————————————————————————					
Renaissance-style	————————————————————————————————————					
Archaeological (other than Classical)	———————————————————————————————————					
Naturalistic-style	——					
Etruscan-style			————————————————————————————			
Algerian (Moorish)-style	—————————————————————————					
Assyrian (Nineveh)-style		————————————————				
Cult of the diamond			————————————————————————			
Sentimental	——					
Celtic (Scottish and Irish)-style	——					
Massive gold jewelry			————————————			
Indian-style		————————————————				
Sporting	——					
Commercial	——					
Aesthetic Movement			————————————————————————————————			

Celtic Revival
Arts and Crafts
Liberty metalwork
Vogue for pearls
Gothic Revival

Japanese-style			————————————————————————

257

Designers and Manufacturers

ASHBEE, CHARLES ROBERT (1863–1942)

Pioneer of Art Nouveau jewelry in England, Ashbee was not by training a jeweler, but through his involvement with the Arts and Crafts Movement he became interested in its design. In 1888, inspired by Ruskin, Ashbee founded the Guild and School of Handicraft in the East End of London. Ashbee, with the help of a practising metalworker, trained the Guildsmen, learning as he went. The amateur quality of much Guild silver, metalwork and jewelry is partly the result of Ashbee's policy of recruitment, which reflected his own philanthropic motives and his dislike of commercial manufacturers. Ashbee was a brilliant designer, creating a style equivalent to Art Nouveau with simple wire forms, embellished with CABOCHONS, ENAMELS and occasionally small precious stones. He translated Cellini's treatises on goldsmiths and sculpture (1898).

Pendant brooch, designed by C. R. Ashbee (1863-1942) for his wife Janet, and made by the Guild of Handicraft, c. 1898. Silver and gold, set with a baroque pearl, pearl blisters, diamonds and a ruby. Victoria and Albert Museum.

BROGDEN, JOHN

Partner in the firm of Watherston & Brogden, of 16 Henrietta Street, Covent Garden, London, and exhibitor at the Great Exhibition of 1851. Brogden subsequently ran the firm under his own name, the Watherstons, father and son, removing to Pall Mall. Brogden is best known for his jewelry in the Classical taste – he also worked in the Greek, Etruscan, Renaissance and Egyptian styles – using gold, ENAMELLING, precious and semi-precious stones. A set of CAMEO jewelry by Brogden, exhibited at Paris in 1867, is in the Victoria & Albert Museum, London. His maker's mark, J.B., is struck on some of his pieces.

BURGES, WILLIAM (1827–81)

English designer responsible for only a few items of jewelry, the most outstanding of which was a set of marriage jewelry made for Lord Bute. But his knowledge of techniques and styles, about which he wrote on several occasions, was a source of inspiration to his fellow-designers in the Arts and Crafts Movement.

CASTELLANI, FORTUNATO PIO (1793–1865)

Italian goldsmith and jeweler, Castellani's great achievement was the rediscovery of the Etruscan technique of GRANAGLIA, long thought to have died out. Castellani, however, found peasant craftsmen in the Umbrian Marches still practising the technique and brought some of them to Rome. Fortunato Pio retired in *c.* 1858, and his business was afterwards managed by his son Augusto (1829–1914), who had the artistic help of his brother Alessandro (1824–83) and of their associate, Michelangelo Caetani, Duke of Sermoneta (1804–83). Alessandro's political views had brought about his imprisonment in the Castel Sant' Angelo. Released in 1858, he was forced to leave Italy temporarily and went first to Paris and then to London. He advised the British Museum and the South Kensington Museum on purchases, selling part of his vast collections to them. The Castellani firm worked mainly, although by no means entirely, in the Antique Classical manner. Their jewelry is marked with crossed Cs.

COLONNA, EDWARD (b. 1862)

Born in Germany but trained as an architect in Brussels, Colonna emigrated to America in 1882, where he worked with Associated Artists, a group of interior decorators headed by the famous LOUIS COMFORT TIFFANY. A theorist as well as designer – he produced an essay on design which anticipates the work of Horta and Van de Velde – he was one of the early exponents of the Art Nouveau style. He also worked in Paris in the 1890s, designing jewelry which was sold by Samuel Bing's shop, L'Art Nouveau.

CUZNER, BERNARD (1877–1956)

English silversmith and jeweler, Cuzner was trained at the Vittoria Street School for Jewelers and Silversmiths, Birmingham, under R. Catterson-Smith and GASKIN. As a very young man, he worked briefly for LIBERTY's Cymric scheme, designing silver and jewelry, but for much of his career he was an independent craftsman.

FROMENT-MEURICE, FRANÇOIS-DESIRÉ (1802–55)

Greatest French jeweler and goldsmith of his age, Froment-Meurice specialized mainly (although not entirely) in work in the Medieval and Renaissance styles. He made much use of the human figure in his work, employing modellers of some distinction for the purpose. In this he and his fellow jewelers in Paris differed from their English counterparts, who rarely attempted to incorporate figures and animals in their works. Froment-Meurice gained the Council Medal, the highest award at the Great Exhibition of 1851. He died just before the opening of the Paris Exhibition of 1855 but the business was continued by his son, Émile.

GARRARD & CO.

Firm was founded by the early Georgian goldsmith, George Wickes, in Panton Street, London, and taken over by Robert Garrard Sr (d. 1818) in the late eighteenth century. After his death, it was run by his sons Robert (d. 1881) and James and Sebastian. Garrard's succeeded Rundell's as Crown Jewelers *c.* 1840, making substantial contributions to the Great Exhibition of 1851 and subsequent international exhibitions.

GASKIN, ARTHUR (1862–1928)

Painter, illustrator, silversmith and jeweler, Gaskin was a member of the Birmingham Group of artists. Together with his wife, he designed and made delicate jewelry in gold and silver which is usually constructed with wires and decorated with precious and semi-precious stones and ENAMELLING. He contributed a few jewelry designs to LIBERTY's Cymric scheme.

GIULIANO, CARLO (d. 1895)

Goldsmith and jeweler of the mid-Victorian period, Carlo Giuliano left Naples for London, where he settled in the early 1860s, probably under the aegis of Alessandro Castellani. Giuliano was certainly afterwards associated with the Castellani firm, although as a working craftsman he was also employed by several London firms. He acquired premises at 115 Piccadilly in the early 1880s, increasingly specializing in elaborately enamelled and gem-set jewelry in the Classical, Renaissance and other styles. Most of his jewelry bears the initials G.C. He was succeeded in the business by his sons, A. and C. Giuliano.

HUNT & ROSKELL

Successors to Storr & Mortimer in New Bond Street, London, Hunt & Roskell were goldsmiths and jewelers employing both French and English designers and craftsmen. They were famous for the high quality of their work and contributed to international exhibitions. The firm was taken over by J. W. Benson towards the end of the nineteenth century.

LALIQUE, RENÉ JULES (1860–1945)
Jeweler, silversmith, designer, glass-maker and the best known and most influential member of the Art Nouveau movement, Lalique briefly studied in London in the late 1870s, returning to Paris to work as a designer for the jewelry trade. He was employed by Boucheron, Cartier and others. He emerged under his own name at the Paris Salon of 1894, having made two sets of jewelry for Sarah Bernhardt. He soon became the leading exponent of Art Nouveau, a style compounded of a variety of influences ranging from Pre-Raphaelite painting to Japanese metalwork and containing marked evidence of the revived Rococo and even the Renaissance manners. Lalique was as daring a technical inventor as he was a designer, using horn, ivory, PASTE, PLIQUE-À JOUR ENAMELLING and glass. The figures and animals in his jewelry were often modelled by his father-in-law and brother-in-law, both named Auguste Ledru. After the First World War, he virtually gave up jewelry to work in glass.

LIBERTY, SIR ARTHUR LASENBY (1843–1917)
Neither a jeweler nor a designer, Sir Arthur Liberty was manager of Farmer & Rogers Oriental department from 1863 to 1875. He subsequently opened his famous shop in Regent Street, specializing in imported exotic wares and Oriental goods and materials. Patronized by Rossetti, Whistler and others, Liberty began to extend the range of his wares. Successful ventures with fabrics, costumes and furniture specially designed and made for the firm encouraged him, in 1899, to launch his Cymric scheme for metalwork and jewelry. Designs were commissioned from promising, although unacknowledged, artists, and most of the wares were produced in the Birmingham factory of W. H. Haseler. Modern in design and attractive, Liberty's mass-produced wares were extremely popular.

MORRIS, WILLIAM (1834–96)
Most influential designer and craftsman of his age, William Morris did not himself design jewelry, although a few of his associates, notably Burne-Jones and Rossetti, are known to have done so. With Ruskin, Morris stood for crafts-manship as opposed to trade or commercial production, and for the dignity of man in labour. His views influenced the younger members of the Arts and Crafts Movement, all of whom turned against

the vulgarity both of expensive gem-set jewelry and of tawdry stamped work, preferring to execute work decorated with CABOCHONS and ENAMELLING.

PHILLIPS, ROBERT (d. 1881)
Goldsmith and jeweler of Cockspur Street, London, Phillips was mainly famous for his splendid coral jewelry, the best of which was made by outstanding craftsmen in Naples. He also sold works in gold in the Classical and other styles. Among others he employed the Italian jeweler, Carlo Doria.

PUGIN, AUGUSTUS WELBY NORTHMORE (1812–52)
Architect, antiquary, designer and writer, a proselytizer of the Gothic, Pugin was a master in that idiom. He designed in all varieties of Gothic, but came to prefer the work of the late style, insisting that his designs were executed in the old manner. He preferred CABOCHON stones and revived and developed the art of CHAMPLEVÉ ENAMELLING, which was otherwise mainly used in the decoration of mourning jewelry. A parure (or set) of jewelry originally designed in 1847–8 for his intended third wife, Miss Helen Lumsden (who jilted him), and given to Jane Knill (whom he married), was executed by John Hardman & Co., of Birmingham, and exhibited in the Medieval Court of the Great Exhibition of 1851. Three items from the set are in the collections of the Victoria and Albert Museum, London.

TIFFANY, LOUIS COMFORT (1848–1933)
Painter, interior designer, jeweler and glass-worker. Son of Charles Lewis Tiffany who began making jewelry in 1848, Louis Comfort Tiffany founded Associated Artists in 1879 (later known as Tiffany Studios). On the death of his father in 1902, Tiffany also became Art Director of Tiffany & Co., New York. Under Charles Lewis Tiffany's direc-

Brooch, Tiffany & Co., c. 1880. Platinum and gold. This brooch in the form of a butterfly was made at the height of Tiffany's success, Associated Artists having been formed in 1879. Private Collection.

tion, the firm's jewelry and silver were strongly influenced by the Japanese style; his son turned it in the direction of Art Nouveau. Tiffany jewelry was sold at Samuel Bing's shop in Paris.

VEVER, HENRI (1854–1942)
One of the most influential French designers of Art Nouveau jewelry and author of an authoritative work on French nineteenth-century jewelry. Together with his brother Paul (1851–1915), he inherited his father's jewelry firm in 1874 and developed a reputation second only to that of Lalique. His characteristic style is somewhat formal and he shows a preference for geometric shapes.

WILSON, HENRY (1864–1934)
Architect, silversmith and jeweler, Wilson developed an increasingly rich style based loosely on Byzantine models. He was a highly skilled craftsman and taught at the Central School of Arts and Crafts and at the Royal College of Art, London. His jewelry is often intricate in design and execution, set with a variety of stones and often also enamelled. He was one of the few English craftsmen to make use of the human figure in his most elaborate designs. He wrote a manual, *Silverwork and Jewelry* (1903).

Glossary

Aigrette
Head ornament of pearls or gems set in gold or silver in the form of a spray or plume. The word is adopted from the French word for heron, *aigrette* – hence the English word 'egret' which was initially applied to the heron's crest and thence to helmet plumes and head-dress in general.

Aiguillette
Jewel for the shoulders.

Amethyst
Transparent violet or purple quartz.

Baguettes
Gems, usually small diamonds, cut in the shape of narrow rectangles; mainly a twentieth-century shape.

Bangle
Solid metal BRACELET in favour throughout much of the later Victorian period. Often in serpent form or decorated with the motifs popular at the time although one of the most popular bracelets of the 1870s was a plain gold bangle.

Benoiton chain
Chain suspended from the bonnet or the coiffure to form a loop on the bosom. *c.* 1866.

Bijouterie
Craft of the enameller and goldsmith as

opposed to the craft of the mounter and gem-setter, which is called *joaillerie*.

Bracelet
One of the most characteristic items of Victorian jewelry, two or three sometimes being worn on each arm. They followed the fashion, serpent bracelets, link bracelets set with enamels or gems and bracelets of plaited hair and of carved coral and ivory being particularly favoured.

Brilliant cut
An elaborate cut mainly used for diamonds, usually with a total of fifty-eight facets, although both more or fewer facets are known.

Brooch
Often designed in the Victorian period with a RING or hook to be interchangeable with a PENDANT. Followed the various fashions of the era, namely Medieval, Egyptian and Etruscan styles, botanical themes etc. Hair brooches were highly favoured especially from *c.* 1840 to 1870 as part of the cult of mourning and sentimental jewelry.

Brooch and earrings, probably English, 1835-40. Gold set with peridots. Brooches were often designed with a ring and hook so they could be interchangeable with a pendant. Victoria and Albert Museum.

Cabochon
Oldest method of cutting gems; the top of the stone is rounded.

Cairngorm
Quartz of a brownish colour found in the mountains of that name in Scotland, although most commercial jewelers used stones mined in South America. Cairn-gorm jewelry was a popular tourist souvenir.

Cameo
Gem or shell carved in relief, the design standing out against a contrasting background (see INTAGLIO). In the mid-Victorian period cameo *habillés* were made, whereby the head carved in the stone was shown wearing a NECKLACE and EARRINGS which were set with tiny stones.

Cannetille
Somewhat coarse type of gold or imitation gold FILIGREE popular in France and elsewhere from *c.* 1811 to 1850. Beads of coiled wire, pyramids and rosettes were much favoured as motifs in this style of decoration.

Carbuncle
Garnet, sometimes an almandine – a violet-red variety of garnet that has been cut *en* CABOCHON.

Chalcedony
Bluish quartz.

Champlevé enamelling
Method of ENAMELLING in which the ground is hollowed out in accordance with the design of the enamel.

Chatelaine
Hook with chain or chains hung from a BROOCH or girdle for carrying keys, seals and other small objects. Originating in the seventeenth century, it declined in popularity at the end of the eighteenth century but was revived as an 'antique' in the 1830s. Steel chatelaines were fashionable from 1845 to 1855 and again from the 1870s onwards when they were sometimes combined with JET and electroplated silver.

Cloisonné enamelling
Method of ENAMELLING in which the design is marked out by metal strips soldered on to the base.

Collet
Metal mount for a stone.

Comb
Hair ornaments were popular throughout the Victorian era, being worn either on the forehead so that the upper part of the comb formed a diadem or placed in the chignon at the back of the head. The body of the comb was generally tortoiseshell; in the 1860s gold-topped combs were fashionable.

Cordonnière
Girdle made to look like cord and tied in front.

Diamanté
White PASTE used to imitate diamonds.

Earrings
With few intermissions, earrings were popular throughout the Victorian period. Their shape in this period depended largely on how the hair was worn. Pendant drop earrings, large in the 1830s and '40s, were made increasingly

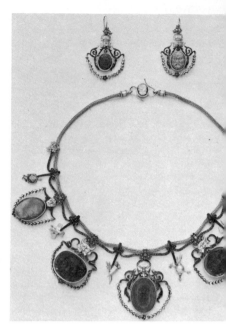

Necklace and earrings, John Brogden, London, c. 1867. Gold, enamelled and hung with cameos in chalcedony and onyx. Victoria and Albert Museum.

longer in the 1860s and by 1870 they sometimes reached the shoulder. In 1890 stud earrings with a screw fitting were favoured.

Enamelling
Powder or paste made from a silicate of glass and powdered metallic oxides and placed on metal to which it is fused in a furnace. A wide variety of colours can be produced and the process calls for great skill.

Ferronière
Narrow chain or band encircling the forehead. Renaissance style, worn in the late Georgian and early Victorian period. The name is taken from Leonardo da Vinci's picture *La Belle Ferronière*. The Victorians who adapted the word to the jewel failed to realize that the word 'ferronière' referred not to the jewel but to the subject of the painting, namely the blacksmith's wife. Highly fashionable between 1837 and 1844 for both daytime and evening wear.

Filigree
Fine gold or silver wire used to make delicate patterns resembling lace.

Girdle
Term for the line dividing the crown and the base of a faceted gem stone.

Granaglia or granulation work
Method of making gold or silver cuttings into minute grains by melting them into a rotating crucible together with charcoal which was subsequently washed away. The technique, which resulted in minute granules used to form a raised surface

decoration, was developed by the Etruscans. The CASTELLANIS and other Victorian jewelry manufacturers adopted the technique.

Hair jewelry
Reaching the peak of its popularity from the 1840s to the 1870s, hair jewelry was frequently worn in remembrance of a loved one or as a token of sentiment. Complete pieces were made of woven hair or a lock of hair was mounted in a BROOCH, BRACELET clasp, etc.

Handkerchief ring
Small gold RING worn on the little finger in the 1870s and connected by a chain with a large ring in which the handkerchief was held.

Intaglio
Carved design hollowed out of the surface of a gem as opposed to a CAMEO in which the background is cut away.

Jet
Of organic origin, jet was mined extensively in the district around Whitby, Yorkshire. Found in a stratum of lias, it is a black substance which takes a high polish and carves well. The jet trade, languishing during the eighteenth century, was revived in the nineteenth century for mourning and other types of jewelry.

Mosaic
Type of decoration in jewelry which became particularly popular in the early-nineteenth century. Made in Italy and bought by the English travellers as souvenir jewelry; also imported, unmounted, for setting by jewelry manufacturers. Designed as small medallions which were generally framed in gold and made up into NECKLACES, BRACELETS, clasps and EARRINGS.

Necklace
In the 1830s and '40s there was a vogue for necklaces of SEED PEARLS or fine gold chains and ribbons crossed at the throat and held with a jeweled button or slide. Many other materials were also favoured, the late 1870s and 1880s seeing the vogue for the silver necklace.

Niello
Black filling for a carving, such as lead, mixed with sulphur, silver and copper. Used to fill engraved work and emphasize the design.

Paste
Glass, usually containing a proportion of lead oxide, used for imitation gems.

Pavé
Setting in which the stones are laid flat on the base to form a 'pavement' showing very little metal between them.

Pendant
Particularly common on NECKLACES from the 1860s to c. 1885, often in the Greek or Etruscan styles, with medallions or a locket enclosing a lock of hair.

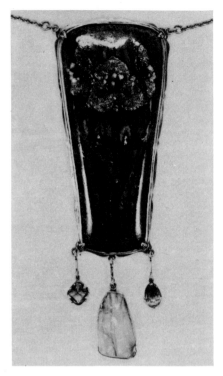

Pendant and chain, designed and made by Nelson Dawson, the enamel by his wife, c. 1900. Gilded copper, set with a painted enamel plaque and hung with pendant drops of opal and amethyst. Victoria and Albert Museum.

Pinchbeck
Alloy of copper and zinc, called after its inventor, Christopher Pinchbeck (d. 1732). It was used from the eighteenth century onwards in imitation jewelry to simulate gold.

Plique-à-jour enamelling
Method of ENAMELLING where the back is attached temporarily during the firing and then removed to let the light shine through.

Posy rings
RING which has a motto or 'poesy' engraved on the inner side.

Regard ring
RING set with a variety of small stones, the initial letters of which spell the word 'regard'. Fashionable tokens of friendship and sentiment.

Ring
Continued to be worn throughout the Victorian period but not particularly distinctive or imaginative in its design. Conventional floral designs, diamond clusters, hearts, serpent rings and stones set in half-hoops were mainly favoured.

Rose cut
Traditional method of cutting stones, especially diamonds. Though largely superseded by the BRILLIANT CUT, introduced in the seventeenth century, it continued to be used in Victorian times. The stones had a flat base and rose to a point, the facets were triangular, and were twenty-four or thirty-six in number.

Seed pearl
Round pearl weighing under a quarter of a grain, popular with the early Victorians for parures and NECKLACES.

Stomacher
Ornament designed for the front of the corsage, being generally based on floral and ribbon patterns and offering an opportunity for the lavish display of diamonds and PASTES.

Bibliography

Birmingham City Museum and Art Gallery. *Birmingham Gold & Silver 1773–1973*, Catalogue of the exhibition held 28 July–16 September 1973, Birmingham, 1973.

BODE, WILHELM. *Kunst und Kunstgewerbe am Ende des XIX Jahrhunderts*, Berlin, 1901

BOHAN, PETER. *American Gold 1700–1860*, monograph based on the exhibition held 2 April–28 June 1963, Yale University Art Gallery, New Haven, Connecticut, 1963

BRUTON, E. *Diamonds*, London, 1970

BURY, SHIRLEY. 'The Silver Designs of Dr Christopher Dresser', *Apollo*, London, December 1962

CLIFFORD SMITH, H. *Jewellery*, second ed., London, 1973

EMANUEL, H. *Diamonds and Precious Stones*, London, 1865

EVANS, J. *A History of Jewellery, 1100–1870*, second ed., London, 1973

FLOWER, M. *Victorian Jewellery*, second ed., London, 1967

FONTENAY, E. *Les Bijoux*, Paris, 1887

JANSON, DORA JANE. *From Slave to Siren: the Victorian Woman and her Jewelry*, Durham, North Carolina, 1971

LEWIS, M. D. S. *Antique Paste Jewellery*, London, 1970

McCLINTON, KATHARINE M. *Collecting American 19th-century Silver*, New York, 1968

ROCHE, J. C. *The History, Development and Organisation of the Birmingham Jewellery and Allied Trades*, supplement to the *Dial*, Birmingham, 1927

ROSET, HIPPONAX (pen name of PAXTON, JOSEPH RUPERT), *Jewelry, The Precious Stones: with a History & Description, etc.*, Philadelphia, 1856

Royal Academy of Arts. *Victorian and Edwardian Decorative Art. The Handley-Read Collection*, Catalogue of the exhibition held 4 March–30 April 1972, London, 1972

VEVER, H. *La Bijouterie française au XIX siècle*, 3 vols, Paris, 1906–8.

Dress

BRITISH

The most remarkable feature of women's dress in the Victorian period was its variety. Whereas in the preceding centuries feminine clothing had always progressed gradually to an apotheosis of its proper style and equally slowly withdrawn from it, during Queen Victoria's reign women's fashions produced, almost without the normal preparatory warning, a succession of sudden and startling changes, each of which transformed the human form into an exotic artifact quite different in character from its predecessor.

This behaviour was, however, in no way true of the dress of men, which, when Queen Victoria came to the throne, had already achieved the rigid form and sombre colour that were to be its chief characteristics when she died.

Throughout the reign, moreover, except in the hunting-field and for one or two other sporting occasions confined to the upper classes, it would be true to say that the dress of the two sexes was more dissimilar than at any other period in history. Corresponding differences were maintained during the first decade that followed Victoria's death, but they began to dissolve when the First World War imposed uniforms on a great many women as well as on men.

Working-class Dress

England never developed a distinctive peasant dress, and even regional differences in the clothing of the working classes have been few and confined almost entirely to one or two remote coastal districts in, for example, Northumberland and Cornwall. Throughout Queen Victoria's reign, therefore, work-

OPPOSITE *Male Dress from* Gazette of Fashion, 1853. *Fashion plate printed in France of men in morning coats, a garment originally designed as a riding coat. Victoria and Albert Museum.*

ing-class women adapted, as best they could, and as they had done in the past, the simpler fashions of the middle class.

Upper part of Surrey smock and detail of smocking, English, nineteenth century. Cotton. This type of yoked shirt was worn by agricultural labourers. Guildford Museum.

Some occupational peculiarities could be found, however, in men's dress: linen smocks, for instance (corresponding to the *blouse* of French peasants but, in England, usually undyed), were worn by most farmers and their employees, while artisans replaced the white shirt — the obligatory wear of gentlemen and clerks — by those of coloured or chequered, coarser stuff. Men employed in heavy labour usually wore strong and

almost waterproof corduroy trousers, while a coloured kerchief, knotted round the neck, was worn by almost all workmen to replace the upper-class collar and tie. Towards the century's end, cloth caps of neutral colour and uniform shape, introduced first for sports' wear, became a badge of the working-class man.

Household and hotel servants of both sexes were either provided with a livery or expected to provide themselves with plain clothing which conformed to a required pattern but was not entirely unrelated to current fashion.

Formal Dress

Regulations governed the dress to be worn on formal occasions at Court. Men wore *levée* dress, consisting of knee-breeches, silk stockings and a cut-away coat in silk or velvet with, in addition, a sword; ladies, a low-cut evening dress with a train of prescribed length attached to the shoulders at the back and three ostrich feathers set far back on the head.

Before examining Victorian dress in closer detail, it should be said that during the whole reign the very concept of fashion as applied to clothing was questioned in a way that had never occurred before; first by doctors, then by artists and finally by a great many, if not the majority, of members of the intelligentsia. This questioning led to attempts to devise forms of clothing which, because they combined artistic with hygienic design, need not, it was argued, be subject to changes of fashion. 'Aesthetic' dress owed a great deal to clothing worn by Pre-Raphaelite painters and members of their circle and successors; 'hygienic' dress reached its climax with the Rational Dress Society's display at the International Health Exhibition of 1884. These movements had virtually worn themselves out by the century's end.

The Crinoline

One of the most dramatic changes in women's dress coincided almost exactly with Queen Victoria's accession. In the early 1830s, fashionable dress had looked flaunting yet brittle; skirts swung 6 in (15 cm) off the ground; hair, with the aid of gum arabic, was stiffened into upstanding loops. Towards the end of the second quarter of the decade, however, women gave up attempting to look like *filles de joie* and, by a sudden transformation, assumed the air of demure virgins. At this moment there began a prolonged period of an almost stable composition consisting of a bodice laced very tightly round the ribs, sleeves set in well below the shoulder-line, a bell-shaped skirt springing from the natural waistline and a small bonnet enclosing a compact style of hairdressing. Outdoors, shawls from India or Paisley were worn by the rich; cheap and sober counterparts by the poor. The shawl remained a distinctive feature of women workers in Lancashire cotton-mills well into the twentieth century.

The bell-shaped skirt was held out over a number of petticoats until, in about 1850, a crinoline undercage was introduced which, besides being considered lighter and much more comfortable, enabled skirts to be expanded to a large circumference. The crinoline remained fashionable until, in 1868, it disappeared almost overnight, unlamented.

The Emergence of the Watteau Toilette

Within months the aspect of women again changed completely. The bell was

The Fashions expressly designed and prepared for The Englishwoman's Domestic Magazine, *February 1866. The skirts are arranged upon Thomson's crinolines. Victoria and Albert Museum.*

replaced by the Watteau toilette, consisting of a dress looped-up into large puffs below the waist at the back but with a line unbroken from breast to knee in front; a pleated frill extended from the knee to the ground. High heels supplanted the early Victorian flat shoes and produced the required 'Grecian bend' which thrust the breasts forward and the hips back, thereby emphasizing the puffed-out crinolette. This was reflected in the chignon, an enormous bouffant mass of intertwined plaits or curls of hair, usually false, pinned to the back of the head. Shawls disappeared, to be replaced by closely fitted jackets ending just below the waist.

Meanwhile, in the masculine wardrobe, the lounge suit appeared, consisting of trousers worn with a short jacket to match but the straight, double-breasted frock coat, reaching the knee, was still obligatory for all but extremely informal occasions. The frock coat was already the standard wear for men when Queen Victoria came to the throne. No generally acceptable alternative to the black, silk-plush top-hat had appeared by the end of the 1870s.

In 1877 the Watteau toilette was superseded by the princess line which, still dispensing with a marked line at the waist, covered the body with a long, moulded sheath, ending in a flared skirt from the calf down. This temporary and inconveniently restricting fashion, which turned women into what a contemporary

described as 'live mummies', lasted only four years. By 1881 a modified version of the Watteau toilette was returning.

This fashion of the 1880s, though distinctive, appears to have been given no label. A projection below the waist at the back reappeared, but now, instead of being softly puffy, it was as rigid as a shelf and from it a skirt hung free from the legs, a feature which was regarded as practical and comfortable. In front, the unbroken line of the Watteau toilette was replaced by a closely fitted bodice which ended at the waist and a straight or stiffly pleated skirt. Apart from its back projection (only later named a bustle), the chief characteristic of this dress was the close smoothness with which it covered the body, as feathers do a well-groomed bird. A neat knot of hair at the back of the head and a compact curly fringe in front were surmounted by a tiny bonnet for formal occasions or, more casually, by a smallish hat.

Bustle, 1884. White figured cotton, openwork embroidery frill; twelve curved steels. An elaborate example of the bustle structure of the mid 1880s. City Art Gallery, Manchester.

Final Developments

The last major change in the appearance of fashionable Victorian women appeared at the end of the 1880s, when a certain degree of soft romanticism was expressed in a loosening of the dressing of the hair, large Gainsborough hats, drooping puffed upper-sleeves (once beloved by the Pre-Raphaelites), and the disappearance of the projecting crinolette. Lace was widely used for fichus and flounces and the conscious introduction of historicism by a high-waisted Empire line, was considered charming when worn by young girls.

A craze for bicycling invaded the 1890s and brought in the masculine Norfolk suit. Usually made of tweed, it consisted of loose breeches held by a band below the knee and a high-buttoned jacket with four vertical box-pleats; it was worn with stockings and a cloth cap. A similar suit was not, by this time, considered shocking when worn strictly for cycling, by women. The Trilby, a soft felt hat, provided, at last, an informal alternative to the top-hat for men.

In spite of continuous protests on grounds of both health and aesthetics, a feature of almost all Victorian feminine fashion was tight lacing, which was as popular at the end of the reign as it had been at the beginning. In the 1890s women regarded an 18 in (45 cm) waist as highly desirable.

An invention which revolutionized dressmaking and enabled the less well-off to appear well dressed, was the sewing-machine, available commercially in the 1860s; it probably also helped to improve the lot of working tailors and dressmakers, whose conditions of over-work and underpay had troubled the consciences of philanthropists throughout the reign.

When Queen Victoria came to the throne, English clothes, including the Queen's, were more stylish than those in France inspired by the dowdy Bourbon monarchy. In the 1850s, however, Charles Worth, the English designer working in Paris, restored the leadership to France, though men's clothes designed and made in England remained the most admired.

Stella Mary Newton

AMERICAN

Not even the richest American was dressed in the latest European fashion during a large part of Queen Victoria's lifetime. French styles took a year to be pirated in England and longer to be imported into America. The Great Western stage-coach took two weeks in 1838. By 1869, the continents were seven days apart; by 1889, five or six days. Americans began to travel in Europe, as adventurous European aristocrats had been doing in America since the 1830s, to hunt or to invest.

Fashion Influences

Until the east and west coasts of America were united by railway in 1869, fashion information travelled by ox-cart, covered wagon, barge or stage-coach, or came round the Horn. As the latest reports crept westward, the clothes became increasingly attenuated and debased by home sewers with few resources. The Grand Duke Alexis, travelling by luxurious Pullman in the 1870s, admitted to finding Denver a most sophisticated city, but by then French gowns could be bought in San Francisco, and many Americans went to France for dresses and to England for tailoring.

Calculating time-lags is the greatest problem in dating American dress. Unless home-produced, the first fabrics had to be imported. Late in the eighteenth century, Samuel Slater had bootlegged printing machinery into New England. By 1800, there were 165 mills operating in three states, and Mrs Slater had developed the first cotton thread.

Itinerant pedlars, often Jewish, and later founders of clothing and department store empires, carried cotton prints to supplement woven checks and stripes of home-spun and dyed fabrics: linen, wool and linsey-woolsie.

From the late eighteenth century, the visit of the itinerant printer was eagerly awaited. With woodblocks and a few permanent colours such as red, blue and black, he stamped prints on linen bed and table furnishings and petticoats, no scrap of which was ever wasted.

Beginnings of Ready-made Clothing

By 1819, the date of Queen Victoria's birth, ready-to-wear clothing had begun to be produced, principally men's clothing and hats, boots and shoes for all, and women's millinery. The need for Civil-War uniforms put the industry on a firm basis.

The Scotsman Charles Mackintosh's waterproof garments which first appeared in England in *c.* 1838, were perfected by the American Charles Goodyear's discovery of vulcanization in 1855. This discovery was to prove valuable for footwear.

Brooks Bros were providing fine tailoring in New York from 1818. Catalogues, principally of men's and boys' wear, were produced by Oak Hall in the 1870s and by Jordan Marsh in the 1880s. Sears Roebuck's 1888 catalogue offered jewelry and diamonds; by 1894–5 they provided (as they still do), practically anything anyone might need to work or play with, or wear, whether on a farm, road, at home or in a machine shop. It was only in women's clothing that Sears Roebuck did not offer the complete wardrobe: shoes and gloves, corsets and underwear, blouses and tailored coats had to be bought from other sources. Women's and girls' clothes were still frequently made at home or by the visiting dressmaker.

Early Fashion Records

At about the time of Queen Victoria's birth the artist John Lewis Krimmel (1787–1821) provided an interesting record of early nineteenth-century American dress. He depicted his family, who appear as a typical middle-class group, in simple, home-made clothes, which are certainly pretty in themselves but equally interesting for the imaginative use of the fabrics which have gone into their design.

A picture of a flax-scutching bee party in Pennsylvania Dutch country (p. 266) illustrates not only how every gathering tended to become a social occasion but also the strong German influence on peasant costume. The women wear bonnets, snoods, a fichu over a close bodice and an apron over a full skirt. All the clothes are home dyed in natural, vegetable dyes, or indigo. The men wear the humbler hat of beaver fur, not the silk top hat of the upper classes.

From 1830 to 1895, *Godey's Lady's Book* offered delightful fashion plates although they were never American in origin, even when labelled 'New York style' or 'Philadelphia fashion'. Rather, they were the imported work of dynasties of European fashion illustrators selected

An Artist and his Family *by John Lewis Krimmel (1787-1821), c. 1820. Oil on canvas, 30 in × 25 in (76 cm × 63 cm). An interesting record of early nineteenth-century American dress. National Gallery of Art, Washington.*

for the American market (see p. 269). New York had *The Monitor of Fashion* in 1853, *Demorest's*, 1866–89, and *Harper's Bazaar*, from 1867 to our time.

The corset and crinoline after their initial fashionable success were resented in America just as they were by the Pre-Raphaelites in England. One of the major stands against this supremely feminine fashion was made by the social reformer, Mrs Amelia Jenks Bloomer, who appeared publicly in 1851 in long, loose pantaloons which gathered at the ankles and showed below full skirts. Bloomers, so-named after their wearer, enjoyed a short-lived success although they were subsequently revived in various forms as for example in the

ABOVE Godey's Unrivalled Winter Fashions *from 'Ladies in Winter Fashions for 1855', Godey's Lady's Book, Vol. 51. Coloured engraving. Fashion plate specifically intended for the American market. British Museum.*

Flax Scutching Bee *by Linton Park (1826-1906), c. 1860. Oil on canvas, 31¾ in × 50½ in (78 cm × 127 cm). An illustration of the strong German influence on peasant costume. National Gallery of Art, Washington.*

baggy knickerbockers worn by women bicyclists in 1890.

Paper Patterns

By 1851, Isaac Singer had improved Elias Howe's original sewing-machine and succeeded in selling 233,000 throughout the world over the next two decades. Concurrent with the improvement of the sewing-machine was the development in the paper-pattern industry. Butterick was one of the first companies to operate in this field, having been founded by Ebenezer Butterick, a former tailor from Massachusetts. By the spring of 1863 Butterick had designed and produced enough graded paper patterns to have them packaged in boxes of one hundred for sale to tailors and dressmakers around his area of the country. By 1872 the Butterick Publishing Co. was selling paper patterns nationally. Patterns were also obtainable through *Smith's Illustrated Pattern Bazaar*, which was published in New York in 1873, and *The Delineator*, of which the thirteenth volume had been brought out by 1879.

Immigrant Influences

Starving Irish immigrants made no such cultural impact in America as did the early German settlers in St Louis, or the Scandinavians in the North West. Between 1870 and 1880, an immense tide of immigrants from all parts of South

Daniel Boone's First View of Kentucky in 1786 *by William Ranney, 1849. Oil on canvas. Fashion had little influence on practical working dress. National Cowboy Hall of Fame.*

Between Decks in an Emigrant Ship *by A. B. Houghton, 1872. Print. Subtitled 'Feeding Time: a Sketch from Life', this picture depicts the clothes of the lower-middle class American. Metropolitan Museum of Art.*

and East Europe changed the whole racial amalgam of America. German-Jewish master-tailors with well-organized factories had taken control of the clothing industry by 1880. The Poles, Russian-Jews and Italians who had arrived on the scene later had to work in sweat-shops or take home piece-work.

At the very time when Americans were wearing impoverished and debased versions of European fashions, their country was also developing the style of the present-day world. It began late in the eighteenth century with travellers and fur trappers, who supplied beaver to overseas importers until felt hats were superseded by silk in about 1838.

Wild-West Dress

Dress in the Wild West changed little over the years. A painting of Daniel Boone viewing Kentucky for the first time in 1786, painted by an artist called William Ranney in 1849 shows that, apart from a soldier's tricorn, fashion had little effect on workaday dress. Their clothes were made of native materials under Indian, Mexican-Spanish or French-Canadian influences. They incorporated practical details such as the seams of the buckskin shirts and breeches which were fringed in an attempt to speed the passage of water off the wearer

and also to supply a ready store of string. Legs, when not protected by boots, were bound in leather stockings, closely tied at the ankle and calf. Mountain-dwellers wadded fur skin around their heads as protection against the cold and a dangling racoon tail was often added for decoration.

Indian Dress

The Indian women's predilection for ornamentation is well displayed in their imaginative use of natural objects. They embellished their moccasins and any plain edge with porcupine quills, seeds, shells, bones and beads; they even used feathers, ermines' tails and bears' claws. In the South West they favoured silver conchos and turquoise and painted or incised Mexican designs on leather. For headbands and necklaces, they used a variety of materials sometimes resorting to tribal warfare in their choice, as in a surviving example of a necklace made of the left middle finger of numerous enemies.

Cowboy Dress

In the Revolution of 1836, the great ranches of the Spanish *hildagos* were broken up and the loose cattle were rounded up by Texan cowboys.

The *vaqueros*, cowboys or cattledrivers ('buckaroos' to the cowboys) were Mexican Indian day-labourers, but master or man, all were superb horsemen. Their gear was of Spanish inspiration, their hats lacquered stiff, with lower crowns than the later cowboys'. Their short

Spanish jackets were worn with long underdrawers, closed into low-heeled shoes which could be covered by hanging strips of cowhide or *armitas*. These developed into side-buttoned leg protection, the antecedent of the contemporary cowboy's chaps. Rolled up behind the saddle was a patterned Mexican blanket, with a centre opening, to be used as a poncho covering.

Chaps (*chaparras*) were separated and seatless leg protection against thorny chaparral, thickets of dwarf evergreen oaks. They had many forms and closed or snapped along the outerseam so that spurs did not have to be removed. They were made of cowhide, fringed leather and, later, of the fur of wild animals and sheeps' skin.

Cowboys' high boots were made loose for ventilation, stitched stiff and high heeled for bracing with pointed toes to catch loose stirrups. Gauntlets, like all their leather gear, were decorated with Mexican patterns and shell-shaped silver conchos. Red, blue or black silk bandanna handkerchiefs served as sweatbands, towels or bandages; they kept dust from the nose or could be used to mask a holdup man.

A broad-brimmed sombrero hat as protection against sun or rain could carry water or fan a fire. In 1870, the Stetson Co., of Philadelphia, began to ship varied forms of a wide-brimmed felt hat, banded in snakeskin, braided hair or leather and decorated with conchos. In South Texan plains the brim was 4 in (10 cm) wide and the crown 7 in (18 cm) high. In south and south-west Texas, the crown was pinched in. In the North, both brim and crown were smaller and the crown dented all around. Side-

'Soapy' Smith's Saloon Bar at Skagway, Alaska, *1898. Photograph. A typical bar scene showing everyday American male dress in the late nineteenth century. Library of Congress.*

rolled edges, now seen on movie sheriffs, appeared very late. Cowboys kept their hats on indoors.

But pioneers needed readymade clothing. In 1850, a gold-digger, Levi Strauss of San Francisco, sent out work pants, slim legged for safety, low slung for comfort and made of brown tent canvas. Later, he used a specially woven blue denim, and in 1872 added copper rivets at points of strain. Until 1890, cowboys would not accept these.

Late twentieth-century Levis are guaranteed to shrink, wrinkle and fade, as they always did, but in the last century they were almost impossible to wear out. Thus, in early photographs, Levis seem characterless, except those occasionally seen in grey or brown stripes.

The Sweet-Orr Co. was founded in 1870 to provide another garment, blue or white: the overall (usually pronounced overhaul). These are trousers with a bib strapped over the shoulders and pockets and straps to hold necessary equipment for various trades. Overalls were designed to be loose enough to wear over warm clothes or to be worn alone in hot weather.

Nowadays, whether for work or recreation, American people still wear many of the garments which were developed in their country during Queen Victoria's lifetime and which have since been made

familiar by the beloved Western movies of cowboys and Indians.

Millia Davenport

Glossary

Adelaide boots, c. 1830–60
Ladies' boots edged with fur or a fringe.

Aesthetic dress, c. 1880
Introduced by the disciples of the Aesthetic Movement, whose aim was to abolish changes of fashion and to devise a dress which would look permanently beautiful. Depicted in *Punch*, it was satirized by W. S. Gilbert in his opera *Patience*.

Agnes Sorel style, 1861
French term for the English PRINCESS DRESS, a dress in which the bodice and skirt were cut in one and closely gored to fit at the waist.

Albert boots, 1840–c. 1870
Boots with side laces, cloth tops and patent-leather toe caps.

Albert driving-cape, or sac, 1860
Loose style of CHESTERFIELD OVERCOAT used as a driving coat. The back usually made without a centre seam.

Albert jacket, c. 1850
Very short-skirted coat just covering the seat, made with a breast pocket and mainly worn in the summer.

Albert overcoat, 1877
Made with a fly-front fastening and a half-circle cape lying flat on the shoulders; a deep back vent. Mid-calf

length with close sleeves and stitched cuffs.

Albert top frock, 1868–1890s
Overcoat in the form of a FROCK COAT, with flapped pockets in the waist seam and a velvet or sealskin collar, 3 in (7.5 cm) deep and lying on the shoulders like a CAPE.

Amazon corset, 1850s
Riding-corset with elastic lacings.

American shoulders, 1880
Coat shoulders padded some 2 in (5 cm) in front of the shoulder seam to produce the effect of 'square', broad shoulders.

American trousers, 1857
Trousers worn without BRACES on which the cloth is gathered into a narrow waistband with a strap and buckle behind.

American vest, 1860
Waistcoat used for business wear, without collar or lapels and buttoned high.

Ankle-jacks, c. 1845
Short boots laced up with ten holes, five a side. Popularly worn in the East End of London.

Antigropolis, 1850s
Gaiter adapted to either walking or riding; generally of leather, similar in shape to the mud boot but fastened at the side by means of a spring. (*The Gentleman's Magazine of Fashion*, 1855.)

Apron
Protection for the wearer's dress, most often secured by strings and ties. Made usually of fine linen, lawn or muslin in the nineteenth century, and often pinned on, it became known as the small tea apron or 'pinner'. Small black aprons, sometimes embroidered in colours, were popularly known as fig leaves.

Artistic dress, c. 1850
Worn by members of the Pre-Raphaelite circle and later (1870–95) crystalized into a dress with sleeves puffed above the elbow, a normal waistline and a skirt which neither trailed on the ground nor was extended over an understructure.

Babet cap, 1836–c. 1848
Muslin morning CAP trimmed with ribbon, the sides shielding the cheeks.

Bachlick, 1868
Cashmere FICHU edged with swansdown, tasselled and with a hood-like point behind.

OPPOSITE October bonnet and collar fashions for 1838, *American. Godey's Lady's Book. The Godey's Lady's Book was virtually a European fashion guide for the American market. British Museum.*

OVERLEAF A Private View *by William Powell Frith (1819–1909). Oil on canvas; 1881. Frith started as an itinerant portrait painter but after 1840 specialized in genre subjects. J. C. Pope Collection.*

Bag-plastron, 1884
PLASTRON, or front panel of a day dress, the plastron sagging in front and forming a bag.

Bags
Slang term for trousers.

Balayeuse, 1870
Broad frilling of stiff white muslin or artificial lace used as protective edging for a skirt and train.

Balmoral jacket, 1867
Day jacket worn by women buttoning up to the throat and simulating a waist-coat with points in front and behind.

Bandanna
Large silk or cotton handkerchief dyed in brilliant coloured spots on a dark ground. Widely used by American cowboys.

Bang, 1880
American term for hair cut in a straight fringe across the forehead.

Basque
Fashionable term for when the upper portion, or corsage, of a woman's dress descended below the waist.

Basquin, 1857
Coat with deep BASQUES and fringed trimming.

Bathing dress
Male. 'Flannels' or voluminous flannel gowns were worn at public baths in the early part of the century, but it was not until *c.* 1870 that brief triangular trunks were introduced for seaside bathing.
Female. A loose ankle-length flannel gown with long sleeves was worn until 1865 when 'the Zouave Marine Swimming Costume' was introduced 'with body and trousers cut in one' and made in dark-blue serge or brown holland. In 1868 an attached knee-length skirt was added; in 1878 the skirt was shortened and became a separate item, the garment subsequently developing into sleeveless knee-length combinations still retaining the short, detachable skirt.

Bavolet, 1830
Soft frill attached to the back of the BONNET to protect the neck.

Bell skirt, 1891
Flared, gored skirt, the skirt edge stiffened with muslin lining, or, for walking, lined throughout. Usually tailor made.

Benjamin
Loose overcoat worn by the lower classes.

Beret, 1820
CAP with a large, flat crown extensively

trimmed with ribbons, flowers and feathers.

Bertha, 1839
CAPE-like collar of varying length and generally made of lace.

Bloomers, 1851
Name applied to a modified form of trousers worn as rational dress by Mrs Amelia Bloomer and her supporters, 1890. Name given to the baggy KNICKER-BOCKERS worn by women bicyclists.

Amelia Bloomer *by T. W. Brown. 1851. After a daguerreotype. Mrs Bloomer made her first appearance in the pantaloons subsequently named after her in 1851. Radio Times Hulton Picture Library.*

Boa
Round tippet made of swansdown, feathers or fur, usually 6 ft–8 ft (1·8 m–2·4 m) long.

Boater
Stiff straw hat worn by men in summer, devised from the hat of a late eighteenth-century sailor.

Bonnet
Generally a form of hat tied by ribbon strings under the chin and brimless at the back. Alternatively, an American Indian headdress of upstanding feathers attached to a head band, with two feathered streamers hanging down the back.

New Autumn Millinery *from 'Bonnets and Hats', The Lady, 24 September 1885. Sketch. The accompanying text reads, 'Fashion has scarcely decided which is to be the bonnet or the hat par excellence of the coming winter'.*

Bowler, c. 1860
Hard dome-shaped felt hat designed by the English hatter, William Bowler. Americans called it a Derby because the Earl of Derby always wore a bowler to the races at Epsom Downs.

Braces
Originally a pair of straps passed over the shoulder and attached by a single BUTTON at the front and back to support breeches or trousers. Later a double-tongued pattern to attach to two buttons at each side at the front began to be used. By 1850 the two straps were united under the shoulder blades.

Brodequin, 1830s
Satin or velvet boots trimmed with a fringe.

Burnouse, 1830s–1865
Evening mantle of cashmere with a serviceable hood attached at the shoulders.

Bust bodice, 1889
Breast support laced front or back and worn above the CORSET.

Button
Used lavishly on the vest, cuff and pockets of the male costume and as both fastenings and dress ornaments on the female costume.

Caban, 1840s
Loose cloak with armholes worn by men.

Cage petticoat, or artificial crinoline, 1856–68
Structure composed of wire or watch-spring hoops increasing in size from the waistband down and forming a dome-

Crinoline frame, 'The Colby Skirt, Patented 6 February 1866'. Braid-covered, hinged wire and braid. This crinoline shows the elaboration evolved just before its decline. City Art Gallery, Manchester.

shaped PETTICOAT resembling a cage to distend the wide skirts of a dress. By 1868, the cage had changed its shape and extended only at the back, to become known as the CRINOLETTE.

Calcarapedes, 1860s
Self-adjusting galoshes made of rubber and worn by men.

Cameleons, 1859
Ladies' boots and shoes perforated to reveal coloured STOCKINGS.

Camisole, c. 1845
Short-sleeved or sleeveless under-bodice worn over STAYS to protect a tight-fitting dress.

Canezou, c. 1830
Short, pointed CAPE. *c.* 1850. Wide and elaborate FICHU of muslin, lace and ribbons. Belted white blouse, corded and puffed, an antecedent of the shirtwaister.

Cap
Head-covering, usually of soft material, fitting neatly to the head. Originally, when worn by men, it implied social inferiority, but in the nineteenth century it was adopted by gentlemen as fashionable and practical wear for the country and sport. The wearing of caps by ladies became gradually less fashionable from the 1850s. By 1880 young women no longer wore caps and by the 1890s they were worn only by old nurses or female domestic servants.

Cape
Short shoulder-cloak.

Capeline, 1863
Hood of light material with attached CAPE used by women for country wear.

Capote, 1830–40
BONNET with soft crown made increasingly to frame and conceal the face in the 1840s.

Chemisette
Under-bodice or 'fill-in' to the cutaway neck of a day dress.

Chesterfield overcoat, 1840
Classic knee-length overcoat, usually with a velvet collar, named after the 6th Earl of Chesterfield.

Chignon
Hair twisted into a knot at the nape or top of the head and often supplemented by false hair. Reached its fashionable climax in the late '60s to mid '70s.

Corset
French word used as a refinement for STAYS to describe the tightly fitted, boned and laced bodice which reached from the bosom to the hips shaping to a small waist, and hooked at the front and laced at the back. The corset of the 1890s was made of heavy cotton and boned to produce the fashionable wasp waist of 18 in (45 cm).

Corset, 1880-90. Cotton twill stiffened by piping. Corsets became longer and more rigid between 1876 and 1890 and then shortened and became more decorative in the 1890s. City Art Gallery, Manchester.

Cowboy boot
Calf-high boot with a high slanting Cuban heel to hold the foot in the stirrup, the top often decorated with appliquéd motifs.

Crinolette, 1868–c. 1873
Modified cage CRINOLINE, hooped only at the rear. See also CAGE PETTICOAT.

Crinoline
Originally a PETTICOAT corded and lined with horsehair and finished with a straw braid at the hem, it developed into the CAGE PETTICOAT (or artificial crinoline) and by 1868 into the CRINOLETTE.

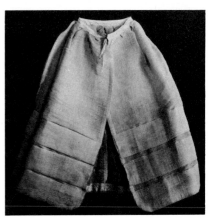

Petticoat, 1840-55. Horsehair. The stiff crinoline petticoat was the basis of the many petticoats supporting the skirt before the introduction of the crinoline frame. City Art Gallery, Manchester.

Dinner jacket
English. Introduced as 'dress lounge' in 1888, the term dinner jacket was used from 1898; a jacket for informal evening wear. (*American* see TUXEDO.)

Dolly Varden dress, 1871
BONNET, CAP, hat and dress derived and fashionably called after the heroine of Dickens' novel *Barnaby Rudge.*

Dolman, 1870–c. 1880
CAPE-like coat with a sleeve cut in one with the side piece and hanging loose.

Dress clothes
Term originally applied to formal social dress for day and evening wear which included a tail coat and a dress coat.

Dressing-gown
Loose-sleeved, full-length wrap generally worn by men with a tasselled skull cap. Early dressing-gowns were usually of white cotton, cambric or wool; later coloured or patterned.

Dux collar, 1860
Narrow, stand-up collar, the corners turned down in front.

Empire dress, c. 1860–90
Certain items of clothing such as the BONNET and high-waisted dress which attempted to revive the then-fashionable Empire style.

Engageantes, c. 1840–65
Detachable white under-sleeves edged with lace or embroidery.

Epaulettes
Ornamental shoulder pieces worn throughout the century but particularly popular in the 1860s.

Fall
Pendant ornament in dress such as a cascade of lace, ruffles or ribbon.

Fan
Ivory, bone, mother-of-pearl and painted fans were fashionable throughout the century. In the 1890s the large folding ostrich-feather fan was introduced.

Fanchon cap, c. 1850
Lace or tulle CAP which extended over the ears.

Fichu
Neckcloth usually of sheer white cotton or muslin draped around the throat and shoulders and usually bunched above the waist.

Flounce
Deep-gathered or pleated frill applied to ladies' clothing as decoration.

Frock coat
Single- or double-breasted coat with skirts joined at the waistline, the back with a vent, side pleat and hip BUTTONS. Of black or Oxford grey cheviot, or unfinished worsted, with striped or checked trousers in grey and black and a matching or contrasting waistcoat.

Gainsborough bonnet, 1877
Generally of velvet trimmed with roses and with a high front brim.

Gaiter
Cloth or leather strap for the ankle or leg generally buttoned at the side with a buckle strap under the foot. Fashionable for women 1820–c. 1840 and also in the 1890s when they were generally made in silk, cashmere or elastic material.

Garibaldi dress, 1860s
Types of dress such as blouse, bodice, jacket, sleeve and vest so-called after Garibaldi's visit to England in 1863, and influenced by his revolutionary dress.

Gibson girl or Shirtwaist girl
Immortalized by the American artist, Charles Dane Gibson (1867–1944), she wore a simple blouse of starched white linen and a cravat with a tailored skirt topped by a sailor hat.

Gladstone overcoat 1870s
Short double-breasted overcoat with a shoulder CAPE and borders trimmed with astrakhan.

Gloves
Male. Always short and until *c.* 1870 often coloured for day, white for evenings, lavender for weddings.
Female. Either wrist length or elbow length, coloured for day and white for evening.

Handkerchief
Men's larger than women's, often coloured for day use. Black edged or completely black, they were worn by both sexes for mourning. For evening, generally silk and often embroidered and edged with lace. For day use, from *c.* 1870 the plain white cambric, cotton or linen handkerchief was generally used.

Henley boater, 1894
Felt hat shaped like a straw BOATER.

Homburg, 1889
Stiff felt hat with a dent in the crown running from front to back.

Inverness, 1859
Originally a large loose overcoat with a deep CAPE, subsequently a sleeveless cloak with a short cape, cloth belt and leather-covered buckle. Made of checked woollen cloth from Inverness, Scotland, and usually worn with CAP of the same cloth.

Isabeau dress, 1860s
Day dress, the bodice and skirt cut in one and gored to fit at the waist like the PRINCESS DRESS.

Kate Greenaway dress, 1880s and 1890s
Style of dress for young girls made popular by the illustrations by the artist of that name.

Knickerbockers, 1860
Loose form of breeches, the name deriving from the (fictional) Dutch founders of New York as described by Washington Irving in his *History of New York* by Dietrick Knickerbocker, 1808.

Jacket, c. 1840
It became socially acceptable and began to replace the coat as part of a gentleman's suit. Worn by ladies mainly for sports wear, or as part of the TAILOR MADE costume, especially in the 1890s.

Jaeger underclothes, 1880s
Always made of wool and introduced by a German, Dr Gustave Jaeger, for both sexes; combinations of natural wool designed on hygienic principles to cover the whole body. Digital socks and stockings.

Langtry hood, 1880s
Detachable hood to any garment of outdoor wear, named after the actress Lily Langtry.

Levis or blue jeans, c. 1850
Strong cotton trousers of indigo blue denim reinforced with copper rivets. Created by Levi Strauss, who went to California in the gold rush.

Little Lord Fauntleroy dress, 1886
Velvet tunic and KNICKERBOCKERS with a wide sash and white lace collar made fashionable by the novelist Frances Hodgson Burnett (1849–1924).

Lounge suit, 1860
Suit for informal wear made up of a lounging jacket, trousers and waistcoat, all in the same material.

Mac(k)intosh, 1836
Short rubber-coated, waterproof overcoat named after Charles Macintosh (1766–1843).

Mitten
Long or short glove and often of net or openwork. In the 1830s and '40s short black mittens were worn with morning dress and, in the evening, long mittens, a fashion which was revived in the 1870s.

Mob cap
Frilled CAP of cambric or muslin for indoor wear.

Moccasin
Soft, leather shoe without a heel. Moccasins worn by North American Indians were embroidered with beads and dyed porcupine quills and had a fold-over cuff tied at the back.

Morning coat
Male garment, originally a riding-coat, it was also adopted by women as a development of the day jacket and worn over a waistcoat with a collar and necktie.

Muff
Soft bag open at either end for warming the hands. Usually small but some from 10 in–11 in (25·3–27·8 cm) long. Fashionable furs were sable, ermine, chinchilla and sealskin. Velvet was also favoured and plush edged with fur.

Muffatee
Small wrist MUFF sometimes worn in winter.

New York surtout, c. 1850
Man's fashionable short, black overcoat with skirts cut straight around and a wide collar braided with black silk.

Newmarket coat, 1830
Tail coat, previously called a riding-coat, often worn open. By 1850 it was generally called a cutaway and in the 1870s it was identified with the MORNING COAT.

Newmarket jacket, 1891
Close-fitting, hip-length jacket worn by women, with the characteristic Newmarket feature of flapped pockets on the hips and close sleeves ending in a cuff or buttoned shirt.

Newmarket overcoat
Male, 1881. Long, skirted overcoat, usually finished with a velvet collar. Worn for riding and driving.
Female, 1889. Tailor made and closed to the waist, the long skirts left open to reach nearly to the ground, the coat was usually faced with a velvet collar, lapels and cuffs.

Nightclothes
Male. Nightshirt resembling a dayshirt with a loose, turned-down collar, or a loose ankle-length nightgown.
Female. Long-sleeve linen, silk or cotton nightgown.

Norfolk jacket, 1880
So-called after the coat of the Duke of Norfolk's hunting-suit which appeared in 1880 with KNICKERBOCKERS. A lounge jacket of mid-thigh length made with box pleats at the front and back under which passes the self-belt and large bellow pockets on the hips. In 1894 a

yoke was often added, the box pleats starting from the yoke.

Ondine crinoline, c. 1860

A CAGE CRINOLINE with the hoops constructed in 'wave-like bands'.

Overalls

English. Loose trousers of white cord or leather worn by men for riding.

American. Loose-fitting over-trousers with a front bib held by a strap around the neck. Made for working wear in dark-blue or brown denim or duck.

Oxford button-overs, c. 1860

'Oxonian shoes which cover the instep and are closed by being buttoned instead of being stringed'. (Mayhew Bros., *London Life and Poor*, 1862.)

Oxford tie, c. 1890

Narrow necktie, equal in width overall, worn by men with a LOUNGE SUIT and by women with a morning blouse. Also low, soft, patent-leather shoes worn by men with evening dress and laced and tied over the instep.

Oxonian boots or collegians, c. 1830–50

Short boots, later black japanned, having a small piece cut out from each side to enable them to be pulled on more easily.

Paddock coat, 1892

Long overcoat without a seam at the waist made with a fly-front and double breasted or single breasted.

Paletot

Traditional French term reintroduced in the 1830s and used to describe a short greatcoat worn by men and a three-quarter length cloak worn by women.

Pamela bonnet, c. 1850

Small straw BONNET, trimmed with ribbons and sometimes flowers, named after the novel by Richardson.

Pannier dress, 1868

Double-skirted day dress, the underskirt trained and trimmed with a FLOUNCE and the upper skirt bunched out round the back and sides by means of a draw-string below.

Parasol

Light decorative UMBRELLA carried by ladies as protection against the sun.

Pardessus, 1840

Outdoor, waisted garment, often made with rounded collar and lace or velvet trimming.

Passementerie

Trimming, usually of gimp or lace, used for dresses.

Pelisse-robe, 1817

Day dress, fastened down the front with concealed hooks and eyes or ribbon bows.

Peplum, 1866, revived in 1890s

Short FLOUNCE or overskirt suspended from a bodice or belt over an underskirt.

Petticoat

Underskirt which gradually became more elaborate in the nineteenth century.

In the 1840s, several were often worn, the undermost being usually of flannel; by the 1890s petticoats were often made of silk or satin and lavishly bordered, frilled or flounced with ribbon and lace.

Piccadilly collar, 1860

Shallow, stand-up collar, the first to be separate from the shirt, fastened to it by a BUTTON at the back and a stud in front.

Plastron

Derived from the French word for a breast plate, the front panel of a bodice of a different colour and material from the rest of the bodice.

Polka, 1844

Short cashmere or velvet ladies' mantle or jacket made with loose sleeves worn as an outdoor garment.

Polonaise

Dress with an overskirt bunched up behind to cover the underskirt, or, in the 1830s, a term used to describe a military REDINGOTE as worn by civilians.

Poncho

Square of rough, woollen cloth hand woven with broad stripes of brilliant colour with a hole in the centre for the head. Worn by both men and women, and largely by Spanish Americans.

Princess dress, 1840

Style of dress made without a seam at the waist, the bodice and skirt being cut in one, and the skirt gored, popularly associated with the Princess of Wales when, *c.* 1878–80, it was at the height of fashion.

Pyjamas, 1870s

Jacket and trousers made in wool or silk and often with a striped design for night wear. 'The doom of the sleeping shirt is written. . . . The pyjama sleeping suit is to take its place. . . . Of oriental origin, of silks etc., generally striped'. (*Tailor and Cutter*, 1897.)

Quilling

Small, round pleats in lace, tulle or ribbon used for trimming dresses.

Raglan boot, c. 1858

Hunting-boot named after Lord Raglan, the Crimean general, reaching to mid thigh.

Raglan cape, 1857

Loose overcoat, commonly made of waterproof material, with sleeves cut to join the garment from underarm to neck and pockets without flaps.

Redingote, 1835–c. 1860

Variation of the PELISSE-ROBE, a close-fitting gown fastening the whole length of the front. In the 1890s the name was applied to a ladies' double-breasted out-door coat with a fitted body and a long, flared skirt.

Reformed dress, 1883

The introduction of greater utility in male and female dress prompted by the exhibition of the Dress Reform Society.

Roseberry collar, 1894

Detachable collar, 3 in (7·5 cm) deep behind and pointed in front but with the corners rounded off, named after the Prime Minister of the day, Lord Roseberry.

Russian jacket, 1865

Short, sleeveless JACKET resembling a bolero, worn over a waistcoat.

Sac overcoat, c. 1843–c. 1875

Loose, knee-length overcoat, the edges bound or double-stitched with large sleeves widening at the wrist.

Safety pin

Pin with a protective sheath covering its point introduced from Denmark in 1878.

Sailor dress

Blouse, hat and suit; worn mainly by English and American children, imitating dress worn in the navy.

Scarborough Ulster, 1892

Sleeveless ULSTER with a CAPE and hood.

Shawl

Square or oblong covering for the neck and shoulder, varying in size and materials. Shawls from Paisley in Scotland were made from 1808 in intricate pomegranate or Persian pear patterns. The design required four months of work, but the actual weaving on British power looms was accomplished in a week. The size of the fashionable shawl increased with the expanding size of the skirt. To wear with the CRINOLINE, they were sometimes made as much as 12 ft (3·7 m) long.

Shooting coat, 1860s–1880s

The name commonly used in these decades for the MORNING COAT.

Smock-frock

Yoked shirt or loose, knee-length gown worn by agricultural labourers. 1880s: an informal ladies' garment worn by women followers of the Aesthetic Movement and their children.

Smoking jacket, 1850

Short lounge coat of velvet, brocade, plush, merino or printed flannel formerly used for smoking at home.

Snood

Coarse hairnet or fabric bag, sometimes attached to a hat, to hold a woman's hair loosely at the back of the neck.

Sombrero

Broad-brimmed felt or straw hat, originally Spanish. Worn by horsemen in the south west of America, South America and Spain. Sometimes referred to by Americans as a ten-gallon hat.

Spat

Short form of cloth garter, after the colonial word spatterdash. Made of white, grey or fawn box-cloth, or canvas cloth, and buttoned at the sides.

Stays

Earlier name for CORSETS.

Stockings
Close-fitting covering for the foot and leg, generally knitted or woven. In the mid-century vivid-coloured PETTICOATS came into fashion with stockings to match, even in horizontal stripes. In the 1890s the vogue was for black stockings worn regardless of the colour of the shoe.

Suspenders
Pair of straps passing over the shoulders to hold up trousers; the accepted name for BRACES in America, and in the trade as an alternative in Britain. In 1878 the elastic suspender which clipped to the border of the CORSET and the top of the STOCKING, began to supersede the garter for women.

Tailor made, 1877
Woman's JACKET and skirt made of a uniform cloth material by a tailor for morning and country wear and constructed on essentially masculine lines.

Talma cloak, 1850
Long CAPE or cloak, sometimes hooded, with a wide turnover collar and a silk lining worn with evening dress and named after the French tragedian, François Joseph Talma (1763–1826).

Tam-o'-shanter, 1880s
Soft, round, brimless hat with a bobble in the centre of the crown, named after a poem by Robert Burns.

Tattersall vest, 1895
Sporting waistcoat made in a heavy woollen material of small plaids and checks.

Teagown, c. 1877
Loose garment, originally worn only by married women in the late afternoon after hunting and before dressing for dinner.

Top frock, 1830
Overcoat cut like a FROCK COAT but usually somewhat longer and generally double breasted.

Top hat
Hat with a tall cylindrical crown reaching its extreme height *c.* 1850 with a crown some 8 in (20·2 cm) high, with a narrow brim usually slightly curled at the side. Usually black, but sporting varieties might be grey, white or brown.

Tourneur, 1830–40
Hip and bustle pads.

Tricorn or tricorne hat
Three-cornered cocked hat.

Trilby, 1895
A soft felt hat with a dent in the crown running from front to back. Named from the novel by George du Maurier and the later play based on it.

Tuxedo, 1898
American term for the English DINNER JACKET, closed with one BUTTON only. The name derives from the design improvised by American millionaires living in Tuxedo Park, New York.

Ulster, 1869
Heavy overcoat with a waistbelt either complete or as a strap across the back, originally worn by men and women in Ulster, Northern Ireland. At first it had a detachable hood but in the 1870s a detachable CAPE was more usual.

Umbrella
Patent tubular metal frames were introduced in *c.* 1835. It was regarded as fashionable to carry an umbrella providing it was rolled up.

Undervest, c. 1840
Feminine undergarment, usually of knitted lisle or silk, worn under the CORSET on the hygienic principle of 'wool next to the skin'.

Unmentionables
One of the many Victorian euphemisms for mens' trousers or breeches. Others included 'Inexpressibles', 'Unwhisperables', 'Don't Mentions' and 'Kicksies'.

Victoria bodice, 1899
Very low, square or round *décolletage* secured by shoulder straps.

Victoria sleeve, c. 1840
Revived in the 1890s. A day sleeve with a large FLOUNCE at the elbow and two smaller ones above, the sleeve tightening below the elbow and ending in a closed cuff.

Victorine, c. 1849
Narrow, flat tippet, tied with ribbon at the throat and edged with fur.

Waterproof, 1880
Name applied to many forms of outdoor garments in which the cloth is sealed against moisture. See MACKINTOSH.

Watteau toilette
Long bodice introduced in Paris in 1868 to replace the CRINOLINE, fastened in front with a skirt edged with deep pleating, an overdress was looped up at the back of the skirt and extended over a CRINOLETTE with a 'Watteau' pleat running from neck to hem.

Wedding dress
White was customary throughout the century, the dress ranging from the semi-*décolleté* style of the 1840s to the high neck of the 1880s. Materials favoured were heavy silk, velvet, satin or white lace over silk or satin.

Wedding suit
In the 1850s the FROCK COAT began to replace the dress coat. By 1860 the costume had become a blue or claret-coloured frock coat, white waistcoat and lavender doeskin trousers. In the 1870s the frock coat was being replaced by the MORNING COAT which by 1886 had become the rule.

Yachting jacket, 1860–80
Short, square-cut outdoor coat or reefer, reaching to hip level.

Zouave coat, 1845
Voluminous coat with velvet collar and cuffs, lined and quilted throughout with silk.

Zouave jacket, c. 1859
Bolero-style jacket with rounded corners of deep-blue Arabian cloth decorated with gold braid and frequently worn by men with red pantaloons. The original design was adopted from the Algerian Zouave troops in the Italian war of 1859. The uniform was copied by some independent companies of the U.S. army in the Civil War and was also followed in feminine fashions of the 1870s.

Bibliography

ARNOLD, JANET. *Patterns of Fashion 1860–1940*, 2 vols, London, 1972

ARNOLD, JANET. *Handbook of Costume*, London, 1973

BALLIN, ADA S. *Science of Dress in Theory and Practice*, London, 1885

CUNNINGTON, C. WILLETT. *English Women's Clothing in the Nineteenth Century*, London, 1937

DAVENPORT, MILLIA. *The Book of Costume*, New York, 1948

Gallery of English Costume. *Women's Costume 1835–1870*, Manchester, 1951

Gallery of English Costume. *Women's Costume 1870–1900*, Manchester, 1953

GERNSHEIM, ALISON. *Fashion and Reality*, London, 1963

HAWEIS, MRS. *The Art of Dress*, London, 1879

LAVER, JAMES. *A Concise History of Costume*, London, 1969

McCELAN, ELIZABETH. *A History of American Costume 1607–1870*, New York, 1969

OLIPHANT, MRS. *Dress*, London, 1878

WAUGH, NORAH. *Corsets and Crinolines*, London, 1954

WAUGH, NORAH. *The Cut of Men's Clothes 1600–1930*, London, 1964

WAUGH, NORAH. *The Cut of Women's Clothes 1600–1930*, London, 1968

Textiles

BRITISH

The Victorian era was a period of great expansion in the textile industry with the development of the Jacquard loom and above all the growth of power-loom weaving, contributing to a vast increase in the production of woven textiles. Machine printing from engraved metal rollers was gradually replacing the slow and laborious process of hand-block printing, particularly for the cheaper ranges and for new export markets. The perfection of new chemical and aniline dyes vastly increased the range of available colours, and designers and manufacturers were quick to exploit these technical advances. New patterns were churned out week by week, one novelty following another in a bewildering variety of styles, drawn from every period of historic ornament, but transformed by the designers into something that was essentially Victorian and that could have belonged to no other age.

Early Victorian Designs

The traditional block-printed floral chintz on a white ground with a glazed finish, was still in favour at the beginning of Queen Victoria's reign, but increasingly after 1840 the drawing became looser, the flowers more luxuriant. Rococo scrolls and cartouches, in the so-called Louis Quatorze style, and Gothic architectural details were introduced into the designs, which became more and more crowded. Huge cabbage roses, hydrangeas, convolvulus, fuchsias, Victoria Regia lilies and other exotic blooms were printed in their full, natural colours both on cotton and on a fine, worsted wool known as challet. These floral chintzes reached the height of their

popularity at the time of the Great Exhibition of 1851. Some of the prize-winning exhibits were, however, only one year later, to be included in an exhibition at the Museum of Ornamental Art at Marlborough House as examples of 'False Principles of Design', the false principle in question being the 'direct imitation of nature'.

The later 1850s and 1860s saw the production of more delicate floral chintzes with rosebuds instead of cabbage roses, violets, harebells, heather and ferns, and diamond-trellis designs with a border of related flowers and leaves.

The roller-printed fabrics presented even more variety. Tartan and paisley patterns and jeweled motifs were combined with flowers in both natural and unnatural colours – some designs would be printed in as many as twenty different colourways. In the 1840s there was a revival of pictorial styles manifest in a whole range of romantic, historical, commemorative and exotic designs with subjects ranging from Crusaders and Saracens to sentimental scenes of children or peasants, or representations of popular figures such as the Duke of Wellington, the young Prince of Wales or Jenny Lind the Swedish Nightingale, vignetted in a floral wreath.

While pictorial styles were not suitable for woven fabrics, the designs were no less eclectic. Modifications of eighteenth-century damask patterns with formalized flowers and leaves, and designs of acanthus leaves and Classical scrolls and ornament, are found throughout the 1830s and 1840s. The Louis Quatorze style, introduced in the 1830s, was characterized by designs with Rococo scrolls and cartouches filled with diaper ornament combined with curling leaves and sprays of flowers, a style which reached its apogee in the mid-1840s.

Formal Gothic patterns, based on fifteenth-century damasks and velvets were introduced by designers such as A. W. N. Pugin together with designs

based on Gothic architectural details such as tracery, crockets and cusps. Floral Gothic designs, of stylized daisies and other flowers, often with exaggerated spiky leaves, persisted well into the 1870s. The first Elizabethan designs appeared in about 1834 and became increasingly popular in the 1840s and early 1850s. Some were purely abstract with bands of strapwork, cartouches and bracket scrolls, sometimes shaded to give a three-dimensional effect, others had flowers introduced into the designs.

The publication of Owen Jones' *Plans, Elevations, Sections and Details of the Alhambra* in 1842 inspired designs with Moorish arabesques, tile diapers and interlaced patterns which appear in both printed and woven fabrics in the late 1840s and 1850s. Publication of Owen Jones' *The Grammar of Ornament* in 1856, which illustrated practically every known style of ornament from prehistoric times onwards, provided the designer of flat pattern with an even greater repertoire and was to become a veritable 'Bible' in the design studios.

Owen Jones was himself a prolific designer, and a distinguished series of furnishing silks with Egyptian, Greek, Etruscan, Persian, Indian and Chinese motifs, were woven from his designs by Benjamin Warner at Spitalfields in the early 1870s. These silks by Benjamin Warner, and others by firms such as Keith & Co., of Spitalfields, and Daniel Walters & Sons, of Braintree, must be classed as luxury goods. The more characteristic furnishing fabrics of the period are the elaborately patterned cotton and worsted, or silk and worsted, damasks woven on the power looms of Yorkshire, in the neighbourhood of Halifax and Bradford.

The patterns of these worsted fabrics generally followed those of the more expensive woven silks but there were more ephemeral, short-lived fashions. For example, in 1852 designs of fruit were introduced, and throughout the year sprays of apple, pear, plum and currants, or bunches of grapes, remained the most popular patterns. After 1855 purely floral patterns were less common and ornamental stripes were introduced with motifs borrowed from a wide range of historic styles.

Distinctive Victorian Designs

Changing fashions in colour as well as in pattern occurred throughout this period. During the 1830s and 1840s, bright, clear colours – scarlet, yellow, turquoise blue and light green – were used for the ground colour, with the pattern in white or natural-coloured thread. In the early 1850s crimson tended to replace scarlet and bottle green was predominant. After 1855 the colours became even heavier and more sombre, with dark maroon, tan and dark bottle or olive greens predominating. Three or four colours were often used in one design. In the 1870s a black worsted ground was often used with the motifs in silk thread, usually in the three primary colours of red, yellow and blue.

Another popular fabric for upholstery was a heavy, stamped velvet known as Utrecht Velvet, not hitherto manufactured in Great Britain, which was introduced by Bennett & Co., of Manchester, in about 1850, and later produced by a number of other firms, including Morris & Co. Plush, chenille, and worsted repps, in plain colours, were also popular for furnishing.

The Japanese influence, which affected all the decorative arts in the 1870s and 1880s, was apparent in the field of textiles at all levels of the trade. Distinguished designs were produced by the architect E. W. Godwin, who based them on sketches made from authentic Japanese ornament, and by Bruce J. Talbert, whose designs were more freely based on Japanese models. His designs were predominantly floral, characterized by stylized flowers with flat, unshaded petals and leaves, butterflies and other Japanese-inspired motifs, and were widely imitated in both printed and woven fabrics, even in the cheapest ranges, throughout the 1870s and 1880s.

Morris and Other Designers

The major influence on textile design during the latter part of the Victorian period was that of William Morris. Although Morris founded his firm in 1861, and designed his first wallpaper the following year, the first textile to be put on the market was *Tulip*, dating from

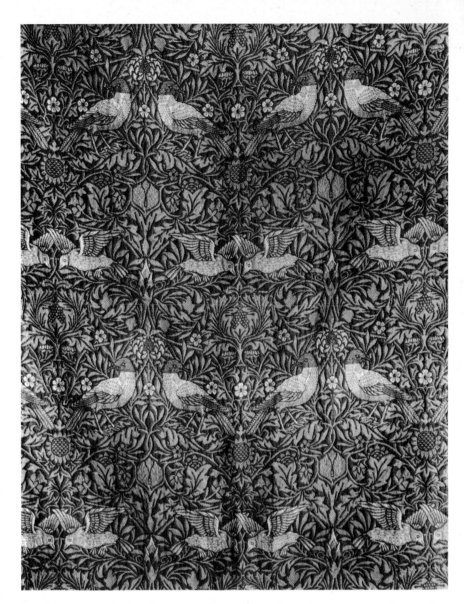

Bird, *William Morris, designed 1878. Woven wool. In 1877 Morris acquired a Jacquard loom so that his fabrics could be woven under his direct supervision. William Morris Gallery.*

1875. Most of Morris' designs, whether for woven or printed fabrics, were floral, combining a deep knowledge of historic pattern structure with a direct observation of nature; designs that were characterized by a feeling for living growth and a sense of one plane behind another. The main pattern of flowers and leaves was often accompanied by a subsidiary small-scale background pattern to stabilize the design (see colour plate p. 281).

Morris' early chintzes were printed by his friend Sir Thomas Wardle, at Leek, who printed them on his tussore silk as well as on cotton. Similarly Morris' early woven fabrics, wool, silk and cotton

damasks, and heavy woollen 'tapestries', were at first woven by outside firms. It was not until 1877, when he installed a Jacquard loom in Ormond Yard, adjoining his Queen Square Workshops, that he was able to weave fabrics under his own direct supervision with a silk weaver from Lyons and an old Spitalfields weaver. The first successful fabric to be woven there was *Flower Garden,* dating from 1879.

Morris was never completely satisfied with the way Wardle printed his designs, but it was not until he found suitable

OPPOSITE ABOVE: Artichoke, *designed by William Morris c. 1875, worked by Mrs Godman.* BELOW: African Marigold, *William Morris, design registered 1876, printed by Sir Thomas Wardle. Hand block-printed cotton. Victoria and Albert Museum.*

premises at Merton Abbey in 1881 that he was able to print his own. There he revived the costly and obsolete method of indigo-discharge printing, the first fabric to be printed by this means being *Strawberry Thief* (1883), perhaps his most famous and popular design. Four of Morris' designs were printed on velveteen, and a number of his designs were woven in madras muslin by Alexander Morton & Co., of Darvel in Ayrshire, Scotland.

By the 1880s Morris' fabrics were so successful that a number of firms sought to imitate them, including Liberty & Co., Regent Street, whose 'art fabrics' were an essential part of the Aesthetic Movement. The firm was founded by Mr Lazenby Liberty in May 1875 and their early fabrics had a distinctly Oriental flavour, being either imported directly from the East or their designs being printed on Indian silks by Thomas Wardle, of Leek. By about 1890, however, they began to commission designs from many of the leading designers of the day, including Lindsay Butterfield (1869–1948), C. F. A. Voysey and Arthur Silver, the founder of the Silver Studios. Many of the Liberty art fabrics were in the Art Nouveau style, and in Italy, the style was so associated with Liberty that it was known as the *Stile Liberty*.

One of the most important designers to be influenced by Morris was A. H. Mackmurdo, who founded the Century Guild in 1882 with the aim of rendering 'all branches of art the sphere no longer of the tradesman but of the artist'. Mackmurdo and one of the co-founders, Herbert Horne, designed printed textiles produced for the Guild by Simpson & Godlee, of Manchester, and woven fabrics produced by A. H. Lee, of Birkenhead. While some of Mackmurdo's textiles and wallpapers, notably *Squirrel*, show a distinct Morris influence, Mackmurdo was soon to evolve a highly personal style with swirling flame-like motifs that were to anticipate the Art Nouveau style by fully a decade.

C. F. A. Voysey's earliest textile designs show the combined influence of Morris and Mackmurdo, but by about 1896 his personal style was fully developed, a style that was to have a great influence on the development of Art Nouveau on the Continent, although Voysey himself stated that he abhorred

OPPOSITE *Lamp mat made in Kennebunkport, Maine,* c. *1850. Berlin woolwork, centre square in cross stitch with raised woolwork flowers in each corner ; border in raised woolwork with flowers in natural colours. Smithsonian Institution.*

TOP *Floral pattern, C. F. A. Voysey (1857-1941), designed* c. *1890, probably printed by Turnbull & Stockdale Ltd. Printed cotton. Voysey's early designs show the influence of Mackmurdo and Morris. Victoria and Albert Museum.*

ABOVE Fairyland, *C. F. A. Voysey, designed 1896 for Alexander Morton & Co. Woven wool and cotton. Whitworth Art Gallery.*

TOP White Poppy *probably by Lindsay Butterfield (1869-1948), designed* c. *1891 for Sir Thomas Wardle of Leek. Butterfield was one of the many talented designers commissioned by Liberty & Co. Whitworth Art Gallery.*

ABOVE *Floral pattern, Lindsay Butterfield, designed* c. *1895 for Sir Thomas Wardle of Leek. Printed silk. Wardle combined his talents as a silk-printer, dyer and designer. Whitworth Art Gallery.*

the latter. Like Morris and Mackmurdo, Voysey often incorporated birds into his designs, but they are highly stylized, being reduced to flat silhouettes. Tulips, chrysanthemums and twisting leaves are among Voysey's most characteristic motifs.

Another important late-nineteenth century textile designer was Lewis F. Day, who published numerous books on art and design and exercised a consider-

able influence through his regular contributions to the *Art-Journal, Magazine of Art* and *The Manchester Guardian.* Most of Day's designs are based on historic ornament or stylized flowers, derived from Jacobean and other embroidery patterns, and were printed by Turnbull & Stockdale, of which he became art director in 1881.

Walter Crane, although a prolific designer of wallpapers, produced relatively few textiles, these few numbering *Four Seasons,* printed by Wardle of Leek, in 1893, and in cotton, *The British Empire*

and *A Fantasy of Fashions* printed by Edmond Potter & Co., of Manchester, to commemorate Queen Victoria's 1887 Jubilee.

The Influence of the Aesthetic Movement

Apart from these fabrics produced by distinguished designers, the influence of William Morris and the Aesthetic Movement had an effect on the general run of production in the late nineteenth cen-

ABOVE: Bolton Abbey in the Olden Time, *Sir Edwin Landseer (1802-73). Berlin woolwork. Designs such as this reproduction were hand coloured on squared paper and copied on to square-meshed canvas. Private Collection.*

tury. Softer, more subdued colours were generally preferred – the 'greenery yallery' range of olives, drab yellows, soft blues and quiet autumn tints. Cretonnes featured poppies, chrysanthemums and daisies, and similar flowers are found on the furnishing silks, together with Art Nouveau designs which, by the turn of the century, was to some extent the dominant style.

Throughout the early Victorian period, undoubtedly the most popular type of embroidery was Berlin woolwork; indeed it virtually ousted all other types. Berlin woolwork was a type of canvas embroidery worked in worsted wools on square-meshed canvas in tent or cross stitches from printed patterns, each square of the printed design representing one square of the canvas. The printed patterns were mostly published in Berlin and were first imported into England in about 1805, and, by 1840, 14,000 different patterns had been published.

The pictorial patterns, intended to be worked as framed pictures or firescreen panels, covered a wide variety of subjects. The paintings of Sir Edwin Landseer were especially popular, but famous masterpieces, such as Leonardo da Vinci's *Last Supper* or Raphael's *Sistine Madonna* also received their share of attention from the Berlin patternmakers. Religious subjects, particularly from the Old Testament, Oriental themes and romantic scenes of peasants and children, were also common. Dogs, notably King Charles spaniels curled up on a cushion, were also prevalent.

For upholstery purposes – chair seats and backs, cushions, footstools and piano fronts – floral designs were most favoured. The early floral patterns were fairly restrained, often worked in silks as well as wool, with the light canvas background left unworked. By 1850 more exuberant patterns of exotic flowers or huge cabbage roses were set against a black background which emphasized the glaring colours of the aniline dyes. Gaudy parrots and baskets of fruit were often incorporated. Added realism was given by working parts of the design – the plumage of the birds or individual flowers – in a series of loops (known as plush stitch) which were then cut to give the effect of the thick velvet pile. As a variant, the Berlin patterns were worked in beads, either in full colour, or in *grisaille*, using crystal, opaque-white, grey and black beads only. This *grisaille* beadwork was much used for hand and banner screens, for upholstery and small articles such as tea cosies, the beadwork being set off by a brilliant red or blue background.

Although the craze for Berlin woolwork persisted well into the 1880s, the 1870s saw a revival of embroidery as an art. The revival was first manifest in church embroidery and the architect G. E. Street showed altar frontals, based on Medieval models, at the 1862 Exhibition.

The Flower Pot, *William Morris, worked by May Morris. Embroidered panel, silk on linen. The patterns sold by Morris & Co. were often designed and worked by Morris' daughter, May. William Morris Gallery.*

William Morris' earliest embroideries were also of Medieval inspiration: in 1866 he produced a series of figure panels, based on Chaucer's *Legend of Good Women* for the Red House, his home at Bexley Heath. Embroideries were among the earliest products of the Morris firm, founded in 1861.

The interest in embroidery engendered by the Church, and above all by William Morris, led to the establishment of a number of bodies for the propagation of needlework as an art. The earliest, and most important, was the Royal School of Art Needlework founded in 1872. The School had the twofold aim of reviving embroidery for domestic purposes and providing employment for distressed gentlewomen. The School commissioned designs from the leading architects and designers of the day including William Morris, Burne-Jones, Walter Crane, Selwyn Image, Sir Frederick Leighton, Sir E. J. Poynter and Alexander Fisher. The range included large figure panels and *portières*, designs for sofa backs and piano fronts, cushions, firescreens and for every domestic article that could conceivably be decorated with embroidery.

As with Berlin woolwork, a high proportion of the designs were floral, but the cabbage roses and exotic blooms were replaced by the flowers beloved of the Aesthetic Movement – sunflowers, daisies, madonna lilies, irises, daffodils and the stiff Crown Imperial. Fruit, especially pomegranates, was also popular, as well as patterns derived from Italian Renaissance, Greek Island and Turkish embroidery. Japanese-style designs, incorporating cranes, herons or peacocks, were much used for three-fold screens. The patterns were worked in crewel wools, often in monochrome shades of brown, or in floss silks.

Both Morris & Co. and the Royal School of Art Needlework sold both finished embroideries and designs for the customers to work for themselves. The patterns sold by Morris & Co. were almost exclusively floral and were designed by Morris himself, his daughter May, or his chief assistant J. H. Dearle.

Barbara Morris

AMERICAN

Two main classes of textiles in the United States in the nineteenth century were those that were machine made and the wide range of needlework items made in the home. There were, in addition, hundreds of yards of fabric imported from Great Britain and other countries in Europe, and from all over the world for home furnishings and dress, reflecting the style and taste of their country of manufacture. Their American use sometimes took the form of a straight copy and sometimes a modified form.

Much of the American taste of this period reflected a subdued or somewhat less elaborate version of the British, for only a small proportion of the American people could afford to use textiles in an extravagant manner. Although textile manufacture had reached an important plateau by the beginning of the Victorian era, and cotton mills were prolific, their products were not luxury items. The expanding agricultural and manufacturing economy, giving rise to a growing middle class, created a market for less expensive goods and increased the leisure time that allowed women to produce decorative quilts and other needlework. The story of textiles in nineteenth-century America is the story of the growth of an emerging middle class.

Textile manufacture had a slow beginning in Colonial America. As an English colony, encouragement had been given to the export of raw materials in exchange for the manufactured goods supplied by the mother country. This was especially true of textile goods, one of Britain's strong industries. Even after political independence had been sought and won, the new United States of America was not economically free. Her would-be industrialists offered rewards and other enticements to interest trained craftsmen, mill operators and others to come with their mechanical and professional skills, which was all that they could bring as no machines, models or plans were allowed to leave England. The transfer of English technology to America had begun.

Textile Production

The 1790 introduction by the English immigrant Samuel Slater of the Ark-wright system for the machine spinning of cotton, together with the information about the power loom gained by Francis Lowell during a visit to England, adapted and introduced by 1814, enabled American cotton manufacturers to reach a highly productive state by the 1820s. The continual lack of sufficient numbers of skilled labourers made it necessary to make machines increasingly automatic, allowing one worker to oversee more than one machine. An early example of this was the invention of the self-acting temple in 1818 by Ira Draper.

The temple is the device on the loom that provides a horizontal tension on the woven goods to ensure uniformity of width. In the early English power loom, the temple of the hand loom was used and the weaver had to move it manually after a few inches of fabric had been woven. Although the early power loom had many limitations, the powered shuttle wove the fabric so quickly that the weaver had to limit his attention to one loom to be certain that the temple was moved at the proper time. In America, with the self-acting temple, the weaver could tend at least two looms. This marked the beginning of a series of improvements to the power loom, and by the end of the nineteenth century one weaver could tend sixteen looms.

Cotton was the fibre most easily handled by machine. By the 1820s the production of checks, sheetings and shirtings – simple fabrics that could be produced in great abundance – was a full-scale industry. However, if it had not been for the introduction of machine, or cylinder, printing, much of the large quantity of plain cotton goods that could be woven on the power loom would have had only a limited market.

Cylinder printing turned out hundreds of yards of printed goods at a rate unequalled by the earlier methods of hand-block printing or copper-plate printing. The deterrent to the use of cylinder printing was the skill and cost of engraving the printing cylinder. The die and mill, an American invention first used to engrave the rollers for printing bank notes, was used to transfer a small pattern repeatedly to the larger printing roller. This method economized on the cost of cylinder engraving and consequently the printing of cottons in America. The simplest type was the one-colour print that used only one roller. This method was, however, practical for patterns of a small repeat only.

The invention in the 1840s of the pantograph machine to transfer larger designs to the roller put the American printing industry in world competition with its moderately priced goods. By the second half of the century prints produced from machines with twelve cylinders were on the market.

In patterned, woven textiles produced in America during this period of the nineteenth century there were two major categories. First there were the products of the hand weavers who continued in the tradition of the eighteenth century but adapted their patterns to the technical improvements that were available, such as the use of the Jacquard head introduced to the American hand loom in the 1820s.

In 1830 there were still many professional hand weavers in America. They worked primarily in the expanding small town and rural areas of Pennsylvania, New York, Ohio, Indiana and the Southern states, producing fabrics directly for the consumer to specific order. Many yards of plain goods were woven, but the best surviving examples are patterned goods such as table linens and bedcovers. A linen, damask tablecloth woven by the weaver S. Butterfield in North Hartford, Oneida County, New York State, in 1837 shows a design of a stylized floral medallion; the corner box pictures George Washington with his name and 'United we stand divided we fall', while 'Under this we prosper' runs along the top and bottom inner border. This identical pattern was used for cotton and wool bedcovers.

The most common type of coverlet was of white cotton and indigo-dyed wool. Usually the cotton was a machine-spun product furnished by the weaver and the wool was a hand-spun product furnished by the person for whom it was woven. These coverlets represent a transition of textile production from the home to the mill and were very common in the second quarter of the nineteenth century. Their production in less accessible places continued even later. The great impact of the railroad on America in the mid-nineteenth century brought goods and

Capture of General la Vega By Captain May, *Zachary Taylor, 1846. Roller print. This and other scenes from the Battle of Resaca de la Palma are depicted on a Mexican War commemorative textile. Smithsonian Institution.*

Jacquard coverlet, 1842. Cotton and wool. Although unmarked, the emblem in the corners, and the end border designs are typical of William Craig, a professional weaver of Indiana. Smithsonian Institution.

people together and the need for local weavers was never felt in the expanding western regions. Important inroads were also being made in the power weaving of patterned textiles in the mills.

As early as 1837 a United States patent was issued for a fancy power loom to William Crompton, another English immigrant who, encouragingly for the Americans, said he could never have invented it if he had not come to America. Although his reason for this statement is not recorded, it probably reflects the encouragement given by the mill owners to those concerned with power-loom improvements. Crompton's patent covered the control of the harnesses necessary to weave small, patterned textiles. The Crompton loom was put into immediate production and patterned cottons were woven by power in Lowell, Massachus-

etts, for the first time. Many later improvements were made by his son, George Crompton.

The expansion of the manufacture to woollens (woven in America on a cotton warp) came with the introduction of cassimere manufacture in 1840. Problems that had been solved relating to the power weaving of cotton fabrics, made the transition to this cotton-warp woollen fabric an easy one. The new, inexpensive woollens were available for use at home and for export. It was to be another twenty years before combing wools and combing machines, necessary for the production of worsted fabrics, were to be introduced. And although good worsted fabrics were woven by the 1860s, the United States never offered any real competition to the British market in this class of textiles. She continued to compete best in the products that represented the full capability of machine production, not in those that required highly skilled labour.

Almost simultaneous with the inventions relating to the power production of fabrics was important work in the field of the power weaving of carpeting.

Erastus Bigelow's earliest patents were concerned with the power weaving of patterned counterpanes and with coach lace. By 1840 he had turned his attention to a power loom for weaving ingrain carpeting on which, when perfected, yards of carpeting could be woven by one weaver and an assistant. Bigelow continued his inventive efforts to produce looms for Brussels, Wilton, and tapestry carpeting for thousands of people who had never previously been able to afford the luxury of a carpet under foot. Once again the rapid growth of the machine-woven carpeting industry and its even cheaper, printed floor-cloth substitutes reflected the purchasing power of the emergent middle-class market.

The last half of the nineteenth century not only brought into focus the new worsted industry but also the manufacture of silk goods. The silk industry had been limited primarily to the production of sewing-silks in the first half of the nineteenth century: the few isolated efforts to produce silk fabrics had been limited to hand-spun yarns on hand looms. Several different projects had been initiated to introduce sericulture to the United States but the necessary cheap, but skilled, labour to reel the cocoons was never available. The gradual change and adaptation to the use of

ABOVE *Ingrain carpet loom, original patent model 2625 issued to Erastus Bigelow (1814-79) on 16 May 1842. The first American power loom for weaving ingrain carpeting. Smithsonian Institution.*

TOP LEFT AND RIGHT *Floral patterns, Paragon Silk Co., New Jersey, c. 1890. The manufacture of silk fabrics in the United States was confined to hand-spun yarns on hand looms until the last quarter of the nineteenth century, when the introduction of power machinery made the industry profitable. American machine-made silks, although of good quality, never really competed with the earlier silk centres of Europe. Smithsonian Institution.*

LEFT *Ingrain carpet patent design (Pat 1144), 1856. This example dating from 1859 is based on the design patent of Elemir J. Ney and is typical of designs of the period. Smithsonian Institution.*

power machinery to weave silk fabrics made this industry profitable by the last quarter of the nineteenth century. The fabrics produced, although of good quality, never competed with those of the earlier silk centres of Great Britain and Europe. By the end of the Victorian period the American textile industry was in every way viable and an economic factor in the world market.

Needlework

As textile production became a mill activity in the nineteenth century, several factors contributed to the rise in the volume of home needlework produced at this time. These factors, to name a few, included an increasing number of urban people with sufficient income so that the women did not have to work outside the home, increasing quantities of cheaper cotton goods to convert into even more decorative items, and the rise of the printed pattern, which enabled women without special training to follow commercial patterns rather than rely on their own artistic skills. Original examples were still produced, but much of the embroidery work was copied directly from a pattern.

One of the most representative examples of American needlework is the patchwork quilt, and the golden era of quilt making in the second quarter of the nineteenth century. Both the patchwork and the appliqué techniques continued to be popular. Although the large, single-motif design was still used, the design of

RIGHT *Crazy patchwork quilt, New York City, 1883. Silk. The crazy patchwork quilt was later reduced in size, covered in silk and elaborate stitching and known as the Victorian Slumber Throw. Smithsonian Institution.*

Bird in floral garland, c. 1868. Berlin woolwork. This design is based on a pattern from Peterson's Magazine. *Smithsonian Institution.*

LEFT *Quilt, c. 1830. Appliquéd cotton. The design represents an adaptation of the Great Seal of the United States. The quilt contains a high proportion of blue printed cotton fabrics, popular at this time. Smithsonian Institution.*

repeated motifs, usually in squared multiples, increased in popularity. The influence of the machine, which made repeated-motif design popular in other kinds of hand work, may have had its influence, but the greater ease with which smaller design-units could be handled while they were being stitched was certainly a factor.

A more common type of embroidery in America is canvas work; this was the counterpart of Berlin woolwork which was so popular in England and often called by the same name in America, since it was also worked with Berlin wool yarn.

Rug hooking was also a favourite pastime, and patterns or stamped burlap were used. Usually narrow strips of fabric would be hooked into the ground fabric, these strips being saved from old fabrics, or they could be purchased.

The silk crazy patch quilt, so popular in America in the late Victorian period, exemplifies the period not only by the rich fabrics, deep colours and elaborate decorative stitching, but also by its name – Victorian Slumber Throw. The quilt was reduced in size, dressed up in the elaborate silks that were now being woven by power, and decorated with fanciful stitches that worked up fast; it was then placed in the parlour. A colourful era was coming to a climactic end.

Grace Cooper

Designers and Manufacturers

BIGELOW, ERASTUS BRIGHAM (1814–79)
American industrialist and developer of the power carpet loom which he invented for INGRAIN carpeting in 1840 at Lowell, Massachusetts. This device was perfected in 1841 and between 1845 and 1851 he produced his greatest invention, the power loom, for Brussels and Wilton carpeting, establishing a carpet mill at Clinton, Massachusetts in 1849. The first power loom could turn out from 10 to 12 yards (9·14–10·97 m) a day, increasing in proportion with the degree of the instrument's refinement and producing up to 25 yards (22 m) per day for the latest model. Bigelow exhibited his Brussels and Wilton carpets at the Great Exhibition of 1851. Handmade, such carpets would be manufactured at the rate of 7 yards (6·4 m) per day with ten to twelve hours work put in by a craftsman assisted by a drawing boy. His inventions aided carpet manufacture in

Europe as well as in the United States. Bigelow also patented improvements in power looms for coach lace and counterpanes.

BURNE-JONES, SIR EDWARD COLEY (1833–98)
English painter and designer of tapestries and stained glass for Morris, Marshall, Faulkner & Co.

CRANE, WALTER (1845–1915)
English designer, painter, book-illustrator and writer on art and design. Produced numerous designs for wallpapers but relatively few for textiles. His textile designs included *Four Seasons* for WARDLE, two Jubilee designs for Edmund Potter, DAMASK designs for John Wilson & Sons, two hand block-printed fabrics for Birch, Gibson & Co., and a woven fabric for WARNER. Also designed embroideries for the Royal School of Art Needlework.

The Four Seasons, *Walter Crane (1845-1915), designed 1890 for Sir Thomas Wardle of Leek. Printed velveteen. One of the relatively few designs for textiles produced by Crane. Museum für Kunst und Gewerbe, Hamburg.*

Floral pattern, Lewis F. Day (1845-1910), designed c. 1898 for Turnbull & Stockdale Ltd. Roller-printed cotton repp. Day was Art Director of Turnbull & Stockdale Ltd. and a prolific designer. Whitworth Art Gallery.

CROMPTON, WILLIAM (1806–91)
English born, American inventor of the first fancy power loom in 1837.

DAY, LEWIS F. (1845–1910)
Prolific English designer of fabrics, and art director of Turnbull & Stockdale from 1881, Lewis Day wrote *Art in Needlework* (1900), in which he ex-

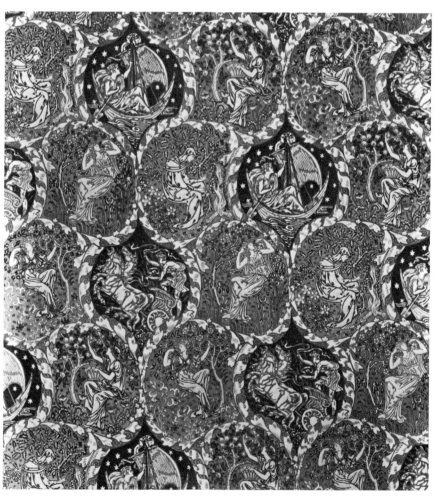

pounds the MORRIS doctrine that art in embroidery could come about only through a knowledge and study of old embroidery. This view had already encouraged, from the 1870s onwards, a serious study of embroidery. Loan exhibitions of both old and modern works were held throughout England, the most important being held at the South Kensington Museum, London, in 1873.

DEARLE, JOHN H. (1860–1932)
Joined the MORRIS firm at the age of eighteen as an apprentice and became Morris' chief assistant. Dearle absorbed his master's personal style so thoroughly that it is almost impossible to tell their work apart.

DRESSER, CHRISTOPHER (1834–1904)
English designer and writer. Published his first book on design, *The Art of Decorative Design* in 1862, followed by a number of volumes on design theory, botany and Japanese art. Produced an enormous number of designs for all media in a wide variety of styles ranging from the strictly functional to the eccentric. Designed textiles for Warner & Sons, Turnbull & Stockdale, WARDLE and Steiner & Co.

GODWIN, E. W. (1833–86)
English architect and designer. Set up in practice in Bristol in 1854. Moved to London in 1865 and designed his first wallpapers the following year. From 1868 designed furniture, wallpapers, carpets and textiles both for commercial production and private commissions. Like TALBERT, Godwin was a leading exponent of the Japanese style, drawing direct inspiration from Japanese ornament.

HAITÉ, GEORGE CHARLES (1855–1954)
Son of George Haité, a leading British designer of Paisley patterns. Designed textiles and wallpapers for most of the leading firms of the day including Warner & Sons, G. P. & J. Baker, Jeffrey & Co.

HORNE, HERBERT (1864–1916)
Co-founder of the Century Guild for which he designed fabrics and wallpaper.

JONES, OWEN (1809–74)
English architect and ornamental designer. By his example and the publication of his *The Grammar of Ornament*, he exercised very great influence on the design of English wallpaper, carpets and furniture. He also produced many illuminated and other works, and an outstanding series of woven silks for Warner & Sons in the early 1870s.

LOWELL, FRANCIS CABOT (1775–1817)
American manufacturer who, after spending three years in Lancashire from 1810 to 1813, put an end to the problem of getting YARN woven into cloth which was occasioned by the acute labour shortage.

At Waltham he introduced his modification of the English power loom which, by 1816, was able to turn out a yard-wide cotton material close to the unbleached cottons of India. His company, the Boston Manufacturing Co., Waltham, soon afterwards expanded and began to manufacture and print calicoes: in 1822, towards this end, the Merrimack Co. was established in an area to be named Lowell in 1824. By 1839 this one company was able to produce more than 1,000,000 yards of print cloth each year.

MACKMURDO, ARTHUR H. (1851–1942)
Scottish architect and designer and founder of the Century Guild, working in England, who for much of his career was a follower of MORRIS. Mackmurdo's style of domestic design in the 1880s was more advanced than anything else in Europe and had a substantial influence on textile design.

Cromer Bird, Arthur H. Mackmurdo (1851-1942), designed 1882 for the Century Guild. Cretonne. Mackmurdo was an innovator who had a substantial influence on European textile designs. William Morris Gallery.

MORRIS, WILLIAM (1834–96)
Morris began his first experiments with embroidery in 1855, while working in the office of STREET. His experimental piece, a repeating pattern of flowering trees and birds, *If I Can*, may be seen with much of his other work at Kelmscott Manor, Oxfordshire. The characteristic 'Morris embroideries' worked chiefly in darning stitches in FLOSS SILKS did not appear until the 1870s when the firm began to produce designs for *portières* (a curtain hung over a door or doorway), coverlets and cushions. Until 1880 most of these designs came from Morris himself, but after this date they tend to come from his daughter or DEARLE. Morris' influence was most widespread

through his designs for flat pattern. He produced forty-four designs for printed fabrics, the first to be put on the market being *Tulip* in 1875, the last, *Compton* in 1896. All his designs were printed by woodblock, the majority in vegetable dyes. The earliest were printed by WARDLE at Leek but after Morris moved to Merton Abbey in 1881, most of his designs were printed there. In 1883 he revived the obsolete and laborious process of INDIGO-DISCHARGE PRINTING, his most famous design *Strawberry Thief* being printed by that method. He also designed some twenty-five woven fabrics, including DAMASKS, heavy woollen tapestries and silk and wool double cloths. His first woven fabrics, *Anemone* and *Honeycomb*, were power-loom woven by H. C. McCrea of Halifax in 1875, but after 1877 Morris was able to weave some of his fabrics under his own supervision. He designed a number of machine-woven carpets in the 1870s and in 1879 embarked on the weaving of the hand-knotted Hammersmith carpets and rugs. He taught himself tapestry weaving in 1879 and set up high warp tapestry looms at Merton Abbey in 1885.

PUGIN, AUGUSTUS WELBY NORTHMORE (1812–52)
English architect, also a designer of furniture, silver, textiles, stained glass and jewelry. As the builder of many new Catholic churches which needed altarfrontals and vestments, Pugin was the main instigator of the revival of church embroidery in England in which from the 1840s both the Anglican and Catholic Churches in England began to take an interest. This, in turn, was accompanied by criticism of the deadening effect of BERLIN WOOLWORK which relied heavily on the use of patterns.

SILVER, ARTHUR (1852–96)
English designer and craftsman. Founded the Silver Studios in 1880 which continued in active production until 1965. Designed fabrics and wallpapers for most of the leading firms of the day including Liberty & Co., Alexander Morton & Co., Warner & Sons and Lightbown, Aspinall & Co. Among the other designers in the Silver Studios were his brother, Harry Silver, his son Rex Silver (1879–1965) and Harry Napper (d. 1930).

SLATER, SAMUEL (1768–1835)
After serving eight years as an apprentice to Jedediah Strutt and as overseer in the Milford Mill, Slater emigrated to America. In 1790, he introduced mechanical CARDING and spinning to Pawtucket, Rhode Island, by successfully transplanting to the United States Arkwright's system of cotton spinning. He has been called the Father of the Cotton Manufacture of America.

STREET, GEORGE EDMUND (1824–81)
Prominent English architect of the Gothic Revival and follower of the Anglo-Catholic Oxford Movement. Together with his sister and his friends, the Blencowes, G. E. Street founded the Ladies' Ecclesiastical Embroidery Society with the aim of maintaining a high standard in church needlework.

TALBERT, BRUCE J. (1838–81)
Trained as an architect, Talbert became a leading English furniture designer of his day and was a prolific designer of printed and woven textiles, carpets and wallpapers. His style, characterized by sharply delineated outlines and flat stylized flowers and leaves, was strongly influenced by Japanese art. His designs were widely imitated throughout the late 1870s and 1880s.

VOYSEY, CHARLES FRANCIS ANNESLEY (1857–1941)
English architect and designer. Set up his own practice in 1882 and designed his first textiles and wallpapers in 1883 under the influence of MACKMURDO. By 1890 Voysey had evolved his own personal style which was characterized by huge papery poppies, twisting leaves and stylized birds, designs which contributed to the development of Art Nouveau both at home and abroad. Voysey continued to design fabrics until 1928.

Floral pattern, C. F. A. Voysey, designed c. 1900 for G. P. & J. Baker. Voysey's designs had a direct influence on the development of Art Nouveau. Museum für Kunst und Gewerbe, Hamburg.

WARDLE, SIR THOMAS (1831–1909)
Silk printer and dyer of Leek, Staffordshire, Sir Thomas Wardle was a lifelong friend and associate of MORRIS. In 1879 his wife founded the Leek Embroidery Society, whose characteristic repeating designs were printed by wood block on TUSSORE SILK specially dyed at Leek; gold thread for this work was imported from China. Some of the designs were by Wardle himself, who adapted a number of patterns from Indian Art, including *Ajunta* for which he drew inspiration directly from the famous cave-frescoes. Leek embroidery achieved its fame primarily in the ecclesiastical field, and during the 1880s and 1890s many churches commissioned embroidery from the Society. Wardle also printed the early fabrics of MORRIS and many of the Liberty art fabrics.

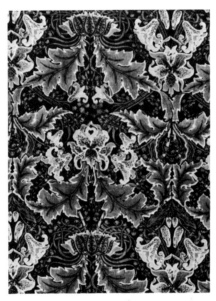

Floral pattern, Sir Thomas Wardle (1831-1909), designed 1895 for Liberty & Co. Wardle printed the early fabrics of Morris and many of the Liberty & Co. art fabrics. Victoria and Albert Museum.

WARNER, BENJAMIN
Firm of weavers of Spitalfields, London, who wove silks to the designs of GODWIN, JONES and SILVER. Such work was the swansong of the great Spitalfields hand-loom weaving industry, the former chief rival to the industries of Genoa and Lyons.

WHEELER, CANDACE THURBER (1828–1923)
Embroideress, designer, writer and lecturer. One of the founders of the first decorative art society in America and of the group, Associated Artists, which was set up on the initiative of Louis Comfort Tiffany in 1879. Designed embroideries, needlewoven tapestries and textiles both for Tiffany and her own organization; these are well represented in the Metropolitan Museum of Art, New York.

Glossary of Materials and Forms

Berlin wool
Fine, WORSTED YARN used for embroidery and knitting, made from the wool of Merino sheep of Saxony and other German states. It was also called German wool.

Burlap
Coarse, plain-woven, CANVAS-like fabric, usually made of jute or hemp. Also called gunny, it was used as the base fabric in RUG HOOKING.

Canvas
Heavy, strong, plain-woven fabric of linen, cotton, silk or a mixture, soft finished or highly sized. Used for interlinings, ART NEEDLEWORK and for stiffening coats and facings; the heavier grades were for seamen's clothing, sails and tents. Berlin canvas signifies in particular, a coarse fabric with square mesh formed by paired threads; it was originally of silk, but also made later of other fabrics.

Cassimere
Woollen cloth with a fine twill weave, closely sheared to give a smooth face. Softer than WORSTED, it is often made with worsted WARP and woollen FILLING and is light or medium in weight.

Challet, challis or challie
Soft, lightweight, WORSTED cloth without gloss, used chiefly for dresses, sleeping-garments, counterpanes and robes. It originated in England in c. 1830, at which time it was usually figured in a delicate floral pattern.

Chenille
French for caterpillar. Victorian chenille cord consisted of silk, cotton, wool or WORSTED, woven on a loom and then cut giving the YARN a tufted, velvet-like pile protruding all around, similiar in appearance to a fuzzy caterpillar. As such it was used for embroidery and tassels. A fabric made with the FILLING of this cord was used for draperies and covers.

Chintz
Originally painted or stained calico, mentioned as early as the twelfth century; later a plain-woven fabric, sometimes glazed, printed with a gay, floral pattern, often in five bright colours. It was used for draperies, slip covers and cushions, etc. The word means varied.

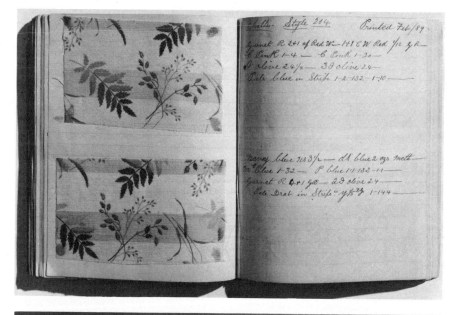

LEFT *Sample book of Thomas Stafford, head colourist at Coheco Manufacturing Co., Dover, New Hampshire, illustrating different colours of printed challis, 1889. Smithsonian Institution.*

BELOW LEFT *Christening dress, c. 1880. Embroidered cotton. The cotton industry flourished in America while much of the embroidery was done at home directly from patterns. Smithsonian Institution.*

Cretonne

Strong, unglazed (as opposed to CHINTZ) medium-weight fabric in a variety of weaves and finishes, printed on one or both sides in large patterns, usually floral. Made of cotton or linen, it was used chiefly for curtains and slip covers. The name probably came from the town in Normandy, France.

Crewel wool

WORSTED YARN, loosely twisted and used for embroidery and fancywork. It was also formerly used for fringes and LACES.

Damask

Firm, reversible, glossy fabric woven in intricate patterns so that one side has a satin WARP design with FILLING face background and the other side is in reverse. It was made on draw looms and JACQUARD LOOMS and used for table linens, upholstery and hangings, and occasionally for garments. The name comes from Damascus, whence the fabric originated. It was first brought to the Western world by Marco Polo in the thirteenth century.

Floss silk

Coarse, tangled silk-fibres from the outside of the cocoon; less lustrous than real silk, but strong.

Ingrain

Fabric of YARNS dyed before being woven or knitted.

Lace

Needlepoint lace is made with a single thread and a needle using embroidery stitches, principally the buttonhole stitch. Pillowlace – so-called from being made on a small pillow – or bobbin lace, comes from a multitude of threads wound for convenience on to bobbins, so that the lace can be created in a range of twists and plaits combining various numbers of threads. In the United States, lacemaking was a homecraft and did not become established on a commercial basis until the introduction of lace machines late in the nineteenth century. In England, on the other hand, the advent of machine-made lace had wide effects on the industry. The traditional centres of handmade lace were at Honiton in Devon, southwest England, and in the East Midlands, especially Buckinghamshire and Northamptonshire. In 1808 John Heathcoat of Nottingham took out the first patent for a bobbin-net machine which precipitated a rapid growth in the production of embroidered net. The designs of handmade laces were copied and adapted and contemporary white embroidery also influenced the technique. Together with the continual reduction of import duties on French and Belgian lace from the end of the Napoleonic Wars up till their final abolition in 1860, this development caused a decline in the handmade side of the lace industry, though some kind of equilibrium between machine- and hand-produced wares was reached in the 1860s. Honiton lace was given a stimulus by royal patronage in the 1840s, beginning with Queen Victoria's wedding-dress which was trimmed with lace to the value of £1,000. The industry consequently experienced a period of prosperity in the 1850s, before a further decline, despite a brave showing at the Great Exhibition of 1851. In the 1870s there was much restoration carried out on seventeenth-century Venetian needlepoint. The East Midlands had always catered for less exalted tastes than Devon, and produced light bobbin lace for the middle classes, mostly trimmings, insertions and borders. At the beginning of the century, it enlarged its scope to include shawls and other more complicated items but after 1815, with the influx of Continental lace and increasing competition from the mills, it too experienced a slump. At the 1862 International Exhibition, following the boom years of 1851 to 1857, the goods produced were mainly of a coarse, Maltese type. By 1878 the struggle between the two techniques of production was over, the *Art-Journal* catalogue of the Paris Exhibition of that year declaring: 'when machine-made is compared with hand-made lace, the superiority of the latter does not seem to the initiated so great as to warrant the enormous difference of cost'. This trend was becoming clear even in the 1840s which witnessed the setting up of a Government School for lace designs in Nottingham and the invention of John Livesey's lace-curtain machine. At the end of the century handmade lace became a suitable branch of fancywork for amateurs, and instruction books on how to make Honiton lace were published as early as the 1870s.

Madras muslin

Muslin is a soft cotton fabric of loose, firm, plain weave, bleached or unbleached, used for dresses, shirts, undergarments, pillowcases and sheets. Madras muslin is heavily figured, sometimes in colour.

Needlework pictures

Fancywork developed from the delicate furniture-coverings of pattern-woven silks and satins at the end of the eighteenth century. The embroidered pictures differed from their predecessors in general spirit and intention, as well as by the materials and techniques employed. The designs ranged from landscape through topography and portraits to mythological subjects – all on a ground material of fine linen, CANVAS, silk or satin. They were usually framed in black glass. The most typical were the mourning pictures, in particular in the United States, for example those dedicated to George Washington. Many of the most elaborate were the work of schoolgirls.

Paisley shawl

By the late 1770s the fashion for shawls, originating in the 'Kashmirs' brought back from India, had caught on in England and Scotland. Import duties were imposed on these exotic articles but demand continued – even with a duty of 81% in 1812 – inspiring English and Continental weavers to try their hand. Paisley, in Renfrewshire, Scotland, having outstripped its rival Edinburgh, became renowned for shawls woven in imitation of Kashmir work. 'Cashmere' wool was used as a substitute for the fine hair of the Tibetan goat used in Kashmir. This came from goats of the same strain, but transported to the less exacting climates of England and North America. By c. 1805, plain-centred shawls might have narrow, floral borders sewn on them, and occasionally the central field was enlivened with a repetitive pattern, known as the spade middle. Geometrical Persian patterns followed in c. 1815 and gradually, Kashmir patterns were imitated, including the Indian pine pattern, but were necessarily restricted in scope until Paisley adopted the JACQUARD LOOM and spouline card action in about 1835. From 1845 to 1860 through the use of Cashmere wool, the patterns were as elaborate as the original Kashmirs and the texture nearly as fine. From then on came a gradual deterioration. The primary colours approved in the shawls of the Regency were replaced in the 1840s by delicate harmonies, but after 1860 a much more violent contrast was preferred, though many shawls were also made in white or black. True Paisleys are woven shawls made on hand looms, though embroidered and printed shawls were made in the town itself. Paisley shawls woven on the Jacquard loom were priced in 1850 at from £5 to £25 guineas. The time required for weaving ranged from three days to a week. By comparison, printed shawls would be made, twenty or thirty in a week, to sell from

7s 6d to £5. Queen Victoria wore a Paisley shawl at a royal christening in 1842.

Patchwork

Mosaic of fragments of materials sewn edge to edge, although some so-called patchwork quilts are made of applied work. In England patchwork quilts originated in the eighteenth century. Most patterns were geometrical or formal, such as *Honeycomb*, which was composed entirely of hexagons, and the most popular design. Other patterns, such as *Shell* and various feather patterns were taken from traditional quilting designs. American patchwork quilts of the eighteenth and nineteenth centuries show an amazing variety of patterns of much greater elaboration than English examples: there are over 300 named designs, many of them with a religious origin. One of the most striking and common traditional patterns is the *Star of Bethlehem*, an eight-pointed star, worked either as a single central motif, surrounded by smaller stars, or as a number of small stars of equal size regularly arranged on a white ground. Other quilts were made with applied colour patches on a white ground elaborately quilted with geometrical, feather or floral designs.

Plush

Woollen or WORSTED pile cloth, the pile being $\frac{1}{8}$ in (3 mm) more in height and longer than velvet. The term is derived through the French *peluche* from Latin *pilus*, meaning a hair. The cloth is compact and bristly and used chiefly for capes, coats and upholstery.

Repp

Fabric with a ribbed effect: the word is a corruption of rib.

Ribbon

Ribbonwork, embroidery in fine, narrow silk ribbons, often combined with CHENILLE thread and aerophane (muslin gauze). Originated in the eighteenth century, and was popular in England and France, especially for dress-trimmings, bags, handscreens and other small articles. As early as the eighteenth century, both plain and figured ribbons were woven on single hand looms in Coventry. In 1823 the JACQUARD LOOM arrived in Coventry, but the French weavers were more practised in its use and with the lifting in 1826 of the prohibition on the import of French silks, figured ribbons from Basle and St Étienne flooded the market. To prove their ability to compete on equal terms, the Coventry weavers produced ribbons for the Great Exhibition of 1851. The ribbons were designed by a pupil of the Coventry School of Design, which had been established for just such a purpose as

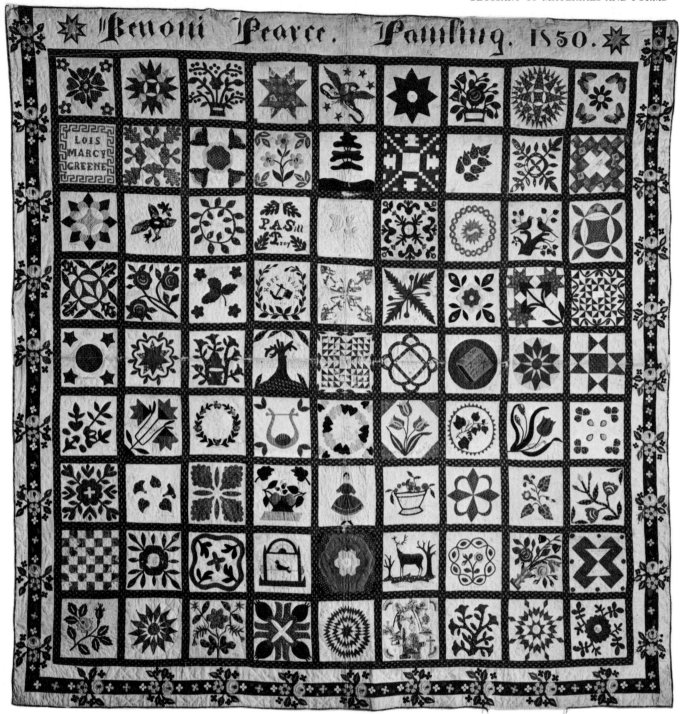

Album quilt, American, 1850. Pierced and appliqued cotton. Each square was made by a friend or relative with a different motif. Smithsonian Institution.

this in 1843. In 1860, with the repeal of duty on imported French goods, many of the Coventry firms went bankrupt with the notable exception of Thomas Stevens, who adapted his looms to weave pictures, book-markers and other novelties. Stevens' woven pictures were sold in cardboard mounts and known as Stevengraphs.

Samplers

Embroidered panels, originally intended as a reference-sheet of stitches and patterns and later as an exercise for beginners. Both English and American Victorian examples are usually square in shape, signed and dated. The introduction of the alphabet, religious texts and mottoes or verses was common. Maps, a common design in England, were much less common in the United States and, when they were made, were frequently of one State only. By the mid-nineteenth century, however, the wide availability of patterns and materials for the popular

BERLIN WOOLWORK put an end to all the more individual expressions in embroidery.

Throw

Light-weight piece of fabric, usually a scarf, shawl or blanket.

Tussore, tusseh, tussah or wild silk

Product of the uncultivated silkworm, which feeds on the leaves of the oak tree, castor oil plant, cherry tree and uncultivated mulberry tree. This produces a strong, flat silk fibre, irregular in diameter and usually undyed. It is not as soft as true silk. The word possibly derives from the form of the cocoon.

Utrecht Velvet
Lower grade of fabric than the ordinary velvet, used in upholstery.

Velveteen
Velvet made from cotton instead of silk and possessing a short, close pile. Used for coats, suits, dresses, children's wraps and draperies. In America, velveteens have a FILLING (weft) pile as opposed to the WARP pile of velvets.

Leaf and Rose, *designed c. 1882 by the Century Guild. Velveteen. The aim of the Guild was 'to render all branches of art the sphere no longer of the tradesman but of the artist'. William Morris Gallery.*

Worsted fabric
Made from worsted YARNS that have been COMBED, laid quite parallel and made of equal length; they are then twisted to make a regular, smooth yarn, which is bright, elastic and very strong. They are easy to dye and used in the manufacture of suitings and dress fabrics including serge. The name comes from the small town of Worstead in Norfolk, England, where a particularly fine wool fabric of that name originated.

Glossary of Techniques, Terms and Inventions

Aniline dye
Aniline or anilin, is a colourless oily compound, used as a base of coal-tar dyes. Aniline dyes began to replace vegetable dyes in English textiles in the 1860s, the first being solferino and magenta. In 1857 Perkins discovered aniline mauve and in 1859 came Vergnin and Regnard's aniline red.

Art needlework
Form of popular embroidery which, by the mid 1870s had replaced BERLIN WOOLWORK almost entirely. Its chief characteristic, whatever the technique, was a use of rather sombre colours, no doubt as a reaction against the harsh and gaudy colours of the BERLIN WOOLS. The most popular form was CREWEL WORK, usually worked in CREWEL WOOLS but also in silk. In the United States the craze was as widespread as in England, although the term 'crewel work' was not in popular use in this country until somewhat later. It was not really suitable for upholstery, but ran riot over tidies for covering the backs and arms of chairs, curtains and *portières*, wall-hangings, counterpanes and coverlets.

Berlin woolwork
Ancient, durable all-over type of embroidery or fancywork in which the principal stitch is CROSS STITCH. Done on CANVAS, it was also called cushion-style, canvas embroidery and canvas work, but since 1820 more usually it has been called after the garishly coloured WORSTEDS imported from Berlin. The first thirty years of the Victorian era were dominated by the fashion for Berlin woolwork and it virtually ousted all other types of decorative needlework.

Rug, English, c. 1860. Berlin woolwork. This needlework was very popular in the Victorian period; sometimes used in conjunction with beadwork although this was less usual in the 1860s. Mayorcas Ltd.

The designs were hand-coloured on squared paper and were copied stitch by stitch on to square-meshed canvas. The first Berlin patterns were published in 1804, and in the 1830s were imported, together with the wool, in great numbers. The designs were mostly flowers or exotic birds. The fashion persisted into the 1870s but by the 1860s a change was coming about in the type of patterns and in the colouring, with geometric designs, ornamental scrolls and formalized acanthus and vine leaves replacing the sprawling naturalistic blooms and the colours changing to browns and softer greens. Parts of the design were often worked in beads or silk. SAMPLERS on long strips of canvas showing various patterns worked in Berlin wools were also to be found.

Carding
Preparation of wool, flax or cotton YARN for spinning, by separating, cleaning and partly straightening the fibres. Carded fibres are spun perpendicular to the alignment of the fibres: both carding and COMBING were done by hand before the invention of a machine.

Combing
Process of removing the short fibres from a long-staple wool and straightening out the long fibres in the lengths. It produces a finer, smoother YARN than CARDING alone: the combed fibres are then spun parallel to the alignment of the fibres. Combing is only used for the best quality yarns of wool and cotton, the latter after 1840.

Combing machine
Between 1790 and 1792 the Rev. Dr Cartwright, who had invented the power loom, tried to invent a machine comber, but was not successful and the first one was patented in 1827 by Platt and Collier in England. In 1846 a Frenchman, Josué Heilmann, took out a patent and in 1851 Donisthorpe & Lister of Manningham, near Bradford, Yorkshire, brought out a patent for what became known as a nip-comber. There were several other rivals in the field in the mid-nineteenth century.

Crewel stitch
Crewel itself is a thin WORSTED YARN used for tapestry and embroidery. Crewel stitch, also known as stem stitch, is an embroidery stitch whose lines follow the outline of the shape being stitched. The needle is brought out each time at the left-hand side of the previous stitch and proceeds upwards. The stitch is even and regular and is used for solid FILLING, imparting a woven appearance to the shape filled. Crewel stitch is not to be confused with crewel work, where Oriental designs, often termed Jacobean, are worked on strong fabric in coloured

WORSTEDS. Many stitches are employed in this sort of embroidery.

Cross stitch

Decorative stitch which forms an X, used on dresses, children's clothes and linens, also on CANVAS in needle tapestry-work and BERLIN WOOLWORK, in which each cross is completed before the next is begun.

Cylinder printing

First successful cylinder printing was done by the Scotsman, Thomas Bell, in 1785 at Monsey, near Preston, England. Already by 1770 he had invented a flat-bed method of printing textiles from engraved copper plates. In cylinder printing the design was transferred by engraving on to copper rollers in a repeat pattern; the rollers were then covered with dye and the material passed over under pressure. In the nineteenth century as many as six colours could be printed at once, using six rollers, each inked with a different dye. The invention is first recorded in the United States as early as 1815, at Philadelphia. It speeded the production of printed fabric from a few hundred yards to thousands of yards per day.

Draw loom

Before the invention of the JACQUARD LOOM the draw loom was used for the production of patterned cloth weaves. All the WARP threads required to make the same movement were tied together in a bunch and each bunch was then attached to one strong cord, which extended upwards to a platform where an assistant, (the 'draw boy'), could raise or lower them as required by the design. One early improvement was that of extending the cords to enable the draw boy to work on the floor at the side of the loom; this was followed by the provision of additional cords, which simplified the work of selecting the HEDDLES. Jacquard's later contribution was to facilitate the weaving of much more intricate patterns and to eliminate the need for a draw boy.

Filling

YARN running crosswise of the woven fabric, at right angles to the WARP. It is also known as the weft. An individual thread of weft is called a pick.

Heddle or heald

Small cords or wires through which the WARP is passed in a loom, by means of which the threads are separated into two sets or more so as to allow the passage of the shuttle bearing the FILLING.

Indigo-discharge printing

First used in c. 1806 and later revived by MORRIS. The cloth was first dyed plain, then the pattern was printed in a 'discharge' chemical which took the dye out of the cloth, leaving a white pattern or a pattern of some colour other than the ground. Indigo itself is the most valuable of the vegetable dyestuffs.

Jacquard loom

Invented by Joseph-Marie Jacquard of

Floral pattern, Lewis F. Day, designed 1898 for Turnbull & Stockdale Ltd. Discharge-printed cotton. Victoria and Albert Museum.

Lyons, France, in 1804, to facilitate the weaving of figured fabrics in the loom. Elaborate cloth weaves were produced by the substitution of perforated strips of cardboard punched according to intricate design for the ordinary and restricted number of HEDDLE frames and pattern chains. These perforations, in connection with rods and cords, regulated the raising of the stationary WARP-threaded mechanisms, thus procuring a

Hooked rug made in Cleveland, Ohio, 1876. Wool. This rug is made from strips of wool fabrics which have been hooked into the ground fabric. Smithsonian Institution.

pattern as the punched cards were fed into the loom in a similar way to that used in a barrel-organ.

Mill and die process
Refinement of CYLINDER PRINTING. One roller, known as the die, is engraved with a fine overall pattern from a drawing. The second cylinder on to which the pattern is transferred in relief from the first is called the mill, which is then used to engrave the design on to the printing cylinder. By using these two, overall repeating background patterns were produced. By 1835, two rollers, usually one inked in black and the other in red,

could be run together, and by about 1840 the machines and dye substances were sufficiently perfected to allow the printing of many colours consecutively as cloth rolled rapidly over the rollers.

Pantograph machine
Apparatus for copying the artist's designs on to a copper printing roller to any scale within the capacity of the device. A dummy point traced over the original drawing moves a series of arms to a stylus that reproduces the traced line in larger or smaller scale. It was first introduced in 1834.

Rug hooking
Technique of rug making popular between 1840 and 1900. The background material was homespun linen, factory-woven cloth or BURLAP. The cloth scraps were cut out in strips and a hook was used to draw these up in loops from the back of the ground fabric. Sometimes the loops were cut when made, sometimes not, and in some rugs the loops varied in length to give a raised or sculptured effect to parts of the design. The best material for the pile was wool. By about 1870 commercial patterns were available.

Tent stitch
Single stitch slanting from left to right over one cross of canvas. Each stitch lies across one vertical and one horizontal thread. It can be worked horizontally or diagonally on the canvas and is also known as *petit point*.

Warp
Series of threads placed lengthways in the loom over any desired width. Also called the chain or twist. An individual thread of warp is called an end.

Weave
Plain weaving is the simplest weave, in which each FILLING YARN passes successively over and under each WARP yarn, to form an even surface. Twill weaving has diagonal ridges, or ribs, produced by causing the filling threads to pass over one and under two or more threads of the warp, instead of over and under in regular progression.

Yarn
Continuous strand of spun fibre, distinct from thread, which is made up of several yarns twisted together.

Bibliography

ALFORD, LADY MARIAN. *Needlework as Art,* London, 1886
APPLETON, NATHAN. *Introduction of the Power Loom and Origin of Lowell,* Lowell, Mass., 1858
ASLIN, ELIZABETH. *The Aesthetic Movement,* London, 1969
ATWATER, MARY M. *The Shuttle-Craft Book of American Hand Weaving,* New York, 1951
BIGELOW-HARTFORD CARPET CO., *A Century of Carpet and Rug-making in America,* New York, 1925
BOLTON, ETHEL STANWOOD, and JOHNSTON COE, EVA. *American Samplers,* Boston, Mass., 1921
BROCHETT, L. P. *The Silk Industry in America,* New York, 1876
CLARK, FIONA. *William Morris,* London, 1974
COLE, ARTHUR HARRISON. *The American Wool Manufacture,* New York, 1926, reprinted, 1969
COOK, CLARENCE. *The House Beautiful,* New York, 1878
COOPER, GRACE ROGERS. *The Copp Family Textiles,* Washington D.C., 1971
FINLEY, RUTH E. *Old Patchwork Quilts and the Women Who Made Them,* Philadelphia, 1929
HARBESON, GEORGIANA BROWN. *American Needlework,* New York, 1938
HAYES, JOHN L. *American Textile Machinery,* Cambridge, Mass., 1879
HENDERSON, PHILIP. *William Morris, His Life, Work and Friends,* London, 1967, reprinted Harmondsworth, 1972
LOCKWOOD and GLAISTER. *Art Embroidery,* London, 1878
MADSEN, S. TSCHUDI. *Art Nouveau,* London, 1967
MONTGOMERY, FLORENCE M. *Printed Textiles,* New York, 1970
MONTGOMERY, JAMES. *A Practical Detail of the Cotton Manufacture of the United States of America and the State of the Cotton Manufacture of that Country Contrasted and Compared with that of Great Britain,* Glasgow, 1840, reprinted, New York, 1968
MORRIS, BARBARA J. *Victorian Embroidery,* London, 1962
MORRIS, BARBARA J. 'Victorian Textiles', *Connoisseur Period Guides,* Early Victorian, 1830-1860, London, 1958
MORTON, JOCELYN. *Three Generations in a Family Textile Firm,* London, 1971
SWYGERT, MRS LUTHER M. (ed.) *Heirlooms from Old Looms,* (Coverlets), Chicago, 1955
WATKINSON, RAYMOND. *William Morris as Designer,* London, 1967
WHITE, GEORGE S. *Memoir of Samuel Slater,* Philadelphia, 1836
WYCKOFF, WILLIAM C. *The Silk Goods of America,* New York, 1880

OPPOSITE *Dining room at 7, Hammersmith Terrace, home of Sir Emery Walker, d. 1930. This London house, belonging to a member of the Arts & Crafts Movement, retains its period interior. Wallpaper Willow; textiles Brother Rabbit, both designed by William Morris.*

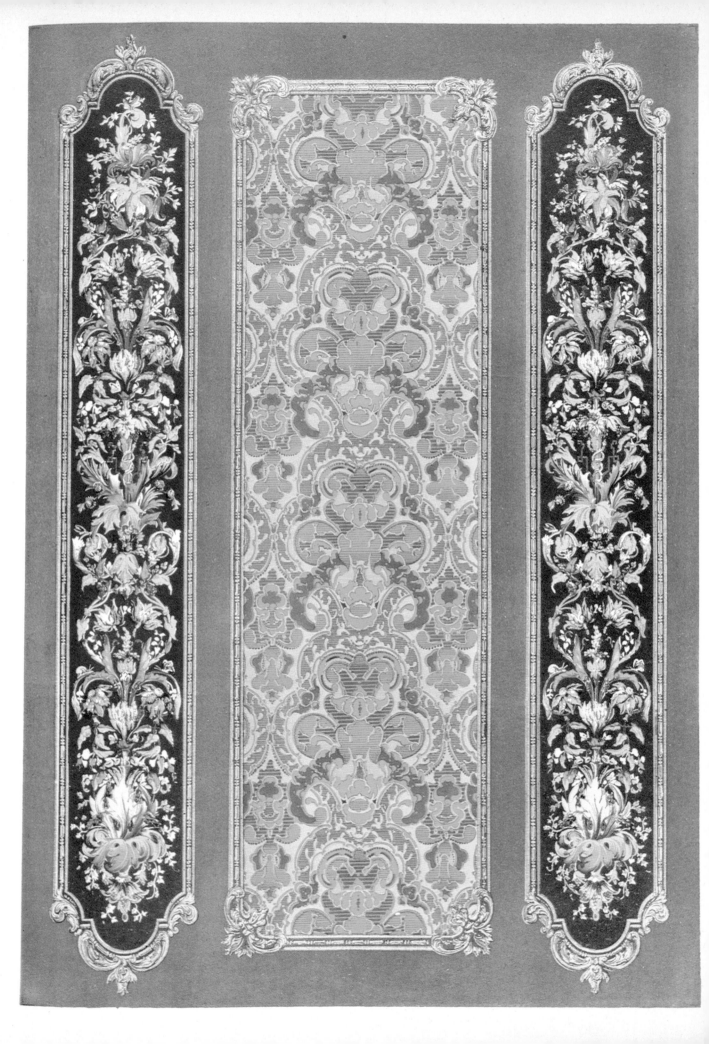

Wallpaper

BRITISH

The rapid change in fashionable nineteenth-century wallpaper design is commented on by writers throughout the Victorian period. In fact, most architects and decorators preferred not to illustrate their comments on wallpaper in books and magazines for fear that the examples shown might become obsolete before the article or book could be published.

Taxes on the production of paper and the printing of wallpapers, in existence since Queen Anne's reign, severely restricted the development of the wallpaper industry in Britain. Although a machine to produce 'endless lengths' instead of sheets was perfected in 1805, because the legislators could not agree on a method of levying taxes, it was not allowed to go into production until 1830. Across the Channel, the absence of restrictive taxation and a congenial attitude towards the services performed by qualified designers led to the production of artistically superior wallpapers of worldwide appeal. British tax laws prohibited any importation of wallpaper into Britain until 1825, when the law was relaxed. At this time an import tax was levied at the rate of 1s per square yard (·86 sq. m), or approximately 7s per piece. These high taxes did not prevent the French product from selling very well.

Expansion of the Industry

Early in Queen Victoria's reign, the development of a truly workable machine to print the recently permitted 'endless lengths' of paper, coupled with the reduction in 1834 and 1846 and eventual elimination in 1861 of the British tax on paper, led to increasing expansion in

wallpaper production, from 1,000,000 pieces in 1834 to 19,000,000 pieces in 1861.

Another contributive factor to this expansion was the series of exhibitions beginning with the Manchester Exhibition of 1846. The third exhibition of this series, the Manchester Exhibition of 1849, was so successful that it inspired the *Journal of Design and Manufactures 1849–1852*, with its tipped-in swatches of wallpapers and fabrics currently in production and led directly to the introduction of a wallpaper section at the Great Exhibition of 1851, where thirty English firms exhibited wallpaper and 25,000 square feet (2,322 sq. m) of wall space were occupied by examples of wallpaper.

The excesses of the early nineteenth-century decorative arts, as depicted in the books of G. Cooper and George Smith, are superbly illustrated by the frequently quoted passage from Maria Edgeworth's *The Absentee* (1812), when Mr Soho describes the variety of available designs of wallpaper to a client. After talking of his 'encoinieres', his 'Turkish Tent Drapery' in apricot cloth, crimson velvet or in fluted crimson satin, his 'Chancelières with chimeras at the corners', his 'Statira Canopy' and his 'Seraglio Ottomans', he unrolls and shows his 'Alhambra hangings', his 'Trebizond Trellice', his 'Chinese Pagoda' and his 'Egyptian Hieroglyphic' papers. All this to be illuminated by his 'Sphynx' candelabras and his 'Phoenix' Argands.

Fashionable Designs

Designs popular in the early years of Queen Victoria's reign included many that had long been standard, particularly the imitations of costly fabrics, including loopings and festoons of drapery, the architectural motifs – mouldings, cornices and dados – and the imitations of marble and woodgrain. The mould-

ings and cornices were frequently printed in order to allow a skilled paperhanger to arrange for proper shadow from natural sources of light in each section of a wall or room. One such narrow architectural border of the 1840s in the collection of Gallier House, New Orleans, is printed sixteen strips to the width and has the same moulding printed in four bands with the light from the top left, four bands with the light from the top right, four bands with the light from the bottom left and four bands with the light from the bottom right. Wallpaper ceiling roses were also printed right through the century.

Judged by today's standards, the least desirable of the architectural papers were those depicting *trompe l'œil* statues of historical or literary figures, complete with plinth, and *trompe l'œil* picture frames containing still lifes of pendant dead game.

The sample-books of the 1830s, '40s and '50s show 'staircase' papers, frequently Gothic in design, in addition to the mock marble, granite and woodgrain papers that were almost *de rigueur* for such use through more than half the century.

Papers for the major reception rooms were frequently flocked, in total or in part, the colours often clear and brilliant (royal blue being among the most popular) and the designs often built around a floral motif. The French mural or landscape papers, so popular in America until about 1860, were never appreciated in the British Isles.

In the 1840s the pilaster-type papers became increasingly fashionable. These had broad floral and strapwork borders and superimposed corners to divide the walls of a room into panels. Numerous examples of this style were shown by both English and French manufacturers at the 1851 and 1862 Exhibitions. One example designed in 1851 by Wm. Woollams & Co. and pictured in M. Digby Wyatt's *Industrial Arts of the Nineteenth Century* required seventy

Ogival pattern probably by William Wool-lams & Co., mid-nineteenth century. Block-printed in distemper and metal gilt with two dense applications of flock. Whitworth Art Gallery.

RIGHT Trellis, *William Morris (1834-96), 1862. Block-printed in distemper. This design was derived from a wooden trellis in the Red House; the birds and insects were drawn by Philip Webb. Whitworth Art Gallery.*

blocks to print the design at the then extravagant cost of £140 for the blocks.

Although machinery to print wallpaper became more and more sophisticated throughout the 1860s, most papers with any pretension to quality were still being printed from woodblocks. Following the severe criticism of three-dimensional, or *trompe l'œil*, designs shown in the 1851 Exhibition, wallpaper designers gradually turned to flatter and less technically ambitious patterns – but the change was very gradual and not fully implemented until sometime after 1862 and the International Exhibition of that year.

Effect of the Arts and Crafts Movement on Wallpaper

William Morris and his friends, dissatisfied with the furnishing items commercially available, founded in 1861 Morris, Marshall, Faulkner & Co., incorporating a team of craftsmen intent on producing furniture, carpets, stained glass, fabrics, wallpapers, etc. to their own specifications. Morris' first wallpaper design, *Trellis*, of 1862, was, as it happened, his third wallpaper design to be printed. Originally appealing to a very limited clientele, the taste for this

type of design soon spread over a broader base to become the foundation for England's supremacy in the decorative arts of the later nineteenth century.

Diaper patterns, large and small, each shown in three or four colours, fill two exciting sample-books of 1865–6 in the collections of the Victoria and Albert Museum, London. Inspiration for these ranges from the vaguely to the decidedly Gothic. All have at least a little gilding in their colour schemes, which although frequently composed of strong colour, do make use of more muted tones than ten years earlier.

Charles L. Eastlake, in his *Hints on Household Taste*, (1868), stated that paperhangings should never be allowed to cover the whole area of a wall from skirting to ceiling; he recommended the use of a chair-rail with a plain dado of 2–3 ft (60–90 cm) in height and a space or frieze just below the ceiling in addition to the side wall paper.

Complementary Wallpaper

In 1875 the first group of dado, fill and frieze papers designed *en suite* was created by Brightwon Binyon and printed by Jeffrey & Co. This consisted of a dado of corn and poppies; a frieze of flying swallows and the filling, a diaper pattern with a dividing border of dragonflies. Walter Crane's second wallpaper design (the first being a nursery paper), the *Margarete* suite of 1876, consisting of the *Alcestis* frieze, *Margarete* filling and *Lily and Dove* dado, also printed by Jeffrey & Co., won two medals and a diploma at the 1876 Centennial Exposition in Philadelphia.

These complementary groups of wallpaper, which also often included a ceiling paper to make four designs *en suite*, continued in popularity until about 1890. The first of these to be designed specifically to fit the rake of a staircase dates from about 1880.

The French never fully accepted the idea of two-dimensional design and continued to publish patterns based on the Empire and Louis styles until the advent of Art Nouveau.

Later Fashions in Wallpaper

Embossing, although first patented as a workable process in 1829 and used regularly since that date, became increasingly important as the century progressed. Linoleum-like wallcoverings with raised designs and exotic names, became legion: patterns were produced

Margarete suite, Walter Crane (1845-1915), 1876. (Top) Alcestis frieze. (Above left) Lily and Dove dado. (Above right) Margarete filling. This was Crane's second wallpaper design and one of the first group of dado, fill and frieze papers to be designed en suite. *Victoria and Albert Museum.*

such as *Tynecastle*, 1874; *Lincrusta Walton*, 1877; *Lignomur*, 1880; *Supercoriam*, 1881; *Anaglypta*, 1887; *Cameoid*, 1888; *Calcorian*, 1892 and *Cordelova*. Many earlier designs included flocking, but after 1885 the concentration was on high relief and the imitation of stamped leathers. Gilded decoration on embossed designs was frequent from 1860 onwards, but this too was most popular at the end of the century when almost every pattern was available in an all gilded colourway.

The taste for 'damask' papers, with their contrast of lustrous grounds and matt designs, or vice versa, reached its apogee in the late 1870s and early 1880s,

Golden Lustre Silks and Crystal Damasks being among the most popular types.

Throughout the century much effort went into attempts to provide a washable, or sanitary, wallpaper. Early patents included a varnish afterprocess of 1802, the use of Japan oil and turpentine in 1828, and baked on hardened distemper in 1851; but the first really practical sanitary paper was one imitating oak grain and printed in oil colours in 1853. Further patents followed in 1863, 1869 and 1871, all for single-colour sanitaries. In 1884 the first multi-colour sanitary was offered.

Crown papers, in which each strip is topped by a separately applied piece of

paper both to terminate the design and to provide a frieze around the top of the wall, had been in irregular use since the 1840s but became high fashion in the last decade of the nineteenth and first decade of the twentieth century. In fact the end of the century could well be labelled the 'frieze period', as design concentration was on the upper portion of all walls.

Surprisingly, following the great advance of technological development by the British artisan in printing, embossing, flocking and gilding wallpaper by machine, the end of the century also saw increased attention paid to hand stencilling and blocking.

Lewis F. Day's comment in 1882 could have been said solely of Victorian wallpapers: 'Our ornament is of its century, in as much as it is prosaic, mechanical, fickle, self assertive and none too lofty in its ambition – nor is it guiltless of the besetting sin of the age we live in, viz cleverness.'

Samuel J. Dornsife

AMERICAN

The French Influence

Surviving advertisements from a wide variety of sources indicate the tremendous popularity of wallpaper among the middle and upper classes in the American Colonies after the middle of the eighteenth century.

Despite the fact that Plunket Fleeson advertised wallpaper in Philadelphia in 1739, the industry was slow to expand in the Colonies and it was not until the last two decades of the eighteenth century that manufacturers became well distributed up and down the East Coast.

Every port had its importers of both English and French wallpapers, who jubilantly advertised their stocks as each shipment from abroad arrived. A large-scale wallpaper dealer in Philadelphia in 1793 advertised 15,000 pieces in 600 different patterns of from two to twenty-six colours each.

Natural Wonders, *A. L. Diament & Co., Philadelphia, first issued in 1834. Panel made up of nine strips printed in tempera colour. One of many scenic and mural wallpapers. A. L. Diament & Co.*

The opinion has been frequently expressed that, in the period between 1780 and 1870, American taste in wallpaper followed French example owing to sympathy with the French for their help in the War of Independence (1776–83). This taste for things French was not, however, seen as strongly in other fields, as would have been expected had this been the case.

A more likely factor would seem to be the exuberance, vitality and artistic achievement of the early nineteenth-century French paper stainers. Besides, it is known that the government policy of heavy taxation (and even the inability over a period of more than twenty years to establish a tax policy), together with poor design-manufacturer relations, restricted and confined the development of the wallpaper industry in Britain.

In any case, French wallpapers must have been as popular in the United States in the early nineteenth century as they were in France itself. The few surviving examples might indicate that this is not true of the fabric papers, which through *trompe l'œil* effects could make a room appear to be hung with silk, satin or velvet complete with swags, fringes, ropes, and tassels; but, contrastingly, the many surviving examples of the mural or scenic type of paper indicate the tremendous popularity of these in the United States.

Scenic Wallpaper

At first, many of these scenic and mural wallpapers illustrated stories from Classical mythology and this may, in itself, provide a clue to their popularity. After all, sympathy with the Greeks in their war for independence led to the full development of the Greek Revival style in architecture in the United States, and to the naming of countless communities as the frontier moved westward across what is now Eastern and East Central United States. *Telemachus, Antenor, Cupid and Psyche, Olympic Fêtes* and

ABOVE The War of Independence, *A. L. Diament & Co., Philadelphia, first issued in 1838. Military skirmishes were super-imposed against the same background that was used for the series,* Scenic America. *A. L. Diament & Co.*

Galerie Mythologique led to *Vues de Suisse, Monuments de Paris, Les Incas* and *Vues d'Italie*, and then to *Scenic America*, with views of the Niagara Falls, West Point, New York Bay, Boston Harbour, Natural Bridge and a dance of the Winnebago Indians, produced in 1834 specifically for the American trade.

Scenic America was so successful that four years later, in 1838, an alternative version entitled *War of Independence* was published using the same background scenes, but superimposing military skir-mishes between English and American troops in place of the civilians at peaceful occupations who featured in *Scenic America*. Both these series have retained their popularity to the present day and are still being printed, in the most part, from the original woodblocks.

A variety of perhaps two hundred such scenic or mural wallpapers was circulated in the United States. Throughout the 1860s wallpaper dealers were selling enough to justify the expense of having blocks made for their advertisements in city directories, which show scenes from the various sets. Concurrent with the hand printing of wallpapers, John Howell of Philadelphia had, in 1844, imported from England the first steam-driven colour-printing machine.

Contemporary Viewpoints on Wallpaper

As in England, there was plenty of criticism for the type of design offered, but little criticism of wallpaper, *per se*. In 1850, Downing said, 'Paperhangings

Advertisement for Finn & Burton's 'paper hanging warehouse', 1849. This fashion-able Philadelphia wallpaper shop was based at its Arch Street address from 1847 to 1850. Author's Collection.

offer so easy, economical and agreeable a means of decorating or furnishing the walls of an apartment.' But he also said, 'avoid all flashy and gaudy' and 'all imitations of church windows'. He recommended that panels of wallpaper in harmonious or contrasting colours, cut in such strips as design and wall areas required, should be laid on walls of a uniform colour, thus giving an effect similar to that produced by a poly-chromatic artist at one fifth the cost; he estimated that a room 24 ft × 18 ft (7·32 m × 5·49 m) should cost $16 finished this way. The pilaster papers offered by most manufacturers would

have provided a similar decoration with a much more professional appearance.

In 1851, Gervase Wheeler makes a similar recommendation, saying: 'En-caustic [sanitary] paper, one colour and without pattern may very easily be used in such a manner as at small cost to produce all the effect of artistic fresco-or oil-painting,' or pilaster paper, 'in simple lines or in larger surfaces in accordance with a prearranged design.'

The catalogue for the 1853 Crystal Palace Exhibition in New York City (officially entitled *New York Exhibition, The Industry of all Nations*) shows two full-page illustrations of elaborate pilaster-type architectural wallpapers with comment in line with criticism by Richard Redgrave, R.A., on items exhi-bited in London in 1851:

We employ this page to represent a specimen of paperhangings exhibited by Jules Desfossé of Paris. The

Pilaster paper, *Morant & Boyd, London, 1853. Exhibited in the New York Crystal Palace Exhibition of 1853 and featured in the exhibition catalogue. It was chosen to appeal to the American market. Author's Collection.*

RIGHT Pilaster paper, *Jules Desfossé, Paris, c. 1853. Described in the New York Crystal Palace Exhibition catalogue as an architectural paper 'designed to cover the wall . . . to the exclusion of all paintings.' Author's Collection.*

opposite page is occupied with another example selected from the contributions of Messrs Morant and Boyd of London. Both of these specimens are examples of architectural decorations, designed to cover the wall and adorn it to the exclusion of all paintings and similar items of taste. Paperhangings of this description are admissible in public halls and saloons and sometimes perhaps in the entrance hall, but not elsewhere, of a private residence.

Cleaveland & Backus comment in 1856:

In apartments of regular shape, plain papers may be used with good effect, the ground being first laid and then surrounded with border strips of different colour in panel fashion. Next to the ceiling a border of contrasting colour should always be placed.

They did not favour grained or marbled papers, or graining on wood.

How different are the suggestions from the samples shown in the sample books. A dealer in New Orleans, in 1857, advertised 'the largest and best stock of paperhanging in this city consisting in part of gold, velvet, fresco, marble, stone, oak, granite, views, statuaries, ornaments and decorations of every description. Also on hand large stock

low and medium priced papers, gold and fancy borders, fire screens, etc.'

In 1859, Fowler & Wells suggest neutral tints such as grey or fawn with a white ceiling and say that an architectural paper must be in the same style as the house – no Gothic papers in Grecian houses.

Throughout the 1860s the critics advocated the use of a two-dimensional design, while the public continued to enjoy such decorative wallpapers as the crimson, garnet and gold velvet paper supplied for the East Room of the White House in 1861 by Carryl, the Philadelphia decorator, who advertised on occasion in *Godey's Lady's Book*.

As in Britain, all through the middle years of the century, mock marble, granite or grained papers were the most frequent choices for halls and stairs

The English Influence

Eastlake's *Hints on Household Taste* was as popular in the United States as in Britain. Whatever aversion may have previously existed to the English taste, it

was Walter Crane's *Margarete* suite which won outstanding acclaim at the Centennial Exhibition. In 1878, H. H. Holly could say that up until that time there had been little encouragement for importation of Morris patterns but that American taste was now improving. Until a few years before designs had often been so large that it was not unusual to do away with an important door in order to avoid interfering with the pattern. He also recommended wallpapers generally, considering them 'cheap, easily hung and highly furnishing in their effect'.

Other comments in 1878, this time by Harriet Spofford, were in favour of the 'powdery bloom' of a paperhanging as compared with a painted wall. She continues, 'France has hitherto produced the best, while Germany and Belgium have given the cheapest papers; but England has lately come to rival France'. Among the varieties available, she cites:

. . . common satin faced ones; the more desirable rough surfaced sort; the gilded, silvered and bronzed grounds; embossed gilt and mica;

imitation of silks and tapestries, cretonnes, chintzes; and raised and stamped velvets; some like delicate embroidered muslins and others like embossed Spanish leathers; thick Japanese papers; and others yet more expensive, thick and heavy; in addition to those for ceilings, dados and for friezes.

The greater number of these papers are conventional in design.

Mrs Jones and H. T. Williams in 1885 are still advising two-dimensional design as opposed to *trompe l'œil* effects and recommend 'lovely greys, pearl, sage, stone or that exquisite "ashes of roses tint" that has been copied from the imported paperhangings of the celebrated Morris Company of London.'

By 1888 Varney's recommendations include bright or brilliant shades for the dining room, bronze shades with slight points of gold for a library, slight soft shades of blue or light grey for bedrooms and rich cream colours with perhaps a little gold for parlours or drawing-rooms. He expressed the opinion that gilded papers were not needed to add to the richness of a room, and comments that *Lincrusta Walton*, recently introduced from England, by that date had a manufactory in Connecticut and an office in New York City at 41 Union Square. Varney also says:

Dados are rarely used upon parlors or drawing rooms; a frieze or border is always used and these are of widths varying from 6 in to 20 in [15·2 cm– 50·8 cm]. Dados are used in a library – not less than 26 in [66 cm] wide or more than 5 ft [1·52 m]; oftenest between 30 in and 40 in [91 cm– 122 cm]. Dining room dados are 30 in to 40 in in height.

The heavy embossed wallcoverings exemplified by *Lincrusta Walton* or *Tynecastle* were extremely popular over a long period of time and were still being shown in wallpaper sample-books of the 1920s.

The fashion for wallpaper was carried across the plains and round the Horn by the pioneers and settlers; contemporary accounts tell how to 'plaster' and apply wallpaper even to the side walls of a sod house.

In 1903 A. S. Jennings recommends the use of hand-stencilled accents on a wallpapered wall and of friezes entirely painted or stencilled above a wallpaper; he claims that, in his opinion, a perfectly plain ingrain or oatmeal paper with a bold, well-designed frieze is the perfection of good decoration, commenting further that while these ingrain papers had been common in the United States for at least fifteen years, they had only

recently become accepted in Great Britain.

For all its delicacy and fragility, especially when it had been stuck to a wall for some time, wallpaper was not easy to remove. Consequently, poor workmen allowed it to accumulate at the rate of about one layer every five years until a series of sixteen to twenty layers – an encyclopedia of wallpaper sequences – could often be found on the walls of older houses. The perfection of the wallpaper steamer in the 1930s, with its considerably easier and less messy removal process, destroyed much information about our nineteenth-century past before it was properly appreciated or documented.

Samuel J. Dornsife

Designers and Manufacturers

M. H. BIRGE & SONS
Firm established in Buffalo, New York, in 1834. It achieved one of the longest traditions among American wallpaper manufacturers specializing in a wide variety of papers, including complex panel decorations. In 1889 it advertised such exotic wares as 'Ecclesiastical Decorations, studied from the Mural paintings of Notre Dame'.

BROPHY, ANDREW FINGAL (d. 1912)
British draughtsman and architect who designed several damask papers and wallhangings in the Adam style.

BUMSTEAD, JOSIAH
Manufacturer established in Boston in 1796. In 1839 Bumstead travelled to Europe and visited the ZUBER factories in Alsace. He produced a large assortment of his own papers, as well as importing from France.

BURGES, WILLIAM (1827–81)
British architect and medievalist, he designed wallpapers exclusively for JEFFREY & CO., as well as jewelry, furniture and other *objets d'art*. His own London house was decorated as a model residence of the fifteenth century.

BUTTERFIELD, LINDSAY (1869–1948)
British designer of several papers for Essex & Co. based on stylized floral patterns such as poppies, tiger lilies and apple-blossom.

WILLIAM COOKE & SONS
Leeds firm who were pioneers in lustre papers. The firm supplied wallpapers to the Royal Family, including a green and gold flock paper for the Prince Consort's bedroom at Balmoral.

COTTERELL BROS LTD
Established in Bristol, Somerset, in 1844, they subsequently opened a branch in Bath. They were among the first to print imitations of wood grains for use as wallpaper, and to utilize a sophisticated block-printing plant. In 1897 they supplied Queen Victoria with a large quantity of papers for Osborne House on the Isle of Wight.

COWTAN & CO.
Old-established firm of Oxford Street, London, whose origins date back to the eighteenth century and who continued well into the twentieth century. It supplied high-quality wallpaper to most of the great historic houses of Britain, including Blenheim Palace and Woburn Abbey. Mawer Cowtan, head of the firm for some years, was himself a distinguished wallpaper designer and critic.

CRACE, JOHN GREGORY (1809–89)
Recognized English authority on the decorative arts, involved in an old-established family firm of decorators, who were one of the most respected houses during the early Victorian period. His father was employed by the Prince Regent on work at Windsor Castle and the Brighton Pavilion. Crace was associated with PUGIN in the execution of the papers for the new Houses of Parliament. His two lectures to the Royal Institution of British Architects in 1839 on the history and manufacture of paperhangings are one of the earliest serious assessments of the subject. The Crace firm was taken over in 1899 by COWTAN & CO.

CRANE, WALTER (1845–1915)
Primarily an English book illustrator and in his youth apprenticed to the wood engraver W. J. Linton. He was an important follower of MORRIS, and his wallpaper designs were among the most popular of the day. His first paper was the nursery hanging *Sing a Song of Sixpence*, designed for JEFFREY & CO. in 1875. He excelled in a naturalistic treatment of the human figure, which, with peacocks, cockatoos and lions, are drawn against a background of intertwining stems and leaves. Usually one colour predominates. His output was large, and among his more famous papers are *Peacocks and Amorini, Sleeping Beauty, Wood Notes* and *Macaw. Margarete*, one of his combination papers (a popular form combining frieze, filling and dado) won awards at the Philadelphia Centennial Exposition in 1876.

DAVIS, OWEN WILLIAM (b. 1838)
English designer of wallpapers for several prominent manufacturers. The reflection in his papers of his interest in the art of Pompeii and the Renaissance, as well

TOP Corona Vita, *Walter Crane, c. 1880. Primarily an English book illustrator, Crane was an important follower of Morris. Whitworth Art Gallery.* ABOVE *Sanitary dado, David Walker, 1895. Machine-printed panel. Victoria and Albert Museum.*

as his commitment to the Gothic Revival, contributed to a broadening in public taste.

DAY, LEWIS FOREMAN (1845–1910)
Prolific English writer and artist, and an expert in the design of stained glass, tiles and chintzes. His wallpapers were all executed by JEFFREY & CO. and display an exceptional boldness of form and aptitude for repeated patterns. Best

known are *Jacobite, Piccolomini* and *Abercorn,* a design for an embossed-leather wall decoration. He held an unrelenting campaign against the vulgarity and eclecticism so often to be found in domestic decoration at that time, and believed that design in this field should be 'frank, honest, unpretending and workmanlike'.

A. L. DIAMENT & CO.
Established in Philadelphia in 1885, the Company produced the series *Antique Scenic Papers of the Western World* and others, based upon the works of artists such as David, Claude and Vernet.

DRESSER, DR CHRISTOPHER (1834–1904)
English scientist, artist and author of *The Art of Decorative Design.* His wallpaper designs were printed by JEFFREY & CO., ARTHUR SANDERSON & SONS and LIGHTBOWN, ASPINALL & CO. and can be recognized by their concern with botanical forms and strong colour tones. His travels in Europe, America and Japan brought varied influences into his style; on one occasion he travelled to Egypt for inspiration and returned with sketch-books full of highly specialized drawings to incorporate into his designs.

DUFOUR, JOSEPH
Manufacturer established in Paris in 1807, later known as Dufour-Leroy. They produced scenic papers that were beyond doubt the most popular to be exported to America, including the Neoclassical masterpiece *Les Amours de Psyché,* of which an original set is in the Bonaparte House in Philadelphia. It was designed by Lafitte, engraved by Mader *père* and required the printing of 1,500 blocks. Their other well-known papers include *Monuments de Paris* and *Vues d'Italie.* The firm was eventually taken over by Desfossé & Karth.

EASTLAKE, CHARLES L. (1836–1906)
Nephew of the great Sir Charles Lock Eastlake and author of *Hints on Household Taste in Furniture and Upholstery* (1868), Charles Eastlake was more of a wallpaper critic than a designer, although his *Solanum* paper, printed by JEFFREY & CO. in 1869, was one of the first designs to break away from formalism.

GODWIN, EDWARD WILLIAM (1835–86)
English artist and architect, who first began to design wallpapers for JEFFREY & CO. in 1866. He also designed carpets, textiles and furniture, and was able to take up commissions for complete decorative schemes, such as that at Dromore Castle, Eire, for the Earl of Limerick. Among his better-known papers are *Sparrows and Bamboo* and *The Peacock.* His work is distinguished by its light touch and Oriental influence.

GREENAWAY, KATE (1846–1901)
One among many of the English artists whose designs were used for delightful nursery papers towards the end of the century. Others include Cecil Aldin, Randolph Caldecott, CRANE and Will Owen. An early nursery paper *c.* 1870 in the Victoria and Albert Museum, London, shows the four seasons framed in a trellis pattern and is attributed to the firm of HEYWOOD, HIGGINBOTTOM & SMITH.

HAITE, GEORGE CHARLES (1855–1924)
English landscape painter and decorative artist who produced several notable wallpaper designs, particularly for raised papers such as *Anaglypta* (see PALMER).

HAYWARD & SON LTD
One of the oldest decorating firms in London, tracing back its origins to the seventeenth century. The firm entered the wallpaper trade in the first half of the nineteenth century and produced an outstanding collection of ecclesiastical papers. They were the pioneers of the art of stencilling as applied to wallpaper and introduced a patent joint in which the paper was trimmed to follow the curved line of the pattern.

HEYWOOD, HIGGINBOTTOM & SMITH
One of the largest British wallpaper manufacturers when at their most active: in 1859 their output was such that they paid £20,000 in paper duty and sent out three million pieces. Their greatest achievement was the development in the 1870s of the SANITARY process, by which engraved rollers pressed the design on to the paper with oil colours, thus producing for the first time a washable paper.

JOHN HOWELL & SONS
The first wallpaper manufacturers to be established in New York State, opening at Albany in 1790 and settling after a series of moves in Philadelphia. The arrival there in 1844 of the first colour-printing machine from England introduced a new era in the wallpaper industry in America.

HUNTINGDON, JAMES (d. 1878)
One of the first commercial designers and brother of the three partners of Huntingdon Frères in Paris. His work is chiefly connected with the firm of POTTERS OF DARWEN, of which he became managing director before his death, and shows a marked French influence and a taste for the Rococo. In 1848 he established in London a large engraving and designing business which produced work for most of the leading wallpaper houses of the day. His remarkable pilaster design was shown at the International Exhibition of 1862.

JEFFREY & CO.
A British firm with an unsurpassed record in its contribution to the artistic

The May Tree, *Walter Crane produced by Jeffrey & Co., 1896. Frieze colour-printed from wood blocks. Crane excelled at the naturalistic treatment of trees with intertwining branches and waving stems. Victoria and Albert Museum.*

RIGHT *Floral pattern, Owen Jones (1809-74), c. 1871. Jones in his* The Grammar of Ornament *influenced both designers and public in their choice of wallpaper. Whitworth Art Gallery.*

side of the wallpaper industry. Founded in 1836, it was one of the first firms to produce the new cylinder-printed papers. In 1862 MORRIS entrusted to them the first of his designs. WARNER, one of the great names in wallpaper manufacture, joined the firm in 1866 and in 1871 became sole proprietor. The firm was an initiator of new styles, and the quality of their work maintained a consistently high standard. Most of the outstanding designers of the nineteenth century had work produced by them.

JONES, OWEN (1809–74)

Pioneer of the Gothic Revival, and Superintendent of Works for the Great Exhibition, Owen Jones did a great deal to bring recognition to wallpaper as a worthwhile medium for design. *The Grammar of Ornament* (1856) had a strong influence on the taste of the period in its appeal against impurity of style. In 1865 he completed the decorations for the Viceroy's Palace in Cairo, one of the most elaborate sets of designs to have been produced for a single building, consisting of Persian-inspired paper hangings for walls, ceilings, dados and borders. His papers combine simple geometric designs with vibrant colours,

and they carry his monogram on the back. The most familiar is probably *Horse Chestnut Leaves* and the notable pilaster design that he submitted to the Paris International Exposition of 1867.

LIGHTBOWN, ASPINALL & CO.

Established in Manchester in 1847, specialists in hand-made marble papers and Cordovan leather papers. They claim to have introduced multiple-colour printing to the popular SANITARY PAPERS in 1884.

MACKMURDO, ARTHUR H. (1851–1942)

British co-founder with Selwyn Image in 1882 of the Century Guild and its magazine *The Hobby Horse*. The wallpapers and cretonnes which he and his associate Herbert Horne designed exerted a strong influence at the end of the nineteenth century, and can often be recognized by their typical colourways of dull rose, browns and yellows.

MORRIS, WILLIAM (1834–96)

The greatest single influence in bringing

everyday domestic design into the field of the arts. Many of the sixty or more wallpapers he designed are more universally familiar than any other Victorian papers. His earlier designs such as *Trellis, The Daisy, Pomegranate* and *Willow* have a quality of freshness and innocence, where simple flowers, birds and leaves combine with delicate colours. From these he progressed to increasingly bold and magnificent papers, which employed a wide range of colours and demanded great technical skill in execution;

The Daisy, *William Morris, printed by Jeffrey & Co. for Morris, Marshall, Faulkner & Co., 1864. Hand-printed. One of Morris' early designs which combines freshness of design with delicate colours. Victoria and Albert Museum.*

Acanthus required two sets of blocks and thirty-two printings. He believed that 'Beauty mingled with invention, founded on the observation of Nature, is the mainspring of design', and he hoped, with the flowing lines and pure colours of his wallpapers, to 'lead the mind out of doors'. His own firm, first registered in 1861 as Morris, Marshall, Faulkner & Co. Fine Art Workmen, had difficulties in mastering the technical problems of wallpaper printing, and all his designs were executed by the great firm JEFFREY & CO. under the close supervision of WARNER. In his protest against commercialism, Morris insisted that his designs should be printed by hand and in pure vegetable colours. A contemporary critic said: 'We owe it to him that simple middle class houses have walls more beautifully decorated than those of kings' palaces used to be.'

Compton, *William Morris, 1896. Block-printed in distemper. Morris' last wallpaper design, designed for L. W. Hodson of Compton Hall, Wolverhampton, and also produced as a chintz. Whitworth Art Gallery.*

MUCHA, ALPHONSE (1860–1939)
Painter and illustrator closely identified with the Art Nouveau movement, he is most famous for his unusual poster designs. He also turned to wallpaper design, and several of his papers were exhibited in Paris in 1897 and 1900 having a marked influence on designers in Britain and the United States. The exhibition of his work in the Victoria and Albert Museum, London, in 1963 included designs for his wallpaper *Poppy*.

PALMER, THOMAS J.
In 1887 Palmer took out a patent in England for embossing pulp on a paper-making machine. He also produced an inexpensive relief wallpaper known as *Anaglypta*.

PERRY, JOHN & CO.
Islington firm, established in 1875, who were the originators of dried mica as applied to wallpapers; these were advertised as untarnishable silver papers.

With satinized and other shiny papers, they were very popular in the nineteenth century.

POTTERS OF DARWEN
First British firm successfully to use machinery for producing wallpapers on a commercial scale. In 1839 Charles Potter, with the help of his chief engineer Walmsley Preston, experimented in printing paper on a calico-printing machine. The method was eventually perfected with the use of paper in continuous lengths (first manufactured by Robert Fourdrinier in 1799) instead of the 12 yard (10·97 m) lengths previously used in hand printing, and created a revolution in the wallpaper industry. HUNTINGDON was a distinguished member of the firm.

PUGIN, AUGUSTUS WELBY (1812–52)
Architect, writer and a leader of the English Gothic Revival. In 1843 the papers he designed for the new Houses of Parliament (executed by SCOTT & CO. under the supervision of CRACE), illustrated his austere belief that fidelity to true Gothic principles was the final end of art and helped to diminish the flood of bad taste which swept over the wallpaper industry with the advent of machinery and mass-production. Pugin also designed papers for many great houses, including Lismore Castle, Eire, Scarisbrick Hall, Lancashire and Banyons Manor, East Anglia.

ARTHUR SANDERSON & SONS
First established in 1860, the firm moved to Berners Street in the West End of London in 1864. In 1885 it introduced to Britain the ingrain papers from America. In their factory at Chiswick they achieved a high standard in modern and scientific methods of production, and by the turn of the century many of the famous old firms had come under their management.

SCOTT, CUTHBERTSON & CO.
Incorporating the distinguished British firms of Eckhardt Bros and later Hinchcliff & Co., they introduced raised flock papers in the 1850s and are famous for their connection with the manufacture of the PUGIN papers for the new Houses of Parliament.

SCOTT MORTON & TYNECASTLE CO.
British firm who introduced in 1874 a form of wall covering in which canvas was pressed into a relief pattern reminiscent of embossed leather, known as *Tynecastle*. Their designs were based on those of the great periods of domestic architecture and were used for walls, friezes and ceilings, often combined with gilding for greater effect. H. Norman Shaw and H. Baillie Scott were among those whose designs were applied in this way.

SEDDING, JOHN DANDO (1838–91)
English author of *Art and Handicraft* and one of the many architects who applied his talents to wallpaper, Sedding's designs were printed by JEFFREY & CO.

SILVER, ARTHUR (1853–96)
English designer of several papers based on conventional floral and plant subjects. Sidney Haward was chief assistant in his studio for a time and later branched out on his own to produce a steady stream of original and talented designs.

SHAND KYDD, WILLIAM
Came to London from Scotland in 1881 to work as a designer for HAYWARD & SON LTD, Shand Kydd later set up as a decorative artist on his own account. The productions of Shand Kydd Ltd, established in 1891, were in the first rank of contemporary wallpapers. All the work, from the first design to the cutting of the blocks, was done on the premises. Shand Kydd specialized in handmade friezes and block and stencil work, and a large proportion of his work was exported to America.

SUMNER, GEORGE HEYWOOD (1853–1940)
British painter, book illustrator and designer of stained glass, Sumner was closely associated with CRANE and DAY. His wallpapers, which appeared towards the end of the century and were printed by JEFFREY & CO. were based on floral motifs and were highly individual. He is probably best known for his *Columbine* paper.

TALBERT, BRUCE J. (1838–81)
British architect, furniture designer, and author of *Gothic Forms* (1867), Bruce Talbert created the famous *Sunflower* paper for JEFFREY & CO., which won the Gold Medal in the Paris Exposition of 1878 and was universally imitated by designers and machine printers. His ornate and individual style was often influenced by Japanese art and had a strong influence on the later development of free and flexible design.

TIFFANY, LOUIS COMFORT (1848–1933)
Son of the founder of the famous New York store. Although Tiffany devoted himself eventually to decorative glassware, he was also associated with wallpaper design.

VOYSEY, CHARLES FRANCIS ANNESLEY (1857–1941)
Architect and designer who devoted his artistic life to a search for simplicity in design, and renewed the fine tradition in English wallpaper initiated by MORRIS. His huge output of over 100 designs was mainly produced before the end of the century and owed much to the influence of MACKMURDO. Most of the great

English manufacturers included his work in their collections, and during his peak period of 1890 to 1900 he was under contract to the newly founded Essex & Co. who dealt almost exclusively with his papers. Bird and floral motifs abound in his work as the titles suggest: *Vulture and Lily*, *Bird and Tulip*, *Buttercup and Daisy*. He held that 'A wallpaper should always be essentially a pattern.' His use of Art Nouveau mannerisms influenced contemporary designers such as BUTTER-FIELD, Arthur Gwatkin, Sydney Mawson and Harry Napper, and on the Continent Henry van de Velde was profoundly impressed by his work.

WALTON, FREDERICK
Englishman who produced in 1877 a strong and very flexible linoleum-based wall hanging called *Lincrusta*.

WARNER, METFORD
Chairman for over fifty years of the British firm JEFFREY & CO., and the great entrepreneur of the wallpaper industry. He was tireless in his search for new talent, and thus contributed more than any other individual, to the place the British wallpaper trade gained in the decorative arts. His patient supervision of the printing of MORRIS' papers showed the value he placed in achieving work of the highest possible quality. Among the artists he persuaded to design for his firm were CRANE, EASTLAKE, GODWIN and the bird and animal artist, Harrison Weir.

WHEELER, CANDACE (1828–1923)
Designer, writer on household decoration and one of the founders of the first decorative-art society in America.

WILLIAM WOOLLAMS & CO.
London firm who were in production for almost the whole of the nineteenth century. They were famous for their handmade papers, and flocks made of goats' hair. By 1890 the Company had secured eighteen gold, silver and bronze medals at important exhibitions. Frédéric Aumonier introduced stamped-gold and embossed-leather papers to the firm, and pioneered the abolition of arsenic from wallpaper processes (see p. 300).

ZUBER, JEAN OF RIXHEIM
One of the most important of the French manufacturers to export a large quantity of scenic papers to America. Among the prominent artists to design for Zuber were Joseph Malaine, Antoine-Pierre Mongin, Ehrmann and Fuchs. His *Paysage à Chasse* (1831) is to be found in the Van Buren house at Kinderhook, New York, above a dado-height *Balustrade*. The highly popular *Scenic America* series was printed in 1834 and *Isola Bella* in 1843. *Eldorado* (1848), of which an original set is in the Salem Club in Massachusetts, was printed from 2,000 hand-engraved blocks.

Glossary of Types

Architectural paper

Friezes and cornices representing architectural embellishments were so devised as to enable the decorator to imitate carving and plasterwork in the cornice or dado of a room. Often the *chiaroscuro* effect would be made to follow the light and shade in a particular room, for which purpose the papers were sometimes sold divided into four strips to the width, with the light in each strip coming from a different angle. Wood and plaster mouldings were included, and even pilasters and stone balustrades. All

Illustration from How to Build, Furnish and Decorate, *American, 1883. A proposal for the arrangement of wallpaper in the decoration of a ceiling from a contemporary magazine. Author's Collection.*

kinds of finishes were used, for example, embossing, varnishing or spangling with mica dust or metallic powders. Wood papers were carefully grained and stone papers were designed to imitate stucco, granite, roughcast and marble with great accuracy. In the United States marbleized paper was widely used in conjunction with inserted painted panels.

Block-printed paper

Blocks used for handprinting were usually 21 in (53 cm) wide; they varied in length and were $3\frac{1}{2}$–4 in (9–10 cm) thick. The pattern was transferred from a tracing and chipped to a relief of about $\frac{1}{8}$–$\frac{1}{4}$ in (3–6 mm).

Ceiling rose

Ceilings were often blackened by the smoke from chandeliers and the central applied paper rose, whether machine or hand-printed, originated as a replaceable solution to the problem.

Combination paper

Known also as dado-filling frieze papers, they were recommended by EASTLAKE and actually introduced into England by JEFFREY & CO.

SCIENCE AGRICULTURE DRAMA MUSIC POETRY PAINTING DESIGN ARCHITECTURE PEACE JUSTICE LIBERTY

The Diamond Jubilee Frieze, *English, 1897. Sanitary machine-printed in six colours. Peace and Justice flank the throne and children bear objects illustrating the blessings of the reign. Whitworth Art Gallery.*

Drape paper
Imitation velvet or silk was caught up at intervals by heavy cords and tassels. The papers were introduced into America in about 1806 by the Frenchman DUFOUR.

Embossed paper
In 1829 the device for embossing and twilling papers was patented in England by Tom Cobb.

Fabric paper
Imitative of the actual texture of gold, silk, chintz, etc. Until the 1870s fabric papers were manufactured by hand, then by machine-operated rotary brushes which laid the colour and mica on evenly and produced a good, durable surface on which to work. Flowered silk designs were always popular but declined in quality towards the mid century. At the end of the Victorian period, satin papers, polished by rubbing with French chalk, were considered a major triumph.

Flock paper
Designed, as in the eighteenth century, to imitate velvet, these were often used to decorate dining rooms. The paper was first given a good varnish ground and the design then printed on by block or stencil. The flock particles were 'strewn' on the prepared paper and the residue removed with a soft camel-hair brush. In 1850 the cheapest flock paper cost about 2s per yard (91 cm). At the International Exhibition of 1862 flock-upon-flock was shown, with the design standing out in heavy relief.

Floral paper
Full-blown roses and other popular flowers were often used to decorate bedrooms.

Foreign paper
Papers imitating the supposed national styles of Italy and other countries. These included Japanese leather papers and 'India hangings', based on the hand-painted papers imported from China.

Historical paper
Based on Elizabethan, Medieval or Queen Anne designs.

Machine-printed paper
Hand machines, working with roller and block, seem to have been used up to 1850. In 1835 BUMSTEAD invented the first colour-printing machine, consisting of a large cylinder round which the paper passed, and many small ones pressing against it, each engraved with different parts of the pattern and inked with different colours. By 1854 such machines could produce per hour 200 pieces, 12 yards (11 m) long and in fifty-four colours.

Morris paper
First appearing in 1862, they reverted from TROMPE L'ŒIL to two-dimensional flatness and did not attempt to hide the mechanized nature of the wallpaper medium. They took their inspiration from the past, for example the diagonal structure of Italian cut velvets. MORRIS' other contributions were freshness of colour and design and the use of hatching to indicate shadow.

Mythological paper
Represented by such series as DUFOUR's *Galerie Mythologique* of 1814, mainly to be seen in America.

Nursery paper
Originating in the second half of the nineteenth century, the first examples were gaudy and badly executed but later designs improved under the influence of such artists as GREENAWAY.

Picture paper
Opulent still-life designs mainly contemporary with the introduction of the printing-machine. Scarcely any memorable event, famous scene or social pastime up to the end of the nineteenth century failed to be recorded. Some designs took their inspiration from old engravings; others included lithographic portraits of the famous in sepia frames.

Sanitary paper
Because of their oily constituents and consequent impermeability, sanitary papers could be sponged and were thus

used in kitchens and halls. They were duller and more lithographic than the brilliant, opaque-surface printed papers.

Scenic paper

Imported by the United States, mainly from France, in the early part of the nineteenth century to cover walls totally, rather than as in the eighteenth century, to be used in panels. They ran above a chair-rail in continuous sequence and with no repetition. Usually sold in twenty to thirty selectable strips, they were brought into prominence by ZUBER and DUFOUR. Often a paper balustrade ran underneath.

Statuary paper

Based on the French panoramic papers, the statues portrayed often had their own niches and plinths. In about 1812, goddesses began to appear in the United States, followed by statesmen, artists and monarchs. When the fashion later reached England, the Muses, Shakespeare and Milton occupied prominent positions.

Trompe l'œil paper

Play of light and shade on flowers, foliage and other subjects was emphasized to give a three-dimensional effect.

Bibliography

ARROWSMITH, H. W. & A. *The House Decorator*, London, 1840

ARROWSMITH, JAMES. *The Paper Hanger's Companion*, Philadelphia, 1852

BIRGE WALLPAPER CO. *A Textbook of Colonial Wallpapers*, Buffalo, New York, n.d. (1930)

CASSELL, PETTER & GALPIN. *Cassell's Illustrated Exhibitor, The International Exhibition of 1862*, London and New York, 1862

CLEAVELAND, H. W. & BACKUS, WM. and S. D. *Village and Farm Cottages*, New York, 1856

COLE, HENRY ed. *The Journal of Design and Manufactures*, London, 1849–1852

COOPER, GEORGE. *Designs for the Decoration of Rooms in the Various Style (sic) of Modern Embellishment*, London, 1807

DOWNING, A. J. *The Architecture of Country Houses*, New York and Philadelphia, 1850

EASTLAKE, CHARLES L. *Hints on Household Taste*, fourth American ed., Boston, 1876

EDIS, R. W. *Decoration and Furniture of Town Houses*, London, 1881

ENTWISLE, E. A. *Wallpapers of the Victorian Era*, Leigh-on-Sea, Essex, 1964

FOWLER & WELLS. *The House, A Pocket Manual on Rural Architecture*, New York, 1859

HOLLY, H. HUDSON. *Modern Dwellings in Town and Country*, New York, 1878

HUNTER, G. L. *Decorative Textiles*, Philadelphia, 1918

JEFFREY & CO. *The Victorian Papers*, 1885

JENNINGS, ARTHUR S. *Wallpapers and Wallcoverings*, New York, 1903

KATZENBACH, L. W. *The Practical Book of American Wallpaper*, Philadelphia, 1951

LOUDON, J. C. *An Encyclopedia of Cottage, Farm and Villa Architecture & Furniture*, London, 1833

LICHTEN, FRANCES. *Decorative Art of Victoria's Era*, New York, 1950

MAYALL, BEARD (ed.). *Tallis's History and Description of the Crystal Palace*, 3 vols, London and New York, n.d. (1851)

McCLELLAND, NANCY. *Historic Wallpapers*, Philadelphia and London, 1924

MUMFORD, LEWIS. *The Brain Decades*, 1955

NORBURY, JAMES. *The World of Victoriana*, London, 1972

SANBORN, KATE. *Old Time Wallpapers*, New York, 1905

SILLIMAN, B. JR, and GOODRICH, C. R. *The World of Science, Art and Industry Illustrated from Examples in the New York Exhibition, 1853–1854*, New York and London, 1854

SHOPPELL, ROBERT W. *How to Build, Furnish and Decorate*, New York, 1883

SMITH, GEORGE, *A Collection of Designs for Household Furniture and Interior Decoration*, London, 1808

SMITH, GEORGE. *The Cabinet Maker's and Upholsterer's Guide*, London, 1826

SMITH, WALTER. *Examples of Household Taste*, Vol. 2, New York, 1877

SPOFFORD, HARRIET P. *Art Decoration Applied to Furniture*, New York, 1878

SUGDEN, A. V. and EDMONDSON, J. L. *A History of English Wallpaper 1509–1914*, London, 1926

TALBERT, B. J. *Gothic Forms, Examples of Ancient and Modern Furniture*, London, 1876

VARNEY, ALMON. *Our Homes and their Adornments*, Detroit, Michigan, 1883

Victoria and Albert Museum, *Catalogue of an Exhibition of Victorian and Edwardian Decorative Arts; The Catalogue of the American Museum of Decorative Art and Design*, London, 1973

WARING, J. B. *Masterpieces of Industrial Art and Sculpture at the International Exhibition, 1862*, 3 vols, London, 1863

WHEELER, GERVASE. *Rural Homes*, New York, 1851

Whitworth Art Gallery, *Catalogue of Historic Wallpapers at the Whitworth Art Gallery*, Manchester, 1972

WYATT, M. DIGBY. *Industrial Arts of the Nineteenth Century at the Great Exhibition 1851*, 2 vols, London, 1853

Juvenilia

BRITISH

By the outset of Queen Victoria's reign there was a marked change of attitude towards children. It was now recognized that they had needs of their own and should not be expected to behave as miniature adults. A number of play-things were being devised to amuse as well as to instruct, coinciding with the introduction of new industrial techniques which made mass production possible. A wide variety of toys to supply the large middle-class families became readily available and from this vast output many dolls and toys have survived for the enjoyment of collectors today.

Dolls

The splendid English wooden dolls of the eighteenth century were on the decline by the early years of the nineteenth century, when mass-produced peg-wooden, or Dutch (a corruption of *Deutsch*) dolls were being imported from Germany. They were well made, and came in many sizes, with peg joints, spoon-like hands and flat, painted feet: even the tiniest one-inch dolls moved at elbows, hips and knees. These dolls were delicately painted over the gesso and varnished, with black hair and wisps of curls round the face. Some had yellow combs on top of their heads, as for example the dolls that the young Princess Victoria dressed in 1830. They were cheap, widely enjoyed throughout the century, and can be found made up as character dolls, pedlars and other novelties.

A new, harder kind of papier mâché made possible the mass production of dolls' heads of a type known as milliner's models. They were play dolls, not

OPPOSITE *Doll, English, c. 1850. Wax over composition with glass eyes, dressed in a white dress with broderie anglaise. Described as 'Queen Victoria at the age of five years'. Victoria and Albert Museum.*

fashion dolls as the name suggests, and were hollow moulded with deep shoulders and the elaborate, top-heavy hairstyles of the 1820s and '30s. They had well-painted faces with black hair and were finished with shiny varnish. The heads were fixed on to simple cloth or kid bodies, with long narrow arms and legs. The forearms were sometimes kid with stitched fingers, sometimes wood with spoon-shaped hands and flat, wooden feet.

Dolls, English, c. 1830. Wooden, heads covered with gesso and painted. These dolls belonged to Queen Victoria. The male doll represents a dancing master; the female, a ballerina. London Museum.

A cheap doll, popular in the 1840s, was one with a waxed papier-mâché head. The heads were crudely modelled and the skin colour and features such as rosy cheeks and smiling mouths were painted on. The heads were then dipped several times in clear wax to produce a glowing complexion. Dark pupil-less eyes were fitted, and a length of hair curled at the ends into fashionable ringlets was pressed into a slit cut on top of the head from front to back and glued in place, so that these dolls became known as 'split-heads'. They must have looked charming when they were new, but owing to the

different rate of contraction between the wax and the base, they easily became crazed. If the crazing has become old and brown, the dolls acquire a macabre look.

There were many variants, and later versions in the 1860s sometimes have the hair, and often a hat as well, modelled in one and painted before being dipped. The cotton bodies are often finished with short wooden forearms and painted boots. Some have squeak boxes inside; others have moving eyes worked by a wire which runs down the body and out at the back or side. Papier-mâché and wax-over dolls were mainly made in Germany.

Pedlar dolls are English and were made throughout the nineteenth century. Often wooden Dutch dolls were used, but the more interesting examples have heads of papier mâché, kid or wax on a home-made body. The normal costume was a print dress with red flannel cloak and brown or black bonnet. Whether male or female pedlars (the majority were female), each carried a large basket filled with all manner of miniature wares – books, sheets of pins, cards of buttons and lace, spools of silk, strings of beads, brushes, combs and minute scissors. Stay laces, skewers and tin graters hung round the edge.

China dolls also came into favour in the 1840s, having been first made in Germany and then in France. The heads were beautifully modelled as if from life and highly glazed with the hair painted black, the eyes blue and the skin left white. Some of these heads, which had shoulder plates with holes at the front and back to which to attach the bodies, were made up on cloth or kid bodies with china arms and legs; other heads were sold separately and sewn on to home-made bodies. By the middle of the century there was a wide variety of glazed heads with different hairstyles and hair ornaments. They continued to be made until the end of the century although the later ones were not so fine.

Pedlar doll, English, c. 1830. Wooden. The normal costume of the English pedlar doll was a print dress, red flannel cloak and brown or black bonnet. Each doll carried a basket filled with wares. London Museum.

In the late 1850s a new unglazed china (bisque) began to be used for dolls with blond hair. At the height of their popularity in the 1870s the dolls' heads were embellished with a profusion of curls, ribbons, flowers and jewelry, painted in pale colours, often rather sugary. Some were partially glazed and touched with lustre, while a few had such refinements as swivel heads and glass eyes.

The poured wax dolls have always been considered an English invention for, although they were also made in other countries, the finest were made in London in the 1850s and '60s by doll makers whose names have long since become famous. Among the best known, although they seldom marked their dolls, were Montanari and Pierotti, Italian wax workers who turned their attention to dolls, Marsh who claimed the title Royal Dollmaker, and Meech and Edwards.

At the Great Exhibition in 1851 Madame Montanari won a prize for a display which included adult dolls, child dolls and baby dolls. Baby dolls became popular from that date, dressed in long robes. The heads, forearms and lower legs were made by pouring warm wax into moulds, and they were finished by hand. Real hair, individually set or in

TOP *Doll's head, European, c. 1850. Porcelain. Originally owned by the late H.M. Queen Mary, the head is highly glazed. Porcelain heads were sometimes sold separately to sew on to home-made bodies. Victoria and Albert Museum.*

ABOVE *Doll, English, c. 1880. Bisque with kid arms and cloth body, dressed as a bride in a satin and lace jacket and separate skirt. An exquisite English luxury doll following the French fashions. Victoria and Albert Museum.*

tufts, was pricked into the wax with a hot needle or a scalpel knife and gently pressed into place. Eyebrows and eyelashes were set in the same way. Stationary glass eyes, usually blue, were fitted into well-defined sockets and the head and limbs were sewn on to calico bodies

through eyelet holes. These wax dolls which were still being made at the end of the century, were surprisingly life-like and when fully dressed made a luxury present for a little girl of well-to-do parents.

In 1860 the French fashion doll arrived on the English market to compete as a luxury doll with its English wax rival. These dolls had fine bisque heads, delicately tinted complexions, realistic glass eyes and wigs of real hair, styled in the current fashion. Tiny ear rings hung from pierced ears. They were exquisitely dressed and often came with a trunk holding a complete wardrobe with every conceivable accessory – jewelry, brush and comb and a powder puff. Their bodies were tailored in kid with gusseted

joints; some had porcelain arms, some had swivel heads. There were lady dolls (*poupées*) and by 1870 new girl dolls (*bébés*) with hollow ball-jointed bodies of wood or composition. There were musical dolls and dolls that walked or talked. Steiner, Jumeau and Bru are three from a host of makers.

By the 1890s the German manufacturers such as Simon & Halbig and Armand Marseille had captured the market with dolls that had sleeping eyes, real eyelashes and well-jointed bodies at a price within the reach of many more families.

OPPOSITE *Selection of toys, British and American, nineteenth century. The group of toys includes pegs, humming tops, American alphabet blocks and a scripture cube game. Bethnal Green Museum.*

Dolls' Houses

Victorian dolls' houses were made for children to play with. Earlier English ones called baby houses had been made for the enjoyment of adults. A few large houses were still being built in the nineteenth century, but instead of a lock, they had a hook or bolt.

The first dolls' houses designed for play were plain and stoutly built with three or four rooms and no staircase; the door and windows were often painted on the front. The dolls' house made for Princess Victoria had one room up and one down, with the minimum of furniture.

From the time of Queen Victoria's accession, dolls' houses were either made at home or on a small-scale commercial basis. The front opened in one, two or even three parts, and, if the house had rooms behind rooms, it opened at the back as well. Some houses were narrow from front to back, large enough to stand on the nursery floor or small enough to stand on the nursery cupboard. They were painted to look like stone or had façades marked to simulate brick or stucco. Inside, there might be a straight-up staircase; the rooms were papered and painted.

From about 1870 a number of attractive, well-constructed dolls' houses were imported from Europe with delightful balconies, porticoes and bay windows, but after 1890 shoddy, factory-made houses came on the market with thin walls and ill-proportioned rooms. The houses were filled with furniture to look like real Victorian homes. A rather superior kind of furniture was made in imitation of gilded rosewood; an attractive type of bedroom furniture including washstands and chests of drawers was made in pale creamy wood with a high gloss. Kitchen ware abounded in wood, china and metal. The drawing rooms were full of all manner of miniature objects; clocks, vases, lamps, coal scuttles, bird-cages, even magazines and sheet music to give reality; and the houses were inhabited by dolls' house families of two or three generations, including servants and domestic pets.

There were dinner sets and teasets made in the Staffordshire potteries with transfer designs of landscapes or scenes of children at play, and dolls'-house food, too large for the dolls' house but the right size for the bigger dolls.

OPPOSITE The Hobby Horse, *American, c. 1840. Oil on canvas. The rocking horse was a popular toy in America, although this example may have been imported. National Gallery of Art, Washington.*

LEFT *Doll's house dressing table, English,* c. *1870. An example of the highly varnished cream furniture from the doll's house of the late H.M. Queen Mary. London Museum.*

BELOW *Group of dolls with 'bathing baby', English,* c. *1860. Porcelain. The dolls are shown with simulated cane furniture and various other miniature pieces. Mary Hillier Collection.*

BOTTOM (above) *Dolls' house food, English,* c. *1850. Plaster painted in bright colours, diam. of plate 1¾ in (5 cm). The dishes represent traditional English food. London Museum.* BOTTOM (below) *Dolls' dinner plate, Staffordshire, late nineteenth century. Blue-and-white pottery, diam. of plate 3½ in (9 cm). London Museum.*

Toy Theatres

When Queen Victoria came to the throne, the boys in middle-class families were busy colouring and cutting out the characters and scenery for their Skelt theatres. The first sheets of paper characters had been published in 1811 and sold for a penny plain and twopence coloured. By the 1830s some uncoloured sheets were being sold for a halfpenny, between ten and forty sheets being required to make up a complete play with characters appearing two or three times in different poses. Proscenium fronts were produced in the same way for mounting on to wooden stages. A book of words was specially adapted for each play, which had already been performed on the London stage.

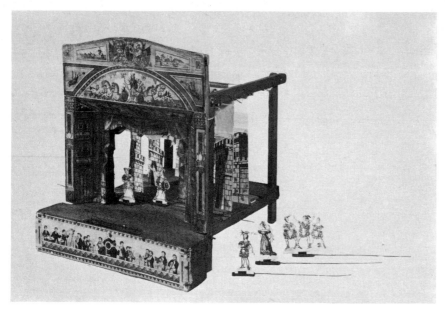

*Toy theatre, Benjamin Pollock, London,
c. 1910 from designs of* c. 1850. *Wood with
hand-coloured paper stage front and orches-
tra, ht 17 in (42 cm). The stage is set with
a scene from* Douglas. *London Museum.*

The cut-out figures were pushed on the
stage in wire slides behind footlights of
spluttering colza oil, while boys de-
claimed the lines; red and blue fire
heightened the dramatic moments. Very
few new plays were published after
1860, but such publishers as Redington,
Pollock and Webb continued to reissue
many of the old plays until the end of the
century and even later.

Jigsaw Puzzles

From the time that John Spilsbury
mounted and dissected the first map of
England and Wales in the 1760s, until
after 1900, jigsaws were known as
dissected puzzles. Only the edges were
interlocking. The earliest puzzles were
made of mahogany but, by 1830, white-
wood which was cheaper, was being
widely used both for puzzles and boxes.
The boxes had sliding lids which were
decorated with large coloured pictures.
In the early years the Dartons and the
Wallis family were using hand-coloured
engravings for didactic puzzles, mainly
maps, genealogical tables and Biblical
subjects. By 1850, such high-class publishers as the Barfoots and William
Spooner were producing, with coloured
lithographs, a wide range of educational
subjects in a more entertaining style.
Puzzles were also produced for sheer
enjoyment, with topics as varied as the
seaside, royal occasions and fairy tales.

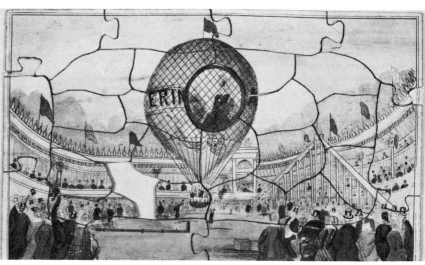

*Dissected puzzle described as 'Balloon
ascent from Batty's Hippodrome opposite
the south end of the Broad Walk, Kensington Gardens', c. 1851. Wooden, 6¾ in ×
11½ in (17 cm × 29 cm). London Museum.*

Many of these publishers were also
responsible for table games, childrens'
books, card games, peepshows or pictures designed for scrap books. Young
children had their own alphabet bricks
or cubic blocks each side of which
carried part of a picture. An unusual set
of bricks, for Sunday amusement, had
the design of a Gothic church on one
side and Biblical texts on the reverse.

Table Games

Parlour games of all kinds played an
important part in Victorian family life.
Teaching and moral games were published by the print sellers up until about
1850; coloured engravings or lithographs
were mounted on linen and folded into a
slip case. You could choose from such
titles as 'Game of Railroad Adventures',
'Wonders of the World', or the 'Principal
Events in English History'. The games
were played with a teetotum but later on
they were mounted on boards as they are
today and played with dice. These later
games were more lighthearted. 'The
Race Game', for example, was a steeple-
chase played with lead horses and riders.
Card games might aim to instruct like
'Counties of England' or 'The London
Post', or merely to amuse like 'Old
Maid' or 'Happy Families'.

Mechanical Toys

The production of popular clockwork
toys began in about 1850. In England, by
the 1880s, the firm of William Britain
was making a number of ingenious
mechanical figures propelled by clockwork or heavy flywheel momentum. An
equestrienne galloped round a circus
ring, and a walking bear lifted up its
head and opened its mouth to show its
teeth. Other mechanical toys were
worked by steam or trickling sand. By
the end of the century a great range of
metal toys, both clockwork and friction
driven, became available at reasonable
prices due to improved methods of mass
production, especially in Germany.

Toy Soldiers

Early wooden soldiers, turned on a lathe,
and paper soldiers were also much
favoured by boys in the first part of the
nineteenth century, but these were
already being superseded by the little tin
soldier. Tin was expensive and brittle,

lead was cheap but too soft to hold the detail, so an alloy was used. German manufacturers produced flat lead soldiers – and civilian figures – and solid rounded soldiers, including many representing British regiments. In 1893 William Britain Jr produced the first hollow-cast toy soldiers. They were light, cheap and well finished, and they captured the market at home and abroad. The first lines to be produced were the Life Guards, the Grenadier Guards and a kilted Highland regiment.

Optical Toys

The thaumatrope was the first of a series of moving-picture toys based on the phenomenon of the persistence of vision. A paper disk with different objects drawn on each side, for example a bird on one side and a cage on the other, was twirled by means of thin cords attached to each side of the disk, with the result that the pictures merged and the bird appeared in the cage. A development of this was a series of pictures drawn in different stages of movement, in the phenakistoscope on a cardboard disk spun in front of a mirror, and in the zoetrope on a paper strip placed inside a spinning metal drum. Other variations were the viviscope and the praxinoscope.

Noah's Ark, German, c. 1850. Carved and painted wood, ht 17 in (42 cm). Made for the English market. The figures totalled 193. The standard of carving on Noah's arks, first made in the mid-eighteenth century, deteriorated in the early nineteenth century. London Museum.

Zoetrope strips, English, late nineteenth century. Paper. These strips show stages of movement. When the drum is rotated and the figures are viewed through the slits, they appear to move. London Museum.

LEFT *Zoetrope, English, late nineteenth century. Black tin drum on mahogany base, ht 12 in (30 cm). Early optical toy based on the phenomenon of the persistence of vision. Other optical toys included the thaumatrope, phenakistoscope and praxinoscope; optical art was later superseded by photography. London Museum.*

Later on photography replaced drawings, and in a mutoscope, based on the flick book principle, one could view a sequence of movements by turning a handle. A stereoscope combined two slightly different views to give a still picture a three-dimensional effect. From about 1840 children had their own magic lanterns with sets of coloured slides to illustrate fairy tales or nursery rhymes. Some slides could be made to produce a moving picture – a boy and girl on a see-saw or a kaleidoscopic pattern.

Wooden toys of every description were also made: constructional sets for farms and forts, toy shops, Noah's arks, boats, horses to pull or lead carts, or splendid rocking horses to ride. Many cheap toys were made in the back-street industries of English towns, often to sell for as little as a penny. Of the thousands of toys produced, only a few have survived: the balls, tops, hoops, kites and guns are almost all lost. Those that remain are mostly the luxury toys or the ones so carefully guarded by parents that they were hardly ever used by the child. The majority were played with, enjoyed, broken and thrown away.

Mary Speaight

AMERICAN

It may be of more than chronological interest to observe that the beginnings of the toy industry in the United States in the 1830s, and the accession of Queen Victoria to the throne of Great Britain in the same decade, are parallel launchings of two institutions which flourished for generations thereafter. It is more than coincidental that the vitality and variety of the Victorian era are reflected in the fanciful and imaginative toys which were made to beguile American children.

Rapid Development of the Toy Industry

Although its early history, unfortunately, is buried in a morass of unsalvaged and possibly unsalvageable, records, it is clear that after 1850 American toy manufacturing greatly accelerated and, following the Civil War, became a sizeable industry. One tin-toy manufacturer, during the 1870s, produced nearly forty million items a year. Such a statistic belies a long-held misconception that there was no real toy industry in the United States before the First World War, and that imports dominated American nurseries. This misconception has also been overturned in the wake of research, in recent years, by a burgeoning horde of antique-toy collectors, who have stockpiled an imposing mass of old catalogues, patent papers and other primary sources, including the toys themselves.

Like the toys of all countries, many of these reflect historic events or personages. A clockwork toy manufactured by E. R. Ives & Co. of Bridgeport, Connecticut, in the late 1870s represents General Grant puffing real smoke from a cigar. A corrupt politician seems a less likely subject for a child's toy, but an iron mechanical bank made by J. & E. Stevens & Co. soon after the downfall in 1871 of 'Boss Tweed' of New York, consists of a stout figure seated in a chair who quickly pockets any coin placed in his hand, bowing politely as he accepts it.

Indigenous subject matter, as might be supposed, is represented in many other ways. In both toys and games, 'Darkies' are present in profusion, and Uncle Sam is a popular figure together with a

celebrated bird, the American Eagle. The variety of fire-fighting equipment available in miniature is attributable not only to the universal excitement of fire fighting which has always ignited small boys, but to the era of wooden structures and great conflagrations, which reduced a full-sized problem to a toy reflection. The toy hose carriages of the 1870s, surprisingly (and charmingly) decorated with flowers and stencilling, had given way by the 1890s, to such practical representations as a substantial firehouse with an iron façade which, when activated, made a bell clang, the doors fly open and the engine start off for the fire.

The Industrial Revolution in the United States, a not particularly beguiling phenomenon in full size, is disarmingly suggested in miniature by a progression of steam toys which were

and are as operable as the toy trains of all persuasions which rushed towards a miniature rendezvous with the future.

Tin and Iron Toys

When in 1869, a Connecticut clock- and toymaker named George W. Brown merged his line of tin toys with the line of iron toys and banks manufactured by J. & E. Stevens & Co. of Cromwell, Connecticut, they were launching not only a successful toy business, but, inadvertently, they were encompassing an assortment of toys which was to gratify a large and assiduous number of American toy collectors less than a century later. With a highly imaginative variety of mechanical and still banks, animated cap pistols, clockwork and bell

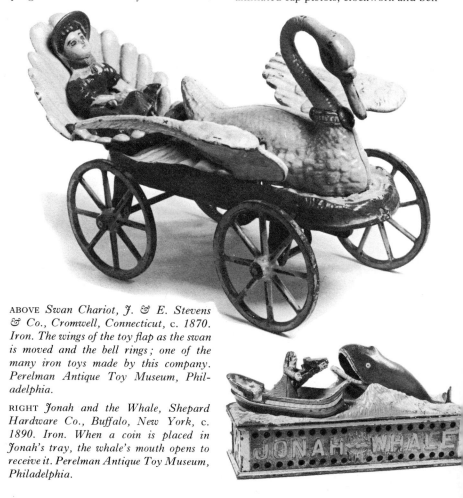

ABOVE *Swan Chariot, J. & E. Stevens & Co., Cromwell, Connecticut, c. 1870. Iron. The wings of the toy flap as the swan is moved and the bell rings; one of the many iron toys made by this company. Perelman Antique Toy Museum, Philadelphia.*

RIGHT *Jonah and the Whale, Shepard Hardware Co., Buffalo, New York, c. 1890. Iron. When a coin is placed in Jonah's tray, the whale's mouth opens to receive it. Perelman Antique Toy Museum, Philadelphia.*

toys, and an infinitude of other playthings, the Stevens & Brown Manufacturing Co. were one of the many manufacturers of such future collecting categories as 'transportation' and 'early tin'.

The latter were made of tin plate imported from England and are undoubtedly among the most beautiful toys made – they include japanned carriages and locomotives and ships which, though their stencilled patterns may be chipped and fading, have the primitive appeal of folk art. Similar toys were manufactured by other companies in New England towns, but were later 'overtaken', according to George Brown's biographer, Edith Barenholtz, by such big-city factory giants as E. R. Ives & Co. of Bridgeport, Connecticut, Althof, Bergmann & Co. of New York, and others.

In 1740, the American tin industry had been launched, and it is believed that toys were among the first products made. However, a century later, in 1838, a fully fledged tin-toy maker, the Philadelphia Tin Toy Company, was known to be in business, and clearly was flourishing in 1848 when its advertisement in the Philadelphia directory pictured several toys. Included were a wheeled platform with a boy mounted on a dog, and waving a flag; and a horse-drawn locomotive named 'Gen. Taylor', made in honour of a Mexican War hero who was elected president of the United States that year. A later catalogue for the firm includes illustrations of steam locomotives and dolls'-house furniture.

If tin toys were of greater delicacy, such iron products as mechanical banks and bell toys often displayed a similarly astonishing blend of realism and fantasy. George Brown's tin chariot pulled by a lion and piloted by a queen, garbed regally in royal blue and complete with crown, is rivalled by an iron chariot (by Stevens) in the form of a swan in which a passenger reclines among the feathers; the swan's wings flap when the toy is pulled.

Mechanical banks and bell toys vie in complexity and ingenuity with clockwork toys. The latter include dressed figures by E. R. Ives & Co., a toy manufacturer of great versatility, who produced such flights of fancy as a monkey churning, Uncle Sam driving a velocipede and a mechanical skeleton dancing. (The latter well calculated, surely, to induce bedtime terrors!)

Ives also made trains: the toy historian, Louis Hertz, points out that the firm pioneered locomotives and trains from the clockwork tin floor models of the 1870s to clockwork and electric-track trains in the twentieth century. There were many other companies making trains, steam toys and friction toys, as well as automobiles from almost the moment the automobile was invented.

Dolls' Houses and Related Toys

Like dolls' houses in Europe during much of the Victorian era, most of the big ones built in the United States – the mansions – were unique examples made by a grandfather, great uncle or family carpenter and, like most dolls' buildings, they reflected the architecture and furnishings of their age. There are many historic and splendid examples of such construction, but there were also, in the

Combination dolls' house, Stirn & Lyon, New York, c. 1860. Wood, pressure-printed in black and red. The combination dolls' house came packed flat, ready to be assembled. Author's Collection.

second half of the century, innumerable commercially-made houses and related buildings which the average dolls' family could afford.

Wood, pressure-printed, was used to build a variety of villas, cottages, churches and stores. Stirn & Lyon manufacturers of New York City, patented many of these as combination buildings which came packed flat and thereby anticipated the life-sized prefabricated houses of generations later. Converse of Winchendon, Massachusetts also made dolls' houses, table and barns similarly embossed on wood.

In lieu of pressure-printing, W. S. Reed of Leominster, Massachusetts, (later Whitney Reed), and R. Bliss & Co. of Pawtucket, Rhode Island, applied lushly-lithographed paper to wood to create a veritable microcosm. R. Bliss & Co. supplied gingerbread firehouses and stables along with villas and cottages, with every gable and turret lovingly rendered in wood, and every spindle and

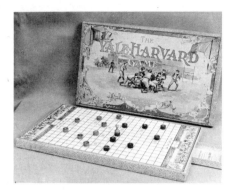

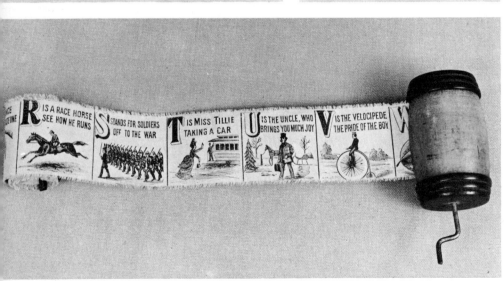

scroll either turned in wood or printed in brilliant colour. W. S. Reed even made a coal yard, and R. Bliss & Co. an 'Adirondack cottage', the latter complete with a surrealistic Indian lurking on a dormer. The lithographed papers were sometimes imported, as the technique itself may well have been.

Wooden Toys and Games

In addition to their miniature architecture, such makers as W. S. Reed and R. Bliss & Co. applied printed paper to boats, trains, blocks and a galaxy of other toys. Reed's 'U.S. Capitol at Washington D.C.' patented in 1884, unreeled, on a movable paper strip beneath the dome, interior views of the Capitol and White House, and the likeness of every president up to Chester A. Arthur. 'Thousands who have never seen this magnificent structure,' the label advised, 'have here an opportunity without the expense of a visit.'

Educational themes appear in a variety of toys and games, beginning with W. & S. B. Ives of Salem, Massachusetts.

OPPOSITE: TOP LEFT *The Yale-Harvard Game, Parker Bros, Salem, Massachusetts, patented 1894. Author's Collection.*

TOP RIGHT *Chiromagica, McLoughlin Bros, New York, late nineteenth century. An educational toy whereby a series of disks, on which are written factual questions, are placed over a magnetic hand which points to the answers on corresponding sheets. Author's Collection.*

CENTRE LEFT *Cob House Blocks, McLoughlin Bros, New York, late nineteenth century. Lithographed paper on wood. The designs represent New York City architecture. Author's Collection.*

CENTRE *Bible Panorama, Milton Bradley Co., Springfield, Massachusetts, c. 1868. This firm marketed a series of 'panoramas' each of which unreeled a series of pictures of historical events. Author's Collection.*

BOTTOM LEFT *The Alphabetical Toy Panorama, Foley & Williams Manufacturing Co., Chicago, patented 1886. The alphabet is pictorially represented on a linen strip. Author's Collection.*

BOTTOM RIGHT *Pedagogue Pencil Box, S. A. Ilsey & Co., Brooklyn, New York, patented 1898. Tin. Designed to hold pencils and to teach multiplication tables by turning the lower section. Author's Collection.*

Milton Bradley & Co. of Springfield, Massachusetts who, along with Parker Bros of Salem, Massachusetts and the McLoughlin Bros of New York City, turned out an immense variety of board and card games, unreeled a box-like series of panoramas less elaborate than Reed's Capitol, but similarly operated, beginning in 1868 with a Historioscope which offered scenes 'from Columbus to the Civil War'.

Considerably earlier, in the 1830s, William S. Tower of Hingham, Massachusetts, a carpenter and part-time toy maker, had organized a guild in which his fellow craftsmen turned out toy versions of their full-sized specialities. The Tower Toy Guild, which made tool chests, dolls' house furniture, boats and many other types of wooden toys, was for decades so successful that a toy trade magazine once described Tower as 'the founder of the toy industry in America'.

If Tower was the founder, two other toymakers, according to toy historian Marshall McClintock, 'stood out above all other nineteenth-century toymen in America, and perhaps in the world. . . .' This sweeping statement was made about two of the eleven Crandalls who, for nearly a century, manufactured toys in the United States. Although these two Crandalls, Jesse A. and Charles M.,

The Acrobats, *Charles M. Crandall, patented 1867. Wooden Toy by Crandall who invented the tongue-and-groove blocks which form its basis. Author's Collection.*

were distantly related, it is believed that they never worked together. Jesse invented nested blocks in his Brooklyn factory, and patented innumerable toys and games. Charles M., who patented his tongue-and-groove blocks in 1867 after he hit upon the idea of making nailless wooden boxes for croquet sets, later translated the process into a number of celebrated toys featuring interchangeable, interlocking parts. These included

Crandall's *District School* and his *Acrobats* made at his factory in Montrose, Pennsylvania. In 1889, after he moved to Waverly, New York, he invented a puzzle, 'Pigs in Clover'. More than a million of these were sold and they became a national craze among adults as well as children.

Dolls

Like many of the other residents of the United States in the nineteenth century, a sizeable percentage of the dolls were immigrants. Of all nineteenth-century American toys, they accounted for the largest share of imports, but despite the relatively small number of native dolls, there was a surprising assortment of individual manufacturers working with a wide variety of materials, though the wax, china and bisque heads used for European dolls were not among them.

Even when the dolls were not immigrants themselves, they were often made by immigrants, whose traditional methods had crossed the ocean with them. The earliest known United States doll patent has such an origin. When this was granted to Ludwig Greiner of Philadelphia in 1858, it was essentially for a modification of a type of head made in his native Thuringia. These heads, made of papier mâché reinforced with linen, were usually brunette in the early years, but were frequently blonde after Greiner improved his patent in 1872. They were often accompanied by bodies manufactured by another Philadelphian, Jacob Lacmann (who was granted patents for doll extremities – fingers in 1871 and feet in 1874). Sometimes a doll was of mixed parentage; with an American body and a European head. Another maker of composition dolls' heads, Philip Goldsmith, who began to make dolls in the late 1860s patented a doll's body in 1885 which ingeniously incorporated a corset.

In 1873, a patent for a wooden doll with mortise-and-tenon joints was granted to Joel Ellis whose native Vermont undoubtedly supplied the maple with which it was made. Features and hair were painted on the pressed wooden heads; hands and feet were of metal. Joel Ellis dolls were made for only a year, but were the forerunners of 'jointed woodens' made by a number of other makers.

Other materials, rubber, celluloid and rag among them, diversified the doll population. A dozen years after Charles Goodyear discovered the hot vulcanization of rubber in 1839, his brother Nelson took out a patent for hard rubber

Doll, Ludwig Greiner, 1858-72, patented 1858. Papier-mâché head and shoulders on a cloth body with leather arms; head reinforced with linen. A very popular doll in the States. Smithsonian Institution.

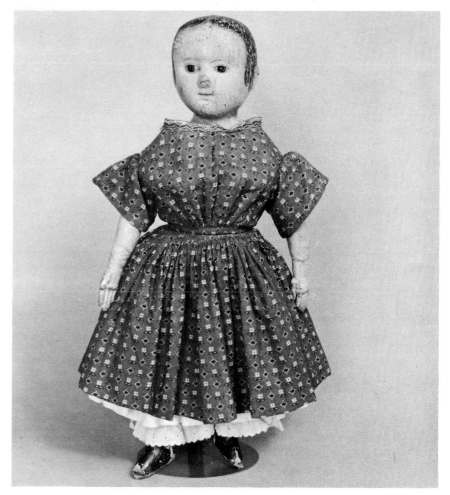

which was impressed on a sizeable assortment of rubber dolls, though relatively few have survived. The Hyatt brothers of New Jersey experimented with celluloid products as early as 1863. Although the year they began to make dolls is unknown, it was clearly before 1880 when William S. Carpenter patented an 'improved' celluloid head.

Martha Chase of Pawtucket, Rhode Island, beginning in the 1880s and continuing for decades, made stockinet dolls inspired by an 'Izannah Walker' she had received as a child. Mrs Walker, of Central Falls, Rhode Island, had patented her original rag doll with a stockinet pressed head in 1873. Both the Walker and Chase dolls were relatively sophisticated rag dolls, layered with other substances as well as cloth.

Although simple rag dolls have existed since the beginning of time, commercially-made versions, euphemistically referred to as 'cloth dolls', were officially recognized in 1886 when a design patent was granted for a printed cut-out rag doll. This was in fact a Santa Claus, but subsequent patentees provided dolls, animals, birds and balls and, indeed, every conceivable shape which could be printed and stuffed.

It is difficult to classify the Auto-peripatetikos, which is as much a clockwork toy as it is a walking doll, but doll collectors seem to have taken it unto

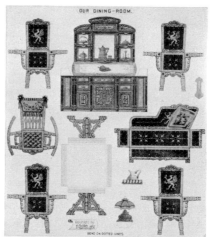

TOP *Doll, Izannah Walker, patented 1873. Rag with a stockinet pressed head. Mrs Walker inspired many makers of rag dolls. Margaret Woodbury Strong Museum Rochester.*

ABOVE *Dolls' house furniture, F. Cairo, Brooklyn, New York, patented 1892. Paper. F. Cairo patented three sheets of furniture for cutting and gluing, a parlour, bedroom and dining room. Author's Collection.*

themselves. Patented in the United States, and then in England in 1862, it might well have been given as a reward to young owners who could pronounce the Greek name of their toy. Other clockwork dolls which are as much toy as doll, include a walking girl pushing a perambulator, invented in 1868 by a Washingtonian named William F. Goodwin, the singing doll, patented in 1882 by William Webber of Massachusetts, and the steel-bodied phonograph doll on which, soon after he introduced the phonograph, Thomas Edison lavished numerous patents between 1878 and 1891.

Surviving American dolls of the Victorian period are rare, some of them, such as the Izannah Walkers, more so than others. Perhaps too well-loved, the composition-headed dolls are, when found, frequently candidates for doll hospitals. The imported bisques and chinas when broken, were discarded, the fragile natives, when bumped or dropped, were likely just to fade away.

Paper dolls and paper furniture and many other paper toys may well be entitled to the last word in a brief summary of American toys. Literally

TOP *Dolls' house cabinet, Bradford Kingman, 1856. Wooden, ht 10⅞ in (27 cm). Kingman, a maker of wooden toys, advertised a similar cabinet in the Maine Business Directory of 1856. Author's Collection.*

ABOVE *Miniature kitchen, probably American, late nineteenth century. Tin, 9½ in × 18 in (24 cm × 46 cm). Popular in the States and on the Continent. Important features were the range and a workable pump. Author's Collection.*

tons of paper toys and children's books were published, beginning early on in the nineteenth century. However, a postscript must allude, at least, to balls, marbles, tops, hoops, Noah's arks, squeak toys – the catalogue is long. It is clear that, during the final seven decades of the nineteenth century, American children were neglected neither by toymakers abroad nor by those at home.

Flora Gill Jacobs

Manufacturers, Retailers and Publishers

ALTHOF, BERGMANN & CO.
New York City jobber and manufacturer of tin toys, beginning in about 1867 and specializing in CLOCKWORK TOYS, dolls' house furniture, etc.

AMERICAN TOY CO.
Wholesale distribution house in New York City, founded by J. & E. Stevens and George W. Brown of Connecticut in 1869 when they merged their lines of iron and tin toys.

AYRES, F. H.
English manufacturer from 1864 of rubber balls and sports goods.

BASSETT-LOWKE
Founded in 1890, the English firm of Bassett-Lowke was primarily renowned for its TOY TRAINS. In 1901, it produced a steam-driven model of Stevenson's *Rocket*, built to scale and to standard gauges defined that year.

BEGGS, EUGENE
Patterson, New Jersey, manufacturer of steam trains, commencing business in *c.* 1870.

BETTS, JOHN
Prolific London publisher, producing mainly maps, Bible stories and puzzles with which he sold a key picture and booklet.

R. BLISS & CO.
Pawtucket, Rhode Island firm, established in 1832, which manufactured wooden toys and games, including tool chests and architectural blocks. In the late nineteenth century, many toys of lithographed paper on wood (dolls' houses, stores, stables, furniture, etc.) were made.

MILTON BRADLEY & CO.
Established in Springfield, Massachusetts in 1860, this firm together with MCLOUGHLIN BROS and PARKER BROS was one of the leading makers of games, puzzles, optical toys, paint sets, etc.

WILLIAM BRITAIN & SONS
Famous as producers of TOY SOLDIERS, although the firm made many ingenious mechanical toys and figures. William Britain, son of William Britain Sr, the Birmingham toy maker, was the real genius of the family. He took out his first patent in 1884 for a clockwork Chinaman; the Equestrienne, for which he took out a patent two years later, was not driven by clockwork but by heavy fly-wheel momentum which Britain called 'friction gear'.

GEORGE W. BROWN & CO.
Manufactured the first CLOCKWORK TOYS made in the United States in 1856

The General, *William Britain & Sons, c. 1880. Lead. When the umbrella is spun the soldier moves. He originally held a sword which was friction-driven from the front wheel of the horse. London Museum.*

at Forestville, Connecticut. In 1869 Brown merged his line of tin toys with the iron toys of J. & E. STEVENS & CO.

CARLISLE & FINCH CO.
Manufacturer of trains, including electric trains and 'electrical novelties', established in 1896 at Cincinnati, Ohio.

CARPENTER, FRANCIS W.
Early maker and popularizer of cast-iron vehicles, based in Port Chester, New York. Patent dates of 1880 and 1883 on Carpenter toys make them easily recognizable.

T. C. CLARK & CO.
English company which established the Shakespeare foundry at Wolverhampton in 1861 and specialized in the production of toys, guns and cannons.

CRANDALL, CHARLES M.
One of eleven Crandalls who manufactured toys in the United States during the nineteenth century, Charles M. Crandall of Covington and Montrose, Pennsylvania, and, later, of Waverly, New York, patented his tongue-and-groove blocks in 1867, later using them as the basis for such celebrated toys as his *District School* and *Acrobats*. Among many other toys, he invented in 1889 a puzzle, *Pigs in Clover* which became a national craze, selling more than a million copies.

CRANDALL, JESSE A.
Beginning in the 1840s, in New York, Jesse Crandall manufactured dolls' carriages, ROCKING HORSES and velocipedes. He took out many patents during

decades of toymaking including a classic one, for nested blocks.

CREMER, W. H. JR
German wholesaler dealing in all types of toys, games, puzzles and dolls. His first warehouse was at 27 Bond Street, London; in 1862 he moved it to 210 Regent Street.

DEAN & SON
London publishers who specialized in juvenile publishing from 1847 and, in particular, toy books with movable characters.

EDLIN, EDWARD C.
Owner from 1807–47 of a juvenile repository specializing in toys and games at 34 New Bond Street, London.

ELLIS, BRITTON & EATON
Springfield, Vermont, toy company, better known as the Vermont Novelty Works, which made wooden toys, including dolls' perambulators, sleighs, dolls' furniture, carts and wagons. In 1869, the firm also advertised 'tin, rubber, pewter and china toys', including tin and iron dolls'-house furniture.

JAMES FALLOWS & SONS
Operated in Philadelphia, c. 1890–5, manufacturing tin and mechanical toys. Previously, Fallows had been the foreman of the Philadelphia Tin Toy Company.

FRANCIS, FIELD & FRANCIS
Also known as the Philadelphia Tin Toy Company. Established as early as 1838, and believed to be the first manufacturer of tin toys in the United States.

GONG BELL MANUFACTURING CO.
Maker of BELL TOYS, founded in 1866, in East Hampton, Connecticut, where there were a number of other factories making bells and bell toys.

J. G. HAMLEY
Famous London toy shop founded in High Holborn in 1763 and first called 'The Noah's Ark' after the sign above the original shop. Later moved to its current location in Regent Street.

N. N. HILL BRASS CO.
Beginning in c. 1889, the Company made BELL TOYS in the bell-making town of East Hampton, Connecticut.

HORNER, W. G.
Manufacturer in Bristol in c. 1860 of ZOETROPES and other optical toys.

HUBLEY MANUFACTURING CO.
Manufacturer from 1894 in Lancaster, Pennsylvania of iron vehicles, stoves and other toys.

HULL & STAFFORD
Manufacturer from Clinton, Connecticut of tin toys. In 1869 the company succeeded the UNION MANUFACTURING CO.

E. R. IVES & CO.
This firm, founded in 1868 in Plymouth, Connecticut and operating later in Bridgeport, Connecticut, made for many

generations, a wide variety of CLOCKWORK TOYS, cast-iron vehicles, trains and other toys.

W. & S. B. IVES
From the 1840s to the 1860s in Salem, Massachusetts, this publisher marketed board and card games and toy books.

JACQUES, J.
London manufacturer and publisher operating from 1849 at 102 Hatton Garden. Produced chessmen in the Staunton style and many games and puzzles. Invented the card game 'Happy Families', for which he commissioned the cartoonist and illustrator Sir John Tenniel to design the cards, and also 'Snap'.

JEWITT, H.
London agent, active from 1870, dealing in toys and games for many American firms.

KENTON HARDWARE CO.
In Kenton, Ohio, founded about 1880, the Kenton Hardware Co. manufactured a well-known line of iron toys and toy banks.

LINES BROS
London firm founded c. 1870 and dealing initially in ROCKING HORSES and wooden toys and later in mechanical toys and Triang toys.

MCLOUGHLIN BROS
John McLoughlin, an American engraver by trade, took his brother into partnership in 1855 to form a company which, for several generations, manufactured juvenile books, games, blocks, paper dolls, dolls' houses and related items.

PARKER BROS
Founded in Salem, Massachusetts in 1883, this firm, which bought the rights to most of the games originally published by W. & S. B. IVES, continues to the present day to publish board games, card games, puzzles, etc.

PETER PIA
New York City manufacturer who started business in 1848 and continued for more than a century producing pewter toys, including dolls'-house furniture.

POLLOCK, BENJAMIN
From 1875 Pollock was the owner of a shop in Hoxton Street in one of the poorer quarters of London from which he sold the famous Pollock toy theatres.

PRATT & LETCHWORTH
Manufacturers in Buffalo, New York, also known as the Buffalo Toy Works, the company produced cast-iron and steel toys, including trains and other vehicles. An 1892 catalogue entitled *The Buffalo Indestructible Iron and Steel Toys*, pictures, among many other toys, a sulky with driver, patented in 1883, and a dray with driver, patented in 1885.

REDINGTON, JOHN
Took over the English publisher J. K. Green's business in about 1857 and reissued nineteen of his plays. In addition Redington designed and etched some of his own which although clumsy and naïve in composition, are remarkable for their dramatic qualities. Succeeded by his son-in-law, POLLOCK.

REED, W. S.
Manufacturer operating from 1875 in Leominster, Massachusetts of wooden toys, blocks, games, trains; often made with lithographed paper applied to the wood.

RILEY BROS
Manufacturers in Bradford, England of magic lanterns, slides and other optical toys.

A. SCHOENHUT & CO.
Philadelphia manufacturer of toy pianos, musical instruments and other toys, established in 1872. After the turn of the century the Company manufactured the celebrated Humpty Dumpty circuses and, later, dolls and dolls' houses.

SECOR, JEROME B.
Bridgeport, Connecticut maker of gun and sewing-machine tools, who patented in 1880, a toy locomotive and a toy pistol, and made clockwork figures, elaborate mechanical birds in cages, etc. Most of Secor's toys were later taken over by E. R. IVES & CO.

SELCHOW & RIGHTER CO.
Founded in 1864, in New York City, the Company operated at a later date in Brooklyn. Manufactured toys and games.

SPEAR, J. W.
Publisher operating in London and Nuremberg from 1878 who specialized in games and puzzles, which he often had printed by the chromo-lithograph method.

SPOONER, WILLIAM
London publisher of high-class workmanship who used hand-coloured lithographs. Contemporary of BETTS.

SPURRIN, E. C.
Successor in 1847 to EDLIN.

J. & E. STEVENS & CO.
Established in 1843 in Cromwell, Connecticut. Manufacturers of iron wheel toys, MECHANICAL BANKS, dolls'-house furniture, etc. See AMERICAN TOY CO.

RAPHAEL TUCK & SONS
Firm with offices in London, Paris and New York who produced all types of juvenilia including puzzles and doll-dressing sets in the latter part of the nineteenth century.

TOWER TOY CO.
Founded in the 1830s as a guild composed of craftsmen in different fields who, by combining their labours and products, offered an extensive line of toys. Head of the enterprise, and a

carpenter by trade, was William S. Tower, who has been described as the founder of the toy industry in America.

UNION MANUFACTURING CO.
From 1854 to 1869, a manufacturer of tin toys in Clinton, Connecticut. Succeeded by HULL & STAFFORD.

VOLTAMP ELECTRIC MANUFACTURING CO.
Manufacturer of TOY TRAINS and train equipment in Baltimore, Maryland.

WALKER, JAMES
Birmingham, England, manufacturer in the 1870 period of tin toys and games.

WALLIS FAMILY
Leading English publishers of children's games and puzzles particularly maps and jigsaws, in the first half of the nineteenth century.

WEEDEN MANUFACTURING CO.
New Bedford, Massachusetts maker of steam engines and other steam toys, beginning in the 1880s and remaining in production for many decades.

WILKINS TOY WORKS
Established in Keene, New Hampshire in 1888, a leading manufacturer of iron and steel toys, including toy banks and CLOCKWORK TOYS.

Doll Marks

The most likely place for a mark on a doll is on the back of the head or shoulders, but equally they may be found inside the head or on the soles of the feet. Marks can be embroidered, incised, pressed, printed, raised, stamped or written. They can be imprinted directly on the doll or affixed by means of a tag, label or ribbon.

Letters or numbers are usually used to indicate the size or mould type. Often, the higher the numeral, the smaller the doll. Initials frequently include the place of manufacture as well as the maker, designer or distributor.

Many initials on dolls stand for 'patented' or 'registered' in various languages. Often doll makers were themselves confused as to whether they had obtained patents, copyrights or trademarks, and this information marked on the doll may not always agree with the company records.

Glossary of Toys and Games

Animated cap pistol
Iron pistol in which the exploding of a cap was accompanied by the movement of animated figures, many of them fanciful, each mounted on a pistol-like framework. Such miscellaneous figures as a sea serpent, George Washington and Punch and Judy were represented.

Bell toy
Highly decorative variety of painted iron toy, usually on a wheeled platform, and featuring an animated figure which accompanied the bell or bells which sounded when the toy was pulled or pushed.

Chromatrope
Lantern slide consisting of two glass disks with linear designs, one rotating in front of the other to give a kaleidoscopic effect.

Chromotrope
Invented in 1876 by a French scientist, Bellair, but exported and sold in Britain and the United States, a chromotrope involved the use of torsion applied to coloured disks. By threading a string through a central hole in the disks, and exploiting its tensile strength by a pulling and relaxing movement, colourful optical effects were produced.

Clockwork toy
Production of popular clockwork toys began about 1870 when factory methods were introduced into Europe and improvements in machine tools and spray painting as well as supplies of very cheap clockwork were made. The first clockwork toys came from Germany. (For British mechanical toys see BRITAIN.)

Friction toys
Such toys as automobiles, street cars, hansom cabs, boats and locomotives, fitted with a heavy fly wheel whose shaft made frictional contact with the wheels of the vehicle. When the toy was pushed, the resulting momentum caused the motion to continue.

Golliwog
Based on a character in a series of picture and verse books by the American author's grandmother, the golliwog first made his appearance in the 1890s. A shock-haired, black-faced rag doll, in the stories he is always partnered by two large Dutch dolls, whose striped and star-patterned dresses were contrived from an American flag, and three smaller peg dolls who contributed to a revival of interest in the old-fashioned wooden doll.

Hot air toys
These have been described as 'the simplest of all movement toys', requiring only the upward flow of hot air, usually from a stove or range, to animate them. An Ives, Blakeslee & Williams catalogue of 1893 shows a mill grinder attached to a stove pipe by a wire. Other subjects included a commercial traveller (tipping his tall hat), a butcher at his chopping block and a cat playing a bass viol.

Kaleidoscope
Named by its inventor, Sir David Brewster in 1817, a kaleidoscope is an optical instrument consisting of from two to four reflecting surfaces placed in a tube at the end of which is a small compartment containing pieces of coloured glass. On looking through the tube, numerous reflections of these are seen, which may be constantly altered by rotation of the instrument.

Mechanical banks
Usually of iron, such banks incorporated one or more figures or objects which were animated by the deposit of a coin. The figures often related to historical (or notorious) personages or events. First appeared about 1870.

Musical box
Mechanical musical instrument consisting of a revolving cylinder with projecting pins which worked upon a resonant comb-like metal plate. Although exceptional examples were produced in England prior to the nineteenth century, notably by James Cox, the Continental makers of automata and mechanical toys dominated this field in the nineteenth century.

Noah's ark
First produced in the mid-eighteenth century, mass-produced arks were made from about 1800–40 with the crudest animals, often just spotted with colour and generally out of scale, unless they were familiar farm animals. The finest arks were made between 1860–70, sometimes with as many as four hundred animals.

Phenakistoscope
Disk invented in c. 1834 whereby figures are arranged radially to represent a moving object in successive positions. On turning the phenakistoscope round rapidly and viewing the figures through a fixed slit (or their reflections in a mirror through radial slits in the disk itself), the successive visual images produce the impression of actual motion.

Praxinoscope
Scientific toy resembling a ZOETROPE whereby the reflections of a series of pictures produce the impression of a moving object.

Praxinoscope theatre
Box with scenery depicted on the lid which remains still while the drum containing the figured slides is revolved. Both are reflected in a mirror, the figures appearing animated against a static background.

Rocking horse
Wooden horse mounted upon rockers for children to ride upon in a rocking motion. Appearing in a simple form

shortly after the middle of the seventeenth century, such improvements were made in the early half of the nineteenth century as double saddle horns, affording the very young a better grip, and sometimes additional seats at the rear. From about 1860, there were many efforts to improve or modify the simple rocker, usually by employing more powerful springs. See colour plate p. 318.

Sand toys
Toys powered by sand falling from open hoppers into the buckets of 'waterwheels' originated in Nuremberg in the early-sixteenth century and made later in England and the United States, but so flimsy and temperamental that they died out in the 1870s and '80s.

Squeak toys
Small figure, usually an animal or bird, of papier mâché or wood situated on a base containing a pair of small bellows which squeaked (or chirped) when pressed.

Stereoscope
Perfected by Sir David Brewster in 1838, the stereoscope has many variants but in its simplest form it is an instrument for obtaining from two pictures of an object taken from slightly different points of view, a single image giving the impression of solidity or relief.

Still banks
As distinguished from MECHANICAL BANKS, which animated one or more figures when a coin was inserted, still banks are inanimate. Although still banks were made of tin and other materials, the most collectable are of iron, often fanciful or historical in subject matter.

Teetotum
Small four-sided disk or die having an initial letter inscribed on each of its sides, and a spindle passing down through it by which it could be twisted, twirled or spun like a small top. The letter which lay uppermost when it fell decided the fortune of the player. Also made as above but with six or eight sides bearing numbers (one to six or one to eight). Used for children's table games in the early-nineteenth century when dice were associated with gambling games.

Toy soldiers
It was not until the eighteenth century that genuine metal toy soldiers appeared, made in considerably larger quantities at the beginning of the nineteenth century since, by the invention of inexpensive metal alloys, metal objects were now available to a much wider section of the public. English children began playing with English-made soldiers in about 1893, the year when a toy maker called William Britain Jr (son

of the toy maker, William Britain of Birmingham) invented the hollow-cast soldier and began to market the toy soldier against German monopoly, German manufacturers having previously made them specifically for the English market.

Toy trains
Although German manufacturers were the first to make and market toy trains, in c. 1860 these rather crude early models were soon rivalled and surpassed by the fine examples produced by the American firm of E. R. IVES & CO. and the English firm of BASSETT-LOWKE, founded in 1890. Model and toy trains are powered by clockwork, electricity or steam but to the collector of early types, the method of propulsion is not as important as whether or not the train is in its original condition.

Zoetrope
Optical toy consisting of an open metal drum with a series of slits round the circumference revolved on a metal spindle in a wooden stand. Paper strips bearing figures representing successive positions of a moving object were arranged one at a time round the inner surface of the drum. These, when viewed through the slits while the cylinder is in steady rotation, produce the impression that the object is actually in motion.

Glossary of Dolls

Bisque doll
Bisque dolls' heads were made from a ceramic material with a hard matt or non-glossy surface that in superior-quality dolls, is virtually translucent. Bisque heads are usually pressed or poured into a mould, those made by the former method being usually earlier in date, rough on the inside and not of uniform thickness. Bisque dolls' heads were popular as early as the 1860s, when they were usually made with hollow shoulders to attach to a stuffed body, and with or without a swivel neck. Bisque was perfected at doll factories in France and Germany but also popular in Britain and the United States, particularly towards the end of the century.

Brownies, 1892–1907
Cut-out rag dolls based on the copyrighted figures of the American designer, Palmer Cox. Twelve different dolls designed to be approximately 7 in (18 cm) tall were made to be cut out of one yard of material. They represented

John Bull, a Canadian, a Chinaman, a Dude, a German, a Highlander, an Indian, an Irishman, a policeman, a sailor, a soldier, and Uncle Sam. Brownies were also made in other materials such as BISQUE and composition on a wire base.

Celluloid doll, c. 1869
Originally an English invention, it was left to two Americans, John Wesley Hyatt and his brother Isaiah Smith Hyatt to manufacture celluloid dolls commercially. They were made of a synthetic material composed of cellulose nitrate, camphor, pigment, fillers, and alcohol, hot steam, being blown into the moulds. Since they were inexpensive, they were collected by children in large numbers, one of the most popular being the Kewpie range.

Character doll
Portrait-type dolls made to represent real people. In the 1890s there were BROWNIES, Steiff and a few other character dolls but the great vogue was in the following century.

China-headed doll
Made of glazed porcelain as opposed to unglazed ceramics which collectors call BISQUE, they achieved great popularity in the 1840s. In the mid-nineteenth century, china heads and limbs were occasionally made for peg-wooden bodies. A superior quality china head is distinguished by its detailed modelling and painting, for example, the details at the hair line and intricate attention to the eyes and nostrils. The red dot in the corner of the eye and the red line over the eye is often lacking in cheaper models. *Harper's Bazaar* referred to china dolls as being old fashioned as early as 1873.

Cloth-bodied doll
Cloth-bodied dolls with little or no articulation were made in the United States and England in the early decades of the nineteenth century. From the 1870s and '80s several patents were taken out relating to the articulation of cloth-bodied dolls.

Composition doll
Dolls' heads and jointed bodies made from a mixture containing mainly glue and wood pulp which was malleable when wet. PAPIER-MÂCHÉ and CELLULOID DOLLS are also often termed composition dolls.

Crying doll
Since an English doll of c. 1760, many different types have been available. The most common means for producing the sound is the use of the bellows and reed pipes.

Dolls' house dolls
Term mainly used to describe small dolls specifically designed for dolls'

houses made in such materials as wood, rag and porcelain.

Frozen Charlotte, c. 1850–c. 1914
Known also as solid china, bathing babies or pillar dolls and made in glazed or unglazed porcelain, they often represented a baby and were sometimes carried in the arms of a larger doll.

Gutta-percha doll
Made widely in the 1850s and subsequently, gutta-percha dolls are often confused with RUBBER DOLLS, although the former is a harder and more fibrous substance.

Horsman doll
Dolls distributed, assembled or made between 1865 and 1901 by Edward Imeson Horsman of New York City, who started primarily as a toy distributor. Horsman began to import from Europe and assemble dolls' heads and bodies from the 1870s, using his famous trademark from 1897.

Infant doll
Dolls dressed as infants showed little difference in conception from those dressed as babies and children. Queen Victoria, when princess, used RAG DOLLS for infants in long dresses, while at a later date, some of the CHINA-HEADED DOLLS, WAX DOLLS, and dolls with papier-mâché heads were dressed in long clothes as infants.

London rag doll, c. 1865–1905
Essentially an English production, the face was made of wax over which a piece of muslin was stretched and the body of calico was stuffed with sawdust. Generally they wore a neat nightcap over a long infant's robe.

Military costume doll
Although the greatest number of military costume dolls were made during or after large-scale wars, such has been their popularity that even in peacetime, many dolls were dressed as soldiers and sailors.

Milliners' model doll
Term usually given by collectors to dolls with papier-mâché heads, kid bodies and wooden limbs, without articulation, thought to have been designed for the use of milliners and hairdressers, hence also known as *coiffure* dolls.

Negro doll
Made in Europe and America for many years, they were particularly popular immediately after the American Civil War, and again in the 1890s when dolls of every nationality were being produced. While some Negro dolls were simply painted black, others displayed Negroid features and had the black pigment mixed in the slip of the bisque.

Papier-mâché doll
Papier-mâché dolls reached the height of their popularity by the mid-nineteenth century, many dolls with heads of papier mâché being exhibited at the Great Exhibition of 1851. Papier mâché began to be used for jointed dolls' bodies in c. 1870, and it continued to be popular well into the twentieth century, although the heads were generally made of ceramics or some other composition.

Parian doll
Dolls made of hard- or soft-paste unglazed porcelain. Untinted bisque dolls are sometimes wrongly referred to as parian. (See PORCELAIN GLOSSARY.)

Patent washable doll, c. 1885
Name applied to certain COMPOSITION DOLLS that were described as washable, a description generally disproved by their young owners.

Phonograph doll, 1878–c. 1925
Manufactured by the American, Thomas Edison, who obtained an English patent for a phonographic doll in 1878, that would produce sound, having a phonet to move its lips. By 1890, about 500 people were engaged in the manufacture of phonography and talking dolls at the Edison establishment: for example eighteen women were employed solely for the recital of the nursery rhymes for the cylinders to go into the clocks.

Rag doll
Commercial rag dolls appeared extensively in the second half of the nineteenth century.

Rubber doll
Charles Goodyear obtained a U.S. patent in 1853 and a British patent in 1855 for moulding toys of India rubber and gutta-percha. Sometimes the entire doll was made of rubber, sometimes only the head and occasionally only the hands.

Stockinet doll
Dolls made with stockinet fabric, but usually reinforced with other materials. Those made from the 1880s by Martha Chase of Pawtucket, Rhode Island, provided a mask with raised features over which the stockinet was stretched. The head and limbs were sized with a coating of glue and/or paste, dyed and painted with oils. The ears and thumbs were applied separately.

Talking doll
Pull-strings, phonographs and reeds were the most common methods used to simulate speech in dolls.

Walking doll
Most nineteenth-century walking dolls were propelled by a clockwork mechanism. In the 1860s, among several patents taken out for walking dolls, the most famous was the Autoperipatetikos by Enoch Rice Morrison. Sometimes the walking mechanism caused the doll's eyes to turn from side to side thus earning the description 'flirty-eyed'.

Wax doll
Luxury dolls of the mid-nineteenth century were provided by the beautifully made wax dolls with inserted hair made by the Pierottis, Montanaris and others. Wax dolls were very fragile, being particularly subject to damage through changes in temperature and scratches. They were also expensive and could seldom boast the latest inventions such as a turning head, or sleeping eyes. From the 1870s, their popularity began to wane, although they continued to be made in limited numbers.

Wooden doll
By the mid-nineteenth century the long-lived wooden doll was becoming cruder, with less carving and often more spherical heads. Heads of other materials such as china and wax were also used on peg-jointed wooden bodies. The relatively small number of American wooden dolls made by the Cooperative Manufacturing Co. were described as 'some unnoticeable toys' when shown at the Vienna Exhibition of 1873.

Bibliography

BELL, R. C. *Board and Table Games*, London, 1969

CARMAN, W. G. *Toy Soldiers*, London, 1972

COLEMAN, DOROTHY. *The Collectors' Encyclopaedia of Dolls*, New York, 1968

COOK, OLIVE. *Movements In Two Dimensions*, London, 1963

CULFF, ROBERT. *The World of Toys*, Feltham, 1969

DAIKEN, LESLIE. *Children's Toys throughout the Ages*, London, 1953

DESMONDE, KAY. *Dolls and Dolls' Houses*, London, 1962

FRASER, ANTONIA. *A History of Toys*, London, 1966

GARRAT, J. G. *A Collector's Guide To Model Soldiers*, London, 1965

GREENE, VIVIAN. *English Dolls' Houses of The Eighteenth and Nineteenth Century*, London, 1965

HANNAS, LINDA. *Two Hundred years of Jigsaw Puzzles*, London, 1968

HANNAS, LINDA. *The English Jigsaw Puzzle*, London, 1972

HILLIER, MARY. *Dolls and Doll Makers*, London, 1968

JACOBS, FLORA GILL. *A History of Dolls Houses*, New York, 1956

NOBLE, JOHN. *Dolls*, New York, 1967, London, 1968

SPEAIGHT, GEORGE. *The History of the English Toy Theatre*, London and New York, 1969

WHITE, GWEN. *European and American Dolls*, London, 1966

WHITEHOUSE, F. R. B. *Table Games of Georgian and Victorian Days*, London, 1971

332

Miscellany

BRITISH

There has been no century to compare with the nineteenth in its enormous production of small articles of a functional, ornamental or memorable nature. No surface could be left unadorned in a Victorian home. The complex nature of the furniture, particularly cabinets with an asymmetrical arrangement of shelves, influenced by Japan, provided the maximum number of display areas for all manner of writing and sewing implements, smoking materials, miniature collections, photographs, or simply knick-knacks and memorabilia. Despite the clutter, it was ordered chaos. 'A place for everything and everything in its place', the saying went.

Homely Disarray

There were a number of social reasons for the increase in production, the first being the growing wealth of the bourgeois classes. They had money to invest in small, decorative objects but they wanted their houses to stay homely, not like the spacious, cold reception rooms of the eighteenth-century upper classes. The family was an important aspect of Victorian life and the security of the family was in the home. Clutter was homely and, in the latter part of the century, the father created for himself a 'cosy corner' with a comfortable chair, his few favourite books arranged between ornamental bookends and within easy reach, as were his footstool, pipe and tobacco. Similarly, the mother of the house had her nook, with her embroidery and darning equipment at hand and her collection of souvenirs and ornaments lovingly arranged within view.

OPPOSITE *Seed picture, American, 1860-75. Seed wreath with feathers, mounted on cloth in a gessoed pine frame, ht 2ft 4½ in (72·4 cm). Greenfield Village and Henry Ford Museum.*

The desire to buy objects both functional and ornamental was encouraged by the great exhibitions, where the best of British crafts and industry, combined with the tastes of Europe and the exotic East, were housed under one roof. There was, furthermore, the notion that everything functional should in some way be picturesque. The nostalgia for past styles and those of other lands resulted in an eclectic jumble of motifs in the decoration of these objects. Besides acquiring paintings, sculpture, coins, glass or ceramics, people collected snuff boxes, silver miniature animals, miniature cups and saucers or quite simply bric-à-brac.

Smoker's companion, English, mid-nineteenth century. Pine, ht approx. 2ft 6in (76·2 cm). This comprises a cigar cutter, two brass ashtrays and two covered boxes. Henry Duke & Son.

In the arrangement of their homes, they were certainly influenced by their great high priestess, the Queen herself, who is shown surrounded by similar objects in photographs of interiors of her private rooms at Windsor, Balmoral and above all Osborne, on the Isle of Wight.

As so many small objects were used in Victorian daily life, it is simplest to divide them into categories: those associated with a lady and her sewing, a gentleman and his smoking, the dressing table, writing table and kitchen. So many craftsmen were involved in different aspects of the production of these objects that it is not possible to single out individual makers. The names of the retailers such as Asprey's, Garrard's, Hennell's and Liberty's appear again and again but the actual production, particularly of metalwork, might come from Elkington & Co. or J. Rodgers & Sons, of Sheffield, and from the many other Birmingham firms.

The Writing Table

The Victorians loved the idea of one piece of furniture that fulfilled numerous functions; for instance, a desk with flaps concealing compartments for correspondence, pigeon holes, drawleaves for writing, rising bookrests for reading, swivelling trays to hold pens, sealing wax or candles and, beneath, a shelf, cupboard and drawers. This offered a variety of surfaces where all manner of accoutrements for correspondence could be gathered. The most popular materials for these were Tunbridgeware and papier mâché. A papier-mâché desk set might comprise a stationery box with sloping lid, perhaps with a view of Windsor or Balmoral, a blotter, inkstand and pen tray, all decorated *en suite*. Alternatively, in Tunbridgeware, there might be the same pieces but perhaps with the addition of a paper knife, paperweights, a candlestand, string box and, the last word in fashion, an orna-

mental obelisk set with compass and thermometer.

Some of the most beautiful desk sets and writing boxes were made in the earlier part of the century of finely figured woods such as bird's eye maple, rosewood or coromandel, and bound with shaped-brass mounts of Gothic form. Perhaps the finest of these are the travelling writing boxes, the interiors lined with pine, the lids with velvet, with silver-topped, glass ink bottles and a lift-out leather-covered writing surface, the exterior complete with brass carrying handles. Blotters and stationery boxes in the latter part of the century were often covered with tooled leather, applied with the owner's initials in engraved silver or gilded metal and with ornate cast and chased corner mounts.

Silver was used for more costly inkstands, often with cut-glass bottles, the mounts cast and chased with flowers. In a silver combined candlestick and inkstand in the Victoria and Albert Museum, London, the notion of disguising the functional as ornamental is carried to the extreme: centred by a tree-trunk candle-holder, the inkwells simulating fruit, the whole rests on a vine leaf. During the rise of the Arts and Crafts Movement, the *avant garde* had pewter desk sets of organic Art Nouveau form, sometimes embellished with panels of enamel, retailed by such firms as Liberty's.

Letter racks, like toast racks, seem to have offered the Victorian designer scope for his imagination. Sometimes rustic in taste, they took the form of crossed tree boughs or even crossed muskets made in silver or porcelain. Then there was the type to hang on the wall; leather or

TOP *Desk set, the bookends stamped Betjemann's Patent Self Closing Book Slide 2797, the mounts of the caskets by Francis Douglas, 1861. Ebonized wood with engraved gilded mounts. Christie's.*

ABOVE *Inkwell in the form of a model Shand Mason horse-drawn fire engine, Shand Mason & Co., London. Silver with engraved inscription, ht 8 in (20·3 cm). The inkwell is beneath the lid of the water tank. Sotheby's Belgravia.*

gilded and metal backed, perhaps with flaps of engraved mother of pearl, with separate sections for Invitations, Accepted, Refused, Bills Unpaid, etc.

Paperweights, copying the French millefiori paperweights of Baccarat and Clichy, were manufactured at Stourbridge and Bristol. But more amusing and collected as souvenirs were their poor cousins, the plain glass domes backed with a tourist view of the pier at Scarborough or Dover Castle, giving the picture a three-dimensional effect.

With the arrival of the daguerreotype,

hotly pursued by other forms of photography, pressed thermoplastic daguerreotype Union cases and photograph frames would also adorn the writing table. The latter were, at their grandest, of cast and chased silver, or when less costly, of pierced gilded metal, ebony, ivory and Tunbridgeware, perhaps with velvet mounts. Some were even embroidered with beadwork or set with shells. To add to this already imposing list, there was probably a silver, or brass, bell in the form of a lady, the striker concealed beneath her skirts, to summon a servant to carry the letters to the post.

The Lady and her Worktable

The Victorian lady was never idle. If she was not devouring the classics, novels or journals, she was probably engaged in some form of handicraft. Thus, for her darning, embroidery, tapestry, patchwork and quilting, all manner of sewing boxes were made, of a variety of materials and with fitted compartments to accommodate the tools.

Tunbridgeware, a mosaic of minute fragments of wood stained in different colours, so named because it originated in the seventeenth century from Tunbridge Wells, was one of the favourite means of decorating workboxes. The most famous firms making Tunbridge-

OPPOSITE *Daguerreotype portrait of George Dolland, hand-tinted and gilt, English, from a travelling case presented to his wife 28 July 1853. Sotheby's Belgravia.*

ware, were Fenner & Nye, of Mount Ephraim, Tunbridge Wells, and Boyce, Brown & Kemp, the latter continuing until 1927, when manufacture ended.

Papier mâché was another popular material for workboxes, essentially feminine in its glossy nature and decoration with the shell and mother-of-pearl 'inlay' of the period 1830–45 and the realistically painted full-blown flowers on black. A further embellishment was the delicate gold and bronze decoration known as the Wolverhampton style. The best-known firm is Jennens & Bettridge, of Birmingham, who, unlike most of the numerous other firms in production, signed their work.

Ladies' workboxes came in original shapes, sometimes in the form of a grand piano or spinet, the lid lifting to reveal an interior of velvet-lined compartments to house the tools of turned ivory, bone or mother of pearl. The highest quality boxes had tools of chased and engraved silver and in the most exotic cases, a musical box hidden underneath.

Tools existed in these boxes that are scarcely heard of today: the steel stiletto, tambour hook, netting tool, tatting shuttle, lucet and thread waxer. Then there were, of course, tape measures, scissors in cases, emeries for cleaning rust off needles and an assortment of reels and spools. The finest scissors and steel tools came from the firm of J. Rodgers & Sons of Sheffield. Turned-ivory spools could have several sections to hold different threads, useful for travelling or in a lady's companion, which she used when about the house. Star-shaped mother-of-pearl disks prevented silk tangling when wound. Thin cases of Tunbridgeware or beadwork held stranded silks.

Thimbles and their cases were produced in enormous variety. Besides the materials already mentioned, they were made of polished horn, brass and turned wood. A very ornate type was the turned-ebony case of chalice shape with ivory appliqués, containing a silver thimble with red stone top. If a daughter pleased her parents with her expertise in needlework, she was sometimes rewarded with a gold thimble – exceedingly rare today.

A workbox often contained a scent flask for toilet water to keep the hands cool, essential for fine embroidery, and also a vinaigrette to revive the vapourish

OPPOSITE *British Victoriana. Included are a shellwork box for gloves, tortoiseshell and silver opera glasses, a turquoise-studded gold thimble and representation of Queen Victoria and Prince Albert. Parry-Crooke Collection.*

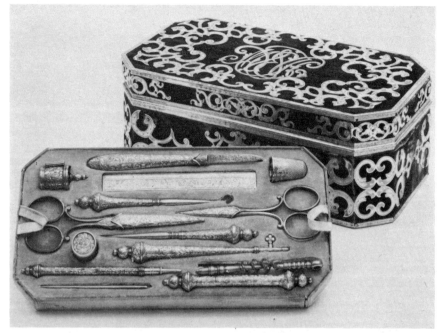

Vinaigrette in the form of a pink, H. W. & L. Dee, 1867. Gilded silver, 3¼ in (8·8 cm). The reviving essence is inhaled by lifting the hinged head of the flower. Sotheby's Belgravia.

TOP *Needlework box, English, c. 1850. Purple velvet with gilded metal strapwork mounts. The gilded items on the tray include a thimble, scissors, needle and pin cases, a pencil and tape measure. Sotheby's Belgravia.*

ABOVE *Scissors, stamped J. Rodgers & Sons, Sheffield. Steel, l 11-12 in (28-30 cm). The decoration of the handles varies from the Neo-Mannerist to the Gothic. Sotheby's Belgravia.*

needlewoman during a stuffy ladies' gathering. Discreet egg-shaped hand coolers of coloured marbles were also used, though not generally catered for in the fitted workbox. They should not be confused with darning mushrooms, sometimes of egg shape and often of wood or porcelain. Another tool, not included

in the workbox but essential in households before the arrival of the sewing machine, was the table clamp. It was used to hold taut linen when being hemmed by hand and was generally made of steel or ivory; it might house a pin cushion on the top. Boxes often had two or three layers, like a trunk, with ribbon loops to lift them out, and a mirror-lined lid.

The Lady and her Dressing Table

Perhaps the most beautiful attributes of the Victorian lady's dressing table were the brush sets. Comprising hair brushes, clothes brushes, hat brush, make-up brush, combs and hand mirror, they were backed with cast and engraved silver, often in the Rococo taste, and were made by the leading silversmiths of the time. Alternatively, they were ivory or tortoiseshell backed, perhaps inlaid with the intricate scrolled initials of the owner in silver. A cheaper substitute for ivory which was invented towards the end of the century was Xylonite, an early form of white plastic retailed by the Xylonite Co. Sadly, few of these brush sets have survived because when the bristles wore out they were discarded.

A lady might have a variety of ceramic or cut-glass powder and cream jars with engraved silver tops. Another essential was a pin tray, again perhaps made of silver, or alternatively Tunbridgeware or papier mâché and equally essential was the dressing-table pin cushion. Here there was no limit to the invention of the Victorian mind; pin cushions were set in silver or brass wheelbarrows, the backs

of animals, carriages and crowns. The loving daughter might sew one for her mother, a favourite type being in the form of flowers, the petals of left-over scraps of material, the centre the cushion. Later in the century cushions were mounted on parian cradles and a variety of other china ornaments such as could be won at the fair.

Pin cushions were often intended for hat pins, particularly when the cartwheel hats of the 1890s became *à la mode*. Hat pins were set with pearls, surrounded by pastes or brilliants, or with china flowers, while ladies in mourning wore pins set with gold-mounted jet.

Fitted jewel cases with secure locks were made of rosewood or other attractively figured woods and decorated with shaped mounts of engraved silver or brass. The interior would be fitted with lift-out trays and velvet-lined compartments. Alternatively, rings were hung on stands of wood or porcelain of simple form with poles rising from a tray, or else in the shape of a hand, the fingers splayed to receive the rings. Articles connected with a lady's toilet which are demoded and thus rarely seen today include button hooks, fan boxes, glove boxes, shoe horns, glove stretchers and glove powder flasks.

When a lady travelled, it was usually with the majority of these articles, and it is perhaps the nineteenth- and early twentieth-century travelling dressing cases that are the last word in fitted boxes. It is almost impossible to list the manufacturers of these portmanteaux because so many craftsmen were involved; the cutter of the glass bottles, the silversmith who cast, chased and engraved the lids and screw tops, the cabinetmaker who made the brass-bound wooden box and the binder who covered the case in crocodile or finest gilded-tooled morocco. However, the cases were usually retailed by such leading silversmiths as Garrard's, Mappin's and Asprey's and bear their stamp.

Dressing case and fitted boxes, W. Leuchars of Piccadilly, London. Walnut with pierced silver mounts in the Medieval style. These were shown at the Great Exhibition of 1851.

Hand mirror in the form of a flounder, H. W. & L. Dee, 1879. Silver, l 7½ in (18·9 cm). This illustrates the Victorian taste for giving functional objects a decorative appearance. Sotheby's Belgravia.

Usually lined with satin or *moiré*, there were holders and compartments for every toilet requisite and maybe a few extras such as writing equipment and a travelling clock.

Smoking Equipment

Queen Victoria heartily disliked the habit and openly condemned cigar smoking at Windsor. However, not even the Duke of Wellington's public condemnation of the addiction in 1845 prevented the craze continuing in gentlemen's homes, where the gentlemen adjourned so that the ladies might not be distressed by the smoke. By the end of the Napoleonic Wars, cigar smoking had almost displaced snuff taking. When the armies returned from the Crimea campaigns, they brought back the habit of cigarette smoking, inherited from the Russians.

As in all other branches of the arts, the Victorian craftsman took the opportunity to stretch his imagination to create decorative, exotic and intricate artifacts for the smoker.

Although snuff was *démodé*, the manufacture of little novelty boxes continued and they were much collected. Scotland carried on the tradition of snuff taking throughout the nineteenth century, sometimes in a purely ceremonial context. The plain horn box was displaced by the snuff mull, made from the curling horn of the mountain ram, of small size and silver mounted for the pocket, or of large size and on a stand for the household. The latter would sometimes be set with a cairngorm in the silver lid and have attached to it by small silver chains, all the tools of snuff taking: a spoon, hare's foot, rake and brush. Scottish snuff mulls are of great interest to collectors and have been retained in many Scottish houses and, indeed, by several British regiments.

Pipes, apart from the early, traditional clay pipes, were carved from meerschaum, imported from Germany or Austria, or were made of porcelain, also usually imported and decorated with ladies of sweet expression. The briar pipe was discovered about the middle of the nineteenth century and has hardly been supplanted since. A gentleman often had a decorative rack, usually made of carved wood, to hold his favourite selection.

As it was desirable to keep the tobacco moist, tobacco jars of traditional form were usually of lead, made from the eighteenth century onwards, or sometimes of pewter, which was considered more attractive because it took a polish.

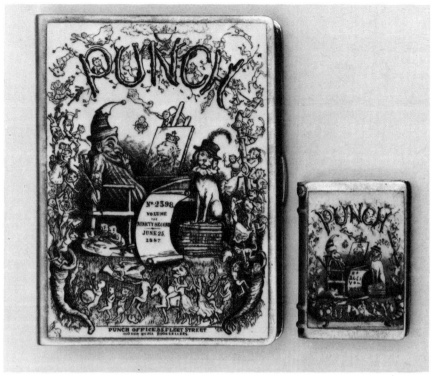

Table lighter in the form of a grizzly bear, J. B. Hennell, 1876. Tooled silver. After the mid century, numerous ingenious and ornamental smoker's accessories were made. Sotheby's Belgravia.

TOP *Cigarette case and matching vesta case in the form of copies of* Punch, *Harrison Bros & Howson, 1886. Black and white enamel, ht 3¼ in (8·2 cm) and 1½ in (3·8 cm). Sotheby's Belgravia.*

ABOVE *Group of Victorian pipes, the bowls probably German and the mounts by Rawlings & Summers, 1847. Porcelain and gilded silver, l 6½ in (16·5 cm). Sotheby's Belgravia.*

On some were depicted subjects of historical or national interest, such as a battle scene from the Crimea; others represented sporting scenes or genre smoking subjects. Sadly, the original presser that goes inside them is almost always lacking.

Matches were still a comparatively new invention and their inflammable nature necessitated a container of fire-proof material. The earliest vesta-cases for the small wax vesta were of silver, slightly shaped, engraved and with a striking edge cast along the bottom; they hung from a gentleman's watch chain. However, it was not long before vesta cases joined the range of novelty boxes, disguised as miniature books, milk churns, animals, pistols, top hats, and even painted tin post boxes. Larger ones for standing on tables, in silver, painted cast iron or brass were often presented as pigs or bears, their rough coats acting as the striking surface. Typically Victorian are pottery match containers in the form of chubby children or young girls with rouged cheeks and over-sweet expressions, some also proffering little dishes for ash.

Cigar cases in their simplest form were made of wood, perhaps sycamore, and decorated with a transfer print or pen-and-ink view. From Scotland again came mauchlineware and tartanware boxes. Drum-shaped containers with tinned interiors to keep the cigars moist were made from Tunbridgeware. An ambitious cigar gadget was the drum-shaped box with central knob which, when lifted, brought up six cigars splayed out, arranged around a spindle, each one supported on a metal tobacco leaf like the opening petals of a flower. All the accessories of cigar smoking suffered the usual disguises; there were cigar cutters in the form of miniature figures, bottles or animals' heads. Also attractive to the collector are papier-mâché cigar cases, designed to take thin cheroots, which are often mistaken for spectacle cases.

Kitchen Objects

The Victorian cook had a positive wealth of gadgets at her disposal in order to create the complicated and lengthy meals that the middle and upper classes enjoyed. The scullery maids cannot have

The Kitchen, *an illustration from* Modern Domestic Cookery *based on the work of Mrs Rundell, 1855. Many kitchen wares of metal, ceramics and glass have survived. Science Museum.*

relished the task of scouring the many tin-lined brass and copper cooking pots, nor the complicated-shaped pastry cutters and jelly moulds.

Food simply was more ornate in the last century; it would be unheard of for butter to arrive at the table without the impression from a wooden butter-printer of a cow or daisy on top. Equally, jellies must come undulating in the shape of fish or wobbling castles, their moulds made either of tin or pottery. Never could the edge of pastry be left plain; it must be scalloped and serrated by a wooden wheel cutter or cut out by a tin or brass pastry cutter. A range of ever-

decreasing sizes and varying shapes of moulds and cutters would be displayed on the kitchen dresser.

The simplest, most traditional and dignified article of kitchen equipment was the pestle and mortar. Made of brass or bronze since time immemorial for the apothecary's purposes, it was usually made of wood, marble or ceramic in the Victorian kitchen with the body of the pestle of sufficient weight to grind and crush herbs and spices. Spices were kept in jars or, more often, tins. The tins were usually attractively painted, having several compartments inside and with a grater for nutmeg.

Among other collectable items not in general use today are marrow scoops, carved-wood bread platters, patent food warmers, toasting forks, chestnut roasters, ale warmers and egg lifters.

Diana Keith Neal

AMERICAN

American Victoriana now commands considerable attention partly, perhaps, because these obsolete objects from an agrarian or early industrial age serve to humanize the twentieth-century environment. In 1837 ties with Europe were still strong, though the production of provincial, or folk art and artifacts had pursued an independent course from early times. By the close of the century 'yankee ingenuity' and the American preoccupation with gadgetry had put

the United States in the forefront of inventiveness.

The Federal period adopted the modes and symbols of the Classical Revival current in Europe with the energy of a new republic acknowledging the first democracy. At this time Britain was emerging as the dominant industrial and mercantile world power. This was inevitably followed by cultural dominance, to which the world paid court at the Great Exhibition of 1851. It is therefore not

inconsistent that America should have had her own Victorian period.

The political independence that America had achieved in the late eighteenth century was not fully confirmed at the cultural level until the Union was a hundred years old and more. Nevertheless, the United States had not gained her independence without also gaining an independent vision which manifested itself outside her 'high art' culture. From the beginning, articles were produced

TOP *Eagle from the stern of a ship, American. Carved, painted and gilded pine, w 4ft 3in (1·3m). The best-known carver of wooden eagles was William Schimmel (1817-90), of Pennsylvania. Arthur and James Ayres Collection.*

ABOVE *Boy's head by Alexander Ames (d. 1847), 1845. Polychrome carved wood, ht 1ft 6in (45·7cm). Life-size statues were a popular folk-art form. New York State Historical Association.*

that were intrinsically new or were manufactured in a new way.

Carved and Household Wares in Wood

American folk art possesses a character all of its own and this is perhaps most evident in the work of artists who worked in wood. The abundance of timber in many regions of the United States had developed a strong tradition in the use of wood for buildings, ships, wagons and household articles.

Some of America's earliest sculptors were woodcarvers – William Rush, Samuel McIntire and the Skillin

RIGHT *Seneca John by Arnold and Peter Ruef, Tiffin, Ohio, c. 1880. The Cigar Store Indian is the most famous of all American shop signs. Greenfield Village and Henry Ford Museum.*

brothers were all active in the late eighteenth and early nineteenth centuries. Architectural woodwork remained important throughout the nineteenth century, but as sail gave way to steam and the iron ship, so the importance of ship-carving waned. Nevertheless, figureheads and sternboards continued to be carved, though some craftsmen, such as Edbury Hatch, were forced by a changing world to abandon the craft. Among earlier craftsmen mention should also be made of Charles A. L. Sampson, of Bath, Maine, John Henry Bellamy, who worked in various New England ports, and perhaps the most famous of all, Laban S. Beecher, of Boston. Some figurehead sculptors carved shop and tavern signs and many turned to this work as their trade in the shipyards declined. In the early nineteenth century, Isaac Fowle is known to have carved a lunette depicting various carpentry tools as the sign for a hardware shop.

Of all American shop signs, the Cigar Store Indians are probably the most famous. They are certainly the most numerous, and in 1937 a total of 585 were recorded in forty-two states. The circus and fairground people were well aware of the effectiveness of carvings for publicity purposes and the greatest showmen of all time, Barnum and Bailey, recognized this to the full. Among the companies that produced such work were the Sebastian Waggon Co. of New York (which employed Samuel Robb) and the Parker Carnival Supply Co. of Abilene, Kansas.

Various toys, including weathervanes and wind toys (known as whirligigs), puppets and marionettes, were also subjects for the nineteenth-century woodcarver. Sculptural qualities may also be discerned in the eagles by William Schimmel and his pupil Aaron Mounts. However, best known, and most readily acquired by the collector today, are decoy ducks which, as works of art, reveal the acute observation of the hunter.

Carved-wood picture frames had for centuries been prepared with gesso as the ground to which water gilding adheres. In the nineteenth century frames continued to be constructed in wood but the decoration, instead of being carved, was usually cast in a gesso composition, or occasionally in lead or pewter, to counterfeit a certain grandeur. For this

Treen, American, nineteenth century. The group includes a butter churn, paddles and mould, a candlestick made from a single branch, a pestle and mortar and a bed wrench. John Judkyn Memorial.

reason some of the most original and interesting nineteenth-century frames are to be found on folk paintings. Edward Hicks is known to have made his own frames and they are frequently painted and lettered with the text that he took for his sermon in paint. The use of natural woods did much to give an individual character to American frame making: curly maple, tiger maple, cedar and cherry were used, or were simulated in paint, and decorated with stencilled designs.

The mazer is a drinking bowl that was made both in Britain and America. It was, for strength and beauty, made from burr (English) or burl (American) maple. The word is derived from the characteristic 'measles' grain. These vessels are among the foremost examples of treen or objects made 'from trees'. Small household objects could readily be made of small tree or shrub wood and popular among those for making spoons, bowls, trenchers, pestles and mortars, piggins and bed wrenches, were the fruit woods of apple, pear, maple, cherry and the hard softwood, yew. The Pennsylvania Germans made mangle boards, spoon racks and small pieces of furniture decorated

ABOVE *Shaker sewing box, given to Anna Case by Sister Mary French in 1879. Pine, maple, walnut, oak and cherry, ht 6¼ in (15.8 cm). Greenfield Village and Henry Ford Museum.*

RIGHT *Cottage organ, Estey Organ Co., Brattleboro, c. 1900. Mahogany with panels of ivory, lacquer and gold paint. The organ case is in the Eastlake style. Grand Rapids Public Museum.*

with chipcarving of the so-called Friesian type. Oval boxes of bentwood were made by the strict religious sect, the Shakers, who traditionally riveted the joint with copper nails and, in accordance with their beliefs, left the boxes undecorated; in contrast, the Pennsylvania-German examples are flamboyantly embellished with paint, and the

join in the bentwood is sewn with wood fibre.

Scrimshaw, Tools and Musical Instruments

Treen was often the product of the amateur working on a small scale and with limited means, and in the same way scrimshaw was made by seamen who in their spare time worked in confined surroundings on walrus, ivory and whale-

Commemorative textile manufactured for the Centennial celebrations of 1876. Printed cotton in imitation of patchwork. The great Centennial Exhibition was held in Philadelphia. John Judkyn Memorial.

bone. Whalers might be away from the home port for years on end and the tooth of the sperm whale was often engraved by the lonely sailor with the image of a girl. At other times a ship or whaling scenes are depicted, together with flags, eagles and other patriotic symbols. The earliest known American specimen is dated 1827, but the Eskimos had been working with the bone and ivory of these Arctic mammals for centuries and may have influenced the work. These Scrimshander articles included busks (corset supports), pastry cutters, rolling pins, 'swifts' or wool-winders, sewing birds, walking-stick handles and oval boxes similar to treen examples.

All these craftsmen needed tools with which to work their materials. In Medieval times the journeyman carpenter could only carry with him on his journey from job to job, the iron or steel elements in his tool kit. Thus the wooden stock of a plane would be made up for use at each stopping place. As travel became easier, it was possible for a carpenter to carry both the iron and the stock. For the purposes of identification such tools were frequently decorated and they are to-day most sought after by collectors.

Industrialization and mass production undermined this tradition, but most nineteenth-century tools once used by the farmer, wheelwright or cabinet-maker are, nevertheless, of great beauty.

Musical instruments followed European precedents: even the Appalachian dulcimer, though elliptical in shape, is ultimately derived from European example. In the late nineteenth century American mass-produced organs with cabinets in the Eastlake style flooded the European market, as had American clocks in the middle of the century. Cottage organs were made by many manufacturers, including Jacob Estey of Brattleboro, the Chicago Cottage Organ Co. and the Sterling Co. of Derby, Connecticut.

Tôle and Commemorative Wares

Tin, or to be precise, tin-plated iron, was popular throughout the nineteenth century and when decorated with paint is usually referred to as tôle (after the French *taule* meaning sheet iron – hence *tôle peinte*). Pennsylvania Germans customarily decorated this ware with flowers on a red ground. Trays, tins, coffee pots, lighting devices, children's toys and many other objects were made of this material. Cookie cutters and candle-moulds, due to the nature of their use, were left undecorated.

In 1853 an international fair was held in New York in a rival building to that of the 1851 Crystal Palace Exhibition in London. On 3 March 1871 Congress passed an Act creating the United States Centennial Commission which was to sponsor 'an international exhibition of the arts, manufactures and products of the soil and mine in the city of Philadelphia in the year 1876'. The Centennial celebrations commemorating the Declaration of Independence of 1776 inspired the production of considerable numbers of commemorative and souvenir items.

On 17 June, 1825, the fiftieth anniversary of the Battle of Bunker Hill, the corner stone of the monument to the Battle was laid in the presence of forty veterans of that engagement. Commemorative items were produced, and at that time and for the next forty years there was a great vogue for pressed-glass cup plates. It was, however, the celebrations of 1876 that really inspired manufacturers. From the beginning, Independence was celebrated by copper-plate printed cottons made in France and England for the export market and in 1876 vast numbers of such commemorative textiles were produced; one enterprising firm went so far as to print an imitation patchwork. The Columbian Exhibition of 1892 was yet another exercise in promoting the sales of all manner of merchandise.

Election campaigns became a selling point for manufacturers as early as 1840, when textiles were printed promoting the presidential campaigns of Harrison and Tyler with the log cabin and hard cider as symbols of the common man. Zachary Taylor (Old Rough and Ready) became, in his 1848 presidential campaign, the subject of innumerable portraits produced by glass-bottle manufacturers and wallpaper and bandbox printers.

Contemporary events were also used as subject-matter for woodblock-printed designs that embellished the simple hat box. Most of these date from the second quarter of the nineteenth century and among the subjects chosen were the opening of the Erie Canal in 1819 and its completion in 1825 and Clayton's balloon ascent from Cincinnati in 1835. The development of tourism in the late nineteenth century, encouraged the manufacture of souvenirs and important among these were the silver spoons bearing emblems associated with particular states or towns.

History in the making is sometimes consciously, at other times unconsciously, commemorated. A wineglass bearing the inscription 'Cherokee Payment,

Grand Rapids carpet sweeper, Bissell, 1895. Wood with painted decoration. This is an early and ornate example of the device, based on a street cleaner of 1842. Science Museum.

July 18, 1894' is an example of the former, while a medal of the Knights of St Patrick, Staten Island, a 'New Testament, Immigrants' Edition' or a thirty-nine star flag are good examples of the latter.

Though the industrialization of America was promoted by the tragedy of the Civil War, a preoccupation with gadgetry was noticeable from the beginning. Apple peelers and early examples of mass-production techniques, such as those employed by Eli Whitney, pointed to the destiny of industrial America. Without these devices, the six shooter

TOP *New Family sewing machine, Singer Sewing Machine Co., 1865. Cast iron. The first sewing machine manufactured by Isaac M. Singer (1811-75) was patented in 1851. Science Museum.*

1874 model typewriter, manufactured by Remington Arms Co., under the Sholes-Glidden patent of 1868. This is one of the earliest mass-produced typewriters. Greenfield Village and Henry Ford Museum.

and barbed wire would not have been present to assist in the winning of the West, and the sewing machine and Bissell carpet sweeper from Grand Rapids would not have released nine-teenth-century women from the ties of the home for the bondage of the type-writer. All these mechanisms, and many others, may be claimed as American developments. One man – Thomas Edison – successfully invented and developed a whole series of items such as the phonograph, the tickatape, the microtasimeter, the cinematograph, car-bon filaments for electric lights, the steam dynamo and other contrivances connected with electricity.

Improvements in plumbing and the invention of the elevator made possible high-rise building developments. The production of petroleum in the third quarter of the nineteenth century, centred on north-west Pennsylvania, meant that mineral oil was largely used for lamps as a natural successor to the candle and whale oil. Louis Comfort Tiffany was one of the first craftsmen to design for electricity, with bronze stan-dard lamps and stained-glass shades. By 1886 William Seward Burroughs had made his adding machine and in the same year George Eastman put his first Kodak on the market. By 1886 printers were using both linotype and half-tone blocks to reproduce the subtleties of the photograph. The completion of the first trans-continental railroad on 10 May 1869 opened up the country and by the 1890s the motor car and the telephone had made their appearance, and the bicycle had become widely popular.

Numerous such objects remain scat-tered throughout the country; they are all important historically, sometimes beautiful aesthetically, and may often be purchased quite cheaply. The agrarian quality of life in pre-Civil War days may be contrasted with industrialized post-Civil War America and these form two distinct areas for the potential collector.

James Ayres

Glossary

Bandbox
Oval or circular box of American origin, at first of thin, split wood and later, in the second quarter of the nineteenth century, of cardboard. Originally used for the storage of bands (ribbons) but later used more generally for articles of clothing,

Bandbox, American, c. 1830. Block-printed paper on wood. The Merchant's Exchange in New York is depicted. Later bandboxes were often of cardboard. Ameri-can Museum in Britain.

especially hats. The most colourful are the ones covered with printed papers de-picting well-known sights and topical and historical events.

Beadwork
FANCYWORK, type of Berlin work, following commercially produced de-signs on squared paper (see TEXTILES GLOSSARY), composed of threaded or stitched coloured-glass beads, imported into England from Germany and Italy. In the United States beadwork was a traditional craft of the American Indians. In both countries it was applied to a net, canvas or wool ground to make anti-macassars, covers for footstools, dress fronts and in particular a range of small female accessories such as purses – the

Beadwork purse, English, mid-nineteenth century. This has a gilded metal mount and clasp. Beadwork was sometimes combined with other forms of needlework. Sotheby's Belgravia.

elongated sacks closed at either end with tassels were known as miser purses – pin cushions and CARD CASES. In the con-text of furniture, beadwork is often found combined with Berlin woolwork on the back of *prie-dieu* chairs, fire screens and cushions.

Card case
Thin, rectangular case for visiting cards, a necessity on both sides of the Atlantic when 'calling'. Made of silver, gold, tortoiseshell, mother of pearl as well as less expensive materials such as PAPIER MÂCHÉ, they were often highly decorated. Ebony cases were particularly fashion-able for mourning.

Chipcarving
The embellishment of a smooth surface whereby the carving tool has been direct-ed alternately at opposing angles to pro-duce a decorative all-over pattern of V-cuts. This kind of work is found in America and Europe. It is sometimes known as Friesian work in America.

Coaster
Receptacle with a baize-covered base or wheels designed to prevent bottles and decanters from marking the polished surface of a dining table and facilitating their movement. Often made in pairs or sets, they are commonly of silver, wood OR PAPIER MÂCHÉ.

Commemorative ware
International exhibitions, royal, political and scientific events and, in the United States, election campaigns gave rise to the manufacture of appropriately decor-ated goods. The fact that they were on the market for a fairly short time meant that they were collected as items from limited, though large, editions. They were also evidence that the owner had attended or witnessed a particular and well-publicized event or had simply been alive when it took place; but above all it was fashionable to buy objects specifi-cally intended to attract tourists, which were first produced in great numbers for the Victorians. Some of the most inter-esting American examples are those that verged on propaganda. In England a surprising number of small, inexpensive objects incorporated mourning details at the time of the death of the Prince Consort in 1861.

Conework
Surface decoration for picture frames, wastepaper baskets and lambrequins, fashionable in the 1870s. Made princi-pally from the scales of pine cones at-tached by putty or sewn to the base, the arrangement might incorporate all man-ner of dried fruits and seeds, husks and twigs. Some were intended to imitate woodcarving.

Daguerreotype case
Having very delicate surfaces, DAGUER-

REOTYPES (see PHOTOGRAPHS GLOSS-
ARY) were generally framed and kept in
cases. In Britain these were most often
of leather or composition; in the United
States, where the daguerreotype was
more popular, the Litchfield Manufacturing Co., of Connecticut, specialized
in PAPIER-MÂCHÉ cases and in 1854
Samuel Peck patented a type of dark-
brown thermoplastic case known as the
Union case.

Decalquage
Transfers applied to any material with a
smooth surface such as glass, plaster of
Paris or paper. Decalcomania was the
name given to the fashion for this type of
home decoration.

Decoy
Carved-wood model of a waterfowl, the
purpose of which was to entice birds to
within range of the hunter. The origin
of the craft of carving decoys in the
United States is Indian: it was a popular
pastime in the mid-nineteenth century.
Later some examples have bodies turned
on a lathe. Floaters were designed to sit
on the water; stickups, resembling wad-
ers, were planted in the ground. While
some might be carefully and realistically
painted, it is not uncommon to find
stylized examples and simple silhouettes.

*Decoy-loon, American, 1850-1900. Pine,
l 1ft 5½ in (44·4cm). That it bears little
resemblance to a loon apparently did not
detract from its efficiency. Abby Aldrich
Rockefeller Folk Art Collection.*

Enamel
Vitreous composition, coloured by
metallic oxides, fused to a base such as
copper or pottery. The technique was
employed by Tiffany's and by craftsmen requiring a delicate surface on small
objects such as CARD CASES and snuff
boxes.

Étui
Portable, often minutely and beautifully
decorated, case for sewing accessories,
the smaller examples intended to be
attached to a châtelaine (see JEWELRY
GLOSSARY). Produced in numerous rare
and inexpensive materials, they were
often tapered to accommodate scissors.

*Box inscribed Louis C. Tiffany (1848-
1933), c. 1901. Iridescent glass and
enamel on copper, l 6in (15·2cm). The
enamelled motifs are red apples and green
leaves. Metropolitan Museum of Art.*

Fancywork
General term for any home handicraft
which employed the time and skill of
Victorian ladies and children. The period
of popularity for any one occupation was
short, and few retained their appeal after
the beginning of the First World War,
when more useful or commercial pas-
times were sought. Characteristically,
fancywork is the creation of a decorative
object, or the decoration of an existing,
manufactured object, using natural
materials such as feathers, shells or pine
cones: these might be collected by the
'artist' at the appropriate season or purchased with accompanying instructions.
The techniques were often demonstrated
at exhibitions and there were also numerous helpful publications such as *Artistic
Amusements*, which appeared in England
in 1877, and in the United States *Lady's
Manual of Fancy Work* by Mrs Pullen.
Often made from delicate, dust-collect-
ing components, fancywork has a tendency to look shabby to the modern collector and examples in good condition
are comparatively rare.

Fretwork
Also known as Sorrento carving and jigsaw work, openwork of thin wood
achieved with a fretsaw following commercially produced patterns. It is often
found made up as wall brackets, wall
pockets and frames.

Japanning
English, and later American, substitute
for Oriental lacquer. Much Victorian
japanning consists of a cheap oil varnish,
thinly applied, although some of the
more expensive Jennens & Bettridge
PAPIER- MÂCHÉ wares acquired an
effective, fine-grained and glossy finish
through extensive baking and hand
polishing. Good quality TÔLE may also
be japanned. Towards the end of the
century there was a considerable interest
in things Oriental and japanning lost

popularity in favour of genuine lacquer
imported from Japan and China.

Mauchline woodware
Decorated boxes and small wooden
keepsakes, usually of sycamore, made
in or near Mauchline, in Scotland. An
early distinction was an integral and
mechanically flawless wooden hinge
incorporated in snuff boxes and tea
caddies. In the nineteenth century the
principal types of decoration on these
wares, which were augmented to include
a range of useful objects, especially those
associated with sewing, knitting and
writing, were pen-and-ink work, varnished transfers and fern patterns. The
latter were made by spraying brown
paint over ferns, which were then removed to leave a silhouette on the wood,
a technique that was also popular in
the United States; printed papers were
substituted for this towards the end of
the century. Some TARTANWARE objects
produced by Scottish makers fall into
the category of Mauchline woodware.

*Wool ball holder, Scottish, mid-nineteenth
century. Sycamore with a transfer-printed
view of the Scott Memorial, Edinburgh.
This type of woodware was made in or
near Mauchline. Sotheby's Belgravia.*

Meerschaum
Magnesium silicate first discovered by
the Black Sea and thought to be petrified
sea foam, or *Meerschaum* in German.
Naturally greyish in colour, tainted by
tobacco smoke it turned amber. Highly
carved examples of meerschaum smok-
ing-equipment – some in dubious taste –
are generally nineteenth century. Pipes
were also made of clay, in particular
those cheaply acquired in public houses
and easily cracked and rejected, and,
towards the end of the century, briar-
wood.

Mother of pearl
Iridescent inner layer of a shell, usually
the nautilus, much favoured by the

Victorians as a decorative inlay. Philip Alsager and George Neville, one-time apprentices with the firm of Jennens & Bettridge, pioneered mother-of-pearl decoration on PAPIER MÂCHÉ which was to become for a time the most popular form of embellishment. Thin layers of the shell were applied to the surface of the object, usually in a flower pattern, and the JAPANNING built up around them. The shell-cutting process was eventually mechanized and the mother of pearl, tinted and combined with other forms of decoration, such as gilding. The shell was also widely used on all manner of small, usually feminine, articles, opera glasses, ÉTUIS and CARD CASES among them.

Nécéssaire

Portable sewing case, larger than an ÉTUI.

Papier mâché

Product principally of the English industrial towns of Birmingham and Wolverhampton; a material manufactured either by shaping paper pulp mixed with chalk and sand in a mould or, after 1772, by compressing the pulp to form a heat-resistant panel which could be sawn and nailed and treated in the same manner as wood. The latter was a particularly suitable base for JAPANNING. The earliest experiments with papier mâché date back to the seventeenth century; the height of its popularity was reached in the early years of Queen Victoria's reign, but by the late 1860s the demand had noticeably declined; by the end of the century commercial production was ceasing. The various techniques for decorating papier mâché include MOTHER-OF-PEARL 'inlay' – a technique for applying nacre to the surface of the object – handpainting, gilding, applying bronze powders, impasto work combined with stencilling, transfer printing, gem laying, marbling and wood graining. The influence of Oriental lacquer decoration was strong, and naturalistic and geometric styles and patterns were also favoured. Firms were apt to specialize in a particular type of ornament – Walton's of Wolverhampton concentrating on church interiors – but flowers, foliage and views of famous landmarks were standard throughout the trade. The foremost makers were Jennens & Bettridge of Birmingham, who presented Queen Victoria with a set of three trays with an apple-green ground at the time of her marriage in 1840. Although the design was cancelled and the green ground remained a comparative rarity, trays remained popular as wedding presents for many years. After the death of the Prince Consort in 1861 a number of pieces decorated with subdued greys and mauves were produced, and an imitation

Tray, Jennens & Bettridge, Birmingham, mid-nineteenth century. Papier mâché. Trays were popular as wedding presents following the gift of a set to Queen Victoria at the time of her marriage in 1840. Sotheby's Belgravia.

jet for dress and hat trimmings was devised. Black was the most common background, though the occasional green- and, rarely, white-grounded examples are found. Objects of every conceivable kind were made of papier mâché, including furniture. 'Blanks', particularly snuff boxes, which received varnished colour lithographs of American patriots on their lids, and some decorated and finished items were exported to the United States, where there was one papier-mâché factory, the Litchfield Manufacturing Co., which operated between 1850 and 1854. Their specialities were DAGUERREOTYPE CASES and clock-cases.

Patent Office model

Small-scale model of a device which, accompanied by detailed drawings, was submitted to the United States Patent Office. Often constructed by a skilled model maker employed by the inventor, the model was required to show all the working parts in miniature. The Patent Office was twice partially destroyed by fire in the nineteenth century and the models replaced. After 1890 it ceased to be necessary to supply them when making an application unless specifically requested, and in 1925 it was decided to disperse the collection, firstly to museums and institutions and then by public auction. Some of the most admired models are those for the domestic and office gadgets that were to change the character of life in the latter part of the century.

Potichimanie

Fashion for pasting drawings and prints on the inside of glass vases and jars, infilled with oil paint, to resemble high-

Patent Office model of a lamp burner, patented by J. A. Frey in 1866, American. These small-scale working models were no longer automatically required after 1890. John Judkyn Memorial.

Scrimshaw, with an etched portrait of Napoleon, English, c. 1835. Whales' teeth, ht 6 in (15·2 cm). Scrimshaw decoration was often topical. Sotheby's Belgravia.

quality decorated porcelain. The skill deteriorated in the United States to the point where coloured figures were pasted to the outside of pottery jars. These were known as Dolly Varden jars.

Scrimshaw

Objects fashioned from whales' teeth or whalebone by whalers in their leisure time at sea. Scrimshaw includes wares for immediate use on board, such as cleats, and presents to be given on their return – busks, swifts for winding yarn, bodkins, wick pickers and crimping wheels for edging pies, as well as numerous articles with scrimshaw parts or decorative details. Most common are sperm whales' teeth etched with patriotic, commemorative, dedicatory or erotic scenes. The incised decoration was often pigmented, and the quality of the carving and detail is occasionally of the very highest. Usually the initial design was made on paper, then transferred to the bone or tooth with pinpricks, which were then joined up and the cross-hatching added. The same decorative technique was applied to small bone and ivory artifacts, very similar to those made earlier in the century by Napoleonic prisoners of war. These included walking-stick handles, paper knives, dominoes, violin pegs and even watch chains.

Shaker boxes

Hand-made boxes produced from the late-eighteenth century in the Shaker communities of the United States for sale or for their own use. Their founder, Mother Ann Lee, emphasized the virtue, not only of simplicity, but also of cleanliness and tidiness: every one of their few possessions must have its allotted place so that it could be found at any time, and many of the boxes were simply for storage. Generally oval with lids, it was usual for several of a similar shape to be made so that one fitted inside another. The wood, maplewood or beech for the sides and pine or sycamore for the bottom and top, was split in strips and steam shaped round a mould. Distinguishing features of all Shaker boxes, whether designed for storage or for more specialized purposes such as berry-collecting or seed-growing, are the overlapping fingers of wood, secured by iron or copper rivets, at the seams. Some are dyed or painted, but they are more usually merely sanded and varnished.

Shellwork

Pastime much recommended for interest and effect by both English and American writers on female recreations. The shells might be collected on the seashore or purchased. Sometimes combined with dried seaweed, the arrangements might

Tea caddy with three canisters, attributed to G. Meekison of Montrose. Sycamore with pen-and-ink and handpainted decoration. Pinto Collection, City Museum and Art Gallery, Birmingham.

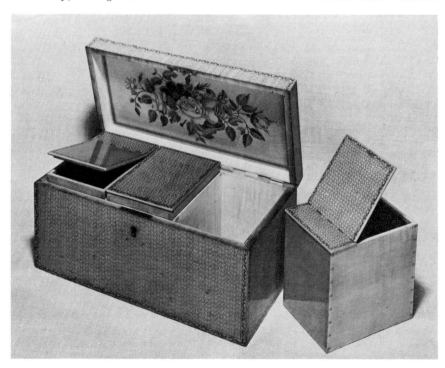

be set under glass domes as mantelpiece ornaments or made up into shell pictures, often on a silk ground. More commonly the shells were applied to a ground of wet plaster and used to embellish looking glasses, picture frames and trinket boxes. A sailor's valentine is a shell mosaic in two parts joined by hinges so that it could be opened and closed like a box. It is probable that at least some of the extant examples were made commercially in the West Indies and sold to English and American sailors. (See colour plate p. 336.)

Tartanware

Wooden item, such as a small box or parasol handle, decorated with a Scottish clan tartan. Hand painted directly on to the base in the 1820s, when they were first produced, it later became the practice to glue mechanically printed paper on to the object, the joins being almost imperceptible. In a general sense, an object in any material and embellished by any means, especially transfer-printing, with tartan decoration. They were particularly popular after 1852, when Queen Victoria acquired Balmoral Castle, in Scotland.

Tea caddy

Box of wood, PAPIER MÂCHÉ, TÔLE or any other material designed to contain tea. While tea was a valuable commodity, the caddy was generally provided with a lock. The tea leaves were stored in canisters, and there was often a mixing-bowl in the middle. The term caddy is derived from the Malay *kati*, a measure of weight. Tea was much less widely drunk in the United States than in

Sailor's valentine, probably made in the West Indies and brought to England. Shell mosaic in an octagonal frame. This is one side of the valentine, which opens like a box. Mallett at Bourdon House Ltd.

Britain and hence fewer accessories for tea making and drinking were produced in America.

Tôle
Tin-plated sheet iron with japanned, painted or stencilled decoration, the name deriving from the French *tôle peinte*; painted sheet iron. In England the firm of Allgood made japanned metalwares at Pontypool in South Wales from 1730, and tôle was still popular for TEA CADDIES and coal scuttles until the late nineteenth century: a number of

items were displayed at the Great Exhibition of 1851. In the United States the nineteenth-century production of decorated tinware was principally in Pennsylvania. It was sold by pedlars and in country stores, and the most common decoration is of fruit and flowers, usually on a black ground, often resembling German folk art. Household wares of tin include spice boxes, teapots and coffee-

349

pots, nutmeg graters, trays, candlesticks and wick trimmers. Document- and cash-boxes were also made, and miniature pieces for children.

Trade and tavern signs

Branch of ornamental painting and woodcarving from which serious painters and sculptors might derive a living. The signs, intended to swing from a bracket, are double sided. They were executed in a primitive manner and brightly coloured to attract the notice of the traveller from a distance. A popular image in the latter years of the nineteenth century was the three-dimensional Cigar-Store Indian of carved wood, holding a cigar, tobacco leaves or snuff.

Treen

General term for small wooden items; objects made from trees, such as butter moulds, marzipan boards and other household and decorative wares.

Tunbridgeware

Wooden mosaic originated and made at Tunbridge Wells, in Kent. The craft developed from the marquetry work produced there in the seventeenth century, which was superseded in about 1830 by a new process known as the end-grain technique, probably devised by Fenner & Co. Fine sticks of various woods, many of them local, were grouped together in bundles and glued according to a pattern. The bundles were then sliced across in thicknesses of approximately $\frac{1}{16}$ in (1·5 mm) and applied as a veneer to brown paper. This was then used to decorate any number of objects including the surface of quite large pieces such as worktables and teapoys. An alternative method used in the making of small pieces involved turning the bundles of wood on a lathe. Known as stickwork, patterns of a geometric nature were made from longitudinal, rather than cross sections, of the wood grain. Among those makers who labelled their work are Edmund Nye, Thomas Barton (the former's apprentice and, later, partner), G. Wise, T. Burrows, J. Friend, A. Talbot, R. License, R. Russell, J. Medhurst, W. Upton, H. Hollamby and Boyce, Brown & Kemp (later the Tunbridge Ware Manufacturing Co. and the last manufacturing firm to close, in 1927); it is not unusual to find the retailer's label on a piece as well. The principal types of decoration were cube patterns, similar to those produced in the previous century, floral patterns resembling BERLIN WOOLWORK (see TEXTILES GLOSSARY) and architectural scenes, often of local interest since Tunbridgeware was particularly admired by visitors to the spa town.

Vinaigrette

Small, usually metal, box with a hinged inner lid, beneath which was placed a sponge scented with a liquid reviving to the female senses. Both the top of the box and the inner grill might be the subject

Vinaigrettes by Birmingham makers. Windsor Castle and castellated mansion, N. Mills, 1837; Newstead Abbey, Taylor & Perry, 1836; Crystal Palace, 1851. Gilded silver. Sotheby's Belgravia.

of fine ornamentation. Introduced in the eighteenth century, the Victorians made them in the form of miniature purses, books and eggs.

Voider

Basket into which dirty plates and cutlery were placed to be removed from the dining room; usually PAPIER MÂCHÉ.

Walking-stick

Functional male accessory and the object of imaginative decorative treatment. For country use, where strength and springiness were of great importance, ash, bamboo, hazel, holly and spindlewood were found to be the most satisfactory woods. For cudgels and shillelaghs, heavy Irish blackthorn with its knobbly exterior was favoured. For town use, more delicate materials such as ebony, ivory, marble and onyx were fashionable. The knob or handle might be of silver, cast and chased, gilded metal in the shape of a Moor's head, or carved from hardstone and set with jewels. The most popular was the malacca cane, possibly sporting a carved ivory head in the form of a snarling lion, hound, horse or clenched fist. Victorian walking-sticks often had additional functions: the heads might conceal compartments for

Lid of a Tunbridgeware playing-card box, English, c. 1850. Wood mosaic. The view is of Malvern Priory; the floral border is in the style of Berlin woolwork. Petrie Collection.

times offered for sale with them. Before about 1880, when the skill fell from favour, mourning wreaths of wax flowers and wax fruit in plaster of Paris baskets were among the most common items.

Bibliography

ANDERE, MARY. *Old Needlework Boxes and Tools,* Newton Abbot, 1971

AYRES, JAMES. *American Antiques,* London and New York, 1973

BUTLER, JOSEPH T. *American Antiques 1800–1900: A Collector's History and Guide,* New York, 1965

CARLISLE, LILIAN BAKER. *Hat Boxes and Bandboxes at the Shelburne Museum,* Shelburne, Vermont, 1960

COMSTOCK, HELEN, (ed.). *The Concise Encyclopaedia of American Antiques,* 2 vols, London, 1958

DAVIDSON, MARSHALL B. (ed.). *The American Heritage History of American Antiques from the Civil War to World War I,* New York, 1969

DE VRIES, LEONARD. *Victorian Inventions,* London, 1973

FIELD, JUNE. *Collecting Georgian and Victorian Crafts,* London, 1973

FRY, P. S. *Collecting Inexpensive Antiques,* London, 1973

GOULD, MARY EARLE. *Early American Wooden Ware and Other Kitchen Utensils,* Rutland, Vermont, 1962

LANGDON, WILLIAM CHAUNCY. *Everyday Things in American Life 1776–1876,* New York, 1941

LICHTEN, FRANCES. *Decorative Art of Victoria's Era,* New York, 1950

LITTLE, NINA FLETCHER. *The Abby Aldrich Rockefeller Folk Art Collection,* Colonial Williamsburg, Virginia, 1957

Metropolitan Museum of Art. *19th-Century America,* Catalogue of the exhibition held 16 April – 7 September 1970, New York, 1970

NORBURY, JAMES. *The World of Victoriana,* London, 1972

PINTO, E. H. and E. R. *Tunbridge and Scottish Souvenir Woodware,* London, 1970

RICHARDS, G. TILGHMAN. *The History and Development of Typewriters,* London, 1964

SLOANE, ERIC. *A Museum of Early American Tools,* New York, 1964

STACKPOLE, EDWARD A. *Skrimshaw at Mystic Seaport,* Mystic, Connecticut, 1958

WOODHOUSE, C. P. *The Victoriana Collector's Handbook,* London, 1970

Group of parasols and walking-sticks with ornamented handles by W. & J. Sangster, of London, illustrated in the catalogue of the Great Exhibition of 1851.

snuff, a compass, or in the case of a doctor's stick, a phial of disinfectant. A button by the head would release a flick knife at the tip, while walking-stick air-guns of steel painted to simulate bamboo were fired by a button trigger. Others unscrewed in the middle to form rifles. These splendid deceptions are now hard to find. Purely decorative are Victorian glass walking sticks, made mainly at Bristol and Nailsea, the stems with col-oured twists of glass and the handles with curling crooks. They are probably glassmakers' apprentice pieces for they are extremely delicate and were surely not intended to be used.

Waxwork

Eighteenth-century skill revived by the Victorians, in particular for modelling flowers. Although in the category of a home occupation, the results were so highly regarded that a section devoted to wax flowers was included in the Great Exhibition of 1851. As with SHELLWORK, the most elaborate arrangements were intended to be enclosed within a glass dome. Pattern books and moulds were available, and the materials were some-

OVERLEAF *Interior at Gallow Hill, Paisley, photographed by Bedford Lemere, 1890s. National Monuments Record.*

351

Contributors

VICTOR ARWAS (British Glass). Art dealer and collector. Author of *Félicien Rops*, 1973, *Chryselephantine Sculpture*, 1974, and, in preparation, books on Art Nouveau and Art Deco glass, ceramics, jewelry, bronzes and several monographs on turn-of-the-century artists.

JAMES AYRES (American Miscellany). Sculptor and Director of The John Judkyn Memorial which from its base at Freshford Manor, Bath, circulates exhibitions about America throughout Britain. Author of *American Antiques*, 1973, and contributor to *Antiques* (New York), *America in Britain* and *Discovering Antiques*.

MARILYNN JOHNSON BORDES (American Furniture). Associate Curator in the American Wing of the Metropolitan Museum of Art, New York. Contributor on furniture to the catalogue of the exhibition *Nineteenth-Century America* held at the Metropolitan in 1970, and to the *Britannia Encyclopedia of American Art*.

SHIRLEY BURY (British Metalwork). Deputy Keeper, Department of Metalwork, Victoria and Albert Museum, London. Head of museum team organizing exhibition *Victorian Church Art* held at Victoria and Albert Museum in 1971 and reorganized the Jewelry Gallery of the Victoria and Albert Museum in 1972. Author of catalogue of exhibition of Victorian church plate, *Copy or Creation*, held at Goldsmiths' Hall, London, in 1967. Contributor on Pugin's marriage jewelry to the Victoria and Albert Museum's Year Book, I, 1969, and introduction to new edition of *Modern English Silverware* by C. R. Ashbee, 1974.

GRACE COOPER (American Textiles). Curator, Division of Textiles, National Museum of History and Technology, Smithsonian Institution, Washington, D.C. Author of *The Scholfield Wool-Carding Machines*, 1959, *The Invention of the Sewing Machine*, 1968, *The Copp Family Textiles*, 1971, *13-Star Flags, Keys to Identification*, 1973. Contributor to and former Department Editor and Advisor (Textiles) of the *Encyclopaedia Britannica*, and contributor to museum and collectors' magazines on a variety of textile subjects including nineteenth-century weavers, carpet bags, woollen mills, textile machines, Centennial prints and handkerchiefs.

JEREMY COOPER (British Sculpture). Head of Furniture and Works of Art Department, Sotheby's Belgravia, London. Author of *Complete Guide to London's Antique Street Markets*, 1974, and *Nineteenth-Century Romantic Bronzes*, 1975.

JOHN CULME (British Silver). Head of Silver and Objects of Vertu from 1825, Department, Sotheby's Belgravia, London. Co-author of *Antique Silver and Silver Collecting*, 1973 and contributor to *Discovering Antiques* and *Art at Auction*.

PHILLIP H. CURTIS (American Porcelain). Curator of Decorative Arts, The Newark Museum, Newark, New Jersey. Author of 'Tucker Porcelain, 1826-1838: a Reappraisal' in *Ceramics in America*, 1972, and *Quilts in the Collection of the Newark Museum*, 1973.

MILLIA DAVENPORT (American Dress). Former theatrical designer. Author of *The Book of Costume*, 1948.

SAMUEL J. DORNSIFE (Wallpaper). Interior designer and member of the American Institute of Interior Designers. Author of 'What do we do with our windows?' in the forthcoming *Winterthur Portfolio*, Vol. 10.

PHILIPPE GARNER (Photographs). Photographic expert, Sotheby's Belgravia, London. Author of *The World of Edwardiana*, 1974, *Art Nouveau*, 1974 and, to be published, *Émile Gallé*.

WILLIAM H. GERDTS (American Sculpture). Curator of the Norfolk Museum, Norfolk, Virginia; Curator of Painting and Sculpture, The Newark Museum, Newark, New Jersey; Professor of Art and Art Gallery Director, The University of Maryland, College Park, Maryland. Author of *The Drawings of Joseph Stella*, 1962, *Painting and Sculpture in New Jersey*, 1964, *American Still-Life Painting*, 1971, *American Neo-Classic Sculpture*, 1973, *The Great American Nude*, 1974, *Revealed Masters*, 1974. Contributor to many periodicals and museum catalogues including *Antiques* (New York), *American Art Journal*, *Art Quarterly*, *Proceedings of the New Jersey Historical Society*.

GEOFFREY GODDEN (British Porcelain). Dealer in ceramics. Author of fifteen books on antiques including *Victorian Painting* 1961, *Encyclopedia of British Pottery and Porcelain Marks*, 1964, *The Handbook of British Pottery and Porcelain Marks*, 1968, *Stevengraphs and Other Victorian Silk Pictures*, 1971, *Jewitt's Ceramic Art of Great Britain, 1800-1900*, 1972, *British Porcelain – an Illustrated Guide*, 1973, *British Pottery, an Illustrated Guide*, 1974.

IAN GRANT (Introduction). Architect, former Secretary of the Victorian Society and currently a member of The Committee of the Victorian Society. Editor of *Great Interiors*, 1967, and, in preparation, a book on the nineteenth-century interior. Contributor to *House and Garden* and *Discovering Antiques*.

MALCOLM HASLAM (British Pottery). Antique dealer and former lecturer in history of design at Birmingham College of Art and Design. Author of forthcoming books on English, Continental and American art pottery. Deputy editor of and contributor to *Discovering Antiques* and contributor to *Antique Finder*, *Art at Auction*, *The Connoisseur* and *Country Life*.

FLORA GILL JACOBS (American Juvenilia). Shortly to open the Washington Dolls' House and Toy Museum. Author of *A History of Dolls' Houses*, 1953 and 1965, *Dolls' Houses in America*, 1974, a children's history of dolls' houses, three children's novels and co-author of *A Book of Dolls and Doll Houses*, 1967.

CEDRIC JAGGER (British Clocks, Watches and Barometers). Assistant Curator responsible for the Collection of Clocks and Watches belonging to the Worshipful Company of Clockmakers, and permanently displayed to the public at the Guildhall, London. Author of *Paul Philip Barraud – a Study of a Fine Chronometer Maker, and of his Relatives, Associates and Successors in the family business: 1750-1929*, 1968, *Clocks*, 1973, and contributor to many periodicals.

DORA JANE JANSON (American Jewelry). Art Historian and Museum docent, Metropolitan Museum of Art, New York and City Art Museum, St Louis, Missouri. Author of the Catalogue of the exhibition *From Slave to Siren: the Victorian Woman and her Jewelry*, held at Duke University Art Museum, Durham, North Carolina, in 1971, 'Omega in Alpha: the Christ Child's Foreknowledge of His Fate' in *Jahrbuch der Hamburger Kunstsammelungen*, Vol. 18, 1973, and co-author of *The Story of Painting for Young People*, 1952, and *The Picture History of Painting*, 1957.

EDWARD JOY (British Furniture). Curator, Ickworth (National Trust), Bury St Edmunds, former Principal Lecturer in History, Shoreditch College of Education. Author of *English Furniture AD 43-1950*, 1962, *Country Life Book of English Furniture*, 1964, *Country Life Book of Clocks*, 1967, *Country Life Book of Chairs*, 1967, *Chippendale*, 1971, *Furniture (The Connoisseur)*, 1972, *English Antique Furniture*, 1973. Contributor to many periodicals including *The Connoisseur, Country Life, Apollo, Burlington Magazine, Antiques* (New York), *Antique Collector, Discovering Antiques, Harper's Bazaar, Furniture History*.

DIANA KEITH NEAL (British Miscellany). Specialist in study of arms and armour and Victorian photographs, formerly with Works of Art Department, Sotheby & Co., London. Contributor to various periodicals including *Discovering Antiques* and *Art at Auction*.

KATHARINE MORRISON MCCLINTON (American Silver). Formerly lecturer on art and interior decoration, University of California, official lecturer and a director of San Diego Fine Arts Gallery. Organized exhibition of Ecclesiastical Art, Dallas Art Museum, Dallas, Texas. Author of over twenty books on antiques including *An Outline of Period Furniture*, 1929, *Collecting American Victorian Antiques*, 1966 and *Collecting American 19th-Century Silver*, 1968. Contributor to many newspapers and periodicals including *Studio International, Country Life, Arts and Decoration, Apollo, The Connoisseur* and *Better Homes and Gardens*.

JAMES R. MITCHELL (American Pottery). Chief Curator, The Carborundum Museum of Ceramics, Niagara Falls, New York, formerly Curator of Decorative Arts, New Jersey State Museum, Trenton, New Jersey. Assistant Curator of the Bennington Museum, Bennington, Vermont. Author of the following exhibition catalogues: 'The American Porcelain Tradition' in *The Connoisseur*, March 1972, 'Ott & Brewer: Etruria in America' in the *Winterthur Portfolio*, Vol. 7, 1972 and for the New Jersey State Museum: *American Pewter, Furniture and Furnishings, Cybis in Retrospect, The American Porcelain Tradition, Ott & Brewer*, and *New Jersey Pottery to 1840*.

BARBARA MORRIS (British Textiles). Assistant Keeper of Circulation at the Victoria and Albert Museum. Author of *Victorian Embroidery*, 1962, and contributor to *The Connoisseur Period Guides* on the Regency and early Victorian periods and to many periodicals including *The Connoisseur, Apollo* and *Discovering Antiques*.

STELLA MARY NEWTON (British Dress). Lecturer and head of the department for the study of the history of dress, Courtauld Institute of Art, University of London, formerly consultant on costume to the National Gallery, London. Author of *Health, Art and Reason: 19th Century Dress Reformers*, 1974, and *Renaissance Theatre Costume*, 1975, and contributor to various periodicals.

KENNETH D. ROBERTS (American Clocks, Watches and Barometers). Formerly Museum Director and Curator, and University Professor of Mechanical Engineering. Author/publisher of *Contributions of Joseph Ives to Connecticut Clock Technology 1810-1862*, 1970, *Elgin Reminiscences*, 1972, *Eli Terry and the Connecticut Shelf Clock*, 1973, and, to be published, *Connecticut Clocks 1840-1880*.

MARY SPEAIGHT (British Juvenilia). Curator, Toys and Dolls, the London Museum. Contributor to *Discovering Antiques*.

FREDERICK WILKINSON (Arms and Militaria). President of the London-based Arms and Armour Society. Author of many books on firearms, edged weapons, military dress, including *Battle Dress*, 1970, *Antique Arms and Armour*, 1972, and of *Castles of England*, 1973.

GEOFFREY WILLS (Metalwork). Author of over twenty books on antiques including *Country Life Book of English China*, 1964, *Book of Copper and Brass*, 1968, *Ivory*, 1968, *English and Irish Glass*, 1968, *Silver*, 1969, *English Furniture* (2 vols.), 1971, *Collecting Antiques*, 1971.

KENNETH M. WILSON (American Glass). Director, Collections and Preservation Greenfield Village and Henry Ford Museum (The Edison Institute), Dearborn, Michigan, formerly Assistant Director and Chief Curator, the Corning Museum of Glass, Corning, New York, Chief Curator, Old Sturbridge Village, Sturbridge, Massachusetts, Assistant Curator, Old Sturbridge Village, Sturbridge, Massachusetts. Author of *New England Glass and Glassmaking*, 1972, *Glass in New England* and contributor to *Antiques* (New York), *Bulletin of the Paperweight Collectors' Association*, *The National Early American Glass Club Bulletin*, *The Chronicle of the Early American Industries Association*, *Journal of Glass Studies*, *Proceedings of the VIIth and VIIIth International Congress in Glass*, *Museum News* and *Discovering Antiques*.

Illustration Acknowledgments

Source credits for the illustrations are given in brief in the captions. The full names are as follows:

Abby Aldrich Rockefeller Folk Art Collection, Colonial Williamsburg
American Museum in Britain, Claverton Manor, Bath
American Watch and Clock Museum, New Haven, Connecticut
Art Museum, Princeton University
Bethnal Green Museum, London
Bodleian Library, Oxford
British Horological Institute, London
British Museum, London
Aubrey Brocklehurst, London
Brooklyn Museum, New York
Brown Collection
Carborundum Museum of Ceramics, Niagara Falls, New York
Chicago Historical Society
Chicago School of Architecture
Christie's, London
City Art Gallery, Manchester
City Museum and Art Gallery, Birmingham
City Museum and Art Gallery, Hanley, Staffordshire
Corning Museum of Glass, New York
Richard Dennis Antiques, London
A. L. Diament & Co., New York
Henry Duke & Son, Dorchester, Dorset
Éditions Graphiques Gallery, London

Fine Art Society Ltd., London
N. Flayderman Collection
Geoffrey A. Godden, F.R.S.A., Worthing, Sussex
Grand Rapids Public Museum, Michigan
Greenfield Village and Henry Ford Museum, Dearborn, Michigan
Guildford Museum, Surrey
K. H. Hayden Collection
Mary Hillier Collection
Historical Society of Pennsylvania, Philadelphia
Hudson River Museum, New York
Flora Gill Jacobs Collection
John Judkyn Memorial, Freshford Manor, Bath
Ken Roberts Publishing Co., New Haven, Connecticut
John Lewis Collection
Library of Congress, Washington D.C.
Trustees of the London Museum, London
Mackintosh Collection, University of Glasgow
Mrs Frank McKenzie Collection
Mallett at Bourdon House Ltd., London
Margaret Woodbury Strong Museum, Rochester, New York
Maryland Historical Society, Baltimore
Mayorcas Ltd., London
Metropolitan Museum of Art, New York
J. R. Mitchell Collection
Mr and Mrs Morrie A. Moss Collection
Museum für Kunst und Gewerbe, Hamburg
Museum of the City of New York

National Army Museum, London
National Cowboy Hall of Fame and Western Heritage Center, Oklahoma City
National Gallery of Art, Washington D.C.
National Museum of Antiquities of Scotland, Edinburgh
National Museum of Ireland, Dublin
National Park Service, Washington D.C.
Negretti & Zambra Ltd, Stocklade, Buckinghamshire
Newark Museum, New Jersey
New Jersey State Museum Collection, Trenton
New York Public Library
New York State Historical Association, Cooperstown
Oglebay Mansion House Museum, Wheeling, West Virginia
Osborne House, Isle of Wight
Michael Parkington Collection
Flavia Petrie Collection
Philadelphia Museum of Art Collection, Pennsylvania
J. C. Pope Collection
Purple Shop, Antiquarius Market, London
Radio Times Hulton Picture Library, London
Science Museum, London
J. S. M. Scott Collection
James R. Seibert Collection
Session of Kippen Parish Church, Stirlingshire
Sheffield Museum
Sherlock Holmes Pub, London
Smithsonian Institution, Washington D.C.
Sotheby & Co, London
Sotheby Parke Bernet, New York
Sotheby's Belgravia, London
Southall Library, Middlesex
Southall Manor, Middlesex
Stourbridge Glass Museum, Worcestershire
Strike One, London
Taft Museum, Cincinnati
Tate Gallery, London
Tradition, London
University Library, Keele
Victoria and Albert Museum, London
Walker Art Gallery, Liverpool
Westminster Public Library, London
Whitworth Art Gallery, Manchester
Frederick Wilkinson Collection
William Morris Gallery, Walthamstow
Worshipful Company of Goldsmiths, London
Yale University Art Gallery, Connecticut

Special credits are due to the following:

p. 18 top Gift of Frederic H. Hatch
p. 20 right National Trust for Historic Preservation, Lyndhurst
p. 24 right and p. 27 The Preservation Society of Newport County
p. 28 Gift of John D. Rockefeller, Jr, 1937
p. 46 Gift of Arthur S. Vernay
p. 47 Rogers Fund, 1969
p. 50 top Gift of the Diocese of Newark, 1941

p. 50 bottom right Gift of Miss Josephine M. Fiala, 1968
p. 51 left Gift of Mrs Charles F. Batchelder
p. 51 top right Edgar J. Kaufmann Charitable Foundation Fund
p. 52 right Gift of Mary J. Kingsland
p. 52 bottom left Anonymous Gift Fund
p. 53 top Emily C. Chadbourne Bequest, 1903
p. 53 bottom Gift of Mrs Frank McCabe
p. 61 bottom Gift of Auguste Pottier and Edgar J. Kaufmann Charitable Foundation Fund
p. 72 top Gift of Mrs John Laimbeer, 1936
p. 72 bottom Gift of Mrs Charles Reginald Leonard, Robert Jarvis Leonard and Charles Reginald Leonard
p. 82 top left and top right Gift of I. N. Phelps Stokes, Edward S. Hawes, Alice Mary Hawes, Marion Augusta Hawes, 1937
p. 83 centre Brady Collection
p. 137 Gifts of Arthur W. Clement
p. 138 top Museum Purchase 73–68
p. 139 Edgar J. Kaufmann Charitable Foundation Fund
p. 141 top The Brewer Collection 354.22
p. 159 bottom (sugar sifter and tapered vase) Gifts of Mrs Frank McKenzie
p. 175 right Gift of Mrs Florence E. Bushie
p. 176 Gift of Mr and Mrs William H. Herriman, 1911
p. 183 top National Collection of Fine Arts
p. 183 bottom and p. 184 left Gift of the Hon. Hamilton Fish, 1894
p. 184 right Gift of James Douglas, 1899
p. 187 Gift of Alfred Corning Clark, 1896
p. 189 right Bequest of Jacob Ruppert, 1939
p. 204 top Bequest of A. T. Clearwater, 1933
p. 204 right Gift of Mrs F. R. Lefferts, 1969
p. 205 top right Anonymous Gift Fund, 1968
p. 207 Gift of William Cullen Bryant, 1877
p. 210 Gift of Mrs Winthrop Atwell
p. 233 bottom Gift of Mrs D. Chester Noyes, 1968
p. 237 top On loan from the Tower of London Armouries
p. 242 below Gift of Mr F. D. Meller
p. 255 top centre Gift of Mrs John Hill Morgan
p. 256 left Gifts of the Mary Flagler Cary Charitable Trust and Mrs August Belmont
p. 258 Lent by Mrs W. E. Ames-Lewis
p. 260 left Joicey Bequest
p. 260 right Gift of Miss Margaret Brearley, 1954
p. 261 Gift of Mrs John Bickerdike and Miss Mary Dawson
p. 267 left Harris Brisbane Dick Fund, 1928, New York
p. 318 Gift of Edward William and Bernice Chrysler Garbisch
p. 326 top left Gift of Mrs J. R. Devereaux
p. 346 top Gift of The Louis Comfort Tiffany Foundation, 1951

Photographic Credits

Introduction
p. 12-13 Bedford Lemere, National Monuments Record, London

p. 14 bottom Country Life, London
p. 15 top Juanita Dugdale, Wesleyan University
p. 15 bottom National Monuments Record, London
p. 16 bottom Historic American Buildings Survey, Washington, D.C.
p. 17 Edwin Smith
p. 18 bottom Cooper-Bridgeman Library, London
p. 20 left Bedford Lemere, National Monuments Record, London
p. 20 right Louis H. Frohman
p. 21 left and right National Monuments Record, London
p. 22 Historic American Buildings Survey, Washington D.C.
p. 24 left English Life Publications Ltd
p. 25 top Country Life, London
p. 25 bottom Sidney Newbery, Cooper-Bridgeman Library, London
p. 26 bottom and p. 30 Historic American Buildings Survey, Washington D.C.

Furniture
p. 34 left Karin Hoddle, Cooper-Bridgeman Library, London
p. 34 right Raymond Fortt Studios, Richmond
p. 35 and p. 36 Cooper-Bridgeman Library, London
p. 50 top Armen
p. 52 top left Jay Cantor
p. 61 top and p. 64 Cooper-Bridgeman Library, London
p. 72 top Armen

Photography
p. 90 top Science Museum, London

Clocks
p. 93 Sperryns Ltd, London
p. 95 John Furley-Lewis, London
p. 96 Cooper-Bridgeman Library, London
p. 109 Rob Matheson, London

Pottery
p. 110 Angelo Hornak, London
p. 111 and p. 113 bottom Cooper-Bridgeman Library, London
p. 115 centre and p. 116 left Leonard & Marcus Taylor Ltd, Middlesex
p. 122 Cooper-Bridgeman Library, London

Porcelain
p. 130 top Cooper-Bridgeman Library, London
p. 135 left and right A. J. Wyatt, staff photographer
p. 138 top and p. 141 top Joseph Crilley

Glass
p. 154 and p. 169 A. C. Cooper Ltd, London
p. 170 Sperryns Ltd, London

Sculpture
p. 177 and p. 178 right Cooper-Bridgeman Library, London

p. 178 left Sotheby's Belgravia, London
p. 179 left and p. 180 left Fine Art Society Ltd, London
p. 181 top right Sotheby's Belgravia, London
p. 191 Cooper-Bridgeman Library, London
p. 192 Gordon Coates
p. 194 Cooper-Bridgeman Library, London

Silver
p. 197 Don Newman, Memphis
p. 200 top right Cooper-Bridgeman Library, London
p. 201 top right Sotheby's Belgravia, London
p. 203 Gorham Co., Providence, Rhode Island
p. 205 bottom left Emanuel Levine Assoc. Inc. Washington D.C.
p. 206 left Gorham Co., Providence, Rhode Island
p. 209 Cooper-Bridgeman Library, London
p. 212 Sotheby's Belgravia, London
p. 214, p. 218 and p. 219 International Silver Co.

Metalwork
p. 220 Cooper-Bridgeman Library, London
p. 222 bottom and p. 224 bottom Grid Studios Ltd, Sheffield
p. 223 right and p. 227 Cooper-Bridgeman Library, London
p. 228 Angelo Hornak, London
p. 233 top Rupert Roddam

Arms and Militaria
p. 236, p. 238 top, centre and bottom and p. 241 left, centre and right Frederick Wilkinson
p. 242 left and p. 243 bottom National Park Service, Washington D.C.
p. 242 centre, p. 243 centre and p. 244 left and right Harold L. Peterson

Jewelry
p. 256 left and right Helga Photo Studio Inc., New York

Dress
p. 266 bottom John R. Freeman (& Co.) Ltd, London
p. 269-72 Cooper-Bridgeman Library, London

Textiles
p. 278, p. 280 and p. 296 Cooper-Bridgeman Library, London
p. 299 John Bethell, London

Wallpaper
p. 303 Cooper-Bridgeman Library, London
p. 306 and p. 311 Vanucci Foto Services, New York

Juvenilia
p. 319 centre Cooper-Bridgeman Library, London
p. 323, p. 324 and p. 325 Allen Bress, Maryland

Miscellany
p. 336 Cooper-Bridgeman Library, London
p. 338 left Angelo Hornak, London
p. 350 bottom Cooper-Bridgeman Library, London
p. 351 Angelo Hornak, London

Index